Cambridge IGCSE™ and O Level

Additional Mathematics

WORKED SOLUTIONS MANUAL

Muriel James

CAMBRIDGE
UNIVERSITY PRESS

Shaftesbury Road, Cambridge CB2 8EA, United Kingdom

One Liberty Plaza, 20th Floor, New York, NY 10006, USA

477 Williamstown Road, Port Melbourne, VIC 3207, Australia

314–321, 3rd Floor, Plot 3, Splendor Forum, Jasola District Centre, New Delhi – 110025, India

103 Penang Road, #05–06/07, Visioncrest Commercial, Singapore 238467

Cambridge University Press is part of the University of Cambridge.

It furthers the University's mission by disseminating knowledge in the pursuit of education, learning and research at the highest international levels of excellence.

www.cambridge.org
Information on this title: www.cambridge.org/9781009299763

First published 2024

20 19 18 17 16 15 14 13 12 11 10 9 8 7 6 5 4 3 2 1

Printed in Dubai by Oriental Press

A catalogue record for this publication is available from the British Library

ISBN 978-1-009-29976-3 Worked Solutions Manual

ISBN 978-1-009-29977-0 Digital Worked Solutions Manual

Additional resources for this publication at www.cambridge.org/go

Endorsement statement

Endorsement indicates that a resource has passed Cambridge International's rigorous quality-assurance process and is suitable to support the delivery of a Cambridge International syllabus. However, endorsed resources are not the only suitable materials available to support teaching and learning, and are not essential to be used to achieve the qualification. Resource lists found on the Cambridge International website will include this resource and other endorsed resources.

Any example answers to questions taken from past question papers, practice questions, accompanying marks and mark schemes included in this resource have been written by the authors and are for guidance only. They do not replicate examination papers. In examinations the way marks are awarded may be different. Any references to assessment and/or assessment preparation are the publisher's interpretation of the syllabus requirements. Examiners will not use endorsed resources as a source of material for any assessment set by Cambridge International.

While the publishers have made every attempt to ensure that advice on the qualification and its assessment is accurate, the official syllabus, specimen assessment materials and any associated assessment guidance materials produced by the awarding body are the only authoritative source of information and should always be referred to for definitive guidance. Cambridge International recommends that teachers consider using a range of teaching and learning resources based on their own professional judgement of their students' needs.

Cambridge International has not paid for the production of this resource, nor does Cambridge International receive any royalties from its sale. For more information about the endorsement process, please visit www.cambridgeinternational.org/endorsed-resources. Cambridge International copyright material in this publication is reproduced under licence and remains the intellectual property of Cambridge University Press and Assessment.

Third party websites and resources referred to in this publication have not been endorsed by Cambridge Assessment International Education.

Contents

How to use this book

This book contains worked solutions to the questions in the *Cambridge International IGCSE Additional Mathematics Coursebook*. Both the book and accompanying digital edition include the solutions to a selection of chapter exercises.

Each solution shows you step-by-step how to solve the question. You will be aware that often questions can be solved by multiple different methods. In this book, we provide a single method for each solution. Do not be disheartened if the working in a solution does not match your own working; you may not be wrong but simply using a different method. It is good practice to challenge yourself to think about the methods you are using and whether there may be alternative methods.

TIP

Additional guidance is included in these boxes throughout the book. These boxes often clarify common misconceptions or areas of difficulty.

> TIP
>
> Continuing the trial and error method to find all factors can be lengthy. Once one factor has been found it may be easier to use division or comparing coefficients to find the other(s).

REMINDER

Key concepts from the corresponding chapter in the coursebook are highlighted in these boxes.

> REMINDER
>
> In question 6 you do not need to convert each angle to degrees.
>
> You should set the angle mode on your calculator to radians.

REMEMBER

These boxes contain key equations, formulae or concepts that you will need to know.

> REMEMBER
>
> - **Collinear** points all lie on a straight line.
> - The equation of a straight line can be written as $y = mx + c$ where 'c' is the y-intercept and 'm' is the gradient.
> - The equation of a straight line with gradient 'm' which passes through the point (x_1, y_1) is:
>
> $y - y_1 = m(x - x_1)$
> - If two lines are parallel then their gradients are equal.
> - If a line has a gradient m, a line perpendicular to it has a gradient $-\frac{1}{m}$.
> - If the gradients of the two perpendicular lines are m_1 and m_2, then $m_1 \times m_2 = -1$

All worked solutions in this resource have been written by the author.

Chapter 1: Functions

Exercise 1.1

1 $x \mapsto x + 1 \quad x \in \mathbb{R}$

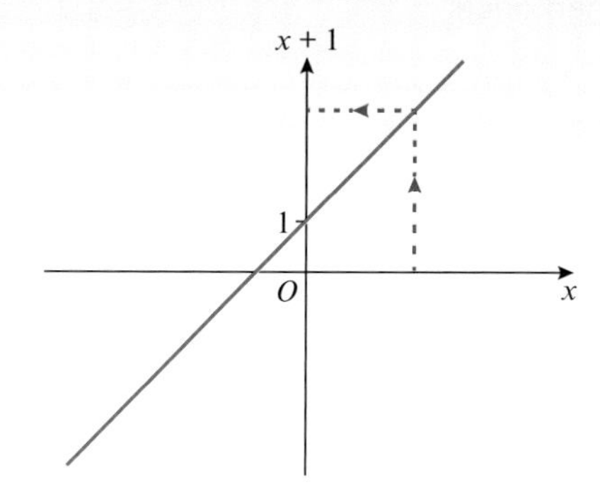

For one input value there is just one output value so this is a **one-one** mapping

2 $x \mapsto x^2 + 5 \quad x \in \mathbb{R}$

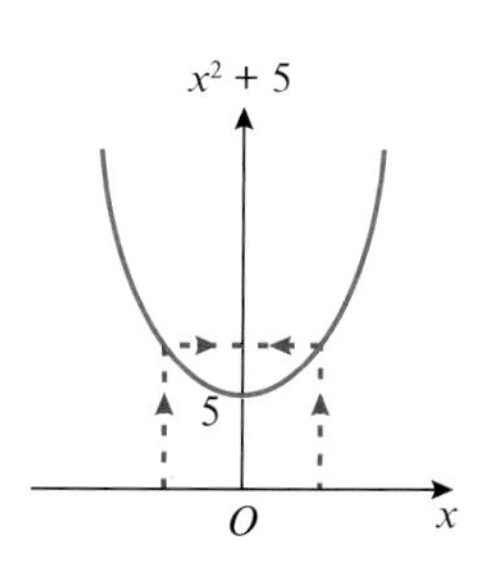

For two input values there is just one output value so this is a **many-one** mapping

3 $x \mapsto x^3 \quad x \in \mathbb{R}$

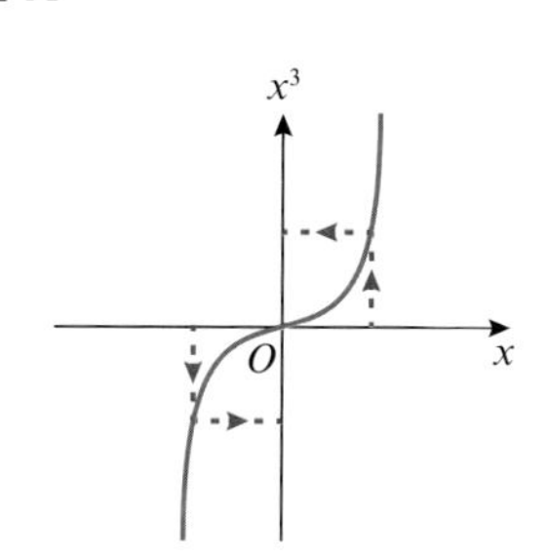

For one input value there is just one output value so this is a **one-one** mapping

4 $x \mapsto 2^x \quad x \in \mathbb{R}$

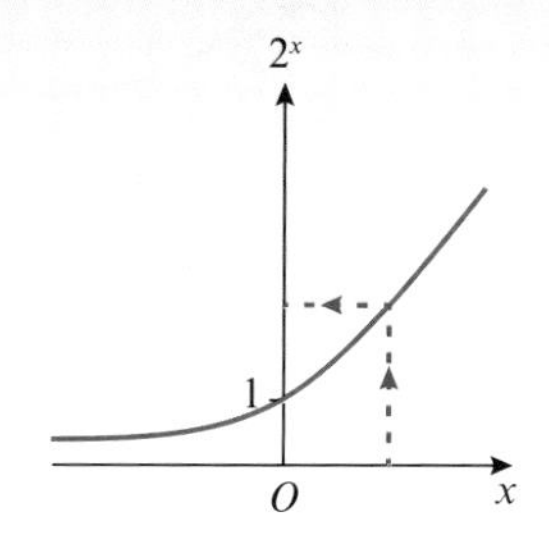

For one input value there is just one output value so this is a **one-one** mapping

5 $x \mapsto \frac{1}{x} \quad x \in \mathbb{R}, x > 0$

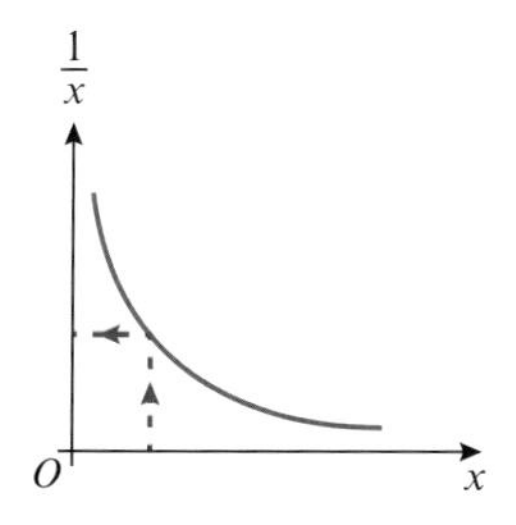

For one input value there is just one output value so this is a **one-one** mapping

6 $x \mapsto x^2 + 1 \quad x \in \mathbb{R}, x \geqslant 0$

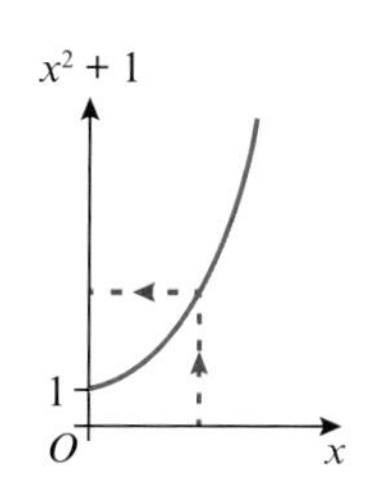

For one input value there is just one output value so this is a **one-one** mapping

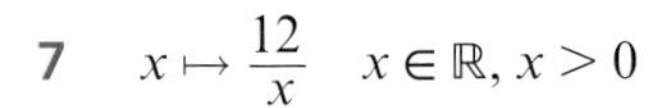

7 $x \mapsto \frac{12}{x} \quad x \in \mathbb{R}, x > 0$

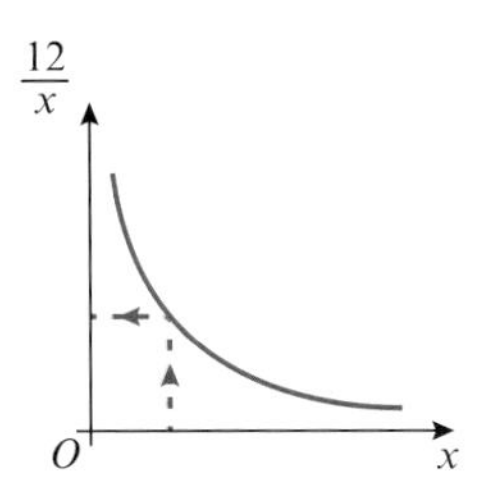

For one input value there is just one output value so this is a **one-one** mapping

8 $x \mapsto \pm x \quad x \in \mathbb{R}, x \geqslant 0$

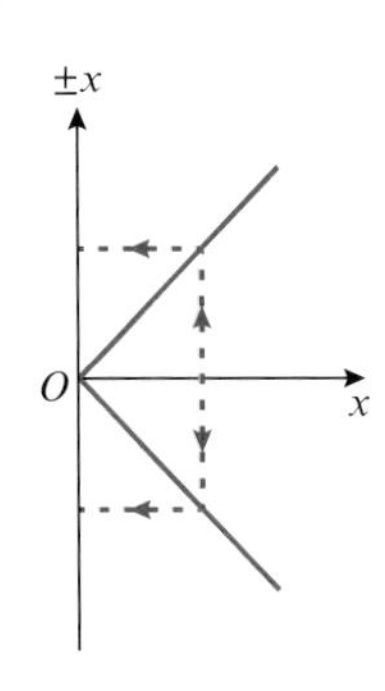

For one input value there are two output values so this is a **one-many** mapping

> **TIP**
>
> One-one mappings and many-one mappings are called functions.

Exercise 1.2

1 The following mappings from Exercise 1.1 are functions:

$x \mapsto x + 1 \quad x \in \mathbb{R},$

$x \mapsto x^2 + 5 \quad x \in \mathbb{R},$

$x \mapsto x^3 \quad x \in \mathbb{R},$

$x \mapsto 2^x \quad x \in \mathbb{R},$

$x \mapsto \frac{1}{x} \quad x \in \mathbb{R}, x > 0,$

$x \mapsto x^2 + 1 \quad x \in \mathbb{R}, x \geqslant 0$

$x \mapsto \frac{12}{x} \quad x \in \mathbb{R}, x > 0$

> **TIP**
>
> If we draw all positive vertical lines on the graph of a mapping, the mapping is:
>
> - a function if each line cuts the graph no more than once
> - not a function if one line cuts the graph more than once.

2 c $f(x) = 7 - 2x, -1 \leqslant x \leqslant 4$

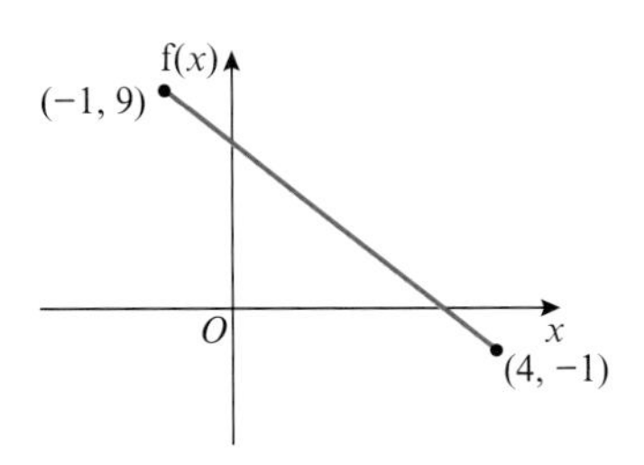

The graph of $y = 7 - 2x$ has a gradient -2 and a y-intercept 7

When $x = -1$, $y = 7 - 2(-1) = 9$

When $x = 4$, $y = 7 - 2(4) = -1$

The range of f is $-1 \leqslant f(x) \leqslant 9$

d $f(x) = x^2, \ -3 \leqslant x \leqslant 3$

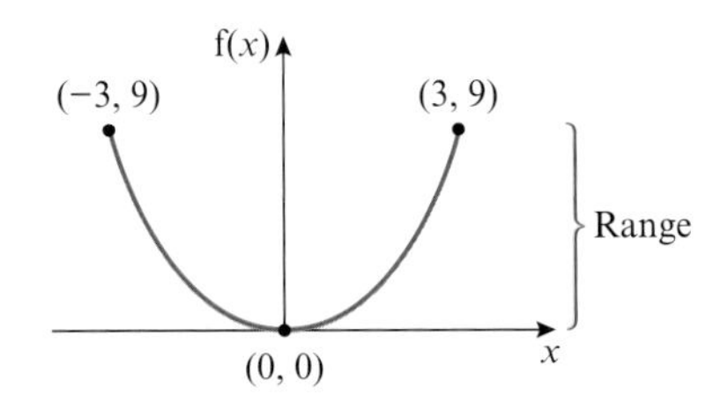

The minimum value of the expression x^2 is 0 which occurs when $x = 0$

The maximum value of the expression x^2 is 9 which occurs when $x = -3$ and $x = 3$

So, the range of the function $f(x) = x^2, -3 \leqslant x \leqslant 3$ is $0 \leqslant f(x) \leqslant 9$

3 $g(x) = x^2 + 2$ for $x \geqslant 0$

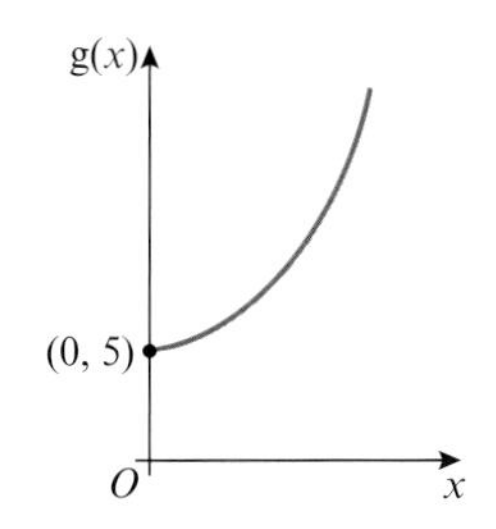

$g(x) = x^2 + 2$ is a positive quadratic function, so the graph will be of the form

The minimum value of the expression $x^2 + 2$ is 2 which occurs when $x = 0$

When $x = 0$, $y = 0^2 + 2 = 2$

There is no maximum value of the expression $x^2 + 2$ for the domain $x \geqslant 0$

The range is $g(x) \geqslant 2$

TIP

The minimum value of an expression of the form $(ax + k)^2$ is 0

The minimum value occurs when $ax + k = 0$,

i.e., when $x = \frac{-k}{a}$

4 $f(x) = x^2 - 4 \quad x \in \mathbb{R}$

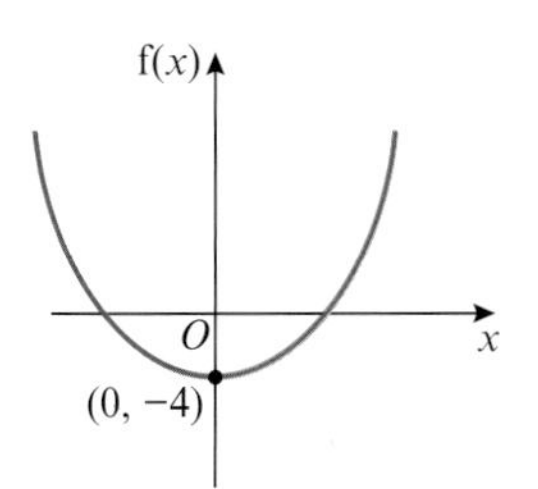

$f(x) = x^2 - 4$ is a positive quadratic function, so the graph will be of the form

The minimum value of the expression $x^2 - 4$ is -4 which occurs when $x = 0$

When $x = 0$, $y = 0^2 - 4 = -4$

There is no maximum value of the expression $x^2 - 4$ for the domain $x \in \mathbb{R}$

The range is $f(x) \geqslant -4$

5 $f(x) = (x - 1)^2 + 5$ for $x \geqslant 1$

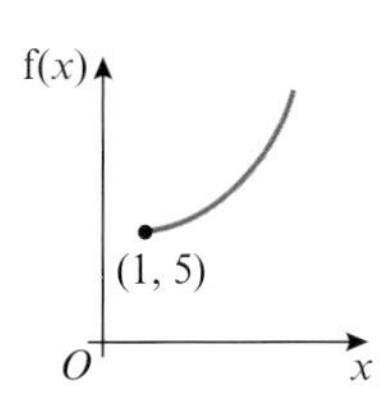

$f(x) = (x - 1)^2 + 5$ is a positive quadratic function, so the graph will be of the form

The minimum value of the expression $(x - 1)^2 + 5$ is 5 which occurs when $x = 1$

When $x = 1$, $y = (1 - 1)^2 + 5 = 5$

There is no maximum value of the expression $(x - 1)^2 + 5$ for the domain $x \geqslant 1$

The range is $f(x) \geqslant 5$

6 $f(x) = (2x + 1)^2 - 5$ for $x \geqslant -\frac{1}{2}$

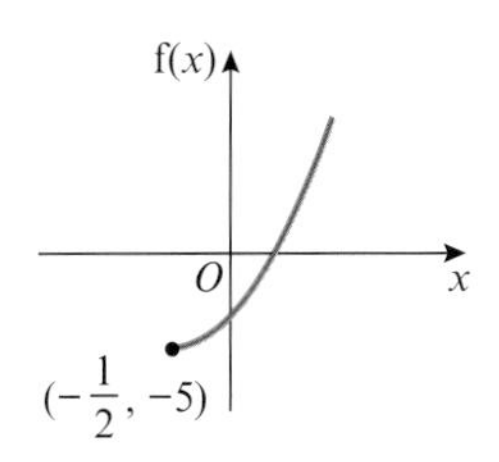

$f(x) = (2x + 1)^2 - 5$ is a positive quadratic function, so the graph will be of the form

The minimum value of the expression $(2x + 1)^2 - 5$ is -5 which occurs when $x = -\frac{1}{2}$

When $x = -\frac{1}{2}$, $y = \left(2 \times -\frac{1}{2} + 1\right)^2 - 5 = -5$

There is no maximum value of the expression $(2x + 1)^2 - 5$ for the domain $x \geqslant -\frac{1}{2}$

The range is $f(x) \geqslant -5$

7 $f : x \mapsto 10 - (x - 3)^2, 2 \leqslant x \leqslant 7$

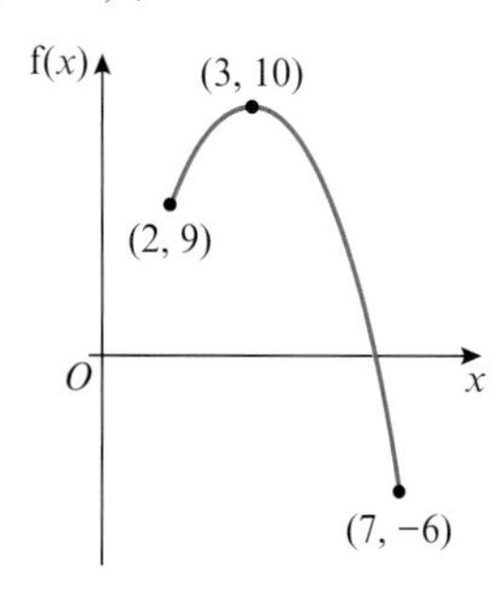

$f : x \mapsto 10 - (x - 3)^2$ is a negative quadratic function, so the graph will be of the form

The maximum value of the expression $10 - (x - 3)^2$ is 10, which occurs when $x = 3$

When $x = 2$, $f : x \mapsto 10 - (2 - 3)^2 = 9$

When $x = 7$, $f : x \mapsto 10 - (7 - 3)^2 = -6$

The range of $f : x \mapsto 10 - (x - 3)^2$ for $2 \leqslant x \leqslant 7$ is $-6 \leqslant f(x) \leqslant 10$

TIP

When finding the range of a function, it is helpful to be familiar with the sketches of graphs of the form $y = \frac{k}{x}$, $y = k\sqrt{x}$, $y = \sqrt{x + k}$, $y = k^x$ etc.

8 $f(x) = 3 + \sqrt{x - 2}$ for $x \geqslant 2$

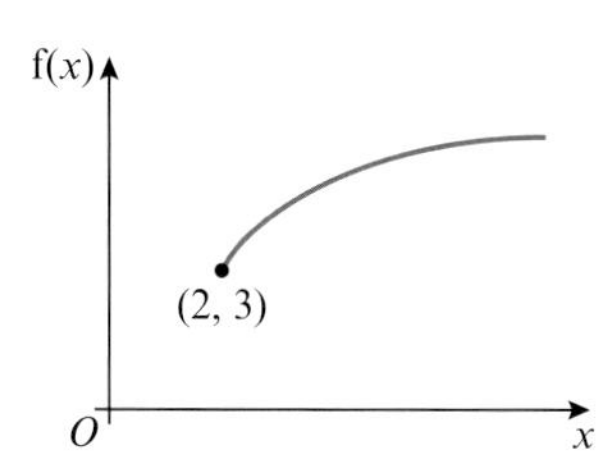

The minimum value of the expression $3 + \sqrt{x - 2}$ is 3, which occurs when $x = 2$

When $x = 2$, $f(x) = 3 + \sqrt{2 - 2} = 3$

There is no maximum value of the expression $3 + \sqrt{x - 2}$ for the domain $x \geqslant 2$

The range is $f(x) \geqslant 3$

Exercise 1.3

1 $fg(2)$ — g acts on 2 first and $g(2) = 2^2 - 1 = 3$

$= f(3)$ — f is the function 'multiply by 2 then add 3'

$= 2(3) + 3$

$= 9$

TIP

To form a composite function, the domain of f must be chosen so that the whole of the range of f is included in the domain of g.

2 $gf(5)$ — f acts on 5 first and $f(5) = 5^2 - 1 = 24$

$= g(24)$ — f is the function 'multiply by 2 then add 3'

$= 2(24) + 3$

$= 51$

3 $f(x) = (x + 2)^2 - 1$ for $x \in \mathbb{R}$

$f^2(3)$ means $ff(3)$

$ff(3)$ — f acts on 3 first and $f(3) = (3 + 2)^2 - 1 = 24$

$= f(24)$ — f is the function 'add 2, square then subtract 1'

$= (24 + 2)^2 - 1$

$= 675$

4 gf(18) f acts on 18 first and $f(18) = 1 + \sqrt{18 - 2} = 5$

$= g(5)$ g is the function 'divide into 10, then subtract 1'

$= \frac{10}{5} - 1$

$= 1$

5 fg(7) g acts on 7 first and $g(7) = \frac{2(7) + 4}{7 - 5} = 9$

$= f(9)$ f is the function 'subtract 1, square then add 3'

$= (9 - 1)^2 + 3$

$= 67$

6 **a** $x \mapsto \sqrt{x} + 2$ is represented by hk

Check: hk(x) means k acts on x first and $k(x) = \sqrt{x}$

$= h(\sqrt{x})$ h is the function 'add 2'

$= \sqrt{x} + 2$

b $x \mapsto \sqrt{x + 2}$ is represented by kh

Check: kh(x) means h acts on x first and $h(x) = x + 2$

$= k(x + 2)$ k is the function 'square root'

$= \sqrt{x + 2}$

7 gf(x) f acts on x first and $f(x) = 3x + 1$

$= g(3x + 1)$ g is the function 'subtract from 2 then divide into 10'

$= \frac{10}{2 - (3x + 1)}$

But $gf(x) = 5$, so $\frac{10}{2 - (3x + 1)} = 5$

Solve $\frac{10}{2 - 3x - 1} = 5$

$\frac{10}{1 - 3x} = 5$

$10 = 5(1 - 3x)$

$10 = 5 - 15x$

$15x = -5$

$x = -\frac{1}{3}$

8 gh(x) h acts on x first and $h(x) = 3x - 5$

$= g(3x - 5)$ g is the function 'square then add 2'

$= (3x - 5)^2 + 2$

But $gh(x) = 51$ so $(3x - 5)^2 + 2 = 51$

Solve $(3x - 5)^2 + 2 = 51$

$(3x - 5)^2 = 49$ square root both sides

$3x - 5 = \pm 7$ (remember $\pm$)

$3x - 5 = 7$ or $3x - 5 = -7$

$3x = 12$ or $3x = -2$

$x = 4$ or $x = -\frac{2}{3}$

9 fg(x) g acts on x first and $g(x) = \frac{3}{x}$

$= f\left(\frac{3}{x}\right)$ f is the function 'square then subtract 3'

$= \left(\frac{3}{x}\right)^2 - 3$

But $fg(x) = 13$ so $\left(\frac{3}{x}\right)^2 - 3 = 13$

Solve $\left(\frac{3}{x}\right)^2 - 3 = 13$

$\left(\frac{3}{x}\right)^2 = 16$ square root both sides

$\frac{3}{x} = \pm 4$

$3 = \pm 4x$

$x = \pm\frac{3}{4}$

However, as $x > 0$, the only solution is $x = \frac{3}{4}$

10 gf(x) f acts on g first and $f(x) = \frac{3x + 5}{x - 2}$

$= g\left(\frac{3x + 5}{x - 2}\right)$ g is the function 'subtract 1 then divide by 2'

$= \frac{\left(\frac{3x + 5}{x - 2} - 1\right)}{2}$

But $gf(x) = 12$ so $\frac{\left(\frac{3x + 5}{x - 2} - 1\right)}{2} = 12$

Solve $\dfrac{\left(\dfrac{3x+5}{x-2}-1\right)}{2}=12$

$\dfrac{3x+5}{x-2}-1=24$

$\dfrac{3x+5}{x-2}=25$

$3x+5=25(x-2)$

$3x+5=25x-50$

$-22x=-55$

$x=2.5$

11 $fg(x)$ g acts on x first and $g(x)=\dfrac{10}{x}$

$=f\left(\dfrac{10}{x}\right)$ f is the function 'add 4, square then add 3'

$=\left(\dfrac{10}{x}+4\right)^2+3$

But $fg(x)=39$ so $\left(\dfrac{10}{x}+4\right)^2+3=39$

Solve $\left(\dfrac{10}{x}+4\right)^2+3=39$

$\left(\dfrac{10}{x}+4\right)^2=36$ square root both sides

$\dfrac{10}{x}+4=\pm6$

$\dfrac{10}{x}+4=6$ or $\dfrac{10}{x}+4=-6$

$\dfrac{10}{x}=2$ or $\dfrac{10}{x}=-10$

$x=5$ or $x=-1$

However, $x>0$ so the only solution is $x=5$

12 $gh(x)$ h acts on x first and $h(x)=2x-7$

$=g(2x-7)$ g is the function 'square then subtract 1'

$=(2x-7)^2-1$

But $gh(x)=0$ so $(2x-7)^2-1=0$

Solve $(2x-7)^2-1=0$

$(2x-7)^2=1$ square root both sides

$2x-7=\pm1$

$2x-7=-1$ or $2x-7=1$

$2x=6$ or $2x=8$

$x=3$ or $x=4$

13 a $x\mapsto(x-1)^3$ is the composite function $fg(x)$

Explanation:

$fg(x)$ means g acts on x first and $g(x)=x-1$

$=f(x-1)$ f is the function 'cube'

$=(x-1)^3$

c $x\mapsto x-2$ is the composite function $gg(x)$ or $g^2(x)$

Explanation:

$gg(x)$ means g acts on x first and $g(x)=x-1$

$=g(x-1)$ g is the function 'subtract 1'

$=(x-1)-1$

$=x-2$

14 $f(x)=\dfrac{x}{x+2}$ for $x\in\mathbb{R}, x\neq-2$

$g(x)=\dfrac{3}{x}$ for $x\in\mathbb{R}, x\neq0$

Finding the domain of $fg(x)$

The domain of $g(x)$ consists of all real numbers except $x\neq0$ (since that input value would result in dividing by 0)

The domain of $f(x)$ consists of all real numbers except $x\neq-2$ (since that input value would result in dividing by 0)

So, we need to exclude from the domain of $g(x)$ the value of x for which $g(x)=-2$

Set $g(x)=-2$

$\dfrac{3}{x}=-2$

$x=-\dfrac{3}{2}$

So the domain of fg(x) is the set of all real numbers except 0 and $-\frac{3}{2}$

This means that $x \in \mathbb{R}, x \neq -\frac{3}{2}, x \neq 0$

15 $f(x) = x^2 - 9$ for $x \in \mathbb{R}, x < 0$

$g(x) = 10 - \frac{x}{2}$ for $x \in \mathbb{R}, x > 6$

Finding the domain of fg(x)

The domain of g(x) consists of all real numbers > 6

The domain of f(x) consists of all real numbers < 0

So $x > 6$ and $g(x) < 0$

Set $10 - \frac{x}{2} < 0$

$10 < \frac{x}{2}$

$x > 20$

Overlap of $x > 6$ and $x > 20$ is $x > 20$

Domain of fg(x) is $x \in \mathbb{R}, x > 20$

Finding the range of fg(x)

$fg(x) = \left(10 - \frac{x}{2}\right)^2 - 9 \quad x \in \mathbb{R}, x > 20$

The graph of $y = fg(x) = \left(10 - \frac{x}{2}\right)^2 - 9$

$x \in \mathbb{R}, x > 20$ looks like:

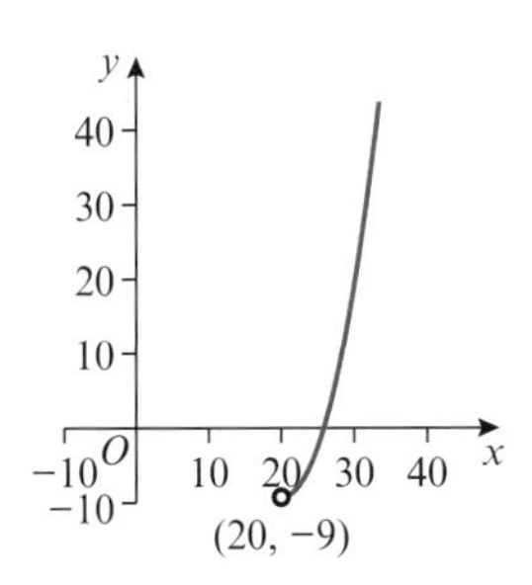

This is a quadratic curve and the turning point occurs when $10 - \frac{x}{2} = 0$

$x = 20$

Hence the turning point is $(20, -9)$

Range is $fg(x) \in \mathbb{R}, fg(x) > -9$

17 $f(x) = 2x - 6$ for $x \in \mathbb{R}$ $\quad g(x) = \sqrt{x}$ for $x \in \mathbb{R}, x \geqslant 0$

a Finding the domain of fg(x)

The domain of f(x) consists of all real numbers

The domain of g(x) consists of all real numbers $x \geqslant 0$

$x \geqslant 0$ and $g(x) \in \mathbb{R}$

So the domain of fg(x) is the set of all real numbers $\geqslant 0$

This means that the domain of fg(x) is $x \in \mathbb{R}, x \geqslant 0$

To find the range of fg(x), first find fg(x)

$fg(x) = 2\sqrt{x} - 6 \quad x \in \mathbb{R}, x \geqslant 0$

The minimum value of the expression $2\sqrt{x} - 6$ is -6, which occurs when $x = 0$

When $x = 0$, $fg(x) = 2\sqrt{0} - 6 = -6$

There is no maximum value of the expression $2\sqrt{x} - 6$ for the domain $x \geqslant 0$.

The range is $fg(x) \in \mathbb{R}, fg(x) \geqslant -6$

b Finding the domain of gf(x)

The domain of f(x) consists of all real numbers.

The domain of g(x) consists of all real numbers $x \geqslant 0$.

$x \in \mathbb{R}$ and $f(x) \geqslant 0$

So $2x - 6 \geqslant 0$

$2x \geqslant 6$

$x \geqslant 3$

So the domain of gf(x) is the set of all real numbers $\geqslant 3$

This means that the domain of gf(x) is $x \in \mathbb{R}, x \geqslant 3$

To find the range of gf(x), first find gf(x)

$gf(x) = \sqrt{2x - 6}$ for $x \in \mathbb{R}, x \geqslant 3$

The minimum value of the expression $\sqrt{2x - 6}$ is 0, which occurs when $x = 3$

When $x = 3$, $gf(x) = \sqrt{2 \times 3 - 6} = 0$

There is no maximum value of the expression $\sqrt{2x - 6}$ for the domain $x \geqslant 3$

The range is $gf(x) \in \mathbb{R}, gf(x) \geqslant 0$

19 $f(x) = 2x + 5$ for $x \in \mathbb{R}, x < 2$
$g(x) = (x - 3)^2$ for $x \in \mathbb{R}, x > 3$

a **i** The graph of $y = 2x + 5$ is a straight line with gradient 2 and a y-intercept of 5

The range of f is $f(x) \in \mathbb{R}, f(x) < 9$
(from substituting $x = 2$ into $f(x) = 2x + 5$)

ii The graph of $g(x) = (x - 3)^2$ is a positive quadratic function. The graph will be U shaped.

$(x - 3)^2$ is a square so it will always be greater or equal to zero. The smallest value it can be is 0. This occurs when $x = 3$ but the domain of $g(x)$ is $x > 3$ so the range of $g(x) > 0$

The range of g is $g(x) \in \mathbb{R}, g(x) > 0$

b Finding $gf(x)$.

f acts on x first and $f(x) = 2x + 5$

$gf(x) = g(2x + 5)$ g is the function 'minus 3 then square'

$gf(x) = (2x + 5 - 3)^2$

$gf(x) = (2x + 2)^2$

c Finding the domain of $gf(x)$

The domain of $g(x)$ consists of all real numbers > 3

The domain of $f(x)$ consists of all real numbers < 2

So $x < 2$ and $f(x) > 3$

Set $2x + 5 > 3$

$2x > -2$

$x > -1$

The overlap of $x > -1$ and $x < 2$ is $-1 < x < 2$

The domain of $gf(x)$ is $x \in \mathbb{R}, -1 < x < 2$

To find the range of $gf(x)$, first find $gf(x)$

$gf(x) = (2x + 2)^2 \quad x \in \mathbb{R}, -1 < x < 2$

The graph of $y = gf(x) = (2x + 2)^2 \quad x \in \mathbb{R}, -1 < x < 2$ looks like:

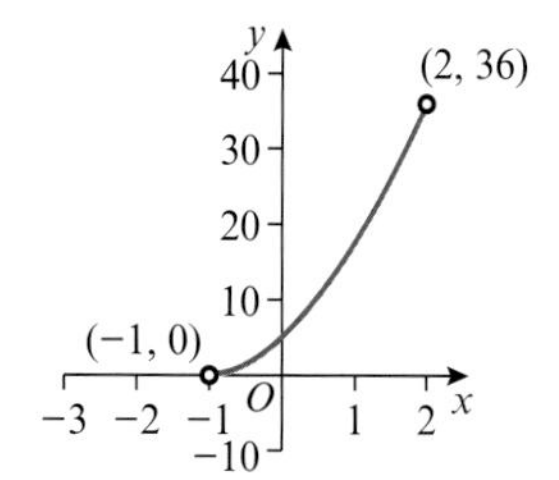

This is a quadratic graph and the turning point is when $2x + 2 = 0$

$x = -1$

Hence the turning point is $(-1, 0)$

Substituting $x = 2$ into $gf(x) = (2x + 2)^2$ gives 36 (which is the maximum value of $gf(x)$)

The range of $gf(x)$ is $gf(x) \in \mathbb{R}, 0 < gf(x) < 36$

Exercise 1.4

1 **c** $|6 - 5x| = 2$

$6 - 5x = 2$ or $6 - 5x = -2$

$-5x = -4$ or $-5x = -8$

$x = \frac{4}{5}$ or $x = \frac{8}{5}$ [or as decimals 0.8 and 1.6]

CHECK: $|6 - 5(0.8)| = 2$ ✓ and $|6 - 5(1.6)| = 2$ ✓

Solution is: $x = 0.8$ or $x = 1.6$

i $|2x - 5| = x$

$2x - 5 = x$ or $2x - 5 = -x$

$x = 5$ or $3x = 5$ so $x = \frac{5}{3}$

CHECK: $|2(5) - 5| = 5$ ✓

and $\left|2\left(\frac{5}{3}\right) - 5\right| = \frac{5}{3}$ ✓

Solution is: $x = 5$ or $x = \frac{5}{3}$

2 **c** $\left|1 + \frac{x + 12}{x + 4}\right| = 3$

$1 + \frac{x + 12}{x + 4} = 3$ or $1 + \frac{x + 12}{x + 4} = -3$

$\frac{x + 12}{x + 4} = 2$ or $\frac{x + 12}{x + 4} = -4$

$x + 12 = 2x + 8$ or $x + 12 = -4x - 16$

$x = 4$ or $5x = -28$

$x = -\frac{28}{5}$

or $x = -5.6$

CHECK: $\left|1 + \frac{4+12}{4+4}\right| = 3$ ✓

or

$$\left|1 + \frac{-5.6+12}{-5.6+4}\right| = \left|1 + \frac{6.4}{-1.6}\right| = \left|1 + \frac{\frac{32}{5}}{\frac{-8}{5}}\right|$$

$$= |1 - 4| = 3 \checkmark$$

Solution is: $x = 4$ or $x = -5.6$

f $9 - |1 - x| = 2x$

$(9 - 2x) = |1 - x|$

$(9 - 2x) = 1 - x$ or $-(9 - 2x) = 1 - x$

$x = 8$ or $-9 + 2x = 1 - x$

$3x = 10$ so $x = \frac{10}{3}$

CHECK:

$9 - |1 - 8| = 2(8)$ and $9 - \left|1 - \frac{10}{3}\right| = 2\left(\frac{10}{3}\right)$

$9 - 7 = 16$ ✗ and $9 - \frac{7}{3} = \frac{20}{3}$ ✓

Solution is: $x = \frac{10}{3}$

3 c $|4 - x^2| = 2 - x$

$4 - x^2 = 2 - x$ or $4 - x^2 = -(2 - x)$

$x^2 - x - 2 = 0$ or $4 - x^2 = -2 + x$

$(x - 2)(x + 1) = 0$ or $x^2 + x - 6 = 0$

$x = 2$ or $x = -1$ or $(x + 3)(x - 2) = 0$

$x = -3$ or $x = 2$

CHECK: If $x = 2$ and CHECK: If $x = -1$

$|4 - 2^2| = 2 - 2$ and $4 - (-1)^2| = 2 - -1$

$0 = 0$ ✓ $3 = 3$ ✓

CHECK: If $x = -3$

$|4 - (-3)^2| = 2 - -3$

$5 = 5$ ✓

Solution is: $x = -3$, $x = -1$ and $x = 2$

g $|2x^2 + 1| = 3x$

$2x^2 + 1 = 3x$ or $2x^2 + 1 = -3x$

$2x^2 - 3x + 1 = 0$ or $2x^2 + 3x + 1 = 0$

$(2x - 1)(x - 1) = 0$ or $(2x + 1)(x + 1) = 0$

$x = 0.5$ or $x = 1$ or $x = -0.5$ or $x = -1$

CHECK:

$|2(0.5)^2 + 1| = 3(0.5)$ and $|2(1)^2 + 1| = 3(1)$

$1.5 = 1.5$ ✓ and $3 = 3$ ✓

CHECK:

$|2(-0.5)^2 + 1| = 3(-0.5)$ and $|2(-1)^2 + 1| = 3(-1)$

$1.5 = -1.5$ ✗ and $3 = -3$ ✗

Solution is: $x = 0.5$ and $x = 1$

4 a $y = x + 4$

$y = |x^2 - 16|$

$|x^2 - 16| = x + 4$

$x^2 - 16 = x + 4$ or $x^2 - 16 = -x - 4$

$x^2 - x - 20 = 0$ or $x^2 + x - 12 = 0$

$(x - 5)(x + 4) = 0$ or $(x + 4)(x - 3) = 0$

$x = 5$ or $x = -4$ or $x = -4$ or $x = 3$

If $x = 5$, substituting into $y = x + 4$

$y = 5 + 4$

$y = 9$

or substituting into $y = |x^2 - 16|$

$y = |5^2 - 16|$

$y = 9$ ✓

If $x = -4$, substituting into $y = x + 4$

$y = -4 + 4$

$y = 0$

or substituting into $y = |x^2 - 16|$

$y = |(-4)^2 - 16|$

$y = 0$ ✓

If $x = 3$, substituting into $y = x + 4$

$y = 3 + 4$

$y = 7$

or substituting into $y = |x^2 - 16|$

$y = |3^2 - 16|$

$y = 7$ ✓

Solutions are: $x = 3$, $y = 7$ and $x = -4$, $y = 0$ and $x = 5$, $y = 9$

b $y = x$

$y = |3x - 2x^2|$

$3x - 2x^2 = x$ or $3x - 2x^2 = -x$

$2x^2 - 2x = 0$ or $2x^2 - 4x = 0$

$2x(x - 1) = 0$ or $2x(x - 2) = 0$

$x = 0$ or $x = 1$ or $x = 0$ or $x = 2$

If $x = 0$, substituting into $y = x$

$y = 0$

or substituting into $y = |3x - 2x^2|$

$y = |3(0) - 2(0)^2|$

$y = 0$ ✓

If $x = 1$, substituting into $y = x$

$y = 1$

or substituting into $y = |3x - 2x^2|$

$y = |3(1) - 2(1)^2|$

$y = 1$ ✓

If $x = 2$, substituting into $y = x$

$y = 2$

or substituting into $y = |3x - 2x^2|$

$y = |3(2) - 2(2)^2|$

$y = 2$ ✓

Solutions are: $x = 0$, $y = 0$ and $x = 1$, $y = 1$ and $x = 2$, $y = 2$

c $y = 3x$

$y = |2x^2 - 5|$

$2x^2 - 5 = 3x$ or $2x^2 - 5 = -3x$

$2x^2 - 3x - 5 = 0$ or $2x^2 + 3x - 5 = 0$

$(2x - 5)(x + 1) = 0$ or $(2x + 5)(x - 1) = 0$

$x = 2.5$ or $x = -1$ or $x = -2.5$ or $x = 1$

If $x = 2.5$, substituting into $y = 3x$

$y = 7.5$

or substituting into $y = |2x^2 - 5|$

$y = |2(2.5)^2 - 5|$

$y = 7.5$ ✓

If $x = -1$, substituting into $y = 3x$

$y = -3$

or substituting into $y = |2x^2 - 5|$

$y = |2(-1)^2 - 5|$

$y = 3$ ✗

If $x = -2.5$, substituting into $y = 3x$

$y = -7.5$

or substituting into $y = |2x^2 - 5|$

$y = |2(-2.5)^2 - 5|$

$y = 7.5$ ✗

If $x = 1$, substituting into $y = 3x$

$y = 3$

or substituting into $y = |2x^2 - 5|$

$y = |2(1)^2 - 5|$

$y = 3$ ✓

Solutions are: $x = 1$, $y = 3$ and $x = 2.5$, $y = 7.5$

Exercise 1.5

1 a

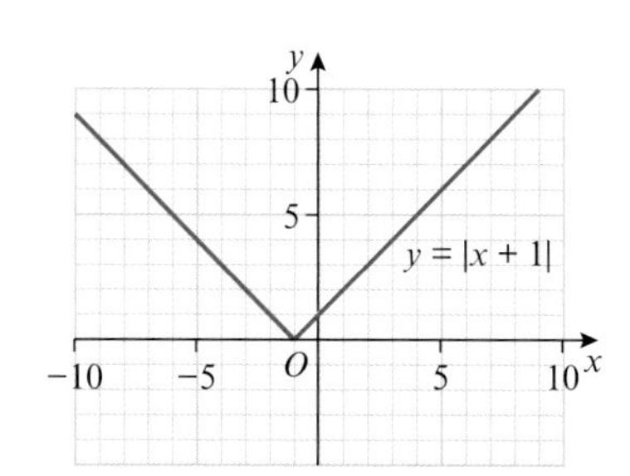

Sketch the graph $y = x + 1$

Reflect in the x-axis the part of the graph that is below the x-axis.

Intercepts at $(-1, 0)$ and $(0, 1)$

e Sketch the graph of $y = 10 - 2x$

Reflect in the x-axis the part of the graph that is below the x-axis.

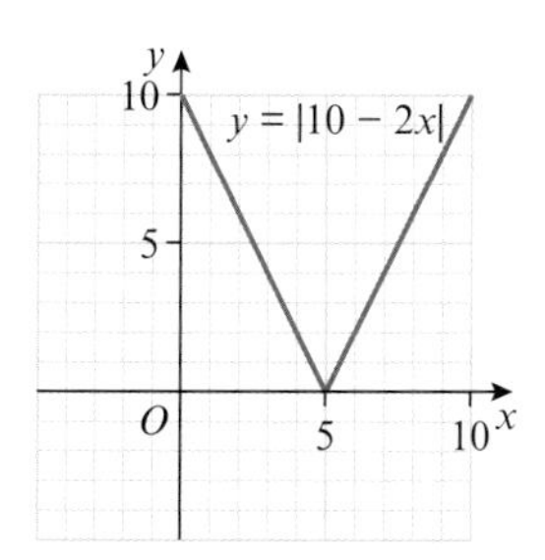

TIP

To sketch the graph of the modulus function $y = |f(x)|$

- Use dotted lines to draw the graph of $y = f(x)$
- Reflect any part of the graph that is below the x-axis in the x-axis
- Use a solid line to draw in the part of the graph that is above the x-axis.

2 a $y = |x - 2| + 3$

x	−2	−1	0	1	2	3	4
y	7	6	5	4	3	4	5

b

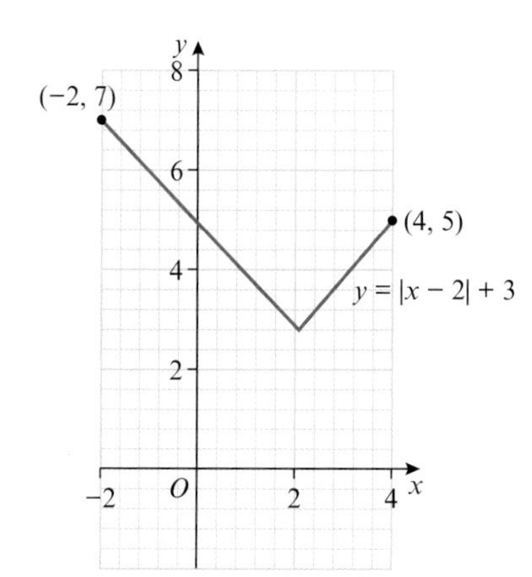

3 c

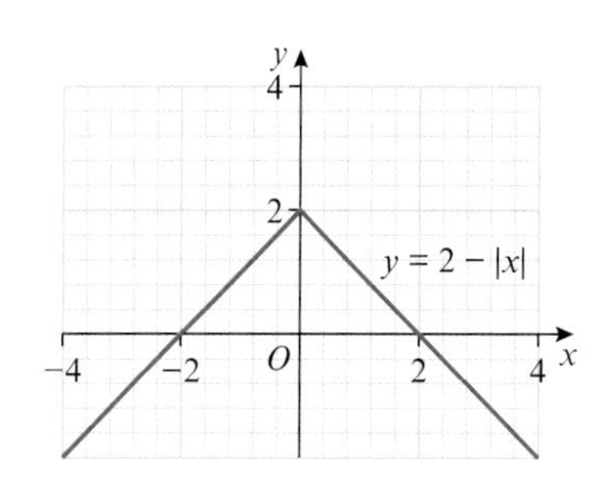

Draw the graph of $y = x$

Reflect in the x-axis the part of the graph that is below the x-axis. (This is the graph of $y = |x|$).

Reflect the graph in the x-axis. (This is the graph of $y = -|x|$).

Transform the graph $\begin{pmatrix} 0 \\ 2 \end{pmatrix}$

e

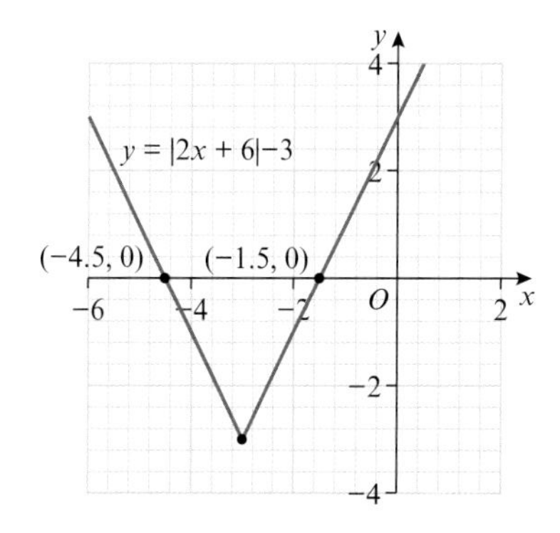

Draw the graph of $y = 2x + 6$

Reflect in the x-axis the part of the graph that is below the x-axis. (This is the graph of $y = |2x + 6|$)

Transform the graph $\begin{pmatrix} 0 \\ -3 \end{pmatrix}$

4 a $f: x \rightarrow 5 - 2x$

The graph of $y = 5 - 2x$ is a straight line with gradient −2 and y-intercept 5

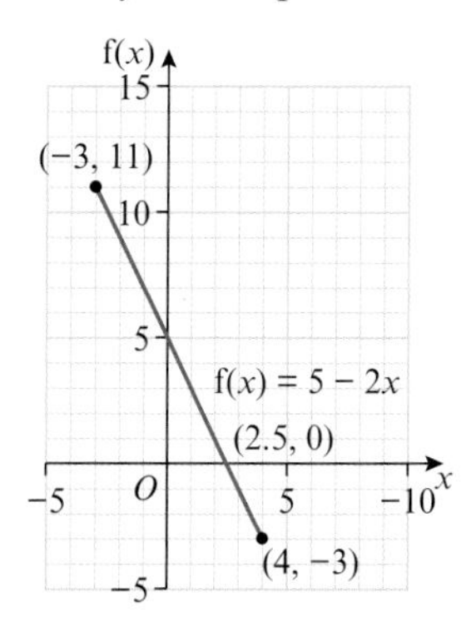

When $x = -3$, $y = 5 - 2(-3) = 11$

When $x = 4$, $y = 5 - 2(4) = -3$

The range of f is $-3 \leqslant \mathrm{f}(x) \leqslant 11$

b $\mathrm{g}: x \rightarrow |5 - 2x|$

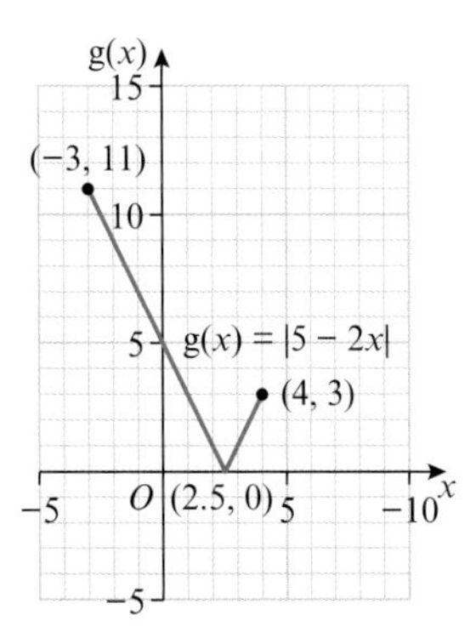

Draw the graph of $y = 5 - 2x$ in the domain $-3 \leqslant x \leqslant 4$

Reflect in the x-axis the part of the graph of $y = 5 - 2x$ that is below the x-axis. (This is the graph of $y = |5 - 2x|$).

The range of g is $0 \leqslant \mathrm{g}(x) \leqslant 11$

c $\mathrm{h}: x \rightarrow 5 - |2x|$

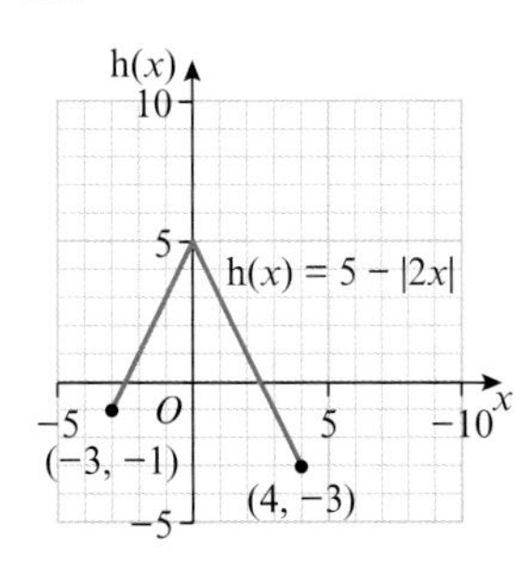

Draw the graph of $y = 2x$

Reflect the part of the graph that is below the x-axis in the x-axis. (This is the graph of $y = |2x|$).

Reflect this graph in the x-axis. (This is the graph of $y = -|2x|$).

Transform the graph $\begin{pmatrix} 0 \\ 5 \end{pmatrix}$

The range of h is $-3 \leqslant \mathrm{h}(x) \leqslant 5$

5

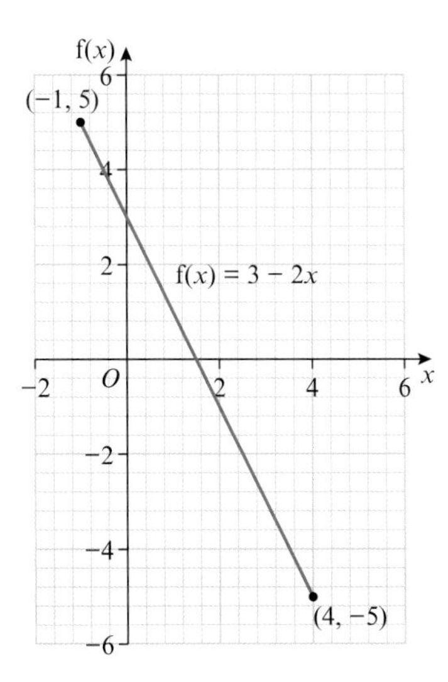

The range of f is $-5 \leqslant \mathrm{f}(x) \leqslant 5$

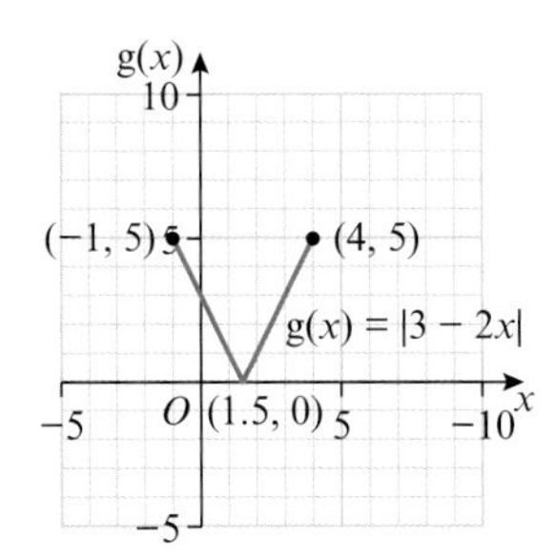

The range of g is $0 \leqslant \mathrm{g}(x) \leqslant 5$

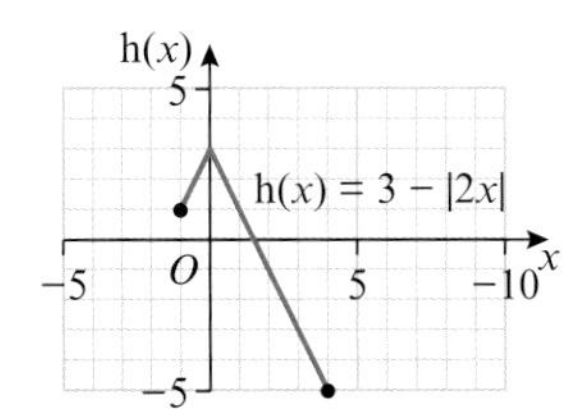

The range of h is $-5 \leqslant \mathrm{h}(x) \leqslant 3$

TIP

It may not be possible to read the intersection point(s) accurately if the solution(s) are not integer values. In this case it may be necessary to use algebra to solve the equations.

6 a Draw the graph of $y = 2x + 4$ in the domain $-6 < x < 2$

Reflect the part of the graph that is below the x-axis in the x-axis. (This is the graph $y = |2x + 4|$).

b

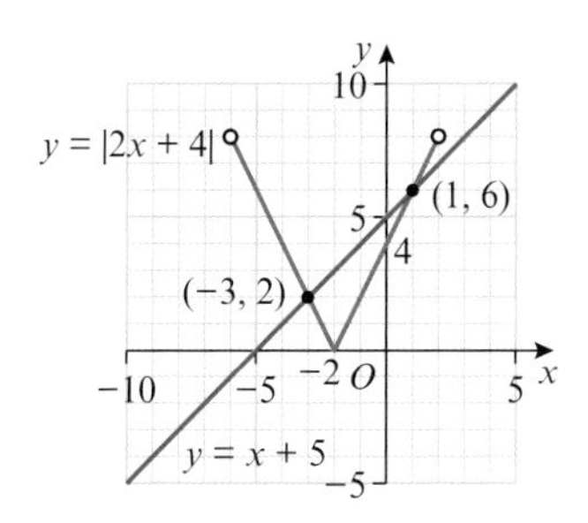

c The equation can be solved by looking at where the two graphs intersect.

$x = -3$ and $x = 1$

7 **a** Draw the graph of $y = 2x - 6$ in the domain $-1 \leqslant x \leqslant 8$

Reflect the part of the graph that is below the x-axis in the x-axis. (This is the graph $y = |2x - 6|$).

Transform the graph by $\begin{pmatrix} 0 \\ -3 \end{pmatrix}$

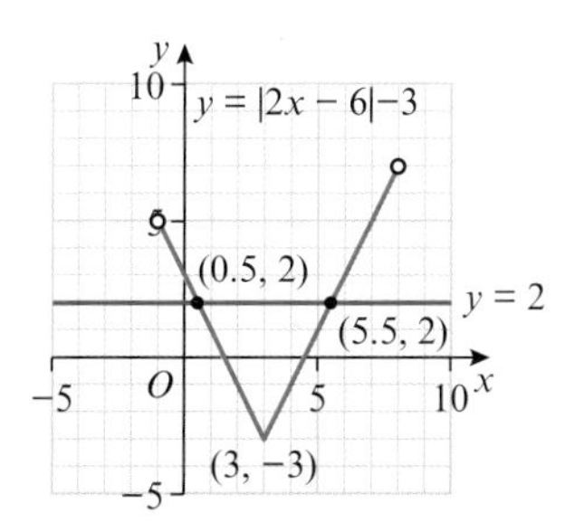

b The range of f is $-3 \leqslant f(x) \leqslant 7$

c The equation can be solved by looking at where the two graphs intersect.

$x = 0.5$ and $x = 5.5$

8 **a** Draw the graph of $y = 3x - 4$ in the domain $-2 < x < 5$

Reflect the part of the graph that is below the x-axis in the x-axis. (This is the graph $y = |3x - 4|$).

b

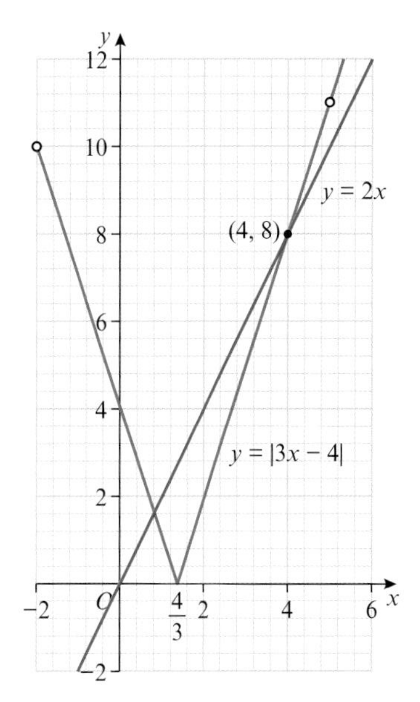

c The equation can be solved by looking at where the two graphs intersect.

$x = \frac{4}{5}$ and $x = 4$

9 **CHALLENGE QUESTION**

a A table of values would be the quickest way to draw the graph.

x	−10	−5	−2	0	2	5	10
y	20	10	4	4	4	10	20

b

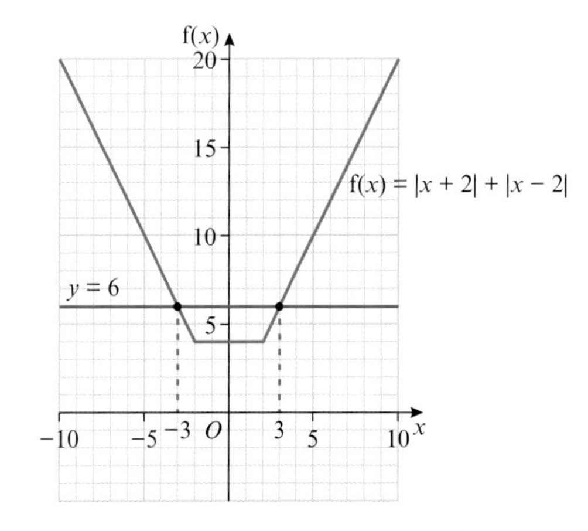

The equation can be solved by looking at where the two graphs intersect.

$x = -3$ and $x = 3$

Exercise 1.6

1 $f(x) = (x + 5)^2 - 7$ for $x > -5$

Step 1

Write the function as $y =$ $\quad y = (x + 5)^2 - 7$

Step 2

Interchange the x and y variables. $\quad x = (y + 5)^2 - 7$

Step 3

Rearrange to make y the subject.

$$x + 7 = (y + 5)^2$$
$$\sqrt{x + 7} = y + 5$$
$$y = \sqrt{x + 7} - 5$$

Therefore $f^{-1}(x) = \sqrt{x + 7} - 5$

2 $f(x) = \dfrac{6}{x + 2}$ for $x > 0$

Step 1

Write the function as $y =$ $\quad y = \dfrac{6}{x + 2}$

Step 2

Interchange the x and y variables. $\quad x = \dfrac{6}{y + 2}$

Step 3

Rearrange to make y the subject.

$$x(y + 2) = 6$$
$$xy + 2x = 6$$
$$xy = 6 - 2x$$
$$y = \frac{6 - 2x}{x}$$

Therefore $f^{-1}(x) = \dfrac{6 - 2x}{x}$

3 $f(x) = (2x - 3)^2 + 1$ for $x \geqslant 1.5$

Step 1

Write the function as $y =$ $\quad y = (2x - 3)^2 + 1$

Step 2

Interchange the x and y variables. $\quad x = (2y - 3)^2 + 1$

Step 3

Rearrange to make y the subject.

$$x - 1 = (2y - 3)^2$$
$$\sqrt{x - 1} = 2y - 3$$
$$2y = 3 + \sqrt{x - 1}$$
$$y = \frac{3 + \sqrt{x - 1}}{2}$$

Therefore $f^{-1}(x) = \dfrac{3 + \sqrt{x - 1}}{2}$

4 $f(x) = 8 - \sqrt{x - 3}$ for $x \geqslant 3$

Step 1

Write the function as $y =$ $\quad y = 8 - \sqrt{x - 3}$

Step 2

Interchange the x and y variables. $\quad x = 8 - \sqrt{y - 3}$

Step 3

Rearrange to make y the subject.

$$\sqrt{y - 3} = 8 - x$$
$$y - 3 = (8 - x)^2$$
$$y = (8 - x)^2 + 3$$

Therefore $f^{-1}(x) = (8 - x)^2 + 3$

5 $f: x \mapsto 5x - 3$ for $x > 0$

Step 1

Write the function as $y =$ $\quad y = 5x - 3$

Step 2

Interchange the x and y variables. $\quad x = 5y - 3$

Step 3

Rearrange to make y the subject.

$$5y = x + 3$$
$$y = \frac{x + 3}{5}$$

Therefore $f^{-1}(x) = \dfrac{x + 3}{5}$

$g(x) = \dfrac{7}{2 - x}$ for $x \neq 2$

Step 1

Write the function as $y =$ $\quad y = \dfrac{7}{2 - x}$

Step 2

Interchange the x and y variables. $\quad x = \dfrac{7}{2 - y}$

Step 3

Rearrange to make y the subject.

$$x(2 - y) = 7$$
$$2x - xy = 7$$
$$xy = 2x - 7$$
$$y = \frac{2x - 7}{x}$$

Therefore $g^{-1}(x) = \frac{2x - 7}{x}$

6 $f : x \to (x + 2)^2 - 5$ for $x > -2$

a **Step 1**

Write the function as $y =$ $\quad y = (x + 2)^2 - 5$

Step 2

Interchange the x and y variables. $x = (y + 2)^2 - 5$

Step 3

Rearrange to make y the subject.

$$x + 5 = (y + 2)^2$$
$$\sqrt{x + 5} = y + 2$$
$$y = \sqrt{x + 5} - 2$$

Therefore $f^{-1}(x) = \sqrt{x + 5} - 2$

b $\sqrt{x + 5} - 2 = 3$

$\sqrt{x + 5} = 5$ $\quad$ square both sides

$x + 5 = 25$

$x = 20$

7 a $f(x) = (x - 4)^2 + 5$ for $x > 4$

Step 1

Write the function as $y =$ $\quad y = (x - 4)^2 + 5$

Step 2

Interchange the x and y variables. $x = (y - 4)^2 + 5$

Step 3

Rearrange to make y the subject.

$$x - 5 = (y - 4)^2$$
$$\sqrt{x - 5} = y - 4$$
$$y = 4 + \sqrt{x - 5}$$

Therefore $f^{-1}(x) = 4 + \sqrt{x - 5}$

b $f^{-1}(x) = f(0)$

$4 + \sqrt{x - 5} = (0 - 4)^2 + 5$

$\sqrt{x - 5} = 17$

$x - 5 = 289$

$x = 294$

8 a $g(x) = \frac{2x + 3}{x - 1}$ for $x > 1$

Step 1

Write the function as $y =$ $\quad y = \frac{2x + 3}{x - 1}$

Step 2

Interchange the x and y variables. $\quad x = \frac{2y + 3}{y - 1}$

Step 3

Rearrange to make y the subject.

$$x(y - 1) = 2y + 3$$
$$xy - x = 2y + 3$$
$$xy - 2y = x + 3$$
$$y(x - 2) = x + 3$$
$$y = \frac{x + 3}{x - 2}$$

Therefore $g^{-1}(x) = \frac{x + 3}{x - 2}$

b $\frac{x + 3}{x - 2} = 5$

$x + 3 = 5x - 10$

$4x = 13$

$x = \frac{13}{4}$

9 $f(x) = \frac{x}{2} + 2$ for $x \in \mathbb{R}$ $\quad g(x) = x^2 - 2x$ for $x \in \mathbb{R}$

a Find $f^{-1}(x)$

Step 1

Write the function as $y =$ $\quad y = \frac{x}{2} + 2$

Step 2

Interchange the x and y variables. $\quad x = \frac{y}{2} + 2$

Step 3

Rearrange to make y the subject. $\quad 2x = y + 4$

$$y = 2x - 4$$

Therefore $f^{-1}(x) = 2x - 4 = 2(x - 2)$

b First find $fg(x)$

$fg(x)$ $\quad$ means g acts on x first and $g(x) = x^2 - 2x$

$= f(x^2 - 2x)$ $\quad$ f is the function 'divide by 2 then add 2'

$fg(x) = \frac{x^2 - 2x}{2} + 2$

Solve $\frac{x^2 - 2x}{2} + 2 = 2x - 4$ multiply each term by 2

$x^2 - 2x + 4 = 4x - 8$ rearrange

$x^2 - 6x + 12 = 0$

Solve using the formula:

$$x = \frac{-(-6) \pm \sqrt{(-6)^2 - 4(1)(12)}}{2(1)}$$

$$x = \frac{6 \pm \sqrt{-12}}{2}$$

There are no solutions to $fg(x) = f^{-1}(x)$

10 $f(x) = x^2 + 2$ for $x \in \mathbb{R}$ $g(x) = 2x + 3$ for $x \in \mathbb{R}$

$gf(x)$ f acts on x first and $f(x) = x^2 + 2$

$gf(x) = g(x^2 + 2)$ g is the function 'multiply by 2 then add 3'

$gf(x) = 2(x^2 + 2) + 3$

$gf(x) = 2x^2 + 7$

Find $g^{-1}(x)$

Step 1

Write the function as $y =$ $y = 2x + 3$

Step 2

Interchange the x and y variables. $x = 2y + 3$

Step 3

Rearrange to make y the subject. $y = \frac{x - 3}{2}$

$g^{-1}(x) = \frac{x - 3}{2}$

$g^{-1}(17) = \frac{17 - 3}{2}$

$g^{-1}(17) = 7$

Solve $gf(x) = g^{-1}(17)$

$2x^2 + 7 = 7$

$2x^2 = 0$

$x = 0.$

11 Find $g^{-1}(x)$

Step 1

Write the function as $y =$ $y = \frac{x - 3}{2}$

Step 2

Interchange the x and y variables. $x = \frac{y - 3}{2}$

Step 3

Rearrange to make y the subject. $2x = y - 3$

$y = 2x + 3$

$g^{-1}(x) = 2x + 3$

Solve $f(x) = g^{-1}(x)$

$\frac{2x + 8}{x - 2} = 2x + 3$

$2x + 8 = (2x + 3)(x - 2)$ expand the brackets

$2x + 8 = 2x^2 - x - 6$ rearrange

$2x^2 - 3x - 14 = 0$ factorise

$(2x - 7)(x + 2) = 0$

$x = 3.5$ or $x = -2$

Solution is: $x = 3.5$ and $x = -2$

TIP

The reflection in the line $y = x$ swaps the range and domain of a function.

12 $f(x) = 3x - 24$ for $x \geqslant 0$. Write down the range of f^{-1}

The range of $f^{-1}(x)$ is the same as the domain of $f(x)$

Range of $f^{-1}(x)$ is $f^{-1}(x) \geqslant 0$

13 $f : x \mapsto x + 6$ for $x \geqslant 0$ $g : x \mapsto \sqrt{x}$ for $x > 0$

Express $x \mapsto x^2 - 6$ in terms of f and g

$f^{-1}(x) = x - 6$

Find $g^{-1}(x)$

Step 1

Write the function as $y =$ $y = \sqrt{x}$

Step 2

Interchange the x and y variables. $x = \sqrt{y}$

Step 3

Rearrange to make y the subject. $y = x^2$

$g^{-1}(x) = x^2$

Looking at $g^{-1}(x) = x^2$ and $f^{-1}(x) = x - 6$

Find $f^{-1}g^{-1}(x)$

$f^{-1}g^{-1}(x)$ means $g^{-1}(x)$ acts on x first and $g^{-1}(x) = x^2$

$= f^{-1}(x^2)$

$= x^2 - 6$

$f^{-1}g^{-1}(x) = x^2 - 6$

14 $f : x \mapsto 3 - 2x$ for $0 \leqslant x \leqslant 5$

$f(x)$ is a one-one function in the given domain so $f^{-1}(x)$ is a one-one function.

$g : x \mapsto |3 - 2x|$ for $0 \leqslant x \leqslant 5$

This is a many-one function so $g^{-1}(x)$ is a one-many mapping and therefore not a function.

$h : x \mapsto 3 - |2x|$ for $0 \leqslant x \leqslant 5$

This is a one-one function in the given domain so $h^{-1}(x)$ is a one-one function.

So f and h have an inverse.

15 a The domain of $f^{-1}(x)$ is the same as the range of $f(x)$

The range of x is $f(x) \geqslant 2$, so the domain of $f^{-1}(x)$ is $x \geqslant 2$

b The range of $g^{-1}(x)$ is the same as the domain of $g(x)$ i.e $x \geqslant 0$

So, $g^{-1}(x) \geqslant 0$

16 a Find $f^{-1}(x)$

Step 1

Write the function as $y =$ $\quad y = 3x - k$

Step 2

Interchange the x and y variables. $\quad x = 3y - k$

Step 3

Rearrange to make y the subject. $\quad 3y = x + k$

$$y = \frac{x + k}{3}$$

$$f^{-1}(x) = \frac{x + k}{3}$$

Find $g^{-1}(x)$

Step 1

Write the function as $y =$ $\quad y = \frac{5x - 14}{x + 1}$

Step 2

Interchange the x and y variables. $\quad x = \frac{5y - 14}{y + 1}$

Step 3

Rearrange to make y the subject.

$$x(y + 1) = 5y - 14$$

$$xy + x = 5y - 14$$

$$x + 14 = 5y - xy$$

$$y(5 - x) = x + 14$$

$$y = \frac{x + 14}{5 - x}$$

$$g^{-1}(x) = \frac{x + 14}{5 - x} \quad x \neq 5$$ (since you cannot divide by zero)

b So, $f^{-1}(5) = \frac{5 + k}{3} = 6$

Solve $\frac{5 + k}{3} = 6$

$$5 + k = 18$$

$$k = 13$$

c $g^{-1}g(x) = x$

Because the graphs of g and g^{-1} are reflections of each other in the line $y = x$. [This is true for all one-one functions and their inverse functions because $gg^{-1}(x) = g^{-1}g(x)$]

17 Find $f^{-1}(x)$ and $g^{-1}(x)$ first

$f^{-1}(x)$

Step 1

Write the function as $y =$ $\quad y = x^3$

Step 2

Interchange the x and y variables. $\quad x = y^3$

Step 3

Rearrange to make y the subject. $\quad y = \sqrt[3]{x}$

$f^{-1}(x) = \sqrt[3]{x}$ or $x^{\frac{1}{3}}$

$g^{-1}(x) = x + 8$

a $x \rightarrow (x - 8)^{\frac{1}{3}}$

Start with $g(x) = x - 8$ and substitute $g(x)$ into $f^{-1}(x) = x^{\frac{1}{3}}$

[i.e. let the range of $g(x)$ become the domain of $f^{-1}(x)$]

This is equivalent to $f^{-1}g(x)$

Answer $f^{-1}g$

b $x \mapsto x^3 + 8$

Start with $f(x) = x^3$ and substitute $f(x)$ into $g^{-1}(x) = x + 8$

[i.e let the range of $f(x)$ become the domain of $g^{-1}(x)$]

This is equivalent to $g^{-1}f(x)$

Answer $g^{-1}f$

c $x \mapsto x^{\frac{1}{3}} - 8$

Start with $f^{-1}(x) = x^{\frac{1}{3}}$ and substitute $f^{-1}(x)$ into $g(x) = x - 8$

[i.e let the range of $f^{-1}(x)$ become the domain of $g(x)$]

This is equivalent to $gf^{-1}(x)$

Answer gf^{-1}

d $x \mapsto (x + 8)^{\frac{1}{3}}$

Start with $g^{-1}(x) = x + 8$ and substitute $g^{-1}(x)$ into $f^{-1}(x) = x^{\frac{1}{3}}$

[i.e let the range of $g^{-1}(x)$ become the domain of $f^{-1}(x)$]

This is equivalent to $f^{-1}g^{-1}(x)$

Answer $f^{-1}g^{-1}$

Exercise 1.7

1 The graph of the inverse of the function is the reflection of the graph of f in the line $y = x$

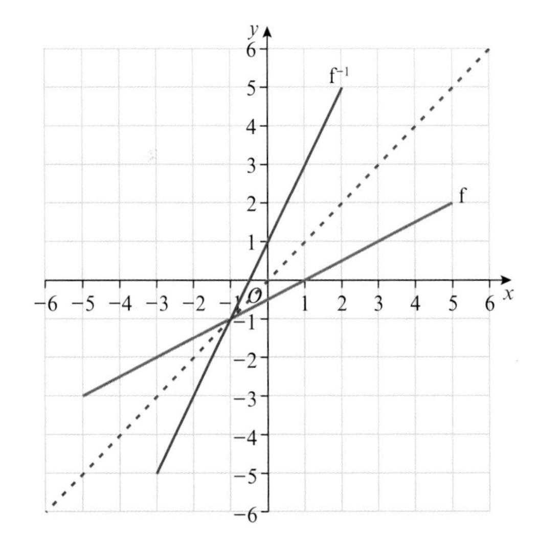

2 The graph of the inverse of the function is the reflection of the graph of g, in the line $y = x$

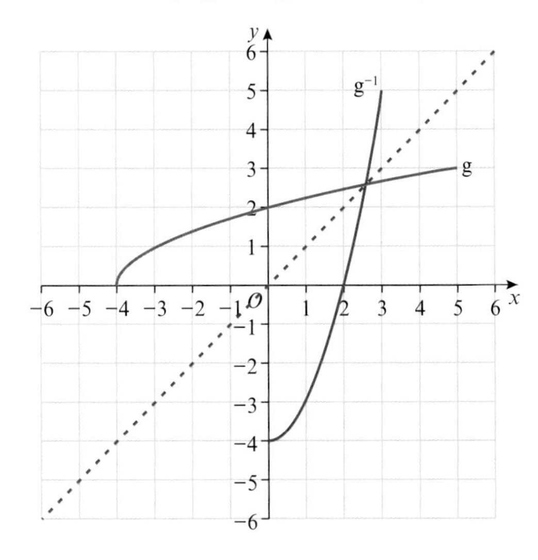

3 $f(x) = x^2 + 3, x \geqslant 0$

The graph of the inverse of the function is the reflection of f in the line $y = x$

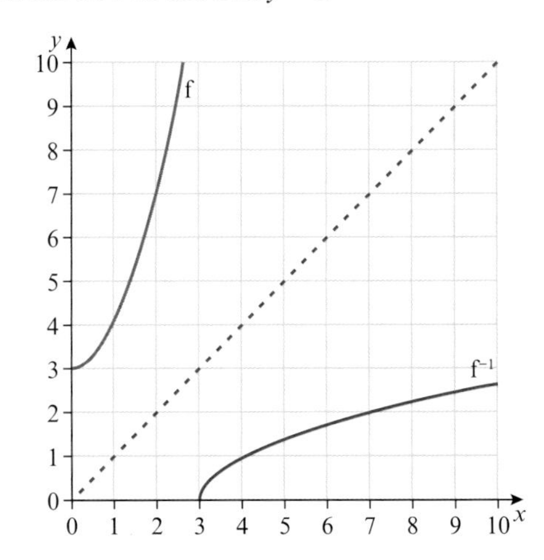

4 The graph of the inverse of the function is the reflection of g in the line $y = x$

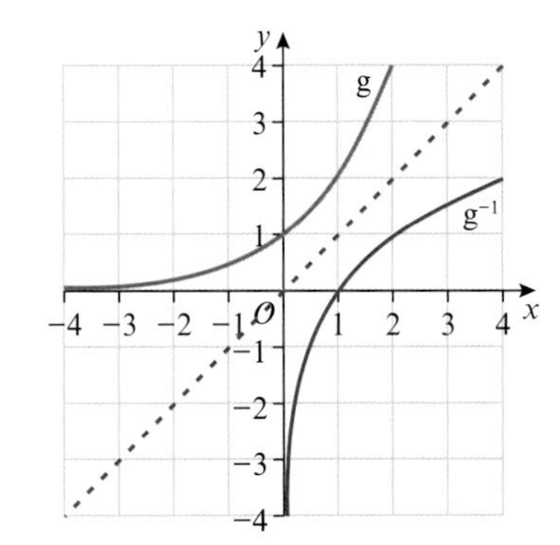

5 The graph of the inverse of the function is the reflection of g in the line $y = x$

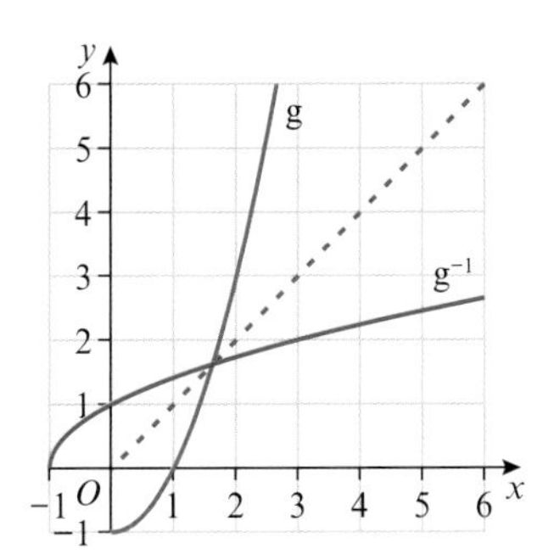

6 The graph of the inverse of the function is the reflection of f in the line $y = x$

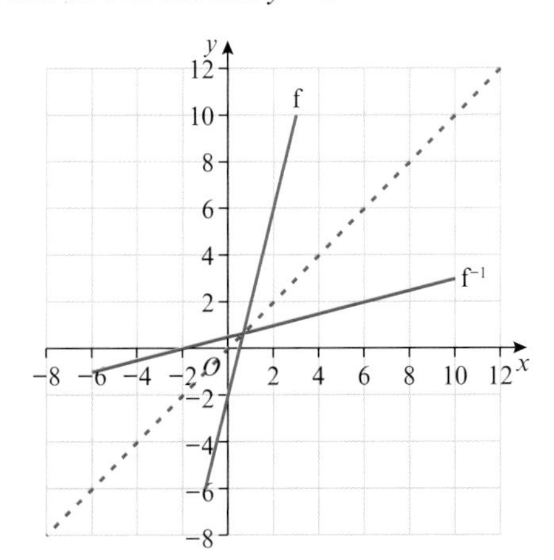

7 a Function f is a one-one function in the given domain. Its inverse will also be a one-one function.

b Find f^{-1}

Step 1

Write the function as $y =$ $\quad y = 3 - (x + 1)^2$

Step 2

Interchange the x and y variables. $x = 3 - (y + 1)^2$

Step 3

Rearrange to make y the subject. $(y + 1)^2 = 3 - x$

$y + 1 = \sqrt{3 - x}$

$y = \sqrt{3 - x} - 1$

Therefore $f^{-1}(x) = \sqrt{3 - x} - 1$

c The graph of the inverse of the function is the reflection of f in the line $y = x$

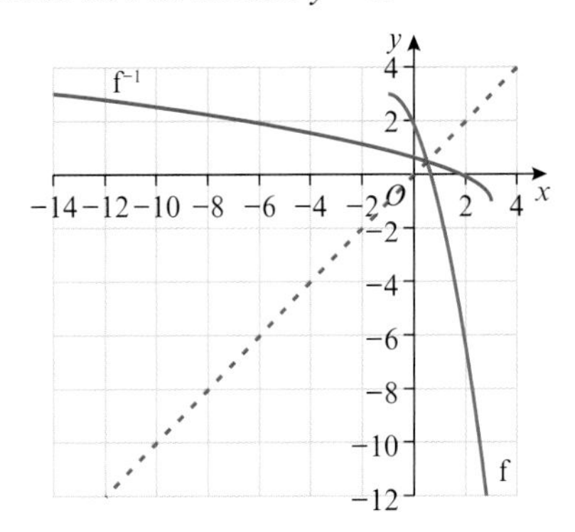

8 **CHALLENGE QUESTION**

$f : x \mapsto \dfrac{2x + 7}{x - 2}$ for $x \neq 2$

Find $f^{-1}(x)$.

a **Step 1**

Write the function as $y =$ $\quad y = \dfrac{2x + 7}{x - 2}$

Step 2

Interchange the x and y variables. $\quad x = \dfrac{2y + 7}{y - 2}$

Step 3

Rearrange to make y the subject.

$x(y - 2) = 2y + 7$

$xy - 2x = 2y + 7$

$xy - 2y = 2x + 7$

$y(x - 2) = 2x + 7$

$y = \dfrac{2x + 7}{x - 2}$

$f^{-1}(x) = \dfrac{2x + 7}{x - 2}$

b $f(x) = f^{-1}(x)$ so $f(x)$ is a self-inverse function.

The curve is symmetrical about the line $y = x$

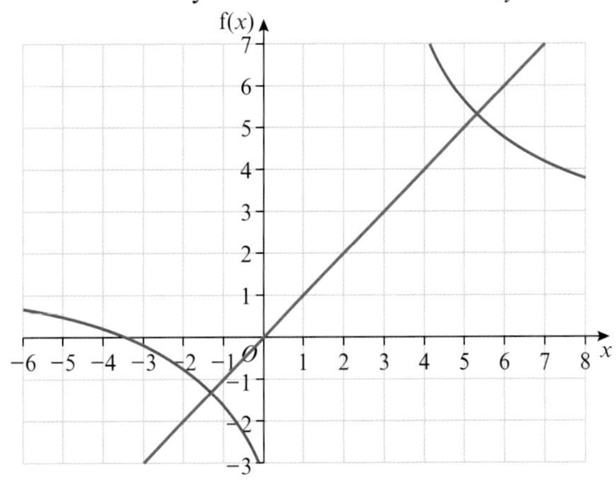

Chapter 2: Simultaneous equations and quadratics

Exercise 2.1

2 $y = x - 6$ (1)

$x^2 + xy = 8$ (2)

Substitute for y in (2)

$x^2 + x(x - 6) = 8$ expand brackets

$x^2 + x^2 - 6x = 8$ simplify and rearrange

$2x^2 - 6x - 8 = 0$ divide both sides by 2

$x^2 - 3x - 4 = 0$ factorise

$(x - 4)(x + 1) = 0$

$x = 4$ or $x = -1$

TIP

Always substitute back into the linear equation not the quadratic.

Substituting $x = 4$ into (1) gives $y = -2$

Substituting $x = -1$ into (1) gives $y = -7$

The solutions are: $x = 4,\ y = -2$ and $x = -1,\ y = -7$

3 $y = x - 1$ (1)

$x^2 + y^2 = 25$ (2)

Substitute for y in (2)

$x^2 + (x - 1)^2 = 25$ expand brackets

$x^2 + x^2 - 2x + 1 = 25$ simplify and rearrange

$2x^2 - 2x - 24 = 0$ divide both sides by 2

$x^2 - x - 12 = 0$ factorise

$(x - 4)(x + 3) = 0$

$x = 4$ or $x = -3$

Substituting $x = 4$ into (1) gives $y = 3$

Substituting $x = -3$ into (1) gives $y = -4$

The solutions are: $x = 4,\ y = 3$ and $x = -3,\ y = -4$

6 $3y = 4x - 5$ (1)

$x^2 + 3xy = 10$ (2)

From (1) $y = \frac{4x - 5}{3}$

Substitute for y in (2):

$x^2 + 3x\left(\frac{4x - 5}{3}\right) = 10$ expand brackets

$x^2 + 4x^2 - 5x = 10$ simplify and rearrange

$5x^2 - 5x - 10 = 0$ divide both sides by 5

$x^2 - x - 2 = 0$ factorise

$(x - 2)(x + 1) = 0$

$x = 2$ or $x = -1$

Substituting $x = 2$ into (1) gives $y = 1$

Substituting $x = -1$ into (1) gives $y = -3$

The solutions are: $x = 2,\ y = 1$ and $x = -1,\ y = -3$

8 $x - y = 2$ (1)

$2x^2 - 3y^2 = 15$ (2)

From (1) $x = 2 + y$

Substitute for x in (2)

$2(2 + y)^2 - 3y^2 = 15$ expand brackets

$8 + 8y + 2y^2 - 3y^2 = 15$ simplify and rearrange

$y^2 - 8y + 7 = 0$ factorise

$(y - 7)(y - 1) = 0$

$y = 7$ or $y = 1$

Substituting $y = 7$ into (1) gives $x = 9$

Substituting $y = 1$ into (1) gives $x = 3$

The solutions are: $x = 3,\ y = 1$ and $x = 9,\ y = 7$

12 $y^2 = 4x$ (1)

$2x + y = 4$ (2)

TIP

Avoid using square roots when solving simultaneous equations.

From (2) $y = 4 - 2x$

Substitute for y in (1)

$(4 - 2x)^2 = 4x$ expand brackets

$16 - 16x + 4x^2 = 4x$ simplify and rearrange

$4x^2 - 20x + 16 = 0$ divide both sides by 4

$x^2 - 5x + 4 = 0$ factorise

$(x - 1)(x - 4) = 0$

$x = 1$ or $x = 4$

Substituting $x = 1$ into (2) gives $y = 2$

Substituting $x = 4$ into (2) gives $y = -4$

The solutions are: $x = 1$, $y = 2$ and $x = 4$, $y = -4$

16 $x - 2y = 1$ (1)

$4y^2 - 3x^2 = 1$ (2)

From (1) $x = 1 + 2y$

Substitute for x in (2)

$4y^2 - 3(1 + 2y)^2 = 1$ expand brackets (be careful with the signs)

$4y^2 - 3 - 12y - 12y^2 = 1$ simplify and rearrange

$8y^2 + 12y + 4 = 0$ divide both sides by 4

$2y^2 + 3y + 1 = 0$ factorise

$(2y + 1)(y + 1) = 0$

$y = -0.5$ or $y = -1$

Substituting $y = -0.5$ into (1) gives $x = 0$

Substituting $y = -1$ into (1) gives $x = -1$

The solutions are: $x = -1$, $y = -1$ and $x = 0$, $y = -0.5$

18 $xy = 12$ (1)

$(x - 1)(y + 2) = 15$ (2)

From (1) $y = \frac{12}{x}$

Substitute for y in (2):

$(x - 1)\left(\frac{12}{x} + 2\right) = 15$ expand brackets

$12 + 2x - \frac{12}{x} - 2 = 15$ multiply both sides by x

$12x + 2x^2 - 12 - 2x = 15x$ simplify and rearrange

$2x^2 - 5x - 12 = 0$ factorise

$(2x + 3)(x - 4) = 0$

$x = -1.5$ or $x = 4$

Substituting $x = -1.5$ into (1) gives $y = -8$

Substituting $x = 4$ into (1) gives $y = 3$

The solutions are: $x = -1.5$, $y = -8$ and $x = 4$, $y = 3$

19 $y = 1 - 2x$ (1)

$x^2 + y^2 = 2$ (2)

Substitute for y in (2):

$x^2 + (1 - 2x)^2 = 2$ expand brackets

$x^2 - 4x + 4x^2 + 1 = 2$ simplify and rearrange

$5x^2 - 4x - 1 = 0$ factorise

$(5x + 1)(x - 1) = 0$

$x = -0.2$ or $x = 1$

Substituting $x = -0.2$ into (1) gives $y = 1.4$

Substituting $x = 1$ into (1) gives $y = -1$

The coordinates are: $(-0.2, 1.4)$ and $(1, -1)$

20 **a** $x + y = 11$ (1)

$xy = 21.25$ (2)

b From (1) $y = 11 - x$

Substitute for y in (2):

$x(11 - x) = 21.25$ expand brackets

$11x - x^2 = 21.25$ multiply both sides by 4

$44x - 4x^2 = 85$ simplify and rearrange

$4x^2 - 44x + 85 = 0$ factorise

$(2x - 5)(2x - 17) = 0$

$x = 2.5$ or $x = 8.5$

Substituting $x = 2.5$ into (1) gives $y = 8.5$

Substituting $x = 8.5$ into (1) gives $y = 2.5$

The possible values of x and y are: $x = 2.5$, $y = 8.5$ and $x = 8.5$, $y = 2.5$

21 Let the lengths of the sides of the squares be x and y.

$x^2 + y^2 = 818$ (1) represents the sum of the areas of both squares

$4x + 4y = 160$ (2) represents the sum of the perimeters of both squares

From (2) $x + y = 40$,

So, $x = 40 - y$

Substitute for x in (1):

$(40 - y)^2 + y^2 = 818$ expand brackets

$1600 - 80y + y^2 + y^2 = 818$ simplify and rearrange

$2y^2 - 80y + 782 = 0$ dividing by 2 gives

$y^2 - 40y + 391 = 0$ factorise

$(y - 23)(y - 17) = 0$

$y = 23$ or $y = 17$

Substituting $y = 23$ into (2) gives $x = 17$

Substituting $y = 17$ into (2) gives $x = 23$

The lengths of the sides of the squares are 17 cm and 23 cm.

22 Find the points of intersection (A and B) of the line and the curve.

$y = 2 - 2x$ (1)

$3x^2 - y^2 = 3$ (2)

Substitute for y in (2):

$3x^2 - (2 - 2x)^2 = 3$ expand brackets

$3x^2 - 4 + 8x - 4x^2 = 3$ simplify and rearrange

$x^2 - 8x + 7 = 0$ factorise

$(x - 1)(x - 7) = 0$

$x = 1$ or $x = 7$

Substituting $x = 1$ into (1) gives $y = 0$

Substituting $x = 7$ into (1) gives $y = -12$

The coordinates of A and B are $(1, 0)$ and $(7, -12)$ (or vice-versa)

The length of the line AB can be found using Pythagoras'

$AB = \sqrt{(1 - 7)^2 + (0 - -12)^2}$

$AB = \sqrt{36 + 144}$ or $\sqrt{180}$ or 13.4164…

$AB = 6\sqrt{5}$ or 13.4 correct to 3 significant figures.

23 Find the points of intersection (A and B) of the line and the curve.

$2x + 5y = 1$ (1)

$x^2 + 5xy - 4y^2 + 10 = 0$ (2)

From (1) $x = \dfrac{1 - 5y}{2}$

Substitute for x in (2):

$\left(\dfrac{1 - 5y}{2}\right)^2 + 5\left(\dfrac{1 - 5y}{2}\right)y - 4y^2 + 10 = 0$ expand brackets

$\dfrac{1 - 10y + 25y^2}{4} + \dfrac{5y - 25y^2}{2} - 4y^2 + 10 = 0$ multiply both sides by 4

$1 - 10y + 25y^2 + 10y - 50y^2 - 16y^2 + 40 = 0$ simplify and rearrange

$41y^2 - 41 = 0$ factorise

$41(y^2 - 1) = 0$

$41(y - 1)(y + 1) = 0$

$y = 1$ or $y = -1$

Substituting $y = 1$ into (1) gives $x = -2$

Substituting $y = -1$ into (1) gives $x = 3$

The coordinates of A and B are $(-2, 1)$ and $(3, -1)$ (or vice-versa)

The midpoint of the line AB is at $\left(\left(\dfrac{-2 + 3}{2}\right), \left(\dfrac{1 + -1}{2}\right)\right)$ or $(0.5, 0)$

24 Find the points of intersection (A and B) of the line and the curve.

$y = x - 10$ (1)

$x^2 + y^2 + 4x + 6y - 40 = 0$ (2)

Substitute for y in (2):

$x^2 + (x - 10)^2 + 4x + 6(x - 10) - 40 = 0$ expand brackets

$x^2 + x^2 - 20x + 100 + 4x + 6x - 60 - 40 = 0$ simplify and rearrange

$2x^2 - 10x = 0$ factorise

$2x(x - 5) = 0$

$x = 0$ or $x = 5$

Substituting $x = 0$ into (1) gives $y = -10$

Substituting $x = 5$ into (1) gives $y = -5$

The coordinates of A and B are $(0, -10)$ and $(5, -5)$ (or vice-versa)

The length of the line AB can be found using Pythagoras'

$AB = \sqrt{(0 - 5)^2 + (-10 - -5)^2}$

$AB = \sqrt{25 + 25}$ or $5\sqrt{2}$ or 7.0710…

$AB = 5\sqrt{2}$ or 7.07 correct to 3 significant figures.

25 Find the points of intersection (A and B) of the line and the curve.

$y = 2x - 2$ (1)

$x^2 - y = 5$ (2)

Substitute for y in (2):

$x^2 - (2x - 2) = 5$ expand brackets

$x^2 - 2x + 2 = 5$ simplify and rearrange

$x^2 - 2x - 3 = 0$ factorise

$(x + 1)(x - 3) = 0$

$x = -1$ or $x = 3$

Substituting $x = -1$ into (1) gives $y = -4$

Substituting $x = 3$ into (1) gives $y = 4$

The coordinates of A are $(-1, -4)$ and B are $(3, 4)$

From the sketch:

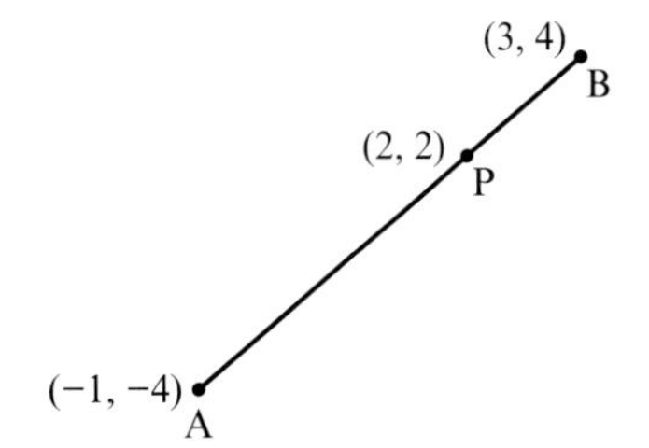

The x-coordinate of P is $\left(\frac{3 - -1}{4}\right) \times 3 + -1 = 2$

The y-coordinate of P is $\left(\frac{4 - -4}{4}\right) \times 3 + -4 = 2$

So P is at $(2, 2)$

26 Find the points of intersection (A and B) of the line and the curve.

$x - 2y = 2$ (1)

$x + y^2 = 10$ (2)

From (1) $x = 2 + 2y$

Substitute for x in (2):

$2 + 2y + y^2 = 10$ simplify and rearrange

$y^2 + 2y - 8 = 0$ factorise

$(y + 4)(y - 2) = 0$

$y = -4$ or $y = 2$

Substituting $y = -4$ into (1) gives $x = -6$

Substituting $y = 2$ into (1) gives $x = 6$

The coordinates of A and B are $(-6, -4)$ and $(6, 2)$ (or vice-versa)

The midpoint of the line AB is at

$\left(\left(\frac{-6 + 6}{2}\right), \left(\frac{-4 + 2}{2}\right)\right)$ or $(0, -1)$

The gradient of the line AB can be found using the formula $\frac{y_2 - y_1}{x_2 - x_1} = \frac{2 - -4}{6 - -6} = \frac{1}{2}$

The gradient of a line that is perpendicular to AB is -2

The equation of any straight line is $y = mx + c$ (where m is the gradient and c is the y-intercept).

The perpendicular bisector of AB has gradient -2 and passes through $x = 0$ and $y = -1$

So, substituting:

$-1 = -2 \times 0 + c$

$c = -1$

The equation of the perpendicular bisector is $y = -2x - 1$

Exercise 2.2

1 a $y = x^2 - 5x - 6$

When $x = 0$, $y = -6$

When $y = 0$,

$x^2 - 5x - 6 = 0$

$(x - 6)(x + 1) = 0$

$x = 6$ or $x = -1$

Axes crossing points are: $(0, -6)$, $(6,0)$ and $(-1, 0)$.

The line of symmetry cuts the x-axis midway between $(6, 0)$ and $(-1, 0)$

So, the line of symmetry is $x = 2.5$

When $x = 2.5$, $y = 2.5^2 - 5(2.5) - 6$

$y = -12.25$

Minimum point $= (2.5, -12.25)$.

e $y = x^2 + 4x + 1$

When $x = 0$, $y = 1$

When $y = 0$,

$x^2 + 4x + 1 = 0$

Using the quadratic formula:

$$x = \frac{-4 \pm \sqrt{4^2 - 4(1)(1)}}{2(1)}$$

$x = -2 - \sqrt{3}$ or $x = -2 + \sqrt{3}$

Axes crossing points are: $(0, 1)$, $(-2 - \sqrt{3}, 0)$ and $(-2 + \sqrt{3}, 0)$.

The line of symmetry cuts the x-axis midway between $(-2 - \sqrt{3}, 0)$ and $(-2 + \sqrt{3}, 0)$.

So, the line of symmetry is $x = -2$

When $x = -2$, $y = (-2)^2 + 4(-2) + 1$

$y = -3$

Minimum point $= (-2, -3)$.

2 b $x^2 - 10x$

$-10 \div 2 = -5$

$x^2 - 10x = (x - 5)^2 - 5^2$

$x^2 - 10x = (x - 5)^2 - 25$

g $x^2 + 9x$

$9 \div 2 = 4.5$

$x^2 + 9x = (x + 4.5)^2 - 4.5^2$

$x^2 + 9x = (x + 4.5)^2 - 20.25$

3 b $x^2 - 10x - 5$

$-10 \div 2 = -5$

$x^2 - 10x - 5 = (x - 5)^2 - 5^2 - 5$

$x^2 - 10x - 5 = (x - 5)^2 - 30$

d $x^2 - 3x + 4$

$-3 \div 2 = -1.5$

$x^2 - 3x + 4 = (x - 1.5)^2 - 1.5^2 + 4$

$x^2 - 3x + 4 = (x - 1.5)^2 + 1.75$

4 c $3x^2 - 12x + 5$

$3x^2 - 12x + 5 = a(x - p)^2 + q$

Expanding the brackets and simplifying gives:

$3x^2 - 12x + 5 = ax^2 - 2apx + ap^2 + q$

Comparing coefficients of x^2, coefficients of x and the constant gives:

$3 = a$ (1)

$-12 = -2ap$ (2)

$5 = ap^2 + q$ (3)

Substituting $a = 3$ in equation (2) gives $p = 2$

Substituting $a = 3$ and $p = 2$ in equation (3) gives $q = -7$

So $3x^2 - 12x + 5 = 3(x - 2)^2 - 7$

h $3x^2 - x + 6 = 3\left[x^2 - \frac{1}{3}x + 2\right]$

$\frac{1}{3} \div 2 = \frac{1}{6}$

$$3\left[\left(x - \frac{1}{6}\right)^2 - \left(\frac{1}{6}\right)^2 + 2\right] = 3\left(x - \frac{1}{6}\right)^2 + 5\frac{11}{12}$$

5 a $6x - x^2 = m - (x - n)^2$

$6x - x^2 = m - (x^2 - 2nx + n^2)$

$6x - x^2 = m - x^2 + 2nx - n^2$

Comparing coefficients of x and the constant gives:

$6 = 2n$ (1)

$0 = m - n^2$ (2)

Substituting $n = 3$ in equation (2) gives $m = 9$

$6x - x^2 = 9 - (x - 3)^2$

c $3x - x^2 = m - (x - n)^2$

$3x - x^2 = m - (x^2 - 2nx + n^2)$

$3x - x^2 = m - x^2 + 2nx - n^2$

Comparing coefficients of x and the constant gives:

$3 = 2n$ (1)
$0 = m - n^2$ (2)

Substituting $n = 1.5$ in equation (2) gives $m = 2.25$

$3x - x^2 = 2.25 - (x - 1.5)^2$

6 b $8 - 4x - x^2 = a - (x + b)^2$

$8 - 4x - x^2 = a - (x^2 + 2bx + b^2)$

$8 - 4x - x^2 = a - x^2 - 2bx - b^2$

Comparing coefficients of x and the constant gives:

$-4 = -2b$ (1)
$8 = a - b^2$ (2)

Substituting $b = 2$ in equation (2) gives $a = 12$

$8 - 4x - x^2 = 12 - (x + 2)^2$

c $10 - 5x - x^2 = a - (x + b)^2$

$10 - 5x - x^2 = a - (x^2 + 2bx + b^2)$

$10 - 5x - x^2 = a - x^2 - 2bx - b^2$

Comparing coefficients of x and the constant gives:

$-5 = -2b$ (1)
$10 = a - b^2$ (2)

Substituting $b = 2.5$ in equation (2) gives $a = 16.25$

$10 - 5x - x^2 = 16.25 - (x + 2.5)^2$

7 a $9 - 6x - 2x^2 = a - p(x + q)^2$

$9 - 6x - 2x^2 = a - p(x^2 + 2qx + q^2)$

$9 - 6x - 2x^2 = a - px^2 - 2pqx - pq^2$

Comparing coefficients of x^2, coefficients of x and the constant gives:

$-2 = -p$ (1)
$-6 = -2pq$ (2)
$9 = a - pq^2$ (3)

Substituting $p = 2$ into equation (2) gives $q = 1.5$

Substituting $p = 2$ and $q = 1.5$ into equation (3) gives $a = 13.5$

$9 - 6x - 2x^2 = 13.5 - 2(x + 1.5)^2$

d $2 + 5x - 3x^2 = a - p(x + q)^2$

$2 + 5x - 3x^2 = a - p(x^2 + 2qx + q^2)$

$2 + 5x - 3x^2 = a - px^2 - 2pqx - pq^2$

Comparing coefficients of x^2, coefficients of x and the constant gives:

$-3 = -p$ (1)
$5 = -2pq$ (2)
$2 = a - pq^2$ (3)

Substituting $p = 3$ into equation (2) gives $q = -\frac{5}{6}$

Substituting $p = 3$ and $q = -\frac{5}{6}$ into equation (3) gives $a = 4\frac{1}{12}$

$2 + 5x - 3x^2 = 4\frac{1}{12} - 3\left(x - \frac{5}{6}\right)^2$

8 a $4x^2 + 2x + 5 = a(x + b)^2 + c$

$4x^2 + 2x + 5 = a(x + b)^2 + c$

$4x^2 + 2x + 5 = ax^2 + 2abx + ab^2 + c$

Comparing coefficients of x^2, coefficients of x and the constant gives:

$4 = a$ (1)
$2 = 2ab$ (2)
$5 = ab^2 + c$ (3)

Substituting $a = 4$ into equation (2) gives $b = \frac{1}{4}$

Substituting $a = 4$, $b = \frac{1}{4}$ into equation (3) gives $c = 4\frac{3}{4}$

$4x^2 + 2x + 5 = 4\left(x + \frac{1}{4}\right)^2 + 4\frac{3}{4}$

b The graph of $y = 4x^2 + 2x + 5$ is a 'U' shaped parabola (because the coefficient of x^2 is positive).

As $y = 4\left(x + \frac{1}{4}\right)^2 + 4\frac{3}{4}$, the minimum value of the expression is $4 \times 0 + 4\frac{3}{4} = 4\frac{3}{4}$

$\left(x + \frac{1}{4}\right)^2$ is a square so it will always be $\geqslant 0$.

The smallest value it can be is 0.

This occurs when $x = -\frac{1}{4}$

So, we can see that the minimum point of the graph is at $\left(-\frac{1}{4}, 4\frac{3}{4}\right)$

The minimum point is above the x-axis so the graph of $y = 4\left(x + \frac{1}{4}\right)^2 + 4\frac{3}{4}$ does not meet the x-axis.

9 a $2x^2 - 8x + 1 = a(x + b)^2 + c$

$2x^2 - 8x + 1 = a(x + b)^2 + c$

$2x^2 - 8x + 1 = ax^2 + 2abx + ab^2 + c$

Comparing coefficients of x^2, coefficients of x and the constant gives:

$2 = a$ (1)

$-8 = 2ab$ (2)

$1 = ab^2 + c$ (3)

Substituting $a = 2$ into equation (2) gives $b = -2$

Substituting $a = 2$, $b = -2$ into equation (3) gives $c = -7$

$2x^2 - 8x + 1 = 2(x - 2)^2 - 7$

b The graph of $y = 2(x - 2)^2 - 7$ is a '∪' shaped parabola (because the coefficient of x^2 is positive). The stationary point (or turning point or minimum point) on the graph of $y = 2(x - 2)^2 - 7$ has the coordinates $(2, -7)$.

10 a $x^2 - x - 5 = (x + b)^2 + c$

$x^2 - x - 5 = x^2 + 2bx + b^2 + c$

Comparing coefficients of x and the constant gives:

$-1 = 2b$ (1)

$-5 = b^2 + c$ (2)

Substituting $b = -0.5$ into equation (2) gives $c = -5.25$

$x^2 - x - 5 = (x - 0.5)^2 - 5.25$

b The graph of $f(x) = (x - 0.5)^2 - 5.25$ is a '∪' shaped parabola (because the coefficient of x^2 is positive).

The minimum point on the graph of $f(x) = (x - 0.5)^2 - 5.25$ has the coordinates $(0.5, -5.25)$

An inverse function $f^{-1}(x)$ can exist if, and only if, the function $f(x)$ is a one to one mapping.

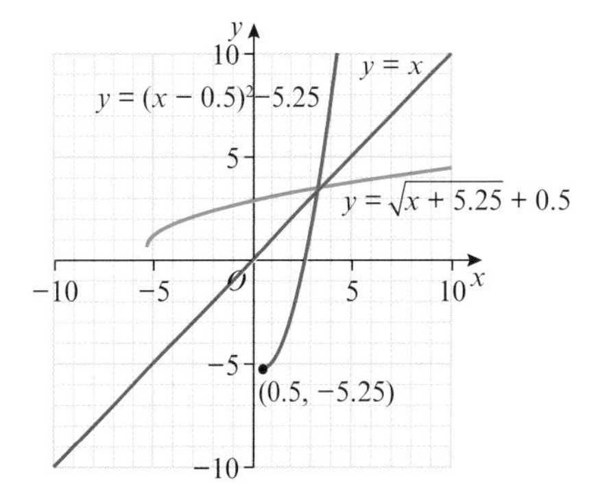

There are an infinite number of domains of $f(x)$ for which $f^{-1}(x)$ can exist ($x \geqslant a$ for any $a \geqslant 0.5$). A suitable choice would be to restrict the domain of $f(x)$ to $x \geqslant 0.5$.

11 a $5 - 7x - 2x^2 = p - 2(x - q)^2$

$5 - 7x - 2x^2 = p - 2(x^2 - 2qx + q^2)$

$5 - 7x - 2x^2 = p - 2x^2 + 4qx - 2q^2$

Comparing coefficients of x and the constant gives:

$-7 = 4q$ (1)

$5 = p - 2q^2$ (2)

$q = -1.75$

Substituting $q = -1.75$ into equation (2) gives $p = 11.125$

$5 - 7x - 2x^2 = 11.125 - 2(x + 1.75)^2$

b The graph of $y = 11.125 - 2(x + 1.75)^2$ is an '∩' shaped parabola (because the coefficient of x^2 is negative). The maximum point of the graph of $y = 11.125 - 2(x + 1.75)^2$ has the coordinates $(-1.75, 11.125)$.

$(x + 1.75)^2$ is a square so it will always be $\geqslant 0$. The smallest value it can be is 0. This occurs when $x = -1.75$.

The maximum value of $11.125 - 2(x + 1.75)^2$ is 11.125.

The range of the function is $f(x) \leqslant 11.125$.

12 a $14 + 6x - 2x^2 = a + b(x + c)^2$

$14 + 6x - 2x^2 = a + b(x^2 + 2cx + c^2)$

$14 + 6x - 2x^2 = a + bx^2 + 2bcx + bc^2$

Comparing coefficients of x^2, coefficients of x and the constant gives:

$-2 = b$ (1)

$6 = 2bc$ (2)

$14 = a + bc^2$ (3)

Substituting $b = -2$ into equation (2) gives $c = -1.5$

Substituting $b = -2$ and $c = -1.5$ into equation (3) gives $a = 18.5$

$14 + 6x - 2x^2 = 18.5 - 2(x - 1.5)^2$

b The stationary point on the graph of $f(x) = 18.5 - 2(x - 1.5)^2$ has the coordinates $(1.5, 18.5)$

c The graph of $f(x) = 18.5 - 2(x - 1.5)^2$ is an '∩' shaped parabola (because the coefficient of x^2 is negative).

$f(x) = 14 + 6x - 2x^2$

When $x = 0$, $f(x) = 14$

When $f(x) = 0$,

$18.5 - 2(x - 1.5)^2 = 0$

$18.5 = 2(x - 1.5)^2$

$9.25 = (x - 1.5)^2$

$x = \pm\sqrt{9.25} + 1.5$

$x = -1.54$ or $x = 4.54$

Axes crossing points are: $(0, 14)$, $(-1.54, 0)$ and $(4.54, 0)$.

The sketch of $y = f(x)$ is:

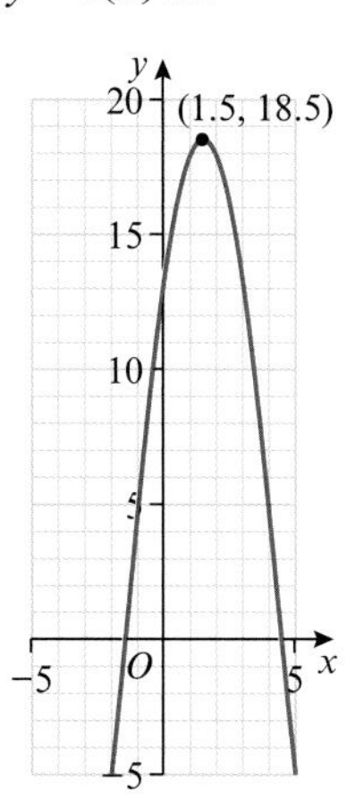

13 a $7 + 5x - x^2 = a - (x + b)^2$

$7 + 5x - x^2 = a - (x^2 + 2bx + b^2)$

$7 + 5x - x^2 = a - x^2 - 2bx - b^2$

Comparing coefficients of x and the constant gives:

$5 = -2b$ (1)

$7 = a - b^2$ (2)

Substituting $b = -2.5$ in equation (2) gives $a = 13.25$

$7 + 5x - x^2 = 13.25 - (x - 2.5)^2$

b The turning point on the graph of $f(x) = 13.25 - (x - 2.5)^2$ has the coordinates $(2.5, 13.25)$. It is a maximum point because the graph of $f(x) = 13.25 - (x - 2.5)^2$ is an '∩' shaped parabola.

c When $x = 7$, $f(7) = 7 + 5(7) - 7^2 = -7$

The sketch of $f(x)$ is:

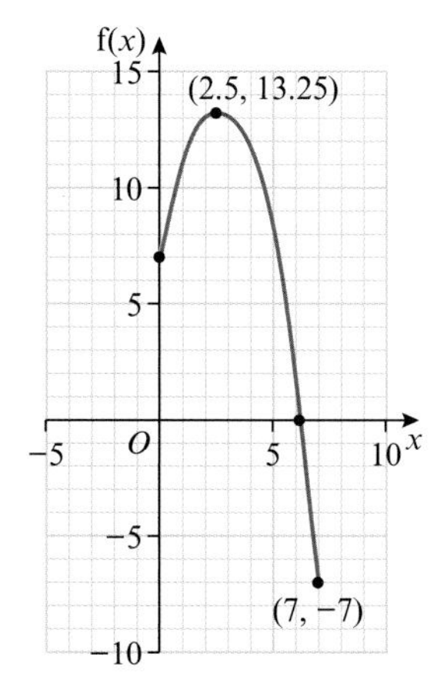

The range of $f(x)$ is $-7 \leqslant f(x) \leqslant 13.25$

d $f(x) = 7 + 5x - x^2$
$0 \leqslant x \leqslant 7$ is a many to one mapping.

Only a one-one function has an inverse that is a function. So, the answer is 'no'.

14 a $2x^2 - 8x + 3$

$2x^2 - 8x + 3 = 2(x + a)^2 + b$

Expanding the brackets and simplifying gives:

$2x^2 - 8x + 3 = 2x^2 + 4ax + 2a^2 + b$

Comparing coefficients of x^2, coefficients of x and the constant gives:

$-8 = 4a$ (1)

$3 = 2a^2 + b$ (2)

Substituting $a = -2$ in equation (2) gives $b = -5$

So $2x^2 - 8x + 3 = 2(x - 2)^2 - 5$.

b The graph of $f(x) = 2(x - 2)^2 - 5$ is a 'U' shaped parabola.

The minimum point of the graph has the coordinates $(2, -5)$

So, a suitable choice would be to restrict the domain to $x \geqslant 2$, which is the largest possible domain for which an inverse exists.

15 $4x^2 + 6x - 8 = 4[x^2 + 1.5x - 2]$

$1.5 \div 2 = 0.75$

$4[(x + 0.75)^2 - 0.75^2 - 2] = 4(x + 0.75)^2 - 10.25$

$f(x) = 4(x + 0.75)^2 - 10.25$

The graph of $f(x) = 4(x + 0.75)^2 - 10.25$ is a 'U' shaped parabola.

The minimum point of the graph has the coordinates

$(-0.75, -10.25)$

An inverse function $f^{-1}(x)$ can exist if, and only if, the function $f(x)$ is a one-to-one mapping.
So, restrict the domain to $x \geqslant -0.75$ i.e., $m = -0.75$

16 a $1 + 4x - x^2 = a - (x + b)^2$

$1 + 4x - x^2 = a - (x^2 + 2bx + b^2)$

$1 + 4x - x^2 = a - x^2 - 2bx - b^2$

Comparing coefficients of x and the constant gives:

$4 = -2b$ (1)

$1 = a - b^2$ (2)

Substituting $b = -2$ in equation (2) gives $a = 5$

$1 + 4x - x^2 = 5 - (x - 2)^2$

b The turning point on the graph of $f(x) = 5 - (x - 2)^2$ has the coordinates $(2, 5)$. It is a maximum point because the graph of $f(x) = 5 - (x - 2)^2$ is an '∩' shaped parabola.

c An inverse function $f^{-1}(x)$ can exist if, and only if, the function $f(x)$ is a one-to-one mapping. The restriction of the domain of $f(x)$ to $x \geqslant 2$ ensures that $f(x)$ is a one-to-one function.

To find the inverse $f^{-1}(x)$, use the completed square form of $f(x)$.

$y = 5 - (x - 2)^2$ swap x and y

$x = 5 - (y - 2)^2$ rearrange

$(y - 2)^2 = 5 - x$ square root both sides

$y - 2 = \sqrt{5 - x}$ add 2 to both sides

$y = 2 + \sqrt{5 - x}$

$f^{-1}(x) = 2 + \sqrt{5 - x}$ where $x \leqslant 5$

Exercise 2.3

1 a $y = |x^2 - 4x + 3|$

First sketch the graph of $y = x^2 - 4x + 3$

When $x = 0$, $y = 3$

So, the y-intercept is 3

When $y = 0$

$x^2 - 4x + 3 = 0$

$(x - 3)(x - 1) = 0$

$x = 3$ or $x = 1$

The x-intercepts are 1 and 3

The x-coordinate of the minimum point
$= \frac{1 + 3}{2} = 2$

The y-coordinate of the minimum point
$= 2^2 - 4(2) + 3 = -1$

The minimum point is $(2, -1)$

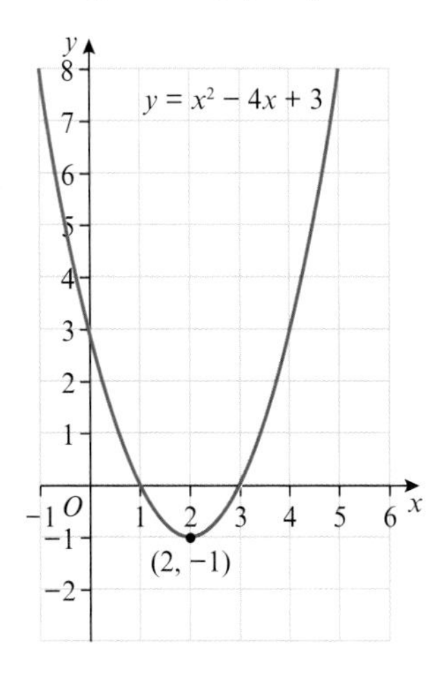

Now reflect in the x-axis the part of the curve $y = x^2 - 4x + 3$ that is below the x-axis.

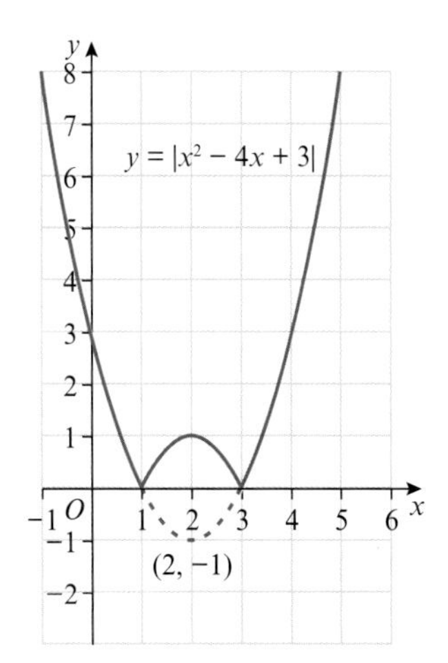

e $y = |2x^2 - 11x - 6|$

First sketch the graph of $y = 2x^2 - 11x - 6$

When $x = 0$, $y = -6$

So, the y-intercept is -6

When $y = 0$

$2x^2 - 11x - 6 = 0$

$(2x + 1)(x - 6) = 0$

$x = -0.5$ or $x = 6$

The x-intercepts are -0.5 and 6

The x- coordinate of the minimum point
$= \frac{-0.5 + 6}{2} = 2.75$

The y- coordinate of the minimum point
$= 2(2.75^2) - 11(2.75) - 6 = -21.125$

The minimum point is $(2.75, -21.125)$

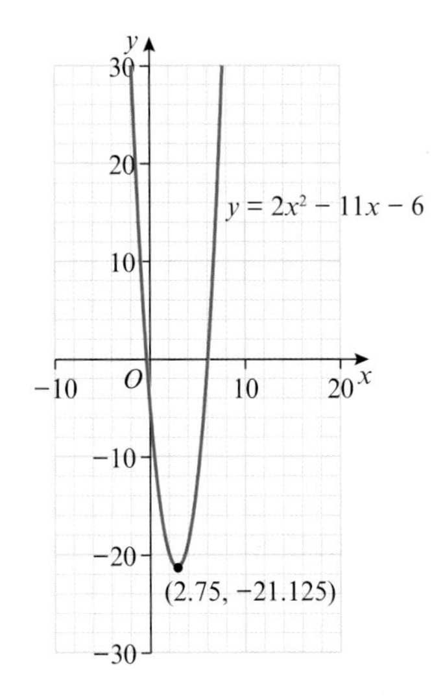

Now reflect in the x-axis the part of the curve $y = 2x^2 - 11x - 6$ that is below the x-axis.

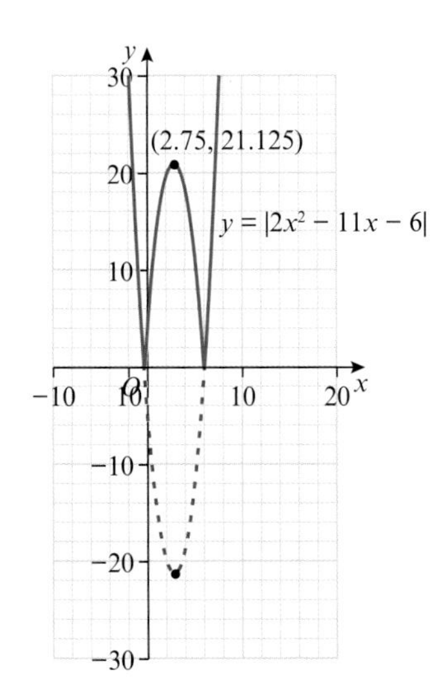

2 **a** $1 - 4x - x^2 = a - (x + b)^2$

$1 - 4x - x^2 = a - (x^2 + 2bx + b^2)$

$1 - 4x - x^2 = a - x^2 - 2bx - b^2$

Comparing coefficients of x and the constant gives:

$-4 = -2b$ (1)

$1 = a - b^2$ (2)

Substituting $b = 2$ in equation (2) gives $a = 5$

$1 - 4x - x^2 = 5 - (x + 2)^2$

$f(x) = 5 - (x + 2)^2$

b The graph of $y = f(x) = 5 - (x + 2)^2$ is an '∩' shaped parabola.

The maximum point is at $(-2, 5)$

$y = 1 - 4x - x^2$

When $x = 0$, $y = 1$

When $y = 0$, $0 = 5 - (x + 2)^2$

$(x + 2)^2 = 5$

$x = \pm\sqrt{5} - 2$

The crossing points are at $(0, 1)$, $(\sqrt{5} - 2, 0)$ and $(-\sqrt{5} - 2, 0)$

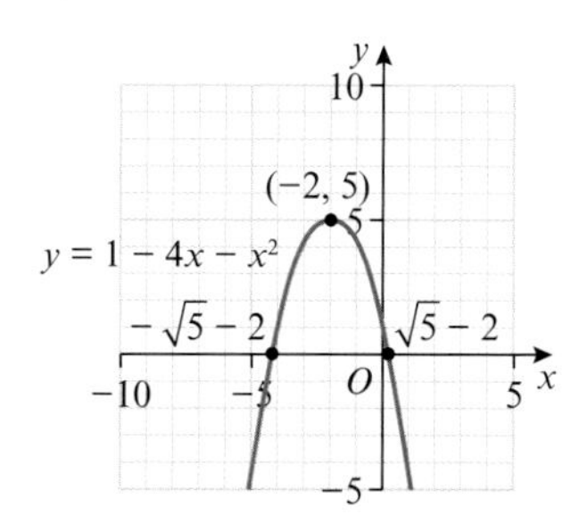

c Now reflect in the x-axis the part of the curve $y = 1 - 4x - x^2$ that is below the x-axis.

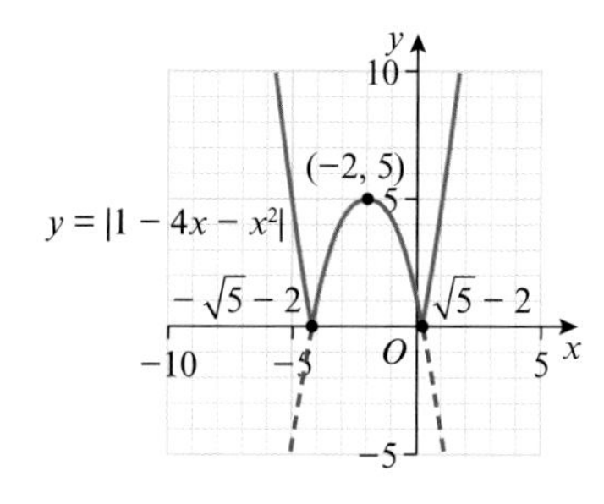

3 **a** $2x^2 + x - 3 = a(x + b)^2 + c$

$2x^2 + x - 3 = ax^2 + 2abx + ab^2 + c$

Comparing coefficients of x^2, coefficients of x and the constant gives:

$2 = a$ (1)

$1 = 2ab$ (2)

$-3 = ab^2 + c$ (3)

Substituting $a = 2$ into equation (2) gives $b = 0.25$

Substituting $a = 2$, $b = 0.25$ into equation (3) gives $c = -3.125$

$2x^2 + x - 3 = 2(x + 0.25)^2 - 3.125$

$f(x) = 2(x + 0.25)^2 - 3.125$

b The graph of $f(x) = 2(x + 0.25)^2 - 3.125$ is a 'U' shaped parabola.

The minimum point is at $(-0.25, -3.125)$

$y = 2x^2 + x - 3$

When $x = 0$, $y = -3$

When $y = 0$, $0 = 2(x + 0.25)^2 - 3.125$

$2(x + 0.25)^2 = 3.125$

$x = \pm\sqrt{1.5625} - 0.25$

The crossing points are at $(0, -3)$, $(1, 0)$ and $(-1.5, 0)$

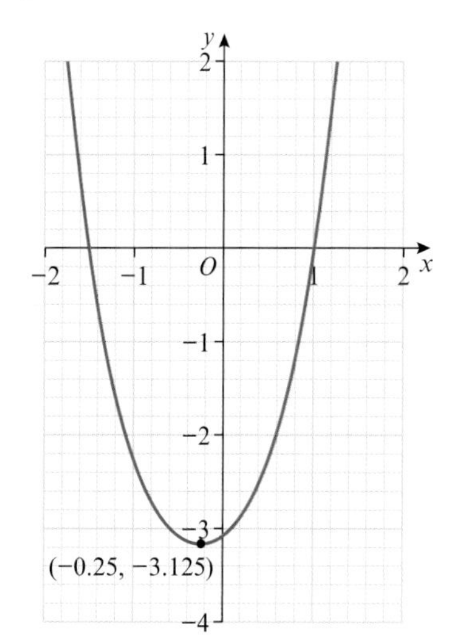

c Now reflect in the x-axis the part of the curve $y = 2x^2 + x - 3$ that is below the x-axis.

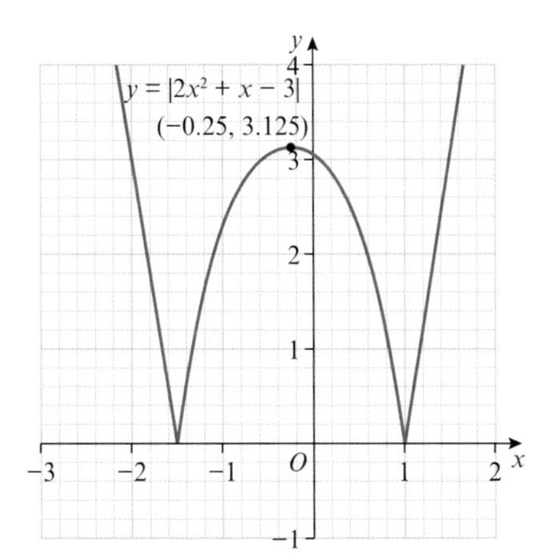

4 a $y = (x - 7)(x + 1)$

When $y = 0$

$(x - 7)(x + 1) = 0$

$x = 7$ and $x = -1$

The crossing points on the x-axis are at $(-1, 0)$ and $(7, 0)$

The graph of $y = (x - 7)(x + 1)$ is a 'U' shaped parabola

The line of symmetry cuts the x-axis midway between $(-1, 0)$ and $(7, 0)$

So, the line of symmetry is $x = 3$

When $x = 3$, $y = (3 - 7)(3 + 1)$

$y = -16$

The stationary point is a minimum point at $(3, -16)$.

When the parts of the graph of $y = (x - 7)(x + 1)$ are reflected in the x-axis to give the graph $y = |(x - 7)(x + 1)|$, the stationary point is at $(3, 16)$

b The graph of $y = |(x - 7)(x + 1)|$ looks like:

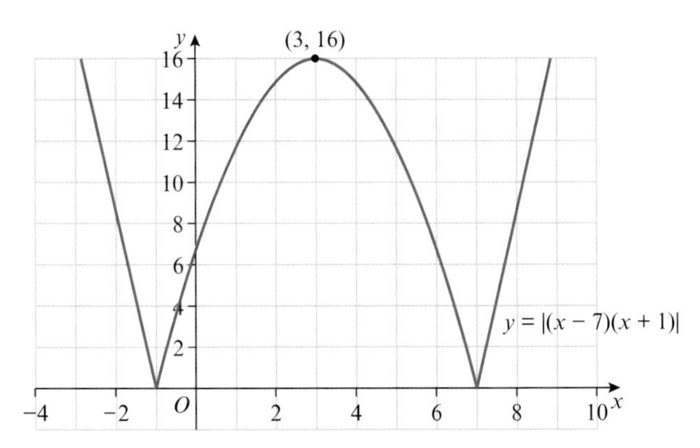

c Looking at the sketch of the graph in **b**, for 4 solutions to

$|(x - 7)(x + 1)| = k, 0 < k < 16$

5 a $y = (x + 5)(x + 1)$

When $y = 0$

$(x + 5)(x + 1) = 0$

$x = -5$ and $x = -1$

The crossing points on the x- axis are at $(-5, 0)$ and $(-1, 0)$

The graph of $y = (x + 5)(x + 1)$ is a 'U' shaped parabola

The line of symmetry cuts the x-axis midway between $(-5, 0)$ and $(-1, 0)$

So, the line of symmetry is $x = -3$

When $x = -3$, $y = (-3 + 5)(-3 + 1)$

$y = -4$

The stationary point is a minimum point at $(-3, -4)$.

When the parts of the graph of $y = (x + 5)(x + 1)$ are reflected in the x-axis to give the graph $y = |(x + 5)(x + 1)|$, the stationary point is at $(-3, 4)$

b The sketch of the graph $y = |(x + 5)(x + 1)|$ looks like:

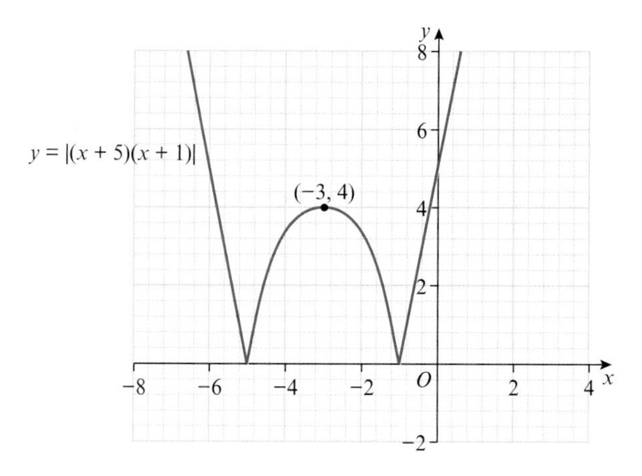

Looking at the sketch, for 2 solutions to $|(x + 5)(x + 1)| = k$, the value of $k > 4$

6 a $y = (x - 8)(x - 3)$

When $y = 0$

$(x - 8)(x - 3) = 0$

$x = 8$ and $x = 3$

The crossing points on the x-axis are at $(8, 0)$ and $(3, 0)$

The graph of $y = (x - 8)(x - 3)$ is a 'U' shaped parabola

The line of symmetry cuts the x-axis midway between $(8, 0)$ and $(3, 0)$

So, the line of symmetry is $x = 5.5$

When $x = 5.5$, $y = (5.5 - 8)(5.5 - 3)$

$y = -6.25$

The stationary point is a minimum point at $(5.5, -6.25)$

When the parts of the graph of $y = (x - 8)(x - 3)$ are reflected in the x-axis to give the graph $y = |(x - 8)(x - 3)|$, the stationary point is at $(5.5, 6.25)$

b The sketch of the graph $y = |(x - 8)(x - 3)|$ looks like:

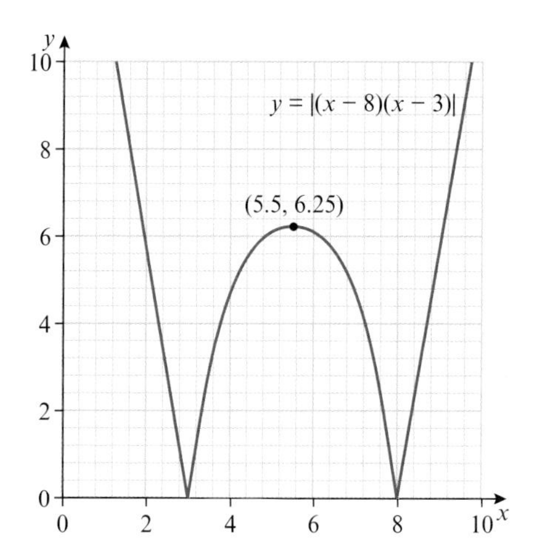

Looking at the sketch, for 3 solutions to $|(x - 8)(x - 3)| = k$, the value of $k = 6.25$

> **TIP**
>
> Solving modulus equations of the type $|f(x)| = k$ usually produces more than one solution.
>
> It is advisable to draw a sketch of $y = |f(x)|$ and $y = k$ on the same axes first.
>
> The number of solutions is the number of intersections of the two graphs.

7 b $|x^2 - 2| = 2$

Sketch the functions of $y = |x^2 - 2|$ and $y = 2$ on the same axes.

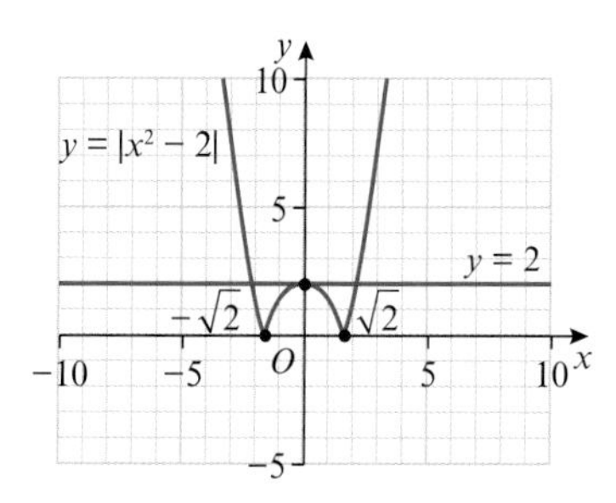

There are 3 points of intersection, so there are 3 solutions to $|x^2 - 2| = 2$

First and second solutions are when $x^2 - 2 = 2$

$x = 2$ and $x = -2$

Third solution is when $x^2 - 2 = -2$

$x = 0$

Check each solution by substituting it back into the original question:

If $x = 2$, $|x^2 - 2| = 2$ becomes $|2^2 - 2| = 2$ which is true.

If $x = -2$, $|x^2 - 2| = 2$ becomes $|(-2)^2 - 2| = 2$ which is true.

If $x = 0$, $|x^2 - 2| = 2$ becomes $|0^2 - 2| = 2$ which is true.

The solutions are $x = 2$, $x = -2$ and $x = 0$

d $|x^2 + 2x| = 24$

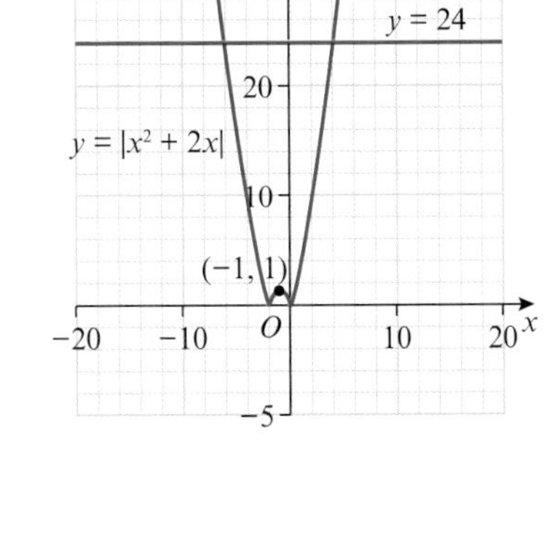

Sketch the functions of $y = |x^2 + 2x|$ and $y = 24$ on the same axes.

Looking at the sketch there are 2 solutions to $|x^2 + 2x| = 24$

$x^2 + 2x = 24$ or $x^2 + 2x = -24$

$x^2 + 2x - 24 = 0$ or $x^2 + 2x + 24 = 0$

$(x + 6)(x - 4) = 0$ or $x = \dfrac{-2 \pm \sqrt{2^2 - 4(1)(24)}}{2(1)}$

no solutions

$x = -6$ or $x = 4$

Check each solution by substituting it back into the original question:

If $x = -6$, $|x^2 + 2x| = 24$ becomes $|(-6)^2 + 2(-6)| = 24$ which is true.

If $x = 4$, $|x^2 + 2x| = 24$ becomes $|4^2 + 2(4)| = 24$ which is true.

The solutions are $x = -6$ and $x = 4$

h $|2x^2 - 3| = 2x$

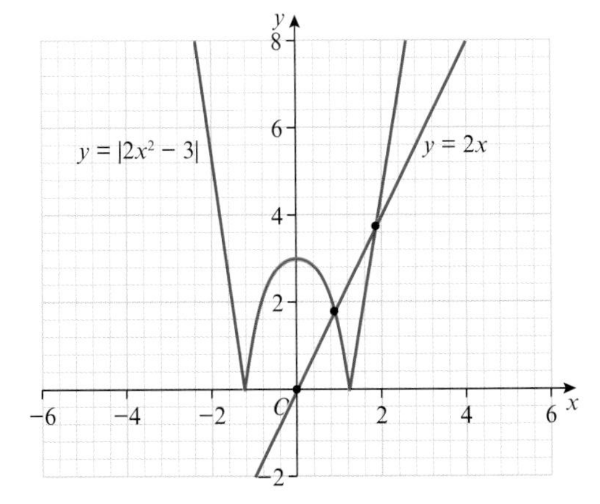

Sketch the functions of $y = |2x^2 - 3|$ and $y = 2x$ on the same axes.

Looking at the sketch there are 2 solutions to $|2x^2 - 3| = 2x$

$2x^2 - 3 = 2x$ or $2x^2 - 3 = -2x$

$2x^2 - 2x - 3 = 0$ or $2x^2 + 2x - 3 = 0$

$x = \dfrac{2 \pm \sqrt{(-2)^2 - 4(2)(-3)}}{2(2)}$ or $x = \dfrac{-2 \pm \sqrt{2^2 - 4(2)(-3)}}{2(2)}$

$x = \dfrac{1 + \sqrt{7}}{2}$ or $x = \dfrac{1 - \sqrt{7}}{2}$ or $x = \dfrac{-1 - \sqrt{7}}{2}$ or $x = \dfrac{-1 + \sqrt{7}}{2}$

Check each solution by substituting it back into the original question:

If $x = \frac{1+\sqrt{7}}{2}$, $|2x^2 - 3| = 2x$ becomes $\left|2\left(\frac{1+\sqrt{7}}{2}\right)^2 - 3\right| = 2\left(\frac{1+\sqrt{7}}{2}\right)$, so $3.646\ldots = -3.646\ldots$ which is true.

If $x = \frac{1-\sqrt{7}}{2}$, $|2x^2 - 3| = 2x$ becomes $\left|2\left(\frac{1-\sqrt{7}}{2}\right)^2 - 3\right| = 2\left(\frac{1-\sqrt{7}}{2}\right)$, so $1.646\ldots = -1.646\ldots$ which is false.

If $x = \frac{-1-\sqrt{7}}{2}$, $|2x^2 - 3| = 2x$ becomes $\left|2\left(\frac{-1-\sqrt{7}}{2}\right)^2 - 3\right| = 2\left(\frac{-1-\sqrt{7}}{2}\right)$, so $3.646\ldots = -3.646\ldots$ which is false.

If $x = \frac{-1+\sqrt{7}}{2}$, $|2x^2 - 3| = 2x$ becomes $\left|2\left(\frac{-1+\sqrt{7}}{2}\right)^2 - 3\right| = 2\left(\frac{-1+\sqrt{7}}{2}\right)$, so $1.646\ldots = 1.646\ldots$ which is true.

The two solutions are $x = \frac{1+\sqrt{7}}{2}$ or $x = \frac{-1+\sqrt{7}}{2}$

8 a $y = x + 1$ (1)

$y = |x^2 - 2x - 3|$ (2)

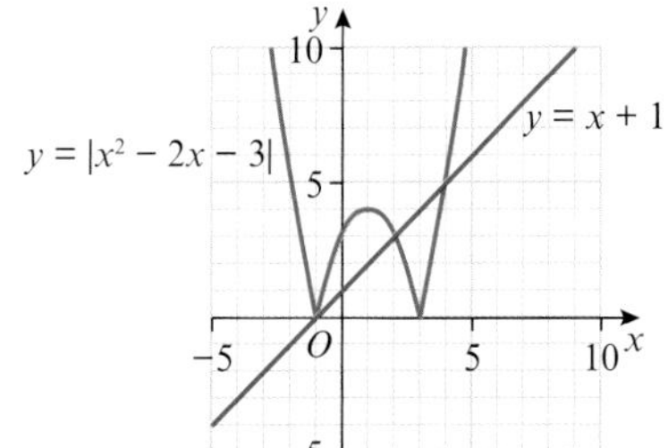

Equating (1) and (2)

Sketch the functions of $y = |x^2 - 2x - 3|$ and $y = x + 1$ on the same axes.

Looking at the sketch there are 3 solutions to $|x^2 - 2x - 3| = x + 1$

$x^2 - 2x - 3 = x + 1$ or $x^2 - 2x - 3 = -(x + 1)$

$x^2 - 3x - 4 = 0$ $\qquad x^2 - 2x - 3 = -x - 1$

$(x - 4)(x + 1) = 0$ $\qquad x^2 - x - 2 = 0$

$x = 4$ or $x = -1$ $\qquad (x - 2)(x + 1) = 0$

$x = 2$ or $x = -1$

Check each solution by substituting it back into the original question:

If $x = 4$, $|x^2 - 2x - 3| = x + 1$ becomes $|4^2 - 2(4) - 3| = 4 + 1$ which is true.

If $x = -1$, $|x^2 - 2x - 3| = x + 1$ becomes $|(-1)^2 - 2(-1) - 3| = -1 + 1$ which is true.

If $x = 2$, $|x^2 - 2x - 3| = x + 1$ becomes $|2^2 - 2(2) - 3| = 2 + 1$ which is true.

The solutions are $x = 4$, $x = -1$ and $x = 2$

Substitute $x = 4$, $x = -1$ and $x = 2$ into $y = x + 1$ to find the corresponding y values.

If $x = 4$, $y = 4 + 1$

$y = 5$

If $x = -1$, $y = -1 + 1$

$y = 0$

If $x = 2$, $y = 2 + 1$

$y = 3$

The solutions are: $x = 4$, $y = 5$ and $x = -1$, $y = 0$ and $x = 2$, $y = 3$.

b 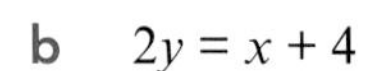

$2y = x + 4$ (1)

$y = \left|\frac{1}{2}x^2 - x - 3\right|$ (2)

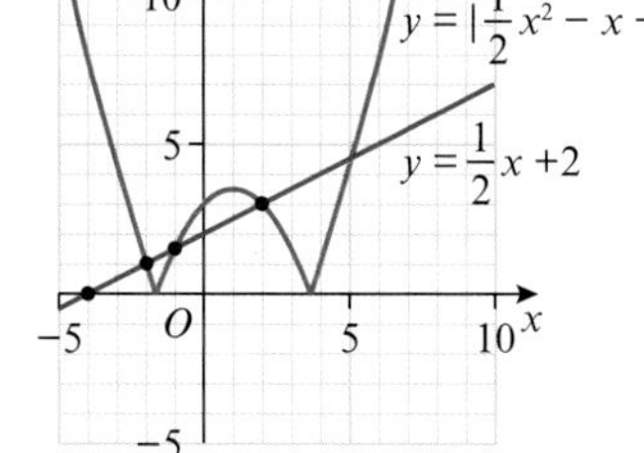

From (1), $y = \frac{1}{2}x + 2$

Equating (1) and (2) $\left|\frac{1}{2}x^2 - x - 3\right| = \frac{1}{2}x + 2$

Sketch the functions of $y = \left|\frac{1}{2}x^2 - x - 3\right|$ and $y = \frac{1}{2}x + 2$ on the same axes.

Looking at the sketch there are 4 solutions to $\left|\frac{1}{2}x^2 - x - 3\right| = \frac{1}{2}x + 2$

$\frac{1}{2}x^2 - x - 3 = \frac{1}{2}x + 2$ or $\frac{1}{2}x^2 - x - 3 = -\left(\frac{1}{2}x + 2\right)$

$x^2 - 2x - 6 = x + 4$ or $x^2 - 2x - 6 = -x - 4$

$x^2 - 3x - 10 = 0$ or $x^2 - x - 2 = 0$

$(x - 5)(x + 2) = 0$ or $(x - 2)(x + 1) = 0$

$x = 5$ or $x = -2$ or $x = 2$ or $x = -1$

Check each solution by substituting it back into the original question.:

If $x = 5$, $\left|\frac{1}{2}x^2 - x - 3\right| = \frac{1}{2}x + 2$ becomes $\left|\frac{1}{2}(5^2) - 5 - 3\right| = \frac{1}{2}(5) + 2$ which is true.

If $x = -2$, $\left|\frac{1}{2}x^2 - x - 3\right| = \frac{1}{2}x + 2$ becomes $\left|\frac{1}{2}(-2)^2 - (-2) - 3\right| = \frac{1}{2}(-2) + 2$ which is true.

If $x = 2$, $\left|\frac{1}{2}x^2 - x - 3\right| = \frac{1}{2}x + 2$ becomes $\left|\frac{1}{2}(2^2) - 2 - 3\right| = \frac{1}{2}(2) + 2$ which is true.

If $x = -1$, $\left|\frac{1}{2}x^2 - x - 3\right| = \frac{1}{2}x + 2$ becomes $\left|\frac{1}{2}(-1)^2 - (-1) - 3\right| = \frac{1}{2}(-1) + 2$ which is true.

Substitute $x = 5$, $x = -2$, $x = 2$ and $x = -1$ into $y = \frac{1}{2}x + 2$ to find the corresponding y values

If $x = 5$, $y = \frac{1}{2}(5) + 2$

$y = 4\frac{1}{2}$

If $x = -2$, $y = \frac{1}{2}(-2) + 2$

$y = 1$

If $x = 2$, $y = \frac{1}{2}(2) + 2$

$y = 3$

If $x = -1$, $y = \frac{1}{2}(-1) + 2$

$y = 1\frac{1}{2}$

The solutions are:

$x = 5, y = 4\frac{1}{2}$ and $x = -2, y = 1$ and $x = 2, y = 3$ and $x = -1, y = 1\frac{1}{2}$

c $y = 2x$ (1)

$y = |2x^2 - 4|$ (2)

Equating (1) and (2) $|2x^2 - 4| = 2x$

Sketch the functions of $y = |2x^2 - 4|$ and $y = 2x$ on the same axes

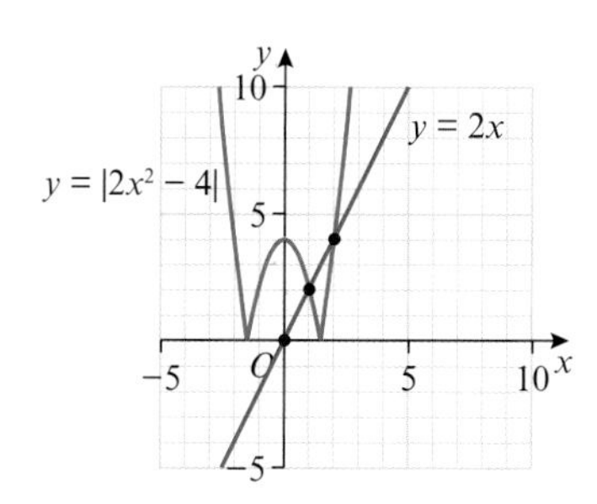

Looking at the sketch there are 2 solutions to $|2x^2 - 4| = 2x$

$2x^2 - 4 = 2x$ or $2x^2 - 4 = -2x$

$2x^2 - 2x - 4 = 0$ or $x^2 + 2x - 4 = 0$

$x^2 - x - 2 = 0$ or $x^2 + x - 2 = 0$

$(x - 2)(x + 1) = 0$ or $(x + 2)(x - 1) = 0$

$x = 2$ or $x = -1$ or $x = -2$ or $x = 1$

Check each solution by substituting it back into the original question.

If $x = 2$, $|2x^2 - 4| = 2x$ becomes $|2(2^2) - 4| = 2(2)$ which is true.

If $x = -1$, $|2x^2 - 4| = 2x$ becomes $|2(-1)^2 - 4| = 2(-1)$ which is false.

If $x = -2$, $|2x^2 - 4| = 2x$ becomes $|2(-2)^2 - 4| = 2(-2)$ which is false.

If $x = 1$, $|2x^2 - 4| = 2x$ becomes $|2(1^2) - 4| = 2(1)$ which is true.

Substitute $x = 2$ and $x = 1$, into $y = 2x$ to find the corresponding y values.

If $x = 2$, $y = 2(2)$

$y = 4$

If $x = 1$, $y = 2(1)$

$y = 2$

The solutions are:

$x = 2$, $y = 4$ and $x = 1$, $y = 2$

Exercise 2.4

1 e $(2x + 1)(x - 4) < 0$

Sketch the graph of $y = (2x + 1)(x - 4)$

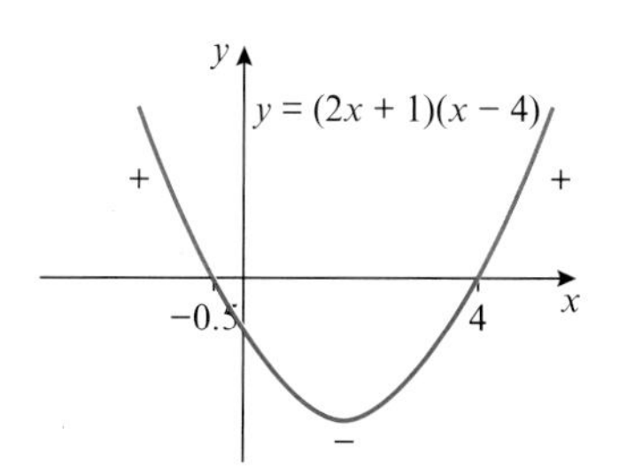

When $y = 0$, $(2x + 1)(x - 4) = 0$

$x = -0.5$ or $x = 4$

So, the x-axis crossing points are -0.5 and 4

For $(2x + 1)(x - 4) < 0$ you need to find the range of values of x for which the curve is negative (below the x-axis).

The solution is $-0.5 < x < 4$

i $(x - 3)^2 \leqslant 0$

Sketch the graph of $y = (x - 3)^2$

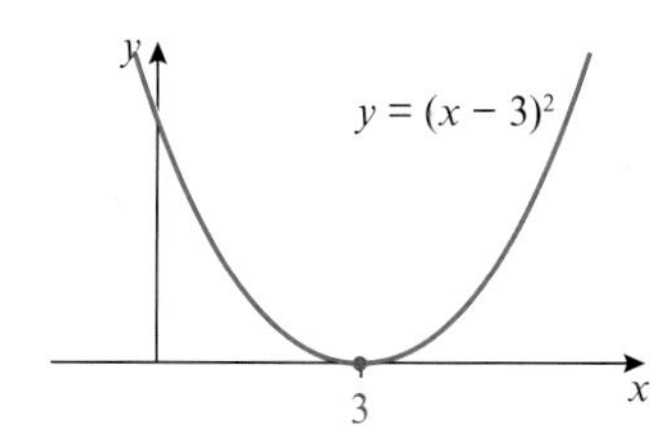

When $y = 0$, $(x - 3)^2 = 0$

$x = 3$

So, the graph touches the x-axis at 3

For $(x - 3)^2 \leqslant 0$ you need to find the range of values of x for which the curve is either zero or negative (below the x-axis).

The solution is $x = 3$.

2 b $x^2 + x - 6 \geqslant 0$

Sketch the graph of $y = x^2 + x - 6$

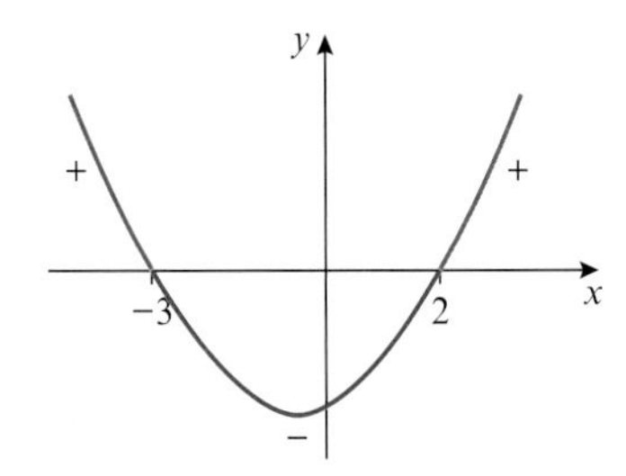

When $y = 0$, $x^2 + x - 6 = 0$

$(x + 3)(x - 2) = 0$

$x = -3$ or $x = 2$

So, the x-axis crossing points are -3 and 2

For $x^2 + x - 6 \geqslant 0$ you need to find the range of values of x for which the curve is either zero or positive (above the x-axis).

The solution is $x \leqslant -3$, $x \geqslant 2$

e $2x^2 - x - 15 \leqslant 0$

Sketch the graph of $y = 2x^2 - x - 15$

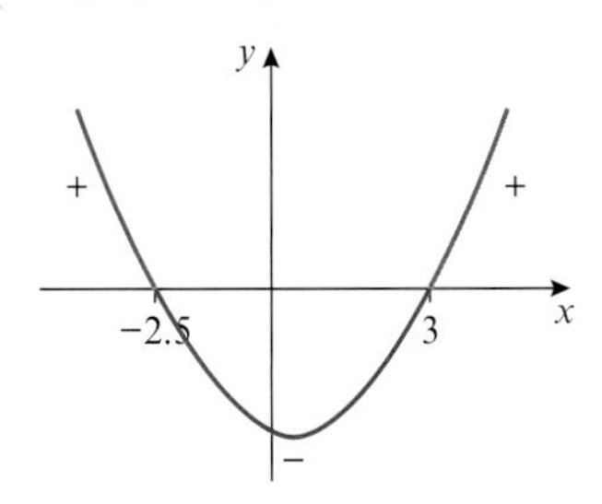

When $y = 0$, $2x^2 - x - 15 = 0$

$(2x + 5)(x - 3) = 0$

$x = -2.5$ or $x = 3$

So, the x-axis crossing points are -2.5 and 3

For $2x^2 - x - 15 \leqslant 0$ you need to find the range of values of x for which the curve is either zero or negative (below the x-axis).

The solution is $-2.5 \leqslant x \leqslant 3$

TIP

There are several methods for solving quadratic inequalities, some alternative methods are shown below.

3 b $12x < x^2 + 35$

Rearranging: $x^2 - 12x + 35 > 0$

Sketch the graph of $y = x^2 - 12x + 35$

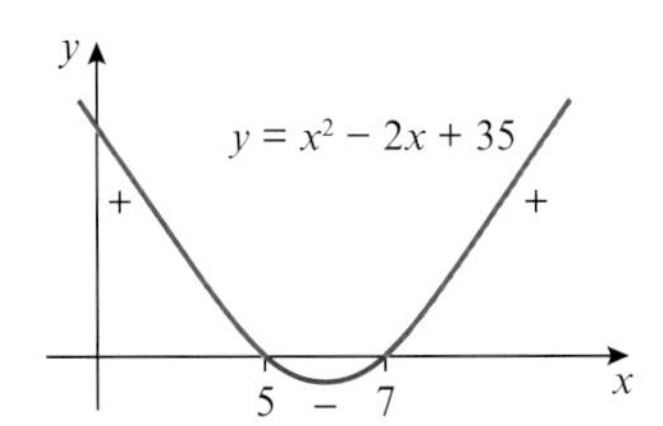

When $y = 0$, $x^2 - 12x + 35 = 0$

$(x - 5)(x - 7) = 0$

$x = 5$ or $x = 7$

So, the x-axis crossing points are 5 and 7

For $x^2 - 12x + 35 > 0$ you need to find the range of values of x for which the curve is positive (above the x-axis).

The solution is $x < 5$, $x > 7$

Method 1

e $(x + 3)(1 - x) < x - 1$

Rearranging: $x^2 + 3x - 4 > 0$

Sketch the graph of $y = x^2 + 3x - 4$

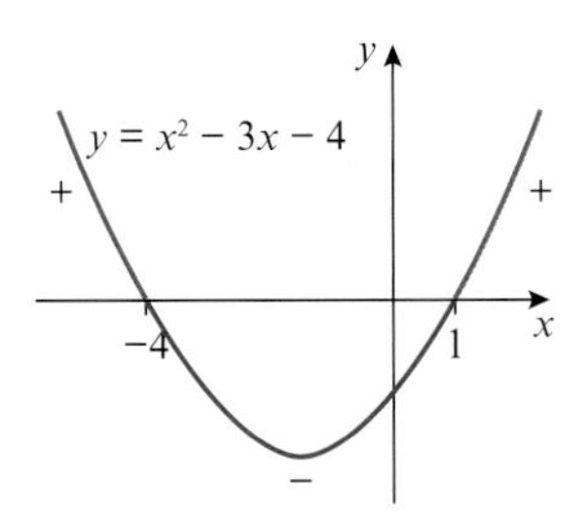

When $y = 0$, $x^2 + 3x - 4 = 0$

$(x - 1)(x + 4) = 0$

$x = 1$ or $x = -4$

So, the x-axis crossing points are 1 and -4

For $x^2 + 3x - 4 > 0$ you need to find the range of values of x for which the curve is positive (above the x-axis).

The solution is $x > 1$, $x < -4$

Method 2

Sketch the graphs of $y = (x + 3)(1 - x)$ and $y = x - 1$ on the same axes.

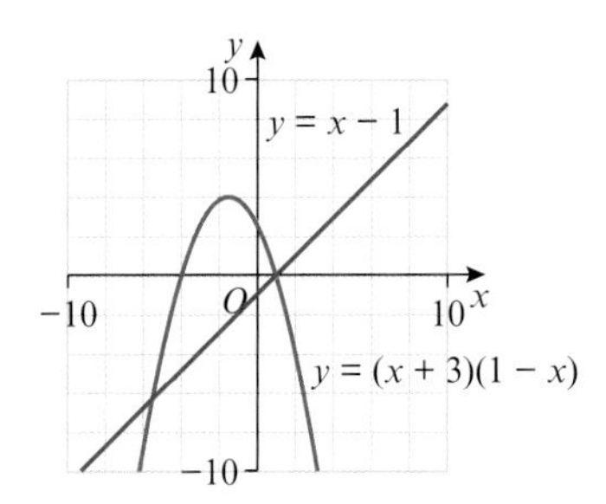

The intersection points of the graphs can be found by solving $(x + 3)(1 - x) = (x - 1)$

Rearranging: $x^2 + 3x - 4 > 0$

When $y = 0$, $x^2 + 3x - 4 = 0$

$(x - 1)(x + 4) = 0$

$x = 1$ or $x = -4$

These solutions are $x = 1$ and $x = -4$

Looking at the two graphs, the graph of $y = (x + 3)(1 - x)$ lies beneath the graph of $y = x - 1$ when $x > 1$ and $x < -4$.

The solution of $(x + 3)(1 - x) < x - 1$ is $x > 1$ and $x < -4$.

4 b $x^2 - 4x \leqslant 12$ (1) and $4x - 3 > 1$ (2)

Rearranging (1): $x^2 - 4x - 12 \leqslant 0$

Now write and solve $x^2 - 4x - 12 = 0$

$(x + 2)(x - 6) = 0$

$x = -2$ or $x = 6$

So, at $x = -2$ and $x = 6$, the value of $x^2 - 4x - 12$ is 0

Now substitute into $x^2 - 4x - 12$, a value of x that is in between -2 and 6,

e.g., $x = 1$

If $x = 1$, we get $1^2 - 4(1) - 12$ which is negative.

So, $x^2 - 4x - 12 \leqslant 0$ for $-2 \leqslant x \leqslant 6$

Rearranging (2): $4x - 4 > 0$

$x > 1$

So, $4x - 3 > 1$ for $x > 1$

Illustrate these two sets of inequalities on number lines:

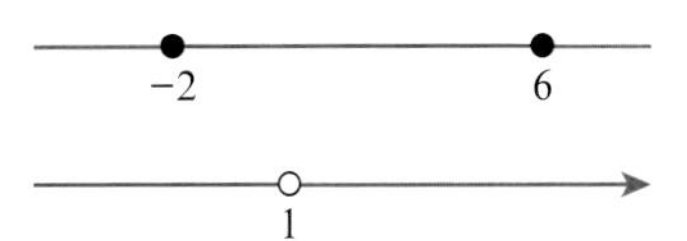

The two inequalities are **both** true for $1 < x \leqslant 6$

e $x^2 + x - 2 > 0$ and $x^2 - 2x - 3 \geqslant 0$

Solve $x^2 + x - 2 = 0$

$(x - 1)(x + 2) = 0$

$x = 1$ or $x = -2$

So, at $x = 1$ and $x = -2$, the value of $x^2 + x - 2$ is 0

Now substitute into $x^2 + x - 2$, a value of x that is in between -2 and 1, e.g, $x = 0$

If $x = 0$, we get $0^2 + 0 - 2$ which is negative.

So, $x^2 + x - 2 > 0$ for $x < -2$ and $x > 1$

Solve $x^2 - 2x - 3 \geqslant 0$

$(x + 1)(x - 3) = 0$

$x = -1$ or $x = 3$

So, at $x = -1$ and $x = 3$, the value of $x^2 - 2x - 3$ is 0

Now substitute into $x^2 - 2x - 3$, a value of x that is in between -1 and 3,

e.g., $x = 1$

If $x = 1$, we get $1^2 - 2(1) - 3$ which is negative.

So, $x^2 - 2x - 3 \geqslant 0$ for $x \leqslant -1$ and $x \geqslant 3$

Illustrate these two sets of inequalities on number lines:

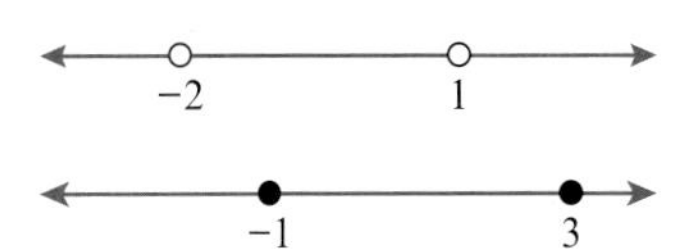

The two inequalities are **both** true for $x < -2$ and $x \geqslant 3$.

5 **a** $|x^2 + 2x - 2| < 13$

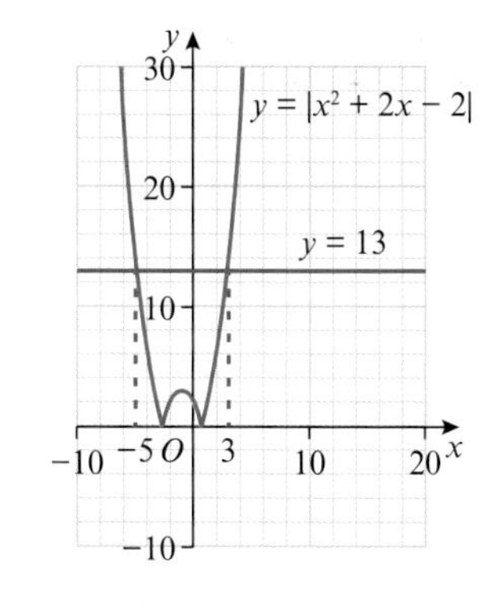

Sketch the graph of $y = |x^2 + 2x - 2|$ and $y = 13$ on the same axes.

Looking at the sketch there are 2 solutions to $|x^2 + 2x - 2| = 13$

$x^2 + 2x - 2 = 13$ or $x^2 + 2x - 2 = -13$

$x^2 + 2x - 15 = 0$ or $x^2 + 2x + 11 = 0$

$(x + 5)(x - 3) = 0$ or $x = \dfrac{-2 \pm \sqrt{2^2 - 4(1)(11)}}{2(1)}$

(no solutions)

$x = -5$ or $x = 3$

We want the solution to $|x^2 + 2x - 2| < 13$

We are looking for the values of x where the graph of $y = |x^2 + 2x - 2|$ is beneath the line $y = 13$.

The solution is $-5 < x < 3$.

c $|x^2 - 6x + 4| < 4$

Sketch the graph of $y = |x^2 - 6x + 4|$ and $y = 4$ on the same axes.

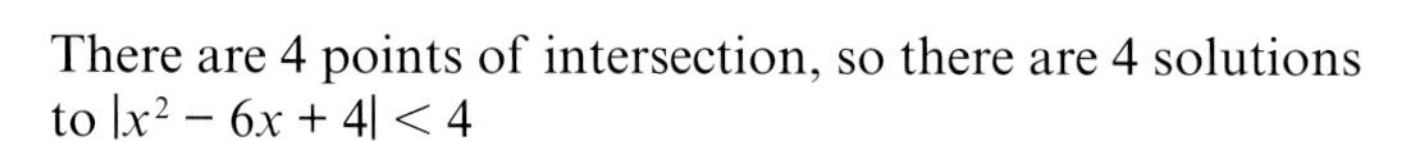

There are 4 points of intersection, so there are 4 solutions to $|x^2 - 6x + 4| < 4$

The first and second solution are when
$$x^2 - 6x + 4 = 4$$
$$x^2 - 6x = 0$$
$$x(x - 6) = 0$$
$$x = 0 \text{ and } x = 6$$

The third and fourth solutions are when
$$x^2 - 6x + 4 = -4$$
$$x^2 - 6x + 8 = 0$$
$$(x - 2)(x - 4) = 0$$
$$x = 2 \text{ and } x = 4$$

We are looking for the values of x for where the graph of $y = |x^2 - 6x + 4|$ is beneath the line $y = 4$

The solution is $0 < x < 2$ and $4 < x < 6$.

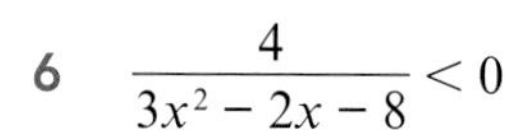

6 $\dfrac{4}{3x^2 - 2x - 8} < 0$

The fraction is undefined when $3x^2 - 2x - 8 = 0$

We need to find the values of x for which the factors are zero.

So, we need to solve $(3x + 4)(x - 2) = 0$

$x = -1\frac{1}{3}$ and $x = 2$ (these are called 'critical points')

Represent these critical values on a number line.

Now substitute x values either side of the critical values, to investigate where $\dfrac{4}{3x^2 - 2x - 8}$ is negative.

Substitute $x = -2$ we get $\frac{4}{3(-2)^2 - 2(-2) - 8}$ which gives a positive value

Substitute $x = 0$ we get $\frac{4}{3(0)^2 - 2(0) - 8}$ which gives a negative value

Substitute $x = 3$ we get $\frac{4}{3(3)^2 - 2(3) - 8}$ which gives a positive value

$\frac{4}{3x^2 - 2x - 8}$ is positive

$-1\frac{1}{3}$ 2 x

$\frac{4}{3x^2 - 2x - 8}$ is negative

So, the solution to $\frac{4}{3x^2 - 2x - 8} < 0$ is $-1\frac{1}{3} < x < 2$.

Exercise 2.5

1 a $x^2 + 4x + 4 = 0$

$$x = \frac{-4 \pm \sqrt{4^2 - 4 \times 1 \times 4}}{2 \times 1}$$

$$x = \frac{-4 \pm \sqrt{0}}{2}$$

$$x = -2$$

The discriminant $b^2 - 4ac$ is **zero** so there are two **equal** roots.

d $x^2 - 3x + 15 = 0$

$$x = \frac{--3 \pm \sqrt{(-3)^2 - 4 \times 1 \times 15}}{2 \times 1}$$

$$x = \frac{--3 \pm \sqrt{-51}}{2}$$

No solutions

The discriminant $b^2 - 4ac$ is **negative** so there are **no real** roots.

h $5x^2 - 2x - 9 = 0$

$$x = \frac{--2 \pm \sqrt{(-2)^2 - 4 \times 5 \times (-9)}}{2 \times 5}$$

$$x = \frac{--2 \pm \sqrt{184}}{10}$$

$$x = \frac{1 + \sqrt{46}}{5} \text{ and } x = \frac{1 - \sqrt{46}}{5}$$

The discriminant $b^2 - 4ac$ is **positive** so there are **two real distinct** roots.

2 $x^2 + kx + 9 = 0$

For two equal roots $b^2 - 4ac = 0$

$k^2 - 4 \times 1 \times 9 = 0$

$(k - 6)(k + 6) = 0$

$k = 6$ and $k = -6$

3 $kx^2 - 4x + 8 = 0$

For two distinct roots $b^2 - 4ac > 0$

$16 - 32k > 0$

$k < 0.5$

4 $3x^2 + 2x + k = 0$

For no roots $b^2 - 4ac < 0$

$2^2 - 4(3)(k) < 0$

$4 - 12k < 0$

$k > \frac{1}{3}$

5 $(k + 1)x^2 + kx - 2k = 0$

For two equal roots $b^2 - 4ac = 0$

$k^2 - 4 \times (k + 1) \times (-2k) = 0$

$k^2 + 8k^2 + 8k = 0$

$9k^2 + 8k = 0$

$k(9k + 8) = 0$

$k = 0$ and $k = -\frac{8}{9}$

6 $kx^2 + 2(k + 3)x + k = 0$

For two distinct roots $b^2 - 4ac > 0$

$[2(k + 3)]^2 - 4 \times k \times k > 0$

$4(k + 3)^2 - 4k^2 > 0$

$4k^2 + 24k + 36 - 4k^2 > 0$

$24k > -36$

$k > -1.5$

7 $3x^2 - 4x + 5 - k = 0$

For two distinct roots $b^2 - 4ac > 0$

$(-4)^2 - 4 \times 3 \times (5 - k) > 0$

$16 - 60 + 12k > 0$

$12k > 44$

$k > 3\frac{2}{3}$

8 $4x^2 - (k - 2)x + 9 = 0$

For two equal roots $b^2 - 4ac = 0$

$[-(k - 2)]^2 - 4 \times 4 \times 9 = 0$

$(k - 2)^2 - 144 = 0$

$(k - 2)^2 = 144$

$k - 2 = 12$ and $k - 2 = -12$

$k = 14$ and $k = -10$

9 $4x^2 + 4(k - 2)x + k = 0$

For two equal roots $b^2 - 4ac = 0$

$16(k - 2)^2 - 16k = 0$

$16k^2 - 64k + 64 - 16k = 0$

$16k^2 - 80k + 64 = 0$

$k^2 - 5k + 4 = 0$

$(k - 4)(k - 1) = 0$

$k = 4$ and $k = 1$

10 $x^2 + (k - 2)x - 2k = 0$

Find the discriminant $b^2 - 4ac$

$(k - 2)^2 - 4 \times 1 \times (-2k)$

$k^2 - 4k + 4 + 8k$

$k^2 + 4k + 4$

$(k + 2)^2$

$(k + 2)^2$ is always greater than or equal to 0, no matter what the value of k.

If k is -2, $(k + 2)^2 = 0$ so $x^2 + (k - 2)x - 2k = 0$ has two equal real roots

For all other values of k, $(k + 2)^2 > 0$ so $x^2 + (k - 2)x - 2k = 0$ has two real distinct roots.

So, the roots of the equation $x^2 + (k - 2)x - 2k = 0$ are real and distinct for all positive real values of k.

11 $kx^2 + 5x - 2k = 0$

Find the discriminant $b^2 - 4ac$

$5^2 - 4 \times k \times (-2k)$

$25 + 8k^2$

If k is negative (or positive) then k^2 is positive and $25 + 8k^2 > 0$ so $kx^2 + 5x - 2k = 0$ has two real distinct roots.

So, the roots of the equation $kx^2 + 5x - 2k = 0$ are real and distinct for all real values of k, $(k \neq 0)$.

Exercise 2.6

1 If $y = kx + 1$ is a tangent to the curve $y = 2x^2 + x + 3$ then they intersect at one point and the equation $2x^2 + x + 3 = kx + 1$ has only one (repeated root).

$2x^2 + x + 3 - kx - 1 = 0$

$2x^2 + x(1 - k) + 2 = 0$

The discriminant $b^2 - 4ac = 0$ for a repeated root.

$(1 - k)^2 - 4 \times 2 \times 2 = 0$

$(1 - k)^2 = 16$

$1 - k = 4$ and $1 - k = -4$

So, $k = -3$ and $k = 5$

2 If the x-axis ($y = 0$) is a tangent to the curve $y = x^2 + (3 - k)x - (4k + 3)$ then they intersect at one point and the equation $x^2 + (3 - k)x - (4k + 3) = 0$ has only one (repeated root).

The discriminant $b^2 - 4ac = 0$ for a repeated root.

$(3 - k)^2 - 4 \times 1 \times -(4k + 3) = 0$

$9 - 6k + k^2 + 16k + 12 = 0$

$k^2 + 10k + 21 = 0$

$(k + 3)(k + 7) = 0$

So, $k = -3$ and $k = -7$

3 If $y = x + c$ is a tangent to the curve $y = 3x + \frac{2}{x}$ then they intersect at one point

and the equation $3x + \frac{2}{x} = x + c$ has only one (repeated root).

$3x + \frac{2}{x} = x + c$ Multiply each term by x

$3x^2 + 2 = x^2 + cx$ Rearrange

$3x^2 - x^2 - cx + 2 = 0$

$2x^2 - cx + 2 = 0$

The discriminant $b^2 - 4ac = 0$ for a repeated root.

$(-c)^2 - 4 \times 2 \times 2 = 0$

$c^2 = 16$

So, $c = \pm 4$

4 If the line $y = 3x + 1$ intersects the curve $y = x^2 + kx + 2$ at two distinct points then the equation $x^2 + kx + 2 = 3x + 1$ has two distinct roots.

$x^2 + kx - 3x + 2 - 1 = 0$

$x^2 + (k - 3)x + 1 = 0$

The discriminant $b^2 - 4ac > 0$ for two distinct roots.

$(k - 3)^2 - 4 \times 1 \times 1 > 0$

$k^2 - 6k + 9 - 4 > 0$

$k^2 - 6k + 5 > 0$

Sketch the graph of $y = k^2 - 6k + 5$

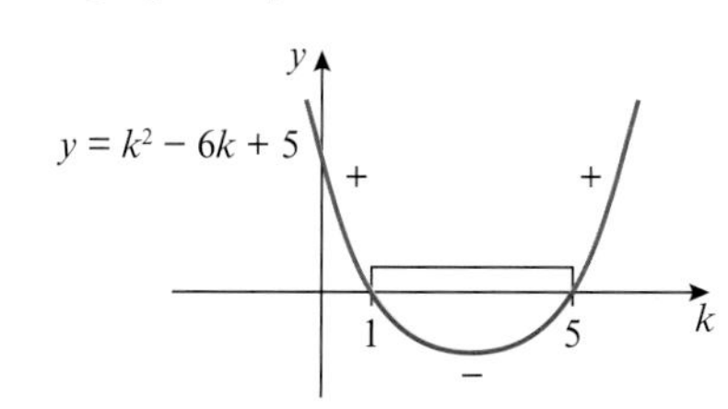

When $y = 0$

$(k - 5)(k - 1) = 0$

$k = 5$ and $k = 1$

So, the k-axis crossing points are $k = 5$ and $k = 1$

For $k^2 - 6k + 5 > 0$ we need to find the range of values of k for which the curve is positive (above the k-axis).

So, $k > 5$ and $k < 1$

5 a If $y = 2x + k$ is a tangent to the curve $x^2 + 2xy + 20 = 0$ then they intersect at one point.

Substituting $y = 2x + k$ into the equation $x^2 + 2xy + 20 = 0$ we get:

$x^2 + 2x(2x + k) + 20 = 0$ which should have only one (repeated root).

$x^2 + 4x^2 + 2kx + 20 = 0$

$5x^2 + 2kx + 20 = 0$

The discriminant $b^2 - 4ac = 0$ for a repeated root.

$(2k)^2 - 4 \times 5 \times 20 = 0$

$4k^2 = 400$

So, $k = \pm 10$

b If $k = 10$ then substituting this into $5x^2 + 2kx + 20 = 0$ we get:

$5x^2 + 20x + 20 = 0$

$x^2 + 4x + 4 = 0$

$(x + 2)^2 = 0$

$x + 2 = 0$

$x = -2$

Substitute $x = -2$ and $k = 10$ into the tangent (linear) equation $y = 2x + k$

$y = 2(-2) + 10$

$y = 6$

So, one intersection point is at $(-2, 6)$

If $k = -10$ then substituting this into $5x^2 + 2kx + 20 = 0$ we get:

$5x^2 - 20x + 20 = 0$

$x^2 - 4x + 4 = 0$

$(x - 2)^2 = 0$

$x - 2 = 0$

$x = 2$

Substitute $x = 2$ and $k = -10$ into the tangent (linear) equation $y = 2x + k$

$y = 2(2) - 10$

$y = -6$

So, the other intersection point is at $(2, -6)$

6 If the line $y = k - x$ intersects the curve $y = x^2 - 7x + 4$ at two distinct points then the equation $x^2 - 7x + 4 = k - x$ has two distinct roots.

$x^2 - 7x + x + 4 - k = 0$

$x^2 - 6x + (4 - k) = 0$

The discriminant $b^2 - 4ac > 0$ for two distinct roots.

$(-6)^2 - 4 \times 1 \times (4 - k) > 0$

$36 - 16 + 4k > 0$

$4k > -20$

$k > -5$

7 We know that the line and the curve intersect but we do not know the number of intersection points.

So, there must be at least one solution to the simultaneous equations:

$y = kx - 10$ (1) and $x^2 + y^2 = 10x$ (2)

Substituting for y in (2)

$x^2 + (kx - 10)^2 = 10x$

$x^2 + k^2x^2 - 20kx + 100 - 10x = 0$

$(1 + k^2)x^2 - (20k + 10)x + 100 = 0$

For at least one solution to this equation, the discriminant $b^2 - 4ac \geqslant 0$

$[-(20k + 10)]^2 - 4 \times (1 + k^2) \times 100 \geqslant 0$

$400k^2 + 400k + 100 - 400 - 400k^2 \geqslant 0$

$400k \geqslant 300$

$k \geqslant 0.75$

8 We know that the line and the curve do not intersect.

So, the equation $x^2 - 5x + 4 = mx - 5$ must have no solutions.

$x^2 - 5x + 4 = mx - 5$

$x^2 - 5x - mx + 9 = 0$

$x^2 - (5 + m) + 9 = 0$

The discriminant $b^2 - 4ac < 0$ for distinct roots or a repeated root.

$[-(5 + m)]^2 - 4 \times 1 \times 9 < 0$

$25 + 10m + m^2 - 36 < 0$

$m^2 + 10m - 11 < 0$

Sketch the graph of $y = m^2 + 10m - 11$

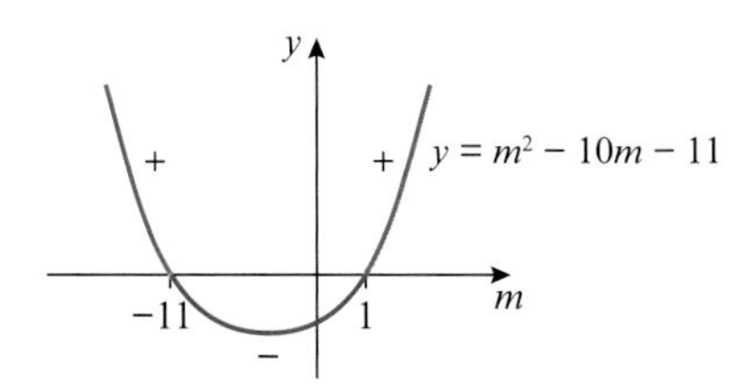

When $y = 0$

$(m - 1)(m + 11) = 0$

$m = 1$ and $m = -11$

So, the m-axis crossing points are $m = 1$ and $m = -11$

For $m^2 + 10m - 11 < 0$ we need to find the range of values of m for which the curve is negative (below the m-axis).

So, $-11 < m < 1$

9 If $y = mx + 6$ is a tangent to the curve $y = x^2 - 4x + 7$ then they intersect at one point and the equation $x^2 - 4x + 7 = mx + 6$ has only one (repeated root).

$x^2 - 4x - mx + 7 - 6 = 0$

$x^2 - (4 + m)x + 1 = 0$

The discriminant $b^2 - 4ac = 0$ for a repeated root.

$[-(4 + m)]^2 - 4 \times 1 \times 1 = 0$

$16 + 8m + m^2 - 4 = 0$

$m^2 + 8m + 12 = 0$

$(m + 2)(m + 6) = 0$

$m = -2$ and $m = -6$

Chapter 3: Factors and polynomials

Exercise 3.1

1 **b** $3\text{P}(x) + \text{Q}(x) = 3(3x^4 + 2x^2 - 1) + 2x^3 + x^2 + 1$

$= 9x^4 + 6x^2 - 3 + 2x^3 + x^2 + 1$

$= 9x^4 + 2x^3 + 7x^2 - 2$

d $\text{P}(x)\text{Q}(x) = (3x^4 + 2x^2 - 1)(2x^3 + x^2 + 1)$

$= 6x^7 + 3x^6 + 3x^4 + 4x^5 + 2x^4 + 2x^2 - 2x^3 - x^2 - 1$

$= 6x^7 + 3x^6 + 4x^5 + 5x^4 - 2x^3 + x^2 - 1$

2 **c** $(3x^2 + 2x - 5)(x^3 + x^2 + 4) = 3x^5 + 3x^4 + 12x^2 + 2x^4 + 2x^3 + 8x - 5x^3 - 5x^2 - 20$

$= 3x^5 + 5x^4 - 3x^3 + 7x^2 + 8x - 20$

f $(3x - 1)^3 = (3x - 1)(3x - 1)(3x - 1)$

$= (9x^2 - 3x - 3x + 1)(3x - 1)$

$= 27x^3 - 9x^2 - 9x^2 + 3x - 9x^2 + 3x + 3x - 1$

$= 27x^3 - 27x^2 + 9x - 1$

3 **b** $(3x + 1)(x^2 + 5x + 2) - [(x^2 - 4x + 2)(x + 3)]$

$= 3x^3 + 15x^2 + 6x + x^2 + 5x + 2 - [x^3 + 3x^2 - 4x^2 - 12x + 2x + 6]$

$= 3x^3 + 15x^2 + 6x + x^2 + 5x + 2 - x^3 - 3x^2 + 4x^2 + 12x - 2x - 6$

$= 2x^3 + 17x^2 + 21x - 4$

c $(2x^3 + x - 1)(x^2 + 3x - 4) - [(x + 2)(x^3 - x^2 + 5x + 2)]$

$= 2x^5 + 6x^4 - 8x^3 + x^3 + 3x^2 - 4x - x^2 - 3x + 4 - [x^4 - x^3 + 5x^2 + 2x + 2x^3 - 2x^2 + 10x + 4]$

$= 2x^5 + 6x^4 - 8x^3 + x^3 + 3x^2 - 4x - x^2 - 3x + 4 - x^4 + x^3 - 5x^2 - 2x - 2x^3 + 2x^2 - 10x - 4$

$= 2x^5 + 5x^4 - 8x^3 - x^2 - 19x$

4 **b** $[\text{f}(x)]^2 = (2x^2 - x - 4)^2$

$= (2x^2 - x - 4)(2x^2 - x - 4)$

$= 4x^4 - 2x^3 - 8x^2 - 2x^3 + x^2 + 4x - 8x^2 + 4x + 16$

$= 4x^4 - 4x^3 - 15x^2 + 8x + 16$

c $f^2(x)$ — $f^2(x)$ means $ff(x)$

$= ff(x)$ — f acts on x first and $f(x) = 2x^2 - x - 4$

$= f(2x^2 - x - 4)$

$= 2(2x^2 - x - 4)^2 - (2x^2 - x - 4) - 4$

$= 2(2x^2 - x - 4)(2x^2 - x - 4) - (2x^2 - x - 4) - 4$

$= 2(4x^4 - 2x^3 - 8x^2 - 2x^3 + x^2 + 4x - 8x^2 + 4x + 16) - 2x^2 + x + 4 - 4$

$= 8x^4 - 4x^3 - 16x^2 - 4x^3 + 2x^2 + 8x - 16x^2 + 8x + 32 - 2x^2 + x + 4 - 4$

$= 8x^4 - 8x^3 - 32x^2 + 17x + 32$

Exercise 3.2

1 d $(x^3 - 3x - 2) \div (x - 2)$

There are no x^2 terms in $x^3 - 3x - 2$, so we write it as $x^3 + 0x^2 - 3x - 2$

Step 1

$$\begin{array}{r|l} & x^2 \\ x - 2 & x^3 + 0x^2 - 3x - 2 \\ & \underline{x^3 - 2x^2} \\ & \quad\; 2x^2 - 3x \end{array}$$

divide the first term of the polynomial by x, $x^3 \div x = x^2$

multiply $(x - 2)$ by x^2

subtract and bring down the $-3x$ from the next column

Step 2

$$\begin{array}{r|l} & x^2 + 2x \\ x - 2 & x^3 + 0x^2 - 3x - 2 \\ & \underline{x^3 - 2x^2} \\ & \quad\; 2x^2 - 3x \\ & \quad\; \underline{2x^2 - 4x} \\ & \qquad\qquad x - 2 \end{array}$$

divide $2x^2$ by x so, $2x^2 \div x = 2x$

multiply $(x - 2)$ by $2x$

subtract and bring down the -2 from the next column

Step 3

$$\begin{array}{r|l} & x^2 + 2x + 1 \\ x - 2 & x^3 + 0x^2 - 3x - 2 \\ & \underline{x^3 - 2x^2} \\ & \quad\; 2x^2 - 3x \\ & \quad\; \underline{2x^2 - 4x} \\ & \qquad\qquad x - 2 \\ & \qquad\qquad \underline{x - 2} \\ & \qquad\qquad\quad 0 \end{array}$$

divide x by x so, $x \div x = 1$

multiply $(x - 2)$ by 1 and subtract

So, $(x^3 - 3x - 2) \div (x - 2) = x^2 + 2x + 1$

f $(x^3 + 2x^2 - 9x - 18) \div (x + 2)$

Step 1

$$\begin{array}{rll} & x^2 & \\ x + 2\big) & \overline{x^3 + 2x^2 - 9x - 18} & \text{divide the first term of the polynomial by } x,\ x^3 \div x = x^2 \\ & \underline{x^3 + 2x^2} & \text{multiply } (x + 2) \text{ by } x^2 \\ & 0 - 9x - 18 & \text{subtract and bring down the } -9x \text{ and the } -18 \text{ from the next columns} \end{array}$$

Step 2

$$\begin{array}{rll} & x^2 \quad -9 & \\ x + 2\big) & \overline{x^3 + 2x^2 - 9x - 18} & \\ & \underline{x^3 + 2x^2} & \\ & 0 - 9x - 18 & \text{divide } -9x \text{ by } x \text{ so, } -9x \div x = -9 \\ & \underline{-9x - 18} & \text{multiply } (x + 2) \text{ by } -9 \\ & 0 & \text{subtract} \end{array}$$

So, $(x^3 + 2x^2 - 9x - 18) \div (x + 2) = x^2 - 9$

2 b $(6x^3 + 11x^2 - 3x - 2) \div (3x + 1)$

Step 1

$$\begin{array}{rll} & 2x^2 & \\ 3x + 1\big) & \overline{6x^3 + 11x^2 - 3x - 2} & \text{divide the first term of the polynomial by } 3x,\ 6x^3 \div 3x = 2x^2 \\ & \underline{6x^3 + 2x^2} & \text{multiply } (3x + 1) \text{ by } 2x^2 \\ & 9x^2 - 3x & \text{subtract and bring down the } -3x \text{ from the next column} \end{array}$$

Step 2

$$\begin{array}{rll} & 2x^2 + 3x & \\ 3x + 1\big) & \overline{6x^3 + 11x^2 - 3x - 2} & \\ & \underline{6x^3 + 2x^2} & \\ & 9x^2 - 3x & \text{divide } 9x^2 \text{ by } 3x \text{ so, } 9x^2 \div 3x = 3x \\ & \underline{9x^2 + 3x} & \text{multiply } (3x + 1) \text{ by } 3x \\ & -6x - 2 & \text{subtract and bring down the } -2 \text{ from the next column} \end{array}$$

Step 3

$$\begin{array}{rll} & 2x^2 + 3x \quad -2 & \\ 3x + 1\big) & \overline{6x^3 + 11x^2 - 3x - 2} & \\ & \underline{6x^3 + 2x^2} & \\ & 9x^2 - 3x & \\ & \underline{9x^2 + 3x} & \\ & -6x - 2 & \text{divide } -6x \text{ by } 3x \text{ so, } -6x \div 3x = -2 \\ & \underline{-6x - 2} & \text{multiply } (3x + 1) \text{ by } -2 \text{ and subtract} \\ & 0 & \end{array}$$

So, $(6x^3 + 11x^2 - 3x - 2) \div (3x + 1) = 2x^2 + 3x - 2$

d $(3x^3 - 21x^2 + 4x - 28) \div (x - 7)$

Step 1

$$\begin{array}{r l}
 & 3x^2 \\
x - 7 \,\big) & \overline{3x^3 - 21x^2 + 4x - 28} \\
 & \underline{3x^3 - 21x^2} \\
 & \qquad\quad 0 + 4x - 28
\end{array}$$

divide the first term of the polynomial by x, $3x^3 \div x = 3x^2$

multiply $(x - 7)$ by $3x^2$

subtract and bring down the $+4x$ and the -28 from the next columns

Step 2

$$\begin{array}{r l}
 & 3x^2 \qquad\quad +4 \\
x - 7) \,\big) & \overline{3x^3 - 21x^2 + 4x - 28} \\
 & \underline{3x^3 - 21x^2} \\
 & \qquad\quad 0 + 4x - 28 \\
 & \qquad\quad \underline{0 + 4x - 28} \\
 & \qquad\qquad\qquad\quad 0
\end{array}$$

divide $4x$ by x so, $4x \div x = 4$

multiply $(x - 7)$ by 4 and subtract

So, $(3x^3 - 21x^2 + 4x - 28) \div (x - 7) = 3x^2 + 4$

3 b $(2x^3 + 9x^2 + 25) \div (x + 5)$

There are no x terms in $2x^3 + 9x^2 + 25$, so we write it as $2x^3 + 9x^2 + 0x + 25$

Step 1

$$\begin{array}{r l}
 & 2x^2 \\
x + 5 \,\big) & \overline{2x^3 + 9x^2 + 0x + 25} \\
 & \underline{2x^3 + 10x^2} \\
 & \qquad -x^2 + 0x
\end{array}$$

divide the first term of the polynomial by x, $2x^3 \div x = 2x^2$

multiply $(x + 5)$ by $2x^2$

subtract and bring down the $+0x$ from the next column

Step 2

$$\begin{array}{r l}
 & 2x^2 - x \\
x + 5 \,\big) & \overline{2x^3 + 9x^2 + 0x + 25} \\
 & \underline{2x^3 + 10x^2} \\
 & \qquad -x^2 + 0x \\
 & \qquad \underline{-x^2 - 5x} \\
 & \qquad\qquad\quad 5x + 25
\end{array}$$

divide $-x^2$ by x so, $-x^2 \div x = -x$

multiply $(x + 5)$ by $-x$

subtract and bring down the $+25$ from the next column

Step 3

$$\begin{array}{r} 2x^2 - x \quad + 5 \\ x+5\overline{)2x^3 + 9x^2 + 0x + 25} \end{array}$$

$\underline{2x^3 + 10x^2}$

$-x^2 + 0x$

$\underline{-x^2 - 5x}$

$5x + 25$ — divide $5x$ by x so, $5x \div x = 5$

$\underline{5x + 25}$ — multiply $(x + 5)$ by 5 and subtract

0

$(2x^3 + 9x^2 + 25) \div (x + 5) = 2x^2 - x + 5$

3 c $(3x^3 - 50x + 8) \div (3x^2 + 12x - 2)$

There are no x^2 terms in $3x^3 - 50x + 8$, so we write it as $3x^3 + 0x^2 - 50x + 8$

Step 1

$$\begin{array}{r} x \qquad\qquad \\ 3x^2 + 12x - 2\overline{)3x^3 + 0x^2 - 50x + 8} \end{array}$$

$3x^3 \div 3x^2 = x$

$\underline{3x^3 + 12x^2 - 2x}$ — multiply $(3x^2 + 12x - 2)$ by x

$-12x^2 - 48x + 8$ — subtract and bring down the $+8$ from the next column

Step 2

$$\begin{array}{r} x \qquad -4 \\ 3x^2 + 12x - 2\overline{)3x^3 + 0x^2 - 50x + 8} \end{array}$$

$\underline{3x^3 + 12x^2 - 2x}$

$-12x^2 - 48x + 8$ — divide $-12x^2$ by $3x^2$ so $-12x^2 \div 3x^2 = -4$

$\underline{-12x^2 - 48x + 8}$ — multiply $(3x^2 + 12x - 2)$ by -4 and subtract

0

So, $(3x^3 - 50x + 8) \div (3x^2 + 12x - 2) = x - 4$

4 a $(x^4 - 1) \div (x + 1)$

There are no x^3, x^2 nor x terms in $x^4 - 1$, so we write it as $x^4 + 0x^3 + 0x^2 + 0x - 1$

Step 1

$$\begin{array}{r} x^3 \qquad\qquad\qquad \\ x+1\overline{)x^4 + 0x^3 + 0x^2 + 0x - 1} \end{array}$$

divide the first term of the polynomial by x, $x^4 \div x = x^3$

$\underline{x^4 + x^3}$ — multiply $(x + 1)$ by x^3

$-x^3 + 0x^2$ — subtract and bring down the $+0x^2$ from the next column

Step 2

$$
\begin{array}{r l}
x^3 - x^2 & \\
x + 1\overline{)x^4 + 0x^3 + 0x^2 + 0x - 1} & \\
\underline{x^4 + x^3} & \\
-x^3 + 0x^2 & \text{divide } -x^3 \text{ by } x,\ -x^3 \div x = -x^2 \\
\underline{-x^3 - x^2} & \text{multiply } (x + 1) \text{ by } -x^2 \\
x^2 + 0x & \text{subtract and bring down the } +0x \text{ from the next column}
\end{array}
$$

Step 3

$$
\begin{array}{r l}
x^3 - x^2 \ + x & \\
x + 1\overline{)x^4 + 0x^3 + 0x^2 + 0x - 1} & \\
\underline{x^4 + x^3} & \\
-x^3 + 0x^2 & \\
\underline{-x^3 - x^2} & \\
x^2 + 0x & \text{divide } x^2 \text{ by } x,\ x^2 \div x = x \\
\underline{x^2 + x} & \text{multiply } (x + 1) \text{ by } x \\
-x - 1 & \text{subtract and bring down the } -1 \text{ from the next column}
\end{array}
$$

Step 4

$$
\begin{array}{r l}
x^3 - x^2 \ + x \ - 1 & \\
x + 1\overline{)x^4 + 0x^3 + 0x^2 + 0x - 1} & \\
\underline{x^4 + x^3} & \\
-x^3 + 0x^2 & \\
\underline{-x^3 - x^2} & \\
x^2 + 0x & \\
\underline{x^2 + x} & \\
-x - 1 & \text{divide } -x \text{ by } x,\ -x \div x = -1 \\
\underline{-x - 1} & \text{multiply } (x + 1) \text{ by } -1 \\
0 & \text{subtract}
\end{array}
$$

$(x^4 - 1) \div (x + 1) = x^3 - x^2 + x - 1$

4 b $(x^3 - 8) \div (x - 2)$

There are no x^2 terms in $x^3 - 8$, so we write it as $x^3 + 0x^2 + 0x - 8$

Step 1

$$\begin{array}{r l}
x^2 \qquad\qquad & \\
x - 2\overline{)x^3 + 0x^2 + 0x - 8} & \text{divide the first term of the polynomial by } x,\ x^3 \div x = x^2 \\
\underline{x^3 - 2x^2} \qquad\qquad & \text{multiply } (x - 2) \text{ by } x^2 \\
2x^2 + 0x \qquad & \text{subtract and bring down the } +0x \text{ from the next column}
\end{array}$$

Step 2

$$\begin{array}{r l}
x^2 + 2x \qquad\quad & \\
x - 2\overline{)x^3 + 0x^2 + 0x - 8} & \\
\underline{x^3 - 2x^2} \qquad\qquad & \\
2x^2 + 0x \qquad & \text{divide the first term of the polynomial by } x,\ 2x^2 \div x = 2x \\
\underline{2x^2 - 4x} \qquad & \text{multiply } (x - 2) \text{ by } 2x \\
4x - 8 & \text{subtract and bring down the } -8 \text{ from the next column}
\end{array}$$

Step 3

$$\begin{array}{r l}
x^2 + 2x + 4 \qquad & \\
x - 2\overline{)x^3 + 0x^2 + 0x - 8} & \\
\underline{x^3 - 2x^2} \qquad\qquad & \\
2x^2 + 0x \qquad & \\
\underline{2x^2 - 4x} \qquad & \\
4x - 8 & \text{divide the first term of the polynomial by } x,\ 4x \div x = 4 \\
\underline{4x - 8} & \text{multiply } (x - 2) \text{ by } 4 \\
0 & \text{subtract}
\end{array}$$

$(x^3 - 8) \div (x - 2) = x^2 + 2x + 4$

Exercise 3.3

1 a Let $f(x) = x^3 - 3x^2 - 6x + 8$ — if $f(4) = 0$, then $x - 4$ is a factor.

$f(4) = (4)^3 - 3(4)^2 - 6(4) + 8$

$= 64 - 48 - 24 + 8$

$= 0$

So, $x - 4$ is a factor of $x^3 - 3x^2 - 6x + 8$

d If $3x + 1$ is a factor then $3x + 1 = 0$

$$3x = -1$$

$$x = -\frac{1}{3}$$

Substituting $x = -\frac{1}{3}$ into $6x^3 + 11x^2 - 3x - 2$ should confirm this.

Let $f(x) = 6x^3 + 11x^2 - 3x - 2$ so if $f\left(-\frac{1}{3}\right) = 0$, then $3x + 1$ is a factor.

$$f\left(-\frac{1}{3}\right) = 6\left(-\frac{1}{3}\right)^3 + 11\left(-\frac{1}{3}\right)^2 - 3\left(-\frac{1}{3}\right) - 2$$

$$= -\frac{6}{27} + \frac{11}{9} + 1 - 2$$

$$= 0$$

So, $3x + 1$ is a factor $6x^3 + 11x^2 - 3x - 2$

2 a Using the factor theorem $f(-1) = 0$

$f(-1) = 0$ gives $6(-1)^3 + 27(-1)^2 + a(-1) + 8 = 0$

$$-6 + 27 - a + 8 = 0$$

$$a = 29$$

b Using the factor theorem $f(-7) = 0$

$f(-7) = 0$ gives $(-7)^3 - 5(-7)^2 - 6(-7) + a = 0$

$$-343 - 245 + 42 + a = 0$$

$$a = 546$$

c If $2x + 3$ is a factor then $2x + 3 = 0$

$$2x = -3$$

$$x = -\frac{3}{2}$$

Substituting $x = -\frac{3}{2}$ into $4x^3 + ax^2 + 29x + 30$ should confirm this.

Using the factor theorem $f\left(-\frac{3}{2}\right) = 0$

$f\left(-\frac{3}{2}\right) = 0$ gives $4\left(-\frac{3}{2}\right)^3 + a\left(-\frac{3}{2}\right)^2 + 29\left(-\frac{3}{2}\right) + 30 = 0$

$$-\frac{27}{2} + \frac{9a}{4} - \frac{87}{2} + 30 = 0$$

$$\frac{9a}{4} = 27$$

$$a = 12$$

3 Using the factor theorem $f(2) = 0$

$f(2) = 0$ gives $(2)^3 + a(2)^2 + b(2) - 4 = 0$

$$8 + 4a + 2b - 4 = 0$$
$$2b = -4 - 4a$$
$$b = -2 - 2a$$

4 a Let $f(x) = x^3 + ax^2 + bx + 30$

If $x^2 + 3x - 10 = (x + 5)(x - 2)$ is a factor of $f(x)$, then $(x + 5)$ and $(x - 2)$ are also factors of $f(x)$

Using the factor theorem:

$f(-5) = 0$ gives $(-5)^3 + a(-5)^2 + b(-5) + 30 = 0$

$$-125 + 25a - 5b + 30 = 0$$
$$25a - 5b = 95$$
$$5a - b = 19 \qquad (1)$$

$f(2) = 0$ gives $(2)^3 + a(2)^2 + b(2) + 30 = 0$

$$8 + 4a + 2b + 30 = 0$$
$$4a + 2b = -38$$
$$2a + b = -19 \qquad (2)$$

Adding (1) and (2) gives $7a = 0$ so $a = 0$

Substituting in (2), $2(0) + b = -19$

$$b = -19$$

So, $a = 0$ and $b = -19$.

b Let $f(x) = ax^3 - 17x^2 + bx - 15$

If $2x^2 - 11x + 5 = (2x - 1)(x - 5)$ is a factor of $f(x)$, then $(2x - 1)$ and $(x - 5)$ are also factors of $f(x)$

Using the factor theorem:

$f\left(\frac{1}{2}\right) = 0$ gives $a\left(\frac{1}{2}\right)^3 - 17\left(\frac{1}{2}\right)^2 + b\left(\frac{1}{2}\right) - 15 = 0$

$$\frac{1}{8}a - \frac{17}{4} + \frac{1}{2}b - 15 = 0 \qquad \text{multiply each term by 8}$$
$$a - 34 + 4b - 120 = 0$$
$$a + 4b = 154 \qquad (1)$$

$f(5) = 0$ gives $a(5)^3 - 17(5)^2 + b(5) - 15 = 0$

$$125a - 425 + 5b - 15 = 0$$
$$125a + 5b = 440$$
$$25a + b = 88 \qquad (2)$$

Multiply (2) by 4 gives $100a + 4b = 352$ (3)

Subtracting (1) from (3) gives $99a = 198$ so $a = 2$

Substituting in (2), $25(2) + b = 88$

$$b = 38$$

So, $a = 2$ and $b = 38$.

c Let $f(x) = 4x^3 + ax^2 + bx + 30$

If $4x^2 - 4x - 15 = (2x + 3)(2x - 5)$ is a factor of $f(x)$, then $(2x + 3)$ and $(2x - 5)$ are also factors of $f(x)$

Using the factor theorem:

$f\left(-\frac{3}{2}\right) = 0$ gives $4\left(-\frac{3}{2}\right)^3 + a\left(-\frac{3}{2}\right)^2 + b\left(-\frac{3}{2}\right) + 30 = 0$

$$-\frac{27}{2} + \frac{9}{4}a - \frac{3}{2}b + 30 = 0$$ multiply each term by 4

$$-54 + 9a - 6b + 120 = 0$$

$$9a - 6b = -66$$ divide each term by 3

$$3a - 2b = -22$$ (1)

$f\left(\frac{5}{2}\right) = 0$ gives $4\left(\frac{5}{2}\right)^3 + a\left(\frac{5}{2}\right)^2 + b\left(\frac{5}{2}\right) + 30 = 0$

$$\frac{125}{2} + \frac{25}{4}a + \frac{5}{2}b + 30 = 0$$ multiply each term by 4

$$25a + 10b = -370$$

$$5a + 2b = -74$$ (2)

Adding (1) and (2) gives $8a = -96$ so $a = -12$

Substituting in (2), $5(-12) + 2b = -74$

$$b = -7$$

So, $a = -12$ and $b = -7$.

5 Let $f(x) = x^3 - 6x^2 + 11x + a$

As $x^2 - 5x + 6 = (x - 3)(x - 2)$ then a factor of $f(x)$ could be $(x - 3)$ or $(x - 2)$ or both.

Using the factor theorem:

$f(3) = 0$ gives $(3)^3 - 6(3)^2 + 11(3) + a = 0$

$$27 - 54 + 33 + a = 0$$

$$a = -6$$

$f(2) = 0$ gives $(2)^3 - 6(2)^2 + 11(2) + a = 0$

$$8 - 24 + 22 + a = 0$$

$$a = -6$$

So, $f(x) = x^3 - 6x^2 + 11x - 6$,

The possible value of a is -6.

6 If $(x - 2)$ is a factor of $3x^3 - (a - b)x - 8$ then $f(2) = 0$

$f(2) = 0$ gives $3(2)^3 - 2(a - b) - 8 = 0$

$$24 - 2a + 2b - 8 = 0$$

$$-2a + 2b = -16 \qquad \text{divide each term by } -2$$

$$a - b = 8 \qquad (1)$$

If $(x - 2)$ is a factor of $x^3 - (a + b)x + 30$ then $f(2) = 0$

$f(2) = 0$ gives $2^3 - 2(a + b) + 30 = 0$

$$8 - 2a - 2b + 30 = 0$$

$$-2a - 2b = -38 \qquad \text{divide each term by } -2$$

$$a + b = 19 \qquad (2)$$

Adding (1) and (2) gives $2a = 27$ so, $a = 13.5$

Substituting in (2) gives $13.5 + b = 19$ so, $b = 5.5$

So, $a = 13.5$ and $b = 5.5$.

7 **a** Let $f(x) = 2x^3 - px^2 - 2qx + q$

As $x - 3$ is a factor of $f(x)$ then using the factor theorem $f(3) = 0$

$f(3) = 0$ gives $2(3)^3 - p(3)^2 - 2q(3) + q = 0$

$$54 - 9p - 6q + q = 0$$

$$-9p - 5q = -54$$

$$9p + 5q = 54$$

As $2x - 1$ is a factor of $f(x)$ then using the factor theorem $f\left(\frac{1}{2}\right) = 0$

$f\left(\frac{1}{2}\right) = 0$ gives $2\left(\frac{1}{2}\right)^3 - p\left(\frac{1}{2}\right)^2 - 2q\left(\frac{1}{2}\right) + q = 0$

$$\frac{1}{4} - \frac{1}{4}p - q + q = 0$$

$$\frac{1}{4}p = \frac{1}{4}$$

$$p = 1$$

Substituting into $9p + 5q = 54$ so, $9 + 5q = 54$

$$q = 9$$

So, $p = 1$ and $q = 9$

b $f(x) = 2x^3 - x^2 - 18x + 9$

If $(x + 3)$ is also a factor of the expression, then using the factor theorem $f(-3) = 0$

$f(-3) = 2(-3)^3 - (-3)^2 - 18(-3) + 9$

$f(x) = -54 - 9 + 54 + 9$

$f(-3) = 0$ so $x + 3$ is also a factor of the expression.

8 a Let $f(x) = x^3 + 8x^2 + 4ax - 3a$

If $x + a$ is a factor of $x^3 + 8x^2 + 4ax - 3a$, then using the factor theorem, $f(-a) = 0$

$f(-a) = (-a)^3 + 8(-a)^2 + 4a(-a) - 3a$

$0 = -a^3 + 8a^2 - 4a^2 - 3a$

$0 = -a^3 + 4a^2 - 3a$

$0 = -a^3 + 4a^2 - 3a$ rearranging

$a^3 - 4a^2 + 3a = 0$ shown

b Solving $a^3 - 4a^2 + 3a = 0$ factorise

$a(a^2 - 4a + 3) = 0$ factorise

$a(a - 3)(a - 1) = 0$

So, the possible values of a are: 0, 1, 3

Exercise 3.4

1 a Let $f(x) = 2x^3 - x^2 - 2x + 1$

If $x - 1$ is a factor of $f(x) = 2x^3 - x^2 - 2x + 1$ then $f(1) = 0$

$f(1) = 2(1)^3 - (1)^2 - 2(1) + 1$

$= 2 - 1 - 2 + 1$

$= 0$

b Since $(x - 1)$ is a factor, $2x^3 - x^2 - 2x + 1 = (x - 1)(ax^2 + bx + c)$

coefficient of x^3 is 2, so $a = 2$ since $1 \times 2 = 2$

constant term is -1, so $c = -1$ since $-1 \times -1 = +1$

$2x^3 - x^2 - 2x + 1 = (x - 1)(2x^2 + bx - 1)$ expand and collect like terms

$2x^3 - x^2 - 2x + 1 = 2x^3 + bx^2 - x - 2x^2 - bx + 1$

$2x^3 - x^2 - 2x + 1 = 2x^3 + (b - 2)x^2 - (1 + b)x + 1$

Equating coefficients of x^2: $b - 2 = -1$

$b = 1$

$f(x) = (x - 1)(2x^2 + x - 1)$

$f(x) = (x - 1)(2x - 1)(x + 1)$

2 a Let $f(x) = x^3 + 2x^2 - 3x - 10$

The positive and negative factors of -10 are $\pm1, \pm2, \pm5, \pm10$

$f(1) = 1^3 + 2(1)^2 - 3(1) - 10 \neq 0$

So, $(x - 1)$ is not a factor of $f(x)$

$f(2) = 2^3 + 2(2)^2 - 3(2) - 10 = 0$

So, $(x - 2)$ is a factor of $f(x)$

The other factors can be found by trial and error, long division or by equating coefficients.

Using long division:

Step 1

x^2	
$x-2\,\overline{)\,x^3+2x^2-3x-10}$	divide the first term of the polynomial by x, $x^3 \div x = x^2$
$\underline{x^3-2x^2}$	multiply $(x-2)$ by x^2
$4x^2-3x$	subtract and bring down the $-3x$ from the next column

Step 2

x^2+4x	
$x-2\,\overline{)\,x^3+2x^2-3x-10}$	
$\underline{x^3-2x^2}$	
$4x^2-3x$	divide $4x^2$ by x so, $4x^2 \div x = 4x$
$\underline{4x^2-8x}$	multiply $(x-2)$ by $4x$
$5x-10$	subtract and bring down the -10 from the next column

Step 3

x^2+4x+5	
$x-2\,\overline{)\,x^3+2x^2-3x-10}$	
$\underline{x^3-2x^2}$	
$4x^2-3x$	
$\underline{4x^2-8x}$	multiply $(x-2)$ by $4x$
$5x-10$	divide $5x$ by x so, $5x \div x = 5$
$\underline{5x-10}$	multiply $(x-2)$ by 5
0	subtract

So, $(x^3 + 2x^2 - 3x - 10) = (x-2)(x^2 + 4x + 5)$

Note that $x^2 + 4x + 5$ cannot be factorised into two further linear factors, since the discriminant < 0

$x^3 + 2x^2 - 3x - 10 = (x-2)(x^2 + 4x + 5)$

TIP

Continuing the trial and error method to find all factors can be lengthy. Once one factor has been found it may be easier to use division or comparing coefficients to find the other(s).

g Let $f(x) = 4x^3 - 8x^2 - x + 2$

The positive and negative factors of $+2$ are ±1, ±2

$f(1) = 4(1)^3 - 8(1)^2 - 1 + 2 \neq 0$

So, $(x-1)$ is not a factor of $f(x)$

$f(2) = 4(2)^3 - 8(2)^2 - 2 + 2 = 0$

So, $(x-2)$ is a factor of $f(x)$

The other factors can be found by trial and error, long division or by equating coefficients.

Comparing coefficients:

Since $(x - 2)$ is a factor, $4x^3 - 8x^2 - x + 2 = (x - 2)(ax^2 + bx + c)$

coefficient of x^3 is 4 , so $a = 4$ since $1 \times 4 = 4$

constant term is -1, so $c = -1$ since $-2 \times -1 = +2$

$4x^3 - 8x^2 - x + 2 = (x - 2)(4x^2 + bx - 1)$ — expand and collect like terms

$4x^3 - 8x^2 - x + 2 = 4x^3 + bx^2 - x - 8x^2 - 2bx + 2$

$4x^3 - 8x^2 - x + 2 = 4x^3 + (b - 8)x^2 - (1 + 2b)x + 2$

Equating coefficients of x^2: $b - 8 = -8$

$b = 0$

$f(x) = (x - 2)(4x^2 - 1)$

$f(x) = (x - 2)(2x - 1)(2x + 1)$

$4x^3 - 8x^2 - x + 2 = (x - 2)(2x - 1)(2x + 1)$

3 d Let $f(x) = 2x^3 + 3x^2 - 17x + 12$

The positive and negative factors of +12 are ±1, ±2, ±3, ±4, ±6, ±12

$f(1) = 2 \times 1^3 + 3(1)^2 - 17(1) + 12 = 0$

So, $(x - 1)$ is a factor of $f(x)$

Use long division to find the other factors:

Step 1

$$\begin{array}{r} 2x^2 \\ x - 1\overline{)2x^3 + 3x^2 - 17x + 12} \\ \underline{2x^3 - 2x^2} \\ 5x^2 - 17x \end{array}$$

divide the first term of the polynomial by x, $2x^3 \div x = 2x^2$

multiply $(x - 1)$ by $2x^2$

subtract and bring down the $-17x$ from the next column

Step 2

$$\begin{array}{r} 2x^2 + 5x \\ x - 1\overline{)2x^3 + 3x^2 - 17x + 12} \\ \underline{2x^3 - 2x^2} \\ 5x^2 - 17x \\ \underline{5x^2 - 5x} \\ -12x + 12 \end{array}$$

divide $5x^2$ by x so, $5x^2 \div x = 5x$

multiply $(x - 1)$ by $5x$

subtract and bring down the -10 from the next column

Step 3

$$\begin{array}{r|l} & 2x^2 + 5x - 12 \\ x - 1) & 2x^3 + 3x^2 - 17x + 12 \end{array}$$

$2x^3 - 2x^2$

$5x^2 - 17x$

$5x^2 - 5x$ — multiply $(x - 1)$ by $4x$

$-12x + 12$ — divide $-12x$ by x so, $-12x \div x = -12$

$-12x + 12$ — multiply $(x - 1)$ by -12

0 — subtract

$f(x) = 2x^3 - x^2 - 2x + 1 = (x - 1)(2x^2 + 5x - 12)$

$= (x - 1)(2x - 3)(x + 4)$

Hence $(x - 1)(2x - 3)(x + 4) = 0$

$x = 1$, $x = 1.5$ or $x = -4$

g Let $f(x) = 4x^3 + 12x^2 + 5x - 6$

The positive and negative factors of -6 are $\pm1, \pm2, \pm3, \pm6$

$f(1) = 4 \times 1^3 + 12(1)^2 + 5(1) - 6 \neq 0$

So, $(x - 1)$ is not a factor of $f(x)$

$f(-2) = 4 \times (-2)^3 + 12(-2)^2 + 5(-2) - 6 = 0$

So, $(x + 2)$ is a factor of $f(x)$

The other factors can be found by equating coefficients:

Since $(x + 2)$ is a factor, $4x^3 + 12x^2 + 5x - 6 = (x + 2)(ax^2 + bx + c)$ — coefficient of x^3 is 4, so $a = 4$ since $1 \times 4 = 4$

constant term is -3, so $c = -3$ since $+2 \times -3 = -6$

$4x^3 + 12x^2 + 5x - 6 = (x + 2)(4x^2 + bx - 3)$ — expand and collect like terms

$4x^3 + 12x^2 + 5x - 6 = 4x^3 + bx^2 - 3x + 8x^2 + 2bx - 6$

$4x^3 + 12x^2 + 5x - 6 = 4x^3 + (b + 8)x^2 - (3 - 2b)x - 6$

Equating coefficients of x^2: $b + 8 = 12$

$b = 4$

$f(x) = (x + 2)(4x^2 + 4x - 3)$

$f(x) = (x + 2)(2x - 1)(2x + 3)$

Hence $(x + 2)(2x - 1)(2x + 3) = 0$

$x = -2$, $x = 0.5$, and $x = -1.5$

4 a Let $f(x) = x^3 + 5x^2 - 4x - 2$

The positive and negative factors of -2 are $\pm1, \pm2$

$f(1) = (1)^3 + 5(1)^2 - 4(1) - 2 = 0$

So, $(x - 1)$ is a factor of $f(x)$

The other factors can be found by long division:

Step 1

$$\begin{array}{r l}
x^2 & \\
x - 1\,\overline{)\,x^3 + 5x^2 - 4x - 2} & \text{divide the first term of the polynomial by } x,\ x^3 \div x = x^2 \\
\underline{x^3 - x^2} & \text{multiply } (x - 1) \text{ by } x^2 \\
6x^2 - 4x & \text{subtract and bring down the } -4x \text{ from the next column}
\end{array}$$

Step 2

$$\begin{array}{r l}
x^2 + 6x & \\
x - 1\,\overline{)\,x^3 + 5x^2 - 4x - 2} & \\
\underline{x^3 - x^2} & \\
6x^2 - 4x & \text{divide the first term of the polynomial by } x,\ 6x^2 \div x = 6x \\
\underline{6x^2 - 6x} & \text{multiply } (x - 1) \text{ by } 6x \\
2x - 2 & \text{subtract and bring down the } -2 \text{ from the next column}
\end{array}$$

Step 3

$$\begin{array}{r l}
x^2 + 6x + 2 & \\
x - 1\,\overline{)\,x^3 + 5x^2 - 4x - 2} & \\
\underline{x^3 - x^2} & \\
6x^2 - 4x & \\
\underline{6x^2 - 6x} & \text{multiply } (x - 2) \text{ by } 4x \\
2x - 2 & \text{divide } 5x \text{ by } x \text{ so, } 5x \div x = 5 \\
\underline{2x - 2} & \text{multiply } (x - 1) \text{ by } 2 \\
0 & \text{subtract}
\end{array}$$

$f(x) = (x - 1)(x^2 + 6x + 2)$

Note that $x^2 + 6x + 2$ cannot easily be factorised into two further linear factors, so use the quadratic formula.

Hence for $(x - 1)(x^2 + 6x + 2) = 0$

$$x = 1 \text{ or } x = \frac{-6 \pm \sqrt{6^2 - 4 \times 1 \times 2}}{2 \times 1}$$

$$x = 1 \text{ or } x = \frac{-6 \pm 2\sqrt{7}}{2}$$

$x = 1$, $x = -3 + \sqrt{7}$ or $x = -3 - \sqrt{7}$

c Let $f(x) = x^3 + 2x^2 - 7x - 2$

The positive and negative factors of -2 are $\pm1, \pm2$

$f(2) = (2)^3 + 2(2)^2 - 7(2) - 2 = 0$

So, $(x - 2)$ is a factor of $f(x)$

The other factors can be found by equating coefficients:

Since $(x - 2)$ is a factor, $x^3 + 2x^2 - 7x - 2 = (x - 2)(ax^2 + bx + c)$

coefficient of x^3 is 1, so $a = 1$ since $1 \times 1 = 1$

constant term is $+1$, so $c = +1$ since $-2 \times 1 = -2$

$x^3 + 2x^2 - 7x - 2 = (x - 2)(x^2 + bx + 1)$ expand and collect like terms

$x^3 + 2x^2 - 7x - 2 = x^3 + bx^2 + x - 2x^2 - 2bx - 2$

$x^3 + 2x^2 - 7x - 2 = x^3 + (b - 2)x^2 - (-1 + 2b)x - 2$

Equating coefficients of x^2: $b - 2 = 2$

$b = 4$

$f(x) = (x - 2)(x^2 + 4x + 1)$

Hence $(x - 2)(x^2 + 4x + 1) = 0$

Note that $x^2 + 4x + 1$ cannot easily be factorised into two further linear factors, so use the quadratic formula.

$x = 2$ or $x = \dfrac{-4 \pm \sqrt{4^2 - 4 \times 1 \times 1}}{2 \times 1}$

$x = 2$ or $x = \dfrac{-4 \pm 2\sqrt{3}}{2}$

$x = 2$, $x = -2 + \sqrt{3}$ or $x = -2 - \sqrt{3}$

5 Let $f(x) = 2x^3 + 9x^2 - 14x - 9$

The positive and negative integer factors of -9 are $\pm1, \pm3, \pm9$

However, substituting each of these factors into the function does not give zero.

Sometimes the roots of a cubic equation are fractional or irrational which makes them harder to spot.

As the coefficient of x^3 is 2, a possible factor for the cubic function could be $(2x \pm p)$ where $p = \pm1, \pm3, \pm9$

In this case, solving $f(x) = 0$, would give $2x \pm p = 0$ so $x = \pm\dfrac{p}{2}$

We therefore need to try substituting fractional values of x, i.e $\pm\dfrac{1}{2}, \pm\dfrac{3}{2}, \pm\dfrac{9}{2}$

$f\left(-\dfrac{1}{2}\right) = 2 \times \left(-\dfrac{1}{2}\right)^3 + 9\left(-\dfrac{1}{2}\right)^2 - 14\left(-\dfrac{1}{2}\right) - 9 = 0$

So, $(2x + 1)$ is a factor of $f(x)$.

Find the other factor(s) by equating coefficients.

Since $(2x + 1)$ is a factor, $2x^3 + 9x^2 - 14x - 9 = (2x + 1)(ax^2 + bx + c)$ — coefficient of x^3 is 2, so $a = 1$ since $2 \times 1 = 2$; constant term is -9, so $c = -9$ since $+1 \times -9 = -9$

$2x^3 + 9x^2 - 14x - 9 = (2x + 1)(x^2 + bx - 9)$ — expand and collect like terms

$2x^3 + 9x^2 - 14x - 9 = 2x^3 + 2bx^2 - 18x + x^2 + bx - 9$

$2x^3 + 9x^2 - 14x - 9 = 2x^3 + (2b + 1)x^2 - (18 - b)x - 9$

Equating coefficients of x^2: $2b + 1 = 9$

$b = 4$

$f(x) = (2x + 1)(x^2 + 4x - 9)$

Note that $x^2 + 4x - 9$ cannot easily be factorised into two further linear factors, so use the quadratic formula.

Hence for $(2x + 1)(x^2 + 4x - 9) = 0$

$x = -0.5$ or $x = \dfrac{-4 \pm \sqrt{4^2 - 4 \times 1 \times -9}}{2 \times 1}$

$x = -0.5$ or $x = \dfrac{-4 \pm 2\sqrt{13}}{2}$

$x = -0.5$, $x = -2 + \sqrt{13}$ or $x = -2 - \sqrt{13}$

6 $x^3 + 8x^2 + 12x = 9$

$x^3 + 8x^2 + 12x - 9 = 0$

Let $f(x) = x^3 + 8x^2 + 12x - 9$

The positive and negative factors of -9 are $\pm 1, \pm 3, \pm 9$

$f(-3) = (-3)^3 + 8(-3)^2 + 12(-3) - 9 = 0$

So, $(x + 3)$ is a factor of $f(x)$

The other factors can be found by equating coefficients:

Since $(x + 3)$ is a factor, $x^3 + 8x^2 + 12x - 9 = (x + 3)(ax^2 + bx + c)$ — coefficient of x^3 is 1, so $a = 1$ since $1 \times 1 = 1$; constant term is -3, so $c = -3$ since $+3 \times -3 = -9$

$x^3 + 8x^2 + 12x - 9 = (x + 3)(x^2 + bx - 3)$ — expand and collect like terms

$x^3 + 8x^2 + 12x - 9 = x^3 + bx^2 - 3x + 3x^2 + 3bx - 9$

$x^3 + 8x^2 + 12x - 9 = x^3 + (b + 3)x^2 + (-3 + 3b)x - 9$

Equating coefficients of x^2: $b + 3 = 8$

$b = 5$

$f(x) = (x + 3)(x^2 + 5x - 3)$

Note that $x^2 + 5x - 3$ cannot easily be factorised into two further linear factors, so use the quadratic formula.

Hence for $(x + 3)(x^2 + 5x - 3) = 0$

$$x = -3 \text{ or } x = \frac{-5 \pm \sqrt{5^2 - 4 \times 1 \times -3}}{2 \times 1}$$

$$x = -3,\ x = \frac{-5 + \sqrt{37}}{2} \text{ or } x = \frac{-5 - \sqrt{37}}{2}$$

$x = -3$, $x = 0.54$ or $x = -5.54$ (to 2 decimal places)

7 **a** Let $f(x) = x^3 - x^2 - x - 2$

If $(x - 2)$ is a factor of $x^3 - x^2 - x - 2$ then substituting $x = 2$ into $f(x)$ will give 0.

$f(2) = 2^3 - 2^2 - 2 - 2 = 0$

So, $(x - 2)$ is a factor of $f(x)$

b The other factors can be found by trial and error, long division or by equating coefficients.

Using long division:

Step 1

$$\begin{array}{r l}
x^2 & \\
x - 2\overline{)x^3 - x^2 - x - 2} & \text{the first term of the polynomial by } x,\ x^3 \div x = x^2 \\
\underline{x^3 - 2x^2} & \text{multiply } (x - 2) \text{ by } x^2 \\
x^2 - x & \text{subtract and bring down the } -x \text{ from the next column}
\end{array}$$

Step 2

$$\begin{array}{r l}
x^2 + x & \\
x - 2\overline{)x^3 - x^2 - x - 2} & \\
\underline{x^3 - 2x^2} & \\
x^2 - x & \text{divide } x^2 \text{ by } x \text{ so, } x^2 \div x = x \\
\underline{x^2 - 2x} & \text{multiply } (x - 2) \text{ by } -1 \\
x - 2 & \text{subtract and bring down the } -2 \text{ from the next column}
\end{array}$$

Step 3

$$\begin{array}{r l}
x^2 + x + 1 & \\
x - 2\overline{)x^3 - x^2 - x - 2} & \\
\underline{x^3 - 2x^2} & \\
x^2 - x & \\
\underline{x^2 - 2x} & \\
x - 2 & \text{divide } x \text{ by } x \text{ so, } x \div x = 1 \\
\underline{x - 2} & \text{multiply } (x - 2) \text{ by } 1 \\
0 & \text{subtract}
\end{array}$$

$f(x) = (x - 2)(x^2 + x + 1)$

Note that $x^2 + x + 1$ cannot be factorised into two further linear factors, since the discriminant < 0.

$x = 2$ or $x = \dfrac{-1 \pm \sqrt{1^2 - 4 \times 1 \times 1}}{2 \times 1}$

$x = \dfrac{-1 \pm \sqrt{-3}}{2 \times 1}$ has no real roots since

$b^2 - 4ac < 0$

So, $x = 2$ is the only real root of $x^3 - x^2 - x - 2 = 0$.

8 a If $f(x) = 0$ and the coefficient of x^3 is 1 then $f(-2) = 0$, $f(1) = 0$, $f(5) = 0$ and $(x + 2)(x - 1)(x - 5) = 0$

So, $f(x) = (x + 2)(x - 1)(x - 5)$

$= (x^2 - 1x + 2x - 2)(x - 5)$

$= (x^2 + x - 2)(x - 5)$

$= x^3 - 5x^2 + x^2 - 5x - 2x + 10$

$= x^3 - 4x^2 - 7x + 10$

b If $f(x) = 0$ and the coefficient of x^3 is 1 then $f(-5) = 0$, $f(-2) = 0$, $f(4) = 0$ and $(x + 5)(x + 2)(x - 4) = 0$

So, $f(x) = (x + 5)(x + 2)(x - 4)$

$= (x^2 + 2x + 5x + 10)(x - 4)$

$= (x^2 + 7x + 10)(x - 4)$

$= x^3 - 4x^2 + 7x^2 - 28x + 10x - 40$

$= x^3 + 3x^2 - 18x - 40$

c If $f(x) = 0$ and the coefficient of x^3 is 1 then $f(-3) = 0$, $f(0) = 0$, $f(2) = 0$ and $(x + 3)(x + 0)(x - 2) = 0$

So, $f(x) = (x + 3)(x)(x - 2)$ or $x(x + 3)(x - 2)$

$= (x^2 + 3x)(x - 2)$

$= x^3 - 2x^2 + 3x^2 - 6x$

$= x^3 + x^2 - 6x$

9 a If $f(x) = 0$ and the coefficient of x^3 is 2 then $f(-0.5) = 0$, $f(2) = 0$, $f(4) = 0$ and $(2x + 1)(x - 2)(x - 4) = 0$

So, $f(x) = (2x + 1)(x - 2)(x - 4)$

$= (2x^2 - 4x + x - 2)(x - 4)$

$= (2x^2 - 3x - 2)(x - 4)$

$= 2x^3 - 8x^2 - 3x^2 + 12x - 2x + 8$

$= 2x^3 - 11x^2 + 10x + 8$

b If $f(x) = 0$ and the coefficient of x^3 is 2 then $f(0.5) = 0$, $f(1) = 0$, $f(2) = 0$ and $(2x - 1)(x - 1)(x - 2) = 0$

So, $f(x) = (2x - 1)(x - 1)(x - 2)$

$= (2x^2 - 2x - x + 1)(x - 2)$

$= (2x^2 - 3x + 1)(x - 2)$

$= 2x^3 - 4x^2 - 3x^2 + 6x + x - 2$

$= 2x^3 - 7x^2 + 7x - 2$

c If $f(x) = 0$ and the coefficient of x^3 is 2 then $f(-1.5) = 0$, $f(1) = 0$, $f(5) = 0$ and $(2x + 3)(x - 1)(x - 5) = 0$

So, $f(x) = (2x + 3)(x - 1)(x - 5)$

$= (2x^2 - 2x + 3x - 3)(x - 5)$

$= (2x^2 + x - 3)(x - 5)$

$= 2x^3 - 10x^2 + x^2 - 5x - 3x + 15$

$= 2x^3 - 9x^2 - 8x + 15$

10 If $f(x) = 0$ and the coefficient of x^3 is 1 then $f(-3) = 0$, $f(1 + \sqrt{2}) = 0$, $f(1 - \sqrt{2}) = 0$ and $f(x) = (x + 3)(x - (1 + \sqrt{2}))(x - (1 - \sqrt{2}))$

$0 = (x + 3)[(x - 1) - \sqrt{2})((x - 1) + \sqrt{2})]$

So, $f(x) = (x + 3)[(x - 1) - \sqrt{2})((x - 1) + \sqrt{2})]$

The square brackets contain an expression for the difference of two squares, so simplifying gives:

$f(x) = (x + 3)[(x - 1)^2 - 2]$

$= (x + 3)[x^2 - 2x + 1 - 2]$

$= (x + 3)[x^2 - 2x - 1]$

$= x^3 - 2x^2 - x + 3x^2 - 6x - 3$

$= x^3 + x^2 - 7x - 3$

11 If $f(x) = 0$ and the coefficient of x^3 is 2 then $f(0.5) = 0$, $f(2 + \sqrt{3}) = 0$, $f(2 - \sqrt{3}) = 0$ and

$f(x) = (x - 0.5)(x - (2 + \sqrt{3}))(x - (2 - \sqrt{3}))$

$0 = (2x - 1)[(x - 2) - \sqrt{3})((x - 2) + \sqrt{3})]$

So, $f(x) = (2x - 1)[(x - 2) - \sqrt{3})((x - 2) + \sqrt{3})]$

The square brackets contain an expression for the difference of two squares, so simplifying gives:

$f(x) = (2x - 1)[(x - 2)^2 - 3]$

$= (2x - 1)[x^2 - 4x + 4 - 3]$

$= (2x - 1)[x^2 - 4x + 1]$

$= 2x^3 - 8x^2 + 2x - x^2 + 4x - 1$

$= 2x^3 - 9x^2 + 6x - 1$

12 a Let $f(x) = 2x^4 + (a^2 + 1)x^3 - 3x^2 + (1 - a^3)x + 3$

If $(2x + 3)$ is a factor of $f(x)$ then $f(-1.5) = 0$

$f(-1.5) = 2(-1.5)^4 + (a^2 + 1)(-1.5)^3 - 3(-1.5)^2 + (1 - a^3)(-1.5) + 3 = 0$

$10.125 - 3.375(a^2 + 1) - 6.75 - 1.5 + 1.5a^3 + 3 = 0$

$10.125 - 3.375a^2 - 3.375 - 6.75 - 1.5 + 1.5a^3 + 3 = 0$

$1.5a^3 - 3.375a^2 + 1.5 = 0$ divide all terms by 1.5

$a^3 - 2.25a^2 + 1 = 0$ multiply all terms by 4

$4a^3 - 9a^2 + 4 = 0$ shown.

b Let $f(a) = 4a^3 - 9a^2 + 4$

The positive and negative factors of +4 are ±1, ±2, ±4

$f(2) = 4(2)^3 - 9(2)^2 + 4 = 0$

So, $(a - 2)$ is a factor of $f(a)$

The other factors can be found by equating coefficients:

Since $(a - 2)$ is a factor, $4a^3 - 9a^2 + 4 = (a - 2)(ba^2 + ca + d)$ coefficient of a^3 is 4 , so $b = 4$ since $1 \times 4 = 4$

constant term is −2, so $d = -2$ since $-2 \times -2 = 4$

$4a^3 - 9a^2 + 4 = (a - 2)(4a^2 + ca - 2)$ expand and collect like terms

$4a^3 - 9a^2 + 4 = 4a^3 + ca^2 - 2a - 8a^2 - 2ca + 4$

$4a^3 - 9a^2 + 4 = 4a^3 - (-c + 8)a^2 + (-2 - 2c)a + 4$

Equating coefficients of a^2: $-c + 8 = 9$

$c = -1$

$f(a) = (a - 2)(4a^2 - 1a - 2)$

Hence $(a - 2)(4a^2 - a - 2) = 0$

Note that $4a^2 - a - 2$ cannot be factorised into two further linear factors, since the discriminant < 0.

$$a = 2 \text{ or } a = \frac{-(-1) \pm \sqrt{(-1)^2 - 4 \times 4 \times -2}}{2 \times 4}$$

$$a = 2 \text{ or } a = \frac{1 \pm \sqrt{33}}{8}$$

$$a = 2,\ a = \frac{1 + \sqrt{33}}{8} \text{ or } a = \frac{1 - \sqrt{33}}{8}$$

Exercise 3.5

1 **a** Let $f(x) = x^3 + 2x^2 - x + 3$

Using the factor theorem:

Remainder $= f(1)$

$= 1^3 + 2 \times 1^2 - 1 + 3$

$= 5$

The remainder is 5.

d Let $f(x) = 2x^3 - x^2 - 18x + 11$

Using algebraic division:

$$\begin{array}{r} x^2 - 9 \\ 2x - 1\overline{)2x^3 - x^2 - 18x + 11} \\ \underline{2x^3 - x^2} \\ -18x + 11 \\ \underline{-18x + 9} \\ 2 \end{array}$$

The remainder is 2.

2 **a** Let $f(x) = x^3 + x^2 + ax - 2$

When $f(x)$ is divided by $(x - 1)$, the remainder is 5 means that: $f(1) = 5$

$1^3 + 1^2 + a(1) - 2 = 5$

$1 + 1 + a - 2 = 5$

$a = 5$

b Let $f(x) = 2x^3 - 6x^2 + 7x + b$

When $f(x)$ is divided by $(x + 2)$, the remainder is 3 means that: $f(-2) = 3$

$2(-2)^3 - 6(-2)^2 + 7(-2) + b = 3$

$-16 - 24 - 14 + b = 3$

$b = 57$

c Let $f(x) = 2x^3 + x^2 + cx - 10$

When $f(x)$ is divided by $(2x - 1)$, the remainder is -4 means that: $f(0.5) = -4$

$2(0.5)^3 + 0.5^2 + c \times 0.5 - 10 = -4$

$0.25 + 0.25 + 0.5c - 10 = -4$

$0.5c = 5.5$

$c = 11$

3 $f(x) = x^3 + ax^2 + bx - 5$

If $(x - 1)$ is a factor of $f(x)$ then $f(1) = 0$

$f(1) = 1^3 + a(1)^2 + b(1) - 5 = 0$

$1 + a + b - 5 = 0$

$a + b = 4$ (1)

When $f(x)$ is divided by $(x + 2)$, the remainder is 3 means that: $f(-2) = 3$

$(-2)^3 + a(-2)^2 + b \times (-2) - 5 = 3$

$-8 + 4a - 2b - 5 = 3$

$4a - 2b = 16$

$2a - b = 8$ (2)

Adding (1) and (2) gives $3a = 12$ so $a = 4$

Substituting into (1) gives $4 + b = 4$ so $b = 0$

$a = 4$ and $b = 0$

4 Let $f(x) = x^3 + ax^2 + 11x + b$

If $(x - 2)$ is a factor of $f(x)$ then $f(2) = 0$

$f(2) = 2^3 + a(2)^2 + 11(2) + b = 0$

$8 + 4a + 22 + b = 0$

$4a + b = -30$ (1)

When $f(x)$ is divided by $(x - 5)$, the remainder is 24 means that: $f(5) = 24$

$5^3 + a \times 5^2 + 11 \times 5 + b = 24$

$125 + 25a + 55 + b = 24$

$25a + b = -156$ (2)

Subtracting (1) from (2) gives $21a = -126$

$a = -6$

Substituting into (1) gives $-24 + b = -30$

$b = -6$

So, $a = -6$ and $b = -6$

5 **a** Let $f(x) = x^3 - 2x^2 + ax + b$

If $(x - 3)$ is a factor of $f(x)$ then $f(3) = 0$

$f(3) = 3^3 - 2(3)^2 + a(3) + b = 0$

$27 - 18 + 3a + b = 0$

$3a + b = -9$ (1)

When $f(x)$ is divided by $(x + 2)$, the remainder is 15 means that: $f(-2) = 15$

$$f(-2) = (-2)^3 - 2(-2)^2 + a(-2) + b = 15$$
$$-8 - 8 - 2a + b = 15$$
$$-2a + b = 31 \qquad (2)$$

Subtracting (2) from (1) gives $5a = -40$

So, $a = -8$

Substituting into (1) gives $-24 + b = -9$

$b = 15$

So, $a = -8$ and $b = 15$

b $f(x) = x^3 - 2x^2 - 8x + 15$

$$\begin{array}{r|l} & x^2 + x - 5 \\ x - 3 & x^3 - 2x^2 - 8x + 15 \\ & \underline{x^3 - 3x^2} \\ & \quad x^2 - 8x \\ & \quad \underline{x^2 - 3x} \\ & \qquad -5x + 15 \\ & \qquad \underline{-5x + 15} \\ & \qquad\qquad 0 \end{array}$$

$f(x) = (x - 3)(x^2 + x - 5)$

Note that $x^2 + x - 5$ cannot be factorised into two further linear factors, since the discriminant < 0.

$$x = 3 \text{ or } x = \frac{-1 \pm \sqrt{1^2 - 4 \times 1 \times -5}}{2 \times 1}$$

$$x = 3,\ x = \frac{-1 + \sqrt{21}}{2} \text{ or } x = \frac{-1 - \sqrt{21}}{2}$$

6 a Let $f(x) = 4x^3 + 8x^2 + ax + b$

If $(2x - 1)$ is a factor of $f(x)$ then $f(0.5) = 0$

$$f(0.5) = 4 \times 0.5^3 + 8 \times 0.5^2 + a(0.5) + b = 0$$
$$0.5 + 2 + 0.5a + b = 0$$
$$0.5a + b = -2.5 \qquad (1)$$

When $f(x)$ is divided by $(x - 2)$, the remainder is 48 means that: $f(2) = 48$

$$f(2) = 4 \times 2^3 + 8 \times 2^2 + a \times 2 + b = 48$$
$$32 + 32 + 2a + b = 48$$
$$2a + b = -16 \qquad (2)$$

Subtracting (1) from (2) gives $1.5a = -13.5$

So, $a = -9$

Substituting into (1) gives $0.5(-9) + b = -2.5$

$b = 2$

So, $a = -9$ and $b = 2$

b $f(x) = 4x^3 + 8x^2 - 9x + 2$

To find the remainder when $f(x)$ is divided by $(x - 1)$, substitute $x = 1$ into $f(x)$

$$f(1) = 4 \times 1^3 + 8 \times 1^2 - 9 \times 1 + 2$$
$$f(1) = 5$$

The remainder is 5

7 $f(x) = 2x^3 + (a + 1)x^2 - ax + b$

When $f(x)$ is divided by $(x - 1)$, the remainder is 5 means that: $f(1) = 5$

$$2 \times 1^3 + (a + 1) \times 1^2 - a(1) + b = 5$$
$$2 + a + 1 - a + b = 5$$
$$b = 2$$

When $f(x)$ is divided by $(x - 2)$, the remainder is 14 means that: $f(2) = 14$

$$2 \times 2^3 + (a + 1) \times 2^2 - a(2) + 2 = 14$$
$$16 + 4a + 4 - 2a + 2 = 14$$
$$2a = -8$$
$$a = -4 \qquad \text{shown}$$

8 $f(x) = ax^3 + bx^2 + 5x - 2$

When $f(x)$ is divided by $(x - 1)$, the remainder is 6 means that: $f(1) = 6$

$$a \times 1^3 + b \times 1^2 + 5 \times 1 - 2 = 6$$
$$a + b + 5 - 2 = 6$$
$$a + b = 3 \qquad (1)$$

When $f(x)$ is divided by $(2x + 1)$, the remainder is -6 means that: $f(-0.5) = -6$

$a \times (-0.5)^3 + b \times (-0.5)^2 + 5 \times (-0.5) - 2 = -6$

$-0.125a + 0.25b - 2.5 - 2 = -6$

$-0.125a + 0.25b = -1.5$ divide each term by -0.125

$a - 2b = 12$ (2)

Subtracting (1) from (2) gives $-3b = 9$

So, $b = -3$

Substituting into (1) gives $a - 3 = 3$

$a = 6$

So, $a = 6$ and $b = -3$

9 a $f(x) = x^3 - 5x^2 + ax + b$

If $(x - 2)$ is a factor of $f(x)$ then $f(2) = 0$

$f(2) = 2^3 - 5(2)^2 + a(2) + b = 0$

$8 - 20 + 2a + b = 0$

$b = 12 - 2a$

b When $f(x)$ is divided by $(x + 1)$, the remainder is -9 means that: $f(-1) = -9$

$(-1)^3 - 5(-1)^2 + a \times (-1) + b = -9$

$-1 - 5 - a + b = -9$

$-a + b = -3$ (1)

Substituting $b = 12 - 2a$ into (1) gives $-a + 12 - 2a = -3$

$a = 5$

Substituting into $b = 12 - 2a$ gives $b = 12 - 2(5)$

$b = 2$.

So, $a = 5$ and $b = 2$

10 a $f(x) = x^3 + ax^2 + bx + c$ (1)

If the roots of $f(x)$ are 2, 3 and k then:

$f(x) = (x - 2)(x - 3)(x - k)$

$f(x) = (x^2 - 5x + 6)(x - k)$

$f(x) = x^3 - kx^2 - 5x^2 + 5kx + 6x - 6k$

$f(x) = x^3 + (-5 - k)x^2 + (6 + 5k)x - 6k$ (2)

Comparing (1) with (2), $a = -5 - k$, $b = 6 + 5k$, $c = -6k$

When $f(x)$ is divided by $(x - 1)$, the remainder is -8 means that: $f(1) = -8$

$1^3 + a \times 1^2 + b \times 1 + c = -8$

$1 + a + b + c = -8$

$a + b + c = -9$

Substituting for a, b and c gives:

$-5 - k + 6 + 5k - 6k = -9$

$-2k = -10$

$k = 5$

b Substituting $k = 5$ into $a = -5 - k$, $b = 6 + 5k$, $c = -6k$ we get:

$a = -10$, $b = 31$ and $c = -30$

So, $f(x) = x^3 - 10x^2 + 31x - 30$

To find the remainder when $f(x)$ is divided by $(x + 1)$, find $f(-1)$

Remainder
$= (-1)^3 - 10 \times (-1)^2 + 31 \times (-1) - 30 = -72$

The remainder is -72

11 a $f(x) = 4x^3 + ax^2 + 13x + b$

If $(2x - 1)$ is a factor of $f(x)$ then $f(0.5) = 0$

$f(0.5) = 4(0.5)^3 + a(0.5)^2 + 13 \times 0.5 + b = 0$

$0.5 + 0.25a + 6.5 + b = 0$

$0.25a + b = -7$ (1)

When $f(x)$ is divided by $(x - 2)$, the remainder is 21 means that: $f(2) = 21$

$4 \times 2^3 + a \times 2^2 + 13 \times 2 + b = 21$

$32 + 4a + 26 + b = 21$

$4a + b = -37$ (2)

Subtracting (2) from (1) from gives $-3.75a = 30$

$a = -8$

Substituting into (2) gives $-32 + b = -37$

$b = -5$

So, $a = -8$ and $b = -5$

b $f(x) = 4x^3 - 8x^2 + 13x - 5$

To find the remainder when $f(x)$ is divided by $(x + 1)$, find $f(-1)$

Remainder
$= 4(-1)^3 - 8 \times (-1)^2 + 13 \times (-1) - 5 = -30$

The remainder is -30

12 $f(x) = x^3 - 8x^2 + kx - 20$

When $f(x)$ is divided by $(x - 1)$, the remainder is R means that: $f(1) = R$

$1^3 - 8 \times 1^2 + k \times 1 - 20 = R$

$1 - 8 + k - 20 = R$

$k - 27 = R$ (1)

When $f(x)$ is divided by $(x - 2)$, the remainder is $4R$ means that: $f(2) = 4R$

$2^3 - 8 \times 2^2 + k \times 2 - 20 = R$

$8 - 32 + 2k - 20 = 4R$

$2k - 44 = 4R$

$k - 22 = 2R$ (2)

Multiplying (1) by 2 gives $2k - 54 = 2R$ (3)

Subtracting (2) from (3) gives $k - 32 = 0$

So $k = 32$

13 a $f(x) = x^3 + 2x^2 - 6x + 9$

When $f(x)$ is divided by $(x + a)$, the remainder is R means that: $f(-a) = R$

$(-a)^3 + 2 \times (-a)^2 - 6 \times -a + 9 = R$

$-a^3 + 2a^2 + 6a + 9 = R$ (1)

When $f(x)$ is divided by $(x - a)$, the remainder is $2R$ means that: $f(a) = R$

$a^3 + 2 \times a^2 - 6 \times a + 9 = 2R$

$a^3 + 2a^2 - 6a + 9 = 2R$ (2)

Multiplying (1) by 2 and then subtracting (2) gives:

$3a^3 - 2a^2 - 18a - 9 = 0$ shown

b Let $f(a) = 3a^3 - 2a^2 - 18a - 9$

The positive and negative factors of -9 are ±1, ±3, ±9

$f(3) = 3(3)^3 - 2(3)^2 - 18 \times 3 - 9 = 0$

So, $(a - 3)$ is a factor of $f(a)$

The other factors can be found by equating coefficients:

Since $(a-3)$ is a factor, $3a^3 - 2a^2 - 18a - 9 = (a-3)(ba^2 + ca + d)$

coefficient of a^3 is 3, so $b = 3$ since $1 \times 3 = 3$

constant term is -9, so $d = 3$ since $-3 \times 3 = -9$

$3a^3 - 2a^2 - 18a - 9 = (a-3)(3a^2 + ca + 3)$ expand and collect like terms

$3a^3 - 2a^2 - 18a - 9 = 3a^3 + ca^2 + 3a - 9a^2 - 3ca - 9$

$3a^3 - 2a^2 - 18a - 9 = 3a^3 - (-c + 9)a^2 + (3 - 3c)a - 9$

Equating coefficients of a^2: $-c + 9 = 2$

$c = 7$

$f(a) = (a-3)(3a^2 + 7a + 3)$

Hence $(a-3)(3a^2 + 7a + 3) = 0$

Note that $3a^2 + 7a + 3$ cannot be factorised into two further linear factors, since the discriminant < 0.

$a = 3$ or $a = \dfrac{-7 \pm \sqrt{7^2 - 4 \times 3 \times 3}}{2 \times 3}$

$a = 3$ or $a = \dfrac{-7 \pm \sqrt{13}}{6}$

$a = 3$, $a = \dfrac{-7 + \sqrt{13}}{6}$ or $a = \dfrac{-7 - \sqrt{13}}{6}$

14 a $f(x) = x^3 + 6x^2 + kx - 15$

When $f(x)$ is divided by $(x - 1)$, the remainder is R means that: $f(1) = R$

$1^3 + 6 \times 1^2 + k \times 1 - 15 = R$

$1 + 6 + k - 15 = R$

$k - 8 = R$ (1)

When $f(x)$ is divided by $(x + 4)$, the remainder is $-R$ means that: $f(-4) = -R$

$(-4)^3 + 6 \times (-4)^2 + k(-4) - 15 = -R$

$-64 + 96 - 4k - 15 = -R$

$-4k + 17 = -R$ (2)

Adding (1) and (2) gives $-3k + 9 = 0$

$k = 3$

b $f(x) = x^3 + 6x^2 + 3x - 15$

To find the remainder when $f(x)$ is divided by $(x + 2)$, find $f(-2)$

Remainder $= (-2)^3 + 6 \times (2)^2 + 3 \times (-2) - 15 = -5$

The remainder is -5

15 $P(x) = 5(x - 1)(x - 2)(x - 3) + a(x - 1)(x - 2) + b(x - 1) + c$

When $P(x)$ is divided by $(x - 1)$, the remainder is 7 means that: $P(1) = 7$

$$P(1) = 5(1 - 1)(1 - 2)(1 - 3) + a(1 - 1)(1 - 2) + b(1 - 1) + c = 7$$
$$c = 7$$

When $P(x)$ is divided by $(x - 2)$, the remainder is 2 means that: $P(2) = 2$

$$P(2) = 5(2 - 1)(2 - 2)(2 - 3) + a(2 - 1)(2 - 2) + b(2 - 1) + 7 = 2$$
$$b + 7 = 2$$
$$b = -5$$

When $P(x)$ is divided by $(x - 3)$, the remainder is 1 means that: $P(3) = 1$

$$P(1) = 5(3 - 1)(3 - 2)(3 - 3) + a(3 - 1)(3 - 2) + (-5)(3 - 1) + 7 = 1$$
$$2a - 10 + 7 = 1$$
$$a = 2$$

16 a $f(x) = x^3 + ax^2 + bx + c$ (1)

If one root is 1 then $f(1) = 1^3 + a \times 1^2 + b \times 1 + c = 0$

$$1 + a + b + c = 0$$
$$a + b + c = -1$$

If the roots of $f(x)$ are 1, k and $k + 1$ then:

$$f(x) = (x - 1)(x - k)(x - (k + 1))$$
$$f(x) = (x^2 - kx - x + k)(x - k - 1)$$
$$f(x) = x^3 - kx^2 - x^2 - kx^2 + k^2x + kx - x^2 + kx + x + kx - k^2 - k$$
$$f(x) = x^3 + (-2k - 2)x^2 + (k^2 + 3k + 1)x - k^2 - k \quad (2)$$

Comparing (1) with (2), $a = -2k - 2$, $b = k^2 + 3k + 1$, $c = -k^2 - k$

When $f(x)$ is divided by $(x - 2)$, the remainder is 20 means that: $f(2) = 20$

$$2^3 + a \times 2^2 + b \times 2 + c = 20$$
$$8 + 4a + 2b + c = 20$$
$$4a + 2b + c = 12 \quad (3)$$

Substituting for a, b and c in (3) gives:

$$4(-2k - 2) + 2(k^2 + 3k + 1) - k^2 - k = 12$$
$$-8k - 8 + 2k^2 + 6k + 2 - k^2 - k = 12$$
$$k^2 - 3k - 18 = 0 \quad \text{shown}$$

b $(k - 6)(k + 3) = 0$

So, $k = 6$ and $k = -3$

Chapter 4: Equations, inequalities and graphs

Exercise 4.1

1 b $|x + 5| = |x - 4|$

Method 1

$x + 5 = x - 4$ or $x + 5 = -(x - 4)$

$0 = -9$ or $2x = -1$

False $\quad x = -0.5$

CHECK: $|-0.5 + 5| = |-0.5 - 4|$ ✓

The solution is $x = -0.5$

Method 2

$|x + 5| = |x - 4|$

$(x + 5)^2 = (x - 4)^2$

$x^2 + 10x + 25 = x^2 - 8x + 16$

$18x = -9$

$x = -0.5$

f $\left|1 - \frac{x}{2}\right| = |3x + 2|$

Method 1

$1 - \frac{x}{2} = 3x + 2$ or $1 - \frac{x}{2} = -(3x + 2)$

$-\frac{7x}{2} = 1$ or $2 - x = -6x - 4$

$7x = -2$ or $5x = -6$

$x = -\frac{2}{7}$ $\quad x = -\frac{6}{5}$

CHECK: $\left|1 + \frac{1}{7}\right| = \left|-\frac{6}{7} + 2\right|$ ✓

$1 + \frac{3}{5} = -\left(-\frac{18}{5} + 2\right)$ ✓

The solutions are $x = -\frac{2}{7}$ and $x = -\frac{6}{5}$

Method 2

$\left|1 - \frac{x}{2}\right| = |3x + 2|$

$\left(1 - \frac{x}{2}\right)^2 = (3x + 2)^2$

$1 - x + \frac{x^2}{4} = 9x^2 + 12x + 4$

$4 - 4x + x^2 = 36x^2 + 48x + 16$

$35x^2 + 52x + 12 = 0$

$(5x + 6)(7x + 2) = 0$

$x = -\frac{6}{5}$ or $x = -\frac{2}{7}$

h $|2x - 1| = 2|3 - x|$

Method 1

$2x - 1 = 2(3 - x)$ or $2x - 1 = -2(3 - x)$

$2x - 1 = 6 - 2x$ or $2x - 1 = -6 + 2x$

$4x = 7$ $\quad x = 5$

$x = \frac{7}{4}$

CHECK: $\left|\frac{7}{2} - 1\right| = 2\left|3 - \frac{7}{4}\right|$ ✓

$|10 - 1| = 2|3 - 5|$ $\quad$ false

The solution is $x = \frac{7}{4}$

Method 2

$|2x - 1| = 2|3 - x|$

$(2x - 1)^2 = [2(3 - x)]^2$

$4x^2 - 4x + 1 = 4(9 - 6x + x^2)$

$4x^2 - 4x + 1 = 36 - 24x + 4x^2$

$20x = 35$

$x = \frac{7}{4}$

2 $y = |x - 5|$ $\quad$ (1)

$y = |8 - x|$ $\quad$ (2)

Equating (1) and (2) gives:

$|x - 5| = |8 - x|$

$(x - 5)^2 = (8 - x)^2$

$x^2 - 10x + 25 = 64 - 16x + x^2$

$6x = 39$

$x = 6.5$ and $y = 1.5$

3 $6|x + 2|^2 + 7|x + 2| - 3 = 0$

Let $y = |x + 2|$

Rewriting the question in terms of y gives:

$6y^2 + 7y - 3 = 0$

$(3y - 1)(2y + 3) = 0$

$y = \frac{1}{3}$ or $y = -\frac{3}{2}$

Substitute $y = \frac{1}{3}$ into $y = |x + 2|$ gives:

$\frac{1}{3} = \lvert x + 2\rvert$	square both sides
$\left(\frac{1}{3}\right)^2 = (x + 2)^2$	expand brackets
$\frac{1}{9} = x^2 + 4x + 4$	multiply all terms by 9
$1 = 9x^2 + 36x + 36$	rearrange
$9x^2 + 36x + 35 = 0$	factorise
$(3x + 7)(3x + 5) = 0$	solve

$x = -\frac{7}{3}$ or $x = -\frac{5}{3}$

4 **a** $x^2 - 6|x| + 8 = 0$ rearrange

$x^2 + 8 = 6|x|$

Either $x^2 + 8 = 6x$

$x^2 - 6x + 8 = 0$

$(x - 4)(x - 2) = 0$

$x = 4$ and $x = 2$

CHECK: $x^2 - 6|x| + 8$

$4^2 - 6|4| + 8 = 0$ ✓

$2^2 - 6|2| + 8 = 0$ ✓

Or $x^2 + 8 = -6x$

$x^2 + 6x + 8 = 0$

$(x + 4)(x + 2) = 0$

$x = -4$ and $x = -2$

CHECK: $x^2 - 6|x| + 8$

$(-4)^2 - 6|-4| + 8 = 0$ ✓

The solutions are $x = \pm 2$ and $x = \pm 4$

b

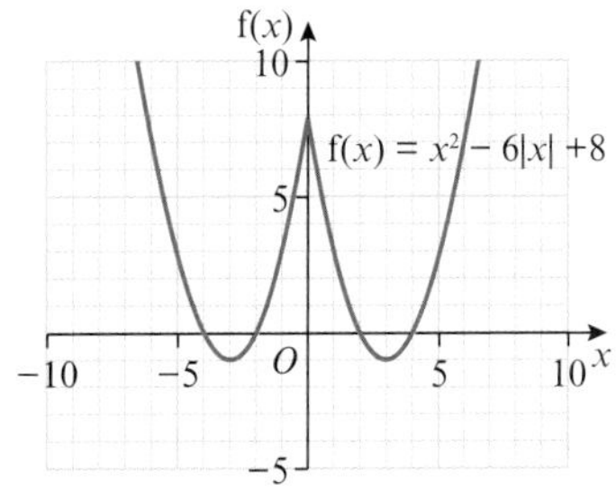

c $f(x) \geqslant -1$

TIP

Solving modulus equations using graphs is not obvious if the solutions are not integers.

Algebraic methods give exact solutions.

5 $|x + 1| + |2x - 3| = 8$

Consider the real number line divided into three intervals by the points where

$x + 1 = 0$ or $x = -1$

$2x - 3 = 0$ or $x = \frac{3}{2}$

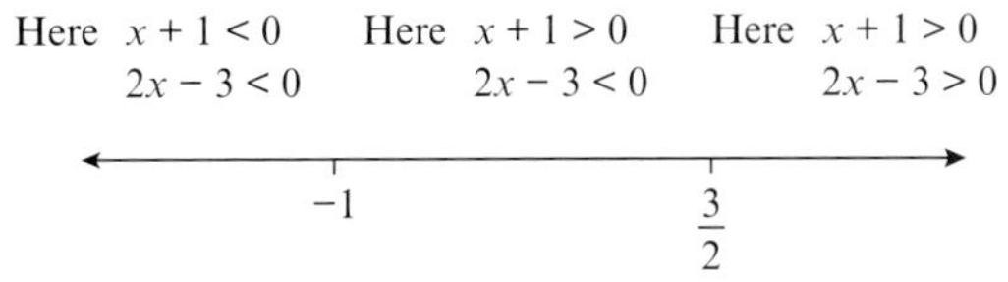

Consider the region $x > \frac{3}{2}$

$|x + 1| = x + 1$

$|2x - 3| = 2x - 3$

The question becomes: $x + 1 + 2x - 3 = 8$

$x = \frac{10}{3}$

This solution **is** in the interval $x > \frac{3}{2}$

Consider the region $-1 < x < \frac{3}{2}$

$|x + 1| = x + 1$

$|2x - 3| = -(2x - 3)$

The equation becomes: $x + 1 - (2x - 3) = 8$

$x = -4$

This **is not** a solution in the interval $-1 < x < \frac{3}{2}$

Consider the region $x < -1$

$|x + 1| = -(x + 1)$

$|2x - 3| = -(2x - 3)$

The equation becomes: $-(x + 1) - (2x - 3) = 8$

$$x = -2$$

This solution **is** in the interval $x < -1$

The solution of $|x + 1| + |2x - 3| = 8$ is $x = \frac{10}{3}$ and $x = -2$

6 $y = |x - 5|$ and $y = |3 - 2x| + 2$

So, $|x - 5| = |3 - 2x| + 2$

$|x - 5| - |3 - 2x| = 2$

Consider the real number line divided into three intervals by the points where

$x - 5 = 0$ or $x = 5$

$3 - 2x = 0$ or $x = \frac{3}{2}$

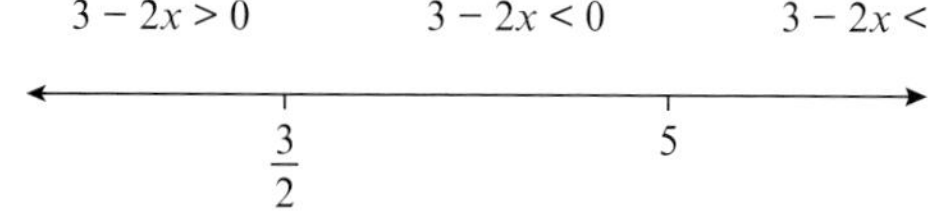

Consider the region $x > 5$

$|x - 5| = x - 5$

$|3 - 2x| = -(3 - 2x) = 2x - 3$

The question becomes: $x - 5 - (2x - 3) = 2$

$$x = -4$$

This solution **is not** in the interval $x > 5$

Consider the region $\frac{3}{2} < x < 5$

$|x - 5| = -(x - 5) = 5 - x$

$|3 - 2x| = -(3 - 2x) = 2x - 3$

The equation becomes: $5 - x - (2x - 3) = 2$

$$x = 2$$

This **is** a solution in the interval $\frac{3}{2} < x < 5$

Consider the region $x < \frac{3}{2}$

$|x - 5| = -(x - 5) = 5 - x$

$|3 - 2x| = 3 - 2x$

The equation becomes: $5 - x - (3 - 2x) = 2$

$$x = 0$$

This solution **is** in the interval $x < \frac{3}{2}$

The solution of $|x - 5| + |3 - 2x| = 2$ is $x = 0$ and $x = 2$

Substituting $x = 0$ into $y = |x - 5|$ gives 5 and $y = |3 - 2x| + 2$ gives 5.

So, $y = 5$ is a solution.

Substituting $x = 2$ into $y = |x - 5|$ gives 3 and $y = |3 - 2x| + 2$ gives 3.

So, $y = 3$ is a solution.

So, the solutions are $x = 0$, $y = 5$ and $x = 2$, $y = 3$

7 $2|3x + 4y - 2| + 3\sqrt{25 - 5x + 2y} = 0$

$25 - 5x + 2y \geqslant 0$ (since you cannot square root a negative number)

However, by definition, $|3x + 4y - 2| \geqslant 0$

The equation $2|3x + 4y - 2| + 3\sqrt{25 - 5x + 2y} = 0$ has a solution **if and only if** $25 - 5x + 2y = 0$ **and** $3x + 4y - 2 = 0$

Solving $5x - 2y = 25$ (1)

and $3x + 4y = 2$ (2)

So, multiplying (1) by 2 then adding (2) gives:

$13x = 52$

$x = 4$

Substitute into (2) gives:

$12 + 4y = 2$

$y = -\frac{5}{2}$

Solution is $x = 4$ and $y = -\frac{5}{2}$

Exercise 4.2

1 To solve the inequality $|x - 2| > |2x - 10|$, find where the graph of the function $y = |x - 2|$ is above the graph of $y = |2x - 10|$

Solution is $4 < x < 8$

2 a Draw a sketch of the graph $y = |3x - 6|$

Draw a sketch of the graph of $y = 3x - 6$

The x-intercept of $y = 3x - 6$ is found by solving $3x - 6 = 0$, i.e, $x = 2$

Reflect the part of the graph that is below the x-axis in the x-axis.

This is the graph of $y = |3x - 6|$

On the same axes:

Draw the graph of $y = |4 - x|$

Draw a sketch of the graph of $y = 4 - x$

The x- intercept of $y = 4 - x$ is found by solving $4 - x = 0$, i.e, $x = 4$

Reflect the part of the graph that is below the x-axis in the x-axis.

This is the graph of $y = |4 - x|$

The graphs of $y = |3x - 6|$ and $y = |4 - x|$ intersect at points A and B

$|3x - 6| = 3x - 6$ if $x \geqslant 2$

$= -(3x - 6)$ if $x < 2$

At A, the line $y = -(3x - 6)$ intersects the line $y = 4 - x$

$$-(3x - 6) = 4 - x$$
$$-3x + 6 = 4 - x$$
$$2x = 2$$
$$x = 1$$

At B, the line $y = (3x - 6)$ intersects the line $y = -(4 - x)$

$$3x - 6 = -(4 - x)$$
$$-3x + 6 = -4 + x$$
$$4x = 10$$
$$x = \frac{5}{2}$$

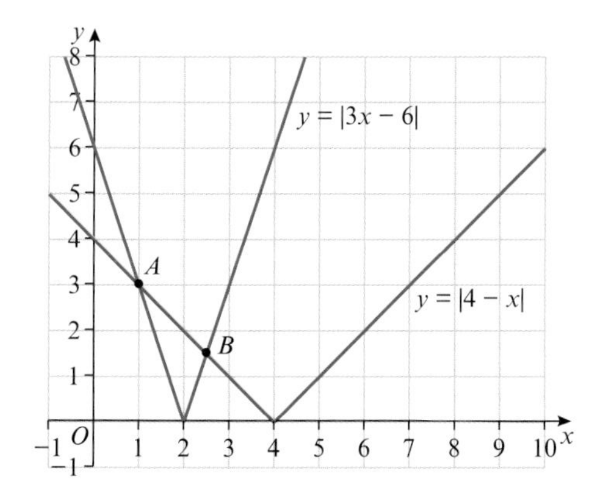

b To solve the inequality $|3x - 6| \geqslant |4 - x|$, find where the graph of the function $y = |3x - 6|$ intersects or is above the graph of $y = |4 - x|$

Solution $x \leqslant 1$ or $x \geqslant \frac{5}{2}$

3 c $|8 - 3x| < 2$

> **REMINDER**
>
> $|p| < q \Leftrightarrow -q < p < q$

$$-2 < 8 - 3x < 2$$

$-2 < 8 - 3x$	and	$8 - 3x < 2$
$-2 < 8 - 3x$	and	$-3x < -6$
$3x < 10$	and	$x > 2$
$x < \frac{10}{3}$	and	$x > 2$

Solution is $2 < x < \frac{10}{3}$

e $|3x + 1| > 8$

> **REMINDER**
>
> $|p| > q \Leftrightarrow p < -q$ or $p > q$

$3x + 1 < -8$	or	$3x + 1 > 8$
$3x < -9$	or	$3x > 7$
$x < -3$	or	$x > \frac{7}{3}$

Solution is $x < -3$ or $x > \frac{7}{3}$

4 a $|2x - 3| \leqslant x - 1$

$$-(x - 1) \leqslant 2x - 3 < x - 1$$

$-(x - 1) \leqslant 2x - 3$	and	$2x - 3 \leqslant x - 1$
$-x + 1 \leqslant 2x - 3$	and	$x \leqslant 2$
$4 \leqslant 3x$		
$\frac{4}{3} \leqslant x$		

Solution is $\frac{4}{3} \leqslant x \leqslant 2$

b $|5 + x| > 7 - 2x$

Sketch the graphs of $y = |5 + x|$ and $y = 7 - 2x$

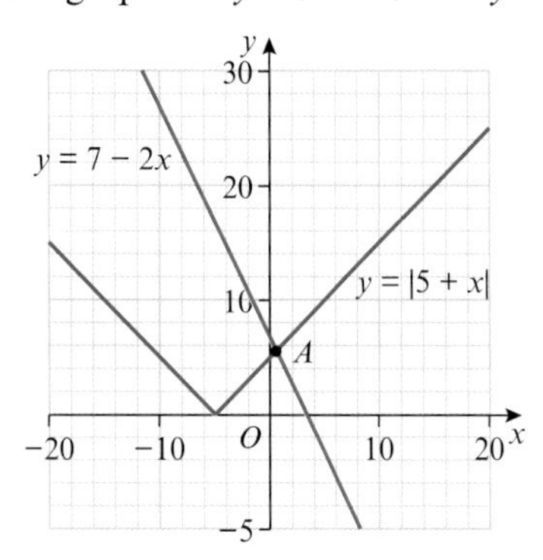

The graphs intersect at point A

At A, $5 + x = 7 - 2x$

$3x = 2$

$x = \frac{2}{3}$ is the x coordinate of A.

To solve the inequality $|5 + x| > 7 - 2x$, find where the graph of the function $y = |5 + x|$ is above the graph of $y = 7 - 2x$

Solution is $x > \frac{2}{3}$

c $|x - 2| - 3x \leqslant 1$ rearrange to isolate the modulus term

Sketch the graphs of $y = |x - 2|$ and $y = 1 + 3x$

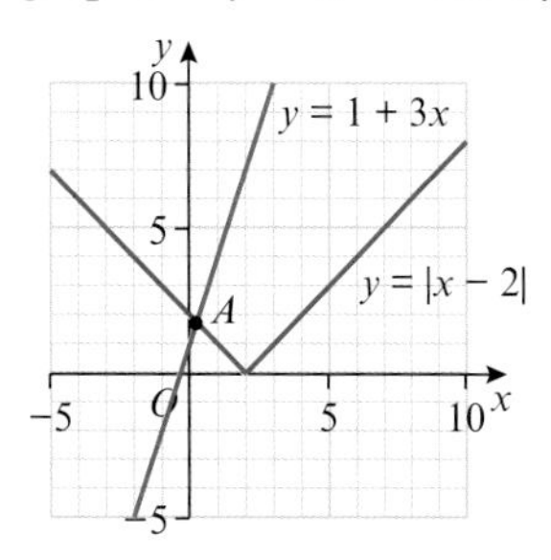

The graphs intersect at point A

At A, $-(x - 2) = 1 + 3x$

$-x + 2 = 1 + 3x$

$x = \frac{1}{4}$ is the x-coordinate of A.

To solve the inequality $|x - 2| \leqslant 1 + 3x$, find where the graph of the function $y = |x - 2|$ intersects or is below the graph of $y = 1 + 3x$

Solution is $x \geqslant \frac{1}{4}$

5 a $|2x - 1| \leqslant |3x|$

Sketch the graphs of $y = |2x - 1|$ and $y = |3x|$

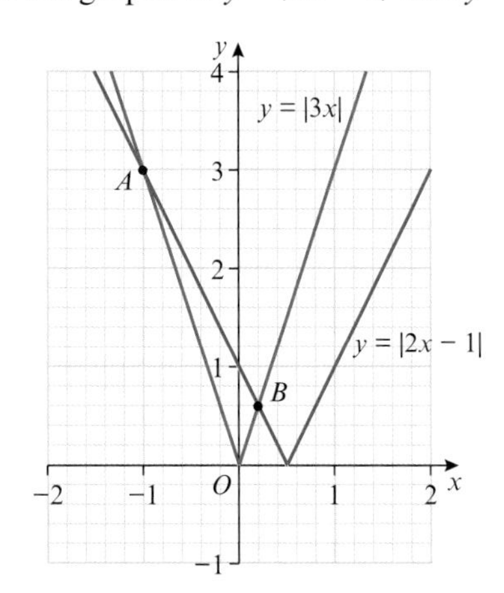

The graphs intersect at points A and B

At A, $-(2x - 1) = -3x$

$-2x + 1 = -3x$

$x = -1$

$x = -1$ is the x-coordinate of A.

At B, $3x = -(2x - 1)$

$3x = -2x + 1$

$x = \frac{1}{5}$ is the x-coordinate of B.

To solve the inequality $|2x - 1| \leqslant |3x|$, find where the graph of the function $y = |2x - 1|$ intersects or is below the graph of $y = |3x|$

Solution is $x \leqslant -1$ and $x \geqslant \frac{1}{5}$

f $|2x| < |x - 3|$

Using algebra square both sides:

$(2x)^2 < (x - 3)^2$

$4x^2 < x^2 - 6x + 9$

$3x^2 + 6x - 9 < 0$

$x^2 + 2x - 3 < 0$

$(x + 3)(x - 1) < 0$

Critical values are 1 and -3

Looking at the sketch, the values of x which satisfy $(x + 3)(x - 1) < 0$ are $-3 < x < 1$

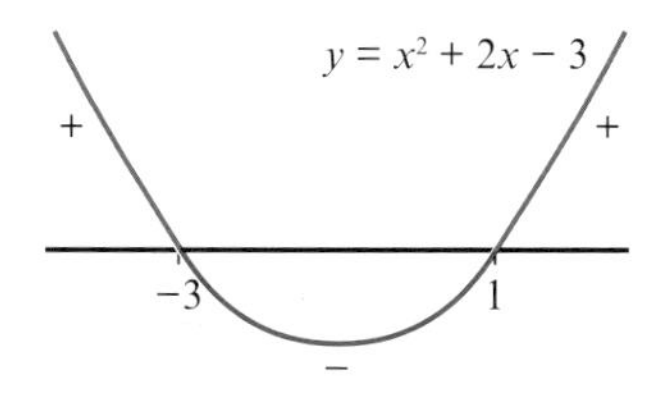

Solution is $-3 < x < 1$

6 b $|x - 2| \geqslant |x + 5|$

Using algebra square both sides:

$$(x - 2)^2 \geqslant (x + 5)^2$$

$$x^2 - 4x + 4 \geqslant x^2 + 10x + 25$$

$$-21 \geqslant 14x$$

Solution is $x \leqslant -\frac{3}{2}$

d $|2x + 3| \leqslant |x - 3|$

Using algebra, square both sides:

$$(2x + 3)^2 \leqslant (x - 3)^2$$

$$4x^2 + 12x + 9 \leqslant x^2 - 6x + 9$$

$$3x^2 + 18x \leqslant 0$$

$$3x(x + 6) \leqslant 0$$

Critical values are 0 and −6

Looking at the sketch, the values of x which satisfy $3x(x + 6) \leqslant 0$ are $-6 \leqslant x \leqslant 0$

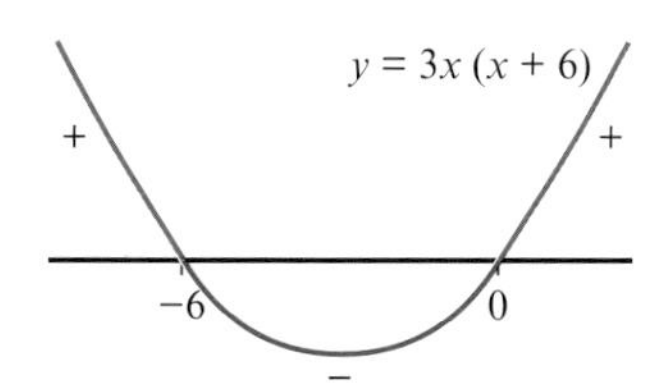

Solution is $-6 \leqslant x \leqslant 0$

7 a $2|x - 3| > |3x + 1|$

Using algebra, square both sides:

$$4(x - 3)^2 > (3x + 1)^2$$

$$4(x^2 - 6x + 9) > 9x^2 + 6x + 1$$

$$4x^2 - 24x + 36 > 9x^2 + 6x + 1$$

$$5x^2 + 30x - 35 < 0$$

$$x^2 + 6x - 7 < 0$$

$$(x + 7)(x - 1) < 0$$

Critical values are −7 and 1

Looking at the sketch, the values of x which satisfy $(x + 7)(x - 1) < 0$ are $-7 < x < 1$

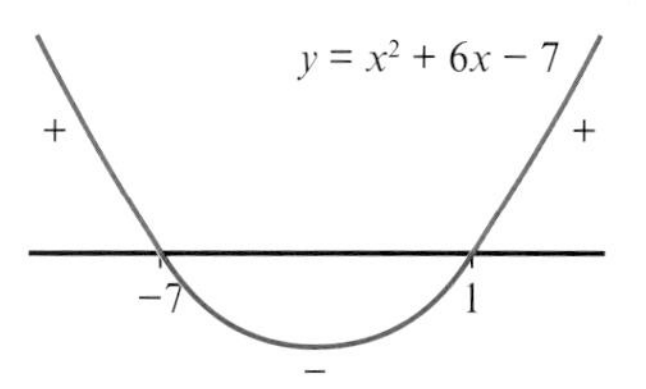

Solution is $-7 < x < 1$

b $3|x - 1| < |2x + 1|$

Using algebra, square both sides:

$$[3(x - 1)]^2 < (2x + 1)^2$$

$$9(x^2 - 2x + 1) < 4x^2 + 4x + 1$$

$$9x^2 - 18x + 9 < 4x^2 + 4x + 1$$

$$5x^2 - 22x + 8 < 0$$

$$(5x - 2)(x - 4) < 0$$

Critical values are $\frac{2}{5}$ and 4

Looking at the sketch, the values of x which satisfy $(5x - 2)(x - 4) < 0$ are $\frac{2}{5} < x < 4$

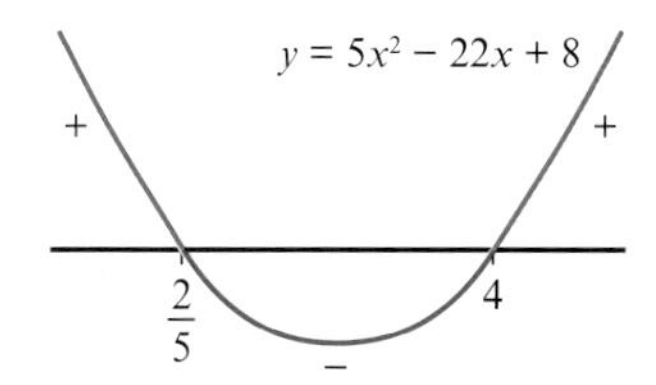

Solution is $\frac{2}{5} < x < 4$

c $|2x - 5| \leqslant 3|2x + 1|$

Using algebra, square both sides:

$$(2x - 5)^2 \leqslant 9(2x + 1)^2$$

$$4x^2 - 20x + 25 \leqslant 9(4x^2 + 4x + 1)$$

$$4x^2 - 20x + 25 \leqslant 36x^2 + 36x + 9$$

$$32x^2 + 56x - 16 \geqslant 0$$

$$4x^2 + 7x - 2 \geqslant 0$$

$$(4x - 1)(x + 2) \geqslant 0$$

Critical values are $\frac{1}{4}$ and −2

Looking at the sketch, the values of x which satisfy $(4x - 1)(x + 2) \geqslant 0$ are $x \leqslant -2$ and $x \geqslant \frac{1}{4}$

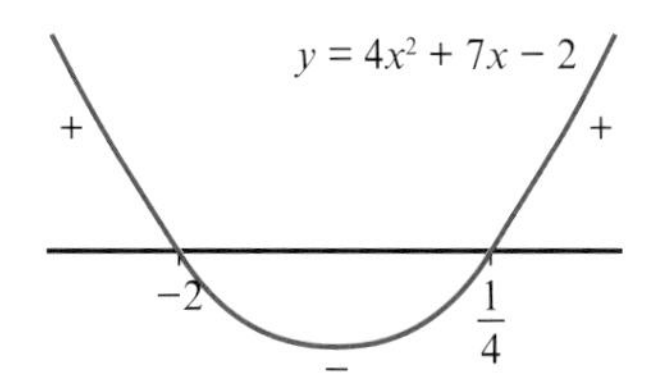

Solution is $x \leqslant -2$ and $x \geqslant \frac{1}{4}$

8 $|x + 2k| \geqslant |x - 3k|$

Using algebra, square both sides:

$$(x + 2k)^2 \geqslant (x - 3k)^2$$

$$x^2 + 4kx + 4k^2 \geqslant x^2 - 6kx + 9k^2$$

$$10kx - 5k^2 \geqslant 0$$

$$5k(2x - k) \geqslant 0$$

k is positive, so $2x - k \geqslant 0$

The critical value is $\frac{k}{2}$

The solution is $x \geqslant \frac{k}{2}$

9 $|x + 3k| < 4|x - k|$

Using algebra, square both sides:

$$(x + 3k)^2 < 16(x - k)^2$$

$$x^2 + 6kx + 9k^2 < 16x^2 - 32kx + 16k^2$$

$$15x^2 - 38kx + 7k^2 > 0$$

$$(5x - k)(3x - 7k) > 0$$

The critical values are $\frac{k}{5}$ and $\frac{7k}{3}$ (k is positive)

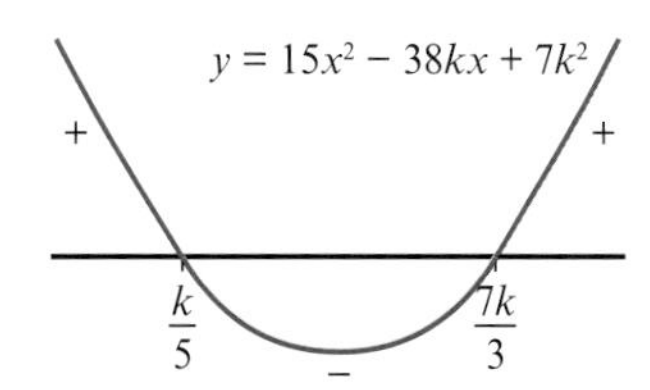

The solution is $x > \frac{7k}{3}$ and $k < \frac{k}{5}$

10 $|3x + 2| + |3x - 2| \leqslant 8$

Rewrite as $|3x + 2| \leqslant -|3x - 2| + 8$

A sketch of the graphs of $y = |3x + 2|$ and $y = |3x - 2|$ looks like:

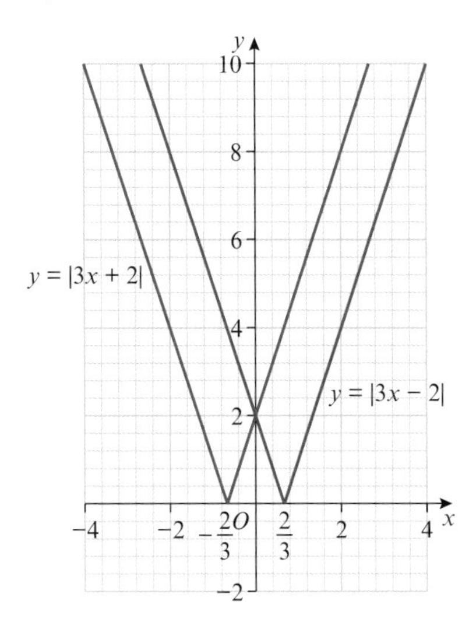

If the graph of $y = |3x - 2|$ is reflected in the x-axis, it is now the graph of $y = -|3x - 2|$

If this graph is now translated $\begin{pmatrix} 0 \\ 8 \end{pmatrix}$, then this is the graph of $y = -|3x - 2| + 8$

A sketch of the graphs of $y = |3x + 2|$ and $y = -|3x - 2| + 8$ looks like:

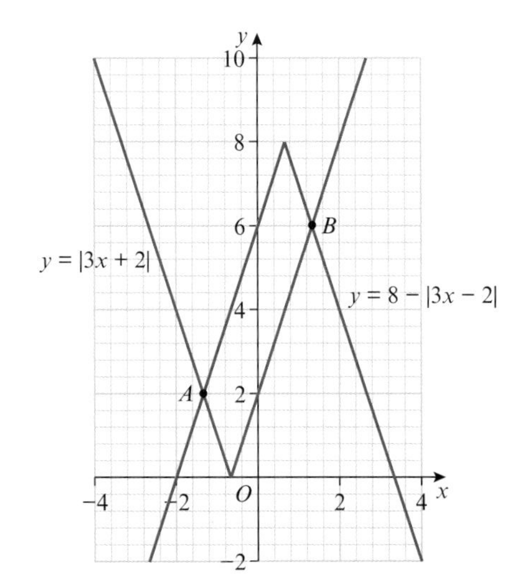

The graphs of $y = |3x + 2|$ and $y = -|3x - 2| + 8$ intersect at two points A and B

At A:

$y = -(3x + 2)$

$y = 8 + (3x - 2)$

Solving $-3x - 2 = 8 + 3x - 2$

$$-6x = 8$$

$$x = -\frac{4}{3}$$

At B:

$y = 3x + 2$

$y = -(3x - 2) + 8$

Solving $3x + 2 = -(3x - 2) + 8$

$$6x = 8$$

$$x = \frac{4}{3}$$

Looking at the sketch, to solve the inequality $|3x + 2| \leqslant -|3x - 2| + 8$ we must find the values of x where the graph of $y = |3x + 2|$ intersects or is below the graph of $y = -|3x - 2| + 8$.

Solution is $-\frac{4}{3} \leqslant x \leqslant \frac{4}{3}$

Exercise 4.3

1 $y = (x - 2)(x + 1)(x - 3)$

When $x = 0$ $y = -2 \times 1 \times -3 = 6$

The curve intercepts the y-axis at $D(0, 6)$

When $y = 0$ $(x - 2)(x + 1)(x - 3) = 0$

$x = 2$, $x = -1$ or $x = 3$

The curve intercepts the x-axis at $A(-1, 0)$, $B(2, 0)$ and $C(3, 0)$

TIP

For a curve with equation $y = k(x - a)(x - b)(x - c)$ the shape of the graph is:

if k is positive

if k is negative

2 a $y = (x - 2)(x - 4)(x + 3)$

has a positive shape. 

When $x = 0$ $y = (0 - 2)(0 - 4)(0 + 3) = 24$

The curve intercepts the y-axis at $(0, 24)$

When $y = 0$ $(x - 2)(x - 4)(x + 3) = 0$

$x = 2$, $x = 4$ or $x = -3$

The curve intercepts the x-axis at $(2, 0)$, $(4, 0)$ and $(-3, 0)$

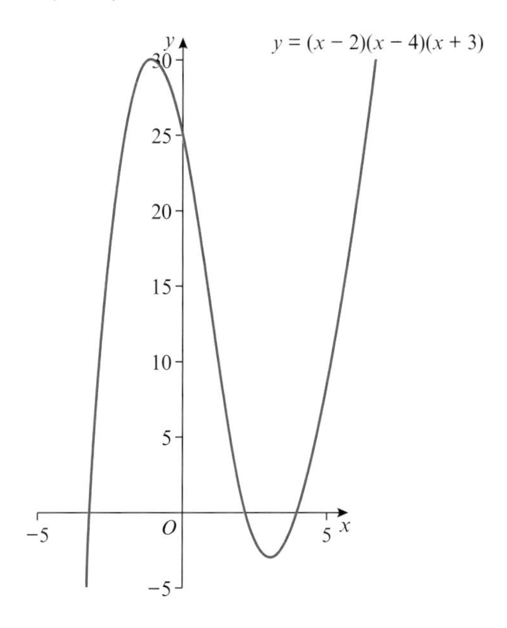

d $y = (3 - 2x)(x - 1)(x + 2)$

has a negative shape. 

When $x = 0$ $y = (3 - 0)(0 - 1)(0 + 2) = -6$

The curve intercepts the y-axis at $(0, -6)$

When $y = 0$ $(3 - 2x)(x - 1)(x + 2) = 0$

$x = 1.5$, $x = 1$ or $x = -2$

The curve intercepts the x-axis at $(1.5, 0)$, $(1, 0)$ and $(-2, 0)$

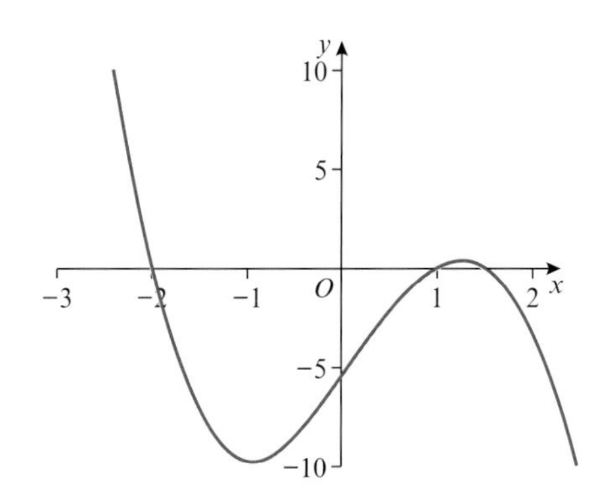

3 $y = 2(x + 1)^2(7 - 2x)$

When $x = 0$ $\quad y = 2(0 + 1)^2(7 - 0) = 14$

The curve intercepts the y-axis at $B(0, 14)$

When $y = 0$ $\quad 2(x + 1)^2(7 - 2x) = 0$

$x = -1$ or $x = 3.5$

The curve intercepts the x-axis at $(-1, 0)$ and $(3.5, 0)$

So, A is at $(3.5, 0)$

4 b $y = x^2(5 - 2x)$ has a negative shape. 

When $x = 0$ $\quad y = 0^2(5 - 0) = 0$

The point $(0, 0)$ lies on the curve.

$y = x^2(5 - 2x)$ can be written as
$y = (x - 0)(x - 0)(5 - 2x)$

When $y = 0$ $\quad y = (x - 0)(x - 0)(5 - 2x) = 0$

So, $x = 0$, $x = 0$ or $x = 2.5$

$x = 0$ is a repeated root.

This indicates that the curve 'touches' the x-axis at $x = 0$ $(y = 0)$

The curve crosses the x-axis at $(2.5, 0)$

$(0, 0)$ is a minimum point.

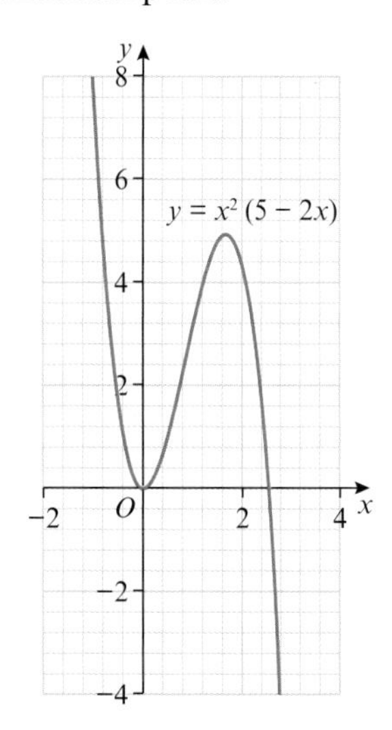

d $y = (x - 2)^2(10 - 3x)$

has a negative shape. 

When $x = 0$ $\quad y = (0 - 2)^2(10 - 0) = 40$

The curve intercepts the y-axis at $(0, 40)$

When $y = 0$ $\quad (x - 2)^2(10 - 3x) = 0$
[or $(x - 2)(x - 2)(10 - 3x)$]

$x = 2$ (repeated root) or $x = \dfrac{10}{3}$

The curve touches the x-axis at $(2, 0)$ and crosses the x-axis at $\left(\dfrac{10}{3}, 0\right)$.

$(2, 0)$ is a minimum point.

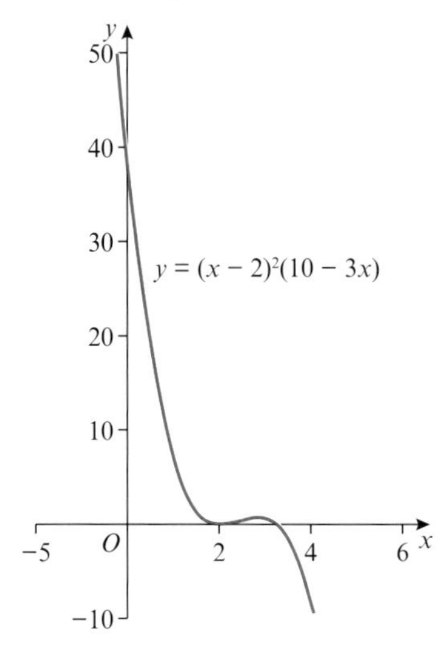

5 b $y = |2(5 - 2x)(x + 1)(x + 2)|$

Sketch the graph of $y = 2(5 - 2x)(x + 1)(x + 2)$

$y = 2(5 - 2x)(x + 1)(x + 2)$

has a negative shape. 

When $x = 0$ $\quad y = 2(5 - 0)(0 + 1)(0 + 2) = 20$

The curve intercepts the y-axis at $(0, 20)$

When $y = 0$ $\quad 2(5 - 2x)(x + 1)(x + 2) = 0$

$x = 2.5$, $x = -1$ or $x = -2$

The curve intercepts the x-axis at $(2.5, 0)$, $(-1, 0)$ and $(-2, 0)$

Reflect in the x-axis, the part of the curve that is below the x-axis.

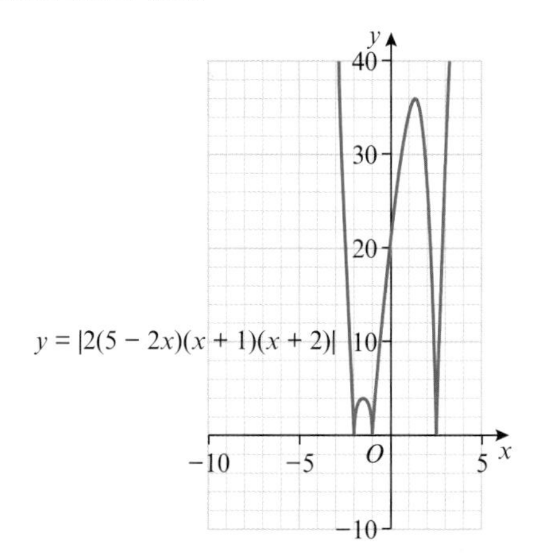

d $y = |3(x-2)^2(x+1)|$

Sketch the graph of $y = 3(x-2)^2(x+1)$

$y = 3(x-2)^2(x+1)$

has a positive shape. 

When $x = 0$ $\quad y = 3(0-2)^2(0+1) = 12$

The curve intercepts the y-axis at (0, 12)

When $y = 0$ $\quad 3(x-2)^2(x+1) = 0$

$x = 2$ (repeated root) or $x = -1$

The curve touches the x-axis at (2, 0) and crosses the x-axis at (−1, 0)

Reflect in the x-axis, the part of the curve that is below the x-axis.

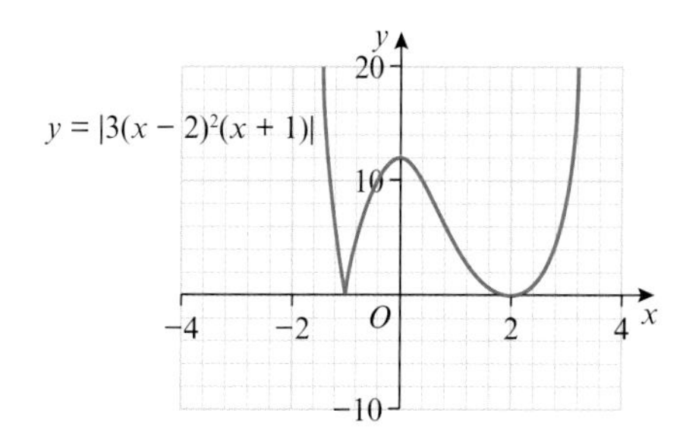

6 a $y = 9x - x^3$

$y = x(9 - x^2)$

$y = x(3 + x)(3 - x)$

$y = x(3 + x)(3 - x)$ has a negative shape.

When $x = 0$ $\quad y = 0(3+0)(3-0) = 0$

The curve intercepts the y-axis at (0, 0)

When $y = 0$ $\quad x(3+x)(3-x) = 0$

$x = 0$, $x = -3$ or $x = 3$

The curve intercepts the x-axis at (0, 0), (−3, 0) and (3, 0)

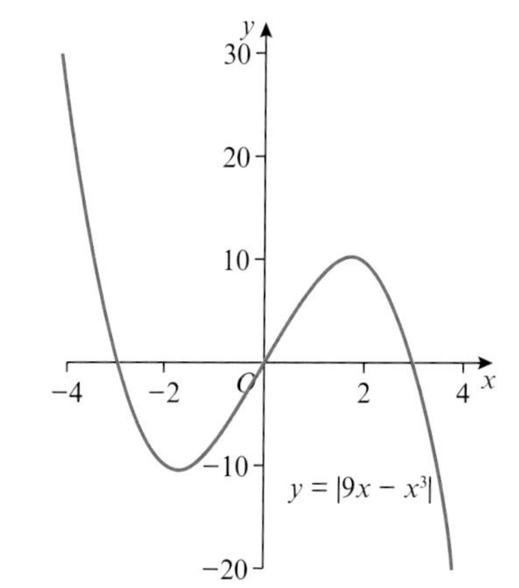

d $y = 2x^3 + 3x^2 - 29x - 60$

The positive and negative factors of −60 are ±1, ±2, ±3 etc

$f(-3) = 2(-3)^3 + 3(-3)^2 - 29(-3) - 60 = 0$

So, $(x + 3)$ is a factor of $f(x)$

The other factors can be found by trial and error, long division or by equating coefficients.

Comparing coefficients:

Since $(x + 3)$ is a factor, $2x^3 + 3x^2 - 29x - 60 = (x+3)(ax^2 + bx + c)$

coefficient of x^3 is 2, so $a = 2$ since $1 \times 2 = 2$

constant term is −60, so $c = -20$ since $3 \times -20 = -60$

$2x^3 + 3x^2 - 29x - 60 = (x+3)(2x^2 + bx - 20)$ — expand and collect like terms

$2x^3 + 3x^2 - 29x - 60 = 2x^3 + bx^2 - 20x + 6x^2 + 3bx - 60$

$2x^3 + 3x^2 - 29x - 60 = 2x^3 + (b+6)x^2 - (20 - 3b)x - 60$

Equating coefficients of x^2: $b + 6 = 3$

$$b = -3$$

$$f(x) = (x + 3)(2x^2 - 3x - 20)$$

$$f(x) = (x + 3)(2x + 5)(x - 4)$$

$$2x^3 + 3x^2 - 29x - 60 = (x + 3)(2x + 5)(x - 4)$$

$$y = (x + 3)(2x + 5)(x - 4)$$

has a positive shape.

When $x = 0$ $\quad y = (0 + 3)(0 + 5)(0 - 4) = -60$

The curve intercepts the y-axis at $(0, -60)$

When $y = 0$ $\quad (x + 3)(2x + 5)(x - 4) = 0$

$x = -3$, $x = -2.5$ or $x = 4$

The curve intercepts the x-axis at $(-3, 0)$, $(-2.5, 0)$ and $(4, 0)$

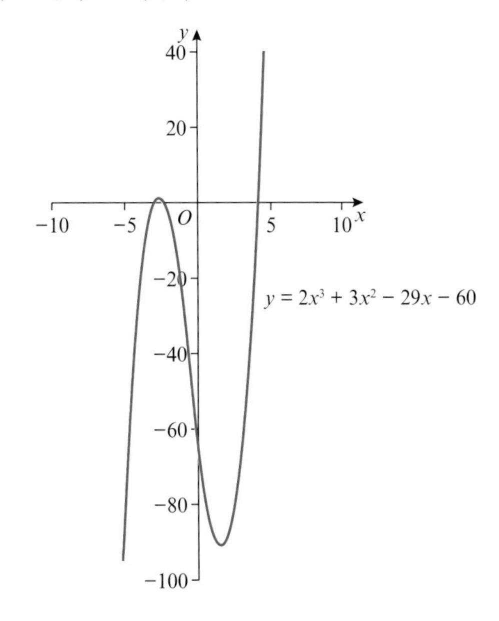

7 a $y = x(x - 5)(x - 7)$

has a positive shape. 

When $x = 0$ $\quad y = 0(0 - 5)(0 - 7) = 0$

The curve intercepts the y-axis at $(0, 0)$

When $y = 0$ $\quad x(x - 5)(x - 7) = 0$

$x = 0$, $x = 5$ or $x = 7$

The curve intercepts the x-axis at $(0, 0)$, $(5, 0)$ and $(7, 0)$

$y = x(7 - x)$ or $y = 7x - x^2$ is an '∩' shaped parabola

When $x = 0$ $\quad y = 0(7 - x) = 0$

The curve intercepts the y-axis at $(0, 0)$

When $y = 0$ $\quad x(7 - x) = 0$

$x = 0$ or $x = 7$

The curve intercepts the x-axis at $(0, 0)$ and $(7, 0)$

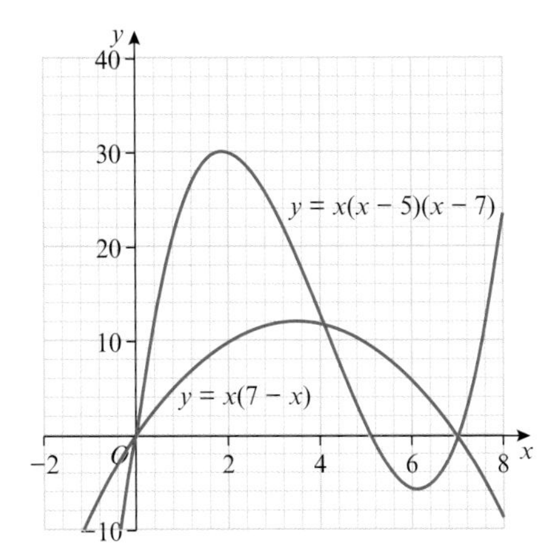

b To find the intersection points of the two graphs we need to solve

$x(x - 5)(x - 7) = x(7 - x)$

TIP

We cannot divide both sides by x since we would lose a solution.

$$x(x - 5)(x - 7) = -x(x - 7)$$

$$x(x - 5)(x - 7) + x(x - 7) = 0$$

$$x(x - 7)[(x - 5) + 1] = 0$$

$$x(x - 7)[x - 4] = 0$$

$x = 0$, $x = 7$ or $x = 4$

Substituting these values into $y = x(7 - x)$ gives the coordinates of the intersection points.

The intersection points are $(0, 0)$, $(4, 12)$ and $(7,0)$.

8 a $y = (2x - 1)(x + 2)(x + 1)$ has a positive shape.

When $x = 0$ $\quad y = (0 - 1)(0 + 2)(0 + 1) = -2$

The curve intercepts the y-axis at $(0, -2)$

When $y = 0$ $\quad (2x - 1)(x + 2)(x + 1) = 0$

$x = 0.5$, $x = -2$ or $x = -1$

The curve intercepts the x-axis at $(0.5, 0)$, $(-2, 0)$ and $(-1, 0)$

$y = (x + 1)(4 - x)$ or $y = -x^2 + 3x + 4$ is an '∩' shaped parabola

When $x = 0$ $\quad y = (0 + 1)(4 - 0) = 4$

The curve intercepts the y-axis at $(0, 4)$

When $y = 0$ $\quad (x + 1)(4 - x) = 0$

$x = -1$ or $x = 4$

The curve intercepts the x-axis at $(-1, 0)$ and $(4, 0)$

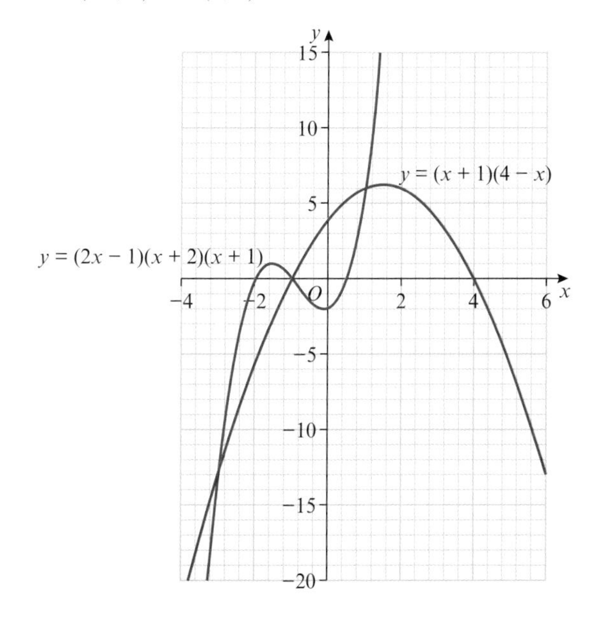

b To find the intersection points of the two graphs we need to solve

$$(2x - 1)(x + 2)(x + 1) = (x + 1)(4 - x)$$

$$(2x - 1)(x + 2)(x + 1) - (x + 1)(4 - x) = 0$$

$$(x + 1)[(2x - 1)(x + 2) - (4 - x)] = 0$$

$$(x + 1)[2x^2 + 3x - 2 - 4 + x] = 0$$

$$(x + 1)[2x^2 + 4x - 6] = 0$$

$$(x + 1)(2x - 2)(x + 3) = 0$$

$x = -1$, $x = 1$ or $x = -3$

Substituting these values into $y = (x + 1)(4 - x)$ gives the coordinates of the intersection points.

The intersection points are: $(-1, 0)$, $(1, 6)$ and $(-3, -14)$.

9 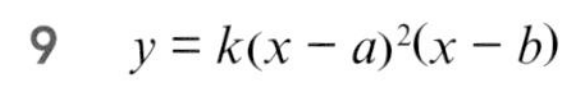
$y = k(x - a)^2(x - b)$

$y = k(x - a)(x - a)(x - b)$

$a = 1$ since the curve touches the x-axis at $x = 1$($x = 1$ is a repeated root).

The curve passes through $(2, 0)$ so $b = 2$

The curve also passes through $(0, 4)$.

Substitute $x = 0,\ y = 4$ into $y = k(x - 1)^2(x - 2)$

$4 = k(0 - 1)^2(0 - 2)$

$k = -2$

10 $y = |k(x - a)(x - b)(x - c)|$

The graph of $y = k(x - a)(x - b)(x - c)$ looks like:

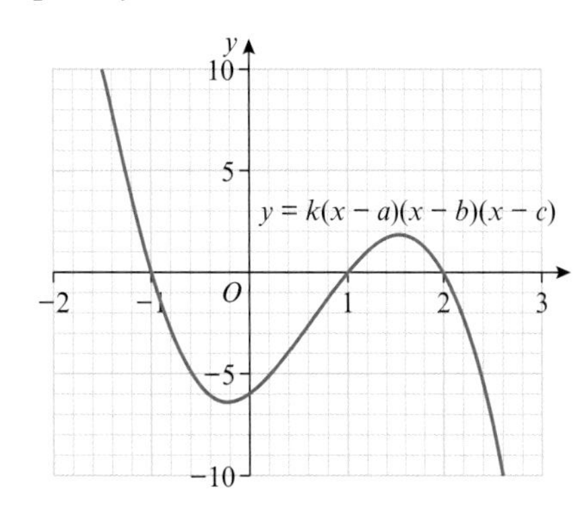

The graph crosses the x-axis at $x = -1$, $x = 1$ and $x = 2$

So, $y = k(x + 1)(x - 1)(x - 2)$, i.e., $a = -1$, $b = 1$ and $c = 2$

The curve $y = k(x + 1)(x - 1)(x - 2)$ also passes through $(0, -6)$

Substitute $x = 0$, $y = -6$ into $y = k(x + 1)(x - 1)(x - 2)$ gives:

$-6 = k \times 1 \times -1 \times -2$

$k = -3$

and $k = 3$ is also a solution since $|-k\text{f}(x)| = |k\text{f}(x)|$.

Exercise 4.4

1 a $x(x - 2)(x + 1) \leqslant 0$

The red sections of the graph represent where the curve $y = x(x - 2)(x + 1)$ is below the x-axis.

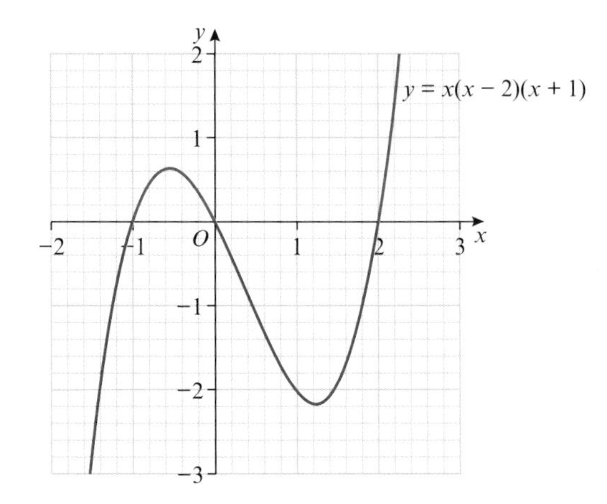

The solution is $x \leqslant -1$ or $0 \leqslant x \leqslant 2$

b $x(x - 2)(x + 1) \geqslant 1$

The red section of the graph represents where the curve $y = x(x - 2)(x + 1)$ is above the line $y = 1$

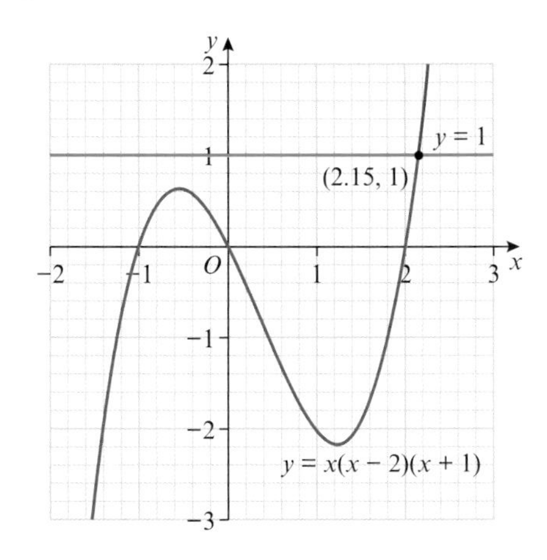

The solution is $x \geqslant 2.1$ (correct to 1 decimal place)

Zooming in further using graphing software gives $x \geqslant 2.15$

c $x(x - 2)(x + 1) \leqslant -2$

The red sections of the graph represent where the curve $y = x(x - 2)(x + 1)$ is below the line $y = -2$

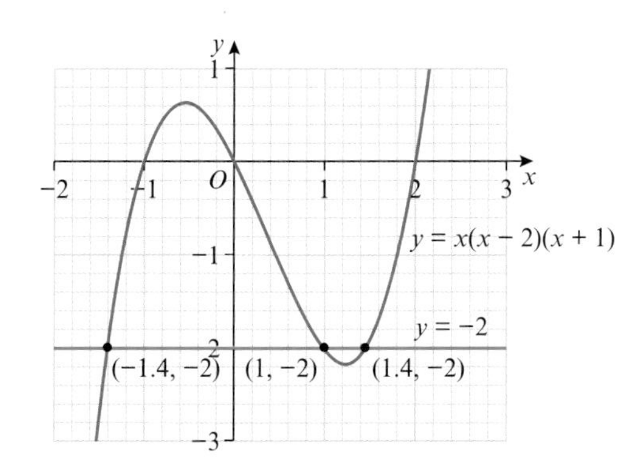

The solution is $x \leqslant -1.4$ or $1 \leqslant x \leqslant 1.4$ (correct to 1 decimal place)

2 a $(x + 1)^2(2 - x) \geqslant 0$

The red section of the graph represents where the curve $y = (x + 1)^2(2 - x)$ is above the x-axis

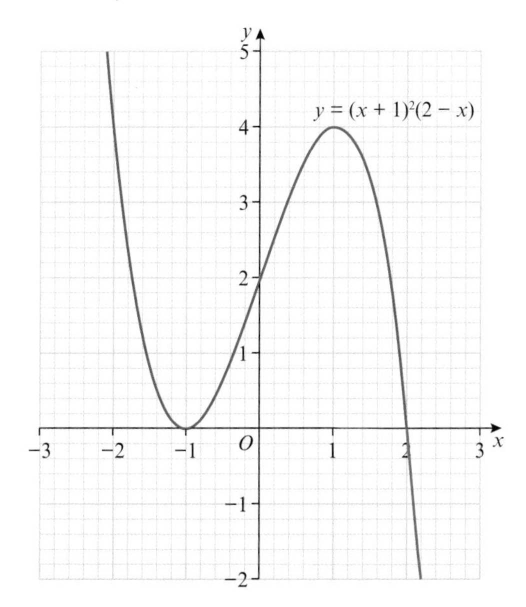

The solution is $x \leqslant 2$

b $(x + 1)^2(2 - x) \leqslant 4$

The red sections of the graph represent where the curve $y = (x + 1)^2(2 - x)$ is below the line $y = 4$

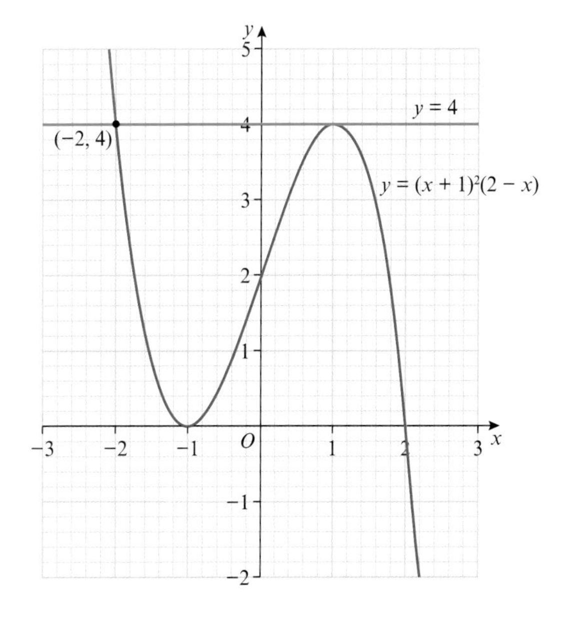

The solution is $x \geqslant -2$

c $(x + 1)^2(2 - x) \leqslant 3$

The red sections of the graph represent where the curve $y = (x + 1)^2(2 - x)$ is

below the line $y = 3$

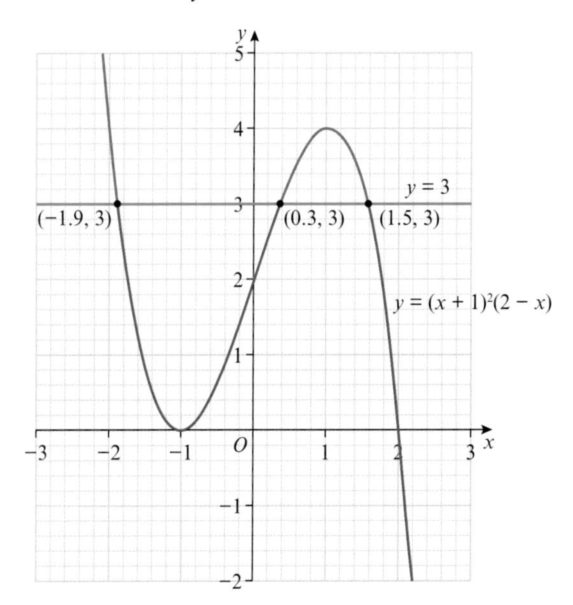

The solution is $-1.9 \leqslant x \leqslant 0.3$ or $x \geqslant 1.5$ (correct to 1 decimal place)

Zooming in further using graphing software gives

$-1.9 \leqslant x \leqslant 0.35$ or $x \geqslant 1.5$

3 a $(1 - x)(x - 2)(x + 1) < -3$

The red sections of the graph represent where the curve $y = (1 - x)(x - 2)(x + 1)$ is below the line $y = -3$

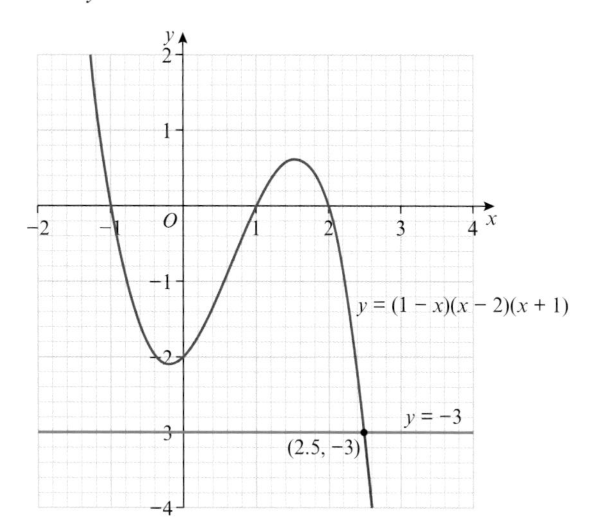

The solution is $x \geqslant 2.5$ (correct to 1 decimal place)

b $(1 - x)(x - 2)(x + 1) \leqslant 0$

The red sections of the graph represent where the curve $y = (1 - x)(x - 2)(x + 1)$ is below the x-axis

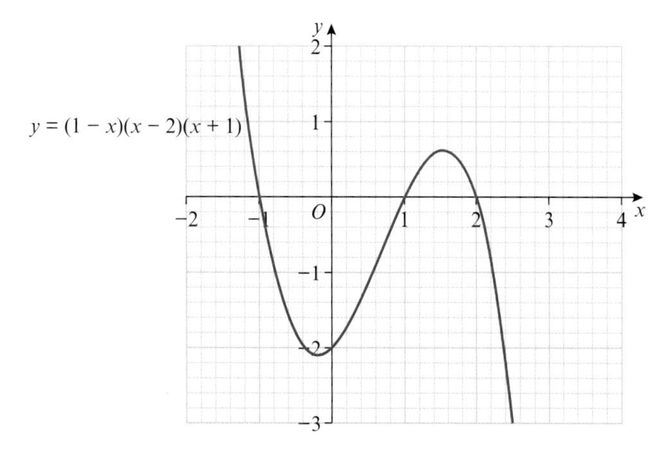

The solution is $-1 \leqslant x \leqslant 1$ or $x \geqslant 2$

c $(1 - x)(x - 2)(x + 1) \geqslant -1$

The red section of the graph represents where the curve $y = (1 - x)(x - 2)(x + 1)$ is above the line $y = -1$

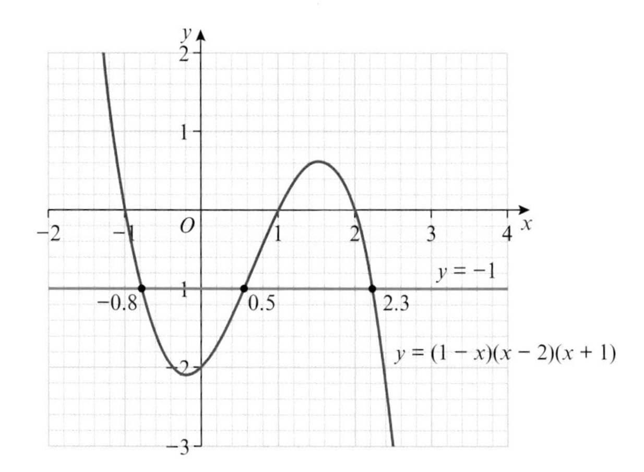

The solution is $x \leqslant -0.8$ or $0.5 \leqslant x \leqslant 2.3$ (correct to 1 decimal place)

Zooming in further using graphing software gives

$0.55 \leqslant x \leqslant 2.32$

Exercise 4.5

1 d

$x^4 + 2x^2 - 8 = 0$ use the substitution $y = x^2$

$y^2 + 2y - 8 = 0$ factorise

$(y + 4)(y - 2) = 0$ solve

$y = -4$ or $y = 2$ substitute x^2 for y

$x^2 = -4$ or $x^2 = 2$

$x = \sqrt{-4}$ (has no solutions) or $x = \pm\sqrt{2}$

$\therefore x = \pm\sqrt{2}$

i

$\frac{8}{x^6} + \frac{7}{x^3} = 1$ multiply each term by x^6

$8 + 7x^3 = x^6$ rearrange

$x^6 - 7x^3 - 8 = 0$ factorise

$(x^3 - 8)(x^3 + 1) = 0$

$x^3 = 8$ or $x^3 = -1$

$x = \sqrt[3]{8}$ or $x = \sqrt[3]{-1}$

$\therefore x = 2$ or $x = -1$

2 c $2x^4 + x^2 - 5 = 0$ — use the substitution $y = x^2$

$2y^2 + y - 5 = 0$ — this does not factorise, so use the quadratic formula

$$y = \frac{-1 \pm \sqrt{1^2 - 4 \times 2 \times -5}}{2 \times 2}$$

$$y = \frac{-1 \pm \sqrt{41}}{4}$$ substitute x^2 for y

$$x^2 = \frac{-1 + \sqrt{41}}{4} \text{ or } x^2 = \frac{-1 - \sqrt{41}}{4}$$

$$x = \sqrt{\frac{-1 + \sqrt{41}}{4}} \text{ or } x = \sqrt{\frac{-1 - \sqrt{41}}{4}} \text{ (no solutions)}$$

$x = 1.1622$ or $x = -1.1622$

$\therefore x = 1.16$ or $x = -1.16$ (to 3 significant figures)

f $2x^8 - 7x^4 - 3 = 0$ — use the substitution $y = x^4$

$2y^2 - 7y - 3 = 0$ — this does not factorise, so use the quadratic formula

$$y = \frac{--7 \pm \sqrt{(-7)^2 - 4 \times 2 \times -3}}{2 \times 2}$$

$$y = \frac{7 \pm \sqrt{73}}{4}$$ substitute x^4 for y

$$x^4 = \frac{7 + \sqrt{73}}{4} \text{ or } x^4 = \frac{7 - \sqrt{73}}{4}$$

$$x = \sqrt[4]{\frac{7 + \sqrt{73}}{4}} \text{ or } x = \sqrt[4]{\frac{7 - \sqrt{73}}{4}} \text{ (no solutions)}$$

$x = 1.404$ or $x = -1.404$

$\therefore x = 1.40$ or $x = -1.40$ (to 3 significant figures)

3 d $\sqrt{x}(2 + \sqrt{x}) = 35$ — expand brackets

$2\sqrt{x} + x - 35 = 0$ — rearrange

$x + 2\sqrt{x} - 35 = 0$ — use the substitution $y = \sqrt{x}$

$y^2 + 2y - 35 = 0$ — factorise

$(y + 7)(y - 5) = 0$ — solve

$y = -7$ or $y = 5$ — substitute $\sqrt{x}$ for y

$\sqrt{x} = -7$ (no solutions) or $\sqrt{x} = 5$

$\therefore x = 25$

h $3\sqrt{x} + \frac{5}{\sqrt{x}} = 16$ — substitute y for $\sqrt{x}$

$3y + \frac{5}{y} = 16$ — multiply all terms by y

$3y^2 + 5 = 16y$	rearrange
$3y^2 - 16y + 5 = 0$	factorise
$(3y - 1)(y - 5) = 0$	solve
$y = \frac{1}{3}$ or $y = 5$	substitute $\sqrt{x}$ for y
$\sqrt{x} = \frac{1}{3}$ or $\sqrt{x} = 5$	
$\therefore x = \frac{1}{9}$ or $x = 25$	

4

$2x^{\frac{2}{3}} - 7x^{\frac{1}{3}} + 6 = 0$	substitute $y = x^{\frac{1}{3}}$
$2y^2 - 7y + 6 = 0$	factorise
$(2y - 3)(y - 2) = 0$	solve
$y = 1.5$ or $y = 2$	substitute $x^{\frac{1}{3}} = y$
$x^{\frac{1}{3}} = 1.5$ or $x^{\frac{1}{3}} = 2$	
$x = \left(\frac{3}{2}\right)^3$ or $x = 2^3$	
$\therefore x = \frac{27}{8}$ or $x = 8$	

5 a

$y = \sqrt{x}$	multiply each term by 5
$5y = 5\sqrt{x}$ and $5y = x + 4$	equate the equations
$5\sqrt{x} = x + 4$	

b

$x - 5\sqrt{x} + 4 = 0$	substitute y for $\sqrt{x}$
$y^2 - 5y + 4 = 0$	factorise
$(y - 4)(y - 1) = 0$	solve
$y = 4$ or $y = 1$	substitute $\sqrt{x}$ for y
$\sqrt{x} = 4$ or $\sqrt{x} = 1$	
$\therefore x = 4^2 = 16$ or $x = 1^2 = 1$	substitute each x value into $y = \sqrt{x}$
$y = \sqrt{16}$ or $y = \sqrt{1}$	
$y = 4$ or $y = 1$	
$P = (16, 4)$ or $Q = (1, 1)$ (or vice-versa).	

6 c

$2(2^{2x}) - 9(2^x) + 4 = 0$	2^{2x} can be written as $(2^x)^2$
$2 \times (2^x)^2 - 9(2^x) + 4 = 0$	use the substitution $y = 2^x$
$2y^2 - 9y + 4 = 0$	factorise
$(2y - 1)(y - 4) = 0$	solve
$y = \frac{1}{2}$ or 4	substitute 2^x for y

$2^x = \frac{1}{2}$ or $2^x = 4$

$\therefore x = -1$ or $x = 2$

d $3^{2x+1} - 28(3^x) + 9 = 0$

3^{2x+1} can be written as $(3^x)^2 \times 3^1$.
If $y = 3^x$ then $(3^x)^2 \times 3^1$ can be written as $y^2 \times 3$ or $3y^2$

So, $3^{2x+1} - 28(3^x) + 9 = 0$ becomes:

$3y^2 - 28y + 9 = 0$ factorise

$(3y - 1)(y - 9) = 0$ solve

$y = \frac{1}{3}$ or $y = 9$ substitute 3^x for y

$3^x = \frac{1}{3}$ or $3^x = 9$

$\therefore x = -1$ or $x = 2$

7 $f(x) = 2^x$ $g(x) = 4x^2 + 7x$

gf(x) means that f acts on x first and $f(x) = 2^x$

$gf(x) = g(2^x) = 4(2^x)^2 + 7(2^x)$

$4(2^x)^2 + 7(2^x) = 2$ substitute y for 2^x

$4y^2 + 7y = 2$ rearrange

$4y^2 + 7y - 2 = 0$ factorise

$(4y - 1)(y + 2) = 0$ solve

$y = \frac{1}{4}$ or $y = -2$ substitute 2^x for y

$2^x = \frac{1}{4}$ or $2^x = -2$ (no solutions)

$2^x = 2^{-2}$

$\therefore x = -2$

8 $f(x) = x^3 - 2$ $g(x) = x^2 - 5x$

gf(x) means that f acts on x first and $f(x) = x^3 - 2$

$gf(x) = g(x^3 - 2) = (x^3 - 2)^2 - 5(x^3 - 2)$

$(x^3 - 2)^2 - 5(x^3 - 2) = 6$ expand brackets

$x^6 - 4x^3 + 4 - 5x^3 + 10 = 6$ simplify

$x^6 - 9x^3 + 8 = 0$ use the substitution $y = x^3$

$y^2 - 9y + 8 = 0$ factorise

$(y - 8)(y - 1) = 0$ solve

$y = 8$ or $y = 1$ substitute x^3 for y

$x^3 = 8$ or $x^3 = 1$

$\therefore x = 2$ or $x = 1$

9 $f(x) = x^2 + 3x$ $g(x) = x^2 - 4x$

gf(x) means that f acts on x first and $f(x) = x^2 + 3x$

$gf(x) = g(x^2 + 3x) = (x^2 + 3x)^2 - 4(x^2 + 3x)$

$(x^2 + 3x)^2 - 4(x^2 + 3x) = 0$	expand brackets
$x^4 + 6x^3 + 9x^2 - 4x^2 - 12x = 0$	simplify
$x^4 + 6x^3 + 5x^2 - 12x = 0$	factorise
$x(x^3 + 6x^2 + 5x - 12) = 0$	(1)

Finding the factors of the cubic expression: $x^3 + 6x^2 + 5x - 12$

The positive and negative factors of -12 are ±1, ±2, ±3 etc

Substituting $x = 1$ into the cubic expression gives:

$(1)^3 + 6(1)^2 + 5(1) - 12$ which is zero.

So, $(x - 1)$ is a factor of $x^3 + 6x^2 + 5x - 12$

The other factors can be found by equating coefficients:

Since $(x - 1)$ is a factor, $x^3 + 6x^2 + 5x - 12 = (x - 1)(ax^2 + bx + c)$	coefficient of x^3 is 1, so $a = 1$ since $1 \times 1 = 1$ constant term is -12, so $c = +12$ since $-1 \times 12 = -12$
$x^3 + 6x^2 + 5x - 12 = (x - 1)(x^2 + bx + 12)$	expand and collect like terms
$x^3 + 6x^2 + 5x - 12 = x^3 + bx^2 + 12x - x^2 - bx - 12$	
$x^3 + 6x^2 + 5x - 12 = x^3 + (b - 1)x^2 + (12 - b)x - 12$	

Equating coefficients of x^2: $b - 1 = 6$

$b = 7$

$(x - 1)(x^2 + 7x + 12)$	factorise the quadratic
$(x - 1)(x + 4)(x + 3)$	substitute into (1) for the cubic
So, from (1), $x(x - 1)(x + 4)(x + 3) = 0$	solve

$x = -4$, $x = -3$, $x = 0$ or $x = 1$

Chapter 5: Logarithmic and exponential functions

Exercise 5.1

1 a

$$1000 = 10^3 \quad \text{take } \log_{10} \text{ of both sides}$$
$$\log_{10} 1000 = \log_{10} 10^3$$
$$\log_{10} 1000 = 3$$

d

$$10^x = 2 \quad \text{take } \log_{10} \text{ of both sides}$$
$$\log_{10} 10^x = \log_{10} 2 \quad \log_{10} 10^x = x \text{ for } x \in \mathbb{R}$$
$$x = \log_{10} 2$$

f

$$10^x = 0.06 \quad \text{take } \log_{10} \text{ of both sides}$$
$$\log_{10} 10^x = \log_{10} 0.06 \quad \log_{10} 10^x = x \text{ for } x \in \mathbb{R}$$
$$x = \log_{10} 0.06$$

> **TIP**
>
> If $y = 10^x$ then $x = \log_{10} y$
>
> And
>
> $\log_{10} y$ can also be written $\lg y$

2 a

$$10^x = 75 \quad \text{take logs to base 10 of both sides}$$
$$\log_{10} 10^x = \log_{10} 75 \quad \log_{10} 10^x = x \text{ for } x \in \mathbb{R}$$
$$x = \log_{10} 75$$
$$x = 1.88 \text{ (3 s.f.)}$$

d

$$10^x = 15.6 \quad \text{take logs to base 10 of both sides}$$
$$\log_{10} 10^x = \log_{10} 15.6 \quad \log_{10} 10^x = x \text{ for } x \in \mathbb{R}$$
$$x = \log_{10} 15.6$$
$$x = 1.19 \text{ (3 s.f.)}$$

f

$$10^x = 0.005 \quad \text{take logs to base 10 of both sides}$$
$$\log_{10} 10^x = \log_{10} 0.005 \quad \log_{10} 10^x = x \text{ for } x \in \mathbb{R}$$
$$x = \log_{10} 0.005$$
$$x = -2.30 \text{ (3 s.f.)}$$

> **TIP**
>
> $\log_a a = 1$
>
> $\log_a 1 = 0$
>
> $\log_a a^x = x$
>
> $a^{\log_a x} = x$
>
> The conditions for $\log_a x$ to be defined are:
>
> - $a > 0$ and $a \neq 1$
> - $x > 0$

3 b

$$\lg 10 = 1 \quad \text{rewrite:}$$
$$\log_{10} 10 = 1 \quad \text{raise each side to a power of 10}$$
$$10^{\log_{10} 10} = 10^1$$
$$10^1 = 10$$

c

$$\lg \frac{1}{1000} = -3 \quad \text{rewrite:}$$
$$\log_{10} 10^{-3} = -3 \quad \text{raise each side to a power of 10}$$
$$10^{\log_{10} 10^{-3}} = 10^{-3}$$
$$10^{-3} = \frac{1}{1000}$$

f $\lg x = -0.8$ rewrite:

$\log_{10} x = -0.8$ raise each side to a power of 10

$10^{\log_{10} x} = 10^{-0.8}$

$x = 10^{-0.8}$

4 a $\lg x = 5.1$

$\log_{10} x = 5.1$

$x = 10^{5.1}$

$x = 125892.5412$

$x = 126000$ (3 s.f.)

d $\lg x = -0.3$

$\log_{10} x = -0.3$

$x = 10^{-0.3}$

$x = 0.5011872336$

$x = 0.501$ (3 s.f.)

f $\lg x = -2.84$

$\log_{10} x = -2.84$

$x = 10^{-2.84}$

$x = 0.0014454\ldots$

$x = 0.00145$ (3 s.f.)

5 c $\lg\sqrt{10}$ rewrite:

$= \log_{10}\sqrt{10}$ write $\sqrt{10}$ as a power of 10

$= \log_{10} 10^{0.5}$

$= 0.5$

e $\lg(10\sqrt{10})$ rewrite:

$= \log_{10}(10\sqrt{10})$ write $\sqrt{10}$ as a power of 10

$= \log_{10} 10^{1.5}$

$= 1.5$

f $\lg\left(\frac{1000}{\sqrt{10}}\right)$ rewrite:

$= \log_{10}\left(\frac{1000}{\sqrt{10}}\right)$ write $\frac{1000}{\sqrt{10}}$ as a power of 10 ($10^3 \div 10^{0.5} = 10^{2.5}$)

$= \log_{10} 10^{2.5}$

$= 2.5$

Exercise 5.2

1 e $2^{-5} = \frac{1}{32}$ — take $\log_2$ of both sides

$\log_2 2^{-5} = \log_2 \frac{1}{32}$

$-5 = \log_2 \frac{1}{32}$

$\log_2 \frac{1}{32} = -5$

g $a^2 = b$ — take $\log_a$ of both sides

$\log_a a^2 = \log_a b$

$2 = \log_a b$

$\log_a b = 2$

i $a^b = c$ — take $\log_a$ of both sides

$\log_a a^b = \log_a c$

$b = \log_a c$

$\log_a c = b$

2 e $\log_{36} 6 = \frac{1}{2}$ — the base is 36. The index is $\frac{1}{2}$

Start to write in exponential form: — write the base and the index first.

so $36^{\frac{1}{2}} = ?$

Complete the exponential form: — $36^{\frac{1}{2}} = 6$

g $\log_x 1 = 0$ — the base is x. The index is 0.

Start to write in exponential form: — write the base and the index first.

$x^0 = ?$

Complete the exponential form: — $x^0 = 1$

i $\log_a b = c$ — the base is a. The index is c.

Start to write in exponential form: — write the base and the index first.

$a^c = ?$

Complete the exponential form: — $a^c = b$

3 b $\log_3 x = 2$ — use if $y = a^x$ then $x = \log_a y$

So, $x = 3^2$

$x = 9$

e $\log_x 144 = 2$ — use if $y = a^x$ then $x = \log_a y$

So, $x^2 = 144$ — square root both sides

$x = 12$

($x \neq -12$ because $\log_{-12}$ is not defined for real numbers)

i $\log_5(2-3x)=3$ — use if $y=a^x$ then $x=\log_a y$

So, $5^3=2-3x$ — solve

$125=2-3x$

$3x=-123$

$x=-41$

4 d $\log_2 0.25$ — $0.25=\frac{1}{4}=\frac{1}{2^2}=2^{-2}$

$=\log_2 2^{-2}$

$=-2$

f $\log_2(8\sqrt{2})$ — $8\sqrt{2}=2^3\times 2^{0.5}=2^{3.5}$

$=\log_2 2^{3.5}$

$=3.5$

i $\log_{64} 8$ — $8=64^{0.5}$

$=\log_{64} 64^{0.5}$

$=0.5$

5 c $\log_x(x\sqrt{x})$ — $x\sqrt{x}=x\times x^{0.5}=x^{1.5}$

$=\log_x x^{1.5}$

$=1.5$

e $\log_x\left(\frac{1}{x^2}\right)^3$ — $\left(\frac{1}{x^2}\right)^3=(x^{-2})^3=x^{-6}$

$=\log_x x^{-6}$

$=-6$

h $\log_x\left(\frac{x\sqrt{x}}{\sqrt[3]{x}}\right)$ — $x\sqrt{x}\div x^{\frac{1}{3}}=x\times x^{\frac{1}{2}}\div x^{\frac{1}{3}}=x^{1+\frac{1}{2}-\frac{1}{3}}=x^{\frac{7}{6}}$

$=\log_x x^{\frac{7}{6}}$

$=\frac{7}{6}$

6 a $\log_3(\log_2 x)=1$ — if $\log_3 y=1$, then $y=3^1$, so $y=3$

$\log_2 x=3$

$x=2^3$

$x=8$

b $\log_2(\log_5 x)=2$ — if $\log_x y=2$ then $y=x^2$

$\log_5 x=2^2$

$\log_5 x=4$

$x=5^4$

$x=625$

Exercise 5.3

1 **c** $3\log_5 2 + \log_5 8$

$= \log_5 2^3 + \log_5 8$

$= \log_5(2^3 \times 8)$

$= \log_5 64$

f $2\log_7\left(\frac{1}{4}\right) + \log_7 8$

$= \log_7\left(\frac{1}{4}\right)^2 + \log_7 8$

$= \log_7\left(\frac{1}{16} \times 8\right)$

$= \log_7\left(\frac{1}{2}\right)$

i $3 - \log_4 10$

$= \log_4 4^3 - \log_4 10$

$= \log_4 \frac{64}{10}$

$= \log_4 6.4$

2 **a** $\log_2 56 - \log_2 7$

$= \log_2 \frac{56}{7}$

$= \log_2 8$

$= \log_2 2^3$

$= 3$

d $\log_3 15 - \frac{1}{2}\log_3 25$

$= \log_3 15 - \log_3 25^{\frac{1}{2}}$

$= \log_3 15 - \log_3 5$

$= \log_3 \frac{15}{5}$

$= \log_3 3$

$= 1$

f $\frac{1}{2}\log_3 16 - 2\log_3 6$

$= \log_3 16^{\frac{1}{2}} - \log_3 6^2$

$= \log_3 4 - \log_3 36$

$= \log_3 \frac{4}{36}$

$= \log_3 \frac{1}{9}$

$= \log_3 1 - \log_3 9$

$= 0 - \log_3 3^2$

$= -2$

3 **a** $2\log_5 3 - \frac{1}{2}\log_5 4 + \log_5 8$

$= \log_5 3^2 - \log_5 4^{\frac{1}{2}} + \log_5 8$

$= \log_5(9 \div 2 \times 8)$

$= \log_5 36$

b $2 + \frac{1}{2}\log_2 49 - \log_2 21$

$= \log_2 2^2 + \log_2 49^{\frac{1}{2}} - \log_2 21$

$= \log_2(4 \times 7 \div 21)$

$= \log_2 \frac{4}{3}$

4 **a** $16 = 2^4$ and $0.25 = \frac{1}{4} = \frac{1}{2^2} = 2^{-2}$

b $\frac{\log_2 16}{\log_2 0.25} = \frac{\log_2 2^4}{\log_2 2^{-2}}$

$= \frac{4}{-2}$

$= -2$

TIP

Be careful! $\frac{\log_x 8}{\log_x 2}$ is not $\frac{8}{2}$ nor $\log_x 4$

Write $\frac{\log_x 8}{\log_x 2} = \frac{\log_x 2^3}{\log_x 2} = \frac{3\log_x 2}{\log_x 2} = 3$

5 **a** $\dfrac{\log_7 4}{\log_7 2} = \dfrac{\log_7 2^2}{\log_7 2} = \dfrac{2\log_7 2}{\log_7 2} = 2$

c $\dfrac{\log_3 64}{\log_3 0.25} = \dfrac{\log_3 4^3}{\log_3 4^{-1}} = \dfrac{3\log_3 4}{-1\log_3 4} = -3$

d $\dfrac{\log_5 100}{\log_5 0.01} = \dfrac{\log_5 10^2}{\log_5 10^{-2}} = \dfrac{2\log_5 10}{-2\log_5 10} = -1$

6 **b**
$$\begin{aligned}\log_5\left(\frac{x}{25}\right) &= \log_5 x - \log_5 25\\ &= \log_5 x - \log_5 5^2\\ &= \log_5 x - 2\log_5 5\\ &= u - 2\end{aligned}$$

d
$$\begin{aligned}\log_5\left(\frac{x\sqrt{x}}{125}\right) &= \log_5 x + \log_5 \sqrt{x} - \log_5 125\\ &= \log_5 x + \log_5 x^{\frac{1}{2}} - \log_5 5^3\\ &= \log_5 x + \frac{1}{2}\log_5 x - 3\log_5 5\\ &= u + \frac{1}{2}u - 3\\ &= \frac{3}{2}u - 3\end{aligned}$$

7 **b**
$$\begin{aligned}\log_4\left(\frac{16}{p}\right) &= \log_4 16 - \log_4 p\\ &= \log_4 4^2 - \log_4 p\\ &= 2\log_4 4 - \log_4 p\\ &= 2 - x\end{aligned}$$

d $\log_4 p = x$ so $p = 4^x$

$\log_4 q = y$ so $q = 4^y$

$$\begin{aligned}pq &= 4^x \times 4^y\\ &= 4^{x+y}\end{aligned}$$

8 **b**
$$\begin{aligned}\log_a\left(\frac{\sqrt{x}}{y}\right) &= \log_a \sqrt{x} - \log_a y\\ &= \log_a x^{\frac{1}{2}} - \log_a y\\ &= \frac{1}{2}\log_a x - \log_a y\\ &= \frac{1}{2} \times 5 - 8\\ &= -5.5\end{aligned}$$

d
$$\begin{aligned}\log_a(x^2y^3) &= \log_a x^2 + \log_a y^3\\ &= 2\log_a x + 3\log_a y\\ &= 2 \times 5 + 3 \times 8\\ &= 34\end{aligned}$$

9 **b**
$$\begin{aligned}\log_a\left(\frac{x^2}{y}\right) &= \log_a x^2 - \log_a y\\ &= 2\log_a x - \log_a y\\ &= 2 \times 12 - 4\\ &= 20\end{aligned}$$

d
$$\begin{aligned}\log_a\left(\frac{y}{\sqrt[3]{x}}\right) &= \log_a y - \log_a \sqrt[3]{x}\\ &= \log_a y - \log_a x^{\frac{1}{3}}\\ &= \log_a y - \frac{1}{3}\log_a x\\ &= 4 - \frac{1}{3} \times 12\\ &= 0\end{aligned}$$

TIP

$\log x + \log x = 2\log x = \log x^2$ [**not** $\log 2x$]

$\log x \times \log x = (\log x)^2$ [**not** $\log x^2$]

Exercise 5.4

1 b $\log_4 2x - \log_4 5 = \log_4 3$ use the division law

$\log_4 \frac{2x}{5} = \log_4 3$ use the equality of logarithms

$\frac{2x}{5} = 3$

$x = 7.5$

Check: when $x = 7.5$, $\log_4 2x - \log_4 5 = \log_4 3$

becomes: $\log_4(2 \times 7.5) - \log_4 5 = \log_4 3$

$\log_4 15$ is defined so $x = 7.5$ is a solution

TIP

$\log_3(x + 3)$ does **not** expand to give $\log_3 x + \log_3 3$

d $\log_3(x + 3) = 2\log_3 4 + \log_3 5$ use the power law

$\log_3(x + 3) = \log_3 4^2 + \log_3 5$ use the multiplication law

$\log_3(x + 3) = \log_3(4^2 \times 5)$ use the equality of logarithms

$x + 3 = 4^2 \times 5$

$x = 77$

2 c **Method 1**

$\log_2(x + 4) = 1 + \log_2(x - 3)$ rearrange

$\log_2(x + 4) - \log_2(x - 3) = 1$ use the division law

$\log_2\left(\frac{x + 4}{x - 3}\right) = 1$ convert to exponential form

$\frac{x + 4}{x - 3} = 2^1$

$x + 4 = 2(x - 3)$

$x + 4 = 2x - 6$

$x = 10$

Method 2

$\log_2(x + 4) = 1 + \log_2(x - 3)$

$\log_2(x + 4) = \log_2 2 + \log_2(x - 3)$ use the multiplication law

$\log_2(x + 4) = \log_2 2(x - 3)$ use the equality of logarithms

$x + 4 = 2(x - 3)$

$x + 4 = 2x - 6$

$x = 10$

f $\lg(4x + 5) + 2\lg 2 = 1 + \lg(2x - 1)$

$\lg(4x + 5) + \lg 2^2 = 1 + \lg(2x - 1)$ — use the power law

$\lg(4x + 5) + \lg 4 = \lg 10 + \lg(2x - 1)$ — rewrite 1 as lg10 and use the multiplication law

$\lg 4(4x + 5) = \lg 10(2x - 1)$ — use the equality of logarithms

$4(4x + 5) = 10(2x - 1)$

$16x + 20 = 20x - 10$

$x = 7.5$

3 b $\log_3 x + \log_3(x - 2) = \log_3 15$ — use the multiplication law

$\log_3[x(x - 2)] = \log_3 15$ — use the equality of logarithms

$x(x - 2) = 15$

$x^2 - 2x - 15 = 0$

$(x - 5)(x + 3) = 0$

$x = 5$ and $x = -3$ (reject) — (for $\log_a x$ to be defined requires $x > 0$)

$x = 5$

f $3 + 2\log_2 x = \log_2(14x - 3)$ — use the power law

$3 + \log_2 x^2 = \log_2(14x - 3)$ — rewrite 3 as $\log_2 2^3$

$\log_2 2^3 + \log_2 x^2 = \log_2(14x - 3)$ — use the multiplication law

$\log_2 8x^2 = \log_2(14x - 3)$ — use the equality of logarithms

$8x^2 = 14x - 3$

$8x^2 - 14x + 3 = 0$

$(4x - 1)(2x - 3) = 0$

$x = \frac{1}{4}$ and $x = \frac{3}{2}$

4 a $\log_x 64 - \log_x 4 = 1$ — use the division law

$\log_x \frac{64}{4} = 1$

$\log_x 16 = 1$ — convert to exponential form

$x^1 = 16$

$x = 16$

d $\log_x 15 = 2 + \log_x 5$ — rearrange

$\log_x 15 - \log_x 5 = 2$ — use the division law

$\log_x \frac{15}{5} = 2$

$\log_x 3 = 2$ — convert to exponential form

$x^2 = 3$

$x = \sqrt{3}$ or $x = -\sqrt{3}$ (reject) — (for $\log_a x$ to be defined requires $x > 0$)

$x = \sqrt{3}$

5 a $(\log_5 x)^2 - 3\log_5(x) + 2 = 0$ can be rewritten as

$(\log_5 x)^2 - 3\log_5 x + 2 = 0$ which can then be written as

$(\log_5 x)^2 - 3(\log_5 x) + 2 = 0$

TIP

Be careful, you cannot write $(\log_5 x)^2$ as $2\log_5 x$ because $2\log_5 x$ is equal to $\log_5 x^2$.

Let $y = \log_5 x$

$y^2 - 3y + 2 = 0$

$(y - 2)(y - 1) = 0$

$y = 2$ and $y = 1$

So, $\log_5 x = 2$ and $\log_5 x = 1$ convert to exponential form

$x = 5^2$ and $x = 5$

$x = 25$ and $x = 5$

d $2(\log_2 x)^2 + 5\log_2(x^2) = 72$ can be rewritten as

$2(\log_2 x)^2 + 5\log_2 x^2 = 72$ which can then be written as

$2(\log_2 x)^2 + 10\log_2 x = 72$

Let $y = \log_2 x$

$2y^2 + 10y = 72$ simplify and rearrange

$y^2 + 5y - 36 = 0$

$(y - 4)(y + 9) = 0$

$y = 4$ and $y = -9$

So $\log_2 x = 4$ and $\log_2 x = -9$ convert to exponential form

$x = 2^4$ and $x = 2^{-9}$

$x = 16$ and $x = \frac{1}{512}$

6 b $2^x = 4^y$ rewrite 4^y as 2^{2y}

$2^x = 2^{2y}$

$x = 2y$ (1)

$2\lg y = \lg x + \lg 5$ use the multiplication law

$2\lg y = \lg 5x$ use the power law

$\lg y^2 = \lg 5x$ use the equality of logarithms

$y^2 = 5x$ (2) using (1), substitute for x in (2)

$y^2 = 10y$

$y^2 - 10y = 0$

$y(y - 10) = 0$

$y = 10$ or $y = 0$ (reject)	(for $\lg y$ to be defined requires $y > 0$)
So, from (1) $x = 20$	
c $\log_4(x + y) = 2\log_4 x$	use the power law

TIP

Note: $\log_4(x + y)$ is **not** equivalent to $\log_4 x + \log_4 y$

$\log_4(x + y) = \log_4 x^2$	use the equality of logarithms
$x + y = x^2$	(1)
$\log_4 y = \log_4 3 + \log_4 x$	use the multiplication law
$\log_4 y = \log_4 3x$	use the equality of logarithms
$y = 3x$	(2) substitute for y in (1)
$x + 3x = x^2$	
$x^2 - 4x = 0$	
$x(x - 4) = 0$	
$x = 4$ and $x = 0$ (reject)	(for $\log_a x$ to be defined requires $x > 0$)
Substituting $x = 4$ into (2) gives $y = 12$	
Solution is $x = 4$ and $y = 12$	

7 a $\lg(x^2 y) = 18$	use the multiplication law
$\lg x^2 + \lg y = 18$	use the power law
$2\lg x + \lg y = 18$	shown
b $\lg(x^2 y) = 18$ or $2\lg x + \lg y = 18$	(1)
$\lg\left(\frac{x}{y^3}\right) = 2$	use the division law
$\lg x - \lg y^3 = 2$	use the power law
$\lg x - 3\lg y = 2$	multiply both sides by 2
$2\lg x - 6\lg y = 4$	(2)
$2\lg x + \lg y = 18$	(1) subtract (1) from (2)
$-7\lg y = -14$	
$\lg y = 2$	convert to exponential form
$y = 10^2$, $y = 100$	
Substitute for y in (1)	
$2\lg x + \lg 100 = 18$	
$2\lg x + 2 = 18$	
$\lg x = 8$	
So, $\lg y = 2$ and $\lg x = 8$	

Exercise 5.5

1 e

$3^{x+1} = 55$ — take logs of both sides

$\lg 3^{x+1} = \lg 55$ — use the power rule

$(x+1)\lg 3 = \lg 55$ — divide both sides by lg3

$$x + 1 = \frac{\lg 55}{\lg 3}$$

$$x = \frac{\lg 55}{\lg 3} - 1$$

$x \approx 2.65$

k

$3^{2x+3} = 5^{3x+1}$ — take logs of both sides

$\lg 3^{2x+3} = \lg 5^{3x+1}$ — use the power rule

$(2x+3)\lg 3 = (3x+1)\lg 5$

Method 1 — divide both sides by lg3 and $3x + 1$

$$\frac{2x+3}{3x+1} = \frac{\lg 5}{\lg 3}$$

$$\frac{2x+3}{3x+1} = 1.4649735\ldots$$

$2x + 3 = 1.4649735(3x + 1)$

$2x + 3 = 4.3949205x + 1.4649735$

$1.5350265 = 2.3949205x$

$x \approx 0.641$

Method 2 — expand the brackets on both sides

$2x \lg 3 + 3 \lg 3 = 3x \lg 5 + \lg 5$ — rearrange

$3 \lg 3 - \lg 5 = 3x \lg 5 - 2x \lg 3$ — factorise

$3 \lg 3 - \lg 5 = x(3 \lg 5 - 2 \lg 3)$

$$x = \frac{3 \lg 3 - \lg 5}{3 \lg 5 - 2 \lg 3}$$

$x \approx 0.641$

2 a

$2^{x+1} - 2^{x-1} = 15$ — replace 2^{x+1} with $2(2^x)$ and 2^{x-1} with $2^{-1}(2^x)$

$$2(2^x) - \frac{1}{2}(2^x) = 15$$

b

$$2(2^x) - \frac{1}{2}(2^x) = 15$$ — use the substitution $y = 2^x$

$$2y - \frac{1}{2}y = 15$$

$1.5y = 15$

$y = 10$

So, $2^x = 10$

c $2^x = 10$ — take logs of both sides

$\lg 2^x = \lg 10$ — use the power rule

$x \lg 2 = \lg 10$

$x \approx 3.32$

3 **c** $3^{x+1} - 8(3^{x-1}) - 5 = 0$ — replace 3^{x+1} with $3(3^x)$ and 3^{x-1} with $3^{-1}(3^x)$

$3(3^x) - 8 \times \frac{1}{3}(3^x) - 5 = 0$ — use the substitution $y = 3^x$

$3y - \frac{8}{3}y - 5 = 0$

$9y - 8y - 15 = 0$

$y = 15$

So, $3^x = 15$ — take logs of both sides

$\lg 3^x = \lg 15$ — use the power rule

$x \lg 3 = \lg 15$

$x = \frac{\lg 15}{\lg 3}$ — remember, this is NOT lg5

$x \approx 2.46$

e $5^x - 5^{x+2} + 125 = 0$ — replace 5^{x+2} with $5^2(5^x)$

$5^x - 25(5^x) + 125 = 0$ — use the substitution $y = 5^x$

$y - 25y + 125 = 0$

$24y = 125$

$y = \frac{125}{24}$

So, $5^x = \frac{125}{24}$ — take logs of both sides

$\lg 5^x = \lg\left(\frac{125}{24}\right)$ — use the power rule

$x \lg 5 = \lg\left(\frac{125}{24}\right)$

$x = \lg\left(\frac{125}{24}\right) \div \lg 5$

$x \approx 1.03$

4 $3^{2x} + 2 = 5(3^x)$ — replace 3^{2x} by $(3^x)^2$ then use the substitution $y = 3^x$

$y^2 + 2 = 5y$ — rearrange

$y^2 - 5y + 2 = 0$ — use the quadratic formula

$y = \frac{--5 \pm \sqrt{(-5)^2 - 4 \times 1 \times 2}}{2 \times 1}$

$y = \frac{5 + \sqrt{17}}{2}$ and $y = \frac{5 - \sqrt{17}}{2}$

So, $3^x = y = \frac{5 + \sqrt{17}}{2}$ and $3^x = y = \frac{5 - \sqrt{17}}{2}$ take logs of both sides

$\lg 3^x = \lg\left(\frac{5 + \sqrt{17}}{2}\right)$ and $\lg 3^x = \lg\left(\frac{5 - \sqrt{17}}{2}\right)$ use the power rule

$x \lg 3 = \lg\left(\frac{5 + \sqrt{17}}{2}\right)$ and $x \lg 3 = \lg\left(\frac{5 - \sqrt{17}}{2}\right)$

$x = \lg\left(\frac{5 + \sqrt{17}}{2}\right) \div \lg 3$ and $x = \lg\left(\frac{5 - \sqrt{17}}{2}\right) \div \lg 3$

$x \approx 1.38$ and $x \approx -0.751$

5 **a** $3^{2x} - 6 \times 3^x + 5 = 0$ replace 3^{2x} by $(3^x)^2$ then use the substitution $y = 3^x$

$y^2 - 6y + 5 = 0$

$(y - 1)(y - 5) = 0$

$y = 1$ and $y = 5$

So, $3^x = 1$, i.e., $x = 0$

and $3^x = 5$ take logs of both sides

$\lg 3^x = \lg 5$ use the power rule

$x \lg 3 = \lg 5$

$x = \frac{\lg 5}{\lg 3}$

$x \approx 1.46$

Solutions are $x = 0$ and $x \approx 1.46$

6 $5^{2x} - 2(5^{x+1}) + 21 = 0$ replace 5^{2x} with $(5^x)^2$ and replace 5^{x+1} with $5(5^x)$

$(5^x)^2 - 2 \times 5(5^x) + 21 = 0$ use the substitution $u = 5^x$

$u^2 - 10u + 21 = 0$

$(u - 7)(u - 3) = 0$

$u = 7$ and $u = 3$

So, $5^x = 7$ take logs of both sides

$\lg 5^x = \lg 7$ use the power rule

$x \lg 5 = \lg 7$

$x = \frac{\lg 7}{\lg 5}$

$x \approx 1.21$

and $5^x = 3$ take logs of both sides

$\lg 5^x = \lg 3$ use the power rule

$x \lg 5 = \lg 3$

$x = \frac{\lg 3}{\lg 5}$

$x \approx 0.683$

7 b $6^{2x} - 6^{x+1} + 7 = 0$ replace 6^{2x} with $(6^x)^2$ and replace 6^{x+1} with $6(6^x)$

$(6^x)^2 - 6(6^x) + 7 = 0$ use the substitution $y = 6^x$

$y^2 - 6y + 7 = 0$ does not factorise so use the quadratic formula

$y = \frac{--6 \pm \sqrt{(-6)^2 - 4 \times 1 \times 7}}{2 \times 1}$

$y = \frac{6 + \sqrt{8}}{2}$ and $y = \frac{6 - \sqrt{8}}{2}$

$y = \frac{6 + 2\sqrt{2}}{2}$ and $y = \frac{6 - 2\sqrt{2}}{2}$

$y = 3 + \sqrt{2}$ and $y = 3 - \sqrt{2}$

So, $6^x = y = 3 + \sqrt{2}$ and $6^x = y = 3 - \sqrt{2}$ take logs of both sides

$\lg 6^x = \lg(3 + \sqrt{2})$ and $\lg 6^x = \lg(3 - \sqrt{2})$ use the power rule

$x \lg 6 = \lg(3 + \sqrt{2})$ and $x \lg 6 = \lg(3 - \sqrt{2})$

$x = \lg(3 + \sqrt{2}) \div \lg 6$ and $x = \lg(3 - \sqrt{2}) \div \lg 6$

$x \approx 0.829$ and $x \approx 0.257$

d $4^{2x+1} = 17(4^x) - 15$ replace 4^{2x+1} with $4(4^x)^2$ and rearrange

$4(4^x)^2 - 17(4^x) + 15 = 0$ use the substitution $y = 4^x$

$(4y - 5)(y - 3) = 0$

$y = 1.25$ and $y = 3$

So, $4^x = 1.25$ take logs of both sides

$\lg 4^x = \lg 1.25$ use the power rule

$x \lg 4 = \lg 1.25$

$x = \frac{\lg 1.25}{\lg 4}$

$x \approx 0.161$

So, $4^x = 3$ take logs of both sides

$\lg 4^x = \lg 3$ use the power rule

$x \lg 4 = \lg 3$

$x = \frac{\lg 3}{\lg 4}$

$x \approx 0.792$

8 b $16^x + 2(4^x) - 35 = 0$ — replace 16^x with $(4^x)^2$ and use the substitution $y = 4^x$

$y^2 + 2y - 35 = 0$

$(y + 7)(y - 5) = 0$

$y = -7$ and $y = 5$

So, $4^x = 5$ — there are no solutions to the equation $4^x = -7$since 4^x is always positive

$\lg 4^x = \lg 5$ — use the power rule

$x \lg 4 = \lg 5$

$x = \dfrac{\lg 5}{\lg 4}$

$x \approx 1.16$

d $25^x + 20 = 12(5^x)$ — replace 25^x with $(5^x)^2$ and rearrange

$(5^x)^2 - 12(5^x) + 20 = 0$ — use the substitution $y = 5^x$

$y^2 - 12y + 20 = 0$

$(y - 10)(y - 2) = 0$

$y = 10$ and $y = 2$

So, $5^x = 10$ — take logs of both sides

$\lg 5^x = \lg 10$ — use the power rule

$x \lg 5 = \lg 10$

$x = \dfrac{\lg 10}{\lg 5}$

$x \approx 1.43$

So, $5^x = 2$ — take logs of both sides

$\lg 5^x = \lg 2$ — use the power rule

$x \lg 5 = \lg 2$

$= \dfrac{\lg 2}{\lg 5}$

$x \approx 0.431$

9 a $3^{2x+1} \times 5^{x-1} = 27^x \times 5^{2x}$ — rearrange

$\dfrac{3^{2x+1}}{27^x} = \dfrac{5^{2x}}{5^{x-1}}$ — replace 27^x with 3^{3x}

$\dfrac{3^{2x+1}}{3^{3x}} = \dfrac{5^{2x}}{5^{x-1}}$ — simplify the fractions using the rules of indices

$3^{2x+1-3x} = 5^{2x-(x-1)}$

$3^{1-x} = 5^{x+1}$ — can be rewritten as

$\dfrac{3^1}{3^x} = 5^x \times 5^1$ — rearrange

$\frac{3^1}{5^1} = 5^x \times 3^x$

$15^x = 0.6$

b $15^x = 0.6$ — take logs of both sides

$\lg 15^x = \lg 0.6$ — use the power rule

$x \lg 15 = \lg 0.6$

$x = \frac{\lg 0.6}{\lg 15}$

$x \approx -0.189$

10 b $|2^{x+1} + 3| = |2^x + 10|$

Either

$2^{x+1} + 3 = 2^x + 10$

$2^{x+1} - 2^x = 7$ — replace 2^{x+1} with 2×2^x

$2 \times 2^x - 2^x = 7$ — factorise

$2^x(2 - 1) = 7$

$2^x = 7$ — take logs of both sides

$\lg 2^x = \lg 7$ — use the power rule

$x \lg 2 = \lg 7$

$x = \frac{\lg 7}{\lg 2}$

$x \approx 2.81$

Or

$2^{x+1} + 3 = -(2^x + 10)$ — rearrange

$2^{x+1} + 2^x = -10$ — replace 2^{x+1} with 2×2^x

$2 \times 2^x + 2^x = -10$ — factorise

$2^x(2 + 1) = -10$

$2^x = \frac{-10}{3}$ — there are no solutions to this equation since 2^x is always positive

The only solution is $x \approx 2.81$

c $3^{2|x|} = 5(3^{|x|}) + 24$

$9^{|x|} = 5 \times 3^{|x|} + 24$ — rearrange

$9^{|x|} - 5 \times 3^{|x|} - 24 = 0$ — factorise

$(3^{|x|} + 3)(3^{|x|} - 8) = 0$

$3^{|x|} + 3 = 0$ or $3^{|x|} - 8 = 0$

So, $3^{|x|} = -3$ has no solutions since for $3^z > 0$ for all $z \in \mathbb{R}$

and $3^{|x|} = 8$ — take logs of both sides

$\lg 3^{|x|} = \lg 8$ — use the power rule

$|x|\lg 3 = \lg 8$ split into two equations

$x = \frac{\lg 8}{\lg 3}$ or $x = -\frac{\lg 8}{\lg 3}$

$x \approx 1.89$ and $x \approx -1.89$

11 $|2^{x+1} - 1| < |2^x - 8|$

Either

$2^{x+1} - 1 < 2^x - 8$

$2^{x+1} - 2^x + 7 < 0$ replace 2^{x+1} with 2×2^x

$2 \times 2^x - 2^x + 7 < 0$ replace 2^x with u

$2u - u + 7 < 0$

$u < -7$

$2^x < -7$ has no solutions since 2^x is always positive

Or

$2^{x+1} - 1 < -2^x + 8$

$2^{x+1} + 2^x - 9 < 0$ replace 2^{x+1} with 2×2^x

$2 \times 2^x + 2^x - 9 < 0$ replace 2^x with u

$2u + u - 9 < 0$

$3u < 9$

$u < 3$

$2^x < 3$ take $\log_2$ of both sides

$\log_2 2^x < \log_2 3$ use the power rule

$x\log_2 2 < \log_2 3$

The only solution is $x < \log_2 3$

Exercise 5.6

REMEMBER

$\log_b a = \frac{\log_c a}{\log_c b}$ and $\log_b a = \frac{\log_{10} a}{\log_{10} b}$

1 **a** $\log_2 10 = \frac{\log_{10} 10}{\log_{10} 2}$

$= \frac{1}{\log_{10} 2}$

$= 3.32$ to 3 s.f.

d $\log_7 0.0025 = \dfrac{\log_{10} 0.0025}{\log_{10} 7}$

$= -3.08$ to 3 s.f.

2 a $\log_x 4 = \dfrac{\log_4 4}{\log_4 x}$

$= \dfrac{1}{\log_4 x}$

$= \dfrac{1}{u}$

d $\log_x 8 = \dfrac{\log_4 8}{\log_4 x}$ $\log_4 8 = \log_4 4^{\frac{3}{2}} = \frac{3}{2}\log_4 4 = \frac{3}{2}$

$= \dfrac{\frac{3}{2}}{\log_4 x}$

$= \dfrac{\frac{3}{2}}{u}$

$= \dfrac{3}{2u}$

3 b $\log_9(9y) = \log_9 9 + \log_9 y$

$= 1 + x$

d $\log_3(81y) = \log_3 81 + \log_3 y$

$= \log_3 3^4 + \dfrac{\log_9 y}{\log_9 3}$

$= 4 + \dfrac{x}{\log_9 9^{\frac{1}{2}}}$

$= 4 + \dfrac{x}{\frac{1}{2}}$

$= 4 + 2x$

4 a $\log_y x = \dfrac{\log_p x}{\log_p y}$

$= \dfrac{20}{5}$

$= 4$

b $\log_X Y = \dfrac{\log_p Y}{\log_p X}$

$= \dfrac{6}{15}$

$= 0.4$

5 $\log_p 2 \times \log_8 p = \dfrac{\log_8 2}{\log_8 p} \times \dfrac{\log_8 p}{\log_8 8}$

$= \dfrac{\log_8 2}{\log_8 8}$

$= \log_8 8^{\frac{1}{3}}$

$= \dfrac{1}{3}$

6 a $\log_9 3 + \log_9(x + 4) = \log_5 25$

$\log_9[3(x + 4)] = 2$ use the multiplication law

$3(x + 4) = 9^2$

$3x + 12 = 81$

$3x = 69$

$x = 23$

b $2\log_4 2 + \log_7(2x + 3) = \log_3 27$ 27 can be written as 3^3

$\log_4 2^2 + \log_7(2x + 3) = \log_3 3^3$

$\log_4 4 + \log_7(2x + 3) = 3\log_3 3$

$1 + \log_7(2x + 3) = 3$

$\log_7(2x + 3) = 2$

$2x + 3 = 7^2$

$x = 23$

7 a $\log_4 x = \dfrac{\log_2 x}{\log_2 4}$

$= \dfrac{\log_2 x}{\log_2 2^2}$

$= \dfrac{\log_2 x}{2\log_2 2}$

$= \dfrac{\log_2 x}{2}$

$= \dfrac{1}{2}\log_2 x$

b $\log_4 x + \log_2 x = 12$

$\dfrac{1}{2}\log_2 x + \log_2 x = 12$

$1.5\log_2 x = 12$

$\log_2 x = 8$

$x = 2^8 = 256$

8 c $5\log_2 x - \log_4 x = 3$ change base of the second term

$$5\log_2 x - \frac{\log_2 x}{\log_2 4} = 3$$

$$5\log_2 x - \frac{\log_2 x}{2} = 3$$

$$4.5\log_2 x = 3$$

$$\log_2 x = \frac{2}{3}$$

$$x = 2^{\frac{2}{3}}$$

$$x = 1.59$$

d $4\log_3 x = \log_9 x + 2$ rearrange

$4\log_3 x - \log_9 x = 2$ change base of the second term

$$4\log_3 x - \frac{\log_3 x}{\log_3 9} = 2$$

$$4\log_3 x - \frac{\log_3 x}{\log_3 3^2} = 2$$

$$4\log_3 x - \frac{\log_3 x}{2} = 2$$

$$3.5\log_3 x = 2$$

$$\log_3 x = \frac{4}{7}$$

$$x = 1.87$$

9 a $\log_x 3 = \dfrac{\log_3 3}{\log_3 x}$

$$\log_x 3 = \frac{1}{\log_3 x}$$

b $\log_3 x = 3 - 2\log_x 3$

$$\log_3 x = 3 - 2 \times \frac{1}{\log_3 x}$$

$\log_3 x = 3 - \dfrac{2}{\log_3 x}$ rearrange

$\log_3 x - 3 + \dfrac{2}{\log_3 x} = 0$ substitute u for $\log_3 x$

$u - 3 + \dfrac{2}{u} = 0$ multiply each term by u

$u^2 - 3u + 2 = 0$ factorise

$$(u - 2)(u - 1) = 0$$

$u = 2$ and $u = 1$

$\log_3 x = 2$ and $\log_3 x = 1$

$x = 3^2$ and $x = 3^1$

$x = 9$ and $x = 3$

10 a $\log_3 x = 9\log_x 3$

$\log_x 3 = \dfrac{\log_3 3}{\log_3 x}$ which means that $\log_x 3 = \dfrac{1}{\log_3 x}$, so substituting gives:

$\log_3 x = \dfrac{9}{\log_3 x}$ let $u = \log_3 x$

$u = \dfrac{9}{u}$

$u^2 = 9$

$u = -3$ and $u = 3$

$\log_3 x = -3$ and $\log_3 x = 3$

$x = 3^{-3}$ and $x = 3^3$

$x = \dfrac{1}{27}$ and $x = 27$

f $\log_5 y = 4 - 4\log_y 5$

$\log_y 5 = \dfrac{\log_5 5}{\log_5 y}$ which means that $\log_y 5 = \dfrac{1}{\log_5 y}$, so substituting gives:

$\log_5 y = 4 - 4 \times \dfrac{1}{\log_5 y}$

$\log_5 y = 4 - \dfrac{4}{\log_5 y}$ let $u = \log_5 y$

$u = 4 - \dfrac{4}{u}$ multiply each term by u

$u^2 = 4u - 4$

$u^2 - 4u + 4 = 0$ factorise

$(u - 2)^2 = 0$

$u = 2$

$\log_5 y = 2$

$y = 5^2$

$y = 25$

11 a $\log_4 x = \dfrac{\log_2 x}{\log_2 4}$

$= \dfrac{\log_2 x}{\log_2 2^2}$

$= \dfrac{\log_2 x}{2\log_2 2}$

$= \dfrac{\log_2 x}{2}$

$= \dfrac{1}{2}\log_2 x$

b $\log_8 y = \dfrac{\log_2 y}{\log_2 8}$

$= \dfrac{\log_2 y}{\log_2 2^3}$

$= \dfrac{\log_2 y}{3\log_2 2}$

$= \dfrac{\log_2 y}{3}$

$= \dfrac{1}{3}\log_2 y$

c First equation: $6\log_4 x + 3\log_8 y = 16$ — substitute $\frac{1}{2}\log_2 x$ for $\log_4 x$ and $\frac{1}{3}\log_2 y$ for $\log_8 y$

$6 \times \frac{1}{2}\log_2 x + 3 \times \frac{1}{3}\log_2 y = 16$ — simplify

$3\log_2 x + \log_2 y = 16$ — (1)

Second equation: $\log_2 x - 2\log_4 y = 4$ — substitute $\frac{1}{2}\log_2 y$ for $\log_4 y$

$\log_2 x - 2 \times \frac{1}{2}\log_2 y = 4$ — simplify

$\log_2 x - \log_2 y = 4$ — multiply each term by 3

$3\log_2 x - 3\log_2 y = 12$ — (2)

Subtract (2) from (1)

$4\log_2 y = 4$

$\log_2 y = 1$

$y = 2$

Substitute into (1) we get:

$3\log_2 x + 1 = 16$

$3\log_2 x = 15$

$\log_2 x = 5$

$x = 2^5$

$x = 32$

Solutions are $x = 32$ and $y = 2$

12 First equation:

$2\log_3 y = \log_5 125 + \log_3 x$ substitute 3 for $\log_5 125$ and rearrange

$2\log_3 y - \log_3 x = 3$

$\log_3 y^2 - \log_3 x = 3$ use the multiplication law

$\log_3\left(\frac{y^2}{x}\right) = 3$

$\frac{y^2}{x} = 3^3$

$y^2 = 27x$ (1)

Second equation:

$2^y = 4^x$ substitute 2^2 for 4

$2^y = (2^2)^x$

$2^y = 2^{2x}$

So $y = 2x$ (2) square both sides

$y^2 = 4x^2$

Substitute for y^2 in (1)

$4x^2 = 27x$

$4x^2 - 27x = 0$

$x(4x - 27) = 0$

$x = 0$ and $x = 6.75$ reject $x = 0$ as $\log_3 0$ has no meaning.
(*for* $\log_a x$ to be defined requires $x > 0$).

Substitute $x = 6.75$ into (2)

$y = 13.5$

Solutions are $x = 6.75$ and $y = 13.5$

Exercise 5.7

REMEMBER

$y = \ln x$ and $y = e^x$ are inverse functions so, if $y = e^{\ln x}$ then $y = x$

3 **b** $e^{\frac{1}{2}\ln 64} = e^{\ln 64^{\frac{1}{2}}} = e^{\ln 8} = 8$

d $-e^{-\ln\frac{1}{2}} = -e^{\ln\left(\frac{1}{2}\right)^{-1}} = -e^{\ln 2} = -2$

4 **b** $\ln e^x = 2.5$ use the power law

$x \ln e = 2.5$

$x = 2.5$

d $e^{-\ln x} = 20$

$e^{\ln x^{-1}} = 20$

$x^{-1} = 20$

$x = 0.05$

5 b $e^{2x} = 28$ take $\log_e$ of both sides

$\ln e^{2x} = \ln 28$

$2x = \ln 28$

$x = \frac{1}{2}\ln 28$

$x = 1.67$ to 3 s.f.

d $e^{2x-1} = 5$ take $\log_e$ of both sides

$\ln e^{2x-1} = \ln 5$

$2x - 1 = 1.6094$

$2x = 2.6094$

$x = 1.30$ to 3 s.f.

6 b $2e^{x} + 1 = 7$

$2e^{x} = 6$

$e^{x} = 3$ take $\log_e$ of both sides

$\ln e^{x} = \ln 3$

$x = \ln 3$

d $\frac{1}{2}e^{3x-1} = 4$

$e^{3x-1} = 8$ take $\log_e$ of both sides

$\ln e^{3x-1} = \ln 8$

$3x - 1 = \ln 8$

$x = \frac{1}{3}(1 + \ln 8)$

7 b $\ln x = -2$

$x = e^{-2} = 0.135$ to 3 s.f.

d $\ln(2x - 5) = 3$

$2x - 5 = e^{3}$

$x = \frac{1}{2}(e^{3} + 5)$

$x = 12.5$ to 3 s.f.

8 a $\ln x^3 + \ln x = 5$ use the multiplication law

$\ln x^4 = 5$

$x^4 = e^5$

$x = \sqrt[4]{e^5}$

$x = 3.49$ to 3 s.f.

b $e^{3x+4} = 2e^{x-1}$ take $\log_e$ of both sides

$\ln(e^{3x+4}) = \ln(2e^{x-1})$

$3x + 4 = \ln 2 + \ln e^{x-1}$

$3x + 4 = \ln 2 + x - 1$ rearrange

$2x = \ln 2 - 1 - 4$

$x = -2.15$ to 3 s.f.

9 c $e^{2x} - 4e^x = 0$ factorise

$e^x(e^x - 4) = 0$

Either $e^x = 0$ (no solutions since e^x is always positive)

Or $e^x - 4 = 0$

$e^x = 4$ take $\log_e$ of both sides

$\ln e^x = \ln 4$

$x = \ln 4$ or $2 \ln 2$ (since $\ln 4 = \ln 2^2 = 2 \ln 2$)

d $e^x = 2e^{-x}$ multiply each term by e^x (remember $e^{-x} \times e^x = e^0 = 1$)

$e^{2x} = 2$ take $\log_e$ of both sides

$\ln e^{2x} = \ln 2$

$2x = \ln 2$

$x = \frac{1}{2}\ln 2$

10 a $e^{2x} - 2e^x - 24 = 0$ replace e^x with u

$u^2 - 2u - 24 = 0$ factorise

$(u - 6)(u + 4) = 0$

$u = 6$ and $u = -4$

So, $e^x = 6$ and $e^x = -4$ no solution for $e^x = -4$ since e^x is always positive

$e^x = 6$ take $\log_e$ of both sides

$\ln e^x = \ln 6$

$x = 1.79$ to 3 s.f.

c $e^x + 2e^{-x} = 80$

$e^x + \frac{2}{e^x} = 80$ replace e^x with u

$u + \frac{2}{u} = 80$ multiply each term by u

$u^2 + 2 = 80u$ rearrange

$u^2 - 80u + 2 = 0$ use the quadratic formula $x = \frac{-b \pm \sqrt{b^2 - 4ac}}{2a}$

$u = \frac{--80 \pm \sqrt{(-80)^2 - 4 \times 1 \times 2}}{2}$

$u = 79.975$ and $u = 0.02501$

So, $e^x = 79.975$ tke $\log_e$ of both sides

$\ln e^x = \ln 79.975$

$x = 4.38$

And $e^x = 0.02501$ take $\log_e$ of both sides

$\ln e^x = \ln 0.02501$

$x = -3.69$

Solutions are $x = 4.38$ and $x = -3.69$ (3 s.f.)

11 a $\ln x = 2 \ln y$ (1)

$\ln y - \ln x = 1$ (2)

Add equations (1) and (2)

$\ln y = 2 \ln y + 1$ subtract $\ln y$ from both sides

$\ln y = -1$

$\log_e y = -1$

$y = e^{-1}$

Substitute into (2)

$\ln e^{-1} - \ln x = 1$

$-1 - \ln x = 1$

$\ln x = -2$

$\log_e x = -2$

$x = e^{-2}$

Solutions are $x = \frac{1}{e^2}$ and $y = \frac{1}{e}$

b $e^{5x-y} = 3e^{3x}$ — take $\log_e$ of both sides and use the multiplication law

$\ln e^{5x-y} = \ln 3 + \ln e^{3x}$

$5x - y = \ln 3 + 3x$ — simplify

$2x - y = \ln 3$ — (1)

$e^{2x} = 5e^{x+y}$ — take $\log_e$ of both sides and use the multiplication law

$\ln e^{2x} = \ln 5 + \ln e^{x+y}$ — simplify

$2x = \ln 5 + x + y$

$x - y = \ln 5$ — (2)

Subtract (2) from (1)

$x = \ln 3 - \ln 5$

$x = \ln 0.6$

Substitute into (2)

$\ln 0.6 - y = \ln 5$

$y = \ln 0.6 - \ln 5$

$y = \ln\frac{0.6}{5}$

Solutions are $x = \ln 0.6$ and $y = \ln 0.12$

12 $5\ln(7 - e^{2x}) = 3$ — divide both sides by 5

$\ln(7 - e^{2x}) = 0.6$

$e^{0.6} = 7 - e^{2x}$ — rearrange

$e^{2x} = 7 - e^{0.6}$

$e^{2x} = 5.17788$ — take $\log_e$ of both sides

$\ln e^{2x} = \ln 5.17788$

$2x = \ln 5.17788$

$x = 0.822$ 3 s.f.

13 $ex - xe^{5x-1} = 0$ — factorise

$x(e - e^{5x-1}) = 0$

Either $x = 0$

Or $e - e^{5x-1} = 0$ — rearrange

$e = e^{5x-1}$ — take $\log_e$ of both sides and use the power law

$\ln e = (5x - 1)\ln e$ — divide both sides by $\ln e$

$1 = 5x - 1$

$x = 0.4$

Solutions $x = 0$ and $x = 0.4$

14 $5x^2 - x^2e^{2x} + 2e^{2x} = 10$ rearrange

$5x^2 - 10 - x^2e^{2x} + 2e^{2x} = 0$ factorise by grouping

$5(x^2 - 2) - e^{2x}(x^2 - 2) = 0$

$(5 - e^{2x})(x^2 - 2) = 0$

Either $5 - e^{2x} = 0$

$e^{2x} = 5$ take $\log_e$ of both sides

$\ln e^{2x} = \ln 5$ use the multiplication law

$2x = \ln 5$

$x = \frac{1}{2}\ln 5$

Or $x^2 - 2 = 0$

$x^2 = 2$

$x = \sqrt{2}$ or $x = -\sqrt{2}$

Solutions are $x = \sqrt{2}$, $x = -\sqrt{2}$ and $x = \frac{1}{2}\ln 5$

Exercise 5.8

1 a $N = 100 \times 2^t$ substitute $t = 12$

$N = 100 \times 2^{12}$

$N = 409600$

b $100 \times 2^t > 10\,000\,000$

$2^t > 100\,000$ take $\log_e$ of both sides

> **TIP**
>
> You could have used logs in other bases, e.g., $\log_a x$ providing $a > 0$ and $a \neq 1, x > 0$.

$\ln 2^t > \ln 100\,000$ use the power law

$t \ln 2 > \ln 100\,000$

$t > \frac{\ln 100\,000}{\ln 2}$

$t > 16.6096$

The time in minutes is 16.61 (2 d.p.)

2 a 'At the beginning', i.e., 2015, $n = 0$ and the population was 50 000

Population when $n = 5$ is $50\,000e^{-0.03(5)}$ or 43 035.39882

Population after 5 years is 43035 to the nearest whole number or 43 000 to 3 s.f.

b $50\,000e^{-0.03n} = 5000$

$e^{-0.03n} = 0.1$ take $\log_e$ of both sides

$\ln e^{-0.03n} = \ln 0.1$ use the power law

$-0.03n = \ln 0.1$

$n = 76.75$ 2 d.p.

At the beginning of the 76th year (i.e 2091), the population will be $50\,000e^{-0.03\times 76} = 5114$

At the beginning of the 77th year (i.e 2092), the population will be $50\,000e^{-0.03\times 77} = 4963$

In 2091 the population will have decreased to 5000.

3 a $V = 2000e^{-kt}$ substitute $v = 1000$, $t = 15$

$1000 = 2000e^{-k\times 15}$

$e^{-15k} = 0.5$ take $\log_e$ of both sides

$\ln e^{-15k} = \ln 0.5$ use the power law

$-15k = \ln 0.5$

$k = -\frac{1}{15}\ln 0.5$

$k = 0.0462$ 3 s.f.

b $V = 2000e^{-22k}$

$V = 2000e^{-22\times 0.0462}$

$V = 723.79$

$V = 724$ 3 s.f.

4 a Given $N = 500e^{-0.3t}$, find the initial population, i.e., substitute $t = 0$

$N = 500e^{-0.3\times 0}$

$N = 500$

The initial population was 500.

b After 6 weeks, substitute $t = 6$ into $N = 500e^{-0.3t}$

$N = 500e^{-0.3\times 6}$

$N = 82.649$

After 6 weeks there are approximately 82 fish.

c Let the number of weeks be w.

Half the number that were initially introduced is 250.

$250 = 500e^{-0.3w}$

$0.5 = e^{-0.3w}$ take $\log_e$ of both sides

$\ln 0.5 = \ln e^{-0.3w}$ use the power law

$\ln 0.5 = -0.3w$

$w = 2.310$

The number of weeks is 2.31 3 s.f.

5 a Given $V = 250\,000e^{an}$, to find the initial value of the house, substitute $n = 0$

$V = 250\,000e^{a \times 0}$

$V = 250\,000$

The initial value was \$250 000

b To find the value of a, substitute $n = 3$, $V = 350\,000$

$350\,000 = 250\,000e^{a \times 3}$

$1.4 = e^{3a}$ take $\log_e$ of both sides

$\ln 1.4 = \ln e^{3a}$ use the power law

$3a = \ln 1.4$

$a = 0.112$ 3 s.f.

c So $V = 250\,000e^{0.112n}$

'Double the value' of the house means that it is worth \$500 000

To find the number of years until its value has doubled, substitute $V = 500\,000$

$500\,000 = 250\,000e^{0.112n}$

$2 = e^{0.112n}$ take $\log_e$ of both sides

$\ln 2 = \ln e^{0.112n}$ use the power law

$\ln 2 = 0.112n$

$n = 6.19$ 3 s.f.

It will take 6.19 years.

6 a $A = A_0 b^n$

Substituting $n = 2$, $A = 1.8$ gives $1.8 = A_0 b^2$ (1)

Substituting $n = 3$, $A = 2.4$ gives $2.4 = A_0 b^3$ (2)

Divide (2) by (1)

$$\frac{2.4}{1.8} = \frac{A_0 b^3}{A_0 b^2}$$

$$b = \frac{4}{3}$$

b $A = A_0 \times \left(\frac{4}{3}\right)^n$ substitute $n = 2$, $A = 1.8$ gives

$$1.8 = A_0 \times \left(\frac{4}{3}\right)^2$$

$$A_0 = 1.8 \div \left(\frac{4}{3}\right)^2$$

$A_0 = \frac{81}{80}$ and A_0 represents the area of the patch at the start of the measurements.

c $A = \frac{81}{80} \times \left(\frac{4}{3}\right)^n$

$\frac{81}{80} \times \left(\frac{4}{3}\right)^n > 7$

$\left(\frac{4}{3}\right)^n > \frac{560}{81}$ take $\log_e$ of both sides

$\ln\left(\frac{4}{3}\right)^n > \ln\frac{560}{81}$ use the power law

$n \ln\left(\frac{4}{3}\right) > \ln\frac{560}{81}$

$n > \ln\frac{560}{81} \div \ln\left(\frac{4}{3}\right)$

$n > 6.72$ 3 s.f.

It would take approximately 6.72 days

Exercise 5.10

1 b $y = 3e^x + 6$

When $x = 0$,

$y = 3e^0 + 6$

$y = 3 + 6$

$y = 9$ hence the y-intercept is (0, 9)

When $y = 0$,

$0 = 3e^x + 6$

$3e^x = -6$

$e^x = -2$ no solutions since e^x is always positive hence the graph does not intersect the x-axis

As $x \to +\infty$, $e^x \to \infty$ so $y \to \infty$

As $x \to -\infty$, $e^x \to 0$ so $y \to 6$ the line $y = 6$ is an asymptote

The sketch graph of $y = 3e^x + 6$ is:

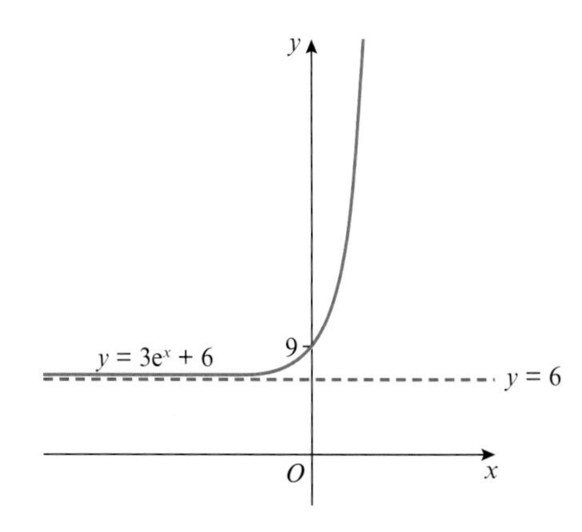

f $y = -2e^{-x} + 4$

When $x = 0$,

$y = -2e^{0} + 4$

$y = -2 + 4$

$y = 2$ hence the y-intercept is $(0, 2)$.

When $y = 0$,

$0 = -2e^{-x} + 4$

$2e^{-x} = 4$

$e^{-x} = 2$ take $\log_e$ of both sides

$\ln e^{-x} = \ln 2$ [or $\log_e(e^{-x}) = \log_e 2$] use the power law

$x = -\ln 2$ hence the x-intercept is $(-\ln 2, 0)$.

As $x \to +\infty$, $e^{-x} \to 0$ so $y \to 4$ hence the asymptote is $y = 4$

As $x \to -\infty$, $e^{-x} \to \infty$ so $y \to \infty$

The sketch graph of $y = -2e^{-x} + 4$ is:

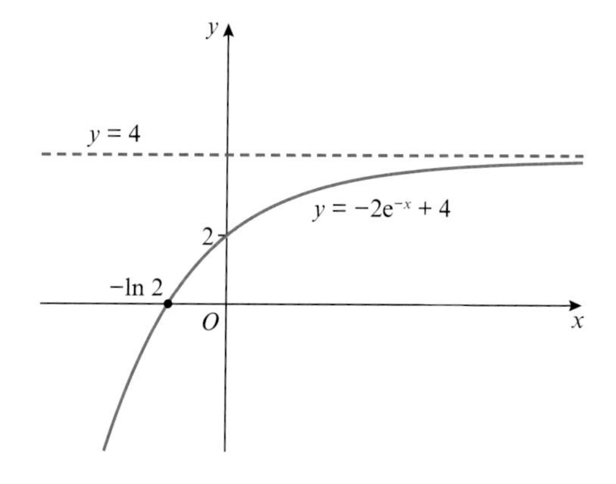

2 c $y = \ln(8 - 2x)$

When $x = 0$,

$y = \ln 8$ hence the y-intercept is $(0, \ln 8)$.

When $y = 0$,

$0 = \ln(8 - 2x)$ $(\log_e(8 - 2x) = 0)$

$e^{0} = 8 - 2x$

$1 = 8 - 2x$

$x = 3.5$ hence the x-intercept is $(3.5, 0)$.

$\ln(8 - 2x)$ only exists for $8 - 2x > 0$

$x < 4$

As $x \to 4$, $y \to -\infty$

As $x \to -\infty$, $y \to \infty$ The line $x = 4$ is an asymptote

The sketch graph of $y = \ln(8 - 2x)$ is:

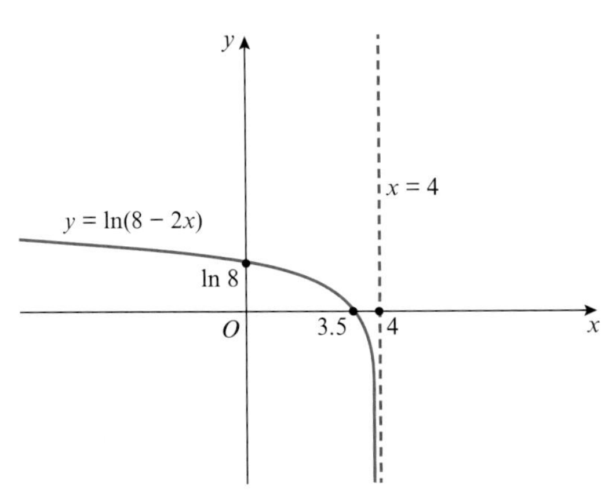

e $y = 4\ln(2x - 4)$

When $x = 0$,

$y = 4\ln(-4)$ $\quad$ $\ln x$ only exists for positive values of x so the graph does not intercept the y axis.

When $y = 0$,

$0 = 4\ln(2x - 4)$

$0 = \ln(2x - 4)$ $\quad$ $(\log_e(2x - 4) = 0)$

$e^0 = 2x - 4$

$1 = 2x - 4$

$x = 2.5$ $\quad$ hence the x-intercept is $(2.5, 0)$.

$4\ln(2x - 4)$ only exists for $2x - 4 > 0$

$x > 2$

As $x \to +\infty$, $y \to \infty$

As $x \to 2$, $y \to -\infty$ $\quad$ The line $x = 2$ is an asymptote.

The sketch graph of $y = 4\ln(2x - 4)$ is:

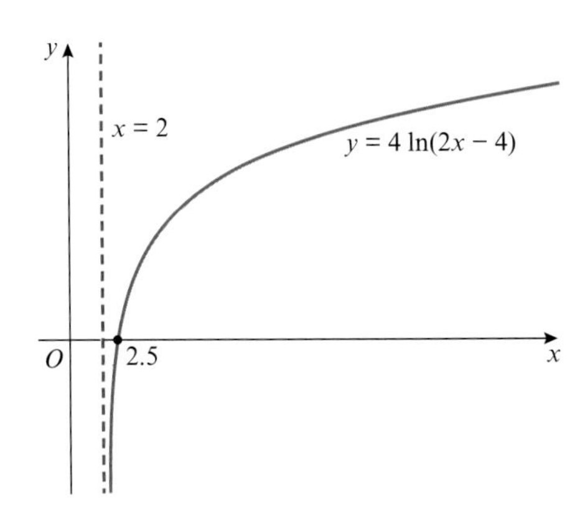

Exercise 5.11

1 d $f(x) = 3e^{2x} + 1$ for $x \in \mathbb{R}$

Step 1 Write the function as $y =$ $\qquad y = 3e^{2x} + 1$

Step 2 Interchange the x and y variables. $\qquad x = 3e^{2y} + 1$

Step 3 Rearrange to make y the subject. $\qquad x - 1 = 3e^{2y}$

$$\frac{x-1}{3} = e^{2y}$$

$$\ln\left(\frac{x-1}{3}\right) = 2y$$

$$y = \frac{1}{2}\ln\left(\frac{x-1}{3}\right)$$

Note: $\log_e\left(\frac{x-1}{3}\right)$ is valid for $x > 1$ $\qquad$ [$\log_a x$ requires $a > 0$ and $a \neq 1$, $x > 0$]

$f^{-1}(x) = \frac{1}{2}\ln\left(\frac{x-1}{3}\right)$ for $x \in \mathbb{R}$ for $x > 1$

h $f(x) = 5 - 2e^{-2x}$ for $x \in \mathbb{R}$

Step 1 Write the function as $y =$ $\qquad y = 5 - 2e^{-2x}$

Step 2 Interchange the x and y variables. $\qquad x = 5 - 2e^{-2y}$

Step 3 Rearrange to make y the subject. $\qquad 5 - x = 2e^{-2y}$

$$\frac{5-x}{2} = e^{-2y}$$

$$\ln\left(\frac{5-x}{2}\right) = -2y$$

$$y = -\frac{1}{2}\ln\left(\frac{5-x}{2}\right)$$

Note: $\log_e\left(\frac{5-x}{2}\right)$ is valid for $x < 5$ $\qquad$ [$\log_a x$ requires $a > 0$ and $a \neq 1$, $x > 0$]

$f^{-1}(x) = -\frac{1}{2}\ln\left(\frac{5-x}{2}\right)$ for $x \in \mathbb{R}$ for $x < 5$

2 c $f(x) = 2\ln(x + 2)$ for $x > -2$

Step 1 Write the function as $y =$ $\qquad y = 2\ln(x + 2)$

Step 2 Interchange the x and y variables. $\qquad x = 2\ln(y + 2)$

Step 3 Rearrange to make y the subject. $\qquad \frac{x}{2} = \ln(y + 2)$

$$e^{0.5x} = y + 2$$

$$y = e^{0.5x} - 2$$

$$f^{-1}(x) = e^{0.5x} - 2$$

f $f(x) = -5\ln(3x - 1)$ for $x > \frac{1}{3}$

Step 1 Write the function as $y =$ $\qquad y = -5\ln(3x - 1)$

Step 2 Interchange the x and y variables. $\qquad x = -5\ln(3y - 1)$

Step 3 Rearrange to make y the subject. $\qquad -0.2x = \ln(3y - 1)$

$$e^{-0.2x} = 3y - 1$$

$$y = \frac{1}{3}(e^{-0.2x} + 1)$$

$$f^{-1}(x) = \frac{1}{3}(e^{-0.2x} + 1)$$

3 a $f(x) = e^{2x} + 1$ for $x \in \mathbb{R}$

$e^{kx} > 0$ for all values of k.

The range of $f(x) > 1$

b $f(x) = e^{2x} + 1\ x \in \mathbb{R}$

Step 1 Write the function as $y = y = e^{2x} + 1$

Step 2 Interchange the x and y variables. $\qquad x = e^{2y} + 1$

Step 3 Rearrange to make y the subject. $\qquad x - 1 = e^{2y}$

$$\ln(x - 1) = 2y$$

$$y = \frac{1}{2}\ln(x - 1)$$

$$f^{-1}(x) = \frac{1}{2}\ln(x - 1)$$

c The domain of $f^{-1}(x)$ is the same as the range of $f(x)$.

The domain of $f^{-1}(x)$ is $x > 1$

d $f^{-1}f(x) = x$

The functions f and f^{-1} are one-one functions (see Chapter 1).

The graphs of f and $f^{-1}$are reflections of each other in the line $y = x$.

$[f^{-1}f(x) = x = ff^{-1}f(x)]$

4 a i $f(x) = e^x$ for $x \in \mathbb{R}$ and $g(x) = \ln 5x$ for $x > 0$

$fg(x)$ $\qquad$ g acts on x first and $g(x) = \ln 5x$

$= f(\ln 5x)$ $\qquad$ f is the function 'e to the power of x'

$= e^{\ln 5x}$

$= 5x$

$fg(x) = 5x$

ii $gf(x)$ — f acts on x first and $f(x) = e^x$

$= g(e^x)$ — g is the function 'multiply by 5 then take $\log_e$ of the result'

$= \ln 5e^x$ — use the multiplication law of logs

$= \ln 5 + \ln e^x$

$= \ln 5 + x$

$gf(x) = x + \ln 5$

b $g(x) = 3f^{-1}(x)$

$f^{-1}(x) = \ln x$

$\ln 5x = 3\ln x$ — use the multiplication law of logs

Either

$\ln 5 + \ln x = 3\ln x$

$2\ln x = \ln 5$

$\ln x = 0.5\ln 5$

$x = e^{0.5\ln 5}$

Solution is $x = 2.24$ to 3 s.f.

Or, if an exact answer required:

$\ln 5x = 3\ln x$

$\ln 5x = \ln x^3$

$5x = x^3$

$x^3 - 5x = 0$ — factorise

$x(x^2 - 5) = 0$

$x = 0$ and $x^2 = 5$

$x = 0$, $x = \sqrt{5}$ and $x = -\sqrt{5}$ *however,* $\log_a x$ *requires* $x > 0$

Solution is $x = \sqrt{5}$

5 **a** i $f(x) = e^{3x}$ for $x \in \mathbb{R}$ and $g(x) = \ln x$ for $x > 0$

$fg(x)$ — g acts on x first and $g(x) = \ln x$

$= f(\ln x)$ — f is the function 'e to the power of $3x$'

$= e^{3\ln x}$

$= e^{\ln x^3}$

$= x^3$

$fg(x) = x^3$

ii $gf(x)$ — f acts on x first and $f(x) = e^{3x}$

$= g(e^{3x})$ — g is the function 'take $\log_e$'

$= 3x$

$gf(x) = 3x$

b $f(x) = 2g^{-1}(x)$

$g^{-1}(x) = e^x$

$e^{3x} = 2e^x$

$\ln e^{3x} = \ln(2e^x)$ use the multiplication law of logs

$\ln e^{3x} = \ln 2 + \ln e^x$

$3x = \ln 2 + x$

$2x = \ln 2$

Solution is $x = \frac{1}{2}\ln 2$

6 a $f(x) = e^{2x}$ for $x \in \mathbb{R}$ and $g(x) = \ln(2x + 1)$ for $x > -\frac{1}{2}$

$fg(x)$ g acts on x first and $g(x) = \ln(2x + 1)$

$= f(\ln(2x + 1))$ f is the function 'e to the power of $2x$'

$= e^{2\ln(2x+1)}$

$= e^{\ln(2x+1)^2}$

$fg(x) = (2x + 1)^2$

b Find $g^{-1}(x)$

Step 1 Write the function as $y =$ $y = \ln(2x + 1)$

Step 2 Interchange the x and y variables. $x = \ln(2y + 1)$

Step 3 Rearrange to make y the subject. $e^x = 2y + 1$

$\frac{1}{2}(e^x - 1) = y$

$y = \frac{1}{2}(e^x - 1)$

$g^{-1}(x) = \frac{1}{2}(e^x - 1)$

Solve $f(x) = 8g^{-1}(x)$

$e^{2x} = 8 \times \frac{1}{2}(e^x - 1)$

$e^{2x} = 4e^x - 4$ rearrange

$e^{2x} - 4e^x + 4 = 0$ factorise

$(e^x - 2)(e^x - 2) = 0$

$e^x - 2 = 0$

$e^x = 2$

$\ln e^x = \ln 2$

$x = \ln 2$

Chapter 6: Straight-line graphs

Exercise 6.1

1 d (−3, 1) and (2, 13)

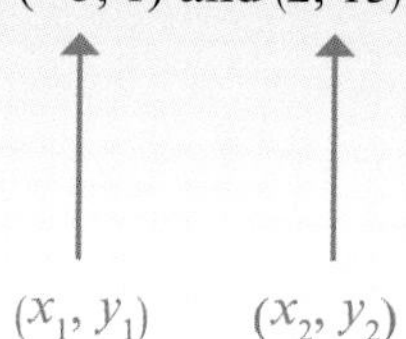

Length of line segment

$= \sqrt{(x_2 - x_1)^2 + (y_2 - y_1)^2}$

$= \sqrt{(2 - -3)^2 + (13 - 1)^2}$

$= 13$

h (−3, −2) and (−1, −5)

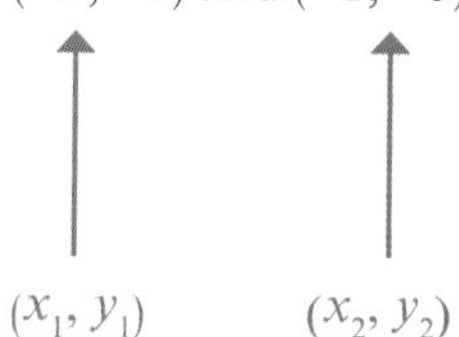

Length of line segment

$= \sqrt{(x_2 - x_1)^2 + (y_2 - y_1)^2}$

$= \sqrt{(-1 - -3)^2 + (-5 - -2)^2}$

$= \sqrt{13}$

2 a $P(3, 11)$ and $Q\,(5, 7)$

$PQ = \sqrt{(5 - 3)^2 + (7 - 11)^2}$

$= \sqrt{20}$ or $2\sqrt{5}$

$P(3, 11)$ and $R\,(11, 10)$

$PR = \sqrt{(11 - 3)^2 + (10 - 11)^2}$

$= \sqrt{65}$

$R(11, 10)$ and $Q\,(5, 7)$

$PQ = \sqrt{(5 - 11)^2 + (7 - 10)^2}$

$= \sqrt{45}$ or $3\sqrt{5}$

$PQ^2 + RQ^2 = (\sqrt{20})^2 + (\sqrt{45})^2 = 65$

$PR^2 = 65$

So, $PQ^2 + RQ^2 = PR^2$ therefore triangle PQR is right-angled at Q.

b $P(-7, 8)$ and $Q(-1, 4)$

$PQ = \sqrt{(-1 - -7)^2 + (4 - 8)^2}$

$= \sqrt{52}$ or $2\sqrt{13}$

$P(-7, 8)$ and $R(5, 12)$

$PR = \sqrt{(5 - -7)^2 + (12 - 8)^2}$

$= \sqrt{160}$ or $4\sqrt{10}$

$R(5, 12)$ and $Q(-1, 4)$

$RQ = \sqrt{(-1 - 5)^2 + (4 - 12)^2}$

$= \sqrt{100}$ or 10

If triangle PQR is right-angled then the hypotenuse would be the longest of the three sides.

The hypotenuse would be PR since $\sqrt{160} > \sqrt{100} > \sqrt{52}$ and the right angle would be at Q.

So $PQ^2 + RQ^2 = PR^2$ should be true

But $(\sqrt{52})^2 + (\sqrt{100})^2 \neq (\sqrt{160})^2$

Triangle PQR is not right-angled.

3 $A(-1, 0)$ and $B(1, 6)$

$AB = \sqrt{(1 - -1)^2 + (6 - 0)^2}$

$= \sqrt{40}$ or $2\sqrt{10}$

$B(1, 6)$ and $C(7, 4)$

$BC = \sqrt{(7 - 1)^2 + (4 - 6)^2}$

$= \sqrt{40}$ or $2\sqrt{10}$

So, $AB = BC$

$A(-1, 0)$ and $C(7, 4)$

$AC = \sqrt{(7 - -1)^2 + (4 - 0)^2}$

$= \sqrt{80}$ or $4\sqrt{5}$

$AB^2 + BC^2 = (\sqrt{40})^2 + (\sqrt{40})^2 = 80$

$AC^2 = (\sqrt{80})^2 = 80$

$AB^2 + BC^2 = AC^2$ therefore triangle ABC is isosceles and right-angled at B.

4 $P = (10, 2b)$, $Q = (b, -5)$ and $PQ = 5\sqrt{10}$

Using $PQ = \sqrt{(x_2 - x_1)^2 + (y_2 - y_1)^2}$ and $PQ = 5\sqrt{10}$

$5\sqrt{10} = \sqrt{(b-10)^2 + (-5-2b)^2}$	square both sides
$250 = (b-10)^2 + (-5-2b)^2$	expand brackets
$250 = b^2 - 20b + 100 + 25 + 20b + 4b^2$	collect terms on one side
$5b^2 - 125 = 0$	divide both sides by 5
$b^2 - 25 = 0$	factorise
$(b-5)(b+5) = 0$	solve
$b = 5$ or $b = -5$	

5 $P = (6, -2)$, $Q = (2a, a)$ and $PQ = 5$

Using $PQ = \sqrt{(x_2 - x_1)^2 + (y_2 - y_1)^2}$

$5 = \sqrt{(2a-6)^2 + (a - -2)^2}$	square both sides
$5^2 = (2a-6)^2 + (a+2)^2$	expand brackets
$25 = 4a^2 - 24a + 36 + a^2 + 4a + 4$	collect terms on one side
$5a^2 - 20a + 15 = 0$	divide by 5
$a^2 - 4a + 3 = 0$	factorise
$(a-3)(a-1) = 0$	solve
$a = 3$ or $a = 1$	

6 **b** Given $(4, 3)$ and $(9, 11)$

Using midpoint $= \left(\frac{x_1 + x_2}{2}, \frac{y_1 + y_2}{2}\right)$

Midpoint $= \left(\frac{4+9}{2}, \frac{3+11}{2}\right) = (6.5, 7)$

f Given $(2a, -3b)$ and $(4a, 5b)$

Using midpoint $= \left(\frac{x_1 + x_2}{2}, \frac{y_1 + y_2}{2}\right)$

Midpoint $= \left(\frac{2a+4a}{2}, \frac{-3b+5b}{2}\right) = (3a, b)$

7 $P = (-8, 2)$, $Q = (a, b)$ and the midpoint $(5, -3)$

Using midpoint $= \left(\frac{x_1 + x_2}{2}, \frac{y_1 + y_2}{2}\right)$

Midpoint $= \left(\frac{-8+a}{2}, \frac{2+b}{2}\right) = (5, -3)$

Equating the x-coordinates gives:

$\frac{-8+a}{2} = 5$

$-8 + a = 10$

$a = 18$

Equating the y-coordinates gives:

$\frac{2+b}{2} = -3$

$2 + b = -6$

$b = -8$

8 $A = (-7, 6)$, $B = (-1, 8)$ and $C = (7, 3)$

a Using midpoint $= \left(\frac{x_1 + x_2}{2}, \frac{y_1 + y_2}{2}\right)$

Midpoint of $AC = \left(\frac{-7+7}{2}, \frac{6+3}{2}\right) = (0, 4.5)$

b As $ABCD$ is a parallelogram, the midpoint of AC is also the midpoint of BD.

Let D have coordinates (a, b)

Midpoint of $BD = \left(\frac{-1+a}{2}, \frac{8+b}{2}\right) = (0, 4.5)$

Equating the x-coordinates gives:

$\frac{-1+a}{2} = 0$

$-1 + a = 0$

$a = 1$

Equating the y-coordinates gives:

$\frac{8+b}{2} = 4.5$

$8 + b = 9$

$b = 1$

The coordinates of $D = (1, 1)$

9 Given: $A = (-2, 4)$, $B = (7, -5)$ and the point $P = (2k, k)$

Length of line segment

$= \sqrt{(x_2 - x_1)^2 + (y_2 - y_1)^2}$

$AP = \sqrt{(2k - -2)^2 + (k - 4)^2}$

$AP = \sqrt{4k^2 + 8k + 4 + k^2 - 8k + 16}$

$AP = \sqrt{5k^2 + 20}$

$BP = \sqrt{(2k - 7)^2 + (k - -5)^2}$

$BP = \sqrt{4k^2 - 28k + 49 + k^2 + 10k + 25}$

$BP = \sqrt{5k^2 - 18k + 74} BP \ = \sqrt{5k^2 - 18k + 74}$

$AP = BP$

$\sqrt{5k^2 + 20} = \sqrt{5k^2 - 18k + 74}$ square both sides

$5k^2 + 20 = 5k^2 - 18k + 74$ solve

$18k = 54$

$k = 3$

10 Let the coordinates of the vertices of triangle ABC be $A = (x_1, y_1)$, $B = (x_2, y_2)$ and $C = (x_3, y_3)$

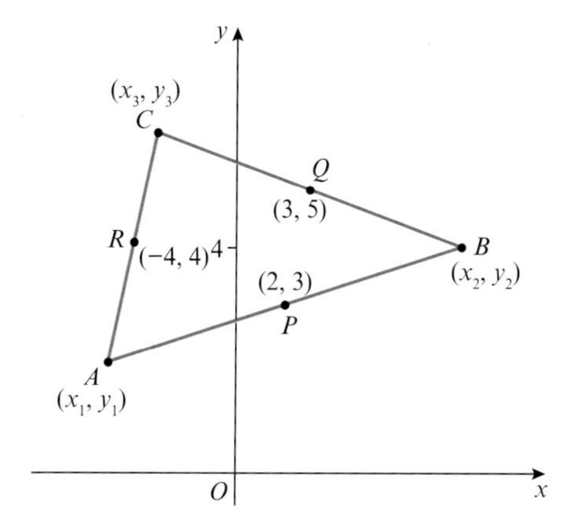

Now $\frac{x_2 + x_3}{2} = 3$ so $x_2 + x_3 = 6$ (1)

Now $\frac{y_2 + y_3}{2} = 5$ so $y_2 + y_3 = 10$ (2)

Now $\frac{x_1 + x_3}{2} = -4$ so $x_1 + x_3 = -8$ (3)

Now $\frac{y_1 + y_3}{2} = 4$ so $y_1 + y_3 = 8$ (4)

Now $\frac{x_1 + x_2}{2} = 2$ so $x_1 + x_2 = 4$ (5)

Now $\frac{y_1 + y_2}{2} = 3$ so $y_1 + y_2 = 6$ (6)

Adding equations (1), (3) and (5) gives:
$2x_1 + 2x_2 + 2x_3 = 2$

Dividing both sides by 2 gives: $x_1 + x_2 + x_3 = 1$

and as $x_1 + x_2 = 4$ then $x_3 = -3$

and as $x_2 + x_3 = 6$ then $x_1 = -5$

and as $x_1 + x_3 = -8$ then $x_2 = 9$

Adding equations (2), (4) and (6) gives:
$2y_1 + 2y_2 + 2y_3 = 24$

Dividing both sides by 2 gives: $y_1 + y_2 + y_3 = 12$

and as $y_1 + y_2 = 6$ then $y_3 = 6$

and as $y_2 + y_3 = 10$ then $y_1 = 2$

and as $y_1 + y_3 = 8$ then $y_2 = 4$

The vertices of triangle ABC are
$A = (-5, 2)$ $B = (9, 4)$ $C = (-3, 6)$

Exercise 6.2

REMEMBER

- **Collinear** points all lie on a straight line.
- The equation of a straight line can be written as $y = mx + c$ where 'c' is the y-intercept and 'm' is the gradient.
- The equation of a straight line with gradient 'm' which passes through the point (x_1, y_1) is:

  $y - y_1 = m(x - x_1)$
- If two lines are parallel then their gradients are equal.
- If a line has a gradient m, a line perpendicular to it has a gradient $-\frac{1}{m}$.
- If the gradients of the two perpendicular lines are m_1 and m_2, then $m_1 \times m_2 = -1$

1 b Let $A = (x_1, y_1)$ and $B = (x_2, y_2)$

and $A = (4, 3)$ $B = (5, 0)$

Using the gradient of a line segment

$AB = \dfrac{y_2 - y_1}{x_2 - x_1}$

Gradient of $AB = \dfrac{0 - 3}{5 - 4} = -3$

f Let $A = (x_1, y_1)$ and $B = (x_2, y_2)$

and $A = (6, -7)$ $B = (2, -4)$

Using the gradient of a line segment

$AB = \dfrac{y_2 - y_1}{x_2 - x_1}$

Gradient of $AB = \dfrac{-4 - -7}{2 - 6} = \dfrac{3}{-4} = -\dfrac{3}{4}$

2 If a line has a gradient m, a line perpendicular to it has a gradient $-\frac{1}{m}$

b A line perpendicular to $-\frac{1}{2}$ has a gradient

$-\dfrac{1}{-\frac{1}{2}} = 2$

d A line perpendicular to $1\frac{1}{4}$ has a gradient

$-\dfrac{1}{1\frac{1}{4}} = -\dfrac{1}{\frac{5}{4}} = -\dfrac{4}{5}$

3 a $A = (3, -5)$ $B = (6, -3)$

For a rectangle the gradient of CD is the same as the gradient of $AB = \dfrac{-3 - -5}{6 - 3} = \dfrac{2}{3}$

b BC and AB are perpendicular so the gradient of BC is $-\dfrac{1}{\text{gradient of } AB} = -\dfrac{1}{\frac{2}{3}} = -\dfrac{3}{2}$

4 $A = (-1, -5)$ $B = (5, -2)$

The gradient of $AB = \dfrac{-2 - -5}{5 - -1} = \dfrac{1}{2}$

AD and AB are perpendicular so the gradient of AD is $-\dfrac{1}{\text{gradient of } AB} = -\dfrac{1}{\frac{1}{2}} = -2$

AB and DC are parallel so the gradient of $DC = \dfrac{1}{2}$

$C = (1, 1)$ so let the coordinates of D be (x, y)

The gradient of $DC = \dfrac{y - 1}{x - 1} = \dfrac{1}{2}$

so $2y - 2 = x - 1$ or $x - 2y = -1$ (1)

The gradient of $AD = \dfrac{y - -5}{x - -1} = -2$

so $y + 5 = -2x - 2$ or $-2x - y = 7$ (2)

Solve equations (1) and (2) simultaneously:

Adding (2) to 2 ×(1) gives $-5y = 5$ so $y = -1$

Substituting into (1) gives $x = -3$

So D is at $(-3, -1)$

5 $P = (-2, 3) \quad Q = (4, -1)$

The gradient of $PQ = \frac{-1 - 3}{4 - -2} = \frac{-4}{6} = -\frac{2}{3}$

The midpoint of $PQ = \left(\frac{-2 + 4}{2}, \frac{3 + -1}{2}\right) = (1, 1)$

So $M = (1, 1)$

As $C = (-1, -2)$ and $M = (1, 1)$ then the gradient of $CM = \frac{1 - -2}{1 - -1} = \frac{3}{2}$

The gradient of $PQ \times$ gradient of $CM = -\frac{2}{3} \times \frac{3}{2} = -1$

So, CM is perpendicular to PQ

6 **a** $A = (-2, 2) \quad B = (3, -1) \quad C = (9, -4)$

The gradient of $AB = \frac{-1 - 2}{3 - -2} = -\frac{3}{5}$

The gradient of $BC = \frac{-4 - -1}{9 - 3} = \frac{-3}{6} = -\frac{1}{2}$

b If A, B and C are collinear then they lie on the same line and the gradient of AB = gradient of BC

As $-\frac{3}{5} \neq -\frac{1}{2}$ then A, B and C are not collinear

7 $A = (-4, 4) \quad B = (k, -2) \quad C = (2k + 1, -6)$

If A, B and C are collinear then the gradient of AB and the gradient of BC should be equal.

The gradient of $AB = \frac{-2 - 4}{k - -4} = \frac{-6}{k + 4}$

The gradient of $BC = \frac{-6 - -2}{2k + 1 - k} = \frac{-4}{k + 1}$

So, $\frac{-6}{k + 4} = \frac{-4}{k + 1}$

$-6k - 6 = -4k - 16$

$k = 5$

8 $A = (-k, -2) \quad B = (k, -4) \quad C = (4, k - 2)$

If the triangle is right-angled at B then the gradient of $AB \times$ gradient of $BC = -1$

The gradient of $AB = \frac{-4 - -2}{k - -k} = \frac{-2}{2k} = -\frac{1}{k}$

The gradient of $BC = \frac{k - 2 - -4}{4 - k} = \frac{k + 2}{4 - k}$

So $-\frac{1}{k} \times \frac{k + 2}{4 - k} = -1$

$\frac{-k - 2}{k(4 - k)} = -1$

$-k - 2 = -k(4 - k)$

$-k - 2 = -4k + k^2$

$k^2 - 3k + 2 = 0$

$(k - 2)(k - 1) = 0$

$k = 1$ or 2

9 $A = (-2, 0) \quad B = (2, 6)$

Let $C = (x, 0)$

The gradient of $AB = \frac{6 - 0}{2 - -2} = \frac{6}{4} = \frac{3}{2}$

The gradient of $BC = \frac{0 - 6}{x - 2} = \frac{-6}{x - 2}$

As angle $ABC = 90°$ then AB is perpendicular to BC

So $\frac{3}{2} \times \frac{-6}{x - 2} = -1$

$\frac{-18}{2x - 4} = -1$

$-18 = -2x + 4$

$x = 11$

C is at $(11, 0)$

Exercise 6.3

1 **a** Using $y - y_1 = m(x - x_1)$ with $m = 3$ $x_1 = 6$ and $y_1 = 5$

$y - 5 = 3(x - 6)$

$y - 5 = 3x - 18$

$y = 3x - 13$

c Using $y - y_1 = m(x - x_1)$ with $m = -\frac{1}{2}$

$x_1 = 8$ and $y_1 = -3$

$y - -3 = -\frac{1}{2}(x - 8)$

$y + 3 = -\frac{1}{2}x + 4$

$y = -\frac{1}{2}x + 1$

2 a (3, 2) and (5, 7)

Gradient of the line segment joining these points $= \frac{7-2}{5-3} = \frac{5}{2}$

Using $y - y_1 = m(x - x_1)$ with $m = \frac{5}{2}$

$x_1 = 3$ and $y_1 = 2$

$y - 2 = \frac{5}{2}(x - 3)$

$2y - 4 = 5x - 15$

$2y = 5x - 11$

c (5, − 2) and (−7, 4)

Gradient of the line segment joining these points $= \frac{4 - -2}{-7-5} = \frac{6}{-12} = -\frac{1}{2}$

Using $y - y_1 = m(x - x_1)$ with $m = -\frac{1}{2}$

$x_1 = 5$ and $y_1 = -2$

$y - -2 = -\frac{1}{2}(x - 5)$

$2y + 4 = -x + 5$

$x + 2y = 1$

3 b The gradient of $x + 2y = 5$ can be found by rearranging the equation to the form $y = mx + c$

$2y = -x + 5$

$y = -\frac{1}{2}x + \frac{5}{2}$ so the gradient is $-\frac{1}{2}$

Any line parallel to this line also has the same gradient.

Using $y - y_1 = m(x - x_1)$ with $m = -\frac{1}{2}$

$x_1 = 2$ and $y_1 = -5$

$y - -5 = -\frac{1}{2}(x - 2)$

$2y + 10 = -x + 2$

$x + 2y = -8$

d The gradient of $4x - y = 6$ can be found by rearranging the equation to the form $y = mx + c$

$y = 4x - 6$ so the gradient is 4

Any line perpendicular to this line also has the gradient $-\frac{1}{4}$

Using $y - y_1 = m(x - x_1)$ with $m = -\frac{1}{4}$

$x_1 = 4$ and $y_1 = -1$

$y - -1 = -\frac{1}{4}(x - 4)$

$4y + 4 = -x + 4$

$x + 4y = 0$

4 a $P = (2, 5)$ $Q = (6, 0)$

The gradient of $PQ = \frac{0-5}{6-2} = \frac{-5}{4}$

A line perpendicular to PQ has gradient

$= -\frac{1}{\frac{-5}{4}} = \frac{4}{5}$

This line passes through point P so:

using $y - y_1 = m(x - x_1)$ with $m = \frac{4}{5}$

$x_1 = 2$ and $y_1 = 5$

$y - 5 = \frac{4}{5}(x - 2)$

$5y - 25 = 4x - 8$

$4x - 5y = -17$

b The line $4x - 5y = -17$ meets the y-axis at R

Set $x = 0$ to find the y-intercept $0 - 5y = -17$

$y = 3.4$

The coordinates of R are (0, 3.4)

c The triangle OPR has 'base' $(OR) = 3.4$ units and perpendicular height 2 units.

Area of triangle $OPR = \frac{1}{2} \times 3.4 \times 2 = 3.4$ units^2

5 a Given (1, 3) and (−3, 1)

The midpoint of these two coordinates is

$\left(\frac{1 + -3}{2}, \frac{3+1}{2}\right) = (-1, 2)$

The gradient of the line segment that joins these two points is $= \frac{1-3}{-3-1} = \frac{-2}{-4} = \frac{1}{2}$

Any line perpendicular to this line has the gradient $-\frac{1}{\frac{1}{2}} = -2$

The perpendicular of the line that joins the two points is found by using:

$y - y_1 = m(x - x_1)$ with $m = -2$

$x_1 = -1$ and $y_1 = 2$

$y - 2 = -2(x - -1)$

$y - 2 = -2x - 2$

$y = -2x$

c Given $(0, -9)$ and $(5, -2)$

The midpoint of these two coordinates is

$\left(\frac{0+5}{2}, \frac{-9+-2}{2}\right) = \left(\frac{5}{2}, -\frac{11}{2}\right)$

The gradient of the line segment that joins these two points is $= \frac{-2 - -9}{5 - 0} = \frac{7}{5}$

Any line perpendicular to this line has the gradient $-\frac{1}{\frac{7}{5}} = -\frac{5}{7}$

The perpendicular of the line that joins the two points is found by using:

$y - y_1 = m(x - x_1)$ with $m = -\frac{5}{7}$

$x_1 = \frac{5}{2}$ and $y_1 = -\frac{11}{2}$

$y - -\frac{11}{2} = -\frac{5}{7}\left(x - \frac{5}{2}\right)$

$14y + 77 = -10x + 25$

$10x + 14y = -52$

$5x + 7y = -26$

6 a Given $A = (-1, 4)$ and $B = (2, 2)$

The midpoint of these two coordinates is

$\left(\frac{-1+2}{2}, \frac{4+2}{2}\right) = \left(\frac{1}{2}, 3\right)$

The gradient of the line segment that joins these two points is $\frac{2-4}{2--1} = \frac{-2}{3}$

Any line perpendicular to this line has the gradient $-\frac{1}{\frac{-2}{3}} = \frac{3}{2}$

The perpendicular bisector of the line that joins the two points is found by using:

$y - y_1 = m(x - x_1)$ with $m = \frac{3}{2}$

$x_1 = \frac{1}{2}$ and $y_1 = 3$

$y - 3 = \frac{3}{2}\left(x - \frac{1}{2}\right)$

$2y - 6 = 3x - \frac{3}{2}$

$4y - 12 = 6x - 3$

$4y - 6x = 9$

The perpendicular bisector intercepts the x-axis where $y = 0$ so $0 - 6x = 9$, $x = -1\frac{1}{2}$

The perpendicular bisector intercepts the y-axis where $x = 0$ so $4y - 0 = 9$, $y = 2\frac{1}{4}$

So $P = \left(-1\frac{1}{2}, 0\right)$ and $Q = (0, 2\frac{1}{4})$

b The length of $PQ = \sqrt{\left(0 - -1\frac{1}{2}\right)^2 + \left(2\frac{1}{4} - 0\right)^2}$

$PQ = \sqrt{\frac{9}{4} + \frac{81}{16}}$

$PQ = \frac{3\sqrt{13}}{4}$ units

c The area of triangle $OPQ = \frac{1}{2} \times$ 'base' (OP) $\times$ 'perpendicular height' (OQ)

$= \frac{1}{2} \times 1\frac{1}{2} \times 2\frac{1}{4}$

$= 1.6875$ units^2

7 a l_1: $3x + 2y = 12$ and l_2: $y = 2x - 1$

Substituting $y = 2x - 1$ into $3x + 2y = 12$ gives:

$3x + 2(2x - 1) = 12$

$3x + 4x - 2 = 12$

$x = 2$

So $y = 2(2) - 1 = 3$

$A = (2, 3)$

b The gradient of l_1 is found by rearranging $3x + 2y = 12$ into the form $y = mx + c$

$2y = -3x + 12$

$y = -\frac{3}{2}x + 6$

l_1 has a gradient $-\frac{3}{2}$

A line perpendicular to l_1 has a gradient $-\frac{1}{-\frac{3}{2}} = \frac{2}{3}$

The equation of the line through A that is perpendicular to l_1 is found by using:

$y - y_1 = m(x - x_1)$ with $m = \frac{2}{3}$

$x_1 = 2$ and $y_1 = 3$

$y - 3 = \frac{2}{3}(x - 2)$

$3y - 9 = 2x - 4$

$3y = 2x + 5$

8 a $A = (1, 5) \quad B = (9, 7) \quad C = (k, -6)$

The midpoint of $AB = \left(\frac{1+9}{2}, \frac{5+7}{2}\right) = (5, 6)$

$M = (5, 6)$

b The gradient of $AB = \frac{7-5}{9-1} = \frac{2}{8} = \frac{1}{4}$

A line perpendicular to AB has a gradient $-\frac{1}{\frac{1}{4}} = -4$

So the gradient of MC is -4

The gradient of $MC = \left(\frac{-6-6}{k-5}\right) = \frac{-12}{k-5}$

So $\frac{-12}{k-5} = -4$

$-12 = -4k + 20$

$k = 8$

9 a $A = (2, -1) \quad B = (3, 7) \quad C = (14, 5)$

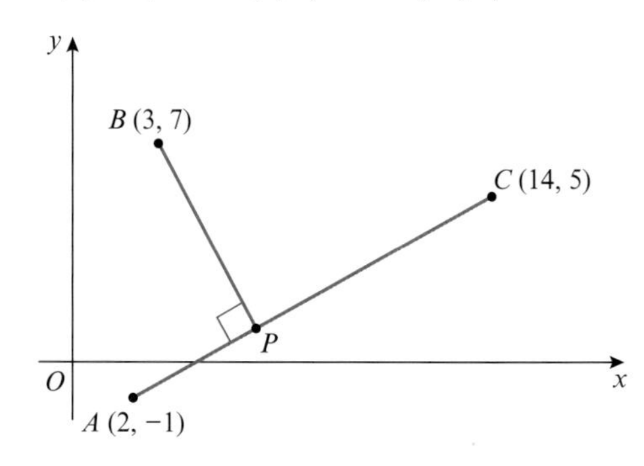

The gradient of $AC = \left(\frac{5 - -1}{14 - 2}\right) = \frac{6}{12} = \frac{1}{2}$

A line perpendicular to AC (such as BP), has a gradient $-\frac{1}{\frac{1}{2}} = -2$

Let the point P be (x, y)

The gradient of $BP = \left(\frac{y-7}{x-3}\right)$

So $\left(\frac{y-7}{x-3}\right) = -2$

$y - 7 = -2x + 6$

$y = -2x + 13$

b Equation of BC can be found using:

$y - y_1 = m(x - x_1)$ with $m = \frac{1}{2}$

$x_1 = 14$ and $y_1 = 5$

$y - 5 = \frac{1}{2}(x - 14)$

$2y - 10 = x - 14$

$2y = x - 4$

Point P is at the intersection of AC and BP.

The coordinates of P can be found by

solving $\quad y = -2x + 13 \quad (1)$

and $\quad 2y = x - 4 \quad (2)$

Use (1) to substitute for y in (2)

$2(-2x + 13) = x - 4$

$-4x + 26 = x - 4$

$5x = 30$

$x = 6$

Substitute for x in (1) gives $y = -2(6) + 13$ so $y = 1$

$P = (6, 1)$

c Length of $AC = \sqrt{(14 - 2)^2 + (5 - -1)^2}$

$AC = \sqrt{144 + 36}$

$AC = 6\sqrt{5}$ units

Length of $BP = \sqrt{(6 - 3)^2 + (1 - 7)^2}$

$BP = \sqrt{9 + 36}$

$BP = 3\sqrt{5}$ units

d Area of triangle $ABC = \frac{1}{2} \times$ 'base' (AC) $\times$ 'perpendicular height' (BD)

$= \frac{1}{2} \times 6\sqrt{5} \times 3\sqrt{5}$

$= 45$ units^2

10 a i $P = (-3, -2)$ $Q = (5, 10)$

The midpoint of these two coordinates is

$\left(\frac{-3+5}{2}, \frac{-2+10}{2}\right) = (1, 4)$

The gradient of the line segment that joins these two points is $= \frac{10 - -2}{5 - -3} = \frac{12}{8} = \frac{3}{2}$

Any line perpendicular to this line has the gradient $-\frac{1}{\frac{3}{2}} = -\frac{2}{3}$

The perpendicular of the line that joins the two points is found by using:

$y - y_1 = m(x - x_1)$ with $m = -\frac{2}{3}$

$x_1 = 1$ and $y_1 = 4$

$y - 4 = -\frac{2}{3}(x - 1)$

$3y - 12 = -2x + 2$

$2x + 3y = 14$

ii $Q = (5, 10)$ $R = (11, -2)$

The midpoint of these two coordinates is

$\left(\frac{5+11}{2}, \frac{10+-2}{2}\right) = (8, 4)$

The gradient of the line segment that joins these two points is $= \frac{-2 - 10}{11 - 5} = \frac{-12}{6} = -2$

Any line perpendicular to this line has the gradient $-\frac{1}{-2} = \frac{1}{2}$

The perpendicular of the line that joins the two points is found by using:

$y - y_1 = m(x - x_1)$ with $m = \frac{1}{2}$

$x_1 = 8$ and $y_1 = 4$

$y - 4 = \frac{1}{2}(x - 8)$

$2y - 8 = x - 8$

$y = \frac{1}{2}x$

b The point that is equidistant from P, Q and R is the point whether the perpendicular bisectors of the sides meet.

Solve $2x + 3y = 14$ (1)

and $y = \frac{1}{2}x$ (2)

Use (2) to substitute for y in (1)

$2x + 3\left(\frac{1}{2}x\right) = 14$

$\frac{7x}{2} = 14$

$x = 4$

Substitute into (2) gives $y = \frac{1}{2}(4) = 2$

The point is $(4, 2)$

Exercise 6.4

REMEMBER

- It may be helpful to familiarise yourself with the properties of special quadrilaterals for example: rhombus, square, trapezium and parallelogram.
- It may help to draw a diagram when solving a coordinate geometry problems.

1 a $A = (-2, 3) \quad B = (0, -4) \quad C = (5, 6)$

Area of a triangle $ABC = \frac{1}{2}|x_1y_2 + x_2y_3 + x_3y_1 - x_2y_1 - x_3y_2 - x_1y_3|$

$= \frac{1}{2}|(-2)(-4) + (0)(6) + (5)(3) - (0)(3) - (5)(-4) - (-2)(6)|$

$= \frac{1}{2}|8 + 15 + 20 + 12|$

$= 27\frac{1}{2}$ units^2

b $P = (-3, 1) \quad Q = (5, -3) \quad R = (2, 4)$

Area of a triangle $PQR = \frac{1}{2}|x_1y_2 + x_2y_3 + x_3y_1 - x_2y_1 - x_3y_2 - x_1y_3|$

$= \frac{1}{2}|(-3)(-3) + (5)(4) + (2)(1) - (5)(1) - (2)(-3) - (-3)(4)|$

$= \frac{1}{2}|9 + 20 + 2 - 5 + 6 + 12|$

$= 22$ units^2

2 a $A = (1, 8) \quad B = (-4, 5) \quad C = (-2, -3) \quad D = (4, -2)$

Area of a quadrilateral $ABCD = \frac{1}{2}|x_1y_2 + x_2y_3 + x_3y_4 + x_4y_1 - x_2y_1 - x_3y_2 - x_4y_3 - x_1y_4|$

$= \frac{1}{2}|(1)(5) + (-4)(-3) + (-2)(-2) + (4)(8) - (-4)(8) - (-2)(5) - (4)(-3) - (1)(-2)|$

$= 54.5$ units^2

3 a $P = (1, 4) \quad Q = (-3, -4) \quad R = (7, k)$

Gradient of $PQ = \frac{-4 - 4}{-3 - 1} = 2$

Gradient of $QR = \frac{k - -4}{7 - -3} = \frac{k + 4}{10}$

Triangle PQR is right-angles at Q so the gradient $PQ \times$ gradient $QR = -1$

$$2 \times \frac{k + 4}{10} = -1$$

$$k + 4 = -5$$

$$k = -9$$

b Area of triangle $PQR = \frac{1}{2} \times PQ \times QR$

Length of $PQ = \sqrt{(-3 - 1)^2 + (-4 - 4)^2} = \sqrt{80}$

Length of $QR = \sqrt{(7 - -3)^2 + (-9 - -4)^2} = \sqrt{125}$

Area $PQR = \frac{1}{2} \times \sqrt{80} \times \sqrt{125}$

$= 50$ units^2

4 a $A = (-4, 0) \quad B = (2, 3)$

$M = \left(\frac{-4+2}{2}, \frac{0+3}{2}\right)$

$M = (-1, 1.5)$

C is at $[(-1 + 3), (1.5 - 6)]$

$C = (2, -4.5)$

b Gradient of $CM = \frac{1.5 - -4.5}{-1 - 2} = -2$

Gradient of $AB = \frac{3 - 0}{2 - -4} = \frac{3}{6} = \frac{1}{2}$

Gradient of $CM \times$ gradient $AB = -2 \times \frac{1}{2} = -1$

Therefore MC is perpendicular to AB

c Triangle ABC has a 'base' length AB and 'perpendicular height' CM

Area of triangle $ABC = \frac{1}{2} \times CM \times AB$

Length of $CM = \sqrt{(-1 - 2)^2 + (1.5 - -4.5)^2} = \sqrt{45}$

Length of $AB = \sqrt{(2 - -4)^2 + (3 - 0)^2} = \sqrt{45}$

Area triangle $ABC = \frac{1}{2} \times \sqrt{45} \times \sqrt{45}$

$= 22.5$ units^2

5 a As BMA is a straight line and M is the midpoint of BA, the coordinates of $B = (4, 5)$

BA is perpendicular to BC so the gradient of $BA \times$ gradient $BC = -1$

Given $B = (4, 5) \quad A = (8, 3) \quad C = (x, y)$

Gradient of $BA = \frac{3 - 5}{8 - 4} = -\frac{1}{2}$

Gradient of $BC = -\frac{1}{-\frac{1}{2}} = 2$

The equation of BC can be found using:

$y - y_1 = m(x - x_1)$ with $m = 2 \quad x_1 = 4 \quad$ and $y_1 = 5$

$y - 5 = 2(x - 4)$

$y = 2x - 3$

The equation of BC is $y = 2x - 3$

The line BC intercepts the y-axis where $x = 0$ so $y = 2(0) - 3$

$C = (0, -3)$

b Triangle ABC is right-angled at B

Area of triangle $ABC = \frac{1}{2} \times BA \times BC$

Length of $BA = \sqrt{(8-4)^2 + (3-5)^2} = \sqrt{20}$

Length of $BC = \sqrt{(0-4)^2 + (-3-5)^2} = \sqrt{80}$

Area triangle $ABC = \frac{1}{2} \times \sqrt{20} \times \sqrt{80}$

$= 20 \text{ units}^2$

6 a $A = (-4, 5) \quad B = (5, 8)$

Gradient of $AB = \frac{8-5}{5--4} = \frac{3}{9} = \frac{1}{3}$

A line perpendicular to AB that passes through points A and C has gradient$= -\frac{1}{\frac{1}{3}} = -3$

The equation of AC can be found using:

$y - y_1 = m(x - x_1)$ with $m = -3 \quad x_1 = -4$ and $y_1 = 5$

$y - 5 = -3(x - -4)$

$y - 5 = -3x - 12$

The equation of AC is $y = -3x - 7$

The line AC intercepts the y-axis where $x = 0$ so $y = -3(0) - 7$

$C = (0, -7)$

b Triangle ABC is right-angled at A

Area of triangle $ABC = \frac{1}{2} \times AB \times AC$

Length of $AB = \sqrt{(5--4)^2 + (8-5)^2} = \sqrt{90}$

Length of $AC = \sqrt{(0--4)^2 + (-7-5)^2} = \sqrt{160}$

Area triangle $ABC = \frac{1}{2} \times \sqrt{90} \times \sqrt{160}$

$= 60 \text{ units}^2$

7 a $ADBC$ is a trapezium.

Gradient of $AB = \frac{3-1}{9-1} = \frac{2}{8} = \frac{1}{4}$

A line perpendicular to AB that passes through point B has gradient $= -\frac{1}{\frac{1}{4}} = -4$

The equation of BC can be found using:

$y - y_1 = m(x - x_1)$ with $m = -4 \quad x_1 = 9$ and $y_1 = 3$

$y - 3 = -4(x - 9)$

$y - 3 = -4x + 36$

The equation of BC is $y = -4x + 39$ (1)

The equation of DC can be found using:

$y - y_1 = m(x - x_1)$ with $m = \frac{1}{4}$ $x_1 = 3.5$ and $y_1 = 8$

$y - 8 = \frac{1}{4}(x - 3.5)$

$4y - 32 = x - 3.5$

The equation of DC is $4y = x + 28.5$ (2)

The coordinates of C can be found by solving (1) and (2) simultaneously

Multiply equation (1) by 4 and subtract (2)

$4y = -16x + 156$

$4y = x + 28.5$

$0 = -17x + 127.5$

$x = 7.5$

The y-coordinate of C is found by substituting $x = 7.5$ into $4y = x + 28.5$

$4y = 7.5 + 28.5$

$y = 9$

$C = (7.5, 9)$

b The area of a trapezium $= \frac{1}{2}(a + b)h$ where a and b are the lengths of the parallel sides and h is the perpendicular height.

Area $ABCD = \frac{1}{2}(DC + AB) \times BC$

Length of $DC = \sqrt{(7.5 - 3.5)^2 + (9 - 8)^2} = \sqrt{17}$

Length of $AB = \sqrt{(9 - 1)^2 + (3 - 1)^2} = \sqrt{68}$

Length of $BC = \sqrt{(7.5 - 9)^2 + (9 - 3)^2} = \sqrt{38.25}$

Area of $ABCD = \frac{1}{2}(\sqrt{17} + \sqrt{68}) \times \sqrt{38.25}$

Area of $ABCD = 38.25$ units^2

8 a $A = (-2, 0)$ $C = (6, 4)$

M is the midpoint of AC

$M = \left(\frac{-2 + 6}{2}, \frac{0 + 4}{2}\right) = (2, 2)$

AC is perpendicular to BM

So, gradient of $AC = \frac{4 - 0}{6 - -2} = \frac{1}{2}$

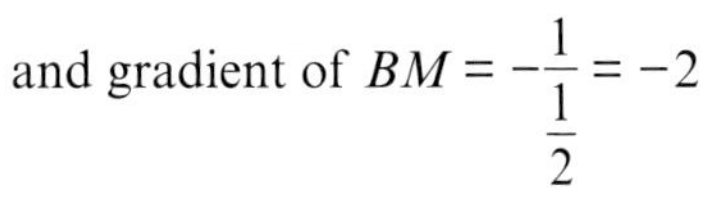

and gradient of $BM = -\frac{1}{\frac{1}{2}} = -2$

also, the gradient of $BM = \frac{2 - y_1}{2 - x_1}$

so $\frac{2 - y_1}{2 - x_1} = -2$

$2 - y_1 = -2(2 - x_1)$

$2 - y_1 = -4 + 2x_1$

$2x_1 + y_1 = 6$ (1)

Angle $ABC = 90°$

Gradient of $BC \times$ gradient $AB = -1$

Gradient $BC = \frac{4 - y_1}{6 - x_1}$

Gradient $AB = \frac{0 - y_1}{-2 - x_1}$

$\frac{4 - y_1}{6 - x_1} \times \frac{0 - y_1}{-2 - x_1} = -1$

$\frac{-y_1(4 - y_1)}{(6 - x_1)(-2 - x_1)} = -1$

$-y_1(4 - y_1) = -1(6 - x_1)(-2 - x_1)$

$-4y_1 + y_1^2 = 12 + 4x_1 - x_1^2$ (2)

Solve (1) and (2) simultaneously

From (1) $y_1 = 6 - 2x_1$

Substitute for y_1 in (2)

$-4(6 - 2x_1) + (6 - 2x_1)^2 = 12 + 4x_1 - x_1^2$

$-24 + 8x_1 + 36 - 24x_1 + 4x_1^2 = 12 + 4x_1 - x_1^2$

$5x_1^2 - 20x_1 = 0$

$5x_1(x_1 - 4) = 0$

$x_1 = 0$ or $x_1 = 4$

If $x_1 = 0$, $y_1 = 6$ and if $x_1 = 4$, $y_1 = -2$

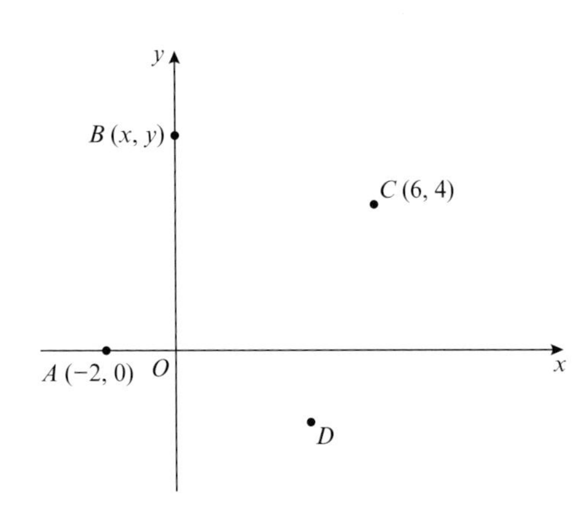

From the diagram, $B = (0, 6)$

The symmetry of the square means that $D = (4, -2)$

b The length of $BC = \sqrt{(6 - 0)^2 + (4 - 6)^2} = \sqrt{40}$

Area of the square $ABCD = \sqrt{40} \times \sqrt{40}$

$= 40$ units^2

9 a $A = (-4, 3)$ $B = (5, -5)$ $C = (15, -1)$

Let the diagonals of the parallelogram bisect each other at M

The midpoint of the diagonal AC is

$\left(\frac{-4 + 15}{2}, \frac{3 + -1}{2}\right) = (5.5, 1)$

b $\overrightarrow{AB} = \begin{pmatrix} 9 \\ -8 \end{pmatrix}$ so $\overrightarrow{CD} = \begin{pmatrix} -9 \\ 8 \end{pmatrix}$

Point D is at $(15 - 9, -1 + 8)$ so $D = (6, 7)$

c The area of the parallelogram can be found using:

Area of a quadrilateral $ABCD = \frac{1}{2}|x_1y_2 + x_2y_3 + x_3y_4 + x_4y_1 - x_2y_1 - x_3y_2 - x_4y_3 - x_1y_4|$

where $A = (-4, 3)$ $B = (5, -5)$ $C = (15, -1)$ $D = (6, 7)$

$= \frac{1}{2}|(-4)(-5) + (5)(-1) + (15)(7) + (6)(3) - (5)(3) - (15)(-5) - (6)(-1) - (-4)(7)|$

$= 116$ units^2

Exercise 6.5

REMEMBER

Use X and Y as the variables in the linear equation to avoid confusion with the original variables x and y in the non-linear equation.

1 c $y = ax^2 - bx$ — divide both sides of the equation by x:

$\frac{y}{x} = ax - b$ — now compare with $Y = mX + c$

The non-linear equation $y = ax^2 - bx$ becomes the linear equation:

$Y = mX + c$ where $Y = \frac{y}{x}$ $\quad X = x \quad m = a \quad c = -b$

h $\frac{1}{y} = a\sqrt{x} - \frac{b}{\sqrt{x}}$ — multiply both sides by $\sqrt{x}$

$\frac{\sqrt{x}}{y} = ax - b$ — now compare with $Y = mX + c$

The non-linear equation $\frac{1}{y} = a\sqrt{x} - \frac{b}{\sqrt{x}}$ becomes the linear equation:

$\frac{\sqrt{x}}{y} = ax - b$ where $Y = \frac{\sqrt{x}}{y}$ $\quad X = x \quad m = a \quad c = -b$

2 e $x^a y^b = e^2$ — take natural logarithms of both sides

$\ln(x^a y^b) = \ln e^2$ — use the multiplication law

$\ln x^a + \ln y^b = \ln e^2$ — use the power law

$a \ln x + b \ln y = 2 \ln e$ — divide both sides by b

$\frac{a}{b}\ln x + \ln y = \frac{2}{b}$ — rearrange

$\ln y = -\frac{a}{b}\ln x + \frac{2}{b}$ — now compare with $Y = mX + c$

The non-linear equation $x^a y^b = e^2$ becomes the linear equation:

$\ln y = -\frac{a}{b}\ln x + \frac{2}{b}$ where $Y = \ln y$ $\quad X = \ln x \quad m = -\frac{a}{b} \quad c = \frac{2}{b}$

TIP

You can take logs of any base in these questions as long as you are consistent.

f $xa^y = b$ take $\log_{10}$ of both sides

$\lg(xa^y) = \lg b$ use the multiplication law

$\lg x + \lg a^y = \lg b$ use the power law

$\lg x + y\lg a = \lg b$ rearrange

$\lg x = -y\lg a + \lg b$ now compare with $Y = mX + c$

The non-linear equation $xa^y = b$ becomes the linear equation:

$\lg x = -y\lg a + \lg b$ where $Y = \lg x$ $X = y$ $m = -\lg a$ $c = \lg b$

Exercise 6.6

TIP

To convert a non-linear equation involving x and y into a linear equation, express the equation in the form $Y = mX + c$ where X and Y are expressions in x and/or y.

1 c The linear equation is $Y = mX + c$, where $Y = y$ and $X = \sqrt{x}$

Gradient $m = \frac{6-3}{5-2} = 1$

Using $Y = mX + c, m = 1, X = 2, Y = 3$

$3 = 1 \times 2 + c$

$c = 1$

Hence $Y = X + 1$

The non-linear equation is $y = \sqrt{x} + 1$

f The linear equation is $Y = mX + c$, where $Y = y$ and $X = \ln x$

Gradient $m = \frac{-2-3}{7-3} = -\frac{5}{4}$

Using $Y = mX + c, m = -\frac{5}{4}, X = 3, Y = 3$

$3 = -\frac{5}{4} \times 3 + c$

$c = \frac{27}{4}$

Hence $Y = -\frac{5}{4}X + \frac{27}{4}$

The non-linear equation is $y = -\frac{5}{4}\ln x + \frac{27}{4}$

2 a i The linear equation is $Y = mX + c$, where $Y = \frac{1}{y}$ and $X = x^2$

Gradient $m = \frac{6-2}{5-1} = 1$

Using $Y = mX + c$, $m = 1$, $X = 1$, $Y = 2$

$2 = 1 \times 1 + c$

$c = 1$

Hence $Y = X + 1$

The non-linear equation is $\frac{1}{y} = x^2 + 1$ rearrange

$1 = y(x^2 + 1)$ divide both sides by $x^2 + 1$

$y = \frac{1}{x^2 + 1}$

ii When $x = 2$, $y = \frac{1}{2^2 + 1}$

$y = \frac{1}{5}$

e i The linear equation is $Y = mX + c$, where $Y = x + y$ and $X = x^2$

Gradient $m = \frac{8 - -2}{10 - 2} = \frac{5}{4}$

Using $Y = mX + c$, $m = \frac{5}{4}$, $X = 10$, $Y = 8$

$8 = \frac{5}{4} \times 10 + c$

$c = -\frac{9}{2}$

Hence $Y = \frac{5}{4} X - \frac{9}{2}$

The non-linear equation is $x + y = \frac{5}{4}x^2 - \frac{9}{2}$

$y = \frac{5}{4}x^2 - x - \frac{9}{2}$

ii when $x = 2$, $y = \frac{5}{4} \times 2^2 - 2 - \frac{9}{2}$

$y = -\frac{3}{2}$

3 The linear equation is $Y = mX + c$, where $Y = \frac{y}{x^2}$ and $X = x^3$

Gradient $m = \frac{12 - 4}{2 - 6} = -2$

Using $Y = mX + c$, $m = -2$, $X = 2$, $Y = 12$

$12 = -2 \times 2 + c$

$c = 16$

Hence $Y = -2X + 16$

The non-linear equation is $\frac{y}{x^2} = -2x^3 + 16$ multiply both sides by x^2

$y = -2x^5 + 16x^2$

4 **a** The linear equation is $Y = mX + c$, where $Y = y^2$ and $X = 2^x$

Gradient $m = 3$

Using $Y = mX + c$, $m = 3$, $X = 8$, $Y = 49$

$49 = 3 \times 8 + c$

$c = 25$

Hence $Y = 3X + 25$

The non-linear equation is $y^2 = 3 \times 2^x + 25$

$y^2 = 3(2^x) + 25$

b When $y = 11$, $11^2 = 3 \times 2^x + 25$

$2^x = 32$

$x = 5$

5 **a** The linear equation is $Y = mX + c$, where $Y = \frac{y}{x}$ and $X = x$

Gradient $m = \frac{-2 - 4}{5 - 2} = -2$

Using $Y = mX + c$, $m = -2$, $X = 2$, $Y = 4$

$4 = -2 \times 2 + c$

$c = 8$

Hence $Y = -2X + 8$

The non-linear equation is $\frac{y}{x} = -2x + 8$ multiply both sides by x

$y = -2x^2 + 8x$

b If $\frac{y}{x} = 3$, then $y = 3x$

Substituting into $y = -2x^2 + 8x$ gives:

$3x = -2x^2 + 8x$ rearrange

$2x^2 - 5x = 0$ factorise

$x(2x - 5) = 0$

$x = 0$ and $x = 2.5$ reject $x = 0$ because $\frac{y}{0}$ is undefined

So $x = 2.5$, $y = 7.5$

6 a The linear equation is $Y = mX + c$, where $Y = e^y$ and $X = x^2$

Gradient $m = \frac{9 - 4}{8 - 3} = 1$

Using $Y = mX + c$, $m = 1$, $X = 3$, $Y = 4$

$4 = 1 \times 3 + c$

$c = 1$

Hence $Y = X + 1$

The non-linear equation is $e^y = x^2 + 1$

b $e^y = x^2 + 1$ take natural logarithms of both sides

$\ln e^y = \ln(x^2 + 1)$

$y = \ln(x^2 + 1)$

7 a The linear equation is $Y = mX + c$, where $Y = \lg y$ and $X = x$

Gradient $m = \frac{8 - 2}{10 - 6} = \frac{3}{2}$

Using $Y = mX + c$, $m = \frac{3}{2}$, $X = 6$, $Y = 2$

$2 = \frac{3}{2} \times 6 + c$

$c = -7$

Hence $Y = \frac{3}{2}X - 7$

The non-linear equation is $\lg y = \frac{3}{2}x - 7$

b $y = 10^{\left(\frac{3}{2}x - 7\right)}$

$y = 10^{\frac{3}{2}x} \times 10^{-7}$

$y = 10^{-7} \times 10^{\frac{3}{2}x}$

8 a The linear equation is $Y = mX + c$, where $Y = \lg y$ and $X = \lg x$

Gradient $m = \frac{14 - 8}{8 - 4} = \frac{3}{2}$

Using $Y = mX + c$, $m = \frac{3}{2}$, $X = 4$, $Y = 8$

$8 = \frac{3}{2} \times 4 + c$

$c = 2$

Hence $Y = \frac{3}{2}X + 2$

The non-linear equation is

$\lg y = \frac{3}{2}\lg x + 2$

$\lg y = \frac{3}{2}\lg x + 2$ rearrange

$\lg y - \frac{3}{2}\lg x = 2$ use the power law

$\lg y - \lg x^{\frac{3}{2}} = 2$ use the division law

$\lg\left(\frac{y}{x^{\frac{3}{2}}}\right) = 2$

$10^2 = \frac{y}{x^{\frac{3}{2}}}$

$y = 100x^{\frac{3}{2}}$

b $y = 100x^{\frac{3}{2}}$

$51.2 = 100x^{\frac{3}{2}}$

$0.512 = x^{\frac{3}{2}}$

$x^3 = (0.512)^2 = 0.262144$

$x = \sqrt[3]{0.262144} = 0.64$

9 a The linear equation is $Y = mX + c$, where $Y = \ln y$ and $X = \ln x$

Gradient $m = \frac{11 - 2}{4 - 1} = 3$

Using $Y = mX + c$, $m = 3$, $X = 1$, $Y = 2$

$2 = 3 \times 1 + c$

$c = -1$

Hence $Y = 3X - 1$

The non-linear equation is $\ln y = 3\ln x - 1$

b $\ln y = 3\ln x - 1$ use the power law

$\ln y = \ln x^3 - 1$ rearrange

$\ln y - \ln x^3 = -1$ use the division law

$\ln\left(\frac{y}{x^3}\right) = -1$

$e^{-1} = \frac{y}{x^3}$

$y = x^3 \times e^{-1}$

$y = \frac{x^3}{e}$

10 a The linear equation is $Y = mX + c$, where $Y = \ln y$ and $X = \ln x$

Gradient $m = \frac{5.3 - 7.7}{3.7 - 2.5} = -2$

Using $Y = mX + c$, $m = -2$, $X = 2.5$, $Y = 7.7$

$7.7 = -2 \times 2.5 + c$

$c = 12.7$

Hence $Y = -2X + 12.7$

The non-linear equation is $\ln y = -2\ln x + 12.7$

When $\ln x = 0$, then $\ln y = 12.7$

b $\ln y = -2\ln x + 12.7$ use the power law

$\ln y = \ln x^{-2} + 12.7$ rearrange

$\ln y - \ln x^{-2} = 12.7$ use the division law

$\ln\left(\frac{y}{x^{-2}}\right) = 12.7$

$\ln(yx^2) = 12.7$

$e^{12.7} = yx^2$ multiply both sides by x^{-2}

$e^{12.7} \times x^{-2} = y$

$y = e^{12.7} \times x^{-2}$ compare with $y = a \times x^b$

$a = e^{12.7}$, $b = -2$

Exercise 6.7

3 a Complete the table for the values, using a calculator to find the values of xy and x^2

x	1	2	3	4	5
y	12.8	7.6	6.4	6.2	6.4
xy	12.8	15.2	19.2	24.8	32
x^2	1	4	9	16	25

Plot the graph of xy against x^2 and join the points with a ruler.

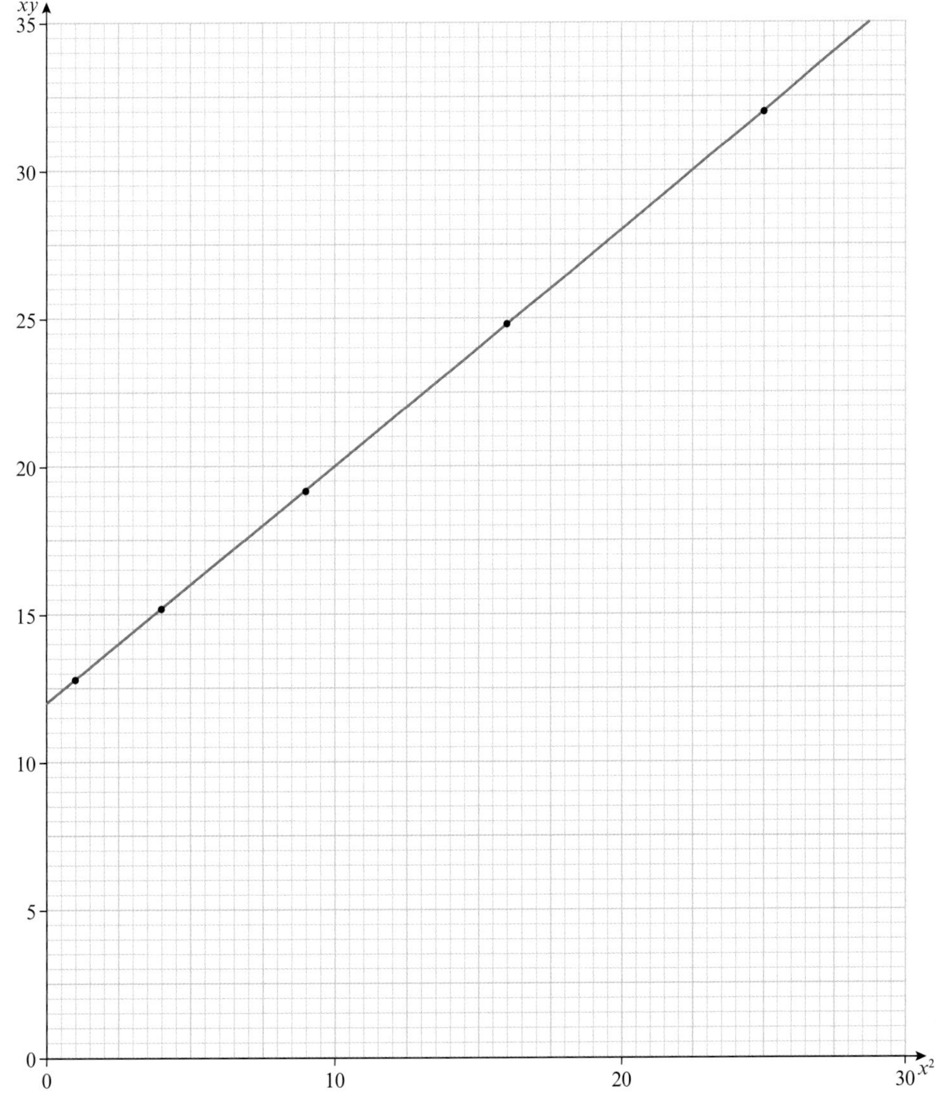

b Gradient of the graph$= \dfrac{32 - 19.2}{25 - 9} = 0.8$ and reading off the graph we can see that the y-intercept is 12.

A straight line has equation $Y = mX + c$ where m is the gradient and c is the y-intercept.

So, $xy = 0.8x^2 + 12$

Divide both sides by x gives: $y = 0.8x + \dfrac{12}{x}$

c Substitute $xy = 12.288$ into $xy = 0.8x^2 + 12$

$12.288 = 0.8x^2 + 12$

$0.8x^2 = 0.288$

$x^2 = 0.36$

$x = 0.6$ and $x = -0.6$

If $x = 0.6$ then substituting into $y = 0.8x + \frac{12}{x}$ gives $y = 0.8 \times 0.6 + \frac{12}{0.6}$ so $y = 20.48$

If $x = -0.6$ then substituting into $y = 0.8x + \frac{12}{x}$ gives $y = 0.8 \times -0.6 + \frac{12}{-0.6}$ so $y = -20.48$

8 a

x	2	4	6	8	10
y	30.0	44.7	66.7	99.5	148.4
$\ln y$	3.40	3.80	4.20	4.60	5.00

Plot the graph of $\ln y$ against x and join the points with a ruler.

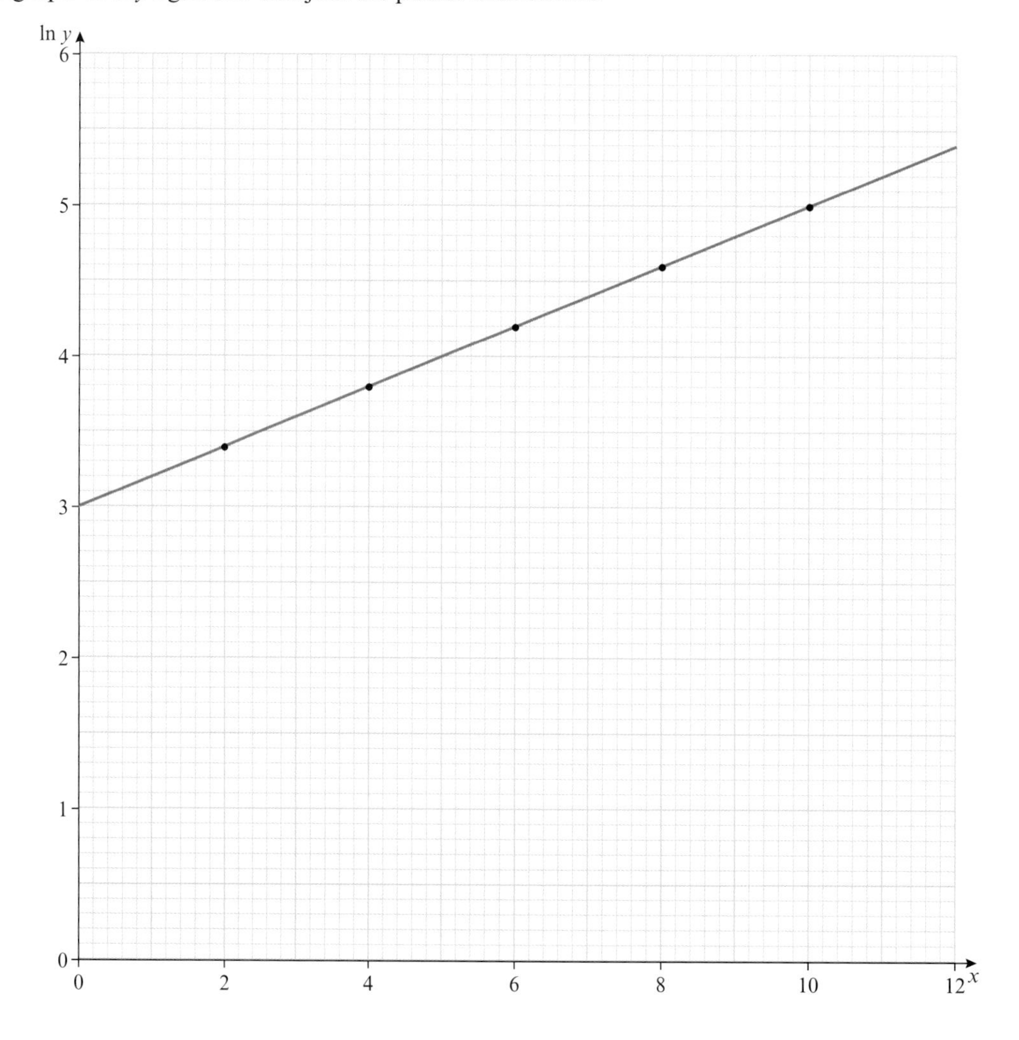

b Gradient of the graph= $\frac{5.0 - 3.8}{10 - 4} = 0.2$ and reading off the graph we can see that the y-intercept is 3.0.

A straight line has equation $Y = mX + c$ where m is the gradient and c is the y-intercept.

So, $\ln y = 0.2x + 3$ (1)

The variables are related by the equation:

$y = e^{ax+b}$ take natural logarithms of both sides

$\ln y = \ln e^{ax+b}$ use the power rule for logarithms

$\ln y = (ax + b)\ln e$

$\ln y = ax + b$ comparing this equation with (1) gives:

$\ln y = 0.2x + 3$

So, $a = 0.2$ and $b = 3$

c When $y = 50$, then substituting into $\ln y = 0.2x + 3$ gives:

$\ln 50 = 0.2x + 3$

$0.2x = \ln 50 - 3$

$x = 4.56$ to 3 significant figures.

Chapter 7: Coordinate geometry of the circle

Exercise 7.1

REMEMBER

The equation of a circle with centre (a, b) and radius r can be written in **completed square form** as:

$(x - a)^2 + (y - b)^2 = r^2$

The expanded form of a circle is $x^2 + y^2 + 2gx + 2fy + c = 0$ where $(-g, -f)$ is the centre and $\sqrt{g^2 + f^2 - c}$ is the radius. This is the equation of a circle written in expanded **general form**.

1 f $(x - 5)^2 + y^2 = 9$

Centre (5, 0), radius $= \sqrt{9} = 3$

j $(x + 3)^2 + (y + 4)^2 = 27$

Centre $(-3, -4)$, radius$= \sqrt{27} = 3\sqrt{3}$

2 b The equation of a circle is $(x - a)^2 + (y - b)^2 = r^2$

Centre $(3, -1)$, radius = 6

$(x - 3)^2 + (y - -1)^2 = 6^2$

$(x - 3)^2 + (y + 1)^2 = 36$

c Centre $(2, -5)$, radius $= 2\sqrt{5}$

$(x - 2)^2 + (y - -5)^2 = (2\sqrt{5})^2$

$(x - 2)^2 + (y + 5)^2 = 20$

3 b $x^2 + y^2 + 14x - 8y + 40 = 0$ is of the form $x^2 + y^2 + 2gx + 2fy + c = 0$

$2g = 14, 2f = -8$

$g = 7, f = -4, c = 40$

Centre $(-7, 4)$, radius $= \sqrt{7^2 + (-4)^2 - 40} = 5$

e $4x^2 + 4y^2 - 4x - 16y + 1 = 0$ divide by 4

$x^2 + y^2 - x - 4y + \frac{1}{4} = 0$ is of the form $x^2 + y^2 + 2gx + 2fy + c = 0$

$2g = -1, 2f = -4$

$g = -\frac{1}{2}, f = -2, c = \frac{1}{4}$

centre $\left(\frac{1}{2}, 2\right)$, radius $= \sqrt{\left(-\frac{1}{2}\right)^2 + (-2)^2 - \frac{1}{4}} = 2$

REMEMBER

If a triangle ABC is right-angled at B, then the points A, B and C lie on the circumference of a circle with AC as diameter.

The perpendicular bisector of a chord passes through the centre of the circle.

If a radius and a line at a point P on the circumference are at right angles, then the line must be a tangent to the curve.

4 A circle centre (3, 2) has an equation $(x - 3)^2 + (y - 2)^2 = r^2$

If the point (7, 5) lies on the circle, then substituting $x = 7$ and $y = 5$ into the equation gives: $(7 - 3)^2 + (5 - 2)^2 = r^2$

$16 + 9 = r^2$

$r = \sqrt{25}$

The equation of the circle is $(x - 3)^2 + (y - 2)^2 = 25$

5 Diameter AB where $A = (5, -3)$ $B = (15, 5)$

The centre of the circle O, is the midpoint of $AB = \left(\frac{5 + 15}{2}, \frac{-3 + 5}{2}\right) = (10, 1)$

The radius of the circle is OA or OB.

Using the distance formula, point $O = (10, 1)$ and $A = (5, -3)$,

The radius $OA = \sqrt{(-3 - 1)^2 + (5 - 10)^2} = \sqrt{41}$

The equation of the circle is $(x - 10)^2 + (y - 1)^2 = 41$

6 $(x - 4)^2 + (y - 5)^2 = 16$

The centre of the circle is (4, 5) and radius $= \sqrt{16} = 4$

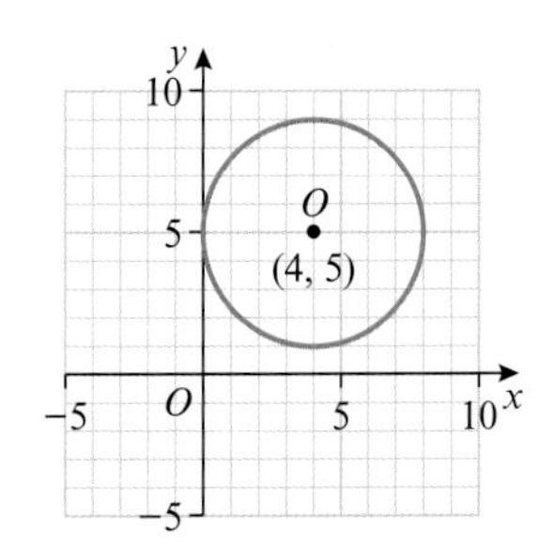

7 If the centre of the circle is $(-3, 2)$ and it touches the y-axis the radius of the circle is 3.

So, the equation of the circle is

$(x - -3)^2 + (y - 2)^2 = 3^2$

$(x + 3)^2 + (y - 2)^2 = 9$

8 $x^2 + y^2 + 8x - 14y = 10$ rearrange

$x^2 + 8x + y^2 - 14y = 10$ complete the squares

$(x + 4)^2 - 4^2 + (y - 7)^2 - 7^2 = 10$

$(x + 4)^2 + (y - 7)^2 = 75$

Centre $(-4, 7)$ radius $= \sqrt{75} = 5\sqrt{3}$

9 $A = (-9, -1) \quad B = (3, -5)$

The midpoint M of $AB = \left(\frac{-9+3}{2}, \frac{-1+-5}{2}\right)$

$M = (-3, -3)$

The gradient of the line segment that passes through $(-9, -1)$ and $(3, -5)$ is $\frac{-5 - -1}{3 - -9} = \frac{-4}{12} = -\frac{1}{3}$

The gradient of the perpendicular bisector of $(-9, -1)$ and $(3, -5)$ is $\frac{-1}{-\frac{1}{3}} = 3$

The equation of the perpendicular bisector that passes through $M = (-3, -3)$ is:

$y - -3 = 3(x - -3)$

$y + 3 = 3x + 9$

$y = 3x + 6$

This perpendicular bisector passes through the centre of the circle.

So, the centre of the circle lies on the line $y = 3x + 6$

10 First find the centre of the circle whose equation is:

$x^2 + y^2 - 4x + 8y - 40 = 0$ rearrange

$x^2 - 4x + y^2 + 8y - 40 = 0$ complete the squares

$(x - 2)^2 - 2^2 + (y + 4)^2 - 4^2 - 40 = 0$

$(x - 2)^2 + (y + 4)^2 = 60$

Its centre is at $(2, -4)$

So, the circle we require has the same centre $(2, -4)$

Its equation is $(x - 2)^2 + (y + 4)^2 = r^2$

As $(5, -2)$ lies on this circle, then substituting $x = 5$ and $y = -2$ will give its radius.

$(5 - 2)^2 + (-2 + 4)^2 = r^2$

$r^2 = 13$

So, $(x - 2)^2 + (y + 4)^2 = 13$

11 $P = (-2, 0) \quad Q = (3, 5) \quad R = (6, 2)$

If PR is a diameter to the circle, angle $PQR = 90°$ (angle in a semi-circle is 90°)

Gradient $PQ = \frac{5 - 0}{3 - -2} = 1$

Gradient $QR = \frac{2 - 5}{6 - 3} = -1$

Gradient $PQ \times$ gradient $QR = 1 \times -1 = -1$

PQ is perpendicular to QR and angle $PQR = 90°$

PR is the diameter of the circle.

The centre of the circle is at M, the midpoint of PR

$M = \left(\frac{-2+6}{2}, \frac{0+2}{2}\right) = (2, 1)$

Using the distance formula, the radius of the circle $MR = \sqrt{(6-2)^2 + (2-1)^2} = \sqrt{17}$

The equation of the circle is $(x - 2)^2 + (y - 1)^2 = 17$

12 The midpoint of $(-1, -4)$ and $(3, 2)$ is $\left(\frac{-1+3}{2}, \frac{-4+2}{2}\right) = (1, -1)$

The gradient of the line segment that passes through $(-1, -4)$ and $(3, 2)$ is $\frac{2 - -4}{3 - -1} = \frac{3}{2}$

The gradient of the perpendicular bisector of $(-1, -4)$ and $(3, 2)$ is $\frac{-1}{\frac{3}{2}} = -\frac{2}{3}$

The equation of the perpendicular bisector that passes through $(1, -1)$ is:

$$y - -1 = -\frac{2}{3}(x - 1)$$

$$3y + 3 = -2x + 2$$

$$3y + 2x = -1$$

This line passes through the centre of the circle (a, b) so $3b + 2a = -1$ (1)

The radius of the circle is $\sqrt{26}$ and this equals the distance between (a, b) and $(3, 2)$

Using the distance formula:

$$\sqrt{26} = \sqrt{(3 - a)^2 + (2 - b)^2}$$

So $(3 - a)^2 + (2 - b)^2 = 26$ (2)

Solve (1) and (2) simultaneously.

$3b + 2a = -1$ (1) rearrange

$$a = \frac{-1 - 3b}{2}$$

Substitute into (2) gives:

$$\left(3 - \left(\frac{-1 - 3b}{2}\right)\right)^2 + (2 - b)^2 = 26$$

$$\left(3 + \frac{1 + 3b}{2}\right)\left(3 + \frac{1 + 3b}{2}\right) + 4 - 4b + b^2 = 26$$

$$9 + 3 + 9b + \frac{(1 + 6b + 9b^2)}{4} + 4 - 4b + b^2 = 26$$

$$13b^2 + 26b - 39 = 0$$

$$b^2 + 2b - 3 = 0$$

$$(b + 3)(b - 1) = 0$$

$b = -3$ and 1 so $a = 4$ and -2

Centre of circle is either $(4, -3)$ or $(-2, 1)$

Equation of the circles are:

$$(x - 4)^2 + (y - -3)^2 = 26$$

$$(x - -2)^2 + (y - 1)^2 = 26$$

The two possible equations are $(x - 4)^2 + (y + 3)^2 = 26$ and $(x + 2)^2 + (y - 1)^2 = 26$

13 The centre of the circle is (a, b), its radius is 5 and $(2, -6)$ lies on the circle.

However, as the y-axis is a tangent to the circle, the centre of the circle could be at $(5, b)$ or $(-5, b)$.

If the circle centre is at $(5, b)$, then the distance between $(5, b)$ and $(2, -6)$ is found using the distance formula:

$$\sqrt{(-6 - b)^2 + (2 - 5)^2} = 5$$

$$(-6 - b)^2 + 9 = 25$$

$$(-6 - b)^2 = 16$$

$-6 - b = +4$ so $b = -10$ or $-6 - b = -4$ so $b = -2$

If the circle centre is at $(-5, b)$, then the distance between $(-5, b)$ and $(2, -6)$ is found

using the distance formula:

$$\sqrt{(-6 - b)^2 + (2 - -5)^2} = 5$$

$$(-6 - b)^2 + 49 = 25$$

$$(-6 - b)^2 = -24$$

There are no solutions to this equation.

So, the centre of the circle could be $(5, -10)$ or $(5, -2)$

Substituting each coordinate into $(x - a)^2 + (y - b)^2 = r^2$ gives the two possible circle

equations: $(x - 5)^2 + (y + 10)^2 = 25$ and $(x - 5)^2 + (y + 2)^2 = 25$

14 If the point $P = (8, 2)$ lies on the circle, then substituting $x = 8$ and $y = 2$ into the left hand side of the equation should give the value 41

$$(x - 4)^2 + (y + 3)^2 = 41$$

$$(8 - 4)^2 + (2 + 3)^2 = 16 + 25 = 41$$

So P does lie on the circle.

The centre of the circle is $(4, -3)$

The gradient of the line that joins $(4, -3)$ and $(8, 2) = \frac{2 - -3}{8 - 4} = \frac{5}{4}$

A radius and a tangent intersect at 90° so the gradient of the tangent at P is $= -\frac{1}{\frac{5}{4}} = -\frac{4}{5}$

The equation of the tangent is found by using:

$y - y_1 = m(x - x_1)$ where $m = -\frac{4}{5}$ $x = 8$ $y = 2$

$$y - 2 = -\frac{4}{5}(x - 8)$$

$$5y - 10 = -4x + 32$$

$$4x + 5y = 42$$

15 The midpoint of (7, 4) and (0, 5) is

$\left(\frac{7+0}{2}, \frac{4+5}{2}\right) = (3.5, 4.5)$

The gradient of the line segment that passes through (7, 4) and (0, 5) is $\frac{5-4}{0-7} = -\frac{1}{7}$

The gradient of the perpendicular bisector of (7, 4) and (0, 5) is $-\frac{1}{-\frac{1}{7}} = 7$

The equation of the perpendicular bisector that passes through (3.5, 4.5) is:

$y - 4.5 = 7(x - 3.5)$

$2y - 9 = 14x - 49$

$14x - 2y = 40 \quad (1)$

This line passes through the centre of the circle.

The line $x + 2y = 5$ (2) also passes through the centre of the circle.

Solve (1) and (2) simultaneously to find the centre of the circle

Adding (1) and (2) gives: $15x = 45$ so $x = 3$

Substituting into (2) gives $y = 1$

The centre of the circle is (3, 1)

To find the radius of the circle, find the distance between the centre (3, 1) and (0, 5)

Using the distance formula: the radius of the circle $= \sqrt{(5-1)^2 + (0-3)^2} = 5$

The circle has equation $(x-3)^2 + (y-1)^2 = 25$

16 a $A = (-1, -4) \quad B = (10, 7) \quad C = (13, 4)$

The gradient of the line joining AB is

$\frac{7 - -4}{10 - -1} = 1$

The gradient of the line joining BC is $\frac{4-7}{13-10} = -1$

The gradient of AB × gradient $BC = 1 \times -1 = -1$ so AB is perpendicular to BC and angle $ABC = 90°$

b AC must be the diameter of the circle (angle in a semi-circle is a right angle)

The midpoint of AC is

$\left(\frac{-1+13}{2}, \frac{-4+4}{2}\right) = (6, 0)$

So, the centre of the circle is (6, 0)

The diameter of the circle can be found using the distance formula:

$AC = \sqrt{(13 - -1)^2 + (4 - -4)^2} = \sqrt{260} = 2\sqrt{65}$

The radius of the circle is $\frac{2\sqrt{65}}{2} = \sqrt{65}$

The equation of the circle is
$(x-a)^2 + (y-b)^2 = r^2$
where $a = 6 \quad b = 0 \quad r = \sqrt{65}$

$(x-6)^2 + y^2 = 65$

17 b Let $A = (0, 5) \quad B = (5, 0) \quad C = (0, -7)$

The midpoint of $AB = \left(\frac{0+5}{2}, \frac{5+0}{2}\right) = (2.5, 2.5)$

The gradient of the line segment that passes through (0, 5) and (5, 0) is $\frac{0-5}{5-0} = -1$

The gradient of the perpendicular bisector of (0, 5) and (5, 0) is $\frac{-1}{-1} = 1$

The equation of the perpendicular bisector that passes through (2.5, 2.5) is:

$y - 2.5 = 1(x - 2.5)$

$y - 2.5 = x - 2.5$

$y = x \quad (1)$

The midpoint of $BC = \left(\frac{5+0}{2}, \frac{0+-7}{2}\right)$

$= (2.5, -3.5)$

The gradient of the line segment that passes through (5, 0) and (0, −7) is $\frac{-7-0}{0-5} = \frac{7}{5}$

The gradient of the perpendicular bisector of (5, 0) and (0, − 7) is $\frac{-1}{\frac{7}{5}} = -\frac{5}{7}$

The equation of the perpendicular bisector that passes through (2.5, −3.5) is:

$y - -3.5 = -\frac{5}{7}(x - 2.5)$

$7y + 24.5 = -5x + 12.5$

$7y + 5x + 12 = 0$ (2)

These two perpendicular bisectors, intersect at the centre of the circle.

Solving (1) and (2) simultaneously by substituting $y = x$ into (2) gives:

$7x + 5x + 12 = 0$

$x = -1$

Substituting into (1) gives: $y = -1$

The centre of the circle is (−1, −1)

The radius of the circle can be found by using the distance formula and the points $A = (0, 5)$ and the centre (−1, −1)

So, radius$= \sqrt{(-1-0)^2 + (-1-5)^2} = \sqrt{37}$

The equation of the circle is
$(x - a)^2 + (y - b)^2 = r^2$
where $a = -1 \quad b = -1 \quad r = \sqrt{37}$

so $(x - -1)^2 + (y - -1)^2 = 37$

or $(x + 1)^2 + (y + 1)^2 = 37$

c Let $A = (0, 0) \quad B = (4, 2) \quad C = (4, 8)$

The midpoint of $AB = \left(\frac{0+4}{2}, \frac{0+2}{2}\right) = (2, 1)$

The gradient of the line segment that passes through (0, 0) and (4, 2) is $\frac{2-0}{4-0} = \frac{1}{2}$

The gradient of the perpendicular bisector of (0, 0) and (4, 2) is $\frac{-1}{\frac{1}{2}} = -2$

The equation of the perpendicular bisector that passes through (2, 1) is:

$y - 1 = -2(x - 2)$

$y - 1 = -2x + 4$

$y + 2x = 5$ (1)

The midpoint of $BC = \left(\frac{4+4}{2}, \frac{2+8}{2}\right) = (4, 5)$

So the equation of the perpendicular bisector that passes through (4, 5) is:

$y = 5$ (2)

These two perpendicular bisectors, intersect at the centre of the circle.

Solve (1) and (2) simultaneously by substituting for y in (1)

$5 + 2x = 5$

$x = 0$

The centre of the circle is (0, 5)

The radius of the circle is the distance between the points $A = (0, 0)$ and the centre (0, 5)

So, radius = 5

The equation of the circle is
$(x - a)^2 + (y - b)^2 = r^2$ where $a = 0 \quad b = 5 \quad r = 5$

$(x - 0)^2 + (y - 5)^2 = 25$

So $x^2 + (y - 5)^2 = 25$

19 a Join the centres A, B, C, D of the red circles and the diagonals AC and BD.

Let the diagonals intersect at M.

$AD = DC = 2$ units

Using Pythagoras, $AC^2 = AD^2 + CD^2$

$AC^2 = 2^2 + 2^2$

$AC = \sqrt{8}$ or $2\sqrt{2}$ units

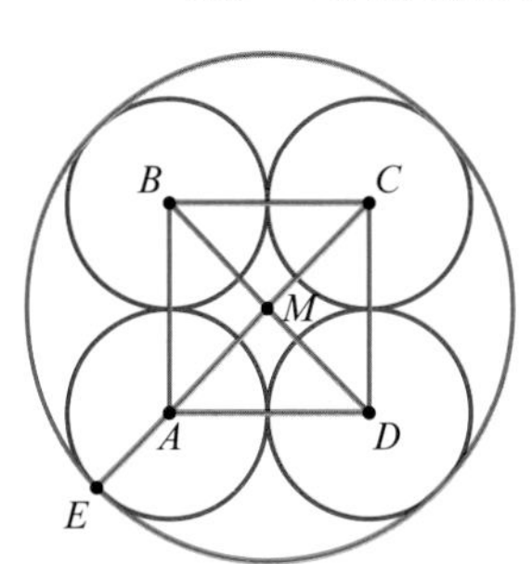

$AM = \frac{1}{2}AC = \sqrt{2}$

Extend CA to E

The radius of the blue circle
$= AM + AE = \sqrt{2} + 1$ units

b Open graphing software such as Desmos and enter the equations of the 5 circles to create an image as shown.

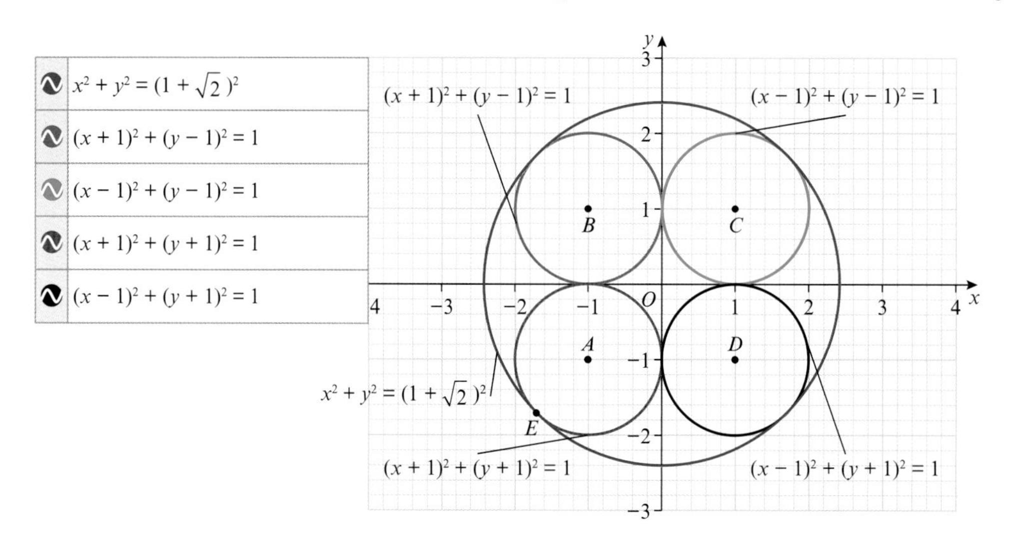

20 Join the centres of the circles A, E and C.

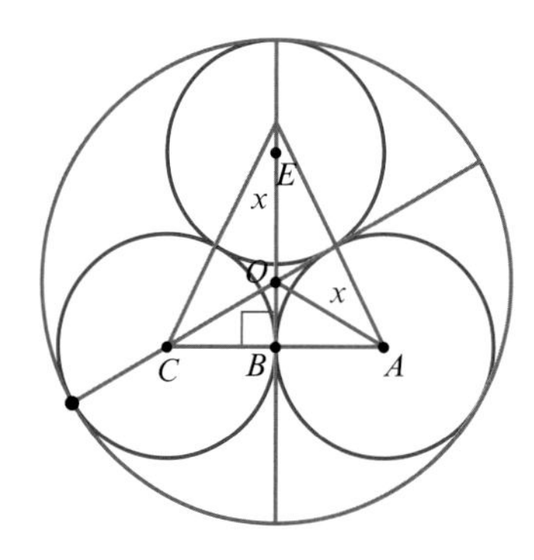

Triangle AEC is equilateral.

The perpendicular bisectors of the sides of the triangle, when extended, meet at the centre of the blue circle, i.e, at O.

Circles with centres A and C touch each other at B.

In triangle EAB, angle $EBA = 90°$, $EA = 2$, $AB = 1$

Using Pythagoras $EA^2 = EB^2 + AB^2$

$$2^2 = EB^2 + 1^2$$

$$EB = \sqrt{3}$$

Let $EO = OA = x$

Using triangle OAE and the fact that $OB = EB - EO$

$OB = \sqrt{3} - x$

Using Pythagoras on triangle OAB:

$OA^2 = AB^2 + OB^2$

$x^2 = 1^2 + (\sqrt{3} - x)^2$

$x^2 = 1^2 + 3 - 2\sqrt{3}x + x^2$ simplify

$2\sqrt{3}x = 4$

$x = \frac{2\sqrt{3}}{3}$

Radius of the large circle $1 + \frac{2\sqrt{3}}{3}$

So, looking at the diagram:

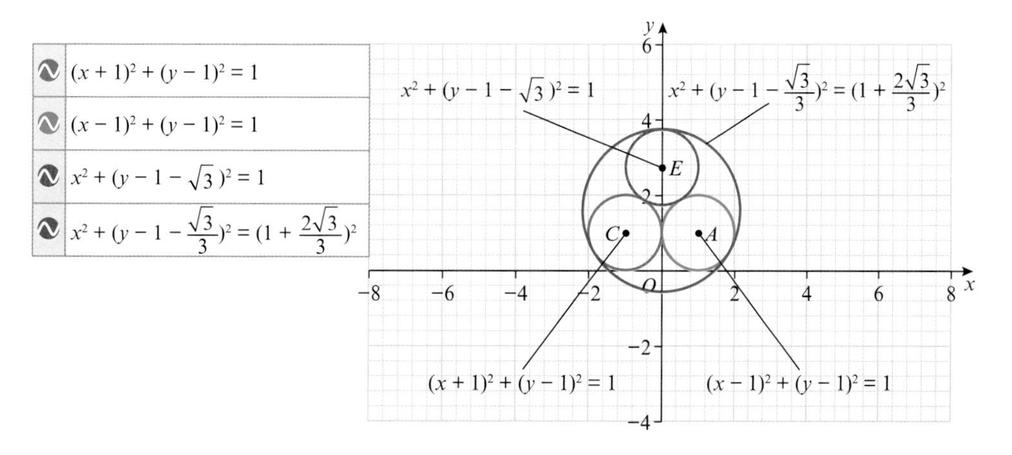

21 a **Method 1**

$A = (-4, -2)$ $B = (-2, 2)$ $C = (5, 1)$

The midpoint of $AB = \left(\frac{-4 + -2}{2}, \frac{-2 + 2}{2}\right) = (-3, 0)$

The gradient of the line segment that passes through $(-4, -2)$ and $(-2, 2)$ is $\frac{2 - -2}{-2 - -4} = 2$

The gradient of the perpendicular bisector of $(-4, -2)$ and $(-2, 2)$ is $\frac{-1}{2} = -\frac{1}{2}$

The equation of the perpendicular bisector that passes through $(-3, 0)$ is:

$y - 0 = -\frac{1}{2}(x - -3)$

$y = -\frac{1}{2}x - 1.5$

$y = -0.5x - 1.5$ (1)

The midpoint of $BC = \left(\frac{-2 + 5}{2}, \frac{2 + 1}{2}\right) = (1.5, 1.5)$

The gradient of the line segment that passes through $(-2, 2)$ and $(5, 1)$ is $\frac{1 - 2}{5 - -2} = -\frac{1}{7}$

The gradient of the perpendicular bisector of $(-2, 2)$ and $(5, 1)$ is $\dfrac{-1}{-\frac{1}{7}} = 7$

The equation of the perpendicular bisector that passes through $(1.5, 1.5)$ is:

$y - 1.5 = 7(x - 1.5)$

$y - 1.5 = 7x - 10.5$

$y = 7x - 9 \qquad (2)$

These two perpendicular bisectors, intersect at the centre of the circle.

Solving (1) and (2) simultaneously by substituting $y = -0.5x - 1.5$ into (2) gives:

$-0.5x - 1.5x = 7x - 9$

$x = 1$

Substituting into (2) gives: $y = -2$

The centre of the circle is $(1, -2)$

The radius of the circle can be found by using the distance formula and the points $A = (-4, -2)$ and the centre $(1, -2)$

So, radius $= \sqrt{(-2 - -2)^2 + (-4 - 1)^2} = 5$

The equation of the circle is
$(x - a)^2 + (y - b)^2 = r^2$
where $a = 1 \quad b = -2 \quad r = 5$

so $(x - 1)^2 + (y - -2)^2 = 25$

or $(x - 1)^2 + (y + 2)^2 = 25 \qquad (3)$

Substituting $D(4, -6)$ into the left-hand side of the circle, i.e, $(x - 1)^2 + (y + 2)^2$ gives:

$(4 - 1)^2 + (-6 + 2)^2 = 25$

$25 = 25$, so the 4th point D does lie on the circle.

Method 2

$A = (-4, -2) \quad B = (-2, 2) \quad C = (5, 1)$

A circle which has a centre (a, b) and radius r has the general equation

$(x - a)^2 + (y - b)^2 = r^2$

- Use points A and B

Substituting $A(-4, -2)$ into $(x - a)^2 + (y - b)^2 = r^2$ gives:

$(x - -4)^2 + (y - -2)^2 = r^2$

$(x + 4)^2 + (y + 2)^2 = r^2$

$x^2 + 8x + 16 + y^2 + 4y + 4 = r^2$

$x^2 + y^2 + 8x + 4y + 20 = r^2 \qquad (1)$

Substituting $B(-2, 2)$ into $(x - a)^2 + (y - b)^2 = r^2$ gives:

$(x - -2)^2 + (y - 2)^2 = r^2$

$(x + 2)^2 + (y - 2)^2 = r^2$

$x^2 + 4x + 4 + y^2 - 4y + 4 = r^2$

$x^2 + y^2 + 4x - 4y + 8 = r^2 \qquad (2)$

Multiplying (1) by -1 gives:

$-x^2 - y^2 - 8x - 4y - 20 = -r^2$ now add (2)

$x^2 + y^2 + 4x - 4y + 8 = r^2$

$-8x - 4y - 20 + 4x - 4y + 8 = 0$ simplify

$-4x - 8y = 12$ divide by 4

$-x - 2y = 3 \qquad (3)$

- Use points C and B

Substituting $C(5, 1)$ into $(x - a)^2 + (y - b)^2 = r^2$ gives:

$(x - 5)^2 + (y - 1)^2 = r^2$

$x^2 - 10x + 25 + y^2 - 2y + 1 = r^2$ simplify

$x^2 + y^2 - 10x - 2y + 26 = r^2 \qquad (4)$

Multiplying (4) by -1 gives:

$-x^2 - y^2 + 10x + 2y - 26 = -r^2$ now add (2)

$x^2 + y^2 + 4x - 4y + 8 = r^2$

$10x + 2y - 26 + 4x - 4y + 8 = 0$ simplify

$14x - 2y = 18 \qquad (5)$

- Solve (3) and (5) simultaneously by subtracting:

$-x - 2y = 3 \qquad (3)$

$14x - 2y = 18 \qquad (5)$

$-15x = -15$

$x = 1$

Substitute into (3) gives:

$-1 - 2y = 3$

$y = -2$

Substitute $x = 1$ and $y = -2$ into (1) gives:

$1^2 + (-2)^2 + 8(1) + 4(-2) + 20 = r^2$

$r = \pm 5$ (reject -5 as a radius has to be positive).

- The equation of a circle that passes through points A, B and C is:

$(x - 1)^2 + (y + 2)^2 = 5^2$

$(x - 1)^2 + (y + 2)^2 = 25$

- Now substitute point $D(4, -2)$ into $(x - 1)^2 + (y + 2)^2 = 25$

$(4 - 1)^2 + (-6 + 2)^2 = 25$

$25 = 25$, so the 4th point D does lie on the circle.

Method 3

If a circle can be drawn through the four points, the quadrilateral they make is called cyclic.

Opposite angles of a cyclic quadrilateral add to 180°.

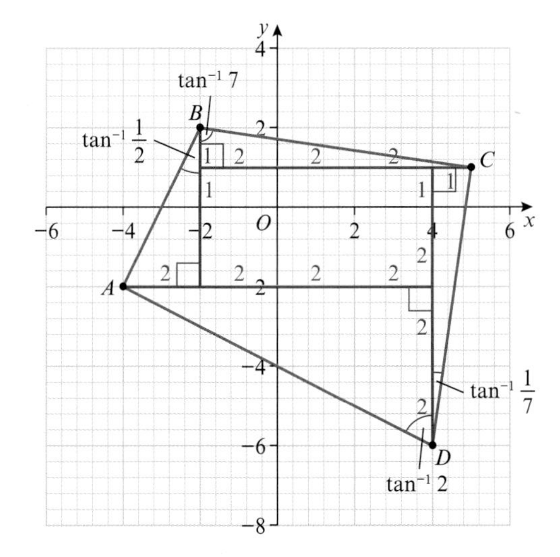

In the diagram,

$$\text{Angle } ABC = \tan^{-1}\left(\frac{1}{2}\right) + \tan^{-1}(7)$$

$$= 26.5651° + 81.8699° = 108.4350°$$

$$\text{Angle } CDA = \tan^{-1}(2) + \tan^{-1}\left(\frac{1}{7}\right)$$

$$= 63.4349° + 8.1301° = 71.5650°$$

$$\text{Angle } ABC + \text{Angle } CDA = 108.435 + 71.565 = 180°$$

Method 4

Use gradient $= \dfrac{y_2 - y_1}{x_2 - x_1}$

Find the gradient of BC

$B = (-2, 2) \quad C = (5, 1)$

Gradient of $BC = \dfrac{1 - 2}{5 - -2} = -\dfrac{1}{7}$

Find the gradient of CD

$C = (5, 1) \quad D = (4, -6)$

Gradient $CD = \dfrac{-6 - 1}{4 - 5} = 7$

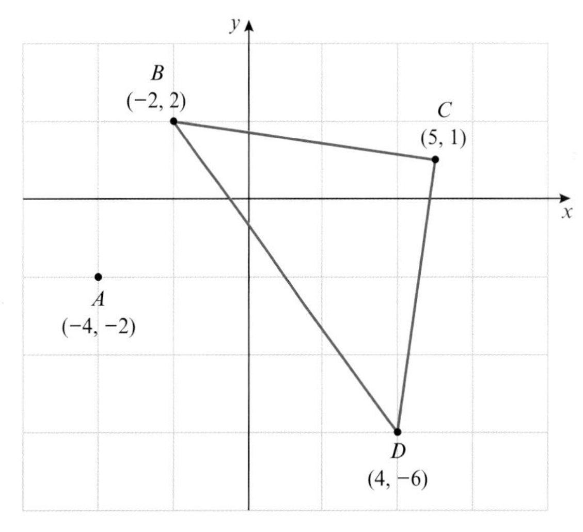

$$\text{Gradient of } BC \times \text{Gradient of } CD = -\frac{1}{7} \times 7 = -1$$

Therefore angle $BCD = 90°$ and so BD must be the diameter of a circle that passes through points B, C and D. (From the circle theorem 'An angle in a semi-circle is 90°')

BD is the hypotenuse of triangle BCD.

The centre of the circle is the midpoint of BD

$$= \left(\frac{-2 + 4}{2}, \frac{2 + -6}{2}\right) = (1, -2)$$

The diameter of the circle is:

Diameter $= \sqrt{(4 - -2)^2 + (-6 - 2)^2} = \sqrt{100} = 10$

So, the radius = 5

The equation of the circle is
$(x - a)^2 + (y - b)^2 = r^2$ where $a = 1$, $b = -2$, $r = 5$

$(x - 1)^2 + (y + 2)^2 = 25$

Substituting point $A = (-4, -2)$ into the left-hand side of the equation gives:

$(4 - 1)^2 + (-6 + 2)^2 = 25$

$25 = 25$ so, the 4th point A does lie on the circle.

b Ptolemy's theorem states that the product of the diagonals of a cyclic quadrilateral equals the sum of the products of the opposite sides

$AC \times BD = AB \times CD + AD \times BC$

In this question, we know that $ABCD$ is a cyclic quadrilateral and $BD = 10$ (Method 4).

The diagonal $AC = \sqrt{(5 - -4)^2 + (1 - -2)^2} = \sqrt{90}$

The product of the diagonals is $\sqrt{90} \times 10 = 30\sqrt{10}$

We need to find the lengths of AB, BC, CD and AD.

$AB = \sqrt{(-2 - -4)^2 + (2 - -2)^2} = \sqrt{20}$

$BC = \sqrt{(5 - -2)^2 + (1 - 2)^2} = \sqrt{50}$

$CD = \sqrt{(4 - 5)^2 + (-6 - 1)^2} = \sqrt{50}$

$AD = \sqrt{(4 - -4)^2 + (-6 - -2)^2} = \sqrt{80}$

Substituting into
$AC \times BD = AB \times CD + AD \times BC$ gives:

$\sqrt{90} \times 10 = \sqrt{20} \times \sqrt{50} + \sqrt{80} \times \sqrt{50}$

$30\sqrt{10} = 10\sqrt{10} + 20\sqrt{10}$

$30\sqrt{10} = 30\sqrt{10}$

So, the points A, B, C and D lie on a circle.

Exercise 7.2

1 a $y = 4$ (1)

$x^2 + y^2 - 4x - 6y + 8 = 0$ (2)

Solve (1) and (2) simultaneously

Substituting for y in (2) gives:

$x^2 + 4^2 - 4x - 6(4) + 8 = 0$

$x^2 - 4x = 0$ Factorise

$x(x - 4) = 0$

$x = 0$ and $x = 4$

The points of intersection are (0, 4) and (4, 4)

c $y = 2x + 3$ (1)

$x^2 + y^2 - 4x + 6y - 12 = 0$ (2)

Solve (1) and (2) simultaneously

Substituting for y in (2) gives:

$x^2 + (2x + 3)^2 - 4x + 6(2x + 3) - 12 = 0$ expand brackets

$x^2 + 4x^2 + 12x + 9 - 4x + 12x + 18 - 12 = 0$ simplify

$5x^2 + 20x + 15 = 0$ divide both sides by 5

$x^2 + 4x + 3 = 0$ factorise

$(x + 3)(x + 1) = 0$

$x = -3$ and $x = -1$

Substitute $x = -3$ into $y = 2x + 3$ gives
$y = 2(-3) + 3 = -3$

Substitute $x = -1$ into $y = 2x + 3$ gives
$y = 2(-1) + 3 = 1$

The points of intersection are $(-3, -3)$ and $(-1, 1)$

2 a Given $x^2 + y^2 = 25$ and
$x^2 + y^2 - 15x + 8y - 75 = 0$

Find the radius of each circle:

Comparing $x^2 + y^2 = r^2$ with $x^2 + y^2 = 25$,

the centre of the circle is (0, 0) and radius is $\sqrt{25} = 5$

Complete the square of

$x^2 + y^2 - 15x + 8y - 75 = 0$

$x^2 - 15x + y^2 + 8y - 75 = 0$

$(x - 7.5)^2 - 7.5^2 + (y + 4)^2 - 4^2 - 75 = 0$

$(x - 7.5)^2 + (y + 4)^2 = \frac{589}{4}$

comparing with $x^2 + y^2 = r^2$

The centre of the circle is $(-7.5, 4)$ and the radius is $\sqrt{\frac{589}{4}}$ or 12.1 to 3 s.f.

The distance between the centres of the circles (0, 0) and $(-7.5, 4)$ can be found using the distance formula.

Use $d = \sqrt{(-7.5 - 0)^2 + (4 - 0)^2}$

$d = 8.5$

The sum of the radii of the two circles is $5 + 12.1 = 17.1$

The distance between the centres of the circles is less than the sum of their radii so the circles intersect.

c $x^2 + y^2 = 25$ and $x^2 + y^2 - 24x - 18y + 125 = 0$

Find the radius of each circle:

Comparing $x^2 + y^2 = r^2$ with $x^2 + y^2 = 25$,

the centre of the circle is (0, 0) and radius is $\sqrt{25} = 5$

Complete the square of

$$x^2 + y^2 - 24x - 18y + 125 = 0$$

$$x^2 - 24x + y^2 - 18y + 125 = 0$$

$$(x - 12)^2 - 12^2 + (y - 9)^2 - 9^2 + 125 = 0$$

$$(x - 12)^2 + (y - 9)^2 = 100$$

comparing with $x^2 + y^2 = r^2$

The centre of the circle is (12, 9) and the radius is $\sqrt{100} = 10$

The distance between the centres of the circles (0, 0) and (12, 9) can be found using the distance formula.

Use $d = \sqrt{(12 - 0)^2 + (9 - 0)^2}$

$d = 15$

The sum of the radii of the two circles is $5 + 10 = 15$

The distance between the centres of the circles is equal to the sum of their radii so the circles touch.

d Given $(x - 8)^2 + y^2 = 4$ and $(x - 2)^2 + (y + 5)^2 = 1$

Find the radius of each circle:

Comparing $x^2 + y^2 = r^2$ with $(x - 8)^2 + y^2 = 4$

the centre of the circle is (8, 0) and radius is $\sqrt{4} = 2$

Comparing $x^2 + y^2 = r^2$ with $(x - 2)^2 + (y + 5)^2 = 1$

the centre of the circle is (2, −5) and radius is $\sqrt{1} = 1$

The distance between the centres of the circles (8, 0) and (2, −5) can be found using the distance formula.

Use $d = \sqrt{(2 - 8)^2 + (-5 - 0)^2}$

$d = \sqrt{61} = 7.81$ to 3 significant figures

The sum of the radii of the two circles is $2 + 1 = 3$

The distance between the centres of the circles is greater than the sum of their radii so the circles do not intersect.

3 Given: a circle $(x - 3)^2 + (y + 2)^2 = 20$ (1) and a straight line $y = x - 3$ (2)

The points P and Q of the intersection of the circle and the line is found by solving (1) and (2) simultaneously.

Use (2) to substitute for y in (1)

$$(x - 3)^2 + (x - 3 + 2)^2 = 20$$

$$(x - 3)^2 + (x - 1)^2 = 20 \quad \text{expand the brackets}$$

$$x^2 - 6x + 9 + x^2 - 2x + 1 = 20 \quad \text{simplify}$$

$$2x^2 - 8x - 10 = 0 \quad \text{divide both sides by 2}$$

$$x^2 - 4x - 5 = 0 \quad \text{factorise}$$

$$(x - 5)(x + 1) = 0$$

So $x = 5$ and $x = -1$

Substituting $x = 5$ into $y = x - 3$ gives:

$y = 2$

Substituting $x = -1$ into $y = x - 3$ gives:

$y = -4$

So $P = (5, 2)$ and $Q = (-1, -4)$ or vice versa

The distance between P and Q can be found using the distance formula.

$PQ = \sqrt{(-1 - 5)^2 + (-4 - 2)^2}$

$PQ = \sqrt{72}$

The distance PQ is $6\sqrt{2}$

4 Given the circle $x^2 + y^2 + 10x - 2y + 9 = 0$ (1) and the line $4y = x + 26$ (2)

Solve (1) and (2) simultaneously.

Use (2) $4y = x + 26$ rearrange

$x = 4y - 26$ now substitute into (1)

$(4y - 26)^2 + y^2 + 10(4y - 26) - 2y + 9 = 0$ expand brackets

$17y^2 - 208y + 676 + 40y - 260 - 2y + 9 = 0$ smplify

$17y^2 - 170y + 425 = 0$ divide both sides by 17

$y^2 - 10y + 25 = 0$

Method 1

Comparing $y^2 - 10y + 25 = 0$ with $ax^2 + bx + c = 0$, $a = 1$ $b = -10$ $c = 25$

The discriminant of the equation is the value of $b^2 - 4ac$

For our equation the discriminant is $10^2 - 4(1)(25) = 0$

As the discriminant is zero then this confirms that the line is a tangent to the circle.

Method 2

Factorise the quadratic $y^2 - 10y + 25 = 0$

$(y - 5)(y - 5) = 0$

$y = 5$ or $y = 5$

There are two equal real roots (which can be described as one repeated (real) root)

Therefore the line is a tangent to the circle.

To find the x- coordinate where they touch, substitute $y = 5$ into $4y = x + 26$

$4(5) = x + 26$

$x = -6$ The touching point is $(-6, 5)$

5 Given $(x + 7)^2 + (y + 2)^2 = 4$ (1) and $(x + 7)^2 + (y + 4)^2 = 16$ (2)

Solve (1) and (2) simultaneously.

From (1) $(x + 7)^2 = 4 - (y + 2)^2$

Substituting for $(x + 7)^2$ in (2) gives:

$4 - (y + 2)^2 + (y + 4)^2 = 16$ expand brackets

$4 - y^2 - 4y - 4 + y^2 + 8y + 16 = 16$ simplify

$4y = 0$

$y = 0$

Substituting into (1) gives $(x + 7)^2 + (0 + 2)^2 = 4$

$(x + 7)^2 = 0$

$x = -7$

The circles touch at one point, i.e., $(-7, 0)$

The centre of the circle $(x + 7)^2 + (y + 2)^2 = 4$ is $(-7, -2)$ and radius $\sqrt{4} = 2$ so $r = 2$

The centre of the circle $(x + 7)^2 + (y + 4)^2 = 16$ is $(-7, -4)$ and radius $\sqrt{16} = 4$ so $r = 4$

If the circles touch internally the distance between the centres should be the same as the difference between their radii.

Distance between the centres $(-7, -2)$ and $(-7, -4)$ is 2 units.

The difference between their radii is $4 - 2 = 2$ so, the circles touch internally.

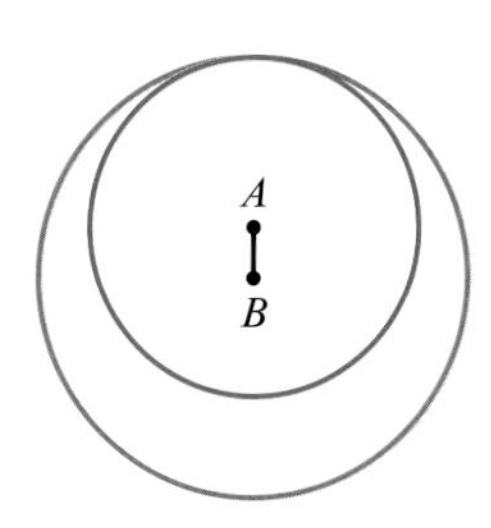

6 a Given $(x - 10)^2 + (y - 5)^2 = 25$ (1) and $(x - 20)^2 + (y - 10)^2 = 100$ (2)

Solve (1) and (2) simultaneously

$(x - 10)^2 + (y - 5)^2 - 25 = (x - 20)^2 + (y - 10)^2 - 100$ rearrange

$(x - 10)^2 - (x - 20)^2 + (y - 5)^2 - (y - 10)^2 + 75 = 0$

Using $a^2 - b^2 = (a - b)(a + b)$

$[(x - 10) - (x - 20)][(x - 10) + (x - 20)] + [(y - 5) - (y - 10)][(y - 5) + (y - 10)] + 75 = 0$

$10(2x - 30) + 5(2y - 15) + 75 = 0$ simplify

$20x + 10y = 300$ divide both sides by 10

$2x + y = 30$ rearrange

So $y = 30 - 2x$

Substitute for y into (1)

$(x - 10)^2 + (30 - 2x - 5)^2 = 25$ simplify bracket

$(x - 10)^2 + (25 - 2x)^2 = 25$ expand

$x^2 - 20x + 100 + 625 - 100x + 4x^2 = 25$ simplify

$5x^2 - 120x + 700 = 0$ divide both sides by 5

$x^2 - 24x + 140 = 0$ factorise

$(x - 10)(x - 14) = 0$

$x = 14$ and $x = 10$

If $x = 14$ then $y = 30 - 2(14) = 2$

If $x = 10$ then $y = 30 - 2(10) = 10$

So $P = (14, 2)$ and $Q = (10, 10)$ or vice versa

The distance $PQ = \sqrt{(10 - 14)^2 + (10 - 2)^2}$

$PQ = 4\sqrt{5}$

b The gradient of the line joining P and $Q = \frac{10 - 2}{10 - 14} = -2$

Using $y - y_1 = m(x - x_1)$ with $m = -2$ $x_1 = 14$ and $y_1 = 2$

$y - 2 = -2(x - 14)$ expand brackets

$y - 2 = -2x + 28$

$y + 2x = 30$

7 Given $y = 2x - 1$ (1) and $x^2 + y^2 + 15x - 11y + 9 = 0$ (2)

Using (1), substitute for y in (2)

$x^2 + (2x - 1)^2 + 15x - 11(2x - 1) + 9 = 0$

$x^2 + (2x - 1)^2 + 15x - 11(2x - 1) + 9 = 0$ expand brackets

$x^2 + 4x^2 - 4x + 1 + 15x - 22x + 11 + 9 = 0$ simplify

$5x^2 - 11x + 21 = 0$

Comparing $5x^2 - 11x + 21 = 0$ with $ax^2 + bx + c = 0$, $a = 5$ $b = -11$ $c = 21$

The discriminant of the equation is the value of $b^2 - 4ac$

For our equation the discriminant is $(-11)^2 - 4(5)(21) = -299$

As the discriminant is negative then the line and the circle do not intersect.

8 a Substitute $x = 7$, $y = 7$ into $x^2 + y^2 - 6x - 8y = 0$

$(7)^2 + (7)^2 - 6(7) - 8(7) = 0$

$0 = 0$ so, $P = (7, 7)$ does lie on the circle.

b Find the centre of the circle $x^2 + y^2 - 6x - 8y = 0$

$x^2 - 6x + y^2 - 8y = 0$ complete the squares

$(x - 3)^2 - 3^2 + (y - 4)^2 - 4^2 = 0$ expand brackets

$(x - 3)^2 + (y - 4)^2 = 25$ simplify

The centre of the circle is at $O = (3, 4)$

The gradient of the line joining P and $O = \frac{4 - 7}{3 - 7} = \frac{3}{4}$

The line OP and the tangent line at P are perpendicular

So the gradient of the tangent at $P = \frac{-1}{\frac{3}{4}} = -\frac{4}{3}$

Using $y - y_1 = m(x - x_1)$ with $m = -\frac{4}{3}$ $x_1 = 7$ and $y_1 = 7$

$y - 7 = -\frac{4}{3}(x - 7)$

$3y - 21 = -4x + 28$

$4x + 3y = 49$

The equation of the tangent at P is $4x + 3y = 49$

9 a Given $2x + y = 6$ (1) and $x^2 + y^2 - 12x - 8y + 27 = 0$ (2)

Using (1), $y = 6 - 2x$

Substitute for y in (2)

$$x^2 + (6 - 2x)^2 - 12x - 8(6 - 2x) + 27 = 0 \quad \text{expand brackets}$$
$$x^2 + 4x^2 - 24x + 36 - 12x - 48 + 16x + 27 = 0 \quad \text{simplify}$$
$$5x^2 - 20x + 15 = 0 \quad \text{divide both sides by 5}$$
$$x^2 - 4x + 3 = 0 \quad \text{factorise}$$
$$(x - 3)(x - 1) = 0$$

$x = 3$ and $x = 1$

Substituting $x = 3$ into $2x + y = 6$ gives $2(3) + y = 6$ so $y = 0$

Substituting $x = 1$ into $2x + y = 6$ gives $2(1) + y = 6$ so $y = 4$

The coordinates of the intersection points are $A = (3, 0)$ and $B = (1, 4)$ or vice versa

b The midpoint of A and B is $\left(\frac{3+1}{2}, \frac{0+4}{2}\right) = (2, 2)$

The gradient of the line AB is $\frac{4-0}{1-3} = \frac{4}{-2} = -2$

The perpendicular bisector has the gradient $-\frac{1}{-2} = \frac{1}{2}$

The equation of the perpendicular of bisector is found by using:

$y - y_1 = m(x - x_1)$ with $m = \frac{1}{2}$ $x_1 = 2$ and $y_1 = 2$

$$y - 2 = \frac{1}{2}(x - 2)$$
$$y - 2 = \frac{1}{2}x - 1$$
$$y = \frac{1}{2}x + 1$$

The equation of the perpendicular of bisector is $y = \frac{1}{2}x + 1$

c To find P and Q, solve $y = \frac{1}{2}x + 1$ (1) and $x^2 + y^2 - 12x - 8y + 27 = 0$ (2) simultaneously

Use (1) to substitute for y in (2)

$$x^2 + \left(\frac{1}{2}x + 1\right)^2 - 12x - 8\left(\frac{1}{2}x + 1\right) + 27 = 0 \quad \text{expand brackets}$$
$$x^2 + \frac{1}{4}x^2 + x + 1 - 12x - 4x - 8 + 27 = 0 \quad \text{multiply both sides by 4}$$
$$4x^2 + x^2 + 4x + 4 - 48x - 16x - 32 + 108 = 0 \quad \text{simplify}$$
$$5x^2 - 60x + 80 = 0 \quad \text{divide both sides by 5}$$
$$x^2 - 12x + 16 = 0$$

Use the quadratic formula to find the solution:

$x = \dfrac{-b \pm \sqrt{b^2 - 4ac}}{2a}$ where $a = 1 \quad b = -12 \quad c = 16$

$x = \dfrac{-(-12) \pm \sqrt{(-12)^2 - 4(1)(16)}}{2(1)}$

$x = \dfrac{12 \pm \sqrt{80}}{2}$

$x = 6 + 2\sqrt{5}$ and $x = 6 - 2\sqrt{5}$

If $x = 6 - 2\sqrt{5}$, substituting into $y = \dfrac{1}{2}x + 1$ gives $y = 4 - \sqrt{5}$

If $x = 6 + 2\sqrt{5}$, substituting into $y = \dfrac{1}{2}x + 1$ gives $y = 4 + \sqrt{5}$

The coordinates of $P = (6 - 2\sqrt{5}, 4 - \sqrt{5})$ and $Q = (6 + 2\sqrt{5}, 4 + \sqrt{5})$

Note: P and Q are not interchangeable since the Shoestring method of calculating the area of a quadrilateral only works if the vertices $APBQ$ are in order.

See diagram.

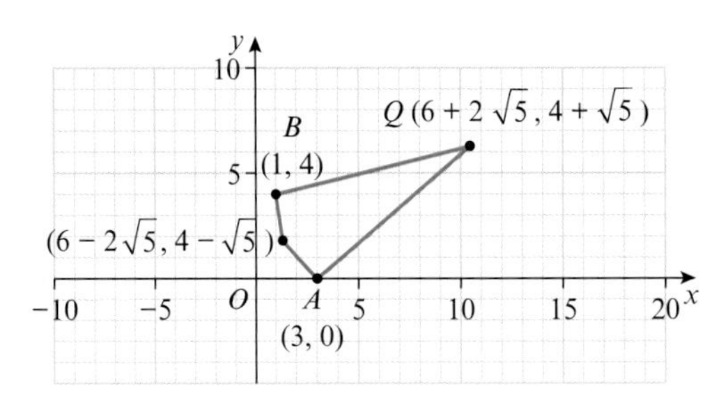

d $A = (3, 0) \qquad P = (6 - 2\sqrt{5}, 4 - \sqrt{5}) \qquad B = (1, 4) \qquad Q = (6 + 2\sqrt{5}, 4 + \sqrt{5})$

Area of a quadrilateral $APBQ = \dfrac{1}{2}|x_1y_2 + x_2y_3 + x_3y_4 + x_4y_1 - x_2y_1 - x_3y_2 - x_4y_3 - x_1y_4|$

$= \dfrac{1}{2}|(3)(4 - \sqrt{5}) + (6 - 2\sqrt{5})(4) + (1)(4 + \sqrt{5}) + (6 + 2\sqrt{5})(0) - (6 - 2\sqrt{5})(0) - (1)(4 - \sqrt{5}) - (6 + 2\sqrt{5})(4) - (3)(4 + \sqrt{5})|$

$= 10\sqrt{5}$ units^2

10 a Given

$x^2 + y^2 - 8x - 4y + 19 = 0$	rearrange
$x^2 - 8x + y^2 - 4y + 19 = 0$	complete the squares
$(x - 4)^2 - 4^2 + (y - 2)^2 - 2^2 + 19 = 0$	simplify
$(x - 4)^2 + (y - 2)^2 - 1 = 0$	rearrange
$(y - 2)^2 = 1 - (x - 4)^2$	(1)

Given $(x - 5)^2 + (y - 2)^2 = 4 \qquad$ (2)

Substitute (1) into (2)

$$(x-5)^2+1-(x-4)^2=4 \qquad \text{expand brackets}$$

$$x^2-10x+25+1-x^2+8x-16-4=0 \qquad \text{simplify}$$

$$2x+6=0$$

$$x=3$$

Substituting into (1) gives:

$(y-2)^2=1-(3-4)^2$

$y-2=0$

$y=2$

As there is one solution, the circles must touch at one point, i.e., (3, 2)

The centre of the circle $(x-4)^2+(y-2)^2=1$ is (4, 2) and radius $\sqrt{1}=1$ so $r=1$

The centre of the circle $(x-5)^2+(y-2)^2=4$ is (5, 2) and radius $\sqrt{4}=2$ so $r=2$

If the circles touch internally the distance between the centres should be the same as the difference between their radii.

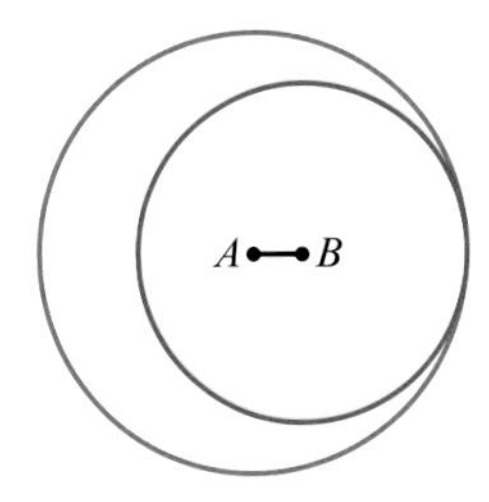

Distance between the centres (4, 2) and (5, 2) is 1 unit.

The difference between their radii is $2-1=1$ so, the circles touch internally.

b First circle equation: $x^2+y^2+6x-4y+3=0$ (1) multiply both sides by -1

$$-x^2-y^2-6x+4y-3=0 \qquad (2)$$

Second circle equation: $x^2+y^2-12x+2y-3=0$ (3)

Adding (2) and (3) gives:

$-18x+6y-6=0$ divide both sides by 6

$-3x+y-1=0$

$y=3x+1$

Substitute for y into (1) gives:

$$x^2+(3x+1)^2+6x-4(3x+1)+3=0 \qquad \text{expand brackets}$$

$$x^2+9x^2+6x+1+6x-12x-4+3=0 \qquad \text{simplify}$$

$$10x^2=0$$

$$x=0$$

Substitute into $y=3x+1$ gives $y=3(0)+1$ so $y=1$

As there is one solution, the circles must touch at one point, i.e., (0, 1)

Given $x^2 + y^2 + 6x - 4y + 3 = 0$ rearrange

$x^2 + 6x + y^2 - 4y + 3 = 0$ complete the squares

$(x + 3)^2 - 3^2 + (y - 2)^2 - 2^2 + 3 = 0$ simplify

$(x + 3)^2 + (y - 2)^2 = 10$

The centre of the circle is $(-3, 2)$ and the radius of the circle $r_1 = \sqrt{10}$

Given $x^2 + y^2 - 12x + 2y - 3 = 0$ rearrange

$x^2 - 12x + y^2 + 2y - 3 = 0$ complete the squares

$(x - 6)^2 - 6^2 + (y + 1)^2 - 1^2 - 3 = 0$

$(x - 6)^2 + (y + 1)^2 = 40$

The centre of the circle is $(6, -1)$ and the radius of the circle $r_2 = 2\sqrt{10}$

The distance between the centres of the circle is $\sqrt{(6 - -3)^2 + (-1 - 2)^2} = \sqrt{90} = 3\sqrt{10}$

The sum of their radii $r_1 + r_2 = \sqrt{10} + 2\sqrt{10} = 3\sqrt{10}$

So the distance between their circles is the same as the sum of their radii so the circles touch externally.

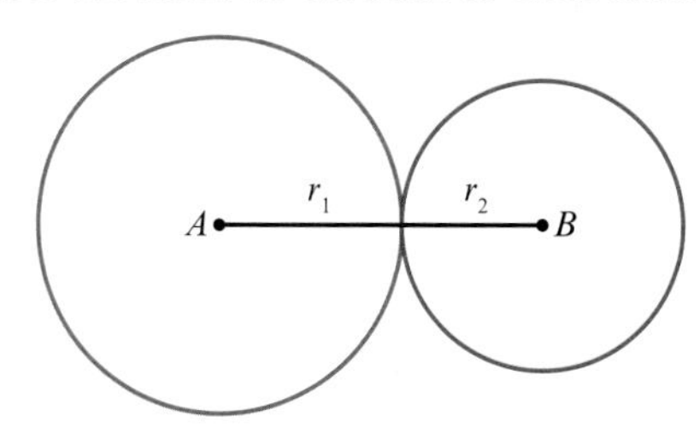

11 Substituting $y = mx + 3$ into $x^2 + y^2 - 10x - 8y + 28 = 0$ gives:

$x^2 + (mx + 3)^2 - 10x - 8(mx + 3) + 28 = 0$ expand brackets

$x^2 + m^2x^2 + 6mx + 9 - 10x - 8mx - 24 + 28 = 0$ factorise

$(1 + m^2)x^2 + (6m - 10 - 8m)x + 9 - 24 + 28 = 0$ simplify

$(1 + m)x^2 + (-2m - 10)x + 13 = 0$

Comparing $(1 + m^2)x^2 + (-2m - 10)x + 13 = 0$ with $ax^2 + bx + c = 0$,

$a = (1 + m^2) \quad b = -2m - 10 \quad c = 13$

The discriminant of the equation is the value of $b^2 - 4ac$

For our equation the discriminant is $(-2m - 10)^2 - 4(1 + m^2)(13)$

For the circle and the line to intersect at two distinct points: $b^2 - 4ac > 0$

So, $(-2m - 10)^2 - 4(1 + m^2)(13) > 0$ expand the brackets

$4m^2 + 40m + 100 - 52 - 52m^2 > 0$

$-48m^2 + 40m + 48 > 0$ divide both sides by -8

$6m^2 - 5m - 6 < 0$ factorise

$(3m + 2)(2m - 3) < 0$

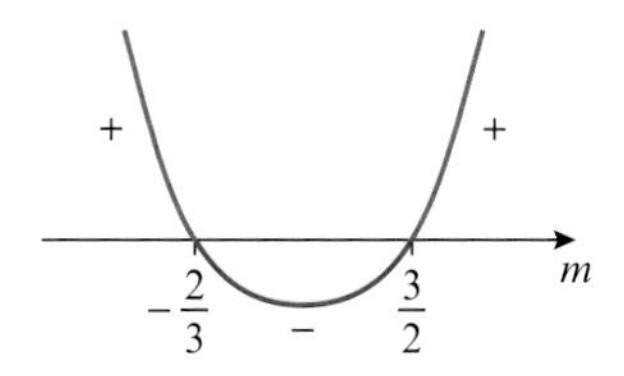

The critical values are $m = -\frac{2}{3}$ or $m = \frac{3}{2}$

The set of values for m are: $-\frac{2}{3} < m < \frac{3}{2}$

12 The equation of a circle is $(x - a)^2 + (y - b)^2 = r^2$ (1)

This circle has a centre at (a, b) and passes through the point (14, 2).

The circle touches the x-axis, so its radius is b

Substituting these values into (1) gives:

$(14 - a)^2 + (2 - b)^2 = b^2$ (2)

The centre of the circle also lies on the line $x + 2y = 28$

Substituting $x = a \quad y = b$ into $x + 2y = 28$ gives:

$a + 2b = 28$ which rearranged is $a = 28 - 2b$ (3)

Using (3), substitute for a in (2)

$$(14 - (28 - 2b))^2 + (2 - b)^2 = b^2$$

$$(14 - 28 + 2b)^2 + (2 - b)^2 = b^2$$

$$(2b - 14)^2 + (2 - b)^2 = b^2 \quad \text{expand brackets}$$

$$4b^2 - 56b + 196 + 4 - 4b + b^2 = b^2 \quad \text{simplify}$$

$$4b^2 - 60b + 200 = 0 \quad \text{divide both sides by 4}$$

$$b^2 - 15b + 50 = 0 \quad \text{factorise}$$

$$(b - 5)(b - 10) = 0$$

$b = 5$ or $b = 10$

Substituting $b = 5$ into (3) gives $a = 28 - 2(5)$ so $a = 18$

Substituting $b = 10$ into (3) gives $a = 28 - 2(10)$ so $a = 8$

One circle has centre (18, 5) and radius 5

The other circle has centre (8, 10) and radius 10

The two circles are: $(x - 18)^2 + (y - 5)^2 = 25$ and $(x - 8)^2 + (y - 10)^2 = 100$

Chapter 8: Circular measure

Exercise 8.1

1 **g** $180° = \pi$ radians

$1° = \frac{\pi}{180}$ radians

$135° = 135 \times \frac{\pi}{180}$ radians

$= \frac{3\pi}{4}$ radians

o $180° = \pi$ radians

$1° = \frac{\pi}{180}$ radians

$210° = 210 \times \frac{\pi}{180}$ radians

$= \frac{7\pi}{6}$ radians

2 **f** π radians $= 180°$

1 radian $= \frac{180°}{\pi}$

$\frac{4\pi}{5}$ radians $= \frac{4\pi}{5} \times \frac{180°}{\pi}$

$= 144°$

n π radians $= 180°$

1 radian $= \frac{180°}{\pi}$

$\frac{8\pi}{3}$ radians $= \frac{8\pi}{3} \times \frac{180°}{\pi}$

$= 480°$

3 **a** $180° = \pi$ radians

$1° = \frac{\pi}{180}$ radians

$32° = 32 \times \frac{\pi}{180}$ radians

$= 0.559$ radians

e $180° = \pi$ radians

$1° = \frac{\pi}{180}$ radians

$247° = 247 \times \frac{\pi}{180}$ radians

$= 4.31$ radians

4 **b** π radians $= 180°$

1 radian $= \frac{180°}{\pi}$

2.5 radians $= 2.5 \times \frac{180°}{\pi}$

$= 143.2°$

d π radians $= 180°$

1 radian $= \frac{180°}{\pi}$

1.83 radians $= 1.83 \times \frac{180°}{\pi}$

$= 104.9°$

5 **a** $180° = \pi$ radians

$1° = \frac{\pi}{180}$ radians

$45° = 45 \times \frac{\pi}{180}$ radians

$= \frac{\pi}{4}$ radians

$90° = 45° \times 2 = \frac{\pi}{2}$ radians

$135° = 135 \times \frac{\pi}{180}$ radians

$= \frac{3\pi}{4}$ radians

$225° = 225 \times \frac{\pi}{180}$ radians

$= \frac{5\pi}{4}$ radians

$270° = 270 \times \frac{\pi}{180}$ radians

$= \frac{3\pi}{2}$ radians

$315° = 315 \times \frac{\pi}{180}$ radians

$= \frac{7\pi}{4}$ radians

b $1° = \frac{\pi}{180}$ radians

$30° = 30 \times \frac{\pi}{180}$ radians

$= \frac{\pi}{6}$ radians

$60° = 60 \times \frac{\pi}{180}$ radians

$= \frac{\pi}{3}$ radians

$90° = 90 \times \frac{\pi}{180}$ radians

$= \frac{\pi}{2}$ radians

$120° = 120 \times \frac{\pi}{180}$ radians

$= \frac{2\pi}{3}$ radians

$150° = 150 \times \frac{\pi}{180}$ radians

$= \frac{5\pi}{6}$ radians

$210° = 210 \times \frac{\pi}{180}$ radians

$= \frac{7\pi}{6}$ radians

$240° = 240 \times \frac{\pi}{180}$ radians

$= \frac{4\pi}{3}$ radians

$270° = 270 \times \frac{\pi}{180}$ radians

$= \frac{3\pi}{2}$ radians

$300° = 300 \times \frac{\pi}{180}$ radians

$= \frac{5\pi}{3}$ radians

$330° = 330 \times \frac{\pi}{180}$ radians

$= \frac{11\pi}{6}$ radians

REMINDER

In question 6 you do not need to convert each angle to degrees.

You should set the angle mode on your calculator to radians.

6 a sin 1.3 radians = 0.964

e $\cos\frac{\pi}{3} = 0.5$

7 **Method 1**

We know that the angle is between 10° and 15° so we use a spreadsheet to generate values of 6 sin 10° and 6 sin 10 (radians)

Angle	6 sin angle (Rad)	6 sin angle (Deg)
10	3.264126665	1.041889066
10.2	4.199248126	1.062508442
10.4	4.966958815	1.083114872
10.6	−5.53665253	1.103708104
10.8	−5.88561738	1.124287888
11	5.999941239	1.144853972
11.2	5.875066375	1.165406107
11.4	5.515971154	1.185944042
11.6	−4.93697157	1.206467527
11.8	4.161150509	1.226976311
12	3.219437508	1.247470145
12.2	2.149375693	1.267948779
12.4	0.993625053	1.288411963
12.6	0.201738283	1.308859448
12.8	1.389058951	1.329290986
13	2.521002221	1.349706326
13.2	3.552441088	1.370105221
13.4	4.44225534	1.390487421

Comparing the values we notice that they are closest between 12.6 and 12.8.

Finding the values of 6 sin 12.6 to 6 sin 12.8 using 2 decimal place intervals for the angles gives:

Angle	6 sin angle (Rad)	6 sin angle (Deg)
12.78	1.272049023	1.327248557
12.79	1.330620517	1.328269791
12.8	1.389058951	1.329290986
12.81	1.447358479	1.330312139

Drawing two graphs of the angle x against 6 sin x in degrees and 6 sin x in radians looks like this:

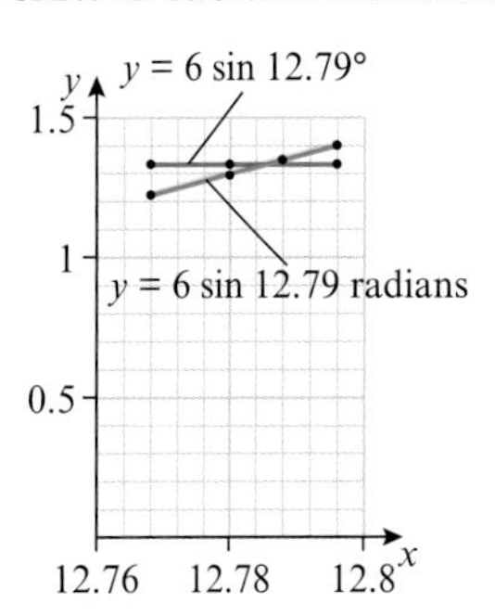

Angle BAC = 12.79° to 2 decimal places.

Method 2

To draw this using graphing software such as Desmos, plot two graphs in degrees mode, $y = 6 \sin x$ and $y = 6 \sin\left(\frac{x \times 180}{\pi}\right)$. The question states that the answer is the same between 10 and 15 degrees and clicking on the intersection point between those values shows 12.79.

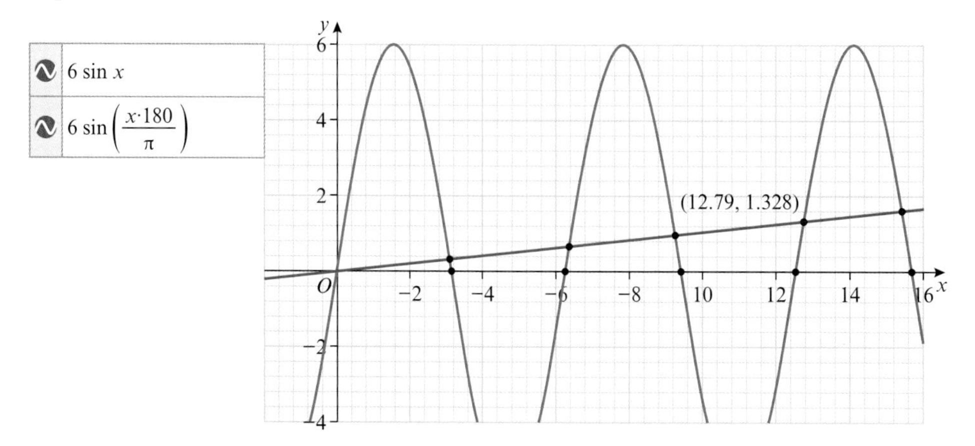

The graphs intersect at BAC =12.79 in degrees.

Angle BAC = 12.79° to 2 decimal places.

Method 3

The graphs shown in Method 2 can also be drawn using a graphical display calculator (GDC). The instructions below use a Casio fx-CG50.

1. Select the graph screen in the main menu.

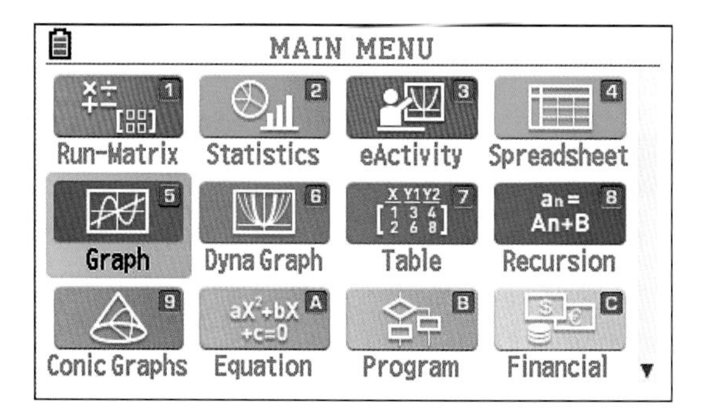

2. Enter the equations of the graphs. Check your GDC is set to degrees mode.

Math Deg Norm1 Real

Graph Func :Y=

Y1 = 6sin x [—]

Y2 = 6sin $\frac{180x}{\pi}$ [—]

Y3: [—]

Y4: [—]

Y5: [—]

SELECT DELETE TYPE TOOL MODIFY DRAW

3. Draw the graphs using your calculators function buttons. For most Casio calculators this is F6. Scroll right using the toggle button until you reach the portion of the x axis between 10 and 15 degrees. Then select the function button that displays graph options. For Casio calculators this is F5.

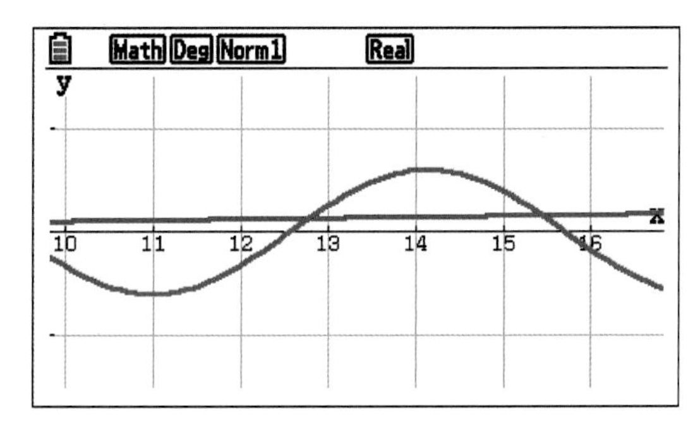

4. Select the intersect function. For most Casio calculators this is F5. Then scroll through the intersection points using the toggle button until you find the point between 10 and 15 degrees.

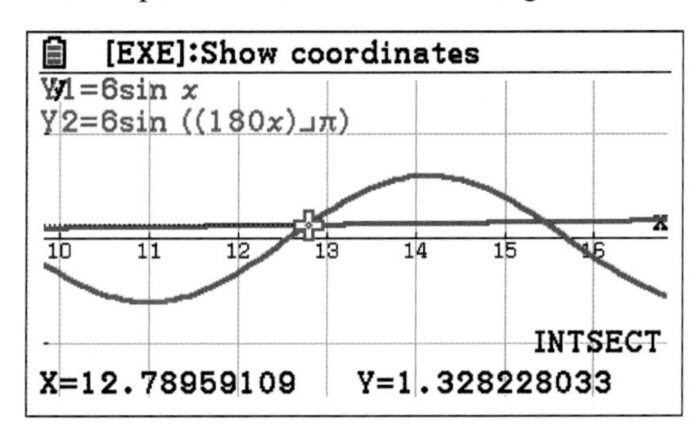

Exercise 8.2

1 a Arc length $= r\theta$

$$= 6 \times \frac{\pi}{4}$$

$$= \frac{3\pi}{2}\text{ cm}$$

d Arc length $= r\theta$

$$= 18 \times \frac{5\pi}{6}$$

$$= 15\pi\text{ cm}$$

TIP

Make sure your calculator is in radian mode for question 2.

2 a Arc length $= r\theta$

$$= 8 \times 1.2$$

$$= 9.6\text{ cm}$$

b Arc length $= r\theta$

$= 2.5 \times 0.8$

$= 2\,\text{cm}$

3 **a** Arc length $= r\theta$

$\theta = \dfrac{\text{arc length}}{r}$

$\theta = \dfrac{5}{4} = 1.25$ radians

b Arc length $= r\theta$

$\theta = \dfrac{\text{arc length}}{r}$

$\theta = \dfrac{13.5}{9} = 1.5$ radians

4 **a** The perimeter of a sector $=$ Arc length $+ 2r$

$= r\theta + 2r$

$= 4 \times 1.1 + 2 \times 4$

$= 12.4\,\text{cm}$

b The perimeter of a sector $=$ Arc length $+ 2r$

$= r\theta + 2r$

$= 8 \times 2 + 2 \times 8$

$= 32\,\text{cm}$

c The perimeter of a sector $=$ Arc length $+ 2r$

$= r\theta + 2r$

$= 5 \times 4.2 + 2 \times 5$

$= 31\,\text{cm}$

5 **a** $BO = \frac{1}{2}BC = \frac{1}{2} \times 16 = 8\,\text{cm}$

Using Pythagoras on triangle ABO:

$AO^2 = AB^2 + BO^2$

$= 6^2 + 8^2$

$= 100$

$AO = \sqrt{100} = 10\,\text{cm}$

b $\tan AOB = \dfrac{6}{8}$ — triangle ABO is right-angled since $ADCB$ is a rectangle

$\tan^{-1}\dfrac{6}{8} = 0.6435011\ldots$ radians — your calculator should be in radian mode

Angle $AOB =$ Angle DOC

Angle $AOD = \pi - 2(0.6435011...) = 1.854590...$ radians

Angle $AOD = 1.85$ radians (3 s.f.)

c The perimeter of a sector = Arc length + $2r$

$$= AO \times \theta + 2 \times AO$$

$$= 10 \times 1.854590... + 2 \times 10$$

$$= 38.5 \text{ cm (3 s.f.)}$$

6 a Arc length $= r\theta$

$$= 10 \times 2.3$$

$$= 23 \text{ cm}$$

b Use the cosine rule to find the length of the chord AB (remember to have your calculator in radian mode).

$$AB^2 = AO^2 + OB^2 - 2 \times AO \times OB \times \cos AOB$$

$$= 10^2 + 10^2 - 2 \times 10 \times 10 \times \cos 2.3$$

$$= 333.255...$$

$$AB = \sqrt{333.255...}$$

$$AB = 18.255...$$

$$AB = 18.3 \text{ cm (3 s.f.)}$$

c The perimeter of the shaded segment = (minor) arc length + AB

$$= r\theta + AB$$

$$= 10 \times 2.3 + 18.255...$$

$$= 41.3 \text{ cm (3 s.f.)}$$

7 a Arc length $GH = r\theta$

$$= 16 \times 0.85$$

$$= 13.6 \text{ cm}$$

b Triangle EFG is isosceles so angle GEF = angle GFE

Angle $EGF = \pi - 0.85 - 0.85 = (\pi - 1.7)$ radians

Use the cosine rule to find the length of EF (remember to have your calculator in radian mode).

$$EF^2 = EG^2 + FG^2 - 2 \times EG \times FG \times \cos EGF$$

$$= 16^2 + 16^2 - 2 \times 16 \times 16 \times \cos(\pi - 1.7)$$

$$= 446.0316...$$

$$EF = \sqrt{446.0316...}$$

$$EF = 21.1194...$$

$$EF = 21.1 \text{ cm (3 s.f.)}$$

c The perimeter of the shaded region = arc length $GH + EG + EH$

$= r\theta + EG + (EF - HF)$

$= 16 \times 0.85 + 16 + (21.1194 - 16)$

$= 34.7194$

$= 34.7 \text{ cm (3 s.f.)}$

Exercise 8.3

1 a Area of a sector $= \frac{1}{2}r^2\theta$

$= \frac{1}{2} \times 6^2 \times \frac{\pi}{3}$

$= 6\pi \text{ cm}^2$

d Area of a sector $= \frac{1}{2}r^2\theta$

$= \frac{1}{2} \times 9^2 \times \frac{5\pi}{6}$

$= \frac{135}{4}\pi \text{ cm}^2$

2 a Area of a sector $= \frac{1}{2}r^2\theta$

$= \frac{1}{2} \times 4^2 \times 1.3$

$= 10.4 \text{ cm}^2$

b Area of a sector $= \frac{1}{2}r^2\theta$

$= \frac{1}{2} \times 3.8^2 \times 0.6$

$= 4.332 \text{ cm}^2$

3 a Area of a sector $= \frac{1}{2}r^2\theta$ multiply both sides by 2

$2 \times$ Area of sector $= r^2\theta$ divide both sides by r^2

$\theta = \frac{2 \times \text{Area of sector}}{r^2}$

$\theta = \frac{2 \times 5}{3^2}$

$\theta = 1.11$ radians (3 s.f.)

b $\theta = \frac{2 \times \text{Area of sector}}{r^2}$

$\theta = \frac{2 \times 30}{7^2}$

$\theta = 1.22448\ldots$

$\theta = 1.22$ radians (3 s.f.)

4 a Arc length $= r\theta$

Angle $POQ = \frac{\text{Arc length } PQ}{\text{radius}}$

$= \frac{8}{10} = 0.8$ radians

b Area of a sector $= \frac{1}{2}r^2\theta$

$= \frac{1}{2} \times 10^2 \times 0.8$

$= 40\,\text{cm}^2$

5 The perimeter of a sector = Arc length + $2r$

$150 = r\theta + 2r$ rearrange

$150 - 2r = r\theta$ divide both sides by r

$\theta = \frac{150 - 2r}{r}$

Area of a sector $= \frac{1}{2}r^2\theta$

$= \frac{1}{2}r^2 \times \frac{150 - 2r}{r}$ simplify

Area of a sector $= r(75 - r)$

6 a $BO = \frac{1}{2}BC = \frac{1}{2} \times 18 = 9\,\text{cm}$

Using Pythagoras on triangle ABO:

$AO^2 = AB^2 + BO^2$

$= 9^2 + 9^2$

$= 162$

$AO = \sqrt{162} = 9\sqrt{2}\,\text{cm}$

b $\tan AOB = \frac{9}{9}$ triangle ABO is right-angled since $ADCB$ is a rectangle

$\tan^{-1} 1 = \frac{\pi}{4}$ radians your calculator should be in radian mode

Angle AOB = Angle DOC

Angle $AOD = \pi - 2 \times \frac{\pi}{4} = \frac{\pi}{2}$ radians c Area of shaded region = Area of sector AOD

$$= \frac{1}{2}r^2\theta$$

$$= \frac{1}{2} \times AO^2 \times \theta$$

$$= \frac{1}{2}(9\sqrt{2})^2 \times \frac{\pi}{2}$$

$$= \frac{81}{2}\pi \text{ cm}^2$$

7 a $\tan POQ = \frac{35}{12}$

$\tan^{-1}\left(\frac{35}{12}\right) = 1.2404\ldots$ radians

$POQ = 1.24$ radians (3 s.f.)

b Area of a sector $= \frac{1}{2}r^2\theta$

Area of sector $POR = \frac{1}{2} \times 12^2 \times 1.2404\ldots$

$= 89.3159\ldots$

$= 89.3 \text{ cm}^2$ (3 s.f.)

c Area of the shaded region = Area of triangle POQ − area of sector POR

$= \frac{1}{2} \times 35 \times 12 - 89.3159\ldots$

$= 120.6840\ldots$

$= 121 \text{ cm}^2$ (3 s.f.)

8 a Let angle $AOB = \theta$ radians

Area of a sector $AOB = \frac{1}{2}r^2\theta$

$$32 = \frac{1}{2} \times 8^2 \times \theta$$

$$\frac{32 \times 2}{8^2} = \theta$$

$\theta = 1$ radian

b AC is a tangent to the circle at A so angle $OAC = 90°$

$$\tan AOC = \frac{AC}{8}$$

$$\tan 1 = \frac{AC}{8}$$

$AC = 8 \tan 1$

Area of triangle $AOC = \frac{1}{2} \times 8 \times 8 \tan 1$

$= 49.8370\ldots$

$= 49.8 \text{ cm}^2$ (3 s.f.)

c Area of the shaded region = Area of triangle AOC − Area of sector OAB

$= 49.8370... - 32$

$= 17.8370...$

$= 17.8\text{ cm}^2$ (3 s.f.)

9 a Area of a sector $HFG = \frac{1}{2}r^2\theta$

$= \frac{1}{2} \times 9^2 \times 0.6$

$= 24.3\text{ cm}^2$

b Triangle EFG is isosceles so angle EFG = angle FEG = 0.6 radians

Angle $EGF = \pi - 0.6 - 0.6 = (\pi - 1.2)$ radians

Area of a non-right-angled triangle $= \frac{1}{2}ab\sin C$

Area of triangle $EFG = \frac{1}{2} \times 9 \times 9 \times \sin(\pi - 1.2)$

$= 37.7475...$

$= 37.7\text{ cm}^2$

c Area of the shaded region = Area of triangle EFG − Area of sector OAB

$= 37.7475... - 24.3$

$= 13.4475...$

$= 13.4\text{ cm}^2$ (3 s.f.)

10 a Arc length $= r\theta$

$$\theta = \frac{\text{arc length}}{r}$$

$$\theta = \frac{9\pi}{12} = \frac{3\pi}{4} \text{ radians}$$

b Area of the shaded region = Area of sector OAB − Area of triangle AOB

$$= \frac{1}{2} \times 12^2 \times \frac{3\pi}{4} - \frac{1}{2} \times 12 \times 12 \times \sin\frac{3\pi}{4}$$

$$= 54\pi - 36\sqrt{2}\text{ cm}^2$$

11 a Let angle $COB = \theta$ radians

Arc length $AD = 4\theta$ cm

Arc length $BC = 10\theta$ cm

$CD = AB = 10 - 4 = 6$ cm

Perimeter of shaded region $= 10\theta + 4\theta + 6 + 6$

$18 = 14\theta + 12$

$14\theta = 6$

$$\theta = \frac{3}{7} \text{ radians}$$

b Shaded area $= \frac{1}{2} \times 10^2 \times \theta - \frac{1}{2} \times 4^2 \times \theta$

$= 42\theta$

Shaded area $= 42 \times \frac{3}{7}$

$= 18\ \text{cm}^2$

12 a $\cos 0.5 = \frac{OD}{5}$

$OD = 5\cos 0.5$

$OD = 4.3879....$

$OD = 4.39\ \text{cm (3 s.f.)}$

b $\sin 0.5 = \frac{CD}{5}$

$CD = 5\sin 0.5$

$CD = 2.3971....$

$CD = 2.40\ \text{cm (3 s.f.)}$

c Arc $AB = 9 \times 0.5 = 4.5\ \text{cm}$

$AD = 9 - 4.3879...$

$AD = 4.6121...$

Perimeter of the shaded region $= BC + \text{arc } AB + AD + CD$

$= 4 + 4.5 + 4.6121... + 2.3971...$

$= 15.5092...$

$= 15.5\ \text{cm (3 s.f.)}$

d Area of the shaded region = Area of sector AOB − Area triangle COD

$= \frac{1}{2} \times 9^2 \times 0.5 - \frac{1}{2} \times 4.3879... \times 2.3971...$

$= 14.9908...$

$= 15.0\ \text{cm}^2\ \text{(3 s.f.)}$

13 Angle $FOG = 1.2$ radians

Shaded area $= \frac{1}{2} \times OG^2 \times 1.2 - \frac{1}{2} \times 5^2 \times 1.2$

$71.4 = \frac{1}{2} \times OG^2 \times 1.2 - \frac{1}{2} \times 5^2 \times 1.2$

$71.4 = 0.6OG^2 - 15$

$OG^2 = \frac{71.4 + 15}{0.6}$

$OG = \sqrt{144} = 12$

So, $HG = EF = (12 - 5) = 7\text{ cm}$

Arc length $HE = 5 \times 1.2 = 6\text{ cm}$

Arc length $GF = 12 \times 1.2 = 14.4\text{ cm}$

Perimeter of shaded region $= 6 + 14.4 + 7 + 7$

$= 34.4\text{ cm}$

14 **a** Area triangle $EOF = \frac{1}{2} \times 10 \times 10 \times \sin 2$

$= 45.4648\ldots$

$= 45.5\text{ cm}^2$

b $OG = EO = OF = 10\text{ cm}$

Angle $FOH = (\pi - 2)$ radians

Area of sector $FOG = \frac{1}{2} \times 10^2 \times (\pi - 2)$

$= 50(\pi - 2)\text{ cm}^2$

$= 57.0796\ldots$

$= 57.1\text{ cm}^2$

c Triangle FEO is isosceles so angle $FEO = \frac{\pi - 2}{2}$

Use triangle FEO and the cosine rule to find EF:

$EF^2 = 10^2 + 10^2 - 2 \times 10 \times 10 \cos 2$

$EF^2 = 283.2293\ldots$

Area of sector $FEH = \frac{1}{2} \times EF^2 \times \left(\frac{\pi - 2}{2}\right)$

$= \frac{1}{2} \times 283.2293\ldots \times \left(\frac{\pi - 2}{2}\right)$

$= 80.8331\ldots$

$= 80.8\text{ cm}^2$ (3 s.f.)

d Area triangle $EOF = \frac{1}{2} \times 10 \times 10 \times \sin 2$

$= 45.4648\ldots\text{ cm}^2$

Area FOH = Area sector FEH − Area triangle EOF

$= 80.8331\ldots - 45.4648\ldots$

$= 35.36832$

Shaded area = Area sector FOG − Area FOH

$= 57.0796\ldots - 35.3683\ldots$

$= 21.7113\ldots$

$= 21.7\text{ cm}^2$ (3 s.f.)

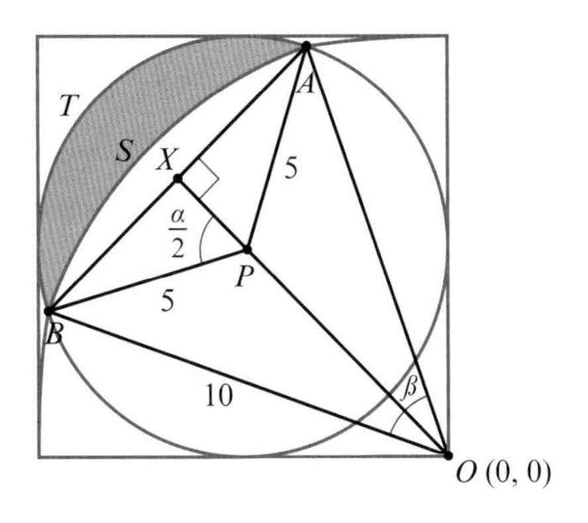

15 Let the bottom right of the square have coordinates (0, 0).

Circle S has radius 10 cm and centre (0, 0) so its equation is $x^2 + y^2 = 100$

Circle T has radius 5 cm and centre (−5, 5) so its equation is $(x + 5)^2 + (y - 5)^2 = 25$

Find the coordinates of where the two circles intersect (i.e A and B) by solving the simultaneous equations:

$x^2 + y^2 = 100$ (1)

$(x + 5)^2 + (y - 5)^2 = 25$ (2)

Expand (2) to give:

$x^2 + 10x + 25 + y^2 - 10y + 25 = 25$

Then subtracting (1) gives:

$10x + 25 - 10y + 25 = -75$ simplify

$10x - 10y = -125$ divide both sides by 10

$x - y = -12.5$ rearrange

$x = y - 12.5$ (3)

Substitute for x in (1)

$(y - 12.5)^2 + y^2 = 100$ expand

$y^2 - 25y + 156.25 + y^2 = 100$ simplify

$2y^2 - 25y + 56.25 = 0$

Use the quadratic formula:

$$y = \frac{-(-25) \pm \sqrt{(-25)^2 - 4 \times 2 \times 56.25}}{2 \times 2}$$

$$y = \frac{25 \pm \sqrt{175}}{4}$$

$$y = \frac{25 - 5\sqrt{7}}{4} \quad \text{and} \quad y = \frac{25 + 5\sqrt{7}}{4}$$

Substitute for y in (3) to find coordinates of points A and B.

$$A = \left[\frac{5}{4}(\sqrt{7} - 5), \frac{5}{4}(\sqrt{7} + 5)\right] \quad \text{and} \quad B = \left[-\frac{5}{4}(\sqrt{7} + 5), -\frac{5}{4}(\sqrt{7} - 5)\right]$$

The chord AB is common to both circles.

The length of the chord is found using the distance formula:

$$AB = \sqrt{\left[\left(-\frac{5}{4}(\sqrt{7} + 5) - \frac{5}{4}(\sqrt{7} - 5)\right)^2\right] + \left[\left(-\frac{5}{4}(\sqrt{7} - 5) - \frac{5}{4}(\sqrt{7} + 5)\right)^2\right]}$$

$$AB = \frac{5\sqrt{14}}{2}$$

Let the point where the perpendicular line from P meets AB be X

At P, let angle $APB = \alpha$ so $BPX = \frac{\alpha}{2}$

So, $\sin BPX = \frac{BX}{5} = \frac{1}{2}AB \div 5$ and

$$\sin\frac{\alpha}{2} = \frac{1}{2}AB \div 5$$

$$\sin\frac{\alpha}{2} = \frac{1}{2} \times \frac{5\sqrt{14}}{2} \div 5$$

$$\sin\frac{\alpha}{2} = \frac{\sqrt{14}}{4}$$

$$\alpha = 2\sin^{-1}\frac{\sqrt{14}}{4} = 2.4188\ldots$$

Area of triangle $APB = \frac{1}{2} \times 5 \times 5 \times \sin\alpha = 12.5\sin\alpha$

Area of sector $PATB = \frac{1}{2} \times 5^2 \times \alpha = 12.5\alpha$

So sector $PATB$ − area of triangle APB = segment $AXTB = 12.5\alpha - 12.5\sin\alpha$

At O, let angle $AOB = \beta$ so angle $XOB = \frac{\beta}{2}$ and $OB = 10$

$\sin XOB = \frac{BX}{OB} = \frac{1}{2}AB \div 10$ and

$$\sin\frac{\beta}{2} = \frac{1}{2}AB \div 10$$

$$\sin\frac{\beta}{2} = \frac{1}{2} \times \frac{5\sqrt{14}}{2} \div 10$$

$$\sin\frac{\beta}{2} = \frac{\sqrt{14}}{8}$$

$$\sin^{-1}\frac{\sqrt{14}}{8} = \frac{\beta}{2}$$

$$\beta = 2\sin^{-1}\frac{\sqrt{14}}{8} = 0.9733\ldots$$

Area of sector $OASB = \frac{1}{2} \times 10 \times 10 \times \beta = 50\beta$

Area of triangle $OAB = \frac{1}{2} \times 10 \times 10 \times \sin\beta = 50\sin\beta$

So, sector $OASB$ − area of triangle OAB = segment $AXBS = 50\beta - 50\sin\beta$

The shaded area = segment $AXBT$ − segment $AXBS$

$$= 12.5\alpha - 12.5\sin\alpha - (50\beta - 50\sin\beta)$$

$$= 12.5 \times 2.4188\ldots - 12.5 \times 0.6614\ldots - (50 \times 0.9733\ldots - 50 \times 0.8267\ldots)$$

$$= 21.9677\ldots - 7.3296\ldots$$

$$= 14.6381\ldots$$

The shaded area is $14.6\,\text{cm}^2$ (3 s.f.)

Chapter 9: Trigonometry

Exercise 9.1

1 c $\sin^2\theta = \sin\theta \times \sin\theta$

The right-angled triangle to represent θ is:

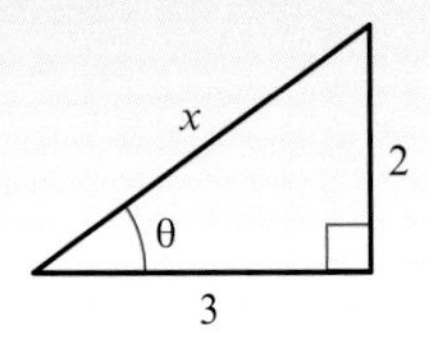

Using Pythagoras' theorem, $x = \sqrt{2^2 + 3^2}$

$$x = \sqrt{13}$$

Hence $\sin\theta = \frac{2}{\sqrt{13}}$

$$\sin^2\theta = \sin\theta \times \sin\theta$$

$$= \frac{2}{\sqrt{13}} \times \frac{2}{\sqrt{13}}$$

$$= \frac{4}{13}$$

e $\frac{2 + \sin\theta}{3 - \cos\theta} = \frac{2 + \frac{2}{\sqrt{13}}}{3 - \frac{3}{\sqrt{13}}}$ multiply the numerator and denominator by $\sqrt{13}$

$= \frac{2\sqrt{13} + 2}{3\sqrt{13} - 3}$ multiply numerator and denominator by $(3\sqrt{13} + 3)$

$= \frac{(2\sqrt{13} + 2)}{(3\sqrt{13} - 3)} \times \frac{(3\sqrt{13} + 3)}{(3\sqrt{13} + 3)}$

$= \frac{78 + 6\sqrt{13} + 6\sqrt{13} + 6}{117 + 9\sqrt{13} - 9\sqrt{13} - 9}$ expand brackets

$= \frac{84 + 12\sqrt{13}}{108}$ simplify

$= \frac{7 + \sqrt{13}}{9}$

2 b 
Given $\sin\theta = \frac{\sqrt{2}}{5}$

The right-angled triangle to represent θ is:

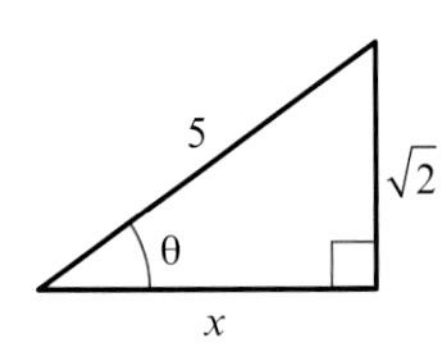

Using Pythagoras' theorem, $x = \sqrt{5^2 - (\sqrt{2})^2}$

$$x = \sqrt{23}$$

Hence $\tan\theta = \frac{\sin\theta}{\cos\theta}$

$$= \frac{\frac{\sqrt{2}}{5}}{\frac{\sqrt{23}}{5}}$$

$= \frac{\sqrt{2}}{\sqrt{23}}$ multiply numerator and denominator by $\sqrt{23}$

$= \frac{\sqrt{2}}{\sqrt{23}} \times \frac{\sqrt{23}}{\sqrt{23}}$

$= \frac{\sqrt{46}}{23}$

e $\frac{\cos\theta - \sin\theta}{\tan\theta} = \frac{\frac{\sqrt{23}}{5} - \frac{\sqrt{2}}{5}}{\frac{\sqrt{46}}{23}}$ multiply numerator and denominator by 115

$= \frac{23\sqrt{23} - 23\sqrt{2}}{5\sqrt{46}}$ multiply numerator and denominator by $\sqrt{46}$

$= \frac{529\sqrt{2} - 46\sqrt{23}}{230}$ divide numerator and denominator by 23

$= \frac{23\sqrt{2} - 2\sqrt{23}}{10}$

3 c Given $\cos\theta = \frac{1}{7}$

The right-angled triangle to represent θ is:

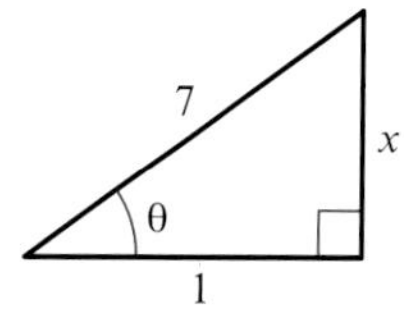

Using Pythagoras' theorem, $x = \sqrt{7^2 - 1^2}$

$x = 4\sqrt{3}$

Hence $\tan\theta = \frac{4\sqrt{3}}{1} = 4\sqrt{3}$

$\tan\theta\cos\theta = 4\sqrt{3} \times \frac{1}{7}$

$= \frac{4\sqrt{3}}{7}$

e $\frac{\cos\theta - \tan\theta}{1 - \cos^2\theta} = \frac{\frac{1}{7} - 4\sqrt{3}}{1 - \left(\frac{1}{7}\right)^2}$

$= \frac{\frac{1}{7} - 4\sqrt{3}}{\frac{48}{49}}$ multiply numerator and denominator by 49

$= \frac{7 - 196\sqrt{3}}{48}$

4 b $\tan^2 60° = \tan 60° \times \tan 60°$

$= \sqrt{3} \times \sqrt{3}$

$= 3$

f $\dfrac{\tan 45° - \sin 30°}{1 + \sin^2 60°} = \dfrac{1 - \frac{1}{2}}{1 + \left(\frac{\sqrt{3}}{2}\right)^2}$ (remember $\sin^2 60$ means $(\sin 60)^2$)

$= \dfrac{\frac{1}{2}}{\frac{7}{4}}$

$= \dfrac{2}{7}$

5 d $\dfrac{5 - \tan\frac{\pi}{3}}{\sin\frac{\pi}{3}} = \dfrac{5 - \sqrt{3}}{\frac{\sqrt{3}}{2}}$ multiply numerator and denominator by 2

$= \dfrac{10 - 2\sqrt{3}}{\sqrt{3}}$ multiply numerator and denominator by $\sqrt{3}$

$= \dfrac{10\sqrt{3} - 6}{3}$

f $\dfrac{\tan\frac{\pi}{4} - \sin\frac{\pi}{4}}{\tan\frac{\pi}{6}\sin\frac{\pi}{6}} = \dfrac{1 - \frac{1}{\sqrt{2}}}{\frac{1}{\sqrt{3}} \times \frac{1}{2}}$ multiply numerator and denominator by $2\sqrt{6}$

$= \dfrac{2\sqrt{6} - 2\sqrt{3}}{\sqrt{2}}$ multiply numerator and denominator by $\sqrt{2}$

$= \dfrac{4\sqrt{3} - 2\sqrt{6}}{2}$

$= 2\sqrt{3} - \sqrt{6}$

Exercise 9.2

2 g $\dfrac{11\pi}{6}$ is in the 4th quadrant

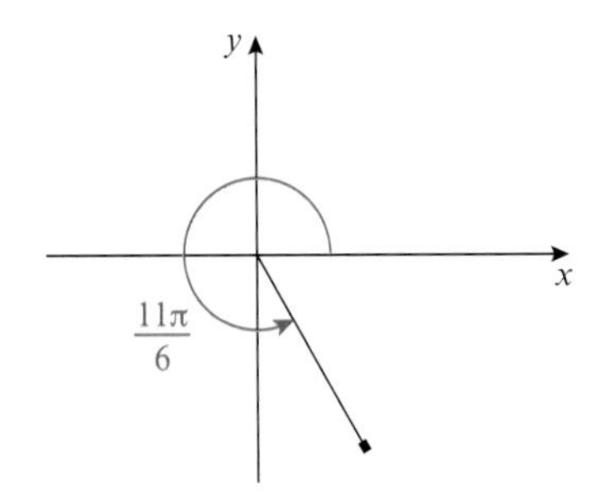

h $-\dfrac{5\pi}{6}$ is in the 3rd quadrant

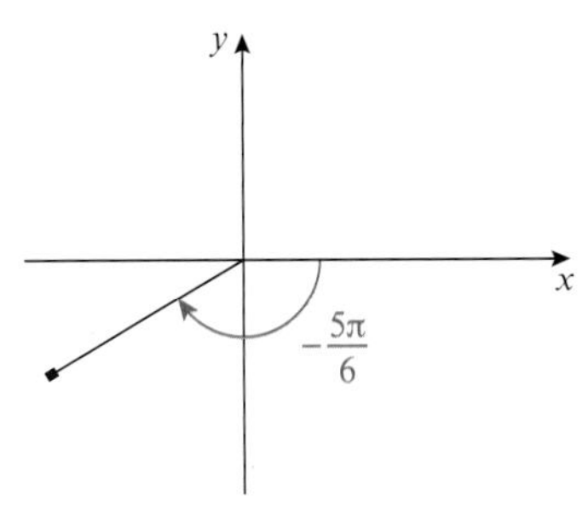

Exercise 9.3

1 c The acute angle made with the positive x-axis is 40°.

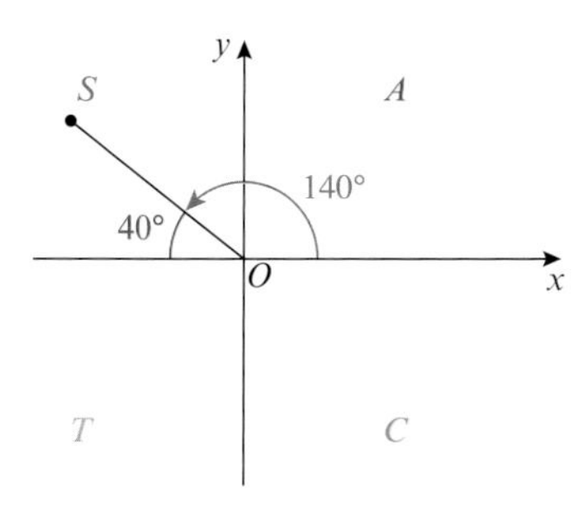

In the second quadrant only sine is positive so tan is negative.

$\tan 140° = -\tan 40°$

j $\frac{9\pi}{4} = 2\pi + \frac{\pi}{4}$

The acute angle made with the positive x-axis is $\frac{\pi}{4}$

In the first quadrant, sine is positive.

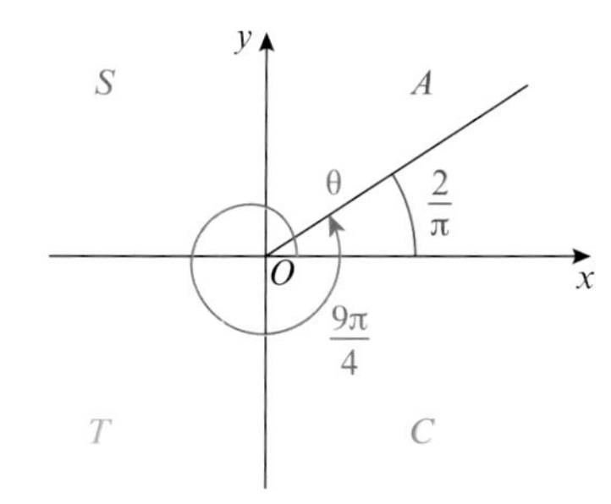

$\sin\frac{9\pi}{4} = \sin\frac{\pi}{4}$

2 a θ is in the 4th quadrant.

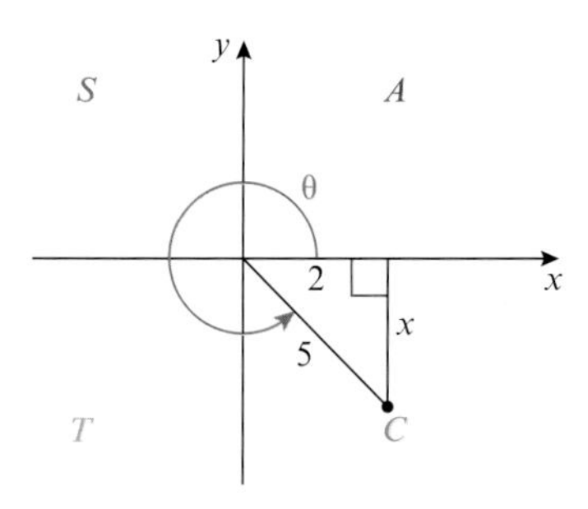

sin is negative and cos is positive in this quadrant

Using Pythagoras:

$x^2 + 2^2 = 5^2$

$x^2 = 5^2 - 2^2$

$x^2 = 21$

$x = \sqrt{21}$

Since $x < 0$, $x = -\sqrt{21}$

$$\tan\theta = \frac{\sin\theta}{\cos\theta} = \frac{\frac{-\sqrt{21}}{5}}{\frac{2}{5}} = -\frac{\sqrt{21}}{2}$$

b θ is in the 4th quadrant.

sin is negative and cos is positive in this quadrant

From part **a**, $\sin\theta = -\frac{\sqrt{21}}{5}$

3 a θ is in the 2nd quadrant.

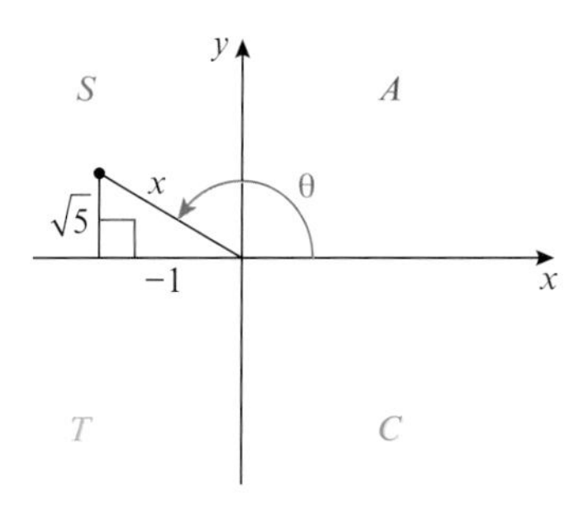

sin is positive and cos is negative in this quadrant.

Using Pythagoras:

$x^2 = (\sqrt{3})^2 + (-1)^2$

$x^2 = 4$

$x = 2$

$\sin\theta = \frac{\sqrt{3}}{2}$

b $\cos\theta = \frac{-1}{2} = -\frac{1}{2}$

4 **a** If θ is obtuse then $90° < \theta < 180°$, i.e., the 2nd quadrant.

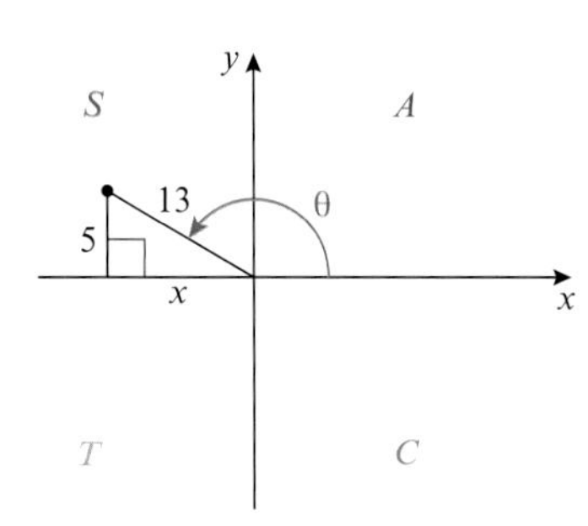

sin is positive and cosine is negative in this quadrant

Using Pythagoras:

$x^2 = 13^2 - 5^2$

$x^2 = 144$

$x = \sqrt{144}$

Since $x < 0$, $x = -\sqrt{144}$

$x = -12$

$\cos\theta = \frac{-12}{13} = -\frac{12}{13}$

b $\tan\theta = \frac{\sin\theta}{\cos\theta} = \frac{\frac{5}{13}}{\frac{-12}{13}} = -\frac{5}{12}$

5 **a** If θ is reflex and $\tan\theta$ is positive then $180° < \theta < 270°$, i.e., the 3rd quadrant.

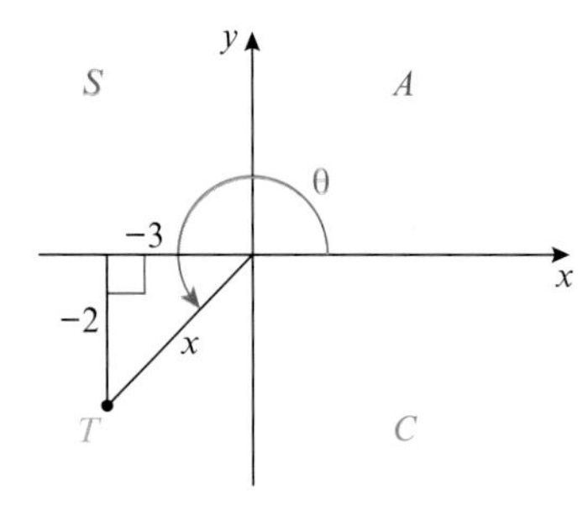

sin is negative and cosine is negative in this quadrant

Using Pythagoras:

$x^2 = (-3)^2 + (-2)^2$

$x^2 = 13$

$x = \sqrt{13}$

$\sin\theta = \frac{-2}{\sqrt{13}} = -\frac{2\sqrt{13}}{13}$

b $\cos\theta = \frac{-3}{\sqrt{13}} = -\frac{3\sqrt{13}}{13}$

6 **a** $\tan A$ is positive in the 1st and 3rd quadrants.

$\cos B$ is negative in the 2nd and 3rd quadrants.

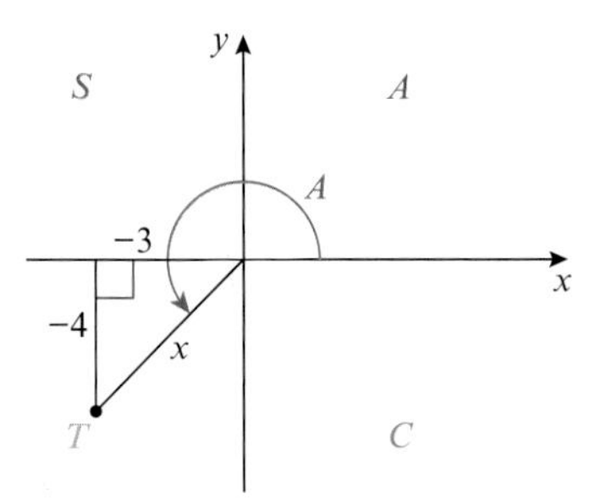

If A and B are in the same quadrants then A and B are in the 3rd quadrant, i.e., $180° < \theta < 270°$.

Using Pythagoras:

$x^2 = (-3)^2 + (-4)^2$

$x^2 = 25$

$x = 5$

$\sin A = \frac{-4}{5} = -\frac{4}{5}$

b $\cos A = \frac{-3}{5} = -\frac{3}{5}$

c Using Pythagoras:

$x^2 = (\sqrt{3})^2 - (-1)^2$

$x^2 = 2$

$x = \sqrt{2}$

Since $x < 0$, $x = -\sqrt{2}$

$\sin B = \frac{-\sqrt{2}}{\sqrt{3}} = -\frac{\sqrt{6}}{3}$

d $\tan B = \frac{-\sqrt{2}}{-1} = \sqrt{2}$

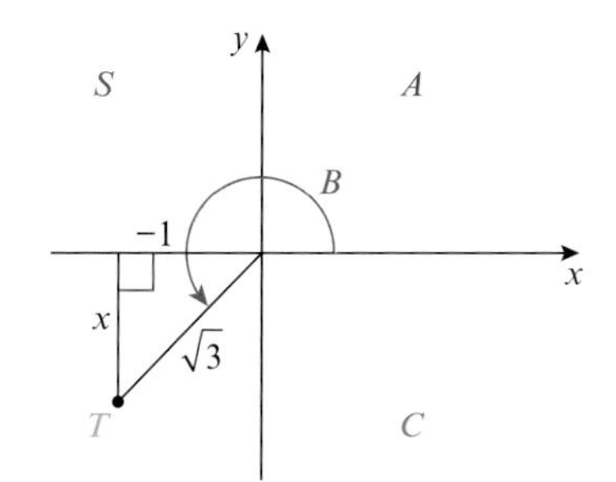

7 a $\sin A$ is negative in the 3rd and 4th quadrants.

$\cos B$ is positive in the 1st and 4th quadrants.

If A and B are in the same quadrants then A and B are in the 4th quadrant, i.e., $270° < \theta < 360°$

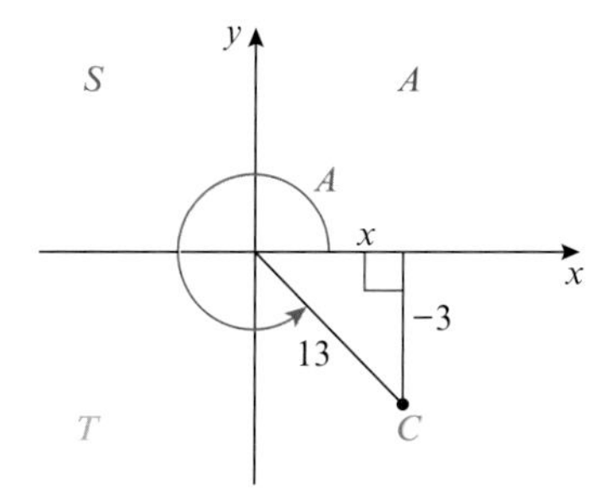

Using Pythagoras:

$x^2 = 13^2 - (-12)^2$

$x^2 = 25$

$x = \sqrt{25}$

Since $x > 0$, $x = 5$

$\cos A = \frac{5}{13}$

b $\tan A = \frac{-12}{5} = -\frac{12}{5}$

c Using Pythagoras:

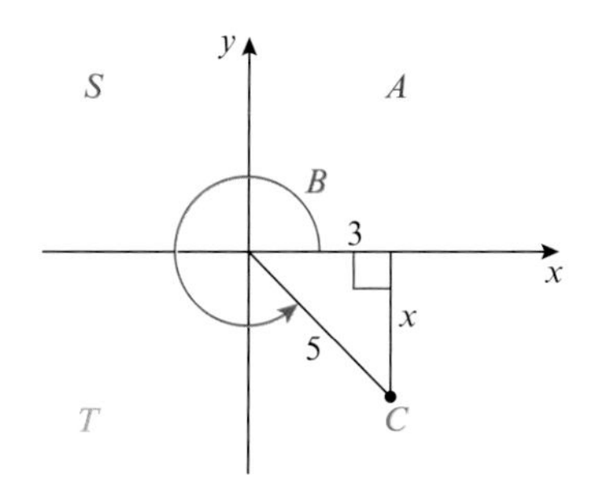

$x^2 = 5^2 - 3^2$

$x^2 = 16$

$x = \sqrt{16}$

Since $x < 0$, $x = -\sqrt{16} = -4$

$\sin B = \frac{-4}{5} = -\frac{4}{5}$

d $\tan B = \frac{-4}{3} = -\frac{4}{3}$

Exercise 9.4

> **TIP**
>
> Horizontal and vertical transformations are independent.
>
> They can be done in any order.

1 a iii $f(x) = 2\cos 3x \quad 0° \leqslant \theta \leqslant 360°$

Amplitude = 2

Period $= \frac{360°}{3} = 120°$

The coordinates of the maximum and minimum points are: (0°, 2), (60°, −2), (120°, 2), (180°, −2), (240°, 2), (300°, −2), (360°, 2).

The sketch of the graph $f(x) = 2\cos 3x$ for $0° \leqslant \theta \leqslant 360°$ can be found in stages:

Start with the sketch of $f(x) = \cos x$ for $0° \leqslant x \leqslant 360°$ which has period 360° and amplitude 1.

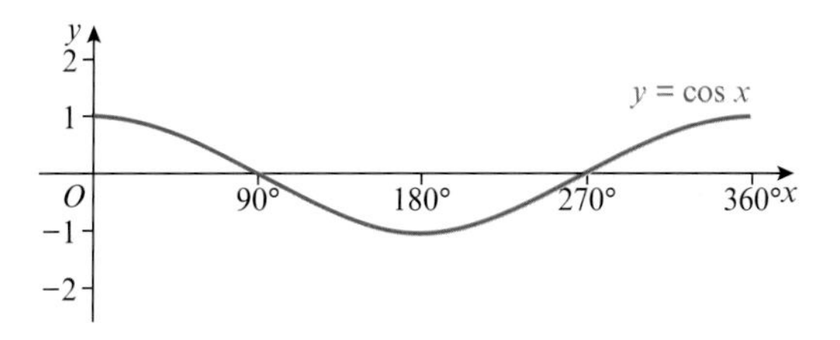

Stretch $y = \cos x$ from the y-axis stretch factor $\frac{1}{3}$.

The period of $y = \cos 3x$ is $\frac{360°}{3} = 120°$.

The amplitude is still 1.

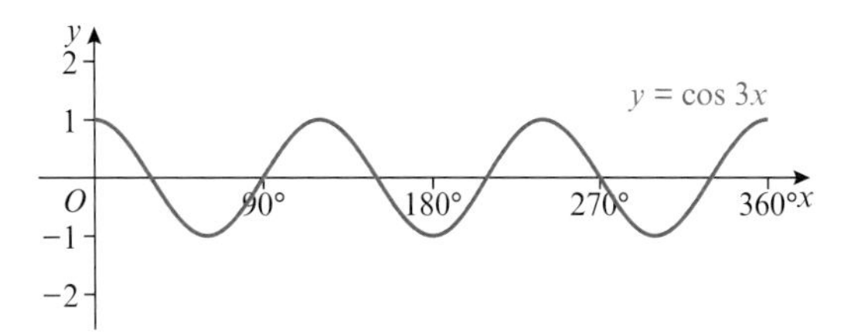

Stretch the graph of $y = \cos 3x$ from the x-axis stetch factor 2.

The period is still 120°.

The amplitude is $1 \times 2 = 2$.

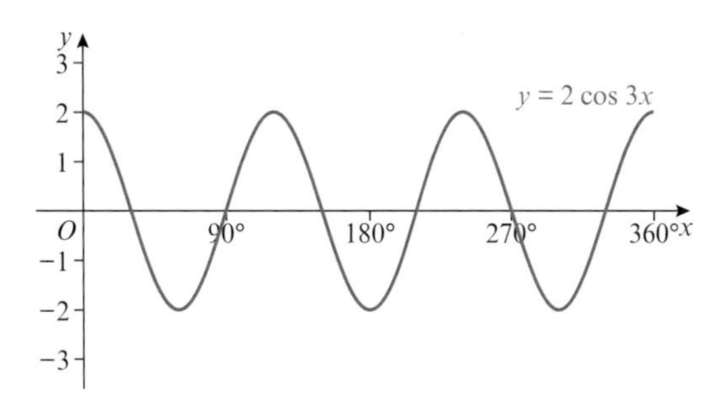

TIP

Horizontal and vertical transformations are independent.

They can be done in any order.

vi $f(x) = 5\sin 2x - 2 \quad 0° \leqslant \theta \leqslant 360°$

Amplitude = 5

Period = $\frac{360°}{2} = 180°$

The coordinates of the maximum and minimum points are: (45°, 3), (135°, −7), (225°, 3), (315°, −7).

The sketch of the graph $f(x) = 5\cos 2x - 2$ for $0° \leqslant \theta \leqslant 360°$ can be found in stages:

Start with the sketch of $f(x) = \sin x$ for $0° \leqslant x \leqslant 360°$ which has period 360° and amplitude 1.

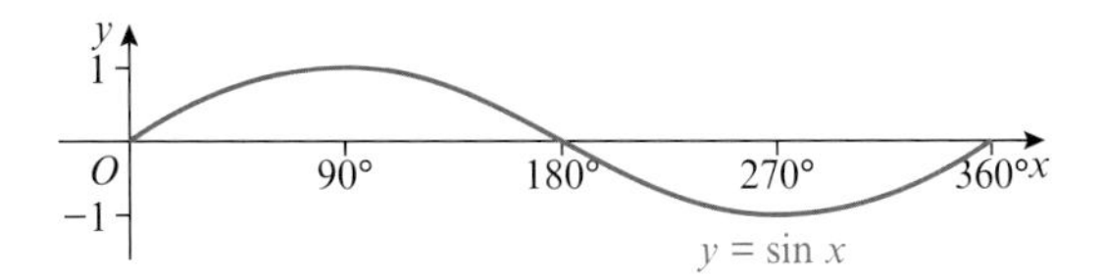

Stretch $y = \sin x$ from the y-axis stretch factor $\frac{1}{2}$.

The period of $y = \sin 2x$ is $\frac{360°}{2} = 180°$.

The amplitude is still 1.

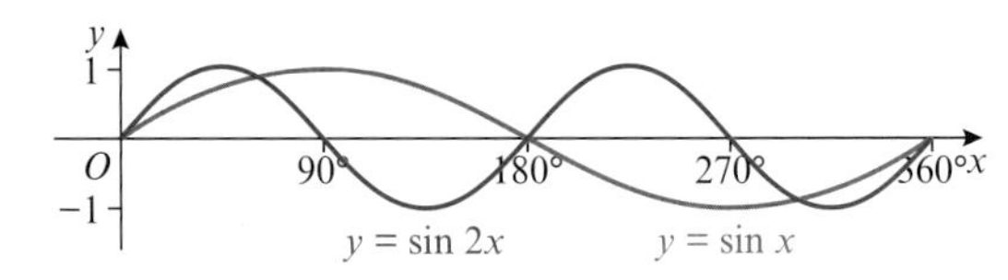

Stretch $y = \sin 2x$ from the x-axis stretch factor 5.

The period of $y = 5\sin 2x$ is still 180°.

The amplitude is $1 \times 5 = 5$.

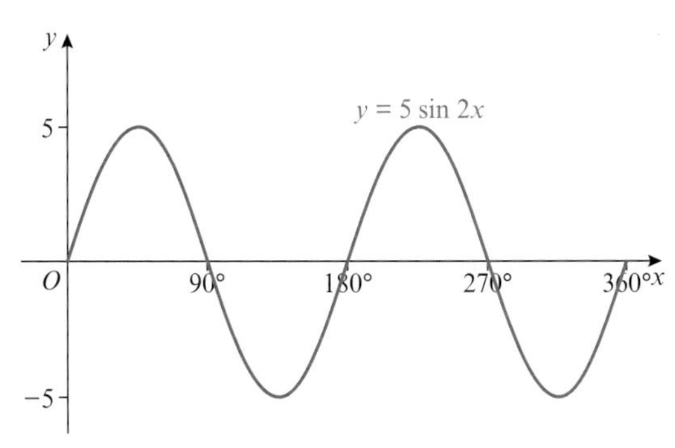

Translate $y = 5\sin 2x$ by the vector $\begin{pmatrix} 0 \\ -2 \end{pmatrix}$

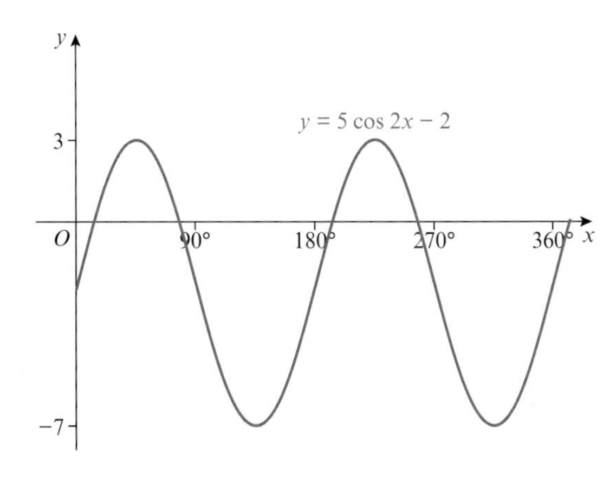

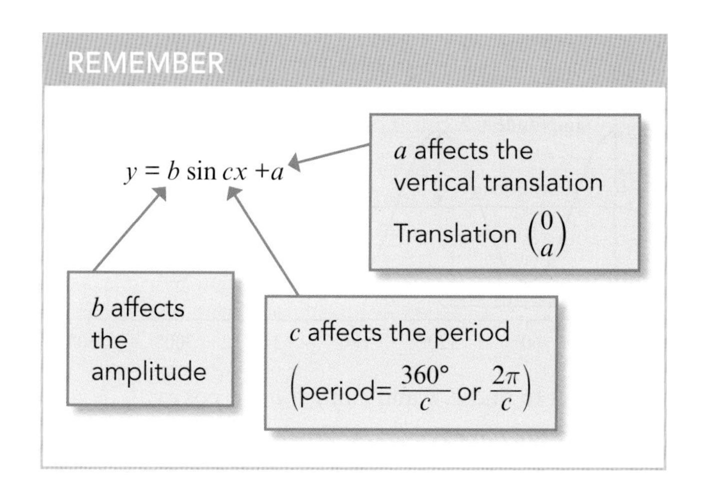

2 a i The graph of $f(x) = \sin x$ has an amplitude 1, period 2π radians and maximum and minimum points at:

$\left(\frac{\pi}{2}, 1\right)$ and $\left(\frac{3\pi}{2}, -1\right)$ respectively.

If the graph of $f(x) = \sin x$ is stretched vertically from the x-axis, stretch factor 4, it becomes the graph of $f(x) = 4 \sin x$. for this graph:

The amplitude is 4.

The period is still 2π radians.

The maximum point is at $\left(\frac{\pi}{2}, 4\right)$ and the minimum point is at $\left(\frac{3\pi}{2}, -4\right)$.

ii The graph of $f(x) = \cos x$ has an amplitude 1, period 2π radians and maximum and minimum points at: $(0, 1)$, $(\pi, -1)$ and $(2\pi, 1)$

If the graph of $f(x) = \cos 3x$ is stretched vertically from the y-axis, stretch factor 3, it becomes the graph of $f(x) = \cos 3x$ for this graph:

The amplitude is still 1.

The period is $\frac{2\pi}{3}$ radians.

The maximum point is at

$(0, 1)$ $\left(\frac{\pi}{3}, -1\right)$ $\left(\frac{2\pi}{3}, 1\right)$, $(\pi, -1)$$\left(\frac{4\pi}{3}, 1\right)$, $\left(\frac{5\pi}{3}, -1\right)$, $(2\pi, 1)$.

b i and ii

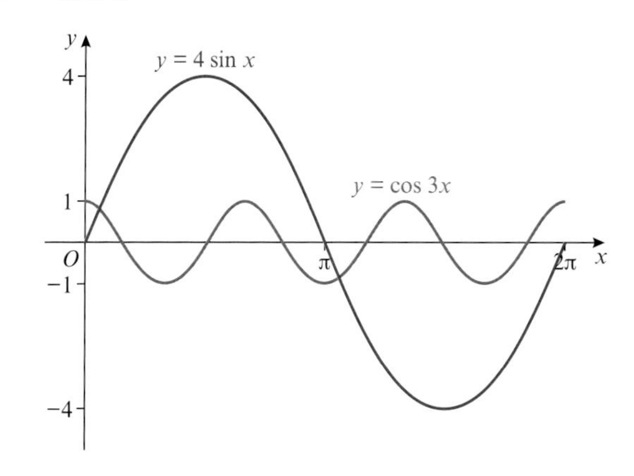

3

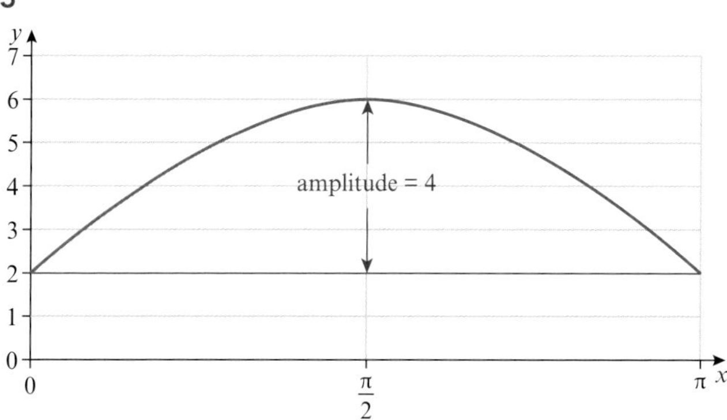

Stages to find a, b and c in $y = a + b \sin cx$:

The midline of the graph of $y = \sin x$ is $y = 0$.

The midline of the graph in this question $y = 2$.

Looking at the diagram, and remembering that the graph of $y = \sin x$ passes through (0 rad, 0), the graph has been transformed 2 units up the y-axis so the vector translation is $\begin{pmatrix} 0 \\ a \end{pmatrix}$ which in this case is $\begin{pmatrix} 0 \\ 2 \end{pmatrix}$.
So $a = 2$.

The amplitude is 4.

The amplitude of a $y = \sin x$ graph is 1.

So, the graph has been stretched vertically, stretch factor 4.

So $b = 4$.

The period of a graph is the length of one repetition or cycle.

The period of a sine graph is 360° or 2π radians.

The period of the given graph is also 2π radians.

So $c = 1$.

Solutions are: $a = 2$, $b = 4$, $c = 1$

4

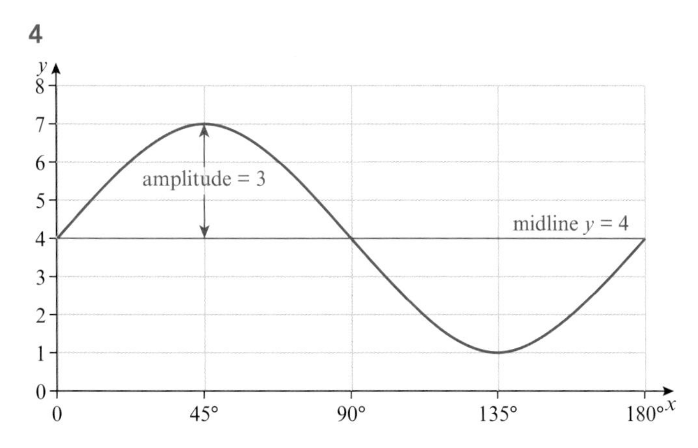

Stages to find a, b and c in $y = a \sin bx + c$:

The midline of the graph of $y = \sin x$ is $y = 0$.

The midline of the graph in this question is $y = 4$.

Looking at the diagram, and remembering that the graph of $y = \sin x$ passes through (0°, 0), the graph has been transformed 4 units up the y-axis so the vector translation is $\begin{pmatrix} 0 \\ c \end{pmatrix}$ which in this case is $\begin{pmatrix} 0 \\ 4 \end{pmatrix}$.

So $c = 4$.

The amplitude is 3.

The amplitude of a $y = \sin x$ graph is 1.

So the graph has been stretched vertically, stretch factor 3.

So $a = 3$.

The period of a graph is the length of one repetition or cycle.

The period of a sine graph is 360° or 2π radians.

The period of the given graph is 180° so $\frac{360°}{180°} = 2$.

So $b = 2$.

The graph is $y = 3 \sin 2x + 4$

Solutions are: $a = 3$, $b = 2$, $c = 4$

5

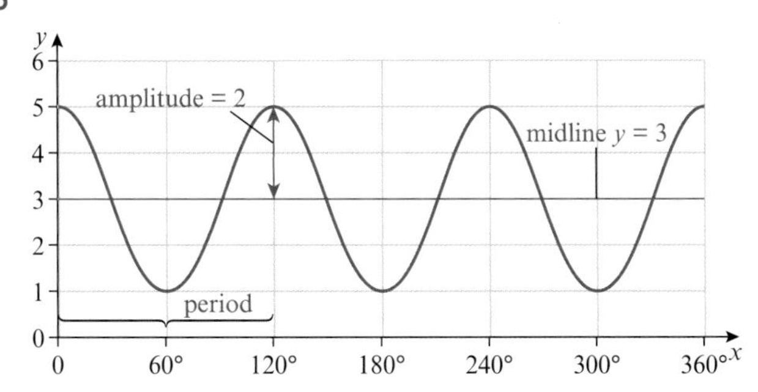

Stages to find a, b and c in $y = a + b \cos cx$:

The midline of the graph of $y = \cos x$ is $y = 0$.

The midline of the graph in this question is $y = 3$.

Looking at the diagram, and remembering that the graph of $y = \cos x$ passes through (0°, 1), the graph has been transformed 3 units up the y-axis so the vector translation is $\begin{pmatrix} 0 \\ a \end{pmatrix}$ which in this case is $\begin{pmatrix} 0 \\ 3 \end{pmatrix}$.

So $a = 3$.

The amplitude is 2.

The amplitude of a $y = \cos x$ graph is 1.

So, the graph has been stretched vertically, stretch factor 2.

So $b = 2$.

The period of a graph is the length of one repetition or cycle.

The period of a cos graph is 360° or 2π radians.

The period of the given graph is 120° so $\frac{360°}{120°} = 3$.

So $c = 3$.

The graph is $3 + 2 \cos 3x$

Solutions are: $a = 3$, $b = 2$, $c = 3$

6 a i

$y = \tan x$ —Stretch from the y-axis→ $y = \tan 2x$

Period 180°   Stretch factor $\frac{1}{2}$ Period $\frac{180°}{2} = 90°$

Asymptotes for $0° \leqslant x \leqslant 360°$ are at $x = 45°$, $x = 135°$, $x = 225°$, $x = 315°$

ii

$y = \tan x$ —Stretch from the y-axis→ $y = \tan\frac{1}{2}x$ —Stretch from the x-axis→ $y = 3\tan\frac{1}{2}x$

Period 180°   Stretch factor 2   Period $\frac{180°}{\frac{1}{2}} = 360°$ Stretch factor 3   Period = 360°

Asymptote for $0° \leqslant x \leqslant 360°$ is at $x = 180°$

iii

$y = \tan x$ —Stretch from the y-axis→ $y = \tan 3x$ —Stretch from the x-axis→ $y = 2\tan 3x$ —Translation by vector→ $y = 2\tan 3x + 1$

Period 180°   Stretch factor $\frac{1}{3}$ Period $\frac{180°}{3} = 60°$ Stretch factor 2   Period = 60° $\begin{pmatrix}0\\1\end{pmatrix}$ Period = 60°

Asymptotes for $0° \leqslant x \leqslant 360°$ are at $x = 30°$, $x = 90°$, $x = 150°$, $x = 210°$, $x = 270°$, $x = 330°$

b

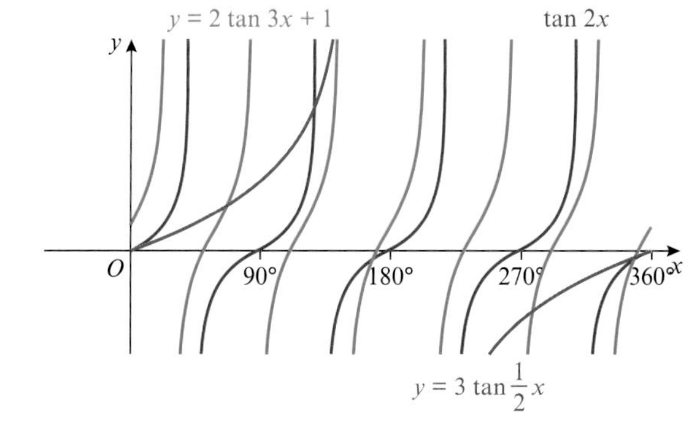

7 a i

$y = \tan x$ —Stretch from the y-axis→ $y = \tan 4x$

Period = π Stretch factor $\frac{1}{4}$ Period = $\frac{\pi}{4}$

Asymptotes for $0 \leqslant x \leqslant 2\pi$ are at:

$x = \frac{\pi}{8}$, $x = \frac{3\pi}{8}$, $x = \frac{5\pi}{8}$, $x = \frac{7\pi}{8}$, $x = \frac{9\pi}{8}$, $x = \frac{11\pi}{8}$, $x = \frac{13\pi}{8}$, $x = \frac{15\pi}{8}$

ii

$y = \tan x$ → (Stretch from the y-axis, Stretch factor $\frac{1}{3}$) → $y = \tan 3x$ → (Stretch from the x-axis, Stretch factor 2) → $y = 2\tan 3x$

Period $= \pi$ → Period $= \frac{\pi}{3}$ → Period $= \frac{\pi}{3}$

Asymptotes for $0 \leqslant x \leqslant 2\pi$ are at:

$x = \frac{\pi}{6},\ x = \frac{\pi}{2},\ x = \frac{5\pi}{6},\ x = \frac{7\pi}{6},\ x = \frac{3\pi}{2},\ x = \frac{11\pi}{6}$

iii

$y = \tan x$ → (Stretch from the y-axis, Stretch factor $\frac{1}{2}$) → $y = \tan 2x$ → (Stretch from the x-axis, Stretch factor 5) → $y = 5\tan 2x$ → (Translation by vector $\begin{pmatrix} 0 \\ -3 \end{pmatrix}$) → $y = 5\tan 2x - 3$

Period $= \pi$ → Period $= \frac{\pi}{2}$ → Period $= \frac{\pi}{2}$ → Period $= \frac{\pi}{2}$

Asymptotes for $0 \leqslant x \leqslant 2\pi$ are at:

$x = \frac{\pi}{4},\ x = \frac{3\pi}{4},\ x = \frac{5\pi}{4},\ x = \frac{7\pi}{4}$

b i

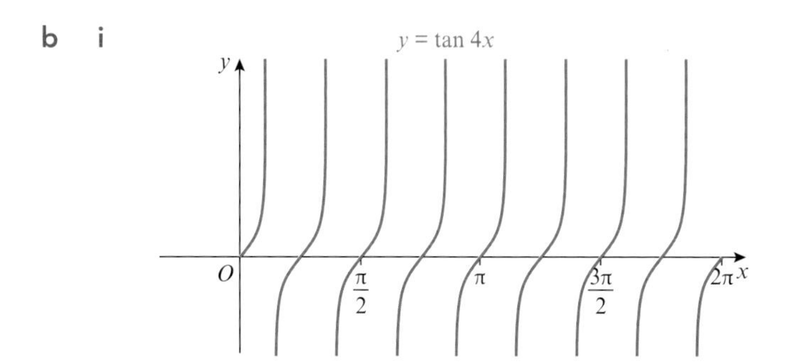

ii

$y = 2\tan 3x$

y
O
π/3
2π/3
π
4π/3
5π/3
2π
x

iii

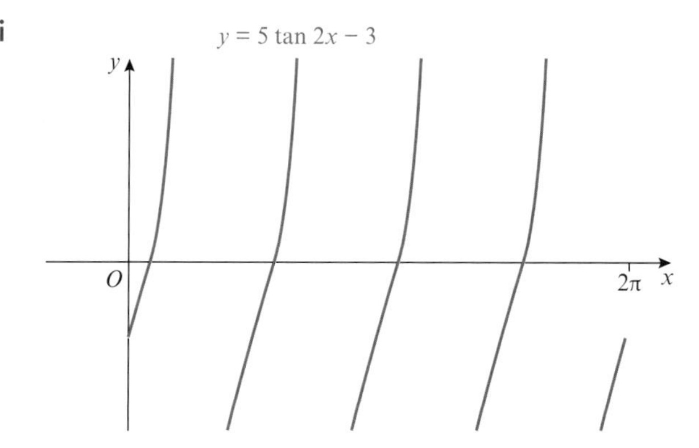

8 $y = A\tan Bx + C$

The asymptotes of the graph of $y = \tan x$ for $0 \leqslant x \leqslant 2\pi$ are $x = \frac{\pi}{2}, x = \frac{3\pi}{2}$

The asymptotes of our graph are also $x = \frac{\pi}{2}, x = \frac{3\pi}{2}$, so the period of the graph is $\frac{\pi}{2}$. Hence $B = 1$

The midline of the graph of $y = \tan x$ is $y = 0$

The midline of our graph is at $y = 3$

The point $\left(\frac{\pi}{4}, 1\right)$ lies on the graph of $y = \tan x$

The point $\left(\frac{\pi}{4}, 4\right)$ lies on our graph so the graph of $y = \tan x$ has been translated vertically by vector $\begin{pmatrix} 0 \\ 3 \end{pmatrix}$ so $C = 3$

The graph has not been vertically stretched so $A = 1$

Solutions are: $A = 1$, $B = 1$, $C = 3$

9 $f(x) = a + b\sin cx$

The amplitude of the function is $\frac{\text{maximum value-minimum value}}{2} = \frac{13 - 5}{2} = 4$

So $b = 4$

The period of the graph is 60° so Period$= \frac{360°}{60°} = 6$

So $c = 6$

The midline is the horizontal line that is midway between the maximum and the minimum points of the graph in this case the midline is at $y = 9$ since $\left(\frac{13 + 5}{2} = 9\right)$

The midline of the graph of $y = \sin x$ is $y = 0$ so our graph has been transformed 9 units up the y-axis, i.e., $\begin{pmatrix} 0 \\ a \end{pmatrix} = \begin{pmatrix} 0 \\ 9 \end{pmatrix}$ therefore $a = 9$

Solutions are: $a = 9$, $b = 4$, $c = 6$

10 a $f(x) = A + 3\cos Bx \ 0° \leqslant x \leqslant 360°$

Comparing our graph with the graph of $y = \cos x$, we notice that:

The period of the $y = \cos x$ graph is 360°

The period of $y = A + 3\cos Bx$ is 72°

So, the period of our graph is $\frac{360°}{72°} = 5$ so, $B = 5$

Therefore $y = A + 3\cos 5x$

The graph of $y = \cos x$ for $0° \leqslant x \leqslant 360°$ has the maximum value 1

The graph of $y = \cos 5x$ has a maximum value of 1

We are told that our graph $y = A + 3\cos 5x$ also has a maximum value 5

$y = A + 3\cos 5x$

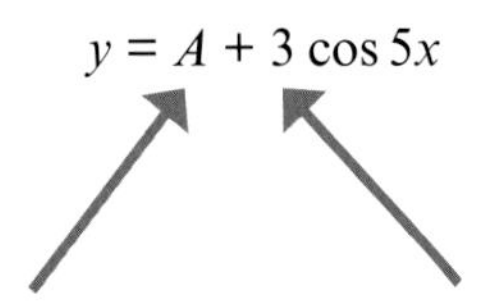

'A' represents a vertical translation

'3' represents a vertical stretch, stretch factor 3

As there are two vertical transformations, does their order matter?

Case 1: If we stretched $y = \cos 5x$ vertically by stretch factor 3 first and then a translation by vector $\begin{pmatrix} 0 \\ 2 \end{pmatrix}$ the maximum value of the graph would be 5.

$y = \cos 5x \xrightarrow[\text{Stretch factor 3}]{\text{Stretch from the } x\text{-axis}} y = 3\cos 5x \xrightarrow[\text{Vector } \begin{pmatrix} 0 \\ 2 \end{pmatrix}]{\text{Translation}} y = 2 + 3\cos 5x$

Case 2: If we translated $y = \cos 5x$ by the vector $\begin{pmatrix} 0 \\ \frac{2}{3} \end{pmatrix}$ first and then stretched vertically by stretch factor 3, the maximum value of the graph is also 5.

Because $y = 3\left(\frac{2}{3} + \cos 5x\right)$ is the same as $y = 2 + 3\cos 5x$

$y = \cos 5x \xrightarrow[\text{Vector } \begin{pmatrix} 0 \\ \frac{2}{3} \end{pmatrix}]{\text{Translation}} y = \frac{2}{3} + \cos 5x \xrightarrow[\text{Stretch factor 3}]{\text{Stretch from the } x\text{-axis}} y = 3\left(\frac{2}{3} + \cos 5x\right)$

Both Case 1 and Case 2 lead to the same solution:

$A = 2, B = 5$

b Amplitude of f is 3

c

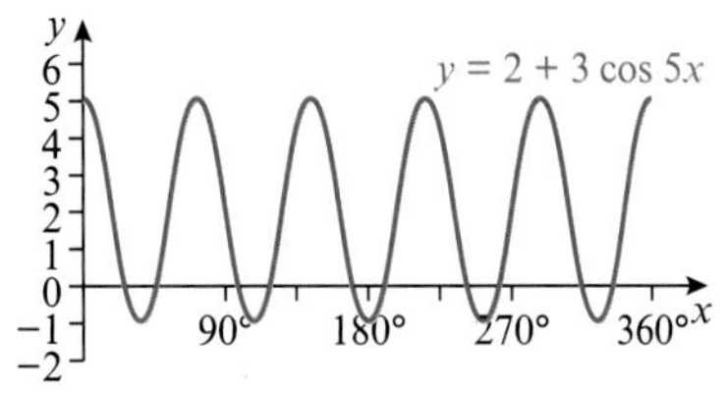

$y = 2 + 3\cos 5x$

y: −2, −1, 0, 1, 2, 3, 4, 5, 6

x: 90°, 180°, 270°, 360°

11 a $f(x) = A + B \sin Cx$

The period of the graph is 90° so as

period$= \frac{360°}{90°} = 4$. Then $C = 4$

The amplitude of our graph is 3, so comparing with the graph of $y = \sin x$ (which has an amplitude 1), our graph has been vertically stretched by scale factor 3.

Hence $B = 3$

The amplitude of the function is 3 so if the minimum value of is -2, the maximum value of f is 4. The midline is the horizontal line that is midway between the maximum and the minimum points of a sine or cosine graph. The midline of $y = \sin x$ is $y = 0$.

The midline of $y = A + 3 \sin 4x$ is $y = 1$

$\left[\text{since } \frac{-2+4}{2} = 1\right]$

So, the graph of $y = 3 \sin 4x$ has been translated

by vector $\begin{pmatrix} 0 \\ 1 \end{pmatrix}$ to give

$y = 1 + 3 \sin 4x$

Solutions are: $A = 1$, $B = 3$, $C = 4$

b

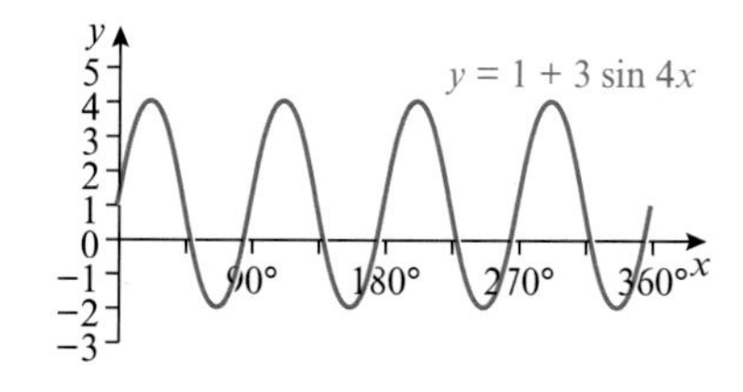

12 a

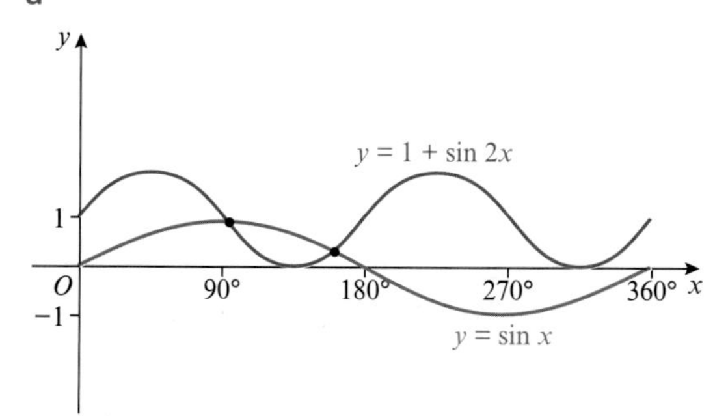

b The graphs $y = \sin x$ and $y = 1 + \sin 2x$ intersect at 2 points.

There are 2 roots to the equation $\sin x = 1 + \sin 2x$ (or $\sin 2x - \sin x + 1 = 0$) for $0° \leqslant x \leqslant 360°$

13 a

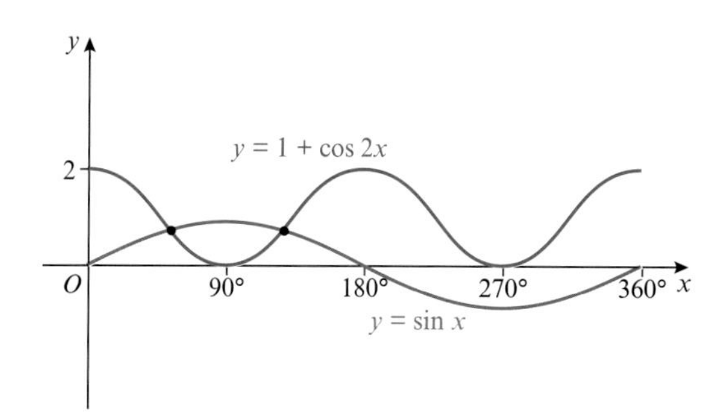

b The graphs $y = \sin x$ and $y = 1 + \cos 2x$ intersect at 2 points.

There are 2 roots to the equation $\sin x = 1 + \cos 2x$ $0° \leqslant x \leqslant 360°$

14 a

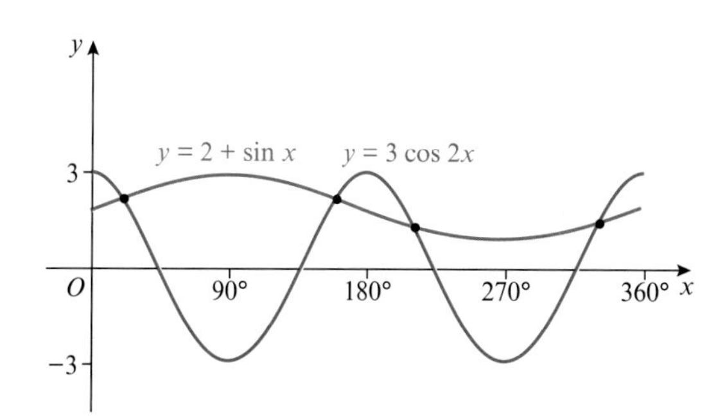

b The graphs $y = 2 + \sin x$ and $y = 3 \cos 2x$ intersect at 4 points.

There are 4 roots to the equation $3 \cos 2x = 2 + \sin x$ for $0° \leqslant x \leqslant 360°$

Exercise 9.5

1 e The range of $f(x) = \left|2 \cos \frac{1}{2}x\right|$ is $0 \leqslant f(x) \leqslant 2$

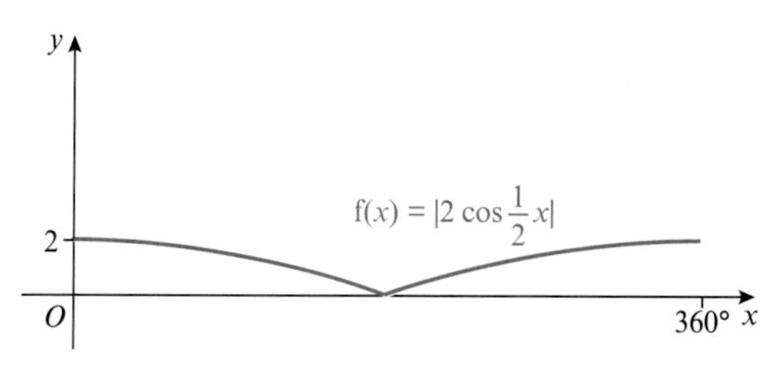

i The range of $f(x) = |4\cos x - 3|$ is $0 \leqslant f(x) \leqslant 7$

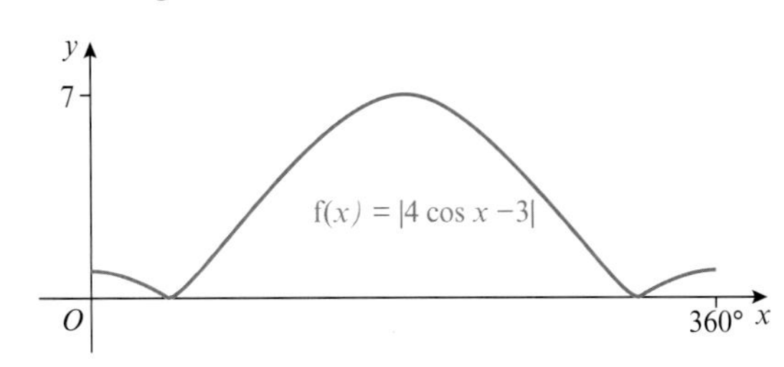

2 a, b

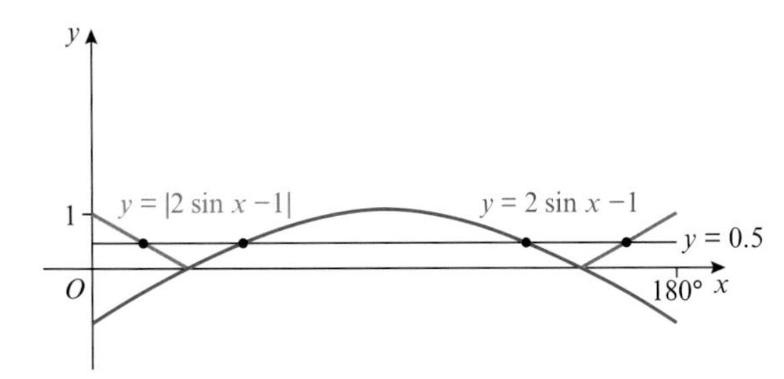

c There are 4 solutions to $|2\sin x - 1| = 0.5$ for $0° \leqslant x \leqslant 180°$

3 a, b

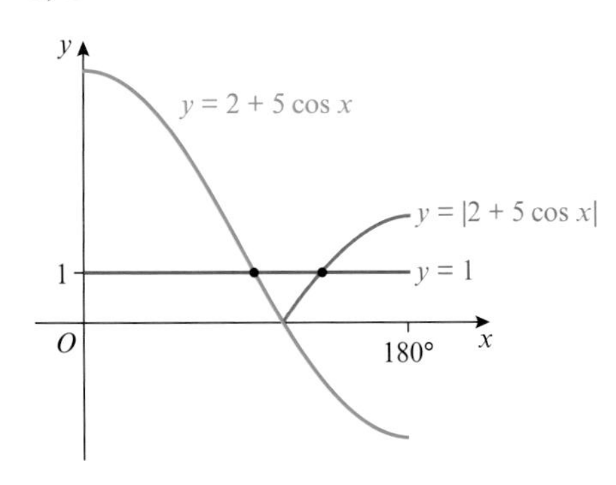

c There are 2 solutions to $|2 + 5\cos x| = 1$ for $0° \leqslant x \leqslant 180°$

4 a, b

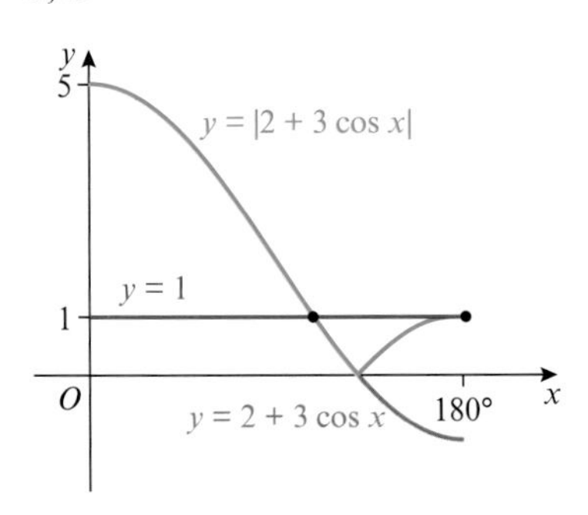

c There are 2 solutions to $|2 + 3\cos x| = 1$ for $0° \leqslant x \leqslant 180°$

5 a

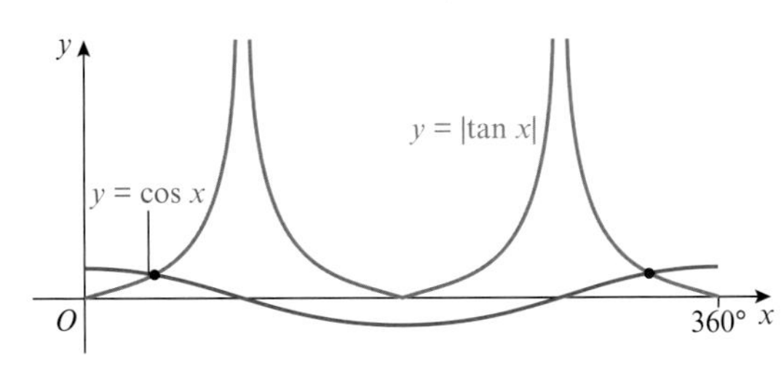

b There are 2 roots to $|\tan x| = \cos x$ for $0° \leqslant x \leqslant 360°$

6 a

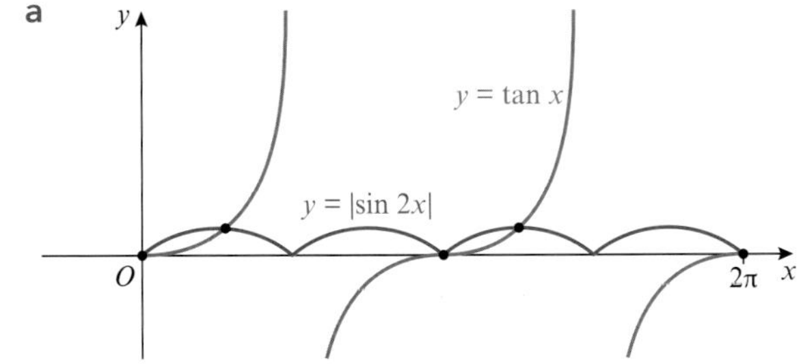

b There are 5 roots to $|\sin 2x| = \tan x$ for $0 \leqslant x \leqslant 2\pi$

7 a

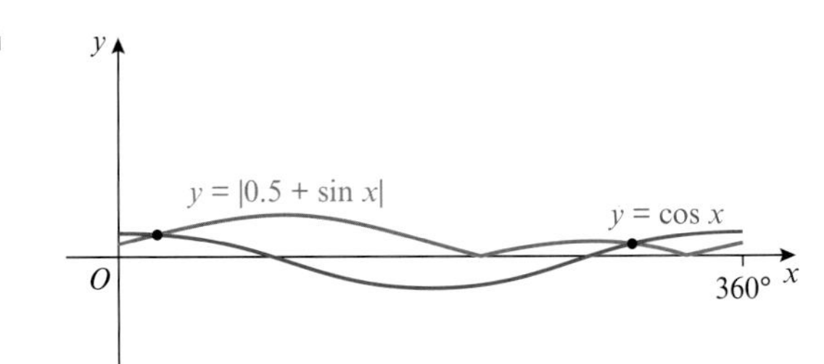

b There are 2 roots to $|0.5 + \sin x| = \cos x$ for $0° \leqslant x \leqslant 360°$

8 a

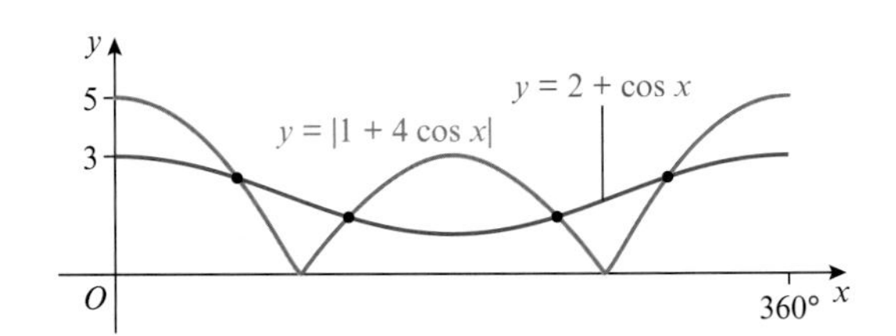

b There are 4 roots to $|1 + 4\cos x| = 2 + \cos x$ for $0° \leqslant x \leqslant 360°$

9 The possible values of k are $1 < k < 5$ in the interval $0 \leqslant x \leqslant 2\pi$

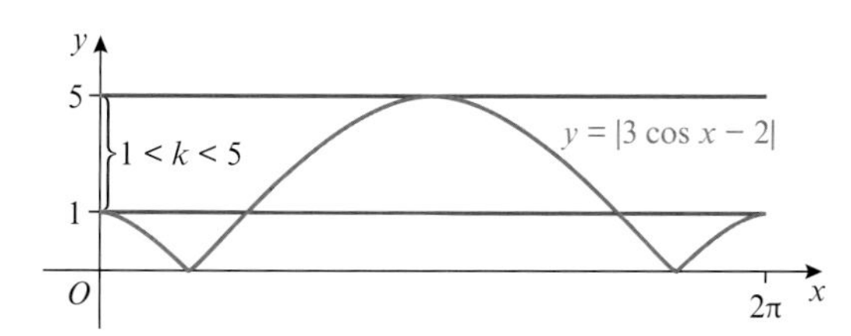

10 Use the graph of $f(x) = |a + b\cos cx|$ to draw the graph of $y = a + b\cos cx$

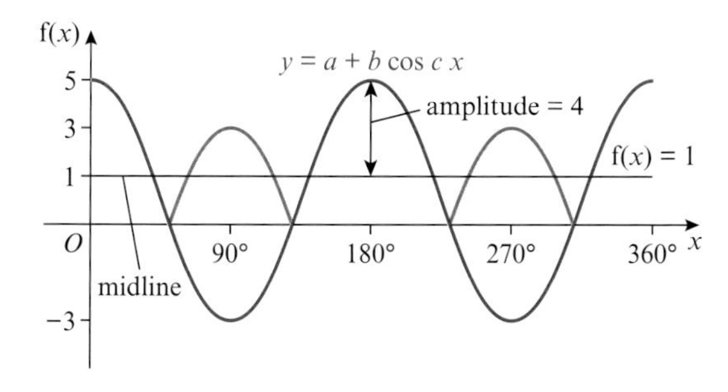

Draw the midline of the graph which has equation $f(x) = 1$.

The amplitude of $y = a + b\cos cx$ is 4 so $b = 4$ (the graph has been stretched vertically stretch factor 4).

The value of $a = 1$ since the graph has been translated by the vector $\begin{pmatrix} 0 \\ 1 \end{pmatrix}$

The period of $y = 1 + 4\cos cx$ is 180° so the graph has been stretched horizontally from the y-axis by stretch factor $\frac{1}{2}$. So $c = 2$.

The graph $y = a + b\cos cx$ is $y = 1 + 4\cos 2x$

Solutions are: $a = 1$, $b = 4$, $c = 2$

Exercise 9.6

1 d $\sin x = -0.6$ use a calculator to find $\sin^{-1}(-0.6)$ to 1 decimal place

$x = -36.9°$

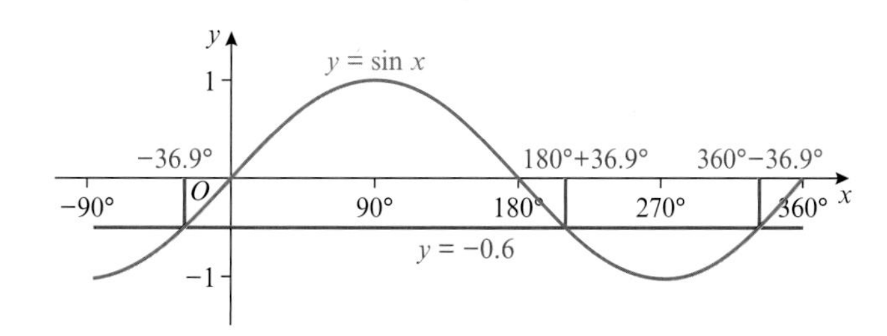

The sketch graph shows there are two values of x, between 0° and 360°, for which $\sin x = -0.6$

Using the symmetry of the curve, the first value is $180° + 36.9° = 216.9°$ and the second value is 323.1°

Hence the solution of $\sin x = -0.6$ for $0° \leqslant x \leqslant 360°$ is

$x = 216.9°$ or $323.1°$ (1 d.p.)

h $2\cos x = 1$ rearrange

$\cos x = -0.5$ use a calculator to find $\cos^{-1}(-0.5)$

$x = 120°$

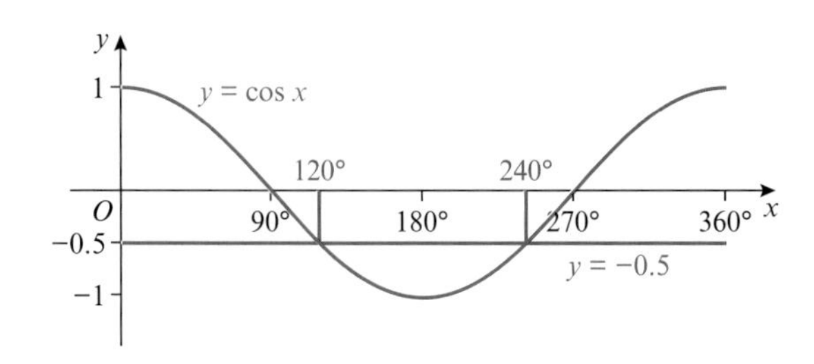

The sketch graph shows there are two values of x, between 0° and 360°, for which $\cos x = -0.5$

Using the symmetry of the curve, the second value is $270° - 30° = 240°$

Hence the solution of $2\cos x = 1$ for $0° \leqslant x \leqslant 360°$ is

$x = 120°$ or $240°$

2 b $\tan x = 0.2$ use a calculator to find $\tan^{-1}(0.2)$

$x = 0.1974$ radians

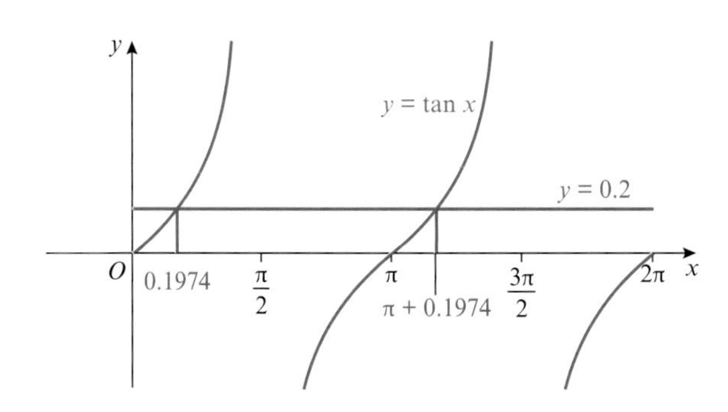

The sketch graph shows there are two values of x, between 0 and 2π, for which $\tan x = 0.2$

Using the symmetry of the curve, the second value is $\pi + 0.1974 = 3.3390$ radians

Hence the solution of $\tan x = 0.2$ for $0 \leqslant x \leqslant 2\pi$ is

$x = 0.197$ radians or 3.34 radians (3 s.f.)

h $5\sin x + 2 = 0$ Rearrange

$\sin x = -0.4$ Use a calculator to find $\sin^{-1}(-0.4)$

$x = -0.4115$ radians

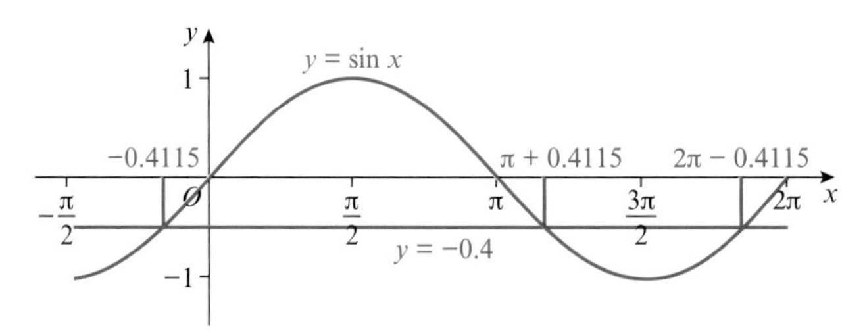

The sketch graph shows there are two values of x, between 0 and 2π, for which $\sin x = -0.4$

Using the symmetry of the curve, the second value is $\pi + 0.4115 = 3.5531$ radians and the third value is $2\pi - 0.4115 = 5.8716$ radians.

Hence the solution of $5 \sin x + 2 = 0$ for $0 \leqslant x \leqslant 2\pi$ is

$x = 3.55$ radians or 5.87 radians (3 s.f.)

3 c $\tan 2x = 2$ for $0° \leqslant x \leqslant 180°$

$\tan 2x = 2$ let $A = 2x$

$\tan A = 2$ use a calculator to find $\tan^{-1}(2)$

$A = 63.43°$

As $A = 2x$, draw the graph of $y = \tan A$ for $0° \leqslant A \leqslant 360°$

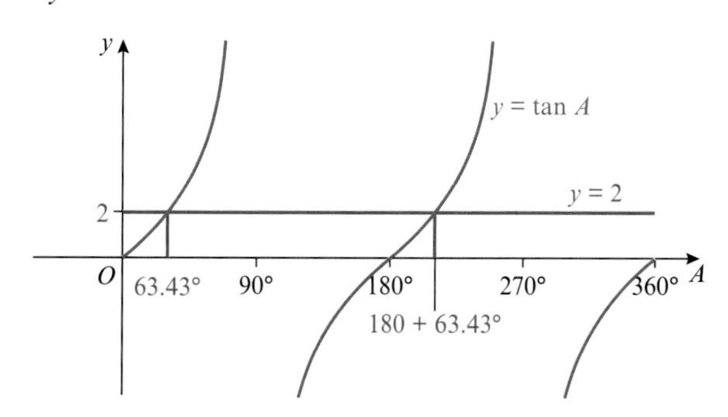

Using the symmetry of the curve, the second value is $180° + 63.43° = 243.43°$

As $A = 2x$, then $x = \frac{A}{2}$

$2x = 63.43$ $2x = 243.43$

$x = 31.7$ $x = 121.7$

Hence the solution of $\tan 2x = 2$ for $0° \leqslant x \leqslant 180°$ is

$x = 31.7°$ or $121.7°$ (1 d.p.)

f $7 \sin 2x = -2$ let $A = 2x$

$\sin 2x = -\frac{2}{7}$

$\sin A = -0.2857$ use a calculator to find $\sin^{-1}(-0.2857)$

$A = -16.60°$

As $A = 2x$, draw the graph of $y = \sin A$ for $-90° \leqslant A \leqslant 360°$

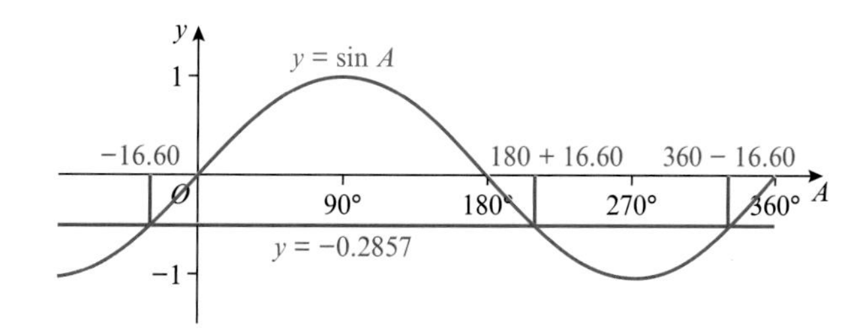

Using the symmetry of the curve

$A = 180 + 16.60$ $A = 360 - 16.60$

$A = 196.60$ $A = 343.4$

As $A = 2x$, then $x = \frac{A}{2}$

$x = 196.60$ $\qquad$ $x = 343.4$

$x = 98.3$ $\qquad$ $x = 171.7$

Hence the solution of $7 \sin 2x = -2$ for $0° \leqslant x \leqslant 180°$ is

$x = 98.3°$ or $171.7°$ (1 d.p.)

4 c Solve $2 \cos\left(\frac{2x}{3}\right) + \sqrt{3} = 0$ for $0° \leqslant x \leqslant 540°$

$2 \cos\left(\frac{2x}{3}\right) + \sqrt{3} = 0$ $\qquad$ rearrange

$\cos\left(\frac{2x}{3}\right) = -\frac{\sqrt{3}}{2}$ $\qquad$ let $A = \frac{2x}{3}$

$\cos A = -\frac{\sqrt{3}}{2}$ $\qquad$ use a calculator to find $\cos^{-1}\left(-\frac{\sqrt{3}}{2}\right)$

$A = 150$

As $A = \frac{2x}{3}$ draw the graph of $y = \cos A$ for $0° \leqslant A \leqslant 360°$

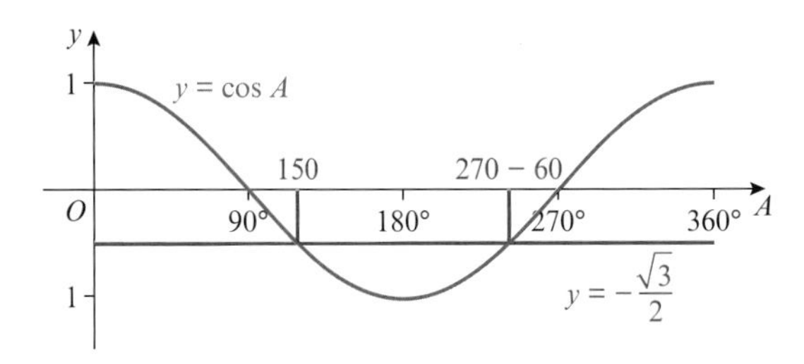

Using the symmetry of the curve

$A = 150$ $\qquad$ $A = 270 - 60$

$A = 210$

As $A = \frac{2x}{3}$ so $x = \frac{3A}{2}$

$x = \frac{3 \times 150}{2}$ $\qquad$ $x = \frac{3 \times 210}{2}$

$x = 225$ $\qquad$ $x = 315$

Hence the solution of $2 \cos\left(\frac{2x}{3}\right) + \sqrt{3} = 0$ for $0° \leqslant x \leqslant 540°$ is

$x = 225°$ or $315°$

f Solving $\sqrt{2}\sin\left(\frac{x}{2}+\frac{\pi}{6}\right)=1$ for $0 \leqslant x \leqslant 4\pi$ radians

$\sqrt{2}\sin\left(\frac{x}{2}+\frac{\pi}{6}\right)=1$ rearrange

$\sin\left(\frac{x}{2}+\frac{\pi}{6}\right)=\frac{1}{\sqrt{2}}$ let $A=\left(\frac{x}{2}+\frac{\pi}{6}\right)$

$\sin A=\frac{1}{\sqrt{2}}$ use a calculator to find $\sin^{-1}\left(\frac{1}{\sqrt{2}}\right)$

$A=\frac{\pi}{4}$

As $A=\left(\frac{x}{2}+\frac{\pi}{6}\right)$, draw the graph of $y=\sin A$ for $\frac{\pi}{6} \leqslant A \leqslant \frac{13\pi}{6}$

$\left[\text{From } \frac{0}{2}+\frac{\pi}{6} \leqslant A \leqslant \frac{4\pi}{2}+\frac{\pi}{6} \text{ which leads to } \frac{\pi}{6} \leqslant A \leqslant \frac{13\pi}{6}\right]$

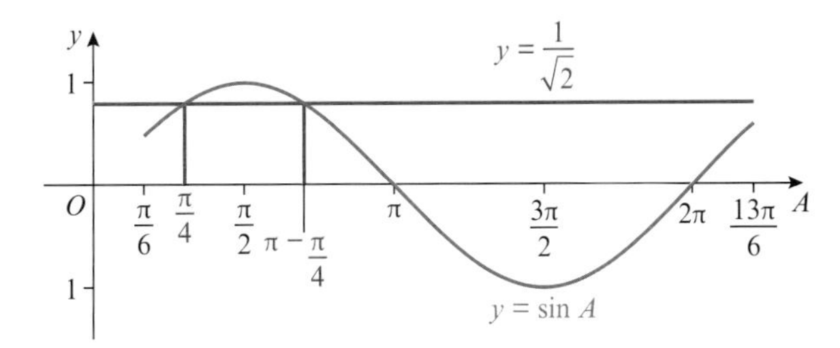

Using the symmetry of the curve:

$A=\frac{\pi}{4}$ $\quad A=\pi-\frac{\pi}{4}$

As $A=\left(\frac{x}{2}+\frac{\pi}{6}\right)$

$A-\frac{\pi}{6}=\frac{x}{2}$

$x=2A-\frac{\pi}{3}$

$x=2\left(\frac{\pi}{4}\right)-\frac{\pi}{3}$ $\quad x=2\left(\pi-\frac{\pi}{4}\right)-\frac{\pi}{3}$

$x=\frac{\pi}{6}$ $\quad x=\frac{7\pi}{6}$

Hence the solution for $\sqrt{2}\sin\left(\frac{x}{2}+\frac{\pi}{6}\right)=1$ for $0 \leqslant x \leqslant 4\pi$ radians is

$x=\frac{\pi}{6}$ radians and $x=\frac{7\pi}{6}$ radians

5 b Solve $3\sin x+4\cos x=0$ for $0° \leqslant x \leqslant 360°$

$3\sin x+4\cos x=0$ divide both sides by $\cos x$

$3\tan x+4=0$ rearrange

$\tan x=-\frac{4}{3}$ use a calculator to find $\tan^{-1}\left(-\frac{4}{3}\right)$

$x=-53.13$

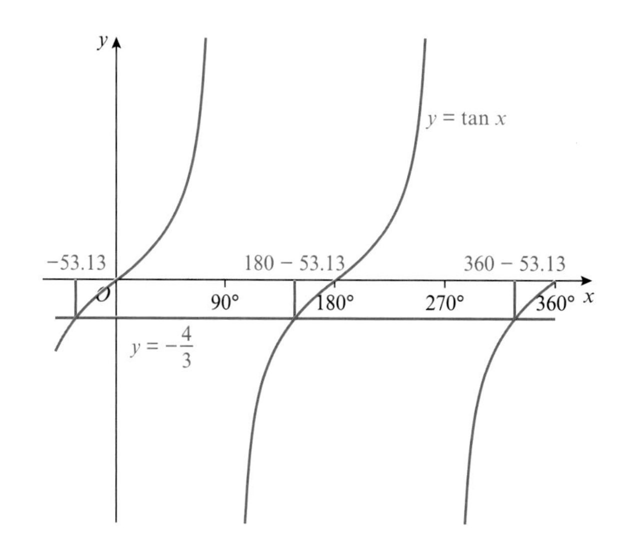

$x = -53.13$ $\quad$ $x = 180 - 53.13$ $\quad$ $x = 360 - 53.13$

$x = 126.9$ $\quad$ $x = 306.9$

Hence the solution of $3 \sin x + 4 \cos x = 0$ for $0° \leqslant x \leqslant 360°$ is

$x = 126.9°$ or $306.9°$ (1 d.p.)

d Solve $5 \cos 2x - 4 \sin 2x = 0$ for $0° \leqslant x \leqslant 360°$

$5 \cos 2x - 4 \sin 2x = 0$ $\quad$ divide both sides by $\cos 2x$

$5 - 4 \tan 2x = 0$ $\quad$ rearrange

$\tan 2x = 1.25$ $\quad$ let $A = 2x$

$\tan A = 1.25$ $\quad$ use a calculator to find $\tan^{-1}(1.25)$

$A = 51.34$

As $A = 2x$, draw the graph of $y = \tan A$ for $0° \leqslant A \leqslant 720°$

[From $2 \times 0° \leqslant A \leqslant 2 \times 360°$ which leads to $0° \leqslant A \leqslant 720°$]

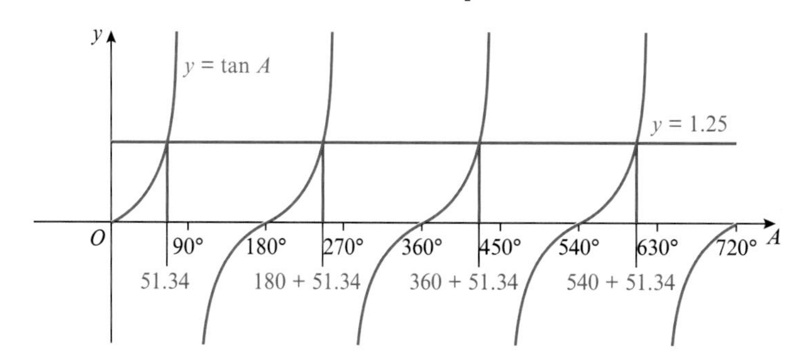

Using the symmetry of the curve

$A = 51.34$ $\quad$ $A = 180 + 51.34$ $\quad$ $A = 360 + 51.34$ $\quad$ $A = 540 + 51.34$

$A = 231.34$ $\quad$ $A = 411.34$ $\quad$ $A = 591.34$

As $A = 2x$ so $x = \dfrac{A}{2}$

$x = 25.7$ $\quad x = 115.7$ $\quad x = 205.7$ $\quad x = 295.7$

Hence the solution of $5\cos 2x - 4\sin 2x = 0$ for $0° \leqslant x \leqslant 360°$ is

$x = 25.7°$ or $x = 115.7°$ or $x = 205.7°$ or $x = 295.7°$ (1 d.p.)

6 Solve $4\sin(2x - 0.4) - 5\cos(2x - 0.4) = 0$ for $0 \leqslant x \leqslant \pi$

$4\sin(2x - 0.4) - 5\cos(2x - 0.4) = 0$ — divide both sides by $\cos(2x - 0.4)$

$4\tan(2x - 0.4) - 5 = 0$ — rearrange

$\tan(2x - 0.4) = 1.25$ — let $A = 2x - 0.4$

$\tan A = 1.25$ — use a calculator to find $\tan^{-1}(1.25)$

$A = 0.8961$

As $A = 2x - 0.4$, draw the graph of $y = \tan A$ for $-0.4 \leqslant A \leqslant 2\pi - 0.4$

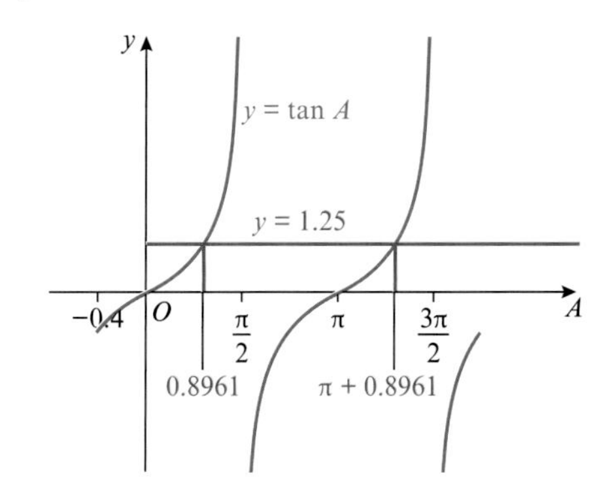

Using the symmetry of the curve

$A = 0.8961$ $\quad A = \pi + 0.8961$

$A = 4.0377$

As $A = 2x - 0.4$ so $x = \dfrac{A + 0.4}{2}$

$x = 0.648$ $\quad x = 2.22$

Hence the solution of $4\sin(2x - 0.4) - 5\cos(2x - 0.4) = 0$ for $0 \leqslant x \leqslant \pi$ is

$x = 0.648$ radians and 2.22 radians (to 3 significant figures)

7 c Solve $3\cos^2 x = \cos x$ for $0° \leqslant x \leqslant 360°$

$3\cos^2 x = \cos x$ — rearrange

TIP

Do not divide both sides by $\cos x$ because some solutions will be missed.

$3\cos^2 x - \cos x = 0$ factorise

$\cos x(3\cos x - 1) = 0$

$\cos x = 0$ or $3\cos x - 1 = 0$

$x = 90$ and 270 $\quad \cos x = \frac{1}{3}$

$x = 70.5$ or $270 + 19.5 = 289.5$

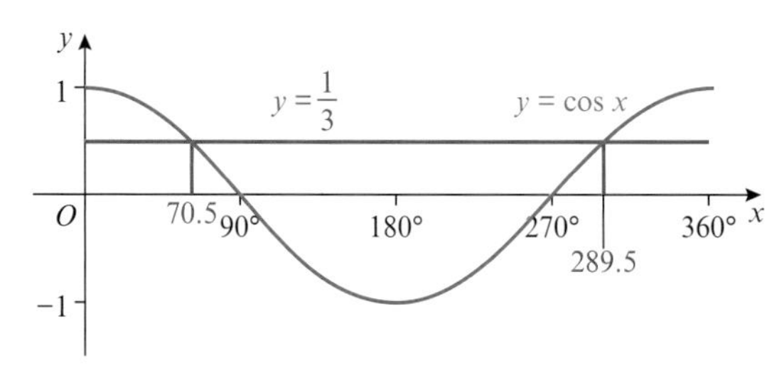

Hence the solution of $3\cos^2 x = \cos x$ for $0° \leqslant x \leqslant 360°$ is

$x = 90°$ or $270°$ or $70.5°$ or $289.5°$(to 1 decimal place)

> **TIP**
>
> It is useful to know the ratios of certain angles as exact values.

f Solve $\sin x \tan x = \sin x$ for $0° \leqslant x \leqslant 360°$

$\sin x \tan x = \sin x$ rearrange

$\sin x \tan x - \sin x = 0$ factorise

$\sin x(\tan x - 1) = 0$

$\sin x = 0$ or $\tan x - 1 = 0$

$x = 0$ or 180 or 360 or $\tan x = 1$

$x = 45$ or 225

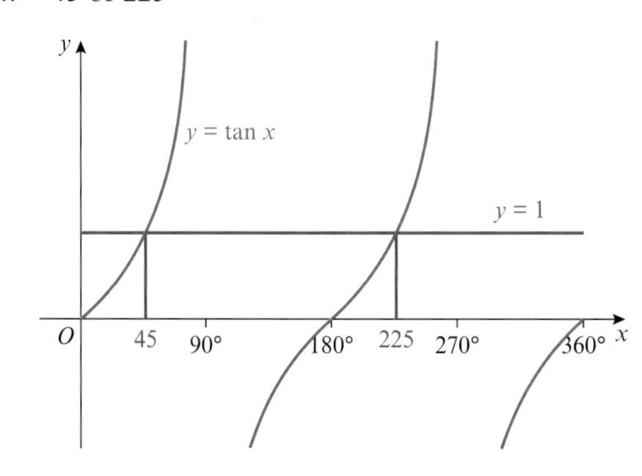

Hence the solution of $\sin x \tan x = \sin x$ for $0° \leqslant x \leqslant 360°$ is

$x = 0°$ or $45°$ or $180°$ or $225°$ or $360°$

8 a Solve $4\sin^2 x = 1$ for $0° \leqslant x \leqslant 360°$

$4\sin^2 x = 1$ rearrange

$\sin^2 x = 0.25$ square root both sides

$\sin x = 0.5$ or $\sin x = -0.5$

$x = 30$ or $x = -30$

$x = 30$ or $x = 180 - 30$ or $x = 180 + 30 = 210$

$= 150$ or $x = 360 - 30 = 330$

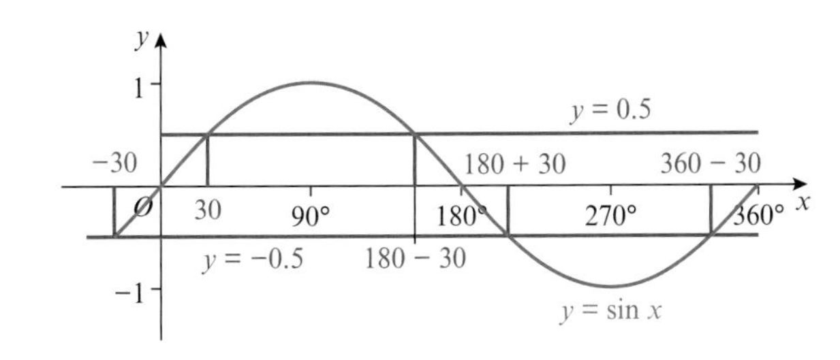

Hence the solution of $4\sin^2 x = 1$ for $0° \leqslant x \leqslant 360°$ is

$x = 30°$ or $150°$ or $210°$ or $330°$

b Solve $25\tan^2 x = 9$ for $0° \leqslant x \leqslant 360°$

$25\tan^2 x = 9$ rearrange

$\tan^2 x = 0.36$ square root both sides

$\tan x = 0.6$ or $\tan x = -0.6$

$x = 30.96$ or $x = -30.96$

$x = 30.96$ or $x = 180 + 30.96$ $\quad x = 180 - 30.96$ or $x = 360 - 30.96$

$x = 211.0$ $\quad x = 149.0$ or $x = 329.0$

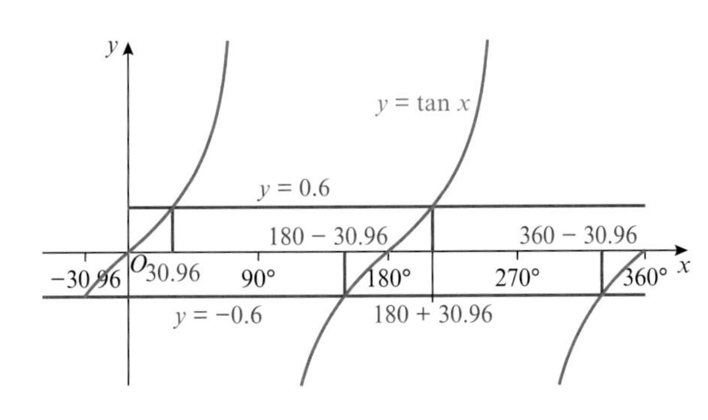

Hence the solution of $25\tan^2 x = 9$ for $0° \leqslant x \leqslant 360°$ is

$x = 31.0°$ or $149.0°$ or $211.0°$ or $329.0°$ (to 1 decimal place)

9 d Solve $2\sin^2 x - \cos x - 1 = 0$ for $0° \leqslant x \leqslant 360°$

$2\sin^2 x - \cos x - 1 = 0$ (1)

As $\sin^2 x + \cos^2 x = 1$

$\sin^2 x = 1 - \cos^2 x$

Substituting for $\sin^2 x$ in (1) gives

$2(1 - \cos^2 x) - \cos x - 1 = 0$ expand brackets and simplify

$2\cos^2 x + \cos x - 1 = 0$ factorise

$(2\cos x - 1)(\cos x + 1) = 0$

$2\cos x - 1 = 0$ or $\cos x + 1 = 0$

$\cos x = 0.5$ or $\cos x = -1$

$x = 60$ or $x = 180$

$x = 60$ or 300

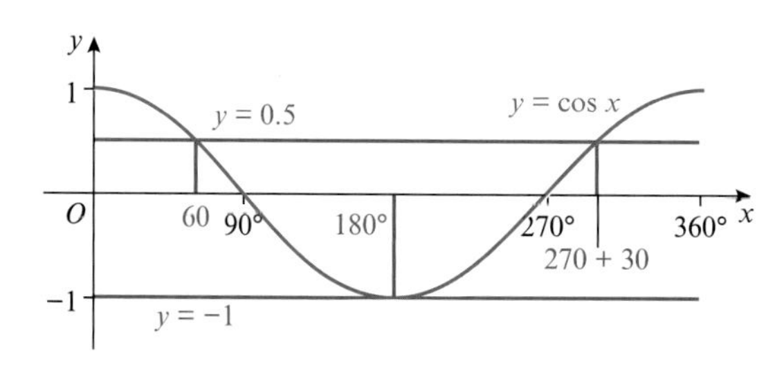

Hence the solution of $2\sin^2 x - \cos x - 1 = 0$ for $0° \leqslant x \leqslant 360°$ is

$x = 60°$ or $180°$ or $300°$

h Solve $1 + \tan x \cos x = 2\cos^2 x$ for $0° \leqslant x \leqslant 360°$

$1 + \tan x \cos x = 2\cos^2 x$ replace $\tan x$ with $\frac{\sin x}{\cos x}$

$1 + \sin x = 2\cos^2 x$ (1)

As $\sin^2 x + \cos^2 x = 1$

$\cos^2 x = 1 - \sin^2 x$

Substituting for $\cos^2 x$ in (1) gives

$1 + \sin x = 2 - 2\sin^2 x$ rearrange

$2\sin^2 x + \sin x - 1 = 0$ factorise

$(2\sin x - 1)(\sin x + 1) = 0$

$2\sin x - 1 = 0$ or $\sin x + 1 = 0$

$\sin x = 0.5$ or $\sin x = -1$

$x = 30$ or $x = 270$

$x = 30$ or 150

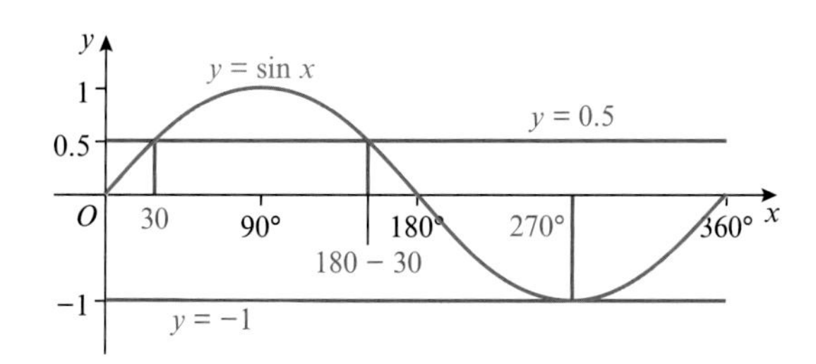

Hence the solution of $1 + \tan x \cos x = 2\cos^2 x$ for $0° \leqslant x \leqslant 360°$ is

$x = 30°$ or $150°$ or $270°$

10 $f(x) = \sin x$ for $0 \leqslant x \leqslant \frac{\pi}{2}$ and $g(x) = 2x - 1$ for $x \in \mathbb{R}$

$gf(x)$ — f acts on x first and $f(x) = \sin x$

$gf(x) = g(\sin x)$ — g is the function 'multiply by 2 then subtract 1'

$gf(x) = 2\sin x - 1$

TIP

To form a composite function, the domain of f must be chosen so that the whole of the range of f is included in the domain of g.

Solve $2\sin x - 1 = 0.5$ for $0 \leqslant x \leqslant \frac{\pi}{2}$

$\sin x = 0.75$

$x = 0.848$ radians

Exercise 9.7

1 b $\dfrac{\cos x \sin x}{\tan x} = 1 - \sin^2 x$

$LHS = \dfrac{\cos x \sin x}{\tan x}$ — use $\tan x = \dfrac{\sin x}{\cos x}$

$= \dfrac{\cos x \sin x}{\frac{\sin x}{\cos x}}$ — multiply numerator and denominator by $\cos x$

$= \dfrac{\cos^2 x \sin x}{\sin x}$

$= \cos^2 x$ — $\sin^2 x + \cos^2 x = 1$ so $\cos^2 x = 1 - \sin^2 x$

$= 1 - \sin^2 x$

$= RHS$

f $\tan^2 x - \sin^2 x = \tan^2 x \sin^2 x$

$LHS = \tan^2 x - \sin^2 x$ — use $\tan x = \frac{\sin x}{\cos x}$

$= \frac{\sin^2 x}{\cos^2 x} - \frac{\sin^2 x}{1}$

$= \frac{\sin^2 x}{\cos^2 x} - \frac{\sin^2 x \cos^2 x}{\cos^2 x}$

$= \frac{\sin^2 x - \sin^2 x \cos^2 x}{\cos^2 x}$ — factorise the numerator

$= \frac{\sin^2 x(1 - \cos^2 x)}{\cos^2 x}$ — $\sin^2 x + \cos^2 x = 1$ so $1 - \cos^2 x = \sin^2 x$

$= \frac{\sin^2 x \times \sin^2 x}{\cos^2 x}$

$= \frac{\sin^2 x}{\cos^2 x} \times \frac{\sin^2 x}{1}$

$= \tan^2 x \sin^2 x$

$= RHS$

2 d $2(1 + \cos x) - (1 + \cos x)^2 = \sin^2 x$

$LHS = 2(1 + \cos x) - (1 + \cos x)^2$ — expand brackets

$= 2 + 2\cos x - (1 + 2\cos x + \cos^2 x)$

$= 2 + 2\cos x - 1 - 2\cos x - \cos^2 x$

$= 1 - \cos^2 x$ — $\sin^2 x + \cos^2 x = 1$ so $\cos^2 x = 1 - \sin^2 x$

$= \sin^2 x$

$= RHS$

f $\cos^4 x + \sin^2 x = \sin^4 x + \cos^2 x$

$LHS = \cos^4 x + \sin^2 x$ — $\sin^2 x + \cos^2 x = 1$ so $\cos^2 x = 1 - \sin^2 x$

$= (1 - \sin^2 x)^2 + \sin^2 x$ — expand brackets

$= 1 - 2\sin^2 x + \sin^4 x + \sin^2 x$

$= \sin^4 x + 1 - \sin^2 x$ — $\sin^2 x + \cos^2 x = 1$ so $\cos^2 x = 1 - \sin^2 x$

$= \sin^4 x + \cos^2 x$

$= RHS$

3 b $\frac{\sin x}{1 + \cos x} + \frac{1 + \cos x}{\sin x} = \frac{2}{\sin x}$

$LHS = \frac{\sin x}{1 + \cos x} + \frac{1 + \cos x}{\sin x}$

$= \frac{\sin^2 x}{\sin x(1 + \cos x)} + \frac{(1 + \cos x)(1 + \cos x)}{\sin x\,(1 + \cos x)}$

$$= \frac{\sin^2 x + (1 + \cos x)(1 + \cos x)}{\sin x(1 + \cos x)}$$

$$= \frac{\sin^2 x + 1 + 2\cos x + \cos^2 x}{\sin x(1 + \cos x)}$$ use $\sin^2 x + \cos^2 x = 1$

$$= \frac{1 + 1 + 2\cos x}{\sin x(1 + \cos x)}$$

$$= \frac{2 + 2\cos x}{\sin x(1 + \cos x)}$$

$$= \frac{2(1 + \cos x)}{\sin x(1 + \cos x)}$$

$$= \frac{2}{\sin x}$$

$= RHS$

c $\frac{\cos^4 x - \sin^4 x}{\cos^2 x} = 1 - \tan^2 x$

$LHS = \frac{\cos^4 x - \sin^4 x}{\cos^2 x}$ factorise the numerator using the difference of two squares

$$= \frac{(\cos^2 x + \sin^2 x)(\cos^2 x - \sin^2 x)}{\cos^2 x}$$ use $\sin^2 x + \cos^2 x = 1$

$$= \frac{\cos^2 x - \sin^2 x}{\cos^2 x}$$ split into two fractions

$$= \frac{\cos^2 x}{\cos^2 x} - \frac{\sin^2 x}{\cos^2 x}$$

$= 1 - \tan^2 x$

$= RHS$

Exercise 9.8

1 a Solve $\cot x = 0.3$ for $0° \leqslant x \leqslant 360°$

$\cot x = 0.3$ use $\cot x = \frac{1}{\tan x}$

$\frac{1}{\tan x} = 0.3$

$\tan x = \frac{10}{3}$

$x = 73.30$

Draw the graph of $y = \tan x$ for $0° \leqslant x \leqslant 360°$

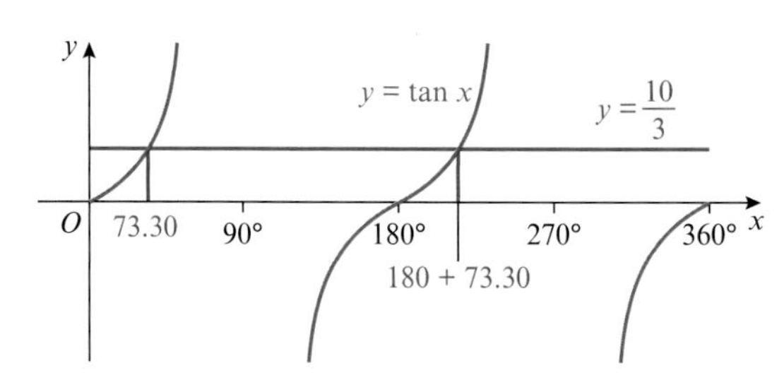

Using the symmetry of the graph:

$x = 73.30$ and $x = 180 + 73.30$

$= 253.3$

Hence the solution of $\cot x = 0.3$ for $0° \leqslant x \leqslant 360°$ is

$x = 73.3°$ or $253.3°$ (to 1 decimal place).

c $\operatorname{cosec} x = -2$ for $0° \leqslant x \leqslant 360°$

$\operatorname{cosec} x = -2$ Use $\operatorname{cosec} x = \frac{1}{\sin x}$

$\frac{1}{\sin x} = -2$

$\sin x = -0.5$

$x = -30$

We need to include the negative angle in our working if we are to use the symmetry of the graph.

Draw the graph of $y = \sin x$ for $0° \leqslant x \leqslant 360°$

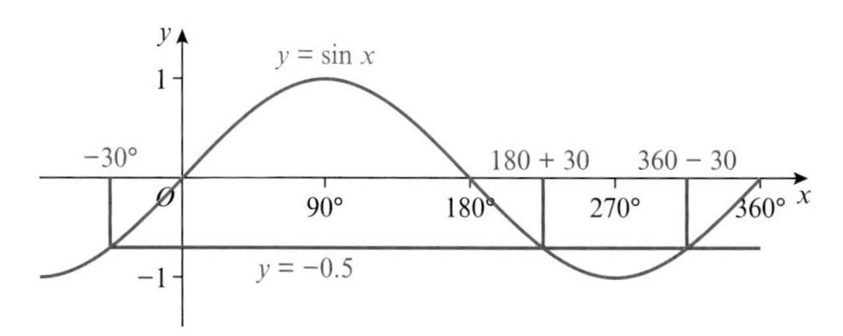

Using the symmetry of the graph:

$x = -30$ $x = 180 + 30$ $x = 360 - 30$

$= 210$ $= 330$

Hence the solution of $\operatorname{cosec} x = -2$ for $0° \leqslant x \leqslant 360°$ is

$x = 210°$ or $x = 330°$

2 c Solve $\sec x = -4$ for $0 \leqslant x \leqslant 2\pi$

$\sec x = -4$ using $\sec x = \frac{1}{\cos x}$

$\frac{1}{\cos x} = -4$

$\cos x = -0.25$

Draw the graph of $y = \cos x$ for $0 \leqslant x \leqslant 2\pi$

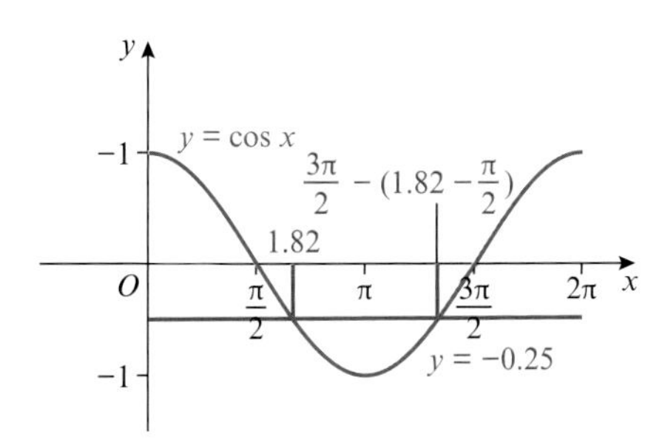

Using the symmetry of the graph:

$x = 1.82$ or $x = \frac{3\pi}{2} - \left(1.82 - \frac{\pi}{2}\right)$

$= 4.46$ radians

Hence the solution to $\sec x = -4$ for $0 \leqslant x \leqslant 2\pi$ is

$x = 1.82$ radians or $x = 4.46$ radians

d Solve $2\cot x + 3 = 0$ for $0 \leqslant x \leqslant 2\pi$

$2\cot x + 3 = 0$

$\cot x = -\frac{3}{2}$ use $\cot x = \frac{1}{\tan x}$

$\frac{1}{\tan x} = -\frac{3}{2}$

$\tan x = -\frac{2}{3}$

$x = -0.5880$

We need to include the negative angle in our working if we are to use the symmetry of the graph.

Draw the graph of $y = \tan x$ for $0 \leqslant x \leqslant 2\pi$

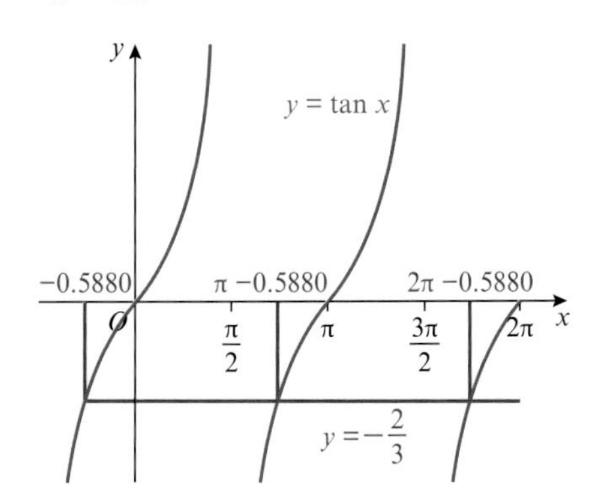

Using the symmetry of the graph:

$x = -0.5880$ or $x = \pi - 0.5880$ or $x = 2\pi - 0.5880$

$= 2.55$ radians $= 5.70$ radians

Hence the solution to $2\cot x + 3 = 0$ for $0 \leqslant x \leqslant 2\pi$ is

$x = 2.55$ radians or $x = 5.70$ radians

3 a Solve $\sec 2x = 1.6$ for $0° \leqslant x \leqslant 180°$

$\sec 2x = 1.6$ let $A = 2x$

$\sec A = 1.6$ using $\sec x = \frac{1}{\cos x}$

$\frac{1}{\cos A} = 1.6$

$\cos A = 0.625$

$A = 51.32$

Draw the graph of $y = \cos A$ for or $0° \leqslant A \leqslant 360°$

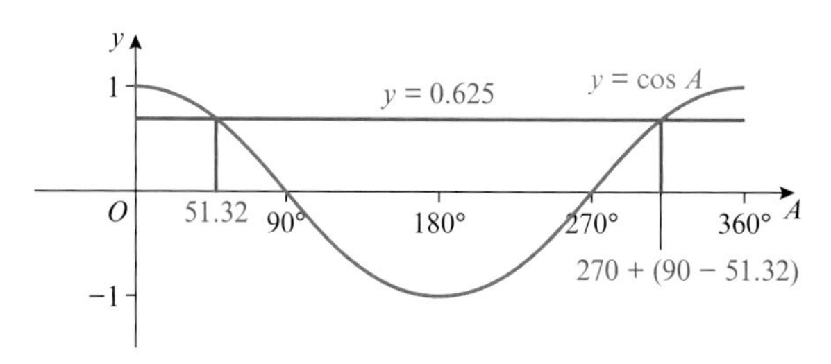

Using the symmetry of the graph:

$A = 51.32$ and $A = 270 + 51.32$

$= 308.68$

As $A = 2x$, then $x = \frac{A}{2}$

$x = 25.7$ or $x = 154.3$

Hence the solution of $\sec 2x = 1.6$ for $0° \leqslant x \leqslant 180°$ is

$x = 25.7°$ or $154.3°$ (to 1 decimal place).

d Solve $5 \operatorname{cosec} 2x = -7$ for or $0° \leqslant x \leqslant 180°$

$5 \operatorname{cosec} 2x = -7$ let $A = 2x$

$5 \operatorname{cosec} A = -7$

$\operatorname{cosec} A = -\frac{7}{5}$ use $\operatorname{cosec} x = \frac{1}{\sin x}$

$\frac{1}{\sin A} = -\frac{7}{5}$

$\sin A = -\frac{5}{7}$

$A = -45.58$

We need to include the negative angle in our working if we are to use the symmetry of the graph.

Draw the graph of $y = \sin A$ for or $0° \leqslant A \leqslant 360°$

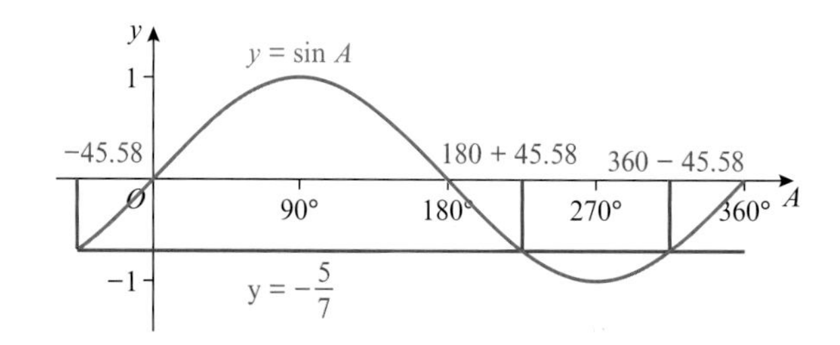

Using the symmetry of the graph:

$A = -45.58$ and $A = 180 + 45.58$ and $A = 360 - 45.58$

$= 225.58$ $\qquad\qquad$ $= 314.42$

As $A = 2x$, then $x = \dfrac{A}{2}$

$x = -22.8$ or $x = 112.8$ or $x = 157.2$

Hence the solution of $5\operatorname{cosec} 2x = -7$ for $0° \leqslant x \leqslant 180°$ is

$x = 112.8°$ or $157.2°$ (to 1 decimal place).

4 b Solve $\operatorname{cosec}(2x + 45°) = -5$ for $0° \leqslant x \leqslant 180°$

$\operatorname{cosec}(2x + 45°) = -5$ $\qquad$ use $\operatorname{cosec} x = \dfrac{1}{\sin x}$

$\dfrac{1}{\sin(2x + 45°)} = -5$

$\sin(2x + 45°) = -0.2$ $\qquad$ let $A = 2x + 45°$

$\sin A = -0.2$

$A = -11.54$

We need to include the negative angle in our working if we are to use the symmetry of the graph.

Draw the graph of $y = \sin A$ for $2 \times 0° + 45° \leqslant A \leqslant 2 \times 180° + 45°$ i.e $45° \leqslant A \leqslant 405°$

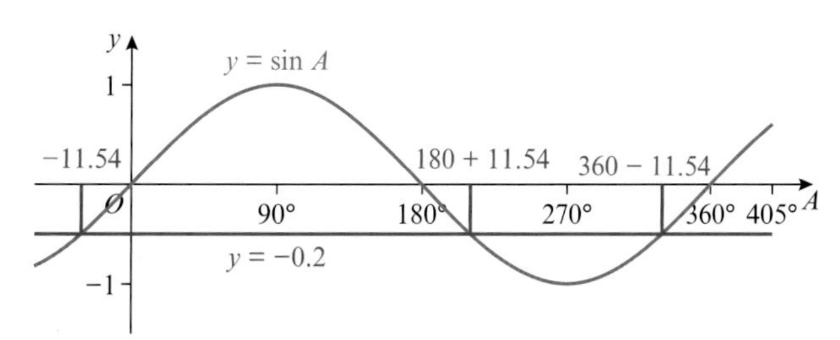

Using the symmetry of the graph:

$A = -11.54$ and $A = 180 + 11.54$ and $A = 360 - 11.54$

$= 191.54$ $\qquad\qquad$ $= 348.46$

As $A = 2x + 45$, then $x = \dfrac{A - 45}{2}$

$x = -28.3$ or $x = 73.3$ or $x = 151.7$

Hence the solution for $\operatorname{cosec}(2x + 45°) = -5$ for or $0° \leqslant x \leqslant 180°$ is

$x = 73.3°$ or $x = 151.7°$ (to 1 decimal place)

c Solve $\cot\left(x + \frac{\pi}{3}\right) = 2$ for $0 \leqslant x \leqslant 2\pi$

$\cot\left(x + \frac{\pi}{3}\right) = 2$ use $\cot x = \frac{1}{\tan x}$

$\frac{1}{\tan\left(x + \frac{\pi}{3}\right)} = 2$

$\tan\left(x + \frac{\pi}{3}\right) = 0.5$ let $A = x + \frac{\pi}{3}$

$\tan A = 0.5$

$A = 0.4636$

Draw the graph of $y = \tan A$ for $0 + \frac{\pi}{3} \leqslant A \leqslant 2\pi + \frac{\pi}{3}$ i.e $\frac{\pi}{3} \leqslant A \leqslant \frac{7\pi}{3}$

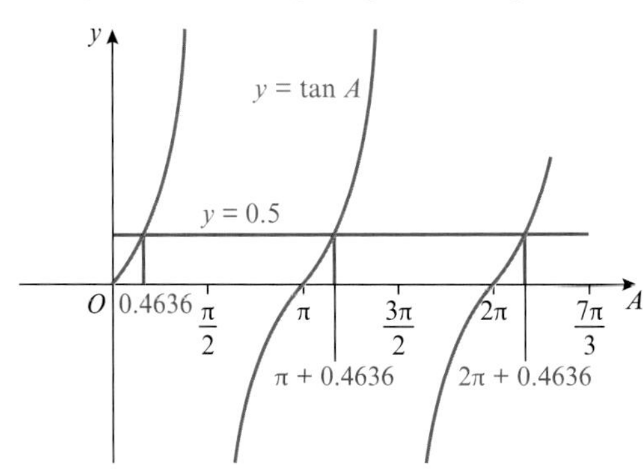

Using the symmetry of the graph:

$A = 0.4636$ and $A = \pi + 0.4636$ and $A = 2\pi + 0.4636$

$= 3.6052$ $= 6.7468$

As $A = x + \frac{\pi}{3}$, then $x = A - \frac{\pi}{3}$

$x = -0.5835$ or $x = 2.56$ or $x = 5.70$

Hence the solution for $\cot\left(x + \frac{\pi}{3}\right) = 2$ for or $0 \leqslant x \leqslant 2\pi$ is

$x = 2.56$ radians or $x = 5.70$ radians (to 3 significant figures)

5 a Solve $\sec^2 x = 4$ for $0° \leqslant x \leqslant 360°$

$\sec^2 x = 4$ square root both sides

$\sec x = 2$ or $\sec x = -2$ using $\sec x = \frac{1}{\cos x}$

$\frac{1}{\cos x} = 2$ or $\frac{1}{\cos x} = -2$

$\cos x = 0.5$ or $\cos x = -0.5$

$x = 60$ or $x = 120$

Draw the graph of $y = \cos x$ for $0° \leqslant x \leqslant 360°$

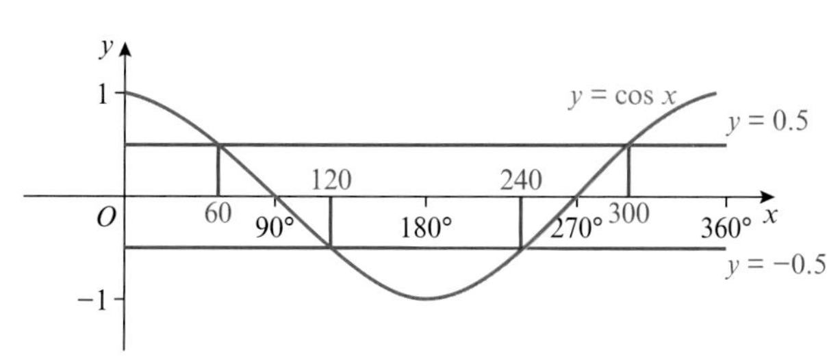

Using the symmetry of the graph:

For $\cos x = 0.5$ then $x = 60$ and $x = 300$

For $\cos x = -0.5$ then $x = 120$ and $x = 240$

Hence the solution of $\sec^2 x = 4$ for $0° \leqslant x \leqslant 360°$ is

$x = 60°$ or $x = 120°$ or $x = 240°$ or $x = 300°$

b Solve $9\cot^2 x = 4$ for $0° \leqslant x \leqslant 360°$

$9\cot^2 x = 4$

$\cot^2 x = \frac{4}{9}$ square root both sides

$\cot x = \frac{2}{3}$ or $\cot x = -\frac{2}{3}$ use $\cot x = \frac{1}{\tan x}$

$\tan x = 1.5$ or $\tan x = -1.5$

$x = 56.31$ or $x = -56.31$

We need to include the negative angle in our working if we are to use the symmetry of the graph.

Draw the graph of $y = \tan x$ for $0° \leqslant x \leqslant 360°$

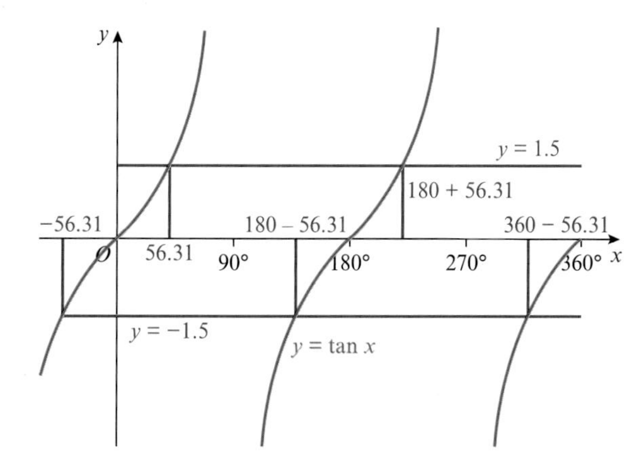

Using the symmetry of the graph:

For $\tan x = 1.5$ then $x = 56.31$ and $x = 180 + 56.31$

$= 236.31$

For $\tan x = -1.5$ then $x = -56.31$ and $x = 180 - 56.31$ and $x = 360 - 56.31$

$= 123.69$ and $= 303.69$

Hence the solution for $9\cot^2 x = 4$ for $0° \leqslant x \leqslant 360°$ is

$x = 56.3°$ or $x = 123.7°$ or $x = 236.3°$ or $x = 303.7°$ (to 1 decimal place)

c Solve $16\cot^2\frac{1}{2}x = 9$ for $0° \leqslant x \leqslant 360°$

$16\cot^2\frac{1}{2}x = 9$

$\cot^2\frac{1}{2}x = \frac{9}{16}$ square root both sides

$\cot\frac{1}{2}x = 0.75$ or $\cot\frac{1}{2}x = -0.75$ let $A = \frac{1}{2}x$

$\cot A = 0.75$ or $\cot A = -0.75$ use $\cot x = \frac{1}{\tan x}$

$\frac{1}{\tan A} = 0.75$ or $\frac{1}{\tan A} = -0.75$

$\tan A = \frac{4}{3}$ or $\tan A = -\frac{4}{3}$

$A = 53.13$ or $A = -53.13$

We need to include the negative angle in our working if we are to use the symmetry of the graph.

Draw the graph of $y = \tan A$ or $0° \leqslant A \leqslant 180°$ since $x = 2A$.

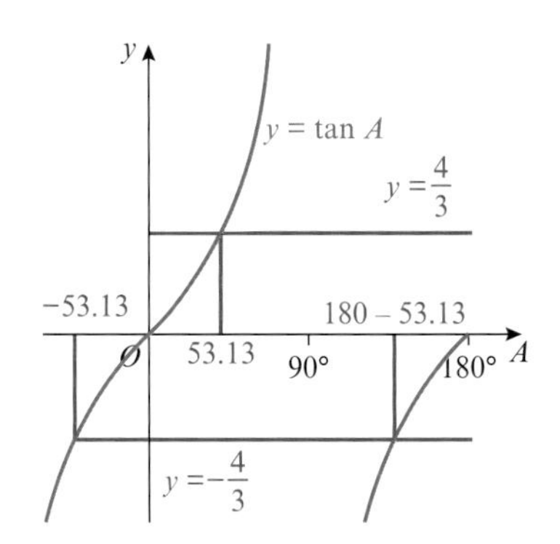

Using the symmetry of the graph:

For $\tan A = \frac{4}{3}$ then $A = 53.13$

For $\tan A = -\frac{4}{3}$ then $A = -53.13$ and $A = 180 - 53.13$

$= 126.87$

As $A = \frac{1}{2}x$ so $x = 2A$

$x = 106.3$ or $x = -106.3$ or $x = 253.7$

Hence the solution for $16\cot^2\frac{1}{2}x = 9$ for $0° \leqslant x \leqslant 360°$ is

$x = 106.3°$ or $x = 253.7°$ (to 1 decimal place)

6 e Solve $6\cos x + 6\sec x = 13$ for or $0° \leqslant x \leqslant 360°$

$6\cos x + 6\sec x = 13$ — using $\sec x = \frac{1}{\cos x}$

$6\cos x + \frac{6}{\cos x} = 13$ — multiply both sides by $\cos x$

$6\cos^2 x + 6 = 13\cos x$ — rearrange

$6\cos^2 x - 13\cos x + 6 = 0$ — factorise

$(2\cos x - 3)(3\cos x - 2) = 0$ — solve

$2\cos x - 3 = 0$ or $3\cos x - 2 = 0$

$\cos x = 1.5$ (no solutions) or $\cos x = \frac{2}{3}$

$x = 48.19$

Draw the graph of $y = \cos x$ for $0° \leqslant x \leqslant 360°$

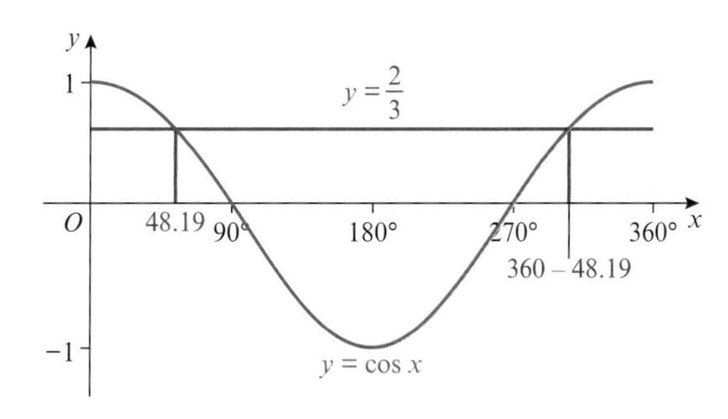

Using the symmetry of the graph:

$x = 48.19$ and $x = 360 - 48.19$

$= 311.81$

Hence the solution for $6\cos^2 x + 6 = 13\cos x$ for $0° \leqslant x \leqslant 360°$ is

$x = 48.2°$ or $x = 311.8°$ (to 1 decimal place)

h Solve $12\sec x - 10\cos x - 9\tan x = 0$ for $0° \leqslant x \leqslant 360°$

$12\sec x - 10\cos x - 9\tan x = 0$ — use $\sec x = \frac{1}{\cos x}$ and $\tan x = \frac{\sin x}{\cos x}$

$\frac{12}{\cos x} - 10\cos x - \frac{9\sin x}{\cos x} = 0$ — multiply both sides by $\cos x$

$12 - 10\cos^2 x - 9\sin x = 0$ — $\sin^2 x + \cos^2 x = 1$ so $\cos^2 x = 1 - \sin^2 x$

$12 - 10(1 - \sin^2 x) - 9\sin x = 0$ — expand brackets

$12 - 10 + 10\sin^2 x - 9\sin x = 0$ — simplify

$10\sin^2 x - 9\sin x + 2 = 0$ — factorise

$(5\sin x - 2)(2\sin x - 1) = 0$ — solve

$5\sin x - 2 = 0$ or $2\sin x - 1 = 0$

$\sin x = 0.4$ or $\sin x = 0.5$

$x = 23.58$ or $x = 30$

Draw the graph of $y = \sin x$ for $0° \leqslant x \leqslant 360°$

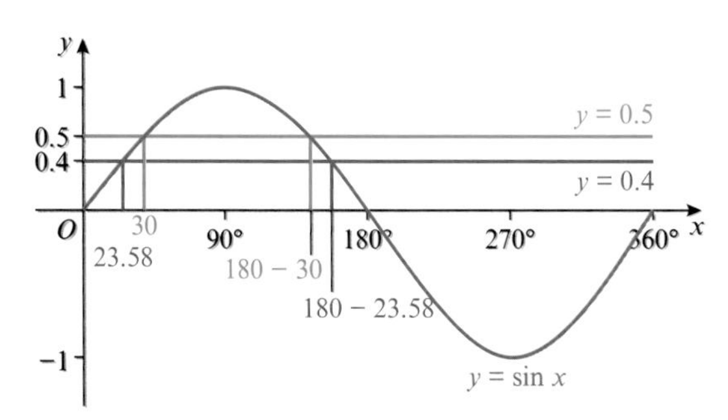

Using the symmetry of the graph

For $\sin x = 0.4$ $\quad x = 23.58$ and $x = 180 - 23.58$

$= 156.42$

For $\sin x = 0.5$ $\quad x = 30$ and $x = 180 - 30$

$= 150$

Hence the solution for $12 \sec x - 10 \cos x - 9 \tan x = 0$ for $0° \leqslant x \leqslant 360°$ is

$x = 23.6°$ or $x = 30°$ or $x = 150°$ or $x = 156.4°$

Exercise 9.9

1 a $\tan x + \cot x = \sec x \operatorname{cosec} x$

$LHS = \tan x + \cot x$ $\quad$ use $\tan x = \frac{\sin x}{\cos x}$ and $\cot x = \frac{\cos x}{\sin x}$

$= \frac{\sin x}{\cos x} + \frac{\cos x}{\sin x}$

$= \frac{\sin^2 x + \cos^2 x}{\cos x \sin x}$ $\quad$ use $\sin^2 x + \cos^2 x = 1$

$= \frac{1}{\cos x \sin x}$

$= \frac{1}{\cos x} \times \frac{1}{\sin x}$ $\quad$ use $\frac{1}{\cos x} = \sec x$ and $\frac{1}{\sin x} = \operatorname{cosec} x$

$= \sec x \operatorname{cosec} x$

$= RHS$

d $\sec x \operatorname{cosec} x - \cot x = \tan x$

$LHS = \sec x \operatorname{cosec} x - \cot x$ $\quad$ use $\frac{1}{\cos x} = \sec x$ and $\frac{1}{\sin x} = \operatorname{cosec} x$

$= \frac{1}{\cos x} \times \frac{1}{\sin x} - \frac{\cos x}{\sin x}$

$= \frac{1}{\cos x \sin x} - \frac{\cos x}{\sin x}$

$= \frac{1}{\cos x \sin x} - \frac{\cos^2 x}{\cos x \sin x}$ $\quad$ simplify

$= \dfrac{1 - \cos^2 x}{\cos x \sin x}$ $\sin^2 x + \cos^2 x = 1$ so $1 - \cos^2 x = \sin^2 x$

$= \dfrac{\sin^2 x}{\cos x \sin x}$ simplify

$= \dfrac{\sin x}{\cos x}$

$= \tan x$

$= RHS$

2 b $(1 + \sec x)(1 - \cos x) = \sin x \tan x$

$LHS = (1 + \sec x)(1 - \cos x)$ expand brackets

$= 1 - \cos x + \sec x - \sec x \cos x$ use $\sec x = \dfrac{1}{\cos x}$

$= 1 - \cos x + \sec x - 1$

$= \sec x - \cos x$

$= \dfrac{1}{\cos x} - \cos x$

$= \dfrac{1}{\cos x} - \dfrac{\cos^2 x}{\cos x}$

$= \dfrac{1 - \cos^2 x}{\cos x}$ $\sin^2 x + \cos^2 x = 1$ so $1 - \cos^2 x = \sin^2 x$

$= \dfrac{\sin^2 x}{\cos x}$

$= \dfrac{\sin x}{1} \times \dfrac{\sin x}{\cos x}$

$= \sin x \tan x$

$= RHS$

d $(\cot x + \tan x)(\cot x - \tan x) = \operatorname{cosec}^2 x - \sec^2 x$

$LHS = (\cot x + \tan x)(\cot x - \tan x)$ expand brackets

$= \cot^2 x - \cot x \tan x + \tan x \cot x - \tan^2 x$

$= \cot^2 x - \tan^2 x$ $1 + \cot^2 x = \operatorname{cosec}^2 x$ so $\cot^2 x = \operatorname{cosec}^2 x - 1$

$= \operatorname{cosec}^2 x - 1 - \tan^2 x$ $1 + \tan^2 x = \sec^2 x$ so $\tan^2 x = \sec^2 x - 1$

$= \operatorname{cosec}^2 x - 1 - (\sec^2 x - 1)$

$= \operatorname{cosec}^2 x - 1 - \sec^2 x + 1$

$= \operatorname{cosec}^2 x - \sec^2 x$

$= RHS$

3 a $\dfrac{1}{\tan x + \cot x} = \sin x \cos x$

$LHS = \dfrac{1}{\tan x + \cot x}$ use $\tan x = \dfrac{\sin x}{\cos x}$ and $\cot x = \dfrac{\cos x}{\sin x}$

$= \dfrac{1}{\dfrac{\sin x}{\cos x} + \dfrac{\cos x}{\sin x}}$ multiply numerator and denominator by $\sin x \cos x$

$= \dfrac{\sin x \cos x}{\sin^2 x + \cos^2 x}$ use $\sin^2 x + \cos^2 x = 1$

$= \sin x \cos x$

$= RHS$

g $\dfrac{\sin x \tan^2 x}{1 + \tan^2 x} = \sin^3 x$

$LHS = \dfrac{\sin x \tan^2 x}{1 + \tan^2 x}$ use $1 + \tan^2 x = \sec^2 x$

$= \dfrac{\sin x \tan^2 x}{\sec^2 x}$ use $\tan x = \dfrac{\sin x}{\cos x}$ and $\sec x = \dfrac{1}{\cos x}$

$= \dfrac{\sin x \times \dfrac{\sin^2 x}{\cos^2 x}}{\dfrac{1}{\cos^2 x}}$ multiply numerator and denominator by $\cos^2 x$

$= \dfrac{\sin^3 x}{1}$

$= RHS$

4 d $\dfrac{\cos x}{1 - \tan x} + \dfrac{\sin x}{1 - \cot x} = \sin x + \cos x$

$LHS = \dfrac{\cos x}{1 - \tan x} + \dfrac{\sin x}{1 - \cot x}$ use $\tan x = \dfrac{\sin x}{\cos x}$ and $\cot x = \dfrac{\cos x}{\sin x}$

$= \dfrac{\cos x}{1 - \dfrac{\sin x}{\cos x}} + \dfrac{\sin x}{1 - \dfrac{\cos x}{\sin x}}$ multiply numerator and denominator of the first fraction by $\cos x$

$= \dfrac{\cos^2 x}{\cos x - \sin x} + \dfrac{\sin x}{1 - \dfrac{\cos x}{\sin x}}$ multiply numerator and denominator of the second fraction by $\sin x$

$= \dfrac{\cos^2 x}{\cos x - \sin x} + \dfrac{\sin^2 x}{\sin x - \cos x}$ multiply numerator and denominator of second fraction by -1

$= \dfrac{\cos^2 x}{\cos x - \sin x} + \dfrac{-\sin^2 x}{\cos x - \sin x}$ add fractions

$= \dfrac{\cos^2 x - \sin^2 x}{\cos x - \sin x}$ factorise the numerator using the difference of two squares

$= \dfrac{(\cos x - \sin x)(\cos x + \sin x)}{\cos x - \sin x}$

$= \sin x + \cos x$

$= RHS$

f $\dfrac{\cos x}{\operatorname{cosec} x + 1} + \dfrac{\cos x}{\operatorname{cosec} x - 1} = 2\tan x$

$LHS = \dfrac{\cos x}{\operatorname{cosec} x + 1} + \dfrac{\cos x}{\operatorname{cosec} x - 1}$ — add the fractions

$= \dfrac{\cos x(\operatorname{cosec} x - 1)}{(\operatorname{cosec} x + 1)(\operatorname{cosec} x - 1)} + \dfrac{\cos x(\operatorname{cosec} x + 1)}{(\operatorname{cosec} x + 1)(\operatorname{cosec} x - 1)}$

$= \dfrac{\cos x(\operatorname{cosec} x - 1) + \cos x(\operatorname{cosec} x + 1)}{(\operatorname{cosec} x + 1)(\operatorname{cosec} x - 1)}$ — expand brackets

$= \dfrac{\cos x \operatorname{cosec} x - \cos x + \cos x \operatorname{cosec} x + \cos x}{\operatorname{cosec}^2 x - 1}$ — $1 + \cot^2 x = \operatorname{cosec}^2 x$ so $\cot^2 x = \operatorname{cosec}^2 x - 1$

$= \dfrac{2\cos x \operatorname{cosec} x}{\cot^2 x}$ — use $\operatorname{cosec} x = \dfrac{1}{\sin x}$ and $\cot x = \dfrac{\cos x}{\sin x}$

$= \dfrac{2\cos x \times \dfrac{1}{\sin x}}{\dfrac{\cos^2 x}{\sin^2 x}}$ — multiply numerator and denominator by $\dfrac{\sin^2 x}{\cos x}$

$= \dfrac{2\sin x}{\cos x}$

$= 2\tan x$

$= RHS$

5 $(3 + 2\sin x)^2 + (3 - 2\sin x)^2 + 8\cos^2 x$ — expand brackets

$= 9 + 12\sin x + 4\sin^2 x + 9 - 12\sin x + 4\sin^2 x + 8\cos^2 x$

$= 18 + 8\sin^2 x + 8\cos^2 x$ — factorise

$= 18 + 8(\sin^2 x + \cos^2 x)$ — use $\sin^2 x + \cos^2 x = 1$

$= 18 + 8$

$= 26$

The expression has a constant value of 26 for all x

6 **a** $5\sin^2 x - 2\cos^2 x$ — $\sin^2 x + \cos^2 x = 1$ so $\cos^2 x = 1 - \sin^2 x$

$= 5\sin^2 x - 2(1 - \sin^2 x)$ — $\sin^2 x + \cos^2 x = 1$ so $\cos^2 x = 1 - \sin^2 x$

$= 5\sin^2 x - 2 + 2\sin^2 x$

$= -2 + 7\sin^2 x$

b $-1 \leqslant \sin x \leqslant 1$ and $0 \leqslant \sin^2 x \leqslant 1$

When $x = 0$, $f(x) = -2 + 7\sin^2 x$ is -2

When $x = 1$, $f(x) = -2 + 7\sin^2 x$ is $-2 + 7 = 5$

The range of the function $f(x) = -2 + 7\sin^2 x$ is $-2 \leqslant f(x) \leqslant 5$

7 a $\sin^2\theta + 4\cos\theta + 2$ — $\sin^2\theta + \cos^2\theta = 1$ so $1 - \cos^2\theta = \sin^2\theta$

$= 1 - \cos^2\theta + 4\cos\theta + 2$ — simplify

$= -\cos^2\theta + 4\cos\theta + 3$ — complete the square

$= -[\cos^2\theta - 4\cos\theta] + 3$

$= -[(\cos\theta - 2)^2 - 2^2] + 3$

$= -[(\cos\theta - 2)^2 - 4] + 3$

$= -(\cos\theta - 2)^2 + 4 + 3$

$= -(\cos\theta - 2)^2 + 7$

$= 7 - (\cos\theta - 2)^2$

b $-1 \leqslant \cos\theta \leqslant 1$

The maximum value of $7 - (\cos\theta - 2)^2$ is $7 -$ minimum value of $(\cos\theta - 2)^2$

The minimum value of $(\cos\theta - 2)^2$ is $(1 - 2)^2 = 1$

So the **maximum** value of $7 - (\cos\theta - 2)^2$ is $7 - 1 = 6$

The minimum value of $7 - (\cos\theta - 2)^2$ is $7 -$ maximum value of $(\cos\theta - 2)^2$

The maximum value of $(\cos\theta - 2)^2$ is $(-1 - 2)^2 = 9$

So the **minimum** value of $7 - (\cos\theta - 2)^2$ is $7 - 9 = -2$

Chapter 10: Permutations and combinations

Exercise 10.1

1 **d** $\dfrac{8!}{5!} = \dfrac{8 \times 7 \times 6 \times \cancel{5} \times \cancel{4} \times \cancel{3} \times \cancel{2} \times \cancel{1}}{\cancel{5} \times \cancel{4} \times \cancel{3} \times \cancel{2} \times \cancel{1}} = 336$

h $\dfrac{5!}{3!} \times \dfrac{7!}{4!} = \dfrac{5 \times 4 \times \cancel{3} \times \cancel{2} \times \cancel{1}}{\cancel{3} \times \cancel{2} \times \cancel{1}} \times \dfrac{7 \times 6 \times 5 \times \cancel{4} \times \cancel{3} \times \cancel{2} \times \cancel{1}}{\cancel{4} \times \cancel{3} \times \cancel{2} \times \cancel{1}} = 4200$

2 **c** $5 \times 4 \times 3 = \dfrac{5 \times 4 \times 3 \times \cancel{2} \times \cancel{1}}{\cancel{2} \times \cancel{1}} = \dfrac{5!}{2!}$

e $\dfrac{10 \times 9 \times 8}{3 \times 2 \times 1} = \dfrac{10 \times 9 \times 8 \times \cancel{7} \times \cancel{6} \times \cancel{5} \times \cancel{4} \times \cancel{3} \times \cancel{2} \times \cancel{1}}{\cancel{7} \times \cancel{6} \times \cancel{5} \times \cancel{4} \times \cancel{3} \times \cancel{2} \times \cancel{1} \times 3 \times 2 \times 1} = \dfrac{10!}{7!3!}$

3 **a** $n(n-1)(n-2)(n-3) = \dfrac{n(n-1)(n-2)(n-3)\cancel{(n-4)(n-5)(n-6)} \times \ldots\ldots.}{\cancel{(n-4)(n-5)(n-6)} \times \ldots\ldots.}$

$= \dfrac{n!}{(n-4)!}$

d $\dfrac{n(n-1)(n-2)(n-3)(n-4)}{3 \times 2 \times 1} = \dfrac{n(n-1)(n-2)(n-3)(n-4)\cancel{(n-5)(n-6)} \times \ldots\ldots.}{3 \times 2 \times 1 \times \cancel{(n-5)(n-6)}\ldots\ldots.}$

$= \dfrac{n(n-1)(n-2)(n-3)(n-4)\cancel{(n-5)(n-6)} \times \ldots\ldots.}{3! \times \cancel{(n-5)(n-6)}\ldots\ldots.}$

$= \dfrac{n!}{3!(n-5)!}$

Exercise 10.2

REMEMBER

The number of ways of arranging n distinct items in a line = $n!$

1 **a** Consider filling 4 spaces. ____ ____ ____ ____

The first person has a choice of 4 spaces

The second person has a choice of 3 spaces

The third person has a choice of 2 spaces

The fourth person fills the last space

The number of arrangements of sitting 4 people is $4 \times 3 \times 2 \times 1 = 4! = 24$

b The number of ways of arranging 7 distinct items in a line = $7! = 5040$

2 a TIGER has no repeating letters so, all the letters are distinct.

The number of ways of arranging 5 distinct items in a line = $5! = 120$

b OLYMPICS has no repeating letters so, all the letters are distinct.

The number of ways of arranging 8 distinct items in a line = $8! = 40320$

c PAINTBRUSH has no repeating letters so, all the letters are distinct.

The number of ways of arranging 10 distinct items in a line = $10! = 3628800$

3 a There are 4 distinct numbers and 4 spaces to fill.

Consider the four spaces: 1st 2nd 3rd 4th

The first number has a choice of 4 spaces

The second number has a choice of 3 spaces

The third number has a choice of 2 spaces

The fourth number fills the last space

The number of arrangements of 4 numbers is $4 \times 3 \times 2 \times 1 = 4! = 24$

Answer 24 arrangements.

b i There is only one possible even number if you arrange 3, 5, 7 and 8.

The 8 must take the last space i.e., the 4th space

The remaining three numbers are all distinct and can be arranged in $3! = 6$ ways.

Answer 6 arrangements.

b ii There is only one number that is greater or equal to 8.

The 8 must take the first space (i.e., in the thousands column)

The remaining three numbers (3, 5 and 7) must fill the hundreds, tens and unit columns. As 3, 5 and 7 are all distinct they can be arranged in $3! = 6$ ways.

Answer 6 numbers.

4 a The seven books are different so, they are all distinct and can be arranged with no restrictions in $7! = 5040$ arrangements.

b The 4 cookery books can be arranged in $4! = 24$ ways.

If the cookery books are kept together then they are one item.

So, the three different history books plus the cookery books make a total of 4 distinct items which can be arranged in $4! = 24$ ways.

So, the number of ways of arranging the books with these restrictions is $24 \times 24 = 576$

Answer 576 arrangements.

5 a The numbers 2, 3, 4, 5 and 6 are distinct numbers.

If they are each used once to make different five digit numbers then they can be arranged in $5! = 120$ ways.

b Three of the numbers out of 2, 3, 4, 5 and 6 are even. These are 2, 4 and 6.

There are 5 spaces to fill.

1st 2nd 3rd 4th 5th

If the last space is filled with a '2', there are four distinct numbers left which can be arranged in 4! ways.

If the last space is filled with a '4', the remaining numbers can be arranged in 4! ways.

Similarly, if the last space is filled with a '6', the remaining numbers can be arranged in 4! ways.

There are $3 \times 24 = 72$ ways to form five even numbers.

Answer 72 arrangements.

c There are 5 spaces to fill.

The first space must be '4' or a '5' or a '6'

If the first space is a '4' then the four remaining numbers (2, 3, 5 and 6) can be arranged in $4! = 24$ ways.

If the first space is a '5' then the four remaining numbers (2, 3, 4 and 6) can be arranged in $4! = 24$ ways.

If the first space is a '6' then the four remaining numbers (2, 3, 4 and 5) can be arranged in $4! = 24$ ways.

There are $3 \times 24 = 72$ ways to form 5 digit numbers that are greater than 40 000.

Answer 72 arrangements.

d Numbers that are even and greater than 40 000, must start with a 4, 5 or 6 and end in a 2, 4 or 6

The possibilities are:

4 ___ ___ ___ 2 The remaining 3 numbers (3, 5 and 6) can be arranged in $3! = 6$ ways

4 ___ ___ ___ 6 The remaining 3 numbers (2, 3 and 5) can be arranged in $3! = 6$ ways

5 ___ ___ ___ 2 The remaining 3 numbers (3, 4 and 6) can be arranged in $3! = 6$ ways

5 ___ ___ ___ 4 The remaining 3 numbers (2, 3 and 6) can be arranged in $3! = 6$ ways

5 ___ ___ ___ 6 The remaining 3 numbers (2, 3 and 4) can be arranged in $3! = 6$ ways

6 ___ ___ ___ 2 The remaining 3 numbers (3, 4 and 5) can be arranged in $3! = 6$ ways

6 ___ ___ ___ 4 The remaining 3 numbers (2, 3 and 5) can be arranged in $3! = 6$ ways

Total number of arrangements is $6 \times 7 = 42$.

6 a There are two groups i.e., girls and boys, within these groups, the girls and boys are distinct.

There are 5 people altogether.

So, we can think of the 5 people as:

$$G_1 \quad G_2 \quad G_3 \quad B_1 \quad B_2$$

But, there is only one way to sit the 5 people if the girls and the boys sit alternately:

$$G \quad B \quad G \quad B \quad G$$

The three girls can sit in $3! = 6$ ways

The two boys can sit in $2! = 2$ ways

There are $3! \times 2! = 12$ ways altogether.

Answer 12 arrangements.

b If the girls sit at the end of each row then there are 6 ways they can sit i.e.

G_1 ___ ___ ___ G_2 or G_1 ___ ___ ___ G_3 etc

The remaining one girl and two boys are all distinct and they sit in the three middle seats in $3! = 6$ ways.

So, if a girl sits at each end then there are $6 \times 6 = 36$ ways to do this.

Answer 36 arrangements.

c There are only two possible arrangements if the girls sit together and the boys sit together. These are GGGBB or BBGGG

The three girls can sit together in $3! = 6$ ways.

The two boys can sit together in $2! = 2$ ways.

So for GGGBB there are $6 \times 2 = 12$ ways

For the BBGGG there are $2 \times 6 = 12$ ways

In total there are $12 + 12 = 24$ ways.

Answer 24 arrangements

7 a The 6 letters of ORANGE are distinct.

The number of ways of arranging n distinct items in a line $= n!$

The number of ways of arranging 6 distinct items in a line $= 6! = 720$ ways

b If the letter 'O' is at the beginning, then there are 5 letters left to be arranged.

There are $5! = 120$ ways to do this.

c There are two possible arrangements that have an 'O' at one end and an 'E at the other.

These are: O ___ ___ ___ E
or E ___ ___ ___ O

The remaining four distinct letters i.e., R, A, N and G can be arranged in $4! = 24$ ways.

There are therefore $2 \times 24 = 48$ ways.

Answer 48 arrangements

8 a The six digits 0, 1, 2, 3, 4, 5 are all distinct.

The first digit can be 1, 2, 3, 4 or 5.

If the first digit is '1', then the remaining 5 distinct digits can be arranged in $5! = 120$ ways.

Similarly if the first digit is a 2, 3, 4 or 5 then each of these represents 120 ways.

So the total number of ways is
$5 \times 120 = 600$ ways.

Answer 600 arrangements.

b The 6 digit even numbers from 0, 1, 2, 3, 4 and 5 are those that end in 0, 2 or 4.

If the last digit is 0 then:

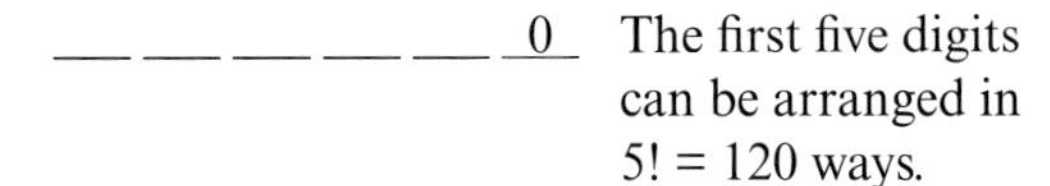

_ _ _ _ _ 0 The first five digits can be arranged in $5! = 120$ ways.

If the last digit is a 2:

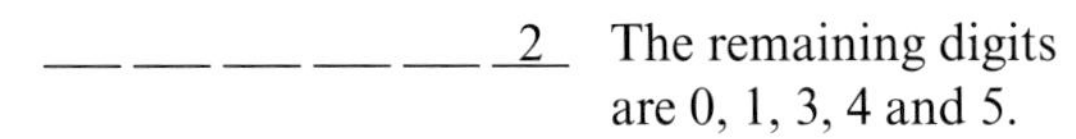

_ _ _ _ _ 2 The remaining digits are 0, 1, 3, 4 and 5.

The left most digit can be 1, 3, 4 or 5:

1 _ _ _ _ 2 The four remaining digits 0, 3, 4 and 5 can be arranged in 4! ways

OR

3 _ _ _ _ 2 The four remaining digits 0, 1, 4 and 5 can be arranged in 4! ways

OR

4 _ _ _ _ 2 The four remaining digits 0, 1, 3 and 5 can be arranged in 4! ways

OR

5 _ _ _ _ 2 The four remaining digits 0, 1, 3 and 4 can be arranged in 4! ways

However if the last digit is a 4

_ _ _ _ _ 4 The remaining digits are 0, 1, 2, 3 and 5

The left most digit can be a 1, 2, 3 or 5

1 _ _ _ _ 4 The four remaining digits 0, 2, 3 and 5 can be arranged in 4! ways

OR

2 _ _ _ _ 4 The four remaining digits 0, 1, 3 and 5 can be arranged in 4! ways

OR

3 _ _ _ _ 4 The four remaining digits 0, 1, 2 and 5 can be arranged in 4! ways

OR

5 _ _ _ _ 4 The four remaining digits 0, 1, 2 and 3 can be arranged in 4! ways

The total number of six-digit numbers is
$120 + 8 \times 4! = 312$

9 There are 3 possible arrangements where 2 boys have 4 girls seated between them:

BGGGGBGG GBGGGGBG GGBGGGGB

The 6 girls can be arranged in $6! = 720$ ways.

The 2 boys can be arranged in $2! = 2$ ways.

Therefore there are $3 \times 720 \times 2 = 4320$ ways.

Exercise 10.3

REMEMBER

The general rule for finding the number of **permutations** of r items from n distinct items is

$$^{n}P_{r} = \frac{n!}{(n-r)!}$$

1 **a** $^{8}P_{5} = \frac{8!}{(8-5)!} = \frac{8!}{3!} = 6720$

c $^{11}P_{8} = \frac{11!}{(11-8)!} = \frac{11!}{3!} = 6\,652\,800$

2 $^{6}P_{4} = \frac{6!}{(6-4)!} = \frac{6!}{2!} = 360$

3 $^{9}P_{5} = \frac{9!}{(9-5)!} = \frac{9!}{4!} = 15\,120$

4 $^{8}P_{3} = \frac{8!}{(8-3)!} = \frac{8!}{5!} = 336$

REMEMBER

In permutations, order matters.

5 The digits are 1, 2, 3, 4, 5, 6 and 7

Method 1

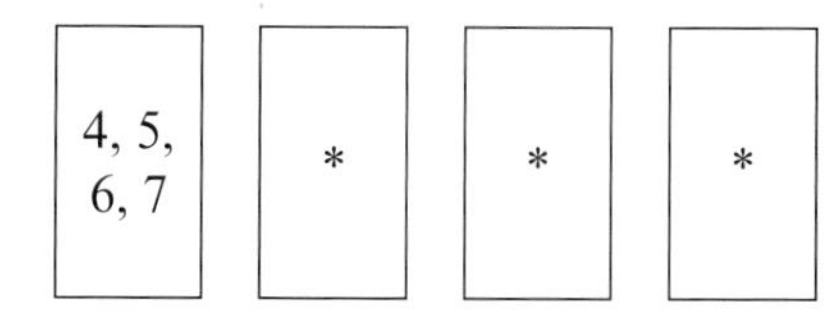

The first digit could be 4, 5, 6 or 7 i.e., $^{4}P_{1}$

There are now three spaces to fill using the remaining 6 digits

So, the number of numbers is $^{4}P_{1} \times {}^{6}P_{3} = 480$

Method 2

Consider the number of choices for filling each of the four spaces:

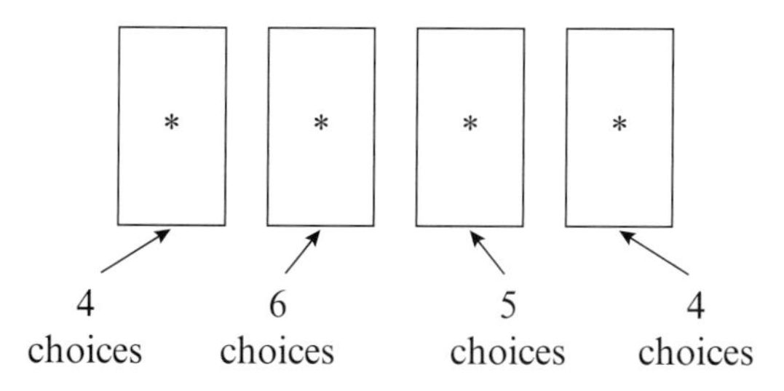

Number of ways of filling the four spaces
$= 4 \times 6 \times 5 \times 4 = 480$

6 The digits are 2, 4, 5, 7 and 8 and we want a four-digit even number.

Method 1

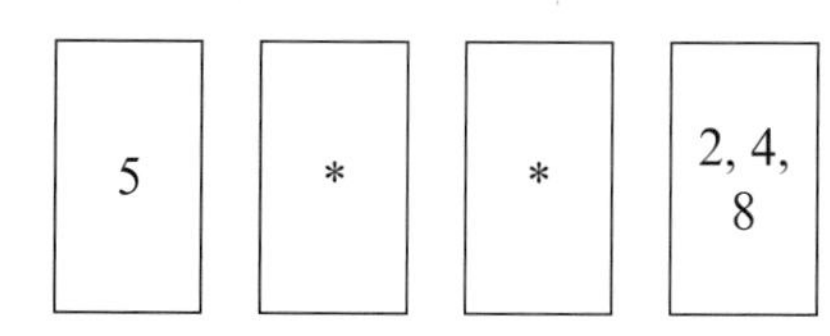

The first digit has to be 5 i.e., $^{1}P_{1}$

The last digit could be 2, 4 or 8 i.e., $^{3}P_{1}$

There are now two remaining spaces to fill i.e., $^{3}P_{2}$

So the number of numbers is $^{1}P_{1} \times {}^{3}P_{1} \times {}^{3}P_{2} = 18$

Method 2

Consider the number of choices for filling each of the four spaces:

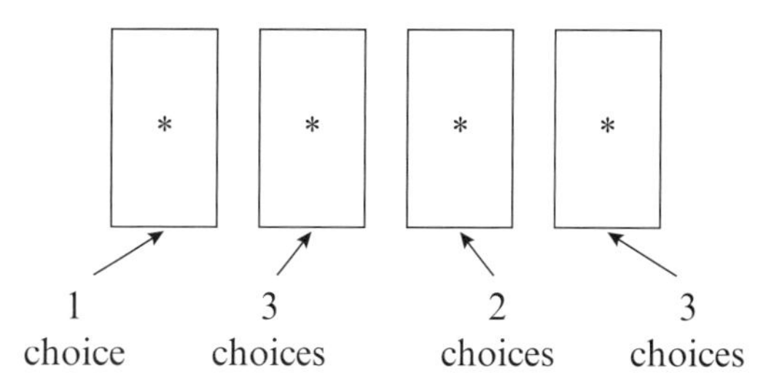

Number of ways of filling the four spaces
$= 1 \times 3 \times 2 \times 3 = 18$

7 Given 1, 2, 3, 4, 5, 6, 7 and 8

a With no restrictions we need to choose 4 digits from 8 digits.

The number of different four-digit numbers is $^{8}P_{4} = 1680$.

b If the four-digit number is odd, then the last digit could be 1, 3, 5 or 7 so $^{4}P_{1}$

There are now three spaces to fill from the seven remaining digits or $^{7}P_{3}$

So the number of numbers is $^{4}P_{1} \times {}^{7}P_{3} = 840$

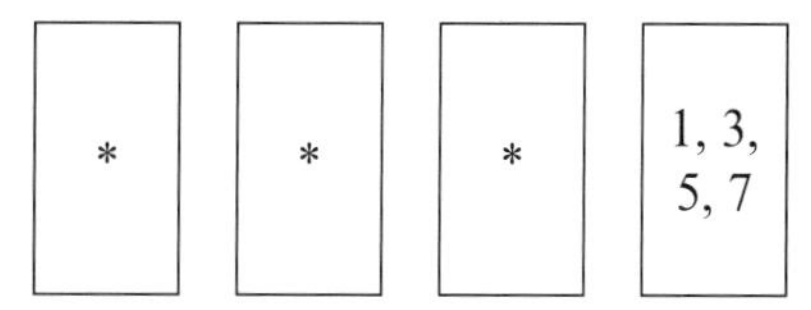

c If the number is to be greater than 6000

Consider the number of choices for filling each of the four spaces:

Number of ways of filling the four spaces
$= 3 \times 7 \times 6 \times 5 = 630$

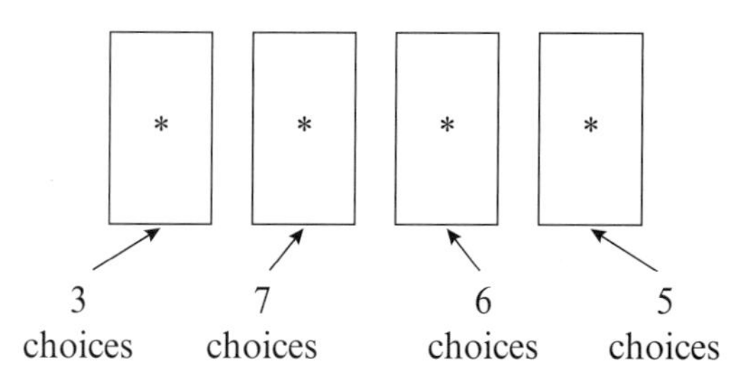

d If the four-digit number is odd and greater than 6000 from 1, 2, 3, 4, 5, 6, 7 and 8

The last digit could be 1, 3, 5 or 7

The first digit could be 6, 7 or 8 BUT if the last digit is 7 then it cannot also be the first digit so we have two cases:

Case 1

If the last digit is 7 (i.e., ${}^1P_1$) then the first digit could be a 6 or an 8 i.e., ${}^2P_1$

So there are now two spaces to be filled from six remaining digits i.e., ${}^6P_2$

So, the number of numbers is ${}^1P_1 \times {}^2P_1 \times {}^6P_2 = 60$

Case 2

If the last digit is a 1 or 3 or 5 (i.e., ${}^3P_1$) then the first digit could be 6, 7 or 8 i.e., ${}^3P_1$

The two remaining spaces need to be filled from the six remaining digits i.e., ${}^6P_2$

So the number of numbers is ${}^3P_1 \times {}^3P_1 \times {}^6P_2 = 270$

The total number of four-digit numbers that are odd and greater than 6000 is $60 + 270 = 330$

8 Given 3, 5, 6, 8 and 9

a The number of three-digit numbers that can be formed is ${}^5P_3 = 60$

b The number of:

three-digit numbers + four-digit numbers + five-digit numbers $= {}^5P_3 + {}^5P_4 + {}^5P_5 = 300$

9 Given 1, 2, 3, 4, 5, 6, 7 and 8

If the four-digit number is even and greater than 2000 from 1, 2, 3, 4, 5, 6, 7 and 8

The last digit could be 2, 4, 6 or 8

The first digit could be 2, 3, 4, 5, 6, 7 or 8 but if the last digit is 2, 4 or 6 or 8 then it cannot also be the first digit so:

Case 1

The last digit is a 2 so the first digit could be 3, 4, 5, 6, 7 or 8 i.e., 6 choices.

The remaining two spaces can then be filled.

The number of ways is $6 \times 6 \times 5 \times 1 = 180$

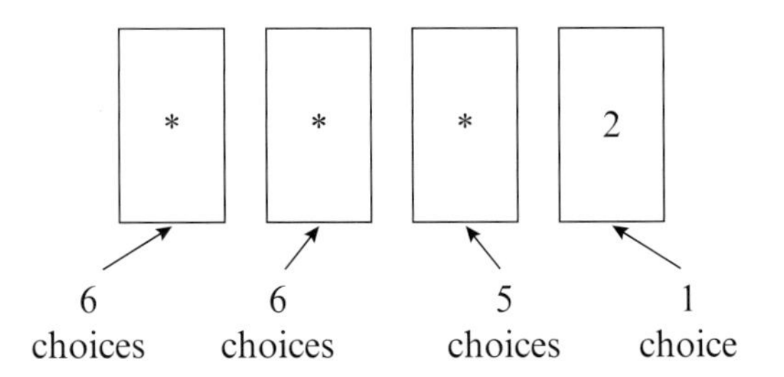

Case 2

The last digit is a 4 so the first digit could be 2, 3, 5, 6, 7 or 8 i.e., 6 choices.

The remaining two spaces can then be filled.

The number of ways is $6 \times 6 \times 5 \times 1 = 180$

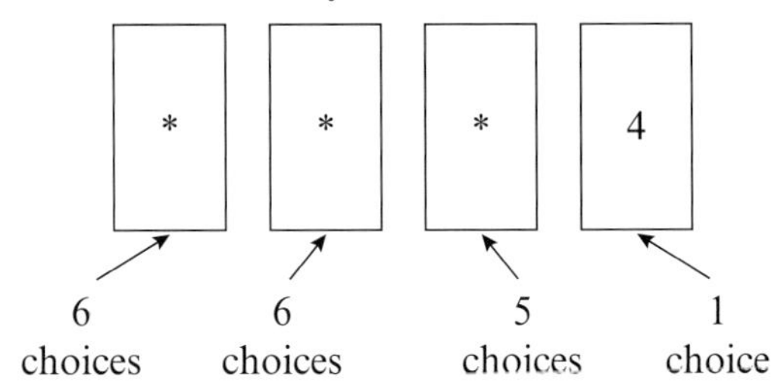

Case 3

The last digit is a 6 so the first digit could be 2, 3, 4, 5, 7 or 8 i.e., 6 choices.

The remaining two spaces can then be filled.

The number of ways is $6 \times 6 \times 5 \times 1 = 180$

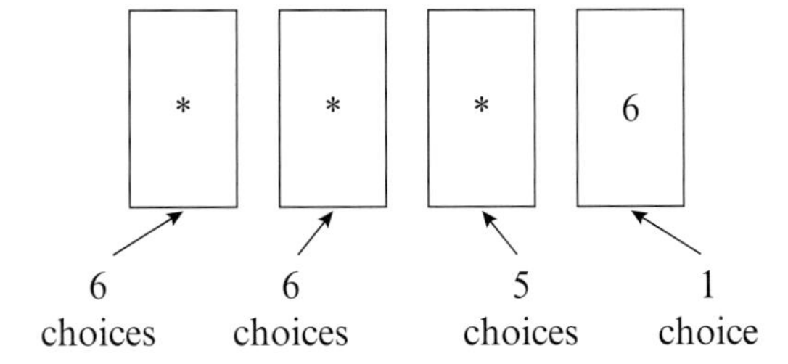

Case 4

The last digit is an 8 so the first digit could be 2, 3, 4, 5, 6, 7 i.e., 6 choices.

The remaining two spaces can then be filled.

The number of ways is $6 \times 6 \times 5 \times 1 = 180$

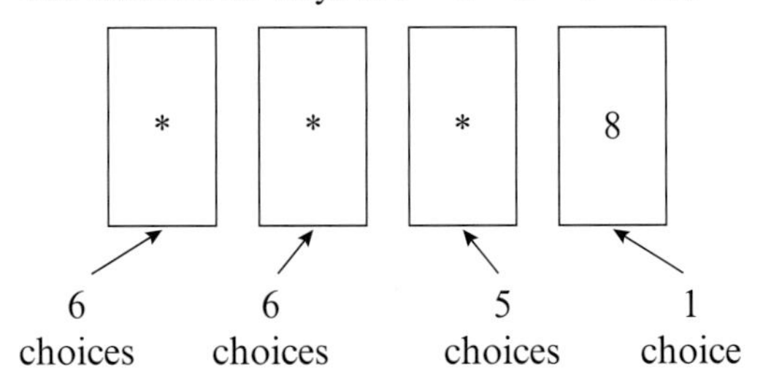

The total number of ways is $4 \times 180 = 720$

10 a Solve ${}^nP_5 = 720$ use ${}^nP_r = \frac{n!}{(n-r)!}$

$$\frac{n(n-1)(n-2)(n-3)(n-4)(n-5)!}{(n-5)!} = 720$$

$$\frac{n(n-1)(n-2)(n-3)(n-4)}{1} = 720$$

$$n(n-1)(n-2)(n-3)(n-4) = 720$$

The 5 factors on the left hand side average to the middle one so:

$(n-2)^5 = 720$ take the fifth root of both sides

$n - 2 = 3.72791\ldots$

$n = 5.72791\ldots$

If $n = 6$ then substitute into $n(n-1)(n-2)(n-3)(n-4) = 720$

$6 \times 5 \times 4 \times 3 \times 2 = 720$

$720 = 720$

Solution is $n = 6$

b Solve ${}^nP_3 = 7n(n-1)$ use ${}^nP_r = \frac{n!}{(n-r)!}$

$$\frac{n(n-1)(n-2)(n-3)!}{(n-3)!} = 7n(n-1)$$

$$\frac{n(n-1)(n-2)}{1} = 7n(n-1)$$

$n(n-1)(n-2) = 7n(n-1)$ expand brackets

$n^3 - 3n^2 + 2n = 7n^2 - 7n$ simplify

$n^3 - 10n^2 + 9n = 0$ factorise

$n(n^2 - 10n + 9) = 0$

$n(n-9)(n-1) = 0$ solve

$n = 0$ [reject as ${}^0P_3$ has no meaning] or

$n = 1$ [reject as ${}^1P_3$ has no meaning] or

$n = 9$

Solution is $n = 9$

c $${}^nP_5 = \frac{n(n-1)(n-2)(n-3)(n-4)\cancel{(n-5)!}}{\cancel{(n-5)!}}$$

$$= \frac{n(n-1)(n-2)(n-3)(n-4)}{1}$$

$$= n(n-1)(n-2)(n-3)(n-4)$$

$${}^nP_4 = \frac{n(n-1)(n-2)(n-3)\cancel{(n-4)!}}{\cancel{(n-4)!}}$$

$$= \frac{n(n-1)(n-2)(n-3)}{1}$$

$$= n(n-1)(n-2)(n-3)$$

$$\frac{\cancel{(n-1)(n-2)(n-3)}(n-4)}{\cancel{(n-1)(n-2)(n-3)}} = 3$$

$n - 4 = 3$

$n = 7$

Solution is $n = 7$

Exercise 10.4

REMEMBER

The general rule for finding the number of combinations of r items from n distinct items is:

$${}^nC_r = \frac{n!}{r!(n-r)!}$$

1 a ${}^5C_1$ represents the number of combinations of 1 from 5

$$= \frac{5!}{1!(5-1)!} = \frac{5 \times \cancel{4} \times \cancel{3} \times \cancel{2} \times \cancel{1}}{1 \times \cancel{4} \times \cancel{3} \times \cancel{2} \times \cancel{1}} = 5$$

f $$\binom{7}{4} = {}^7C_4 = \frac{7!}{4!(7-4)!}$$

$$= \frac{7 \times 6 \times 5 \times \cancel{4} \times \cancel{3} \times \cancel{2} \times \cancel{1}}{\cancel{4} \times \cancel{3} \times \cancel{2} \times \cancel{1} \times 3 \times 2 \times 1} = 35$$

REMEMBER

In combinations, order does not matter.

2 $^8C_3 = \frac{8!}{3!(8-3)!} = \frac{8 \times 7 \times 6 \times \cancel{5} \times \cancel{4} \times \cancel{3} \times \cancel{2} \times \cancel{1}}{3 \times 2 \times 1 \times \cancel{5} \times \cancel{4} \times \cancel{3} \times \cancel{2} \times \cancel{1}} = 56$

$^8C_5 = \frac{8!}{5!(8-5)!} = \frac{8 \times 7 \times 6 \times \cancel{5} \times \cancel{4} \times \cancel{3} \times \cancel{2} \times \cancel{1}}{\cancel{5} \times \cancel{4} \times \cancel{3} \times \cancel{2} \times \cancel{1} \times 3 \times 2 \times 1} = 56$

So $^8C_3 = {}^8C_5$

3 a Number of ways of choosing 3 photographs from 10 photographs is $^{10}C_3 = 120$

b Number of ways of choosing 5 books from 7 books is $^7C_5 = 21$

c Number of ways of choosing a team of 11 footballers from 14 footballers is $^{14}C_{11} = 364$

4 The five letters P, Q, R, S and T are distinct.

There are $^5C_3 = 10$ ways of choosing 3 letters from 5 letters.

5 Number of ways of choosing 5 toys for box A is the same as the number of ways of choosing 3 toys for box B.

The number of ways of choosing 5 toys from 8 toys to go in box A is $^8C_5 = 56$

6 The number of ways of choosing 4 pencils from 8 is $^8C_4 = 70$

The number of ways of choosing 3 pens from 5 is $^5C_3 = 10$

The number of ways of selecting the pens and the pencils is $70 \times 10 = 700$

7 All the letters in PAINTBRUSH are distinct.

a If there is no restriction on the letters selected, the number of ways to select 4 letters from 10 letters is $^{10}C_4 = 210$

b The letter T must be selected in $^1C_1 = 1$ way.

We now need to select 3 more letters from the remaining 9.

The number of ways doing this is $^9C_3 = 84$.

So, the number of ways of selecting four letters from PAINTBRUSH if the letter T must be selected is $1 \times 84 = 84$.

8 a The number of ways of answering 10 questions correctly from 30 questions is $^{30}C_{10} = 30\,045\,015$

b The number of ways of answering 25 questions correctly from 30 questions is $^{30}C_{25} = 142\,506$

9 Choosing 3 long distance runners from 10 long distance runners can be done in $^{10}C_3$ ways

Choosing 5 sprinters from 8 sprinters can be done in $^8C_5$ ways

Choosing 2 jumpers from 5 jumpers can be done in $^5C_2$ ways

The team can be selected in $^{10}C_3 \times {}^8C_5 \times {}^5C_2 = 120 \times 56 \times 10 = 67\,200$ ways.

10 a If there are no restrictions then 5 men + 3 women = 8 people.

All 8 people have an equal chance of being chosen.

The number of ways of choosing 5 members from 8 is $^8C_5 = 56$

b 3 men can be chosen from 5 men in $^5C_3$ ways

2 women can be chosen from 3 women in $^3C_2$ ways

A team of 3 men and 2 women can be chosen in $^5C_3 \times {}^3C_2 = 10 \times 3 = 30$ ways

c If the team does not have more than one woman then the team can be:

5 men and 0 women $^5C_5 \times {}^3C_0 = 1 \times 1 = 1$ way or

4 men and 1 woman $^5C_4 \times {}^3C_1 = 5 \times 3 = 15$ ways

The total number of ways is $1 + 15 = 16$

11 a If there are no restrictions then 7 men + 6 women = 13 people.

All 13 people have an equal chance of being chosen.

The number of ways of choosing 5 members from 13 is $^{13}C_5 = 1287$

b If the team has more men than women then the team can be:

3 men and 2 women ${}^7C_3 \times {}^6C_2 = 35 \times 15$
$= 525$ ways

4 men and 1 woman ${}^7C_4 \times {}^6C_1 = 35 \times 6$
$= 210$ ways

5 men and 0 women ${}^7C_5 \times {}^6C_0 = 21 \times 1$
$= 21$ ways

The total number of ways is $525 + 210 + 21 = 756$

12 The 6 person committee can be made up of:

1 man and 5 women ${}^6C_1 \times {}^7C_5 = 6 \times 21 = 126$ ways

2 men and 4 women ${}^6C_2 \times {}^7C_4 = 15 \times 35 = 525$ ways

3 men and 3 women ${}^6C_3 \times {}^7C_3 = 20 \times 35 = 700$ ways

4 men and 2 women ${}^6C_4 \times {}^7C_2 = 15 \times 21 = 315$ ways

5 men and 1 woman ${}^6C_5 \times {}^7C_1 = 6 \times 7 = 42$ ways

6 men and 0 women ${}^6C_6 \times {}^7C_0 = 1 \times 1 = 1$ way

The total number of ways is
$126 + 525 + 700 + 315 + 42 + 1 = 1709$

13 a If there are no restrictions then
4 teachers + 7 students = 11 people.

All 11 people have an equal chance of being chosen.

The number of ways of choosing 5 members from 11 is ${}^{11}C_5 = 462$

b The 5 person committee can be made up of:

1 teacher and 4 students ${}^4C_1 \times {}^7C_4 = 4 \times 35$
$= 140$ ways

2 teachers and 3 students ${}^4C_2 \times {}^7C_3 = 6 \times 35$
$= 210$ ways

The total number of ways of choosing the committee is $140 + 210 = 350$

14 a If there are no restrictions then:

4 trigonometry questions + 6 algebra questions
= 10 questions

These 10 questions have an equal chance of being chosen.

The number of ways of choosing 8 questions from 10 questions is ${}^{10}C_8 = 45$

b The 8 questions can be made up of:

4 trigonometry and 4 algebra
${}^4C_4 \times {}^6C_4 = 1 \times 15 = 15$ ways

3 trigonometry and 5 algebra
${}^4C_3 \times {}^6C_5 = 4 \times 6 = 24$ ways

2 trigonometry and 6 algebra
${}^4C_2 \times {}^6C_6 = 6 \times 1 = 6$ ways

The total number of selections is
$15 + 24 + 6 = 45$

15 a If there are no restrictions then:

4 comedy movies + 3 thriller movies + 3 science fiction movies = 10 movies

All 10 movies have an equal chance of being chosen

The number of ways of choosing 5 movies from 10 movies is ${}^{10}C_5 = 252$

b The selection can be made up from his favourite thriller movie and 4 other movies

If we take out his favourite thriller movie from the 10 movies, we now have to choose

4 other movies from the 9 movies left. So the number of ways is ${}^9C_4 = 126$

c The selection can be made up from:

3 comedy and 2 thriller and 0 science fiction
$= {}^4C_3 \times {}^3C_2 \times {}^3C_0 = 4 \times 3 \times 1 = 12$

3 comedy and 1 thriller and 1 science fiction
$= {}^4C_3 \times {}^3C_1 \times {}^3C_1 = 4 \times 3 \times 3 = 36$

3 comedy and 0 thriller and 2 science fiction
$= {}^4C_3 \times {}^3C_0 \times {}^3C_2 = 4 \times 1 \times 3 = 12$

4 comedy and 1 thriller and 0 science fiction
$= {}^4C_4 \times {}^3C_1 \times {}^3C_0 = 1 \times 3 \times 1 = 3$

4 comedy and 0 thriller and 1 science fiction
$= {}^4C_4 \times {}^3C_0 \times {}^3C_1 = 1 \times 1 \times 3 = 3$

The total number of ways is
$12 + 36 + 12 + 3 + 3 = 66$

16 There need to be 6 entertainers.

The group can be made up of:

4 singers and 1 guitarist and 1 comedian
$= {}^6C_4 \times {}^5C_1 \times {}^4C_1 = 15 \times 5 \times 4 = 300$

3 singers and 2 guitarists and 1 comedian
$= {}^6C_3 \times {}^5C_2 \times {}^4C_1 = 20 \times 10 \times 4 = 800$

3 singers and 1 guitarist and 2 comedians
$= {}^6C_3 \times {}^5C_1 \times {}^4C_2 = 20 \times 5 \times 6 = 600$

2 singers and 1 guitarist and 3 comedians
$= {}^6C_2 \times {}^5C_1 \times {}^4C_3 = 15 \times 5 \times 4 = 300$

The total number of ways is
$300 + 800 + 600 + 300 = 2000$

17 $45 \times {}^nC_4 = (n+1) \times {}^{n+1}C_5$

$$45 \times \frac{n!}{4!(n-4)!} = (n+1) \times \frac{(n+1)!}{5!(n+1-5)!}$$

$$45 \times \frac{n(n-1)(n-2)(n-3)(n-4)!}{4 \times 3 \times 2 \times 1 \times (n-4)!} = \frac{(n+1)(n+1)n(n-1)(n-2)(n-3)(n-4)!}{5 \times 4 \times 3 \times 2 \times 1(n-4)!}$$

$$\frac{45 \times n(n-1)(n-2)(n-3)}{24} = \frac{(n+1)(n+1)n(n-1)(n-2)(n-3)}{120}$$

$$\frac{45}{24} = \frac{(n+1)(n+1)}{120}$$

$$225 = (n+1)(n+1)$$

$n + 1 = \pm 15$

$n + 1 = -15$ or $n + 1 = 15$

$n = -16$ (reject) or $n = 14$

$n = 14$

Chapter 11: Series

Exercise 11.1

REMEMBER

Pascal's triangle

First Line:			1		
Second Line:		1		1	
Third Line:	1		2		1

1 The 6th row of Pascal's triangle is 1, 6, 15, 20, 15, 6, 1

The 7th row of Pascal's triangle is 1, 7, 21, 35, 35, 21, 7, 1

2 i $(x-2y)^3$ — the index = 3 so use the 3rd row in Pascal's triangle

The 3rd row of Pascal's triangle is 1, 3, 3, 1

$(x-2y)^3 = 1(x)^3 + 3(x)^2(-2y) + 3(x)(-2y)^2 + 1(-2y)^3$ — use the expansion of $(a+b)^3$

$= x^3 - 6x^2y + 12xy^2 - 8y^3$ — be careful with the negative numbers

j $(3x-4)^4$

The 4th row of Pascal's triangle is 1, 4, 6, 4, 1

$(3x-4)^4 = 1(3x)^4 + 4(3x)^3(-4) + 6(3x)^2(-4)^2 + 4(3x)(-4)^3 + 1(-4)^4$ — use the expansion of $(a+b)^3$

$= 81x^4 - 432x^3 + 864x^2 - 768x + 256$ — be careful with the negative numbers

3 e $(x-2)^5$

The 5th row of Pascal's triangle is 1, 5, 10, 10, 5, 1

The term in $x^3 = 10x^3(-2)^2 = 40x^3$

The coefficient of x^3 is 40

h $\left(3-\frac{1}{2}x\right)^4$

The 4th row of Pascal's triangle is 1, 4, 6, 4, 1

The term in $x^3 = 4(3)\left(-\frac{1}{2}x\right)^3 = -\frac{3}{2}x^3$

The coefficient of x^3 is $-\frac{3}{2}$

4 The 5th row of Pascal's triangle is 1, 5, 10, 10, 5, 1

Expand 0 $(4+x)^5$ and $(4-x)^5$

$(4+x)^5 = 1(4)^5 + 5(4)^4(x) + 10(4)^3(x)^2 + 10(4)^2(x)^3 + 5(4)(x)^4 + 1(x)^5$

$(4-x)^5 = 1(4)^5 + 5(4)^4(-x) + 10(4)^3(-x)^2 + 10(4)^2(-x)^3 + 5(4)(-x)^4 + 1(-x)^5$

Adding the previous two lines we get:

$= 2(4)^5 + 20(4)^3(x)^2 + 10(4)(x)^4$

$= 2048 + 1280x^2 + 40x^4$

Comparing with $A + Bx^2 + Cx^4$ then $A = 2048 \quad B = 1280 \quad C = 40$

5 $(1 + 2x)(1 + 3x)^4$

$(1 + 3x)^4 = 1(1)^4 + 4(1)^3(3x) + 6(1)^2(3x)^2 + 4(1)(3x)^3 + 1(3x)^4$

$= 1 + 12x + 54x^2 + 108x^3 + 81x^4$

$(1 + 2x)(1 + 12x + 54x^2 + 108x^3 + 81x^4) =$

$1 + 12x + 54x^2 + 108x^3 + 81x^4 + 2x + 24x^2 + 108x^3 + 216x^4 + 162x^5$

$= 1 + 14x + 78x^2 + 216x^3 + 297x^4 + 162x^5$

6 The 3rd row of Pascal's triangle is 1, 3, 3, 1

$(2 + ax)^3 = 1(2)^3 + 3(2)^2(ax) + 3(2)(ax)^2 + 1(ax)^3$

$= 8 + 12ax + 6a^2x^2 + a^3x^3$

The coefficient of x is 96 so $12a = 96$

$a = 8$

7 a The 4th row of Pascal's triangle is 1, 4, 6, 4, 1

$(3 + x)^4 = 1(3)^4 + 4(3)^3(x) + 6(3)^2(x)^2 + 4(3)(x)^3 + 1(x)^4$

$= 81 + 108x + 54x^2 + 12x^3 + x^4$

b Comparing $(3 + x)^4$ with $(3 + \sqrt{5})^4$, $x = \sqrt{5}$

Replacing x with $\sqrt{5}$ in the expansion we get:

$81 + 108\sqrt{5} + 54(\sqrt{5})^2 + 12(\sqrt{5})^3 + (\sqrt{5})^4$

$81 + 108\sqrt{5} + 270 + 60\sqrt{5} + 25$

$376 + 168\sqrt{5}$

8 a The 5th row of Pascal's triangle is 1, 5, 10, 10, 5, 1

$(1 + x)^5 = 1(1)^5 + 5(1)^4(x) + 10(1)^3(x)^2 + 10(1)^2(x)^3 + 5(1)(x)^4 + 1(x)^5$

$= 1 + 5x + 10x^2 + 10x^3 + 5x^4 + x^5$

b i Comparing $(1 + x)^5$ with $(1 + \sqrt{3})^5$, $x = \sqrt{3}$

Replacing x with $\sqrt{3}$ in the expansion we get:

$1 + 5\sqrt{3} + 10(\sqrt{3})^2 + 10(\sqrt{3})^3 + 5(\sqrt{3})^4 + (\sqrt{3})^5$

$1 + 5\sqrt{3} + 30 + 30\sqrt{3} + 45 + 9\sqrt{3} = 76 + 44\sqrt{3}$

ii Comparing $(1 + x)^5$ with $(1 - \sqrt{3})^5$, $x = -\sqrt{3}$

Replacing x with $-\sqrt{3}$ in the expansion we get:

$1 + 5(-\sqrt{3}) + 10(-\sqrt{3})^2 + 10(-\sqrt{3})^3 + 5(-\sqrt{3})^4 + (-\sqrt{3})^5$

$1 - 5\sqrt{3} + 30 - 30\sqrt{3} + 45 - 9\sqrt{3}$

$76 - 44\sqrt{3}$

c $(1 + \sqrt{3})^5 + (1 - \sqrt{3})^5 = 76 + 44\sqrt{3} + 76 - 44\sqrt{3}$

Answer: 152

9 a The 4th row of Pascal's triangle is 1, 4, 6, 4, 1

$(2 - x^2)^4 = 1(2)^4 + 4(2)^3(-x^2) + 6(2)^2(-x^2)^2 + 4(2)(-x^2)^3 + 1(-x^2)^4$

$= 16 - 32x^2 + 24x^4 - 8x^6 + x^8$

b $(1 + 3x^2)(2 - x^2)^4 = (1 + 3x^2)(16 + 32x^2 + 24x^4 - 8x^6 + x^8)$

We are interested in the coefficient of the x^6 terms so we do not need the full expansion to find the x^6 terms

$(1 + 3x^2)(16 + 32x^2 + 24x^4 - 8x^6 + x^8)$

The x^6 terms are: $-8x^6 + 72x^6 = 64x^6$

Therefore the coefficient of x^6 is 64

10 The 5th row of Pascal's triangle is 1, 5, 10, 10, 5, 1

$$\left(x - \frac{3}{x}\right)^5 = 1(x)^5 + 5(x)^4\left(-\frac{3}{x}\right) + 10(x)^3\left(-\frac{3}{x}\right)^2 + 10(x)^2\left(-\frac{3}{x}\right)^3 + 5(x)\left(-\frac{3}{x}\right)^4 + 1\left(-\frac{3}{x}\right)^5$$

The term $10(x)^3\left(-\frac{3}{x}\right)^2 = 90x$

The coefficient of this term is 90.

11 The 3rd row of Pascal's triangle is 1, 3, 3 and 1

$$\left(x^2 + \frac{1}{2x}\right)^3 = 1(x^2)^3 + 3(x^2)^2\left(\frac{1}{2x}\right) + 3(x^2)\left(\frac{1}{2x}\right)^2 + 1\left(\frac{1}{2x}\right)^3$$

The term independent of x in the expansion is $3(x^2)\left(\frac{1}{2x}\right)^2 = 3x^2 \times \frac{1}{4x^2} = \frac{3}{4}$

Answer: $\frac{3}{4}$

12 a The 5th row of Pascal's triangle is 1, 5, 10, 10, 5, 1

$(2 + y)^5 = 1(2)^5 + 5(2)^4(y) + 10(2)^3(y)^2 + \ldots$

The first three terms are: $32 + 80y + 80y^2$

b Replacing y with $3x - 4x^2$ in these terms we get:

$32 + 80(3x - 4x^2) + 80(3x - 4x^2)^2$

$32 + 80(3x - 4x^2) + 80(3x - 4x^2)(3x - 4x^2)$

The terms in x^2 come from the products:

$80 \times -4x^2 = -320x^2$ and $80 \times 3x \times 3x = 720x^2$

So the coefficient of x^2 is $-320 + 720 = 400$

13 The 5th row of Pascal's triangle is 1, 5, 10, 10, 5, 1

$(3 + ax)^5 = 1(3)^5 + 5(3)^4(ax) + 10(3)^3(ax)^2 + 10(3)^2(ax)^3 + 5(3)(ax)^4 + 1(x)^5$

The term in x^3 is $10(3)^2(ax)^3 = 90a^3x^3$

The coefficient of this term is $90a^3$

The 4th row of Pascal's triangle is 1, 4, 6, 4, 1

$$\left(1 + \frac{ax}{2}\right)^4 = 1(1)^4 + 4(1)^3\left(\frac{ax}{2}\right) + 6(1)^2\left(\frac{ax}{2}\right)^2 + 4(1)\left(\frac{ax}{2}\right)^3 + 1\left(\frac{ax}{2}\right)^4$$

The term in x^2 is $6(1)^2\left(\frac{ax}{2}\right)^2 = \frac{3a^2}{2}x^2$

The coefficient of this term is $\frac{3a^2}{2}$

As $90a^3$ is twelve times $\frac{3a^2}{2}$, so:

$90a^3 = 12 \times \frac{3a^2}{2}$

$5a^3 = a^2$

$5a^3 - a^2 = 0$ factorise

$a^2(5a - 1) = 0$ solve

$a^2 = 0$ or $5a - 1 = 0$

$a = 0$ (reject) or $a = \frac{1}{5}$

Solution is $a = \frac{1}{5}$

14 a The 3rd row of Pascal's triangle is 1, 3, 3, 1

$$\left(x^2 + \frac{4}{x}\right)^3 = 1(x^2)^3 + 3(x^2)^2\left(\frac{4}{x}\right) + 3(x^2)\left(\frac{4}{x}\right)^2 + 1\left(\frac{4}{x}\right)^3$$

$$= x^6 + 12x^3 + 48 + \frac{64}{x^3}$$

$$\left(x^2 - \frac{4}{x}\right)^3 = 1(x^2)^3 + 3(x^2)^2\left(-\frac{4}{x}\right) + 3(x^2)\left(-\frac{4}{x}\right)^2 + 1\left(-\frac{4}{x}\right)^3$$

$$= x^6 - 12x^3 + 48 - \frac{64}{x^3}$$

So, $\left(x^2+\frac{4}{x}\right)^3-\left(x^2-\frac{4}{x}\right)^3=24x^3+\frac{128}{x^3}$

However, $24x^3+\frac{128}{x^3}=ax^3+\frac{b}{x^3}$

Answer: $a=24$ and $b=128$

b Comparing $\left(x^2+\frac{4}{x}\right)^3-\left(x^2-\frac{4}{x}\right)^3$ with $\left(2+\frac{4}{\sqrt{2}}\right)^3-\left(2-\frac{4}{\sqrt{2}}\right)^3$ we see that $x=\sqrt{2}$

So $\left(2+\frac{4}{\sqrt{2}}\right)^3-\left(2-\frac{4}{\sqrt{2}}\right)^3=24(\sqrt{2})^3+\frac{128}{(\sqrt{2})^3}$

$=48\sqrt{2}+\frac{128}{2\sqrt{2}}$

$=48\sqrt{2}+\frac{64}{\sqrt{2}}$

$=48\sqrt{2}+\frac{64}{\sqrt{2}}\times\frac{\sqrt{2}}{\sqrt{2}}$

$=48\sqrt{2}+32\sqrt{2}$

$=80\sqrt{2}$

15 a $y^3=\left(x+\frac{1}{x}\right)^3=1(x)^3+3(x)^2\left(\frac{1}{x}\right)+3(x)\left(\frac{1}{x}\right)^2+1\left(\frac{1}{x}\right)^3$

$y^3=x^3+3x+\frac{3}{x}+\frac{1}{x^3}$ rearrange and factorise

$y^3=x^3+\frac{1}{x^3}+3\left(x+\frac{1}{x}\right)$

$y^3=x^3+\frac{1}{x^3}+3y$ rearrange

$y^3-3y=x^3+\frac{1}{x^3}$

Answer: $x^3+\frac{1}{x^3}=y^3-3y$

b $y^5=\left(x+\frac{1}{x}\right)^5=1(x)^5+5(x)^4\left(\frac{1}{x}\right)+10(x)^3\left(\frac{1}{x}\right)^2+10(x)^2\left(\frac{1}{x}\right)^3+5(x)\left(\frac{1}{x}\right)^4+1\left(\frac{1}{x}\right)^5$

$y^5=x^5+5x^3+10x+\frac{10}{x}+\frac{5}{x^3}+\frac{1}{x^5}$ rearrange and factorise

$y^5=x^5+\frac{1}{x^5}+10\left(x+\frac{1}{x}\right)+5\left(x^3+\frac{1}{x^3}\right)$ substitute y for $x+\frac{1}{x}$ and y^3-3y for $x^3+\frac{1}{x^3}$

$y^5=x^5+\frac{1}{x^5}+10y+5(y^3-3y)$

$y^5=x^5+\frac{1}{x^5}+10y+5y^3-15y$

$$y^5 = x^5 + \frac{1}{x^5} + 5y^3 - 5y$$

$$y^5 - 5y^3 + 5y = x^5 + \frac{1}{x^5}$$

Answer: $x^5 + \frac{1}{x^5} = y^5 - 5y^3 + 5y$

Exercise 11.2

REMEMBER

$(a + b)^n = a^n + {}^3C_1\, a^{n-1}b + {}^3C_2\, a^{n-2}b^2 + {}^3C_3\, a^{n-3}b^3 + \ldots + {}^3C_4\, a^{n-r}b^r + \ldots + b^n$

or

$(a + b)^n = a^n + \binom{n}{1} a^{n-1}b + \binom{n}{2} a^{n-2}b^2 + \binom{n}{3} a^{n-3}b^3 + \ldots + \binom{n}{r} a^{n-r}b^r + \ldots + b^n$

1 a Row 3 is ${}^3C_0, {}^3C_1, {}^3C_2, {}^3C_3$

b Row 4 is ${}^4C_0, {}^4C_1, {}^4C_2, {}^4C_3, {}^4C_4$

c Row 5 is ${}^5C_0, {}^5C_1, {}^5C_2, {}^5C_3, {}^5C_4, {}^5C_5$

2 g $(a - 2b)^4 = a^4 + {}^4C_1\, a^3(-2b) + {}^4C_2\, a^2(-2b)^2 + {}^4C_3\, a^1(-2b)^3 + {}^4C_4\,(-2b)^4$

$= a^4 - 8a^3b + 24a^2b^2 - 32ab^3 + 16b^4$

k $\left(x - \frac{3}{x}\right)^5$

$= (x)^5 + {}^5C_1(x)^4\left(-\frac{3}{x}\right) + {}^5C_2(x)^3\left(-\frac{3}{x}\right)^2 + {}^5C_3(x)^2\left(-\frac{3}{x}\right)^3 + {}^5C_4(x)^1\left(-\frac{3}{x}\right)^4 + {}^5C_5\left(-\frac{3}{x}\right)^5$

$= x^5 - 15x^3 + 90x - \frac{270}{x} + \frac{405}{x^3} - \frac{243}{x^5}$

3 e $(1 - x)^6$

$(1)^6 + {}^6C_1(1)^5(-x) + {}^6C_2(1)^4(-x)^2 + {}^6C_3(1)^3(-x)^3 + {}^6C_4(1)^2(-x)^4 + {}^6C_5(1)(-x)^5 + {}^6C_6(-x)^6$

$= 1 - 6x + 15x^2 - 20x^3 + 15x^4 - 6x^5 + x^6$

The term containing x^3 is ${}^6C_3(1)^3(-x)^3 = -20x^3$

h Given $(4 - 5x)^{15}$

There are 16 terms in this expansion. It is not necessary to write them all down.

Write out the first few terms until the term in x^3 is spotted.

Alternatively go straight to the term in x^3.

$(4)^{15} + {}^{15}C_1(4)^{14}(-5x) + {}^{15}C_2(4)^{13}(-5x)^2 + {}^{15}C_3(4)^{12}(-5x)^3 + {}^{15}C_4(4)^{11}(-5x)^4 + \ldots$

${}^{15}C_3(4)^{12}(-5x)^3 = 455 \times 16\,777\,216 \times -125x^3$

$= -954\,204\,160\,000x^3$

REMEMBER

$$(1 + x)^n = 1 + nx + \frac{n(n-1)}{2!}x^2 + \frac{n(n-1)(n-2)}{3!}x^3 + \frac{n(n-1)(n-2)(n-3)}{4!}x^4 + \ldots$$

4 c $(1 - 3x)^7 = 1 + 7(-3x) + \frac{7 \times 6}{2!}(-3x)^2 + ..$ replace x by $-3x$ and n by 7 in the formula

The first three terms are: $1 - 21x + 189x^2$

g $(5 - x^2)^9 = \left[5\left(1 - \frac{x^2}{5}\right)\right]^9$ the formula is for $(1 + x)^n$ so take out a factor of 5.

$= 5^9\left(1 - \frac{x^2}{5}\right)^9$ replace x by $\left(-\frac{x^2}{5}\right)$ and n by 9

$= 5^9\left[1 + 9\left(-\frac{x^2}{5}\right) + \frac{9 \times 8}{2!}\left(-\frac{x^2}{5}\right)^2 + \ldots\right]$ multiply terms in brackets by 5^9.

$= 5^9\left[1 - \frac{9x^2}{5} + \frac{36}{25}x^4 + \ldots\right]$

The first three terms are: $1953125 - 3515625x^2 + 2812500x^4$

5 a $(1 + 2x)^6 = (1)^6 + {}^6C_1(1)^5(2x) + {}^6C_2(1)^4(2x)^2 + {}^6C_3(1)^3(2x)^3 + \ldots$

The first four terms are: $1 + 12x + 60x^2 + 160x^3$

b $\left(1 - \frac{x}{3}\right)(1 + 2x)^6 = \left(1 - \frac{x}{3}\right)(1 + 12x + 60x^2 + 160x^3\ldots)$

The coefficient of x^3 comes from the products: $(1 \times 160) + \left(-\frac{1}{3} \times 60\right) = 140$

Answer: 140

6 a $\left(1 + \frac{x}{2}\right)^{13} = 1^{13} + {}^{13}C_1(1)^{12}\left(\frac{x}{2}\right) + {}^{13}C_2(1)^{11}\left(\frac{x}{2}\right)^2 + {}^{13}C_3(1)^{10}\left(\frac{x}{2}\right)^3 + \ldots$

The first four terms are $1 + \frac{13}{2}x + \frac{39}{2}x^2 + \frac{143}{4}x^3$

b $(1 + 3x)\left(1 + \frac{13}{2}x + \frac{39}{2}x^2 + \frac{143}{4}x^3\ldots\right)$

The coefficient of x^3 comes from the products: $\left(1 \times \frac{143}{4}\right) + \left(3 \times \frac{39}{2}\right) = \frac{377}{4}$

Answer: $\frac{377}{4}$

7 a $(1 - 3x)^{10} = 1 + 10(-3x) + \frac{10 \times 9}{2!}(-3x)^2 + \frac{10 \times 9 \times 8}{3!}(-3x)^3 + \ldots$

The first four terms are: $1 - 30x + 405x^2 - 3240x^3$

b $(1 - 4x)(1 - 30x + 405x^2 - 3240x^3...)$

The coefficient of x^3 comes from the products: $(1 \times -3240) + ((-4) \times 405) = -4860$

Answer: -4860

8 a $(1 + 2x)^7 = (1)^7 + {}^7C_1(1)^6(2x) + {}^7C_2(1)^5(2x)^2 + ...$

The first three terms are: $1 + 14x + 84x^2$

b $(1 + 14x + 84x^2)(1 - 3x + 5x^2)$

The coefficient of x^2 comes from the products: $(1 \times 5) + (14 \times (-3)) + (84 \times 1) = 47$

Answer: 47

9 a $(1 + x)^7 = (1)^7 + {}^7C_1(1)^6(x) + {}^7C_2(1)^5(x)^2 + {}^7C_3(1)^4(x)^3 + ...$

The first 4 terms are: $1 + 7x + 21x^2 + 35x^3$

b Comparing $(1 + x)^7$ with $(1 + (y - y^2))^7$ and replacing x with $y - y^2$ in the first four terms gives:

$1 + 7(y - y^2) + 21(y - y^2)^2 + 35(y - y^2)^3$

$1 + 7(y - y^2) + 21(y - y^2)(y - y^2) + 35(y - y^2)(y - y^2)(y - y^2)$

$1 + 7y - 7y^2 + 21(y^2 - 2y^3 + y^4) + 35(y - y^2)(y^2 - 2y^3 + y^4)$

$1 + 7y - 7y^2 + 21y^2 - 42y^3 + 21y^4 + (35y - 35y^2)(y^2 - 2y^3 + y^4)$

The coefficient of y^3 comes from: $-42 + 35 = -7$

Answer: -7

10 $\left(x - \frac{3}{x}\right)^7 = (x)^7 + {}^7C_1(x)^6\left(-\frac{3}{x}\right) + {}^7C_2(x)^5\left(-\frac{3}{x}\right)^2 + {}^7C_3(x)^4\left(-\frac{3}{x}\right)^3 + ...$

The term in x is ${}^7C_3(x)^4\left(-\frac{3}{x}\right)^3 = 35 \times x^4 \times -\frac{27}{x^3} = -945x$

Answer: -945

11 $\left(x + \frac{1}{2x^2}\right)^9 = (x)^9 + {}^9C_1(x)^8\left(\frac{1}{2x^2}\right) + {}^9C_2(x)^7\left(\frac{1}{2x^2}\right)^2 + {}^9C_3(x)^6\left(\frac{1}{2x^2}\right)^3 + ...$

The term independent of x is: ${}^9C_3(x)^6\left(\frac{1}{2x^2}\right)^3 = 84x^6 \times \frac{1}{8x^6} = \frac{21}{2}$

Answer: $\frac{21}{2}$

12 $(1 + ax)^n = (1)^n + {}^nC_1(1)^{n-1}(ax) + {}^nC_2(1)^{n-2}(ax)^2 + {}^nC_3(1)^{n-3}(ax)^3 + \ldots$

Or

$1 + n(ax) + \frac{n(n-1)}{2!}(ax)^2 + \frac{n(n-1)(n-2)}{3!}(ax)^3 + \ldots$

The coefficient of x^2 is: $\frac{n(n-1)}{2} \times a^2$

The coefficient of x^3 is: $\frac{n(n-1)(n-2)}{6} \times a^3$

So, $\frac{n(n-1)}{2} \times a^2 = \frac{n(n-1)(n-2)}{6} \times a^3$ multiply both sides by $\frac{6}{a^2 n(n-1)}$ $[n \neq 0]$

$3 = (n-2)a$

$a = \frac{3}{n-2}$

Exercise 11.3

REMEMBER

The nth term of an arithmetic progression is $a + (n-1)d$

The sum of an arithmetic progression, $S_n = \frac{n}{2}(a + l)$ or $S_n = \frac{n}{2}[2a + (n-1)d]$

a = first term, d = common difference, l = last term, n = number of terms

1 The fifth term is $a + 4d$

The fourteenth term is $a + 13d$

2 **b** $20 + 11 + 2 + \ldots$ so $a = 20$, $d = -9$, $n = 20$

Use $S_n = \frac{n}{2}[2a + (n-1)d]$

$S_{20} = \frac{20}{2}[2 \times 20 + (20-1) \times -9]$

$S_{20} = 10[40 - 171]$

$S_{20} = -1310$

d $-2x - 4x - 8x$ so $a = -2x$, $d = -3x$, $n = 40$

$S_n = \frac{n}{2}[2a + (n-1)d]$

$S_{40} = \frac{40}{2}[2 \times (-2x) + (40-1) \times -3x]$

$S_{40} = 20[-4x - 117x]$

$S_{40} = 20[-121x]$

$S_{40} = -2420x$

3 **a** $n\text{th term} = a + (n - 1)d$ — use $a = 23$, $d = 4$ and nth term $= 159$

$159 = 23 + (n - 1) \times 4$ — solve

$n - 1 = 34$

$n = 35$

There are 35 terms

$S_n = \frac{n}{2}(a + l)$ — use $a = 23$, $n = 35$ and $l = 159$

$S_{45} = \frac{35}{2}(23 + 159)$

The sum is 3185

b $n\text{th term} = a + (n - 1)d$ — use $a = 28$, $d = -17$ and nth term $= -210$

$-210 = 28 + (n - 1) \times -17$ — solve

$n - 1 = 14$

$n = 15$

There are 15 terms

$S_n = \frac{n}{2}(a + l)$ — use $a = 28$, $n = 15$ and $l = -210$

$S_{15} = \frac{15}{2}(28 - 210)$ — solve

The sum is -1365

4 $S_n = \frac{n}{2}[2a + (n - 1)d]$ — use $a = 2$, $S_{12} = 618$, and $n = 12$

$618 = \frac{12}{2}[2 \times 2 + (12 - 1)d]$ — solve

$618 = 6[4 + 11d]$

$d = 9$

The common difference is 9

5 **a** $-13 + 19d = 82$ — solve

$d = 5$

The common difference is 5

$n\text{th term} = a + (n - 1)d$ — use $a = -13$, $d = 5$, and last term $= 112$

$112 = -13 + (n - 1) \times 5$ — solve

$n - 1 = 25$

$n = 26$

There are 26 terms

b $S_n = \frac{n}{2}(a + l)$ use $a = -13$, $n = 26$, $l = 112$

$S_{26} = \frac{26}{2}(-13 + 112)$ solve

The sum is 1287

6 The common difference d is $46 - 57 = -11$

nth term $= a + (n - 1)d$ use $a = 57$, $d = -11$, and nth term $= -207$

$-207 = 57 + (n - 1) \times -11$

$n - 1 = 24$

$n = 25$

$S_n = \frac{n}{2}(a + l)$ use $a = 57$, $n = 25$, $l = -207$

$S_{25} = \frac{25}{2}(57 - 207)$ solve

The sum is -1875

7 The common difference d is $5 - -2 = 7$

nth term$= a + (n - 1)d$ use $a = -2$, $d = 7$

If the last term is (the only term) greater than 200 then:

$-2 + 7(n - 1) > 200$

$-2 + 7n - 7 > 200$

$7n > 209$

$n > 29.857\ldots$

So $n = 30$

$S_n = \frac{n}{2}[2a + (n - 1)d]$ $a = -2$, $d = 7$, $n = 30$

$S_{30} = \frac{30}{2}[2 \times -2 + (30 - 1)7]$

$S_{30} = 2985$

The sum of all the terms is 2985

8 $S_n = \frac{n}{2}[2a + (n - 1)d]$ use $a = 8$, $S_6 = 58$, and $n = 6$

$58 = \frac{6}{2}[2 \times 8 + (6 - 1)d]$ solve

$d = \frac{2}{3}$

nth term$= a + (n - 1)d$ use $a = 8$, $d = \frac{2}{3}$, nth term $= 34$

$34 = 8 + (n - 1) \times \frac{2}{3}$

$n = 40$

There are 40 terms

9 Multiples of 6 are 6, 12, 18… so $d = 6$ and $a = 6$

The first multiple of 6 that is greater than 100 is 102 so $a = 102$.

The last multiple of 6 less than 400 is 396 so $l = 396$

nth term $= a + (n - 1)d$ use $a = 102$, $d = 6$, nth term $= 396$

$396 = 102 + (n - 1) \times 6$

$n - 1 = 49$

$n = 50$ so, there are 50 terms in this sequence

$S_n = \frac{n}{2}(a + l)$

$S_{50} = \frac{50}{2}(102 + 396)$

$= 12\,450$

The sum is 12 450

10 nth term $= a + (n - 1)d$ use $a = 7$, $n = 11$, nth term $= 32$

$32 = 7 + (11 - 1)d$

$d = 2.5$

$S_n = \frac{n}{2}[2a + (n - 1)d]$ use $a = 7$, $S_n = 2790$

$2790 = \frac{n}{2}[2 \times 7 + (n - 1) \times 2.5]$ solve

$5580 = n[14 + 2.5n - 2.5]$

$5580 = n[11.5 + 2.5n]$

$2.5n^2 + 11.5n - 5580 = 0$

Use the quadratic formula $n = \dfrac{-b \pm \sqrt{b^2 - 4ac}}{2a}$ $a = 2.5$, $b = 11.5$, $c = -5580$

$n = \dfrac{-11.5 \pm \sqrt{(11.5)^2 - 4 \times 2.5 \times -5580}}{2 \times 2.5}$

$n = -49.6$ (reject, since n has to be a positive integer) or $n = 45$

There are 45 terms

11 The 31 payments are in an arithmetic progression.

$S_n = \frac{n}{2}[2a + (n - 1)d]$ use $a = 140$, $S_n = 15500$ and $n = 31$

$15500 = \frac{31}{2}[2 \times 140 + (31 - 1)d]$ solve

$15500 = 15.5[280 + 30d]$

$d = 24$

The fifth payment is found by using:

nth term$= a + (n - 1)d$ $a = 140$, $n = 5$, $d = 24$

Fifth term$= 140 + (5 - 1) \times 24$

Fifth term is \$236

12 **a** $n\text{th term} = a + (n - 1)d$ use $n = 20$, $n = 8$

$-10 = a + (8 - 1) \times d$

$a + 7d = -10$ (1)

use $S_{20} = -350$, and $n = 20$

$-350 = \frac{20}{2}[2a + (20 - 1)d]$

$-350 = 10[2a + 19d]$

$2a + 19d = -35$ (2)

Subtract (2) from (1)× 2

$-5d = 15$

$d = -3$

Substituting for d in (1) gives:

$a = 11$

The first term is 11 and the common difference is −3.

b $n\text{th term} = a + (n - 1)d$ use $d = -3$, $a = 11$, nth term $= -97$

$-97 = 11 + (n - 1) \times -3$

$n - 1 = 36$

$n = 37$

There are 37 terms

13 $S_n = 4n^2 + 2n$

$S_1 = 4(1)^2 + 2(1) = 6 \longrightarrow$ first term = 6

$S_2 = 4(2)^2 + 2(2) = 20 \longrightarrow$ first term + second term = 20

Second term = 20 − 6 = 14

The first term is 6 and the common difference is 8

14 $S_n = -3n^2 - 2n$

$S_1 = -3(1)^2 - 2(1) = -5 \longrightarrow$ first term = −5

$S_2 = -3(2)^2 - 2(2) = -16 \longrightarrow$ first term + second term = −16

Second term = −16 − −5 = −11

The first term is −5 and the common difference is −6

15 $S_n = \frac{n}{12}(4n + 5)$

$S_1 = \frac{1}{12}(4(1) + 5) \longrightarrow$ first term $= \frac{9}{12}$

$S_2 = \frac{2}{12}(4(2) + 5) = \frac{13}{6} \longrightarrow$ first term + second term $= \frac{26}{12}$

Second term $= \frac{26}{12} - \frac{9}{12} = \frac{17}{12}$

$\frac{17}{12} = \frac{9}{12} + d$ so $d = \frac{8}{12}$

nth term$= a + (n - 1)d$ use $a = \frac{9}{12}, d = \frac{8}{12}$

$n\text{th term} = \frac{9}{12} + (n - 1) \times \frac{8}{12}$

$n\text{th term} = \frac{9}{12} + \frac{8}{12}n - \frac{8}{12}$

$= \frac{1}{12} + \frac{8}{12}n$

$= \frac{1}{12}(8n + 1)$

The nth term is $\frac{1}{12}(8n + 1)$

16 Smallest sector is a and the largest sector is $6.5a$

The total angles= 360 so, $S_{12} = 360$

$S_n = \frac{n}{2}[a + l]$

$360 = \frac{12}{2}[a + 6.5a]$

$a = 8$

The angle of the smallest sector is 8°

17 **a** $S_n = \frac{n}{2}[2a + (n - 1)d]$

$S_{25} = \frac{25}{2}[2a + (25 - 1)d]$

$S_{25} = 25a + 300d$

$S_4 = \frac{4}{2}[2a + (4 - 1)d]$

$S_4 = 4a + 6d$

As the sum of the first 25 terms is fifteen times the sum of the first 4 terms:

$25a + 300d = 15(4a + 6d)$

$35a = 210d$

$a = 6d$

b The nth term $= a + (n - 1)d$ use $d = \frac{a}{6}, n = 55$

The 55th term $= a + (55 - 1) \times \frac{a}{6}$

$= 10a$

18 nth term $= a + (n - 1)d$

8th term $= a + (8 - 1)d$ so 8th term $= a + 7d$

3rd term $= a + (3 - 1)d$ so 3rd term $= a + 2d$

The 8th term = 3 × 3rd term

$a + 7d = 3 \times (a + 2d)$

$a + 7d = 3a + 6d$

$d = 2a$

$S_n = \frac{n}{2}[2a + (n - 1)d]$

$S_8 = \frac{8}{2}[2a + (8 - 1)d]$ and $S_4 = \frac{4}{2}[2a + (4 - 1)d]$

$S_8 = 8a + 28d$ and $S_4 = 4a + 6d$

Substitute $d = 2a$ into S_8 and S_4

$S_8 = 8a + 56a = 64a$ and $S_4 = 4a + 12a = 16a$

$64a = 4 \times 16a$

So, the sum of the first 8 terms is 4 times the sum of the first 4 terms

19 a 1st term = $\cos^2 x$ 2nd term = 1

So $d = 1 - \cos^2 x$

nth term = $a + (n - 1)d$ use $n = 7$, $d = 1 - \cos^2 x$

7th term = $\cos^2 x + (7 - 1)(1 - \cos^2 x)$

7th term = $\cos^2 x + 6 - 6\cos^2 x$

7th term = $6 - 5\cos^2 x$

b $S_n = \frac{n}{2}[2a + (n - 1)d]$ use $a = \cos^2 x$ and $n = 20$, $d = 1 - \cos^2 x$

$S_{20} = \frac{20}{2}[2\cos^2 x + (20 - 1)(1 - \cos^2 x)]$

$S_{20} = 10[19 - 17\cos^2 x]$

$S_{20} = 190 - 170\cos^2 x$ use $\sin^2 x + \cos^2 x = 1$, $\cos^2 x = 1 - \sin^2 x$

$S_{20} = 190 - 170(1 - \sin^2 x)$

$S_{20} = 190 - 170 + 170\sin^2 x$

$S_{20} = 20 + 170\sin^2 x$

The sum of the first 20 terms is $20 + 170\sin^2 x$

20 a The sum of the digits for 15 is $1 + 5 = 6$

16 is $1 + 6 = 7$

17 is $1 + 7 = 8$

18 is $1 + 8 = 9$

The sum of these digits $6 + 7 + 8 + 9 = 30$

Or use the formula $S_n = \frac{n}{2}[2a + (n - 1)d] = \frac{4}{2}[2(6) + (4 - 1)(1)] = 30$

b Write the numbers from 1 to 100 and then in reverse

Set A	1 + 2 + 3 + 4 + 5 + 6 + 7 + 8 + 9 + 10
	100 + 99 + 98 + 97 + 96 + 95 + 94 + 93 + 92 + 91
Digit sum	2 20 20 20 20 20 20 20 20 11
Set B	11 + 12 + 13 + 14 + 15 + 16 + 17 + 18 + 19 + 20
	90 + 89 + 88 + 87 + 86 + 85 + 84 + 83 + 82 + 81
Digit sum	11 20 20 20 20 20 20 20 20 11
Set C	91 + 92 + 93 + 94 + 95 + 96 + 97 + 98 + 99 + 100
	10 + 9 + 8 + 7 + 6 + 5 + 4 + 3 + 2 + 1
Digit sum	11 20 20 20 20 20 20 20 20 2

In the digit sums for set B, there are eight 20's and two 11's, i.e., a digit sum of 182 for the set.

For the numbers from 11 to 90, there are 8 similar sets so $182 \times 8 =$ a digit sum of 1456

In set A there are $8 \times 20 + 11 + 2 =$ a digit sum of 173

In set C there are $8 \times 20 + 11 + 2 =$ a digit sum of 173

In total, $1456 + 173 + 173 = 1802$ but we need to divide by 2 as each number appears twice.

The total digit sum is $1802 \div 2 = 901$

Or

The sum of the digits 0 to 9 is $S_n = \frac{n}{2}[2a + (n - 1)d] = \frac{10}{2}[2(0) + (10 - 1)(1)] = 5 \times 9 = 45$

If the numbers from 0 to 100 are arranged in rows of 10 then there are 10 columns of digits 0 to 9 based on the number of tens in the column and 10 rows of the digits 0 to 9 based on the number of ones in the row. So, there are 20 sums of the digits 0 to 9 in total plus $1 + 0 + 0$ from 100.

So, the total digit sum is $20(45) + 1 = 901$

Exercise 11.4

REMEMBER

nth term of a geometric progression $= ar^{n-1}$ $a =$ first term, $r =$ common ratio

that the sum of a geometric progression, S_n, can be written as:

$S_n = \frac{a(1 - r^n)}{1 - r}$ or $S_n = \frac{a(r^n - 1)}{r - 1}$

Either formula can be used but it is usually easier to

- use the first formula when $-1 < r < 1$.
- use the second formula when $r > 1$ or when $r < -1$.

TIP

These formulae are not defined when $r = 1$.

1 **b** $-1 \quad 4 \quad -16 \quad 64$

$\times -4 \quad \times -4 \quad \times -4$

This sequence is geometric.

The common ratio is -4 and the eighth term is $ar^{n-1} = -1 \times (-4)^{8-1} = 16384$

e 2, 0.4, 0.08, 0.16

$\frac{0.4}{2} = 0.2 \quad \frac{0.08}{0.4} = 0.2 \quad \frac{0.16}{0.08} = 2$

The ratios are not the same so this is not a geometric sequence.

2 ar^{n-1} use $a = a$ and $r = r$

The ninth term ($n = 9$) is $ar^{9-1} = ar^8$

The twentieth term is ($n = 20$) is $ar^{20-1} = ar^{19}$

3 If $n = 3$ then ar^{n-1} is $ar^{3-1} = ar^2 = 108$ (1)

If $n = 6$ then ar^{n-1} is $ar^{6-1} = ar^5 = -32$ (2)

Dividing (2) by (1) gives:

So, $\frac{ar^5}{ar^2} = \frac{-32}{108}$

$r^3 = -\frac{8}{27}$ cube root both sides

$r = -\frac{2}{3}$

Substituting $r = -\frac{2}{3}$ into equation (1) gives $a\left(-\frac{2}{3}\right)^2 = 108$

So $a = 243$

The first term is 243

4 $a = 75$

If $n = 3$ and $a = 75$ then ar^{n-1} is $75r^{3-1} = 75r^2$

$75r^2 = 27$ divide both sides by 75

$r^2 = \frac{27}{75}$ square root both sides

$r = \pm\frac{3}{5}$

The 4th term is $75\left(\frac{3}{5}\right)^{4-1} = 16.2$ or $75\left(-\frac{3}{5}\right)^3 = -16.2$

5 If $n = 2$ then ar^{n-1} is $ar^{2-1} = ar = 12$ (1)

If $n = 4$ then ar^{n-1} is $ar^{4-1} = ar^3 = 27$ (2)

Dividing (2) by (1) gives:

So, $\frac{ar^3}{ar} = \frac{27}{12}$

$r^2 = \frac{27}{12} = \frac{9}{4}$ square root both sides

$r = \pm\frac{3}{2}$ (reject $-\frac{3}{2}$ as all the terms are positive)

$r = \frac{3}{2}$

Substituting $r = \frac{3}{2}$ into equation (1) gives $a\left(\frac{3}{2}\right) = 12$ or $a = 8$

The common ratio is $\frac{3}{2}$ and first term is 8

6 If $n = 6$ then ar^{n-1} is $ar^{6-1} = ar^5 = \frac{5}{2}$ (1)

If $n = 13$ then ar^{n-1} is $ar^{13-1} = ar^{12} = 320$ (2)

Dividing (2) by (1) gives:

So, $\frac{ar^{12}}{ar^5} = \frac{320}{\frac{5}{2}}$

$r^7 = 128$ 7th root both sides

$r = 2$

Substituting $r = 2$ into equation (1) gives $a(2)^5 = \frac{5}{2}$ or $a = \frac{5}{64}$

The 10th term is $ar^{n-1} = \frac{5}{64} \times (2)^{10-1} = 40$

The common ratio is 2, the first term is $\frac{5}{64}$ and the 10th term is 40

7 The sum of the second and third terms is $ar^{2-1} + ar^{3-1} = 30$

$ar + ar^2 = 30$ factorise

$ar(1 + r) = 30$ (1)

$a - ar = 9$ factorise

$a(1 - r) = 9$ (2)

Divide (1) by (2) gives:

$\frac{ar(1 + r)}{a(1 - r)} = \frac{9}{30}$ simplify

$3r^2 + 13r - 10 = 0$ factorise and solve

$(3r - 2)(r + 5) = 0$

$r = \frac{2}{3}$ or $r = -5$ all terms are positive $\longrightarrow r > 0$

$r = \frac{2}{3}$

Substituting $r = \frac{2}{3}$ into (1) gives:

$a \times \frac{2}{3}\left(1 + \frac{2}{3}\right) = 30$

$a = 27$

The 1st term is 27

8 $\frac{x+6}{x} = \frac{x+9}{x+6}$ multiply both sides by $x(x+6)$

$(x+6)^2 = x(x+9)$ expand brackets

$x^2 + 12x + 36 = x^2 + 9x$ simplify and solve

$x = -12$

9 $r = \frac{4}{2} = 2$, $a = \frac{1}{4}$, substitution into $ar^{n-1} > 500\,000$ gives:

$\frac{1}{4}(2)^{n-1} > 500\,000$

$2^{n-1} > 2\,000\,000$

$2^n > 4\,000\,000$

Either:

Take $\log_{10}$ of both sides:

$\log_{10} 2^n > \log_{10} 4\,000\,000$ use the power rule of logs

$n \log_{10} 2 > \log_{10} 4\,000\,000$

$n > 21.931\ldots$

So $n = 22$

Or:

If $n = 21$ then $2^{21} = 2\,097\,152$ and $2^n < 4\,000\,000$

If $n = 22$ then $2^{22} = 4\,194\,304$ and $2^n > 4\,000\,000$

So the 22nd term is the first term to exceed 500 000

10 $r = \frac{32}{64} = \frac{1}{2}$, $a = 256$, substitution into $ar^{n-1} < 0.001$ gives:

$256\left(\frac{1}{2}\right)^{n-1} < 0.001$ solve

$256\,(2^{-1})^{n-1} < 0.001$

$256(2^{1-n}) < 0.001$

$\frac{2^1}{2^n} < \frac{0.001}{256}$

$0.001 \times 2^n > 256 \times 2^1$

$$2^n > \frac{256 \times 2}{0.001}$$

$2^n > 512\,000$

Either:

Take $\log_{10}$ of both sides:

$\log_{10} 2^n > \log_{10} 512\,000$ use the power rule of logs

$n \log_{10} 2 > \log_{10} 512\,000$

$n > 18.965\ldots$

So $n = 19$

Or:

If $n = 18$ then $2^{18} = 262\,144$ and $2^n < 512\,000$

If $n = 19$ then $2^{19} = 524\,288$ and $2^n > 512\,000$

So the 19th term is the first term that is less than 0.001

11 a $r = \frac{8}{4} = 2$ so $r > 1$ use $S_n = \frac{a(r^n - 1)}{r - 1}$, $a = 4$ and $n = 8$

$$S_8 = \frac{4(2^8 - 1)}{2 - 1} = 1020$$

b $r = \frac{243}{729} = \frac{1}{3}$ so $-1 < r < 1$ use $S_n = \frac{a(1 - r^n)}{1 - r}$, $a = 729$ and $n = 8$

$$S_8 = \frac{729\left(1 - \left(\frac{1}{3}\right)^8\right)}{1 - \left(\frac{1}{3}\right)} = 1093\frac{1}{3}$$

12 $r = 3$, so $r > 1$ so, use $S_n = \frac{a(r^n - 1)}{r - 1}$, $a = 1$, $S_n > 2\,000\,000$

$$\frac{1(3^n - 1)}{3 - 1} > 2\,000\,000$$

$3^n - 1 > 4\,000\,000$

$3^n > 4\,000\,001$

Either:

Take $\log_{10}$ of both sides:

$\log_{10} 3^n > \log_{10} 4\,000\,001$ use the power rule of logs

$n \log_{10} 3 > \log_{10} 4\,000\,001$

$n > 13.837\ldots$

So $n = 14$

Or:

If $n = 13$ then $3^{13} = 1\,594\,323$ and $3^n < 4\,000\,001$

If $n = 14$ then $3^{14} = 4\,782\,969$ and $3^n > 4\,000\,001$

The 14th term is the first term to exceed 2 000 000

13 a $a = 10$, $r = \frac{4}{5}$, after n bounces, the ball rises to a height of $ar^n = 10\left(\frac{4}{5}\right)^n$ metres

b As $r = \frac{4}{5}$, this means that $r < 1$ so use $S_n = \frac{a(1 - r^n)}{1 - r}$

The ball travels up 10 m then down 10 m before the first bounce.

10 m ↑↓ 10 m	↑↓	↑↓	↑↓	↑↓
1st bounce	2nd bounce	3rd bounce	4th bounce	5th bounce
10 + 10	8 + 8	6.4 + 6.4	5.12 + 5.12	4.096 + 4.096

From being first thrown until the 5th bounce the ball travels:

$10 + 10 + 8 + 8 + 6.4 + 6.4 + 5.12 + 5.12 + 4.096 + 4.096 = 67.232$ metres

Or use n to calculate the sum of the first 5 terms of the progression.

$2S_n = 2\left(\frac{a(1 - r^n)}{1 - r}\right) = 2\left(\frac{10\left(1 - \left(\frac{4}{5}\right)^5\right)}{1 - \left(\frac{4}{5}\right)}\right) = 67.232$ m where the sum is doubled as the ball travels up and down.

14 The 3rd term is $ar^{3-1} = ar^2$ and the 1st term is a.

$ar^2 = 9a$ divide both sides by a. $(a \neq 0)$

$r^2 = 9$

$r = \pm 3$

The sum of the first 4 terms if $r = -3$ is found by using $S_n = \frac{a(r^n - 1)}{r - 1}$ and $n = 4$

$$S_4 = \frac{a((-3)^4 - 1)}{-3 - 1}$$

Then $\frac{80a}{-4} = ka$

so $k = -20$

The sum of the first 4 terms if $r = 3$ is found by using $S_n = \frac{a(r^n - 1)}{r - 1}$ and $n = 4$

$$S_4 = \frac{a(3^4 - 1)}{3 - 1}$$

Then $\frac{80a}{2} = ka$ so $k = 40$

The values of k are -20 and 40

15 $a = 4$ $r = 1.05$ so $r > 1$ then use $S_n = \dfrac{a(r^n - 1)}{r - 1}$, $n = 10$

The total time taken is:

$$\frac{4(1.05^{10} - 1)}{1.05 - 1} = 50.311\ldots \text{ minutes}$$

50 minutes 19 seconds to the nearest second

16 $S_n = \dfrac{a(r^n - 1)}{r - 1}$, $S_{3n} = \dfrac{a(r^{3n} - 1)}{r - 1}$, $S_{2n} = \dfrac{a(r^{2n} - 1)}{r - 1}$

$$\frac{S_{3n} - S_{2n}}{S_n} = \frac{\dfrac{a(r^{3n} - 1)}{r - 1} - \dfrac{a(r^{2n} - 1)}{r - 1}}{\dfrac{a(r^n - 1)}{r - 1}}$$ multiply numerator and denominator by $\dfrac{r - 1}{a}$

$$= \frac{(r^{3n} - 1) - (r^{2n} - 1)}{(r^n - 1)}$$

$$= \frac{r^{3n} - r^{2n}}{r^n - 1}$$

$$= \frac{r^{2n}(r^n - 1)}{r^n - 1}$$

$$= r^{2n}$$

17 This sequence is made up of two sequences:

1st sequence: $1, 3, 9, 27, 81 \ldots$ which has $a = 1$, $r = 3$, $n = n$

2nd sequence: $1, \dfrac{1}{3}, \dfrac{1}{9}, \dfrac{1}{27}, \dfrac{1}{81} \ldots$ which has $a = 1$, $r = \dfrac{1}{3}$, $n = n$

For the **1st sequence** use $S_n = \dfrac{a(r^n - 1)}{r - 1}$

$$S_n = \frac{1(3^n - 1)}{3 - 1} = \frac{3^n - 1}{2} = \frac{1}{2}(3^n - 1)$$

For the **2nd sequence** use $S_n = \dfrac{a(1 - r^n)}{1 - r}$

$$S_n = \frac{1\left(1 - \left(\frac{1}{3}\right)^n\right)}{1 - \frac{1}{3}}$$ as $\left(\dfrac{1}{3}\right)^n = (3^{-1})^n = 3^{-n}$ so:

$$S_n = \frac{1 - 3^{-n}}{\frac{2}{3}}$$ multiply numerator and denominator by $\dfrac{3}{2}$

$$S_n = \frac{3}{2} - \frac{3}{2} \times \frac{3^{-n}}{1}$$ simplify

$$S_n = \frac{3}{2} - \frac{3^{1-n}}{2}$$ factorise

$$S_n = \frac{3}{2}(1 - 3^{-n}) = \frac{1}{2}(3 - 3^{1-n})$$

The total for the two sequences is $\frac{1}{2}(3^n - 1) + \frac{1}{2}(3 - 3^{1-n})$

$= \frac{1}{2}(3^n - 1 + 3 - 3^{1-n})$

$= \frac{1}{2}(3^n - 3^{1-n} + 2)$

18 6 can be written as 6×10^0

66 can be written as $6 \times 10^1 + 6 \times 10^0$

666 can be written as $6 \times 10^2 + 6 \times 10^1 + 6 \times 10^0$

6666 can be written as $6 \times 10^3 + 6 \times 10^2 + 6 \times 10^1 + 6 \times 10^0$

The sequence is not geometric because there is no common ratio. It can be written as:

$S_n = 6(1 + 11 + 111 + \ldots \text{ to } n \text{ terms})$

$= \frac{6}{9}(9 + 99 + 999 + \ldots \text{ to } n \text{ terms})$

$= \frac{2}{3}[(10 - 1) + (100 - 1) + (1000 - 1) + \ldots \text{ to } n \text{ terms}]$

$= \frac{2}{3}[(10 + 10^2 + 10^3 + \ldots \text{ to } n \text{ terms}) - n]$ This converts the sequence to geometric form

Apply $S_n = \frac{a(r^n - 1)}{r - 1}$ to the progression in brackets, with $a = 10$, $r = 10$

So, $S_n = \frac{2}{3}\left[\left(\frac{10(10^n - 1)}{9}\right) - n\right]$ expand brackets and simplify

$S_n = \frac{2(10^{n+1} - 10 - 9n)}{27}$

Exercise 11.5

REMEMBER

$S_\infty = \frac{a}{1 - r}$ provided that $-1 < r < 1$

1 **a** $a = 3$ $r = \frac{1}{3}$ use $S_\infty = \frac{a}{1 - r}$

$S_\infty = \frac{3}{1 - \frac{1}{3}} = 4.5$

d $a = -162$ $r = \frac{108}{-162} = -\frac{2}{3}$ use $S_\infty = \frac{a}{1 - r}$

$S_\infty = \frac{-162}{1 - -\frac{2}{3}} = -97.2$

2 $a = 10 \quad r = \frac{8}{10} \quad$ use $S_\infty = \frac{a}{1-r}$

$$S_\infty = \frac{10}{1 - \frac{8}{10}} = 50$$

3 $a = 300$, the nth term $= ar^{n-1}$

4th term, $n = 4$ so:

$$300 \times r^{4-1} = -2\frac{2}{5}$$

$$r^3 = \frac{-2\frac{2}{5}}{300} = -\frac{1}{25}$$ take the cube root of both sides

$$r = -\frac{1}{5}$$

use $S_\infty = \frac{a}{1-r}$, $a = 300$, $r = -\frac{1}{5}$

$$S_\infty = \frac{300}{1 - -\frac{1}{5}} = 250$$

The common ratio is $-\frac{1}{5}$ and the sum to infinity is 250.

4 $r = \frac{0.8^2}{1} = 0.64 \quad a = 1 \quad$ use $S_\infty = \frac{a}{1-r}$

$$S_\infty = \frac{1}{1 - 0.64} = 2\frac{7}{9}$$

5 a $0.\dot{4}\dot{2} = 0.424242\ldots\ldots = 0.42 + 0.0042 + 0.000042 = \frac{42}{100} + \frac{42}{10000} + \frac{42}{1000000} + \ldots$

b $r = \frac{42}{10000} \div \frac{42}{100} = \frac{1}{100} \quad a = \frac{42}{100} \quad$ use $S_\infty = \frac{a}{1-r}$

$$S_\infty = \frac{\frac{42}{100}}{1 - \frac{1}{100}} = \frac{14}{33}$$

6 Use $S_\infty = \frac{a}{1-r} \quad a = -120, S_\infty = -72$

$$-72 = \frac{-120}{1-r}$$

$$1 - r = \frac{-120}{-72}$$

$$r = -\frac{2}{3}$$

Use $S_n = \frac{a(1 - r^n)}{1 - r}$ for $n = 3$, $r = -\frac{2}{3}$, $a = -120$

$$S_3 = \frac{-120\left(1 - \left(-\frac{2}{3}\right)^3\right)}{1 - -\frac{2}{3}} = -93\frac{1}{3}$$

The common ratio is $-\frac{2}{3}$ and the sum of the first three terms is $-93\frac{1}{3}$

7 The second term is $ar^{2-1} = 6.5$ so $ar = 6.5$ or $a = \frac{6.5}{r}$

Use $S_\infty = \frac{a}{1 - r}$ $\quad a = \frac{6.5}{r}$, $S_\infty = 26$

$$\frac{\frac{6.5}{r}}{1 - r} = 26 \qquad \text{solve}$$

$$\frac{6.5}{r} = 26(1 - r)$$

$$6.5 = 26r(1 - r)$$

$26r^2 - 26r + 6.5 = 0$ use $r = \frac{-b \pm \sqrt{b^2 - 4ac}}{2a}$ where $a = 26$, $b = -26$, $c = 6.5$

$r = \frac{--26 \pm \sqrt{(-26)^2 - 4 \times 26 \times 6.5}}{2 \times 26} = \frac{26}{52} = \frac{1}{2}$ as the discriminant is zero.

The common ratio $r = 0.5$

The first term $a = \frac{6.5}{0.5} = 13$

8 **a** The second term is $ar^{2-1} = -96$ so:

$ar = -96$ (1)

The fifth term is $ar^{5-1} = 40.5$ so:

$ar^4 = 40.5$ (2)

Dividing (2) by (1)

$$\frac{ar^4}{ar} = \frac{40.5}{-96}$$

$$r^3 = -\frac{27}{64}$$

$$r = -0.75$$

$$ar = -96$$

$$a = \frac{-96}{-0.75} = 128$$

The common ratio is -0.75 and the first term is 128

b Use $S_\infty = \frac{a}{1-r}$ $a = 128$, $r = -0.75$

$S_\infty = \frac{-128}{1 - -0.75} = 73\frac{1}{7}$

9 a $\frac{k}{175} = \frac{63}{k}$ solve

$k^2 = 11025$ square root both sides

$k = \pm 105$ (reject the negative value since all terms are positive)

$k = 105$

b The progression is 175, 105, 63 so $r = \frac{105}{175} = 0.6$ $a = 175$ use $S_\infty = \frac{a}{1-r}$

$S_\infty = \frac{175}{1-0.6} = 437.5$

10 a The second term is $ar^{2-1} = 18$ so:

$ar = 18$ (1)

The fourth term is $ar^{4-1} = 1.62$ so:

$ar^3 = 1.62$ (2)

Dividing (2) by (1) gives:

$\frac{ar^3}{ar} = \frac{1.62}{18}$

$r^2 = 0.09$

$r = \pm 0.3$ (reject -0.3 since the common ratio is positive)

The common ratio is $0.3 = \frac{3}{10}$

The first term is $\frac{18}{0.3} = 60$

b Use $S_\infty = \frac{a}{1-r}$ $a = 60$, $r = \frac{3}{10}$

$S_\infty = \frac{60}{1-0.3} = 85\frac{5}{7}$

11 a $\frac{k}{k+15} = \frac{k-12}{k}$

$k^2 = (k-12)(k+15)$ expand brackets

$k^2 = k^2 + 3k - 180$

$3k = 180$

$k = 60$

b The progression is 75, 60, 48 so $r = \frac{60}{75} = 0.8$ $a = 75$

Use $S_\infty = \frac{a}{1-r}$

$S_\infty = \frac{75}{1-0.8} = 375$

12 The fourth term is $ar^{4-1} = 48$ so:

$ar^3 = 48$ so $a = \frac{48}{r^3}$

Use $S_\infty = \frac{a}{1-r}$ $S_\infty = 3a, r = r, a = \frac{48}{r^3}$

$$3a = \frac{\frac{48}{r^3}}{1-r}$$

$$3 \times \frac{48}{r^3} = \frac{\frac{48}{r^3}}{1-r}$$ divide both sides by $\frac{48}{r^3}$

$$3 = \frac{1}{1-r}$$

$$1 - r = \frac{1}{3}$$

$$r = \frac{2}{3}$$

The first term is $a = \frac{48}{\left(\frac{2}{3}\right)^3} = 162$

13 Use $S_n = \frac{a(1-r^n)}{1-r}$ $n = 3, S_3 = 62$

$$62 = \frac{a(1-r^3)}{1-r}$$

$$62(1-r) = a(1-r^3) \quad (1)$$

$$S_\infty = \frac{a}{1-r} = 62.5$$

$$62.5(1-r) = a \quad (2)$$

Dividing (2) by (1) gives:

$$\frac{62.5(1-r)}{62(1-r)} = \frac{a}{a(1-r^3)}$$

$$\frac{62.5}{62} = \frac{1}{1-r^3}$$

$$1 - r^3 = \frac{124}{125}$$

$$r^3 = \frac{1}{125}$$

The common ratio is $\frac{1}{5}$

The first term is $a = 62.5\left(1 - \frac{1}{5}\right) = 50$

14 $a = 1, r = \frac{2\sin x}{1} = 2\sin x$ for $-\frac{\pi}{2} < x < \frac{\pi}{2}$ $(-1.57 < x < 1.57$ to 3 significant figures).

REMEMBER

If the progression converges to a finite number when summed to infinity, then it is said to be convergent.

The formula $S_\infty = \frac{a}{1-r}$ is valid for $-1 < r < 1$

$$-1 < 2\sin x < 1$$

$$\frac{-1}{2} < \sin x < \frac{1}{2}$$

$$\sin^{-1}\left(-\frac{1}{2}\right) < x < \sin^{-1}\left(\frac{1}{2}\right)$$

$-\frac{\pi}{6} < x < \frac{\pi}{6}$ is the set of values for which the progression is convergent.

15 After the first bounce the ball rises to $\frac{3}{4} \times 12 = 9$ metres

From the start, the ball travels:

$12 + 9 + 9 + 6.75 + 6.75 + \ldots$ or $12 + 2[9 + 6.75 + \ldots]$

For the progression in brackets, $r = 0.75$, $a = 9$ (so $-1 < r < 1$)

Using $S_\infty = \frac{a}{1-r}$

$$S_\infty = \frac{9}{1-0.75} = 36$$

The ball travels a total vertical distance of $12 + 2 \times 36 = 84$ metres

16 a Pattern 1 has a perimeter $3 \times 1x = 3x \longrightarrow 3 \times 2^0 \times \left(\frac{1}{3}\right)^0 x$

Pattern 2 has a perimeter $12 \times \frac{1}{3}x = 4x \longrightarrow 3 \times 2^2 \times \left(\frac{1}{3}\right)^1 x$

Pattern 3 has a perimeter $48 \times \frac{1}{9}x = \frac{16}{3}x \longrightarrow 3 \times 2^4 \times \left(\frac{1}{3}\right)^2 x$

Pattern 4 has a perimeter $192 \times \frac{1}{27}x = \frac{64}{9}x \longrightarrow 3 \times 2^6 \times \left(\frac{1}{3}\right)^3 x$

Pattern n has a perimeter $3 \times 2^{2n-2} \times \left(\frac{1}{3}\right)^{n-1} x$

$$\frac{\text{Perimeter of Pattern } n}{\text{Perimeter of Pattern } n-1} = \frac{3 \times 2^{2n-2} \times \left(\frac{1}{3}\right)^{n-1} x}{3 \times 2^{2(n-1)-2} \times \left(\frac{1}{3}\right)^{(n-1)-1} x}$$

$$= \frac{3 \times 2^{2n-2} \times (3^{-1})^{n-1} x}{3 \times 2^{2(n-1)-2} \times (3^{-1})^{(n-1)-1} x}$$

$$= \frac{3 \times 2^{2n-2} \times 3^{-1(n-1)}x}{3 \times 2^{2(n-1)-2} \times 3^{-1[(n-1)-1]}x}$$

$$= \frac{3 \times 2^{2n-2} \times 3^{1-n}x}{3 \times 2^{2n-4} \times 3^{2-n}x}$$ divide numerator and denominator by $3x$

$$= \frac{2^{2n-2} \times 3^{1-n}}{2^{2n-4} \times 3^{2-n}}$$ simplify using the rules of indices

$$= 2^{2n-2-(2n-4)} \times 3^{(1-n)-(2-n)}$$

$$= 2^2 \times 3^{-1}$$

$$= \frac{4}{3}$$

The common ratio is $\frac{4}{3}$ so $r > 1$

As the value of n approaches infinity, the terms of the series become larger and larger.

For a series to converge, $-1 < r < 1$ so the Koch perimeter series diverges to infinity.

b The Koch snowflake triangles are all equilateral.

The area of an equilateral triangle $= \frac{1}{2} \times ab\sin C$

The area of the patterns are:

Pattern 1 $1 \times \frac{\sqrt{3}}{4} \times (x)^2$ would be $1 \times \left(\frac{1}{3^0}\right)^1 \times \left(\frac{\sqrt{3}}{4}x^2\right)$ or $1 \times \left(\frac{1}{9}\right)^0 \times \left(\frac{\sqrt{3}}{4}x^2\right)$

Pattern 2 $3 \times \frac{\sqrt{3}}{4} \times \left(\frac{x}{3}\right)^2$ would be $3 \times \left(\frac{1}{3^2}\right)^1 \times \left(\frac{\sqrt{3}}{4}x^2\right)$ or $3 \times \left(\frac{1}{9}\right)^1 \times \left(\frac{\sqrt{3}}{4}x^2\right)$

Pattern 3 $12 \times \frac{\sqrt{3}}{4} \times \left(\frac{x}{9}\right)^2$ would be $12 \times \left(\frac{1}{3^4}\right)^1 \times \left(\frac{\sqrt{3}}{4}x^2\right)$ or $12 \times \left(\frac{1}{9}\right)^2 \times \left(\frac{\sqrt{3}}{4}x^2\right)$

Pattern 4 $48 \times \frac{\sqrt{3}}{4} \times \left(\frac{x}{27}\right)^2$ would be $48 \times \left(\frac{1}{3^6}\right)^1 \times \left(\frac{\sqrt{3}}{4}x^2\right)$ or $48 \times \left(\frac{1}{9}\right)^3 \times \left(\frac{\sqrt{3}}{4}x^2\right)$

This is a geometric sequence.

To find the common ratio find $\frac{\text{Area of Pattern 4}}{\text{Area of Pattern 3}} = \frac{48 \times \frac{\sqrt{3}}{4} \times \left(\frac{x}{27}\right)^2}{12 \times \frac{\sqrt{3}}{4} \times \left(\frac{x}{9}\right)^2} = \frac{48 \times \frac{x^2}{729}}{12 \times \frac{x^2}{81}} = \frac{\frac{48}{729}}{\frac{12}{81}} = \frac{4}{9}$

If the area of the first triangle is 1 unit^2, then the sequence of the areas could be written as:

$$1 \times \left(\frac{1}{9}\right)^0, 3 \times \left(\frac{1}{9}\right)^1, 12 \times \left(\frac{1}{9}\right)^2, 48 \times \left(\frac{1}{9}\right)^3 \ldots\ldots$$

Or $1, 3 \times \left(\frac{1}{9}\right)^1, 12 \times \left(\frac{1}{9}\right)^2, 48 \times \left(\frac{1}{9}\right)^3 \ldots\ldots$

The series sum $= 1 + \frac{a}{1-r}$ where $a = \frac{1}{3}$ and $r = \frac{4}{9}$

We can use this formula because $-1 < r < 1$, so the progression for the area of the snowflake converges.

$= 1 + \dfrac{\frac{1}{3}}{1 - \frac{4}{9}}$

$= \dfrac{8}{5}$

So, the area of the Koch triangle converges to $\frac{8}{5}$ times the area of the original triangle.

17 a Let the radius of the large circle be R, the radius of the small circle be r and the hypotenuse of the small right-angled triangle be x.

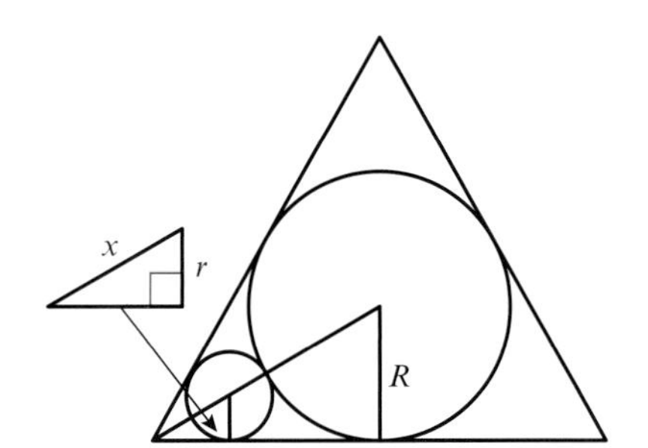

So, $\sin 30° = \frac{1}{2} = \frac{r}{x}$

$x = 2r$

So, for a 30° right-angled triangle the hypotenuse is twice the height.

Consider the relationship between one circle and the next:

The hypotenuse for the large right-angled triangle is:

$x + r + R = 2R$ substitute for x

$2r + r + R = 2R$

$R = 3r$

The radius of each subsequent circle is $\frac{1}{3}$ of the radius of the previous circle.

The circumferences are:

$2\pi R + 3 \times \left[2\pi\left(\frac{R}{3}\right) + 2\pi\left(\frac{R}{9}\right) + 2\pi\left(\frac{R}{27}\right) + \ldots\right]$ or $2\pi R + 3 \times 2\pi R\left(\frac{1}{3} + \frac{1}{9} + \frac{1}{27} + \ldots\right)$

Find the sum to infinity of $\left(\frac{1}{3} + \frac{1}{9} + \frac{1}{27} + \ldots\right)$

Use $S_\infty = \dfrac{a}{1 - r}$ $r = \frac{1}{3}, a = \frac{1}{3}$

$S_\infty = \dfrac{\frac{1}{3}}{1 - \frac{1}{3}} = \dfrac{1}{2}$

$R = 1$

So $2\pi R + 3 \times 2\pi R\left(\frac{1}{3} + \frac{1}{9} + \frac{1}{27} + \ldots\right) = 2\pi + 3 \times 2\pi \times \frac{1}{2}$

So, the sum to infinity of the circumferences of the circles is 5π units

b The sum of the areas of the circles is:

$\pi R^2 + 3\left(\pi\left(\frac{R}{3}\right)^2 + \pi\left(\frac{R}{9}\right)^2 + \pi\left(\frac{R}{27}\right)^2 + \ldots\right)$ or $\pi R^2 + 3\pi R^2\left(\frac{1}{9} + \frac{1}{81} + \frac{1}{729} + \ldots\right)$

Find the sum to infinity of $\left(\frac{1}{9} + \frac{1}{81} + \frac{1}{729} + \ldots\right)$

Use $S_\infty = \dfrac{a}{1-r}$ $r = \dfrac{1}{9}$, $a = \dfrac{1}{9}$

$$S_\infty = \frac{\frac{1}{9}}{1-\frac{1}{9}} = \frac{1}{8}$$

So $\pi R^2 + 3\pi R^2\left(\dfrac{1}{9} + \dfrac{1}{81} + \dfrac{1}{729} + \ldots\right) = \pi R^2 + 3\pi R^2 \times \dfrac{1}{8}$ substitute $R = 1$:

$\pi + 3\pi \times \dfrac{1}{8}$

So, the sum to infinity of the areas of the circles is $\dfrac{11}{8}\pi$ units^2

Exercise 11.6

1 a The common difference $d = 12 - 8 = 4$, $a = 8$, $n = 6$

Use $S_n = \dfrac{n}{2}[2a + (n-1)d]$

$S_6 = \dfrac{6}{2}[2 \times 8 + (6-1) \times 4] = 108$

b The common ratio is $\dfrac{12}{8} = 1.5$ $a = 8$, $r = 1.5$, $n = 6$

Use $S_n = \dfrac{a(r^n - 1)}{r - 1}$

$S_6 = \dfrac{8(1.5^6 - 1)}{1.5 - 1} = 166.25$

2 a The common ratio is $\dfrac{20}{25} = 0.8$ $a = 25$

Use $S_\infty = \dfrac{a}{1-r}$

$S_\infty = \dfrac{25}{1-0.8} = 125$

b The common difference, $d = 20 - 25 = -5$, $a = 25$, $S_n = -1550$

Use $S_n = \dfrac{n}{2}[2a + (n-1)d]$

$-1550 = \dfrac{n}{2}[2 \times 25 + (n-1) \times -5]$

$-3100 = n[50 - 5n + 5]$

$-3100 = 55n - 5n^2$

$5n^2 - 55n - 3100 = 0$ divide both sides by 5

$n^2 - 11n - 620 = 0$ factorise

$(n - 31)(n + 20) = 0$ solve

$n = 31$ or $n = -20$ (reject)

There are 31 terms.

3 **a** The geometric progression has:

common ratio r

1st term $a = 48$

2nd term $= 48r$

3rd term $= 48r^2$

The arithmetic progression has:

common difference d,

1st term $a = 48$,

5th term $= 48 + 4d$

11th term $= 48 + 10d$

So, if the 2nd term of the geometric progression is the same as the 5th term of the arithmetic progression:

$48r = 48 + 4d$ divide both sides by 4

$12r = 12 + d$

$d = 12r - 12$ (1)

and, if the 3rd term of the geometric progression is the same as the 11th term of the arithmetic progression:

$48r^2 = 48 + 10d$ (2)

From (1), substitute for d into (2):

$48r^2 = 48 + 10(12r - 12)$ expand brackets

$48r^2 = 48 + 120r - 120$ rearrange

$48r^2 - 120r + 72 = 0$ divide both sides by 24

$2r^2 - 5r + 3 = 0$ factorise

$(2r - 3)(r - 1) = 0$ solve

$r = 1.5$ or $r = 1$ (reject as $r \neq 1$)

$r = 1.5$

b The 6th term of the **geometric** progression is $ar^{n-1} = 48 \times 1.5^{6-1} = 364.5$

The value of d in the **arithmetic** progression is:

$d = 12r - 12$ substitute $r = 1.5$

$d = 12 \times 1.5 - 12$

$d = 6$

Use nth term $= a + (n - 1)d$ $a = 48$, $d = 6$, $n = 6$

6th term $= 48 + (6 - 1) \times 6 = 78$

The 6th term of the **arithmetic** progression is 78

4 The geometric progression has $n = 6$, $a = 486$ and a common ratio $r = \frac{2}{3}$

Use $S_n = \frac{a(1 - r^n)}{1 - r}$

$$S_6 = \frac{486\left(1 - \left(\frac{2}{3}\right)^6\right)}{1 - \frac{2}{3}} = 1330$$

The arithmetic progression has $n = 35$ and a common difference $d = \frac{3}{2}$,

Use $S_{35} = \frac{35}{2}\left[2a + (35 - 1) \times \frac{3}{2}\right] = 1330$

$2660 = 70a + 1785$

$a = 12.5$

The 1st term of the arithmetic progression is 12.5

The 35th term of the arithmetic progression $= 12.5 + (35 - 1) \times \frac{3}{2} = 63.5$

5 **a** The geometric progression has:

common ratio r

1st term $a = 200$

2nd term $= 200r$

3rd term $= 200r^2$

The arithmetic progression has:

common difference d,

1st term $a = 200$,

5th term $= 200 + 4d$

8th term $= 200 + 7d$

So, if the 2nd term of the geometric progression is the same as the 5th term of the arithmetic progression:

$200r = 200 + 4d$ divide both sides by 4

$50r = 50 + d$

$d = 50r - 50$ (1)

and, if the 3rd term of the geometric progression is the same as the 8th term of the arithmetic progression:

$200r^2 = 200 + 7d$ (2)

From (1), substitute for d into (2):

$200r^2 = 200 + 7(50r - 50)$ expand brackets

$200r^2 = 200 + 350r - 350$ rearrange

$200r^2 - 350r + 150 = 0$ divide both sides by 50

$4r^2 - 7r + 3 = 0$ factorise

$(4r - 3)(r - 1) = 0$ solve

$r = 0.75$ or $r = 1$ (reject as $r \neq 1$)

$r = 0.75$ or $\frac{3}{4}$

b The 4th term of the **geometric** progression is $ar^{n-1} = 200 \times 0.75^{4-1} = 84.375$

The value of d in the **arithmetic** progression is:

$d = 50r - 50$ substitute $r = 0.75$

$d = 50 \times 0.75 - 50$

$d = -12.5$

Use nth term $= a + (n - 1)d$ $a = 200$, $d = -12.5$, $n = 4$

4th term $= 200 + (4 - 1) \times -12.5 = 162.5$

The 4th term of the **arithmetic** progression is 162.5

c Use $S_\infty = \frac{a}{1 - r}$

$S_\infty = \frac{200}{1 - 0.75} = 800$

The sum to infinity is 800

6 a Use $S_n = \frac{n}{2}[2a + (n - 1)d]$ $a = 12$, $S_{16} = 282$

$\frac{16}{2}[2 \times 12 + (16 - 1)d] = 282$

$8[24 + 15d] = 282$

$192 + 120d = 282$

$d = 0.75$

The common difference $d = 0.75$

b The geometric progression has:

common ratio r

1st term $a = 12$

2nd term $= 12r$

3rd term $= 12r^2$

The arithmetic progression has:

common difference 0.75,

1st term $a = 12$,

5th term $= 12 + 4 \times 0.75 = 15$

nth term $= 12 + (n - 1) \times 0.75$ or $0.75n + 11.25$

So, if the 2nd term of the geometric progression is the same as the 5th term of the arithmetic progression:

$12r = 15$

$r = \frac{5}{4}$

The common ratio of the geometric progression is $\frac{5}{4}$

If the 3rd term of the geometric progression is the same as the nth term of the arithmetic progression:

$12r^2 = 0.75n + 11.25$ substitute $r = \frac{5}{4}$

$12 \times \left(\frac{5}{4}\right)^2 = 0.75n + 11.25$

$0.75n = 7.5$

$n = 10$

There are 10 terms

7 Geometric progression 1st term = 80 and 2nd term = 64

The common ratio is $= \frac{64}{80} = 0.8$

The 3rd term of the geometric progression is $64 \times 0.8 = 51.2$

Arithmetic progression

1st term = 80 and 11th term = $80 + (11 - 1)d$ and the nth term= $80 + (n - 1)d$

So, if the 2nd term of the geometric progression is the same as the 11th term of the arithmetic progression:

$64 = 80 + 10d$

$d = -1.6$

The common difference of the arithmetic progression is -1.6

If the 3rd term of the geometric progression is the same as the nth term of the arithmetic progression:

$51.2 = 80 + (n - 1) \times -1.6$

$n - 1 = 18$

$n = 19$

8 **a** For the arithmetic progression, the first term + common difference = second term so:

$5x + 24 = x^2$ solve

$x^2 - 5x - 24 = 0$ factorise

$(x - 8)(x + 3) = 0$

$x = 8$ or $x = -3$

The first three terms of the arithmetic progression are $5x$, $5x + 24$, $5x + 48$

If $x = 8$ the 3rd term is $5 \times 8 + 48 = 88$

If $x = -3$ the 3rd term is $5 \times -3 + 48 = 33$

The 3rd term is either 88 or 33

b The geometric progression is $5x, x^2, -\frac{8}{5}$

$\frac{x^2}{5x} = \frac{-\frac{8}{5}}{x^2}$ multiply both sides by $5x^3$

$x^4 = -\frac{8}{5} \times 5x$

$x^4 + 8x = 0$ factorise

$x(x^3 + 8) = 0$

So $x = 0$ (reject)

Or $x^3 + 8 = 0$

$x^3 = -8$ cube root both sides

$x = -2$

The 1st term of the geometric progression is $5 \times -2 = -10$

The 2nd term of the geometric progression is $(-2)^2 = 4$

The common ratio is $\frac{4}{-10} = -\frac{2}{5}$ or -0.4

Use $S_\infty = \frac{a}{1-r}$

$S_\infty = \frac{-10}{1 - -0.4} = -7\frac{1}{7}$

Chapter 12: Calculus – Differentiation 1

Exercise 12.1

REMEMBER

If $y = x^n$, then $\frac{dy}{dx} = nx^{n-1}$

$\frac{d}{dx}[kf(x)] = k\frac{d}{dx}[f(x)]$

$\frac{d}{dx}[f(x) \pm g(x)] = \frac{d}{dx}[f(x)] \pm \frac{d}{dx}[g(x)]$

1 e Rewrite $\frac{1}{x}$ as x^{-1}

Differentiate with respect to x:

i.e., $\frac{d}{dx}(x^{-1}) = -1x^{-2}$ or $-x^{-2}$ or $-\frac{1}{x^2}$

t Rewrite $\frac{x\sqrt{x}}{x^3}$ as $\frac{x^1 \times x^{\frac{1}{2}}}{x^3}$ or $\frac{x^{\frac{3}{2}}}{x^3} = x^{\frac{3}{2}} \times x^{-3} = x^{-\frac{3}{2}}$

Differentiate with respect to x:

i.e., $\frac{d}{dx}(x^{-\frac{3}{2}}) = -\frac{3}{2}x^{-\frac{5}{2}}$ or $-\frac{3}{2\sqrt{x^5}}$ or $-\frac{3}{2(x^{\frac{1}{2}})^5}$

TIP

It is useful to be able to express expressions with fractional indices in alternative ways.

2 i Rewrite $\frac{x^2 - x - 1}{\sqrt{x}}$ gives:

$= \frac{x^2}{\sqrt{x}} - \frac{x}{\sqrt{x}} - \frac{1}{\sqrt{x}}$

$= \frac{x^2}{x^{\frac{1}{2}}} - \frac{x}{x^{\frac{1}{2}}} - \frac{1}{x^{\frac{1}{2}}}$

$= x^{\frac{3}{2}} - x^{\frac{1}{2}} - x^{-\frac{1}{2}}$

Differentiating with respect to x:

i.e., $\frac{d}{dx}\left(x^{\frac{3}{2}} - x^{\frac{1}{2}} - x^{-\frac{1}{2}}\right) = \frac{3}{2}x^{\frac{1}{2}} - \frac{1}{2}x^{-\frac{1}{2}} + \frac{1}{2}x^{-\frac{3}{2}}$

n Rewrite $(1 - x^3)^2$ as $(1 - x^3)(1 - x^3)$ which is $1 - 2x^3 + x^6$

Differentiating with respect to x:

i.e., $\frac{d}{dx}(1 - 2x^3 + x^6) = -6x^2 + 6x^5$

3 b $y = 4 - 2x^2$

$\frac{dy}{dx} = -4x$

At the point $x = -1$, $\frac{dy}{dx} = -4(-1)$

$\frac{dy}{dx} = 4$ at $(-1, 2)$

f Rewrite $y = \frac{x-3}{\sqrt{x}}$ as $y = \frac{x}{\sqrt{x}} - \frac{3}{\sqrt{x}}$

or $y = x^{\frac{1}{2}} - 3x^{-\frac{1}{2}}$

$\frac{dy}{dx} = \frac{1}{2}x^{-\frac{1}{2}} + \frac{3}{2}x^{-\frac{3}{2}}$

At the point $x = 9$, $\frac{dy}{dx} = \frac{1}{2}(9)^{-\frac{1}{2}} + \frac{3}{2}(9)^{-\frac{3}{2}}$

$\frac{dy}{dx} = \frac{1}{2} \times \frac{1}{3} + \frac{3}{2} \times \left(\frac{1}{3}\right)^3$

$= \frac{1}{6} + \frac{1}{18}$

$\frac{dy}{dx} = \frac{2}{9}$ at $(9, 2)$

4 $y = 2x^2 - x - 1$

The gradient at any point on the curve can be found by differentiation:

$\frac{dy}{dx} = 4x - 1$

If the gradient at a point on the curve is 7 then:

$4x - 1 = 7$

$x = 2$

Substitute $x = 2$ into the equation of the **curve** $y = 2x^2 - x - 1$

$y = 2(2)^2 - 2 - 1$

$y = 5$

The point is $(2, 5)$

5 To find where the curve $y = \frac{x-4}{x}$ crosses the x-axis, substitute $y = 0$

$0 = \frac{x-4}{x}$

$x = 4$ so the curve crosses the x-axis at $x = 4$.

Rewrite $y = \frac{x-4}{x}$ as $y = 1 - 4x^{-1}$ and differentiate:

$\frac{dy}{dx} = 4x^{-2}$

At $x = 4$, $\frac{dy}{dx} = 4(4)^{-2}$ or 0.25

The gradient is 0.25

6 To find where the curve $y = x^3 - 2x^2 + 5x - 3$ crosses the y-axis, substitute $x = 0$

$y = (0)^3 - 2(0)^2 + 5(0) - 3$

$y = -3$ so the curve crosses the y-axis at $(0, -3)$.

$\frac{dy}{dx} = 3x^2 - 4x + 5$

At $x = 0$, $\frac{dy}{dx} = 3(0)^2 - 4(0) + 5$

$\frac{dy}{dx} = 5$

The gradient is 5

7 The x-coordinates of P and Q can be found by solving $y = 2x^2 + 7x - 4$ and $y = 5$ simultaneously:

$2x^2 + 7x - 4 = 5$

$2x^2 + 7x - 9 = 0$

$(2x + 9)(x - 1) = 0$

$2x + 9 = 0$ or $x - 1 = 0$

$x = -4.5$ or $x = 1$

So P and Q are at $x = -4.5$ and $x = 1$

$\frac{dy}{dx} = 4x + 7$

At $x = 4.5$, $\frac{dy}{dx} = 4(-4.5) + 7 = -11$

At $x = 1$, $\frac{dy}{dx} = 4(1) + 7 = 11$

The gradients at points P and Q are -11 and 11

8 $y = ax^2 + bx$

$\frac{dy}{dx} = 2ax + b$

When $x = 2$, $\frac{dy}{dx} = 8$

$4a + b = 8$ (1)

When $x = -1$, $\frac{dy}{dx} = -10$

$-2a + b = -10$ (2)

Subtract (2) from (1)

$6a = 18$

$a = 3$

Substituting into (1) gives:

$4(3) + b = 8$

$b = -4$

Answer $a = 3$, $b = -4$

9 As $(-1, -3)$ lies on the curve, substituting $x = -1$, $y = -3$ into $y = ax + \frac{b}{x}$ gives:

$a(-1) + \frac{b}{-1} = -3$

$a + b = 3$ (1)

$y = ax + \frac{b}{x}$ can be written as $y = ax + bx^{-1}$

$\frac{dy}{dx} = a - bx^{-2}$ or $\frac{dy}{dx} = a - \frac{b}{x^2}$

Substitute $x = -1$ and $\frac{dy}{dx} = -7$ into $\frac{dy}{dx} = a - \frac{b}{x^2}$ gives:

$a - \frac{b}{(-1)^2} = -7$ simplify

$a - b = -7$ (2)

Adding (1) and (2) gives:

$2a = -4$

$a = -2$

Substitute into (1) gives:

$-2 + b = 3$

$b = 5$

Answer $a = -2$, $b = 5$

10 $y = \frac{x^3}{3} - \frac{5x^2}{2} + 6x - 1$

$\frac{dy}{dx} = x^2 - 5x + 6$

To find the points on the curve where the gradient is 2, solve:

$x^2 - 5x + 6 = 2$

$x^2 - 5x + 4 = 0$ factorise

$(x - 4)(x - 1) = 0$

$x - 4 = 0$ or $x - 1 = 0$

$x = 4$ or $x = 1$

Substituting $x = 4$ into the equation of the **curve**

$y = \frac{4^3}{3} - \frac{5(4)^2}{2} + 6(4) - 1$

$y = 4\frac{1}{3}$

Substituting $x = 1$ into the equation of the **curve**

$y = \frac{1^3}{3} - \frac{5(1)^2}{2} + 6(1) - 1$

$y = 2\frac{5}{6}$

The points are $\left(1, 2\frac{5}{6}\right)$ and $\left(4, 4\frac{1}{3}\right)$

11 a Solve $y = \frac{1}{3}x^3 - 2x^2 - 8x + 5$ and $y = x + 5$ simultaneously.

$\frac{1}{3}x^3 - 2x^2 - 8x + 5 = x + 5$

$\frac{1}{3}x^3 - 2x^2 - 9x = 0$ multiply both sides by 3

$x^3 - 6x^2 - 27x = 0$ factorise

$x(x^2 - 6x - 27) = 0$

$x(x - 9)(x + 3) = 0$

$x = 0$ or $x - 9 = 0$ or $x + 3 = 0$

$x = 0, x = 9, x = -3$

Substitute these x values into $y = x + 5$

If $x = 0$ $y = 5$

If $x = 9$, $y = 14$

If $x = -3$, $y = 2$

The points of intersection are: $A = (-3, 2)$, $B = (0, 5)$, $C = (9, 14)$

b $\frac{dy}{dx} = x^2 - 4x - 8$

Substituting $x = -3$ gives:

$\frac{dy}{dx} = (-3)^2 - 4(-3) - 8 = 13$

Substituting $x = 0$ gives:

$\frac{dy}{dx} = (0)^2 - 4(0) - 8 = -8$

Substituting $x = 9$ gives:

$\frac{dy}{dx} = (9)^2 - 4(9) - 8 = 37$

12 a $y = 4x^3 + 3x^2 - 6x - 1$

$\frac{dy}{dx} = 12x^2 + 6x - 6$

b Solve $12x^2 + 6x - 6 \geqslant 0$

Sketch the graph of $y = 12x^2 + 6x - 6$

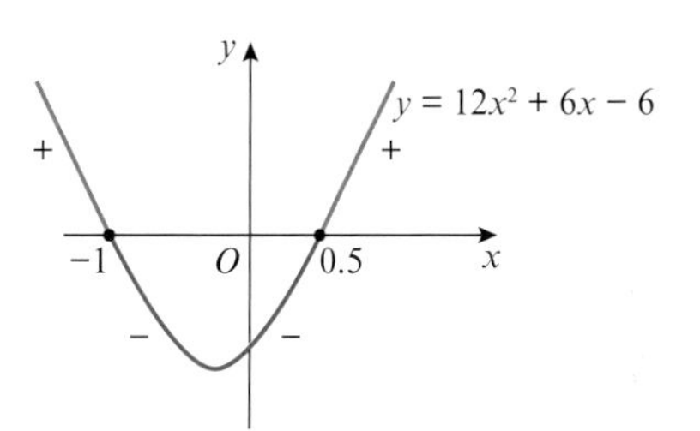

When $y = 0$, $12x^2 + 6x - 6 = 0$

Use the quadratic formula: $x = \frac{-b \pm \sqrt{b^2 - 4ac}}{2a}$

$x = \frac{-6 \pm \sqrt{6^2 - 4 \times 12 \times -6}}{2 \times 12}$

$x = 0.5$ or $x = -1$

So the x-axis crossing points are at 0.5 and -1

For $12x^2 + 6x - 6 \geqslant 0$ you need to find the range of values of x for which the curve is zero or positive (on or above the x-axis).

The solution is $x \leqslant -1$ and $x \geqslant 0.5$

So, the range of values of x for which $\frac{dy}{dx} \geqslant 0$ is $x \leqslant -1$ and $x \geqslant 0.5$

13 a 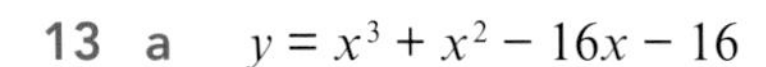

$y = x^3 + x^2 - 16x - 16$

$\frac{dy}{dx} = 3x^2 + 2x - 16$

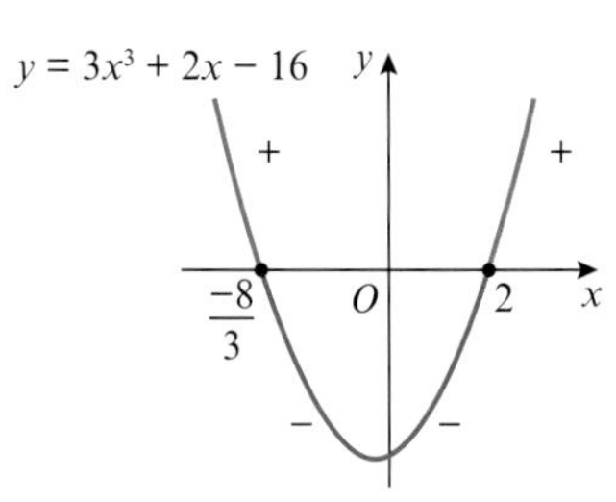

b Solve $3x^2 + 2x - 16 \leqslant 0$

Sketch the graph of $y = 3x^2 + 2x - 16$

When $y = 0$, $3x^2 + 2x - 16 = 0$

So, $(3x + 8)(x - 2) = 0$

$3x + 8 = 0$ or $x - 2 = 0$

$x = -\frac{8}{3}$ or $x = 2$

So, the x-axis crossing points are at $-\frac{8}{3}$ and 2

For $3x^2 + 2x - 16 \leqslant 0$ you need to find the range of values of x for which the curve is zero or negative (on or below the x-axis).

The solution is $-\frac{8}{3} \leqslant x \leqslant 2$

So, the range of values of x for which $\frac{dy}{dx} \leqslant 0$ is $-\frac{8}{3} \leqslant x \leqslant 2$

14 $y = x^5 - 5x^3 + 25x^2 + 145x + 10$

$\frac{dy}{dx} = 5x^4 - 15x^2 + 50x + 145$

We want to prove that $\frac{dy}{dx}$ is never negative

$5x^4 - 15x^2 + 50x + 145$ factorise

$5(x^4 - 3x^2 + 10x + 29)$

$5(x^4 - 4x^2 + x^2 + 10x + 29)$ complete the square

$5[(x^2 - 2)^2 - 4 + x^2 + 10x + 29]$

$5[(x^2 - 2)^2 + x^2 + 10x + 25]$ complete the square

$5[(x^2 - 2)^2 + (x + 5)^2]$

$(x^2 - 2)^2$ and $(x + 5)^2$ are always greater than or equal to 0.

So, $5[(x^2 - 2)^2 + (x + 5)^2]$ is always $\geqslant 0$.

Therefore the gradient i.e. $\frac{dy}{dx}$ is never negative.

Exercise 12.2

REMEMBER

The chain rule: $\frac{dy}{dx} = \frac{dy}{du} \times \frac{du}{dx}$

1 d $y = \left(\frac{1}{2}x - 7\right)^4$

Let $u = \frac{1}{2}x - 7$ and $y = u^4$

$\frac{du}{dx} = \frac{1}{2}$ and $\frac{dy}{du} = 4u^3$

$\frac{dy}{dx} = \frac{dy}{du} \times \frac{du}{dx}$

$= \frac{1}{2} \times 4u^3$

$= 2\left(\frac{1}{2}x - 7\right)^3$

i $y = (x^2 + 2)^4$

Let $u = x^2 + 2$ and $y = u^4$

$\frac{du}{dx} = 2x$ and $\frac{dy}{du} = 4u^3$

$\frac{dy}{dx} = \frac{dy}{du} \times \frac{du}{dx}$

$= 2x \times 4u^3$

$= 8x(x^2 + 2)^3$

2 e $y = \frac{4}{(x^2 - 2x)}$

Let $u = (x^2 - 2x)$ and $y = 4u^{-1}$

$\frac{du}{dx} = 2x - 2$ and $\frac{dy}{du} = -4u^{-2}$

$\frac{dy}{dx} = \frac{dy}{du} \times \frac{du}{dx}$

$= (2x - 2) \times -4u^{-2}$

$= (-8x + 8)(x^2 - 2x)^{-2}$

$= -\frac{8x - 8}{(x^2 - 2x)^2}$

h $y = \frac{1}{2(3x - 2)^4}$

Let $u = (3x - 2)$ and $y = \frac{1}{2}u^{-4}$

$\frac{du}{dx} = 3$ and $\frac{dy}{du} = -2u^{-5}$

$\frac{dy}{dx} = \frac{dy}{du} \times \frac{du}{dx}$

$= 3 \times -2u^{-5}$

$= -6(3x - 2)^{-5}$

$= -\frac{6}{(3x - 2)^5}$

3 a Differentiate with respect to x

$\sqrt{x + 2}$

Remember that this can be rewritten as:

$(x + 2)^{\frac{1}{2}}$ as $x^{\frac{m}{n}} = \sqrt[n]{x^m}$

Let $u = (x + 2)$ and $y = u^{\frac{1}{2}}$

$\frac{du}{dx} = 1$ and $\frac{dy}{du} = \frac{1}{2}u^{-\frac{1}{2}}$

$\frac{dy}{dx} = \frac{dy}{du} \times \frac{du}{dx}$

$= 1 \times \frac{1}{2}u^{-\frac{1}{2}}$

$= \frac{1}{2}(x + 2)^{-\frac{1}{2}}$, which can be rewritten as:

$= \frac{1}{2(x + 2)^{\frac{1}{2}}}$ or as $\frac{1}{2\sqrt{x + 2}}$

h $\frac{3}{\sqrt[3]{2 - 5x}}$

Let $u = 2 - 5x$ and $y = 3u^{-\frac{1}{3}}$

$\frac{du}{dx} = -5$ and $\frac{dy}{du} = -1u^{-\frac{4}{3}}$

$\frac{dy}{dx} = \frac{dy}{du} \times \frac{du}{dx}$

$= -5 \times -1u^{-\frac{4}{3}}$

$= 5u^{-\frac{4}{3}}$

$= \frac{5}{(2 - 5x)^{\frac{4}{3}}}$

4 Given $y = (2x - 5)^4$

Let $u = 2x - 5$ and $y = u^4$

$\frac{du}{dx} = 2$ and $\frac{dy}{du} = 4u^3$

$\frac{dy}{dx} = \frac{dy}{du} \times \frac{du}{dx}$

$= 2 \times 4u^3$

$= 8(2x - 5)^3$

At the point (3, 1), $x = 3$

Substitute $x = 3$ into the result of $\frac{dy}{dx}$

$= 8(2(3) - 5)^3$

$= 8(6 - 5)^3$

$= 8(1)^3$

$= 8$

The gradient of the curve at the point (3, 1) is 8.

5 Given $y = \frac{8}{(x - 2)^2}$

Let $u = x - 2$ and $y = 8u^{-2}$

$\frac{du}{dx} = 1$ and $\frac{dy}{du} = -16u^{-3}$

$\frac{dy}{dx} = \frac{dy}{du} \times \frac{du}{dx}$

$\frac{dy}{dx} = -16u^{-3} \times 1$

$\frac{dy}{dx} = \frac{-16}{(x - 2)^3}$

Remember that a curve crosses the y-axis where $x = 0$.

Substituting $x = 0$ into $\frac{dy}{dx} = \frac{-16}{(x - 2)^3}$ gives:

$\frac{dy}{dx} = \frac{-16}{(0 - 2)^3} = 2$

The gradient of the curve at the x-intercept is 2

6 Given $y = x + \frac{4}{x - 5}$

First find the points where the curve crosses the x-axis

Substituting $y = 0$ gives:

$0 = x + \frac{4}{x - 5}$ multiply both sides by $x - 5$

$0 = x(x - 5) + 4$ expand the brackets and rearrange

$x^2 - 5x + 4 = 0$ factorise

$(x - 1)(x - 4) = 0$

$x = 1$ or $x = 4$

The curve crosses the x-axis at $x = 1$ and $x = 4$

Now differentiate $y = x + \frac{4}{x-5}$ Start with the fraction: $\frac{4}{x-5}$

Let $u = x - 5$ and $y = 4u^{-1}$

$\frac{du}{dx} = 1$ and $\frac{dy}{du} = -4u^{-2}$

$\frac{dy}{dx} = \frac{dy}{du} \times \frac{du}{dx}$

$\frac{dy}{dx} = -4u^{-2} \times 1$

$\frac{dy}{dx} = \frac{-4}{(x-5)^2}$

The gradient at any point on the curve is given as

$\frac{dy}{dx} = 1 - \frac{4}{(x-5)^2}$

Substitute $x = 1$ and $x = 4$ into $\frac{dy}{dx}$ to find the gradients at these points:

If $x = 1$, $\frac{dy}{dx} = 1 - \frac{4}{(1-5)^2}$ or 0.75

If $x = 4$, $\frac{dy}{dx} = 1 - \frac{4}{(4-5)^2}$ or -3

The gradient at the x-intercepts are 0.75 and -3.

7 Rewrite $y = \sqrt{x^2 - 6x + 13}$ as $y = (x^2 - 6x + 13)^{0.5}$

Let $u = x^2 - 6x + 13$ and $y = u^{0.5}$

$\frac{du}{dx} = 2x - 6$ and $\frac{dy}{du} = 0.5u^{-0.5}$

$\frac{dy}{dx} = \frac{dy}{du} \times \frac{du}{dx}$

$\frac{dy}{dx} = (2x - 6) \times 0.5u^{-0.5}$

$\frac{dy}{dx} = \frac{(2x-6) \times 0.5}{(x^2 - 6x + 13)^{0.5}}$ or $\frac{x-3}{(x^2 - 6x + 13)^{0.5}}$

The gradient is zero, so solve $\frac{x-3}{(x^2 - 6x + 13)^{0.5}} = 0$

$\frac{x-3}{(x^2 - 6x + 13)^{0.5}} = 0$ multiply both sides by $(x^2 - 6x + 13)^{0.5}$

$x - 3 = 0$

$x = 3$

To find the y-coordinate of this point, substitute $x = 3$ into the curve equation:

So $y = (x^2 - 6x + 13)^{0.5}$ or $y = (3^2 - 6(3) + 13)^{0.5}$

$y = 2$

The point is at (3, 2)

8 Given $y = \frac{a}{\sqrt{bx+1}}$, find $\frac{dy}{dx}$

Let $u = bx + 1$ and $y = au^{-0.5}$

$\frac{du}{dx} = b$ and $\frac{dy}{du} = -0.5au^{-1.5}$

$\frac{dy}{dx} = \frac{dy}{du} \times \frac{du}{dx}$

$\frac{dy}{dx} = -0.5au^{-1.5} \times b$

$\frac{dy}{dx} = \frac{-0.5ab}{(bx+1)^{1.5}}$

The curve passes through the point (1, 4) so substituting $x = 1$, $y = 4$ into $y = \frac{a}{\sqrt{bx+1}}$ gives:

$4 = \frac{a}{\sqrt{b+1}}$ or $a = 4\sqrt{b+1}$ or $a = 4(b+1)^{0.5}$ (1)

The gradient at the point $x = 1$ is $-\frac{3}{2}$, so substituting into $\frac{dy}{dx} = \frac{-0.5ab}{(bx+1)^{1.5}}$ gives:

$\frac{-0.5ab}{(b+1)^{1.5}} = -\frac{3}{2}$ multiply both sides by $2(b+1)^{1.5}$

$-ab = -3(b+1)^{1.5}$ substitute a from (1) gives:

$-4(b+1)^{0.5} \times b = -3(b+1)^{1.5}$ divide both sides by $(b+1)^{0.5}$

$-4b = -3(b+1)$ expand brackets

$-4b = -3b - 3$

$b = 3$

Substituting $b = 3$ into $a = 4(b+1)^{0.5}$ gives:

$a = 4(3+1)^{0.5}$

$a = 8$

Solution $a = 8$, $b = 3$

Exercise 12.3

REMEMBER

To differentiate the product of two functions you can use the **product rule**

$$\frac{d}{dx}(uv) = u\frac{dv}{dx} + v\frac{du}{dx}$$

It is easier to remember this rule as

'(first function × derivative of second function) + (second function × derivative of first function)'

1 g $y = x^2\sqrt{x+3}$

$$\frac{dy}{dx} = x^2\frac{d}{dx}(x+3)^{\frac{1}{2}} + (x+3)^{\frac{1}{2}}\frac{d}{dx}x^2$$

$$= (x^2)\left[\frac{1}{2}(x+3)^{-\frac{1}{2}}\right] + (x+3)^{\frac{1}{2}}(2x)$$

$$= \frac{1}{2}x^2(x+3)^{-\frac{1}{2}} + 2x(x+3)^{\frac{1}{2}}$$

Rewrite this equation

$$= \frac{x^2}{2\sqrt{x+3}} + 2x(\sqrt{x+3})$$

Create a single fraction

$$= \frac{x^2 + 2x[2(x+3)]}{2\sqrt{x+3}}$$

$$= \frac{x^2 + 2x(2x+6)}{2\sqrt{x+3}}$$

$$= \frac{x^2 + 4x^2 + 12x}{2\sqrt{x+3}}$$

$$= \frac{5x^2 + 12x}{2\sqrt{x+3}}$$

i $y = (2x+1)(x^2+5)$

$$\frac{dy}{dx} = (2x+1)\frac{d}{dx}(x^2+5) + (x^2+5)\frac{d}{dx}(2x+1)$$

$$= (2x+1)2x + (x^2+5)(2)$$

$$= (4x^2+2x) + (2x^2+10)$$

$$= 6x^2 + 2x + 10$$

$$= 2(3x^2 + x + 5)$$

2 $y = x^2\sqrt{(x+2)}$

Rewrite as $y = x^2(x+2)^{\frac{1}{2}}$

$$\frac{dy}{dx} = x^2\frac{d}{dx}(x+2)^{\frac{1}{2}} + (x+2)^{\frac{1}{2}}\frac{d}{dx}x^2$$

$$= x^2\left[\frac{1}{2}(x+2)^{-\frac{1}{2}}\right] + (x+2)^{\frac{1}{2}}(2x)^*$$

$$= \frac{x^2}{2\sqrt{(x+2)}} + 2x(\sqrt{(x+2)})$$

TIP

Sometimes it is easier to make a numerical substitution in an unsimplified expression to avoid algebraic errors when simplifying. For example, in question two it is possible to substitute $x = 2$ after (*). Try it out and check that you get the same result.

Create a single fraction:

$$= \frac{x^2 + 2(2x)(x+2)}{2\sqrt{(x+2)}}$$

$$= \frac{x^2 + 4x(x+2)}{2\sqrt{(x+2)}}$$

$$= \frac{x^2 + 4x^2 + 8x}{2\sqrt{(x+2)}}$$

$$= \frac{5x^2 + 8x}{2\sqrt{(x+2)}}$$

Substitute $x = 2$

$$= \frac{5(4) + 8(2)}{2\sqrt{(2)+2}}$$

$$= \frac{20 + 16}{4}$$

$$= 9$$

3 $y = (x-1)^3(x+3)^2$

To find the gradient of the curve at $x = 2$, we first need to differentiate with respect to x.

$$\frac{dy}{dx} = (x-1)^3\frac{d}{dx}(x+3)^2 + (x+3)^2\frac{d}{dx}(x-1)^3$$

$$\frac{dy}{dx} = (x-1)^3 \times 2(x+3) + (x+3)^2 \times 3(x-1)^2$$

$$\frac{dy}{dx} = 2(x-1)^3(x+3) + 3(x+3)^2(x-1)^2$$

When $x = 2$,

$$\frac{dy}{dx} = 2(2-1)^3(2+3) + 3(2+3)^2(2-1)^2$$
$$= 85$$

The gradient at $x = 2$ is 85.

4 $y = (x+2)(x-5)^2$

The curve crosses the x axis at $x = -2$ and $x = 5$

To find the gradient of the curve at these given points of x, we need to differentiate with respect to x.

$$\frac{dy}{dx} = (x+2)\frac{d}{dx}(x-5)^2 + (x-5)^2\frac{d}{dx}(x+2)$$
$$= (x+2)[2(x-5)] + (x-5)^2(1)$$

$(x-5)$ is a common factor, meaning we can re-write the equation as:

$$\frac{dy}{dx} = (x-5)[2(x+2) + x - 5]$$
$$= (x-5)[2x + 4 + x - 5]$$
$$= (x-5)(3x-1)$$

Substitute the earlier values of x for the x-coordinate at which the curve crosses the axis.

When $x = -2$

$$\frac{dy}{dx} = (-2-5)(-6-1)$$
$$= (-7)(-7)$$
$$= 49$$

When $x = 5$

$$\frac{dy}{dx} = (15-1)(5-5)$$
$$= 14(0)$$
$$= 0$$

Therefore, the gradient of the curve at the points where it meets the x-axis are: 49 and 0

5 Given $y = (2x-3)^2(x+2)^4$

Differentiating with respect to x gives:

$$\frac{dy}{dx} = (2x-3)^2\frac{d}{dx}(x+2)^4 + (x+2)^4\frac{d}{dx}(2x-3)^2$$
$$= (2x-3)^2 \times 4(x+2)^3 + (x+2)^4 \times \underbrace{2(2x-3)^1(2)}_{\text{use the chain rule}}$$
$$= 4(2x-3)^2(x+2)^3 + 4(x+2)^4(2x-3)^1 \quad \text{factorise}$$
$$= 4(2x-3)(x+2)^3[2x - 3 + x + 2] \quad \text{simplify}$$
$$= 4(2x-3)(x+2)^3(3x-1)$$

To find where the gradient is zero, write:

$$\frac{dy}{dx} = 4(2x-3)(x+2)^3(3x-1) = 0 \quad \text{solve}$$

$2x - 3 = 0 \quad \text{or } x + 2 = 0 \quad \text{or } 3x - 1 = 0$

$x = 1.5 \quad \text{or} \quad x = -2 \quad \text{or} \quad x = \frac{1}{3}$

The gradient is zero at the points $x = 1.5$, $x = -2$, and $x = \frac{1}{3}$

6 Given $y = (x + 3)\sqrt{4 - x}$

Rewrite as $y = (x + 3)(4 - x)^{0.5}$

Differentiating with respect to x gives:

$$\frac{dy}{dx} = (x + 3)\frac{d}{dx}(4 - x)^{0.5} + (4 - x)^{0.5}\frac{d}{dx}(x + 3)$$

$$\frac{dy}{dx} = (x + 3) \times \underbrace{0.5(4 - x)^{-0.5}(-1)}_{\text{use the chain rule}} + (4 - x)^{0.5} \times 1 \qquad \text{simplify}$$

$$\frac{dy}{dx} = -0.5(x + 3)(4 - x)^{-0.5} + (4 - x)^{0.5} \qquad \text{factorise}$$

$$\frac{dy}{dx} = (4 - x)^{-0.5}[-0.5(x + 3) + (4 - x)^{1}] \qquad \text{simplify}$$

$$\frac{dy}{dx} = \frac{2.5 - 1.5x}{(4 - x)^{0.5}}$$

To find where the gradient is zero, write:

$$\frac{2.5 - 1.5x}{(4 - x)^{0.5}} = 0 \qquad \text{solve}$$

$2.5 - 1.5x = 0$

$x = 1\frac{2}{3}$

The gradient is zero at the point $x = 1\frac{2}{3}$

Exercise 12.4

REMEMBER

To differentiate the quotient of two functions you can use the quotient rule

$$\frac{d}{dx}\left(\frac{u}{v}\right) = \frac{v\frac{du}{dx} - u\frac{dv}{dx}}{v^2}$$

It is easier to remember this rule as

$$\frac{(\text{denominator} \times \text{derivative of numerator}) - (\text{numerator} \times \text{derivative of denominator})}{(\text{denominator})^2}$$

1 a Use the quotient rule to differentiate with respect to x

$$y = \frac{1 + 2x}{5 - x}$$

$$\frac{dy}{dx} = \frac{(5 - x)\frac{d}{dx}(1 + 2x) - (1 + 2x)\frac{d}{dx}(5 - x)}{(5 - x)^2}$$

$$= \frac{(5 - x)(2) - (1 + 2x)(-1)}{(5 - x)^2}$$

$$= \frac{10 - 2x + 1 + 2x}{(5 - x)^2}$$

$$= \frac{11}{(5 - x)^2}$$

d Use the quotient rule to differentiate with respect to x

$$y = \frac{5x - 2}{3 - 8x}$$

$$\frac{dy}{dx} = \frac{(3 - 8x)\frac{d}{dx}(5x - 2) - (5x - 2)\frac{d}{dx}(3 - 8x)}{(3 - 8x)^2}$$

$$= \frac{(3 - 8x)(5) - (5x - 2)(-8)}{(3 - 8x)^2}$$

$$= \frac{15 - 40x + 40x - 16}{(3 - 8x)^2}$$

$$= -\frac{1}{(3 - 8x)^2}$$

2 Use the quotient rule to differentiate with respect to x

$$y = \frac{x + 3}{x - 1}$$

$$\frac{dy}{dx} = \frac{(x - 1)\frac{d}{dx}(x + 3) - (x + 3)\frac{d}{dx}(x - 1)}{(x - 1)^2}$$

$$= \frac{(x - 1) - (x + 3)}{(x - 1)^2}$$

$$= -\frac{4}{(x - 1)^2}$$

Substitute the value of the coordinate of $x = 2$ to find the gradient at this point

$$\frac{dy}{dx} = -\frac{4}{(2 - 1)^2}$$

$$= -\frac{4}{1}$$

$$= -4$$

3 Use the quotient rule to differentiate with respect to x

$$y = \frac{x^2}{2x - 1}$$

$$\frac{dy}{dx} = \frac{(2x - 1)\frac{d}{dx}x^2 - x^2\frac{d}{dx}(2x - 1)}{(2x - 1)^2}$$

$$= \frac{(2x - 1)(2x) - x^2 \times 2}{(2x - 1)^2}$$ simplify

$$= \frac{2x^2 - 2x}{(2x - 1)^2}$$

$= 0$ so:

$$\frac{2x^2 - 2x}{(2x - 1)^2} = 0$$ solve

$2x^2 - 2x = 0$ factorise

$2x(x - 1) = 0$

$2x = 0$ or $x - 1 = 0$

$x = 0$ or $x = 1$

The y-coordinates can be found by substituting these values into the curve equation $y = \frac{x^2}{2x - 1}$

If $x = 0$, $y = \frac{0^2}{2(0) - 1}$ $y = 0$

If $x = 1$, $y = \frac{1^2}{2(1) - 1}$ $y = 1$

Solution (0, 0) and (1, 1)

4 Given $y = \frac{7x - 2}{2x + 3}$, the curve crosses the y-axis at $x = 0$.

Use the quotient rule to differentiate with respect to x

$$\frac{dy}{dx} = \frac{(2x + 3)\frac{d}{dx}(7x - 2) - (7x - 2)\frac{d}{dx}(2x + 3)}{(2x + 3)^2}$$

$$= \frac{(2x + 3) \times 7 - (7x - 2) \times 2}{(2x + 3)^2}$$

$$= \frac{(14x + 21) - (14x - 4)}{(2x + 3)^2}$$

$$= \frac{25}{(2x + 3)^2}$$

At $x = 0$, $\frac{dy}{dx} = \frac{25}{(2(0) + 3)^2}$

$$\frac{dy}{dx} = \frac{25}{9}$$

The gradient is $\frac{25}{9}$

5 a Differentiate with respect to x.

$$\frac{\sqrt{x}}{2x+1}$$

$$\frac{dy}{dx} = \frac{(2x+1)\frac{d}{dx}x^{\frac{1}{2}} - x^{\frac{1}{2}}\frac{d}{dx}(2x+1)}{(2x+1)^2}$$

$$= \frac{\frac{2x+1}{2\sqrt{x}} - 2\sqrt{x}}{(2x+1)^2}$$

$$= \frac{2x+1-4x}{2\sqrt{x}(2x+1)^2}$$

$$= \frac{-2x+1}{2\sqrt{x}(2x+1)^2}$$

$$= \frac{1-2x}{2\sqrt{x}(2x+1)^2}$$

b $\frac{x}{\sqrt{1-2x}}$

$$\frac{dy}{dx} = \frac{(1-2x)^{\frac{1}{2}}\frac{d}{dx}x - x\frac{d}{dx}(1-2x)^{\frac{1}{2}}}{(\sqrt{1-2x})^2}$$

$$= \frac{\sqrt{1-2x} - x[-1(1-2x)^{-\frac{1}{2}}]}{1-2x}$$

$$= \frac{\sqrt{1-2x} + \frac{x}{\sqrt{1-2x}}}{1-2x}$$

$$= \frac{1-2x+x}{(\sqrt{1-2x})(1-2x)}$$

$$= \frac{1-x}{(1-2x)^{\frac{3}{2}}}$$

c Use the quotient rule to differentiate with respect to x

$$\frac{x^2}{\sqrt{x^2+2}}$$

$$\frac{dy}{dx} = \frac{\sqrt{x^2+2}\frac{d}{dx}x^2 - x^2\frac{d}{dx}\sqrt{x^2+2}}{(\sqrt{x^2+2})^2}$$

$$= \frac{(2x)(\sqrt{x^2+2}) - x^2\left(\frac{x}{(\sqrt{x^2+2})}\right)}{x^2+2}$$

$$= \frac{(2x)(x^2+2) - x^2(x)}{(\sqrt{x^2+2})(x^2+2)}$$

$$= \frac{2x^3+4x-x^3}{(x^2+2)^{\frac{3}{2}}}$$

$$= \frac{x^3+4x}{(x^2+2)^{\frac{3}{2}}}$$

$$= \frac{x(x^2+4)}{(x^2+2)^{\frac{3}{2}}}$$

d Use the quotient rule to differentiate with respect to x

$$y = \frac{5\sqrt{x}}{3+x} \text{ or } y = \frac{5x^{0.5}}{3+x}$$

$$\frac{dy}{dx} = \frac{(3+x)\frac{d}{dx}(5x^{0.5}) - 5x^{0.5}\frac{d}{dx}(3+x)}{(3+x)^2}$$

$$= \frac{(3+x)2.5x^{-0.5} - 5x^{0.5}\times 1}{(3+x)^2}$$

$$= \frac{7.5x^{-0.5} + 2.5x^{0.5} - 5x^{0.5}}{(3+x)^2}$$ multiply numerator and denominator by $x^{0.5}$

$$= \frac{7.5+2.5x-5x}{x^{0.5}(3+x)^2}$$ multiply numerator and denominator by 2 and simplify numerator

$$= \frac{15-5x}{2x^{0.5}(3+x)^2} \text{ or } \frac{dy}{dx} = \frac{5(3-x)}{2\sqrt{x}(3+x)^2} \text{ or } \frac{dy}{dx} = \frac{-5(x-3)}{2\sqrt{x}(3+x)^2}$$

6 Use the quotient rule to differentiate with respect to x

$$y = \frac{x-2}{\sqrt{x+5}}$$

$$\frac{dy}{dx} = \frac{(x+5)^{\frac{1}{2}}\frac{d}{dx}(x-2) - (x-2)\frac{d}{dx}((x+5)^{\frac{1}{2}})}{\left(\sqrt{(x+5)}\right)^2}$$

$$= \frac{\sqrt{x+5} - \frac{x-2}{2\sqrt{x+5}}}{(x+5)}$$

$$= \frac{2(x+5) - (x-2)}{2\sqrt{x+5}\,(x+5)}$$

$$= \frac{2x+10-x+2}{2\sqrt{x+5}\,(x+5)}$$

$$= \frac{x+12}{2\sqrt{x+5}\,(x+5)}$$

Substitute the value of x

$$\frac{dy}{dx} = \frac{-4+12}{2\sqrt{-4+5}\,(-4+5)}$$

$$= \frac{8}{2\sqrt{1}\,(1)}$$

$$= \frac{8}{2}$$

$$= 4$$

7 Use the quotient rule to differentiate with respect to x

$$y = \frac{2(x-5)}{\sqrt{x+1}} \text{ or } y = \frac{2x-10}{(x+1)^{0.5}}$$

$$\frac{dy}{dx} = \frac{(x+1)^{0.5}\frac{d}{dx}(2x-10) - (2x-10)\frac{d}{dx}(x+1)^{0.5}}{((x+1)^{0.5})^2}$$

$$= \frac{(x+1)^{0.5}(2) - (2x-10)(0.5)(x+1)^{-0.5}}{x+1}$$

$$= \frac{2(x+1)^{0.5} - (x-5)(x+1)^{-0.5}}{x+1}$$ multiply numerator and denominator by $(x+1)^{0.5}$

$$= \frac{2(x+1) - (x-5)}{(x+1)^{1.5}}$$ simplify numerator

$$= \frac{x+7}{(x+1)^{1.5}}$$

The gradient at a point on the curve is $\frac{5}{4}$ so:

$\frac{x+7}{(x+1)^{1.5}} = \frac{5}{4}$ solve

$4(x+7) = 5(x+1)^{1.5}$ square both sides

$16(x+7)^2 = 25(x+1)^3$ expand brackets

$16x^2 + 224x + 784 = 25[(x+1)(x+1)(x+1)]$

$16x^2 + 224x + 784 = 25[(x^2+2x+1)(x+1)]$

$16x^2 + 224x + 784 = 25x^3 + 75x^2 + 75x + 25$ simplify

$25x^3 + 59x^2 - 149x - 759 = 0$

Substituting $x = 3$ into the equation gives: $25 \times 3^3 + 59 \times 3^2 - 149 \times 3 - 759 = 0$

So, $x - 3$ is a factor of $25x^3 + 59x^2 - 149x - 759$

$$\begin{array}{r|l} & 25x^2 + 134x + 253 \\ x-3 & 25x^3 + 59x^2 - 149x - 759 \\ & 25x^3 - 75x^2 \\ & \quad 134x^2 - 149x \\ & \quad 134x^2 - 402x \\ & \qquad 253x - 759 \\ & \qquad 253x - 759 \\ & \qquad\qquad 0 \end{array}$$

$(x-3)(25x^2 + 134x + 253) = 0$

$x - 3 = 0$ or $25x^2 + 134x + 253 = 0$

Use the quadratic formula to solve $25x^2 + 134x + 253 = 0$

$x = \frac{-b \pm \sqrt{b^2 - 4ac}}{2a}$

$x = \frac{-134 \pm \sqrt{134^2 - 4 \times 25 \times 253}}{2 \times 25}$

$x = \frac{-134 \pm \sqrt{-7344}}{2 \times 25}$ which has no further solutions, therefore $x = 3$ is the only solution

$x = 3$

Find the y-coordinate by substituting $x = 3$ into the curve equation:

$y = \frac{2(3-5)}{\sqrt{3+1}}$

$y = -2$

The coordinates of the point are $(3, -2)$

8 a $5x - 5y = 2$ rearrange

$5y = 5x - 2$

$y = \frac{5x-2}{5}$

Substituting for y in $x^2y - 5x + y + 2 = 0$ gives:

$x^2\left(\frac{5x-2}{5}\right) - 5x + \frac{5x-2}{5} + 2 = 0$ multiply by 5 and expand brackets

$5x^3 - 2x^2 - 25x + 5x - 2 + 10 = 0$

$5x^3 - 2x^2 - 20x + 8 = 0$ factorise

Substituting $x = 2$ gives $5(2)^3 - 2(2)^2 - 20(2) + 8 = 0$

So, $x - 2$ is a factor of $5x^3 - 2x^2 - 20x + 8 = 0$

$$\begin{array}{r}
5x^2 + 8x - 4 \\
x - 2\,\overline{)\,5x^3 - 2x^2 - 20x + 8} \\
\underline{5x^3 - 10x^2} \\
8x^2 - 20x \\
\underline{8x^2 - 16x} \\
-4x + 8 \\
\underline{-4x + 8} \\
0
\end{array}$$

$(x - 2)(5x^2 + 8x - 4) = 0$ factorise

$(x - 2)(5x - 2)(x + 2) = 0$

$x - 2 = 0$ or $5x - 2 = 0$ or $x + 2 = 0$

$x = 2$ or $x = 0.4$ or $x = -2$

Substitute each x value into $5y = 5x - 2$ gives:

If $x = 2$ then $5y = 8$ so $y = 1.6$

If $x = 0.4$ then $5y = 0$ so $y = 0$

If $x = -2$ then $5y = -12$ so $y = -2.4$

The three points of intersection are: $(-2, -2.4)$, $(0.4, 0)$, $(2, 1.6)$

b Given $x^2y - 5x + y + 2 = 0$ rearrange

$y(x^2 + 1) = 5x - 2$

$y = \frac{5x-2}{x^2+1}$

Use the quotient rule to find $\frac{dy}{dx}$

$$\frac{dy}{dx} = \frac{(x^2+1)\frac{d}{dx}(5x-2) - (5x-2)\frac{d}{dx}(x^2+1)}{(x^2+1)^2}$$

$$\frac{dy}{dx} = \frac{(x^2+1)5 - (5x-2) \times 2x}{(x^2+1)^2}$$

$$\frac{dy}{dx} = \frac{5x^2 + 5 - 10x^2 + 4x}{(x^2+1)^2}$$

$$\frac{dy}{dx} = \frac{-5x^2 + 4x + 5}{(x^2+1)^2}$$

Substitute $x = -2$ into $\frac{dy}{dx}$ gives $\frac{-5(-2)^2 + 4(-2) + 5}{((-2)^2 + 1)^2} = -\frac{23}{25}$

Substitute $x = 0.4$ into $\frac{dy}{dx}$ gives $\frac{-5(0.4)^2 + 4(0.4) + 5}{((0.4)^2 + 1)^2} = \frac{125}{29}$

Substitute $x = 2$ into $\frac{dy}{dx}$ gives $\frac{-5(2)^2 + 4(2) + 5}{((2)^2 + 1)^2} = -\frac{7}{25}$

Answers $-\frac{23}{25}, \frac{125}{29}, -\frac{7}{25}$

Exercise 12.5

REMEMBER

The line perpendicular to the tangent at the point A is called the normal at A.

If the value of $\frac{dy}{dx}$ at the point (x_1, y_1) is m , then the equation of the tangent is given by

$y - y_1 = m(x - x_1)$

The normal at the point (x_1, y_1) is perpendicular to the tangent, so the gradient of the normal is $-\frac{1}{m}$ and the equation of the normal is given by

$y - y_1 = -\frac{1}{m}(x - x_1) \quad m \neq 0$

1 b $y = x^2 + 3x + 2$

$\frac{dy}{dx} = 2x + 3$

When $x = -2$, $y = (-2)^2 + 3(-2) + 2 = 0$

and $\frac{dy}{dx} = 2(-2) + 3 = -1$

Tangent: passes through the point $(-2, 0)$ and gradient $= -1$

$y - 0 = -1(x - -2)$

$y = -x - 2$

e $y = (x - 3)(2x - 1)^2$

Use the quotient rule to find $\frac{dy}{dx}$

$\frac{dy}{dx} = (x - 3)\frac{d}{dx}(2x - 1)^2 + (2x - 1)^2\frac{d}{dx}(x - 3)$

$\frac{dy}{dx} = (x - 3) \times \underbrace{2(2x - 1)^1(2)}_{\text{use the chain rule}} + (2x - 1)^2 \times 1$

$\frac{dy}{dx} = 4(x - 3)(2x - 1) + (2x - 1)^2$

When $x = 2$, $y = (2 - 3)(2(2) - 1)^2 = -9$

and $\frac{dy}{dx} = 4(2 - 3)(2(2) - 1) + (2(2) - 1)^2 = -3$

Tangent: passes through the point $(2, -9)$ and gradient $= -3$

$y - -9 = -3(x - 2)$

$y = -3x - 3$

2 d Rewrite $y = 4 - \frac{2}{x^2}$ as $y = 4 - 2x^{-2}$

$\frac{dy}{dx} = 4x^{-3}$

When $x = -2$, $y = 4 - 2(-2)^{-2} = 3.5$

and $\frac{dy}{dx} = 4(-2)^{-3} = -0.5$

Normal: passes through the point $(-2, 3.5)$ and gradient $= 2$

$\left[\text{The gradient of the normal} = \frac{-1}{\text{gradient of the tangent}}\right]$

$y - 3.5 = 2(x - -2)$

$y = 2x + 7.5$

f $y = \frac{x + 2}{x - 2}$

Use the quotient rule to find $\frac{dy}{dx}$

$$\frac{dy}{dx} = \frac{(x - 2)\frac{d}{dx}(x + 2) - (x + 2)\frac{d}{dx}(x - 2)}{(x - 2)^2}$$

$$\frac{dy}{dx} = \frac{(x - 2)(1) - (x + 2)(1)}{(x - 2)^2}$$

$$\frac{dy}{dx} = \frac{-4}{(x - 2)^2}$$

When $x = 6$, $y = \frac{6 + 2}{6 - 2} = 2$

and $\frac{dy}{dx} = \frac{-4}{(6 - 2)^2} = -\frac{1}{4}$

Normal: passes through the point $(6, 2)$ and gradient $= 4$

$\left[\text{The gradient of the normal} = \frac{-1}{\text{gradient of the tangent}}\right]$

$y - 2 = 4(x - 6)$

$y = 4x - 22$

3 $y = 5x - 3x^{-1}$

$\frac{dy}{dx} = 5 + 3x^{-2}$

When $x = 1$, $y = 5(1) - 3(1)^{-1} = 2$

and $\frac{dy}{dx} = 5 + 3(1)^{-2} = 8$

Tangent: passes through the point (1, 2) and gradient = 8

$y - 2 = 8(x - 1)$

$y = 8x - 6$

Normal: passes through the point (1, 2) and gradient = $-\frac{1}{8}$

$\left[\text{The gradient of the normal} = \frac{-1}{\text{gradient of the tangent}}\right]$

$y - 2 = -\frac{1}{8}(x - 1)$

$y = -\frac{1}{8}x + \frac{17}{8}$

4 $y = x^3 - 2x + 1$

$\frac{dy}{dx} = 3x^2 - 2$

When $x = 2$, $\frac{dy}{dx} = 3(2)^2 - 2 = 10$

Normal: passes through the point (2, 5) and gradient = $-\frac{1}{10}$

$\left[\text{The gradient of the normal} = \frac{-1}{\text{gradient of the tangent}}\right]$

$y - 5 = -\frac{1}{10}(x - 2)$

$y = -\frac{1}{10}x + \frac{26}{5}$

The normal intersects the y-axis where $x = 0$

Substituting $x = 0$ into $y = -\frac{1}{10}x + \frac{26}{5}$ gives:

$y = -\frac{1}{10}(0) + \frac{26}{5}$ so $y = 5.2$

P is at (0, 5.2)

5 The curve $y = \frac{x - 1}{\sqrt{x + 4}}$ crosses the y-axis where $x = 0$

So, $y = \frac{0 - 1}{\sqrt{0 + 4}}$ or $y = -\frac{1}{2}$

The curve intersects the y-axis at $\left(0, -\frac{1}{2}\right)$

Rewrite $y = \frac{x - 1}{\sqrt{x + 4}}$ as $y = \frac{x - 1}{(x + 4)^{0.5}}$

Use the quotient rule to find $\frac{dy}{dx}$

$$\frac{dy}{dx} = \frac{(x + 4)^{0.5}\frac{d}{dx}(x - 1) - (x - 1)\frac{d}{dx}(x + 4)^{0.5}}{(x + 4)}$$

$$\frac{dy}{dx} = \frac{(x + 4)^{0.5}(1) - (x - 1) \times 0.5(x + 4)^{-0.5}}{(x + 4)}$$

$$\frac{dy}{dx} = \frac{(x + 4)^{0.5} - 0.5(x - 1)(x + 4)^{-0.5}}{(x + 4)}$$

At $x = 0$, $\frac{dy}{dx} = \frac{(0 + 4)^{0.5} - 0.5(0 - 1)(0 + 4)^{-0.5}}{(0 + 4)} = \frac{9}{16}$

Tangent: passes through the point $\left(0, -\frac{1}{2}\right)$ and gradient $= \frac{9}{16}$

$$y - -\frac{1}{2} = \frac{9}{16}(x - 0)$$

$$y = \frac{9}{16}x - \frac{1}{2}$$

Normal: passes through the point $\left(0, -\frac{1}{2}\right)$ and gradient $= -\frac{16}{9}$

$$y - -\frac{1}{2} = -\frac{16}{9}(x - 0)$$

$$y = -\frac{16}{9}x - \frac{1}{2}$$

6 Find the equations of the two tangents.

$y = x^2 - 5x + 4$

$\frac{dy}{dx} = 2x - 5$

When $x = 1$, $\frac{dy}{dx} = 2(1) - 5 = -3$

Tangent: passes through the point $(1, 0)$ and gradient $= -3$

$y - 0 = -3(x - 1)$

$y = -3x + 3 \quad (1)$

When $x = 3$, $\frac{dy}{dx} = 2(3) - 5 = 1$

Tangent: passes through the point $(3, -2)$ and gradient $= 1$

$y - -2 = 1(x - 3)$

$y = x - 5 \quad (2)$

Solve equations (1) and (2) simultaneously:

$-3x + 3 = x - 5$

$x = 2$

Substitute into (2) $y = -3$

Q has coordinates $(2, -3)$

7 The gradient of the line $y = 2x - 5$ is 2.

Any line parallel to $y = 2x - 5$ also has a gradient 2.

$y = 3x^2 - 10x - 8$

$\frac{dy}{dx} = 6x - 10$

The gradient of the curve at P, has a gradient 2 so

$6x - 10 = 2$

$x = 2$

The x-coordinate of P is 2.

To find the y-coordinate of P, substitute $x = 2$ into the equation of the curve:

$y = 3(2)^2 - 10(2) - 8$

$y = -16$

$P = (2, -16)$

Tangent: passes through the point $(2, -16)$ and gradient = 2

$y - -16 = 2(x - 2)$

Tangent equation is $y = 2x - 20$

8 **a** $y = x^3 - x + 6$

$\frac{dy}{dx} = 3x^2 - 1$

When $x = -1$, $\frac{dy}{dx} = 3(-1)^2 - 1 = 2$

Tangent: passes through the point $(-1, 6)$ and gradient = 2

$y - 6 = 2(x - -1)$

$y = 2x + 8$

b The tangent at P has gradient 2, so the tangent at Q also has a gradient 2

Solve $3x^2 - 1 = 2$

$3x^2 = 3$

$x = \pm 1$

P is at $x = -1$ so Q is at $x = 1$

The y-coordinate of Q is found by substituting $x = 1$ into the curve equation:

$y = (1)^3 - 1 + 6$

$y = 6$

Q is at $(1, 6)$

c Normal: passes through the point $(1, 6)$ and gradient $= -\frac{1}{2}$

$y - 6 = -\frac{1}{2}(x - 1)$

Normal equation is $y = -\frac{1}{2}x + \frac{13}{2}$

9 $y = 4 + (x - 1)^4$

Differentiate with respect to x using the chain rule:

Let $u = x - 1$ and $y = 4 + u^4$

$\frac{du}{dx} = 1$ and $\frac{dy}{du} = 4u^3$

$\frac{dy}{dx} = \frac{dy}{du} \times \frac{du}{dx}$

$= 4u^3 \times 1$

$= 4(x - 1)^3$

The gradient of the **tangent** line at $P(1, 4)$ is found by substituting $x = 1$ into $\frac{dy}{dx} = 4(x - 1)^3$

$\frac{dy}{dx} = 4(1 - 1)^3 = 0$ (the tangent line at P is zero, so it is a horizontal line).

The **normal** at P is a vertical line that passes through $(1, 4)$ i.e., it has equation $x = 1$

The gradient of the **tangent** line at Q $(2, 5)$ is found by substituting $x = 2$ into $\frac{dy}{dx} = 4(x - 1)^3$

$\frac{dy}{dx} = 4(2 - 1)^3 = 4$

The gradient of the **normal** line at Q has a gradient $-\frac{1}{4}$

So the **normal** line passes through the point $(2, 5)$ and has gradient $= -\frac{1}{4}$

$y - 5 = -\frac{1}{4}(x - 2)$

$y = -\frac{1}{4}x + \frac{11}{2}$

R is at the intersection of $x = 1$ and $y = -\frac{1}{4}x + \frac{11}{2}$

Substituting $x = 1$ into $y = -\frac{1}{4}x + \frac{11}{2}$ gives:

$y = -\frac{1}{4} + \frac{11}{2} = 5.25$

R has coordinates $(1, 5.25)$

10 a $y = (2 - x^{0.5})^4$

Differentiate with respect to x using the chain rule:

Let $u = 2 - x^{0.5}$ and $y = u^4$

$\frac{du}{dx} = -0.5x^{-0.5}$ and $\frac{dy}{du} = 4u^3$

$\frac{dy}{dx} = \frac{dy}{du} \times \frac{du}{dx}$

$= 4u^3 \times -0.5x^{-0.5}$

$= -2x^{-0.5}(2 - x^{0.5})^3$

The gradient of the **tangent** line at $P(1, 1)$ is found by substituting $x = 1$ into

$\frac{dy}{dx} = -2x^{-0.5}(2 - x^{0.5})^3$

$= -2(1)^{-0.5}(2 - (1)^{0.5})^3 = -2$

The **normal** at $P(1, 1)$ has a gradient $\frac{1}{2}$

$y - 1 = \frac{1}{2}(x - 1)$

The **normal** line at P has equation $y = \frac{1}{2}x + \frac{1}{2}$

The gradient of the **tangent** line at $Q(9, 1)$ is found by substituting $x = 9$ into

$\frac{dy}{dx} = -2x^{-0.5}(2 - x^{0.5})^3$

$\frac{dy}{dx} = -2(9)^{-0.5}(2 - (9)^{0.5})^3 = \frac{2}{3}$

The gradient of the **normal** line at Q has a gradient $-\frac{3}{2}$

So the **normal** line passes through the point $(9, 1)$ and has gradient $= -\frac{3}{2}$

$y - 1 = -\frac{3}{2}(x - 9)$

$y = -\frac{3}{2}x + \frac{29}{2}$

R is at the intersection of $y = \frac{1}{2}x + \frac{1}{2}$ (1) and $y = -\frac{3}{2}x + \frac{29}{2}$ (2)

Equating (1) and (2) gives:

$\frac{1}{2}x + \frac{1}{2} = -\frac{3}{2}x + \frac{29}{2}$ multiply both sides by 2

$x + 1 = -3x + 29$

$x = 7$

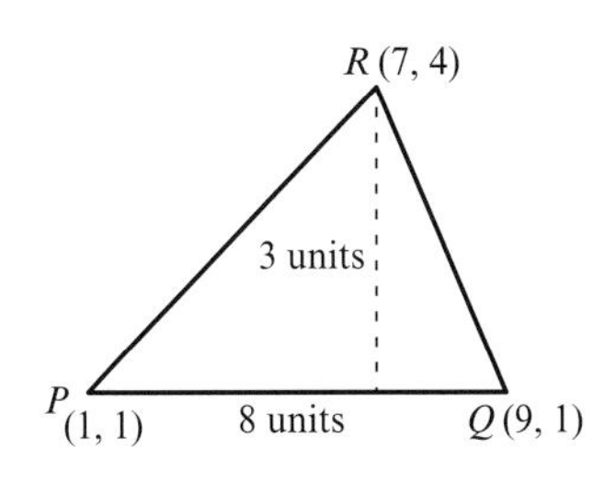

Substituting $x = 7$ into (1) gives:

$y = \frac{1}{2} \times 7 + \frac{1}{2}$

$y = 4$

R is at (7, 4)

b Area of triangle $PQR = \frac{1}{2} \times 8 \times 3 = 12$ units^2

11 a Rewrite $y = \sqrt{x}(x - 2)^3$ as $y = x^{0.5}(x - 2)^3$

Use the product rule to differentiate with respect to x

$u = x^{0.5}$ and $v = (x - 2)^3$

$\frac{du}{dx} = 0.5x^{-0.5}$ and $\frac{dv}{dx} = 3(x - 2)^2$

$\frac{d}{dx}(uv) = u\frac{dv}{dx} + v\frac{du}{dx}$

$\frac{dy}{dx} = x^{0.5} \times 3(x - 2)^2 + (x - 2)^3 \times 0.5x^{-0.5}$

$\frac{dy}{dx} = 3x^{0.5}(x - 2)^2 + 0.5x^{-0.5}(x - 2)^3$ factorise

$\frac{dy}{dx} = 0.5x^{-0.5}(x - 2)^2(6x + x - 2)$

$\frac{dy}{dx} = \frac{(x - 2)^2(7x - 2)}{2\sqrt{x}}$

The gradient of the tangent at $x = 3$ is:

$\frac{dy}{dx} = \frac{(3 - 2)^2(7(3) - 2)}{2\sqrt{3}} = \frac{19}{2\sqrt{3}} = \frac{19\sqrt{3}}{6}$

Tangent: passes through the point $(3, \sqrt{3})$ and gradient $= \frac{19\sqrt{3}}{6}$

$y - \sqrt{3} = \left(\frac{19\sqrt{3}}{6}\right)(x - 3)$ expand brackets

$y - \sqrt{3} = \frac{19\sqrt{3}}{6}x - \frac{19\sqrt{3}}{2}$

$y = \frac{19\sqrt{3}}{6}x - \frac{17\sqrt{3}}{2}$

b To find the gradient of the tangent line at $Q(1, -1)$, substitute $x = 1$ into

$\frac{dy}{dx} = \frac{(x - 2)^2(7x - 2)}{2\sqrt{x}}$

$\frac{dy}{dx} = \frac{(1 - 2)^2(7(1) - 2)}{2\sqrt{1}} = \frac{5}{2}$

The gradient of the normal line at $Q(1, -1)$ is $-\frac{2}{5}$

Normal: passes through the point $(1, -1)$ and has gradient $= -\frac{2}{5}$

$y - -1 = -\frac{2}{5}(x - 1)$

$y = -\frac{2}{5}x - \frac{3}{5}$ or

$y = -0.4x - 0.6$

12 $y = \frac{x^2}{x + 2}$

Use the quotient rule to differentiate with respect to x

$$\frac{dy}{dx} = \frac{(x + 2)\frac{d}{dx}(x^2) - (x^2)\frac{d}{dx}(x + 2)}{(x + 2)^2}$$

$$\frac{dy}{dx} = \frac{(x + 2) \times 2x - x^2(1)}{(x + 2)^2}$$

$$\frac{dy}{dx} = \frac{x^2 + 4x}{(x + 2)^2}$$

When $x = -3$, $y = \frac{(-3)^2}{-3 + 2} = -9$

and $\frac{dy}{dx} = \frac{(-3)^2 + 4(-3)}{(-3 + 2)^2} = -3$

Tangent: passes through the point $(-3, -9)$ and gradient $= -3$

$y - -9 = -3(x - -3)$

$y = -3x - 18$

The tangent line intersects the y axis where $x = 0$ so

$y = 3(0) - 18$

So, $M = (0, -18)$

Normal: passes through $(-3, -9)$ and has gradient $= \frac{1}{3}$

$y - -9 = \frac{1}{3}(x - -3)$

$y = \frac{1}{3}x - 8$

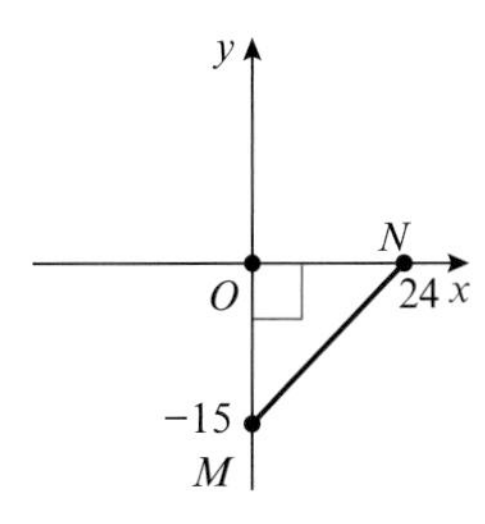

The normal meets the x-axis where $y = 0$

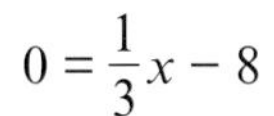

$0 = \frac{1}{3}x - 8$

$x = 24$

So, $N = (24, 0)$

Area of triangle $MNO = \frac{1}{2} \times 24 \times 18$

$= 216$ units^2

13 $y = \dfrac{x-3}{x+2}$ intersects the x-axis where $y = 0$

$0 = \dfrac{x-3}{x+2}$

$x = 3$

$P = (3, 0)$

Use the quotient rule to differentiate with respect to x

$\dfrac{dy}{dx} = \dfrac{(x+2)\dfrac{d}{dx}(x-3) - (x-3)\dfrac{d}{dx}(x+2)}{(x+2)^2}$

$\dfrac{dy}{dx} = \dfrac{(x+2)\times(1) - (x-3)(1)}{(x+2)^2}$

$\dfrac{dy}{dx} = \dfrac{5}{(x+2)^2}$

When $x = 3$, $\dfrac{dy}{dx} = \dfrac{5}{(3+2)^2} = \dfrac{1}{5}$

Normal: passes through (3, 0) and has gradient $= -5$

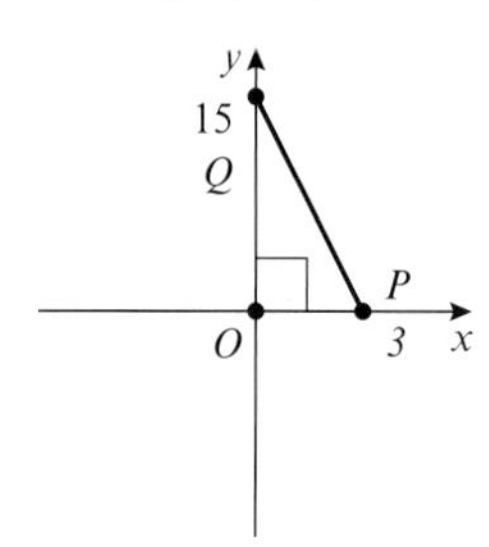

$y - 0 = -5(x - 3)$

$y = -5x + 15$

The normal meets the y-axis where $x = 0$

$y = -5(0) + 15$

$y = 15$

So, $Q = (0, 15)$

Area of triangle $POQ = \dfrac{1}{2} \times 3 \times 15$

$= 22.5 \text{ units}^2$

Exercise 12.6

1 $y = 2x^3 - 3x$

$\dfrac{dy}{dx} = 6x^2 - 3$

When $x = 2$, $\dfrac{dy}{dx} = 6(2)^2 - 3 = 21$

Using $\dfrac{\delta y}{\delta x} \approx \dfrac{dy}{dx}$

$\dfrac{\delta y}{0.01} \approx 21$

$\delta y \approx 21 \times 0.01$

$\delta y \approx 0.21$

2 $y = 5x^2 - \dfrac{8}{x^3}$ can be written as $y = 5x^2 - 8x^{-3}$

$\dfrac{dy}{dx} = 10x + 24x^{-4}$ or $\dfrac{dy}{dx} = 10x + \dfrac{24}{x^4}$

When $x = 1$, $\dfrac{dy}{dx} = 10(1) + \dfrac{24}{(1)^4} = 34$

Using $\dfrac{\delta y}{\delta x} \approx \dfrac{dy}{dx}$

$\dfrac{\delta y}{0.02} \approx 34$

$\delta y \approx 34 \times 0.02$

$\delta y \approx 0.68$

3 $x^2y = 400$ can be written as $y = 400x^{-2}$

$\dfrac{dy}{dx} = -800x^{-3}$ or $\dfrac{dy}{dx} = \dfrac{-800}{x^3}$

When $x = 10$, $\dfrac{dy}{dx} = \dfrac{-800}{10^3} = -0.8$

Using $\dfrac{\delta y}{\delta x} \approx \dfrac{dy}{dx}$

$\dfrac{\delta y}{p} \approx -0.8$

$\delta y \approx -0.8 \times p$

$\delta y \approx -0.8p$

4 $y = \left(\dfrac{1}{3}x - 2\right)^6$

Use the chain rule to differentiate with respect to x

Let $u = \dfrac{1}{3}x - 2$ and $y = u^6$

$\dfrac{du}{dx} = \dfrac{1}{3}$ and $\dfrac{dy}{du} = 6u^5$

$\dfrac{dy}{dx} = \dfrac{dy}{du} \times \dfrac{du}{dx}$

$\dfrac{dy}{dx} = 6u^5 \times \dfrac{1}{3}$

$$\frac{dy}{dx} = 2\left(\frac{1}{3}x - 2\right)^5$$

When $x = 9$, $\frac{dy}{dx} = 2\left(\frac{1}{3}(9) - 2\right)^5 = 2$

Using $\frac{\delta y}{\delta x} \approx \frac{dy}{dx}$

$\frac{\delta y}{p} \approx 2$

$\delta y \approx 2 \times p$

$\delta y \approx 2p$

5 $y = (x + 1)(2x - 3)^4$

Use the product rule to differentiate with respect to x

$$\frac{dy}{dx} = (x + 1)\frac{d}{dx}(2x - 3)^4 + (2x - 3)^4\frac{d}{dx}(x + 1)$$

$$\frac{dy}{dx} = (x + 1) \times \underbrace{4(2x - 3)^3(2)}_{\text{use the chain rule}} + (2x - 3)^4 \times 1$$

$$\frac{dy}{dx} = 8(x + 1)(2x - 3)^3 + (2x - 3)^4$$

When $x = 2$, $\frac{dy}{dx} = 8(2 + 1)(2(2) - 3)^3 + (2(2) - 3)^4 = 25$

Using $\frac{\delta y}{\delta x} \approx \frac{dy}{dx}$

$\frac{\delta y}{p} \approx 25$

$\delta y \approx 25 \times p$

$\delta y \approx 25p$

6 Rewrite $y = (x - 2)\sqrt{2x + 1}$ as $y = (x - 2)(2x + 1)^{0.5}$

Use the product rule to differentiate with respect to x

$$\frac{dy}{dx} = (x - 2)\frac{d}{dx}(2x + 1)^{0.5} + (2x + 1)^{0.5}\frac{d}{dx}(x - 2)$$

$$\frac{dy}{dx} = (x - 2) \times \underbrace{0.5(2x + 1)^{-0.5}(2)}_{\text{use the chain rule}} + (2x + 1)^{0.5} \times 1$$

$$\frac{dy}{dx} = (x - 2)(2x + 1)^{-0.5} + (2x + 1)^{0.5}$$

When $x = 4$,

$$\frac{dy}{dx} = (4 - 2)(2(4) + 1)^{-0.5} + (2(4) + 1)^{0.5} = \frac{11}{3}$$

Using $\frac{\delta y}{\delta x} \approx \frac{dy}{dx}$

$\frac{\delta y}{p} \approx \frac{11}{3}$

$\delta y \approx \frac{11}{3} \times p$

$\delta y \approx \frac{11}{3}p$

7 $T = 2\pi\sqrt{\frac{L}{10}}$ can be written as $T = 2\pi(0.1L)^{0.5}$

$$\frac{dT}{dL} = 0.1\pi(0.1L)^{-0.5}$$

When $L = 40$, $\frac{dT}{dL} = 0.1\pi(0.1 \times 40)^{-0.5} = \frac{\pi}{20}$

Using $\frac{\delta T}{\delta L} \approx \frac{dT}{dL}$

$\frac{\delta T}{1} \approx \frac{\pi}{20}$

$\delta T \approx \frac{\pi}{20} \times 1$

$\delta T \approx \frac{\pi}{20}$

8 a Volume $= 2x \times x \times y$

$360 = 2x^2y$

$x^2y = 180$

$y = 180x^{-2}$ or $y = \frac{180}{x^2}$

b $A = 2 \times x \times 180x^{-2} + 2 \times 2x \times 180x^{-2} + 2 \times 2x \times x$

$A = \frac{360}{x} + \frac{720}{x} + 4x^2$

$A = 4x^2 + \frac{1080}{x}$

c $A = 4x^2 + 1080x^{-1}$

$$\frac{dA}{dx} = 8x - 1080x^{-2}$$

When $x = 2$, $\frac{dA}{dx} = 8(2) - 1080(2)^{-2} = -254$

Using $\frac{\delta A}{\delta x} \approx \frac{dA}{dx}$

$\frac{\delta A}{p} \approx -254$

$\delta A \approx -254 \times p$

$\delta A \approx -254p$

The approximate change in A is $254p$ and it is a decrease.

Exercise 12.7

1 $y = x^2 - 5x$

$\frac{dy}{dx} = 2x - 5$

When $x = 4$, $\frac{dy}{dx} = 3$

$\frac{dx}{dt} = 0.05$

$\frac{dy}{dt} = \frac{dy}{dx} \times \frac{dx}{dt} = 3 \times 0.05 = 0.15$

The rate of change of y is 0.15 units per second

2 $y = x + \sqrt{x - 5}$

$\frac{dy}{dx} = 1 + \frac{1}{2}(x - 5)^{-\frac{1}{2}}$

$= 1 + \frac{1}{2\sqrt{x - 5}}$

When $x = 9$, $\frac{dy}{dx} = 1\frac{1}{4} = \frac{5}{4}$

$\frac{dx}{dt} = 0.1$

$\frac{dy}{dt} = \frac{dy}{dx} \times \frac{dx}{dt} = \frac{5}{4} \times 0.1 = 0.125$

The rate of change of y is 0.125 units per second

3 $y = (x - 3)(x + 5)^3$

$\frac{dy}{dx} = (x - 3)\frac{d}{dx}(x + 5)^3 + (x + 5)^3\frac{d}{dx}(x - 3)$

$= (x - 3)3(x + 5)^2 + (x + 5)^3(1)$

$= 3x - 9 + x + 5(x + 5)^2$

$= (4x - 4)(x + 5)^2$

When $x = -4$, $\frac{dy}{dx} = -20$

$\frac{dx}{dt} = 0.2$

$\frac{dy}{dt} = \frac{dy}{dx} \times \frac{dx}{dt} = -20 \times 0.2 = -4$

The rate of change of y is -4 units per second

4 $y = \frac{5}{2x - 1}$

$\frac{dy}{dx} = \frac{(2x - 1)\frac{d}{dx}5 - 5\frac{d}{dx}(2x - 1)}{(2x - 1)^2}$

$= \frac{-5(2)}{(2x - 1)^2}$

$= \frac{-10}{(2x - 1)^2}$

When $x = -2$, $\frac{dy}{dx} = -\frac{10}{25} = -\frac{2}{5}$

$\frac{dy}{dt} = \frac{dy}{dx} \times \frac{dx}{dt}$

$\frac{dy}{dt} = 0.1$

$0.1 = -\frac{2}{5} \times \frac{dx}{dt}$

$\frac{dx}{dt} = 0.1 \div -\frac{2}{5} = -0.25$

The rate of change of x is -0.25 units per second

5 $y = \frac{2x}{x^2 + 3}$

$\frac{dy}{dx} = \frac{(x^2 + 3)\frac{d}{dx}2x - 2x\frac{d}{dx}(x^2 + 3)}{(x^2 + 3)^2}$

$= \frac{2(x^2 + 3) - 2x(2x)}{(x^2 + 3)^2}$

$= \frac{2x^2 + 6 - 4x^2}{(x^2 + 3)^2}$

$= \frac{-2x^2 + 6}{(x^2 + 3)^2}$

When $x = 1$, $\frac{dy}{dx} = \frac{4}{16} = \frac{1}{4}$

$\frac{dx}{dt} = 2$

$\frac{dy}{dt} = \frac{dy}{dx} \times \frac{dx}{dt} = \frac{1}{4} \times 2 = 0.5$

The rate of increase of y is 0.5 units per second

6 $y = \frac{2x - 5}{x - 1}$

$\frac{dy}{dx} = \frac{(x - 1)\frac{d}{dx}(2x - 5) - (2x - 5)\frac{d}{dx}(x - 1)}{(x - 1)^2}$

$\frac{dy}{dx} = \frac{(x - 1)(2) - (2x - 5)(1)}{(x - 1)^2}$

$\frac{dy}{dx} = \frac{3}{(x - 1)^2}$

When $y = 1$, $1 = \frac{2x - 5}{x - 1}$

$x - 1 = 2x - 5$

$x = 4$

When $x = 4$, $\frac{dy}{dx} = \frac{3}{(4 - 1)^2} = \frac{1}{3}$

$\frac{dx}{dt} = 0.02$

$\frac{dy}{dt} = \frac{dy}{dx} \times \frac{dx}{dt} = \frac{1}{3} \times 0.02 = \frac{1}{150}$

The rate of change of y is $\frac{1}{150}$ units per second

7 $\frac{1}{y} = \frac{1}{8} - \frac{2}{x}$

$\frac{1}{y} = \frac{x - 16}{8x}$

$y = \frac{8x}{x - 16}$

$\frac{dy}{dx} = \frac{(x - 16)\frac{d}{dx}(8x) - (8x)\frac{d}{dx}(x - 16)}{(x - 16)^2}$

$\frac{dy}{dx} = \frac{(x - 16)(8) - (8x)(1)}{(x - 16)^2}$

$\frac{dy}{dx} = \frac{-128}{(x - 16)^2}$

When $x = 8$, $\frac{dy}{dx} = \frac{-128}{(8 - 16)^2} = -2$

$\frac{dx}{dt} = 0.01$

$\frac{dy}{dt} = \frac{dy}{dx} \times \frac{dx}{dt} = -2 \times 0.01 = -0.02$

The rate of change of y is -0.02 units per second

8 $A = x^2$

When $A = 16$, $x = 4$

$\frac{dA}{dx} = 2x$

When $x = 4$, $\frac{dA}{dx} = 2 \times 4 = 8$

$\frac{dA}{dt} = 0.2$

$\frac{dx}{dt} = \frac{dx}{dA} \times \frac{dA}{dt} = \frac{1}{8} \times 0.2 = 0.025$

The rate of increase in x is 0.025 cm per second

9 $V = x^3$

When $V = 512$, $x^3 = 512$ so $x = 8$

$\frac{dV}{dx} = 3x^2$

When $x = 8$, $\frac{dV}{dx} = 3(8)^2 = 192$

$\frac{dV}{dt} = 2$

$\frac{dx}{dt} = \frac{dx}{dV} \times \frac{dV}{dt} = \frac{1}{192} \times 2 = \frac{1}{96}$

The rate of increase of x is $\frac{1}{96}$ cm per second

10 $V = \frac{4}{3}\pi r^3$

When $V = 972\pi$, $\frac{4}{3}\pi r^3 = 972\pi$

$r^3 = 972 \times \frac{3}{4}$

$r = 9$

$\frac{dV}{dr} = 4\pi r^2$

When $r = 9$, $\frac{dV}{dr} = 4\pi(9)^2 = 324\pi$

$\frac{dr}{dt} = \frac{1}{\pi}$

$\frac{dV}{dt} = \frac{dV}{dr} \times \frac{dr}{dt} = 324\pi \times \frac{1}{\pi} = 324$

The rate of increase of the volume is 324 cm^3 per second

11 Volume of the cuboid $= x \times x \times 5x = 5x^3$

$V = 5x^3$

$\frac{dV}{dx} = 15x^2$

When $x = 4$, $\frac{dV}{dx} = 15(4)^2 = 240$

$\frac{dV}{dt} = 0.5$

$\frac{dx}{dt} = \frac{dx}{dV} \times \frac{dV}{dt} = \frac{1}{240} \times 0.5 = \frac{1}{480}$

The rate of increase of x is $\frac{1}{480}$ cm per second

12 Volume of a cone $= \frac{1}{3}\pi r^2 h$

$V = \frac{1}{3} \times \pi \times r^2 \times 18$

$V = 6\pi r^2$

$\frac{dV}{dr} = 12\pi r$

When $r = 10$, $\frac{dV}{dr} = 12\pi(10) = 120\pi$

$\frac{dr}{dt} = 0.1$

$\frac{dV}{dt} = \frac{dV}{dr} \times \frac{dr}{dt} = 120\pi \times 0.1 = 12\pi$

The rate of change of volume is 12π cm^3 per second

13 a $V = \frac{1}{12}\pi h^3$

$\frac{dV}{dh} = \frac{1}{4}\pi h^2$

When $h = 5$, $\frac{dV}{dh} = \frac{1}{4}\pi(5)^2 = \frac{25\pi}{4}$

$\frac{dV}{dt} = 5$

$\frac{dh}{dt} = \frac{dh}{dV} \times \frac{dV}{dt} = \frac{4}{25\pi} \times 5 = \frac{4}{5\pi}$

The rate of increase in h is $\frac{4}{5\pi}$ cm per second

b $\frac{dV}{dh} = \frac{1}{4}\pi h^2$

When $h = 10$, $\frac{dV}{dh} = \frac{1}{4}\pi(10)^2 = 25\pi$

$\frac{dV}{dt} = 5$

$\frac{dh}{dt} = \frac{dh}{dV} \times \frac{dV}{dt} = \frac{1}{25\pi} \times 5 = \frac{1}{5\pi}$

The rate of increase in h is $\frac{1}{5\pi}$ cm per second

14 a $V = 8\pi h^2 - \frac{1}{3}\pi h^3$

$\frac{dV}{dh} = 16\pi h - \pi h^2$

When $h = 2$, $\frac{dV}{dh} = 16\pi(2) - \pi(2)^2 = 28\pi$

$\frac{dV}{dt} = 4\pi$

$\frac{dh}{dt} = \frac{dh}{dV} \times \frac{dV}{dt} = \frac{1}{28\pi} \times 4\pi = \frac{1}{7}$

The rate of increase in h is $\frac{1}{7}$ cm per second

b $\frac{dV}{dh} = 16\pi h - \pi h^2$

When $h = 4$, $\frac{dV}{dh} = 16\pi(4) - \pi(4)^2 = 48\pi$

$\frac{dV}{dt} = 4\pi$

$\frac{dh}{dt} = \frac{dh}{dV} \times \frac{dV}{dt} = \frac{1}{48\pi} \times 4\pi = \frac{1}{12}$

The rate of increase in h is $\frac{1}{12}$ cm per second

Exercise 12.8

REMEMBER

$\frac{dy}{dx}$ is called the **first derivative** of y with respect to x.

If you differentiate $\frac{dy}{dx}$ with respect to x you obtain $\frac{d}{dx}\left(\frac{dy}{dx}\right)$ which can also be written as $\frac{d^2y}{dx^2}$

$\frac{d^2y}{dx^2}$ is called the **second derivative** of y with respect to x.

1 d $y = (4x + 1)^5$

$\frac{dy}{dx} = \underbrace{5(4x + 1)^4(4)}_{\text{use the chain rule}}$

$\frac{dy}{dx} = 20(4x + 1)^4$

$\frac{d^2y}{dx^2} = \underbrace{(4)(20)(4x + 1)^3(4)}_{\text{use the chain rule}}$

$\frac{d^2y}{dx^2} = 320(4x + 1)^3$

f $y = \frac{4}{(x + 3)^{0.5}}$ or $y = 4(x + 3)^{-0.5}$

Use the chain rule to differentiate with respect to x

$\frac{dy}{dx} = (4)(-0.5)(x + 3)^{-1.5}(1)$

$\frac{dy}{dx} = -2(x + 3)^{-1.5}$

$\frac{d^2y}{dx^2} = (-2)(-1.5)(x + 3)^{-2.5}$

$\frac{d^2y}{dx^2} = 3(x + 3)^{-2.5}$

$\frac{d^2y}{dx^2} = \frac{3}{(x + 3)^{\frac{5}{2}}}$

2 b Rewrite $y = \frac{4x - 1}{x^2}$ as $y = 4x^{-1} - x^{-2}$

$\frac{dy}{dx} = -4x^{-2} + 2x^{-3}$

$\frac{d^2y}{dx^2} = 8x^{-3} - 6x^{-4}$

$\frac{d^2y}{dx^2} = \frac{8}{x^3} - \frac{6}{x^4}$

$\frac{d^2y}{dx^2} = \frac{8x}{x^4} - \frac{6}{x^4}$

$\frac{d^2y}{dx^2} = \frac{8x - 6}{x^4}$

TIP

There are alternative ways to differentiate this question:

- Use the quotient rule or
- rewrite the question as $x^{-2}(4x - 1)$ and use the product rule.

f $y = \frac{2x + 5}{3x - 1}$

$\frac{dy}{dx} = \frac{(3x - 1)\frac{d}{dx}(2x + 5) - (2x + 5)\frac{d}{dx}(3x - 1)}{(3x - 1)^2}$

$\frac{dy}{dx} = \frac{(3x - 1)(2) - (2x + 5)(3)}{(3x - 1)^2}$

$\frac{dy}{dx} = \frac{-17}{(3x - 1)^2}$ or $\frac{dy}{dx} = \underbrace{-17(3x - 1)^{-2}}_{\text{use the chain rule}}$

$\frac{d^2y}{dx^2} = -17(-2)(3x - 1)^{-3}(3)$

$\frac{d^2y}{dx^2} = 102(3x - 1)^{-3}$

$\frac{d^2y}{dx^2} = \frac{102}{(3x - 1)^3}$

3 a $f(1) = 1^3 - 7(1)^2 + 2(1) + 1 = -3$

b $f'(x) = 3x^2 - 14x + 2$

$f'(1) = 3(1)^2 - 14(1) + 2 = -9$

c $f''(x) = 6x - 14$

$f''(1) = 6(1) - 14 = -8$

4 a $y = 4x^3 + 3x^2 - 6x - 1$

$\frac{dy}{dx} = 12x^2 + 6x - 6$

$12x^2 + 6x - 6 = 0$ divide both sides by 6

$2x^2 + x - 1 = 0$

$(2x - 1)(x + 1) = 0$

$2x - 1 = 0$ or $x + 1 = 0$

$x = 0.5$ and $x = -1$

b $\frac{d^2y}{dx^2} = 24x + 6$

When $x = -1$, $\frac{d^2y}{dx^2} = 24(-1) + 6 = -18$

When $x = 0.5$, $\frac{d^2y}{dx^2} = 24(0.5) + 6 = 18$

5 $y = 2x^3 - 15x^2 + 24x + 6$

$\frac{dy}{dx} = 6x^2 - 30x + 24$

Values are: 24, 0, −12, −12, 0, 24

$\frac{d^2y}{dx^2} = 12x - 30$

Values are: −30, −18, −6, 6, 18, 30

x	0	1	2	3	4	5
$\frac{dy}{dx}$	+	0	−	−	0	+
$\frac{d^2y}{dx^2}$	−	−	−	+	+	+

6 $y = 2x^3 + 3x^2 - 36x + 5$

$\frac{dy}{dx} = 6x^2 + 6x - 36$ divide both sides by 6

$= x^2 + x - 6$

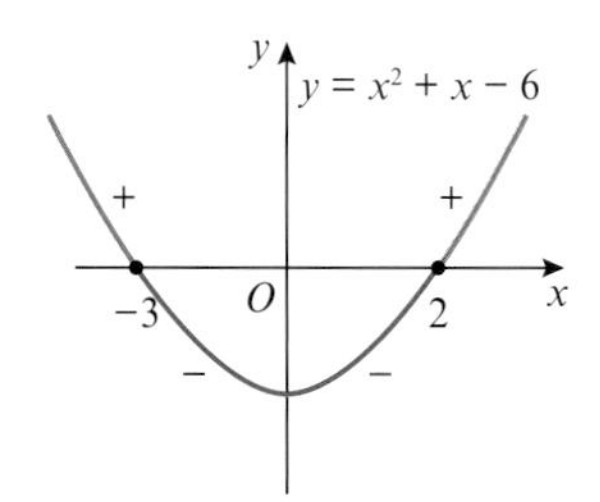

Sketch the graph of $y = x^2 + x - 6$

When $y = 0$, $x^2 + x - 6 = 0$

$(x + 3)(x - 2) = 0$

$x + 3 = 0$ $x - 2 = 0$

$x = -3$ or $x = 2$

So the x-axis crossing points are at −3 and 2

For $x^2 + x - 6 > 0$ you need to find the range of values of x for which the curve is positive (above the x-axis). The solution is $x < -3$ and $x > 2$

So, the range of values of x for which $\frac{dy}{dx} > 0$ is $x < -3$ and $x > 2$

$\frac{d^2y}{dx^2} = 12x + 6$

$12x + 6 > 0$

$x > -\frac{1}{2}$

So, the range of values of x for which $\frac{d^2y}{dx^2} > 0$ is $x > -\frac{1}{2}$

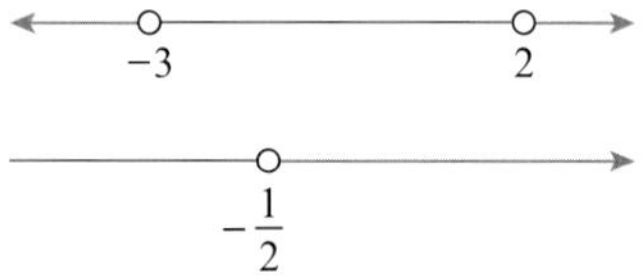

The values of x that satisfy both inequalities are $x > 2$

7 $y = x^2 - 2x + 5$

$\frac{dy}{dx} = 2x - 2$

$\frac{d^2y}{dx^2} = 2$

So, $4\frac{d^2y}{dx^2} + (x - 1)\frac{dy}{dx} = 4(2) + (x - 1)(2x - 2)$

$= 8 + 2x^2 - 4x + 2$

$= 2x^2 - 4x + 10$

$= 2(x^2 - 2x + 5)$

$= 2y$

8 Rewrite $y = 8\sqrt{x}$ as $y = 8x^{0.5}$

$\frac{dy}{dx} = 4x^{-0.5}$

$\frac{d^2y}{dx^2} = -2x^{-1.5}$

So, $4x^2\frac{d^2y}{dx^2} + 4x\frac{dy}{dx} = 4x^2(-2x^{-1.5}) + 4x(4x^{-0.5})$

$= -8x^{0.5} + 16x^{0.5}$

$= -8x^{0.5} + 2(8x^{0.5})$ substitute y for $8x^{0.5}$

$= -y + 2y$

$= y$

Exercise 12.9

REMEMBER

If $\frac{dy}{dx} = 0$ and $\frac{d^2y}{dx^2} < 0$, then the point is a maximum point.

If $\frac{dy}{dx} = 0$ and $\frac{d^2y}{dx^2} > 0$, then the point is a minimum point.

1 d $y = x^3 + x^2 - 16x - 16$

$\frac{dy}{dx} = 3x^2 + 2x - 16$

For stationary points, $\frac{dy}{dx} = 0$.

$3x^2 + 2x - 16 = 0$

$(3x + 8)(x - 2) = 0$

$x = -\frac{8}{3}$ or $x = 2$

When $x = -\frac{8}{3}$, $y = \left(-\frac{8}{3}\right)^3 + \left(-\frac{8}{3}\right)^2 - 16\left(-\frac{8}{3}\right) - 16 = \frac{400}{27}$

When $x = 2$, $y = (2)^3 + (2)^2 - 16(2) - 16 = -36$

The stationary points are $\left(-\frac{8}{3}, 14\frac{22}{27}\right)$ and $(2, -36)$.

$\frac{d^2y}{dx^2} = 6x + 2$

When $x = -\frac{8}{3}$, $\frac{d^2y}{dx^2} = -14$ which is < 0

When $x = 2$, $\frac{d^2y}{dx^2} = 14$ which is > 0

So $\left(-\frac{8}{3}, 14\frac{22}{27}\right)$ is a maximum point and $(2, -36)$ is a minimum point.

f $y = (x - 1)(x^2 - 6x + 2)$

$y = x^3 - 6x^2 + 2x - 1x^2 + 6x - 2$

$y = x^3 - 7x^2 + 8x - 2$

$\frac{dy}{dx} = 3x^2 - 14x + 8$

For stationary points, $\frac{dy}{dx} = 0$.

$3x^2 - 14x + 8 = 0$

$(3x - 2)(x - 4) = 0$

$x = \frac{2}{3}$ or $x = 4$

When $x = \frac{2}{3}$, $y = \left(\frac{2}{3}\right)^3 - 7\left(\frac{2}{3}\right)^2 + 8\left(\frac{2}{3}\right) - 2 = \frac{14}{27}$

When $x = 4$, $y = (4)^3 - 7(4)^2 + 8(4) - 2 = -18$

The stationary points are $\left(\frac{2}{3}, \frac{14}{27}\right)$ and $(4, -18)$.

$\frac{d^2y}{dx^2} = 6x - 14$

When $x = \frac{2}{3}$, $\frac{d^2y}{dx^2} = -10$ which is < 0

When $x = 4$, $\frac{d^2y}{dx^2} = 10$ which is > 0

So $\left(\frac{2}{3}, \frac{14}{27}\right)$ is a maximum point and $(4, -18)$ is a minimum point.

2 c $y = \frac{4}{x} + \sqrt{x}$ can be rewritten as:

$y = 4x^{-1} + x^{0.5}$

$\frac{dy}{dx} = -4x^{-2} + 0.5x^{-0.5}$

For stationary points, $\frac{dy}{dx} = 0$.

$-4x^{-2} + 0.5x^{-0.5} = 0$ factorise

$-0.5x^{-2}(8 - x^{1.5}) = 0$

$-0.5x^{-2} = 0$ so $-\frac{0.5}{x^2} = 0$ no solutions

$8 - x^{1.5} = 0$ so $x^{\frac{3}{2}} = 8$ and $x = 8^{\frac{2}{3}}$ so $x = 4$

When $x = 4$, $y = y = \frac{4}{4} + \sqrt{4} = 3$

$\frac{d^2y}{dx^2} = 8x^{-3} - 0.25x^{-1.5}$

When $x = 4$, $\frac{d^2y}{dx^2} = 8(4)^{-3} - 0.25(4)^{-1.5} = \frac{3}{32}$ which is > 0

So $(4, 3)$ is a minimum point.

f $y = \frac{x^2 - 5x + 3}{x + 1}$

$$\frac{dy}{dx} = \frac{(x+1)\frac{d}{dx}(x^2 - 5x + 3) - (x^2 - 5x + 3)\frac{d}{dx}(x+1)}{(x+1)^2}$$

$$\frac{dy}{dx} = \frac{(x+1)(2x-5) - (x^2 - 5x + 3)(1)}{(x+1)^2}$$

$$\frac{dy}{dx} = \frac{x^2 + 2x - 8}{(x+1)^2}$$

For stationary points, $\frac{dy}{dx} = 0$.

$$\frac{x^2 + 2x - 8}{(x+1)^2} = 0$$

$$x^2 + 2x - 8 = 0$$

$$(x - 2)(x + 4) = 0$$

$$x = 2 \text{ or } x = -4$$

When $x = 2$, $y = \frac{2^2 - 5(2) + 3}{(2 + 1)} = -1$

When $x = -4$, $y = \frac{(-4)^2 - 5(-4) + 3}{(-4 + 1)} = -13$

The stationary points are $(2, -1)$ and $(-4, -13)$.

$$\frac{d^2y}{dx^2} = \frac{(x+1)^2\frac{d}{dx}(x^2 + 2x - 8) - (x^2 + 2x - 8)\frac{d}{dx}(x+1)^2}{(x+1)^4}$$

$$\frac{d^2y}{dx^2} = \frac{(x+1)^2(2x+2) - (x^2 + 2x - 8)(2)(x+1)^1(1)}{(x+1)^4}$$

$$\frac{d^2y}{dx^2} = \frac{(x+1)^2(2x+2) - 2(x^2 + 2x - 8)(x+1)^1}{(x+1)^4}$$ divide numerator and denominator by $(x + 1)$

$$\frac{d^2y}{dx^2} = \frac{(x+1)(2x+2) - 2(x^2 + 2x - 8)}{(x+1)^3}$$

$$\frac{d^2y}{dx^2} = \frac{2x^2 + 4x + 2 - 2x^2 - 4x + 16}{(x+1)^3}$$

$$\frac{d^2y}{dx^2} = \frac{18}{(x+1)^3}$$

TIP

It is not necessary to simplify $\frac{d^2y}{dx^2}$ before substitution.

When $x = 2$, $\frac{d^2y}{dx^2} = \frac{2}{3}$ which is > 0

When $x = -4$, $\frac{d^2y}{dx^2} = -\frac{2}{3}$ which is < 0

So $(2, -1)$ is a minimum point and $(-4, -13)$ is a maximum point.

3 $y = \frac{2x + 5}{x + 1}$

$\frac{dy}{dx} = \frac{(x + 1)\frac{d}{dx}(2x + 5) - (2x + 5)\frac{d}{dx}(x + 1)}{(x + 1)^2}$

$\frac{dy}{dx} = \frac{(x + 1)(2) - (2x + 5)(1)}{(x + 1)^2}$

$\frac{dy}{dx} = \frac{-3}{(x + 1)^2}$

For stationary points $\frac{dy}{dx} = 0$

$\frac{-3}{(x + 1)^2} = 0$ has no solutions so the curve has no turning points.

4 $y = 2x^3 + ax^2 - 12x + 7$

$\frac{dy}{dx} = 6x^2 + 2ax - 12$

For stationary points, $\frac{dy}{dx} = 0$, so substitute $x = -2$ into $\frac{dy}{dx}$

$6(-2)^2 + 2a(-2) - 12 = 0$

$24 - 4a - 12 = 0$

$a = 3$

5 **a** $y = x^3 + ax + b$

$\frac{dy}{dx} = 3x^2 + a$

If there is a stationary point at (1, 3) then

substitute $x = 1$ into $\frac{dy}{dx} = 0$

$3(1)^2 + a = 0$

$a = -3$

So, $y = x^3 - 3x + b$

Substituting $x = 1$ and $y = 3$ into $y = x^3 - 3x + b$ gives:

$3 = 1^3 - 3(1) + b$

$b = 5$

b $y = x^3 - 3x + 5$

$\frac{dy}{dx} = 3x^2 - 3$

$\frac{d^2y}{dx^2} = 6x$

When $x = 1$, $\frac{d^2y}{dx^2} = 6 \times 1 = 6$ which is > 0

So (1, 3) is a minimum point.

c $y = x^3 - 3x + 5$

$\frac{dy}{dx} = 3x^2 - 3$

For stationary points, $\frac{dy}{dx} = 0$.

$3x^2 - 3 = 0$

$3x^2 = 3$

$x = \pm 1$

The other stationary point is at $x = -1$

Substitute $x = -1$ into $y = x^3 - 3x + 5$

$y = (-1)^3 - 3(-1) + 5 = 7$

The other stationary point is at (−1, 7)

$\frac{d^2y}{dx^2} = 6x$

When $x = -1$, $\frac{d^2y}{dx^2} = -6$ which is < 0

So (−1, 7) is a maximum point.

6 **a** Rewrite $y = x^2 + \frac{a}{x} + b$

$y = x^2 + ax^{-1} + b$

$\frac{dy}{dx} = 2x - ax^{-2}$ or $\frac{dy}{dx} = 2x - \frac{a}{x^2}$

As there is a stationary point at (1, −1),

substitute $x = 1$ into $\frac{dy}{dx} = 0$

$2(1) - \frac{a}{1^2} = 0$

$a = 2$

Substituting $x = 1$ and $y = -1$ into $y = x^2 + \frac{2}{x} + b$ gives:

$-1 = 1^2 + \frac{2}{1} + b$

$b = -4$

b $\frac{dy}{dx} = 2x - \frac{2}{x^2}$ or $\frac{dy}{dx} = 2x - 2x^{-2}$

$\frac{d^2y}{dx^2} = 2 + 4x^{-3}$ or $\frac{d^2y}{dx^2} = 2 + \frac{4}{x^3}$

When $x = 1$, $\frac{d^2y}{dx^2} = 2 + \frac{4}{1^3} = 6$ which is > 0

So $(1, -1)$ is a minimum point.

7 a Rewrite $y = ax + \frac{b}{x^2}$

$y = ax + bx^{-2}$

$\frac{dy}{dx} = a - 2bx^{-3}$ or $\frac{dy}{dx} = a - \frac{2b}{x^3}$

As there is a stationary point at $(-1, -12)$, substitute $x = -1$ into $\frac{dy}{dx} = 0$

$a - \frac{2b}{(-1)^3} = 0$

$a + 2b = 0$ (1)

Substituting $x = -1$ and $y = -12$ into $y = ax + \frac{b}{x^2}$ gives:

$-12 = (-1)a + \frac{b}{(-1)^2}$

$-a + b = -12$ (2)

Adding (1) and (2) gives:

$3b = -12$

$b = -4$

Substitute for b into (1) gives:

$a = 8$

b $\frac{dy}{dx} = 8 + 8x^{-3}$

$\frac{d^2y}{dx^2} = -24x^{-4}$

When $x = -1$, $\frac{d^2y}{dx^2} = -24(-1)^4 = -24$ which is < 0

So $(-1, -12)$ is a maximum point.

8 a $y = 2x^3 - 3x^2 + ax + b$

$\frac{dy}{dx} = 6x^2 - 6x + a$

As there is a stationary point at $(3, -77)$, substitute $x = 3$ into $\frac{dy}{dx} = 0$

$6(3)^2 - 6(3) + a = 0$

$a = -36$

Substitute $x = 3$, $y = -77$ into $y = 2x^3 - 3x^2 - 36x + b$

$-77 = 2(3)^3 - 3(3)^2 - 36(3) + b$

$-77 = 54 - 27 - 108 + b$

$b = 4$

To find the other stationary point, solve $\frac{dy}{dx} = 0$

$6x^2 - 6x - 36 = 0$ divide both sides by 6

$x^2 - x - 6 = 0$ factorise

$(x - 3)(x + 2) = 0$

$x = 3$ or $x = -2$

The other stationary point is at $x = -2$

Substituting $x = -2$ into $y = 2x^3 - 3x^2 - 36x + 4$ gives:

$y = 2(-2)^3 - 3(-2)^2 - 36(-2) + 4 = 48$

$(-2, 48)$ is the other stationary point.

$\frac{d^2y}{dx^2} = 12x - 6$

When $x = 3$, $\frac{d^2y}{dx^2} = 12(3) - 6 = 30$ which is > 0

When $x = -2$, $\frac{d^2y}{dx^2} = 12(-2) - 6 = -30$ which is < 0

$(3, -77)$ is a minimum point and $(-2, 48)$ is a maximum point.

d We want the point on the curve where the **gradient** is a minimum

TIP

Be careful!

Do not confuse the point where the gradient is a minimum with the minimum point on the curve!

$y = 2x^3 - 3x^2 - 36x + 4$

$\frac{dy}{dx} = 6x^2 - 6x - 36$ factorise

$= 6[x^2 - x - 6]$ complete the square

$= 6[(x - 0.5)^2 - 0.5^2 - 6]$

$= 6[(x - 0.5)^2 - 6.25]$

The minimum value of the gradient is the minimum value of $6[(x - 0.5)^2 - 6.25]$

The minimum value of $(x - 0.5)^2$ is zero which occurs when $x = 0.5$

The minimum value of the gradient is $6[0 - 6.25] = -37.5$

Substitute $x = 0.5$ into the equation of the **curve** to find the y-coordinate:

$y = 2(0.5)^3 - 3(0.5)^2 - 36(0.5) + 4 = -14.5$

The point where the gradient has the minimum value is $(0.5, -14.5)$.

Exercise 12.10

1 a $x + y = 8$

$y = 8 - x$

b i $P = xy$

$P = x(8 - x)$ or $P = 8x - x^2$

ii $\frac{dP}{dx} = 8 - 2x$

The maximum value of P occurs when $\frac{dP}{dx} = 0$

$8 - 2x = 0$

$x = 4$

Substituting $x = 4$ into $P = 8x - x^2$ gives:

$P = 8(4) - 4^2 = 16$

Maximum value of P is 16.

c i $S = x^2 + y^2$ substituting $y = 8 - x$ gives:

$S = x^2 + (8 - x)^2$

ii $\frac{dS}{dx} = 4x - 16$

The minimum value of S is when $\frac{dS}{dx} = 0$

$4x - 16 = 0$

$x = 4$

Substitute $x = 4$ into $S = x^2 + (8 - x)^2$

$S = (4)^2 + (8 - 4)^2 = 32$

The minimum value of S is 32

2 a The width of the garden fence is $\frac{100 - x}{2}$ metres.

The area of the rectangular garden is $x \times \frac{(100 - x)}{2}$ metres

So $A = x \times \frac{(100 - x)}{2}$

$A = \frac{1}{2}x(100 - x)$

b The maximum value of A occurs when $\frac{dA}{dx} = 0$

$A = 50x - 0.5x^2$

$\frac{dA}{dx} = 50 - x$

$50 - x = 0$

$x = 50$

Substitute $x = 50$ into $A = \frac{1}{2}x(100 - x)$ gives:

$A = \frac{1}{2} \times 50(100 - 50) = 1250$

The maximum area is $1250\,\text{m}^2$ and occurs when $x = 50$

3 a The volume of the cuboid is $2x \times x \times y = 2x^2y$

$2x^2y = 576$

$y = \frac{288}{x^2}$

b The surface area of the cuboid is $2 \times 2x \times x + 2 \times 2x \times y + 2 \times x \times y$

$A = 4x^2 + 4xy + 2xy$

$A = 4x^2 + 6xy$

Substituting for y gives:

$A = 4x^2 + 6x\left(\frac{288}{x^2}\right)$

$A = 4x^2 + \frac{1728}{x}$

c The maximum value of A occurs when $\frac{dA}{dx} = 0$

$A = 4x^2 + 1728x^{-1}$

$\frac{dA}{dx} = 8x - 1728x^{-2}$ or $\frac{dA}{dx} = 8x - \frac{1728}{x^2}$

$8x - \frac{1728}{x^2} = 0$ multiply both sides by x^2

$8x^3 - 1728 = 0$

$x^3 = 216$

$x = 6$

The dimensions of the cuboid when $x = 6$ are 6 cm by 12 cm by $\frac{288}{6^2} = 8$ cm

Substituting $x = 6$ into $A = 4x^2 + \frac{1728}{x}$ gives:

$A = 4(6)^2 + \frac{1728}{6} = 432$

The maximum value of A is 432 cm^2 when the dimensions are 6 cm by 12 cm by 8 cm

4 a Volume of the cuboid is $V = 4x \times x \times h$

$h = \frac{V}{4x^2}$

b The surface area of the cuboid is 400 cm^2

So, $2 \times 4x \times x + 2 \times 4x \times h + 2 \times x \times h = 400$

$8x^2 + 10hx = 400$ (1)

Substitute for h in (1)

$8x^2 + 10\left(\frac{V}{4x^2}\right)x = 400$

$8x^2 + \frac{5V}{2x} = 400$ multiply both sides by $2x$

$16x^3 + 5V = 800x$ rearrange

$5V = 800x - 16x^3$

$V = 160x - \frac{16}{5}x^3$

c V has a maximum value when $\frac{dV}{dx} = 0$

$\frac{dV}{dx} = 160 - \frac{48}{5}x^2$

$160 - \frac{48}{5}x^2 = 0$

$x^2 = \frac{800}{48}$

$x = \pm\frac{5\sqrt{6}}{3}$ (reject the negative value of x)

$x = \frac{5\sqrt{6}}{3}$

The value of x is $\frac{5\sqrt{6}}{3}$

5 a The length of the arc of the sector $= r\theta$

The perimeter of the sector is $r\theta + 2r$

$r\theta + 2r = 60$

$\theta = \frac{60 - 2r}{r}$ or $\theta = \frac{60}{r} - 2$

b Area of a sector $A = \frac{1}{2}r^2\theta = \frac{1}{2}r^2\left(\frac{60}{r} - 2\right)$

$A = 30r - r^2$

c $\frac{dA}{dr} = 30 - 2r$

$\frac{d^2A}{dr^2} = -2$

d A stationary value of A is when $\frac{dA}{dr} = 0$

$30 - 2r = 0$

$r = 15$

The value of r for which there is a stationary value is 15 cm

e Substituting $r = 15$ into $A = 30r - r^2$ gives:

$A = 30(15) - 15^2$

$A = 225$

$\frac{d^2A}{dr^2} = -2$ which is < 0 so the curve $A = 30r - r^2$ has a maximum value

The maximum value of the area is 225 cm^2

6 a The perimeter of the window is a semi-circle $\frac{2\pi r}{2}$ plus the rectangle $2r + h + h$

$\frac{2\pi r}{2} + 2r + h + h = 6$

$\pi r + 2r + 2h = 6$

$2h = 6 - 2r - \pi r$

$h = 3 - r - \frac{\pi r}{2}$

$h = 3 - \frac{1}{2}r(\pi + 2)$

b The surface area $A = \frac{\pi r^2}{2} + 2r \times h$

Substituting for h in $A = \frac{\pi r^2}{2} + 2r \times h$ gives:

$$A = \frac{\pi r^2}{2} + 2r\left[3 - \frac{1}{2}r(\pi + 2)\right]$$

$$A = \frac{\pi r^2}{2} + 6r - \pi r^2 - 2r^2$$

$$A = 6r - 2r^2 - \frac{1}{2}\pi r^2$$

c $\frac{dA}{dr} = 6 - 4r - \pi r$

$\frac{d^2A}{dr^2} = -4 - \pi$

d There is a stationary value for A when $\frac{dA}{dr} = 0$

$6 - 4r - \pi r = 0$

$r(4 + \pi) = 6$

$r = \frac{6}{4 + \pi}$

e $\frac{d^2A}{dr^2} = -4 - \pi$ is < 0 so the stationary point is a maximum point.

The maximum value of A is found by substituting $r = \frac{6}{4 + \pi}$ into $A = 6r - 2r^2 - \frac{1}{2}\pi r^2$

$$A = 6\left(\frac{6}{4 + \pi}\right) - 2\left(\frac{6}{4 + \pi}\right)^2 - \frac{1}{2}\pi\left(\frac{6}{4 + \pi}\right)^2$$

$$A = \frac{36}{4 + \pi} - \frac{72}{(4 + \pi)^2} - \frac{18\pi}{(4 + \pi)^2}$$

$$A = \frac{36(4 + \pi)}{(4 + \pi)^2} - \frac{72}{(4 + \pi)^2} - \frac{18\pi}{(4 + \pi)^2}$$

$$A = \frac{36(4 + \pi) - 72 - 18\pi}{(4 + \pi)^2}$$

$$A = \frac{144 + 36\pi - 72 - 18\pi}{(4 + \pi)^2}$$

$$A = \frac{72 + 18\pi}{(4 + \pi)^2}$$

$$A = \frac{18(4 + \pi)}{(4 + \pi)^2}$$

The maximum value of A is $\frac{18}{4 + \pi}$ m^2

7 a

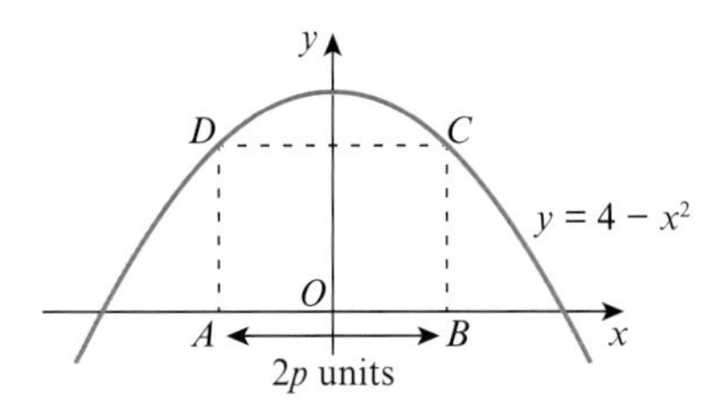

The coordinates of B are $(p, 0)$

Substituting $x = p$ into $y = 4 - x^2$ gives:

$y = 4 - p^2$

So, the coordinates of $BC = (0, 4 - p^2)$

$BC = 4 - p^2$

b The area of the rectangle $ABCD$ is $AB \times BC = 2p \times (4 - p^2) = 2p(4 - p^2)$

c Let A be the area of $ABCD$. A stationary value of A is when $\frac{dA}{dp} = 0$

$A = 2p(4 - p^2)$ expand brackets

$A = 8p - 2p^3$

$\frac{dA}{dp} = 8 - 6p^2$ if $\frac{dA}{dp} = 0$ then:

$8 - 6p^2 = 0$

$p = \pm\sqrt{\frac{4}{3}}$ or $p = \pm\frac{2}{\sqrt{3}}$ or $p = \pm\frac{2\sqrt{3}}{3}$ (reject the negative value)

$p = \frac{2\sqrt{3}}{3}$

d The stationary value of area A is found by substituting $p = \frac{2\sqrt{3}}{3}$ into $A = 2p(4 - p^2)$

$$A = 2 \times \frac{2\sqrt{3}}{3}\left[4 - \left(\frac{2\sqrt{3}}{3}\right)^2\right]$$

$$A = \frac{4\sqrt{3}}{3} \times \frac{8}{3}$$

$$A = \frac{32\sqrt{3}}{9}$$

To determine the nature of this stationary point, find $\frac{d^2A}{dp^2}$

$\frac{dA}{dp} = 8 - 6p^2$

$\frac{d^2A}{dp^2} = -12p$

Substituting $p = \frac{2\sqrt{3}}{3}$ into $\frac{d^2A}{dp^2}$ gives:

$\frac{d^2A}{dp^2} = -12 \times \frac{2\sqrt{3}}{3} = -8\sqrt{3}$ which is < 0

The stationary point is a maximum point.

8 a Volume of a cylinder $= \pi r^2 h$

$\pi r^2 h = 250\pi$ divide both sides by πr^2

$h = \frac{250}{r^2}$

b Total surface area = curved surface area + area of 2 circular ends

$A = 2\pi rh + 2 \times \pi r^2$ substituting $h = \frac{250}{r^2}$ gives:

$A = 2\pi r\left(\frac{250}{r^2}\right) + 2\pi r^2$

$A = 2\pi r^2 + \frac{500\pi}{r}$ or $A = 2\pi r^2 + 500\pi r^{-1}$

c $\frac{dA}{dr} = 4\pi r - 500\pi r^{-2}$

$\frac{dA}{dr} = 4\pi r - \frac{500\pi}{r^2}$

$\frac{d^2A}{dr^2} = 4\pi + 1000\pi r^{-3}$

$\frac{d^2A}{dr^2} = 4\pi + \frac{1000\pi}{r^3}$

d There is a stationary value for A when $\frac{dA}{dr} = 0$

$4\pi r - \frac{500\pi}{r^2} = 0$ multiply both sides by r^2

$4\pi r^3 - 500\pi = 0$

$4r^3 = 500$

$r^3 = 125$

$r = 5$

e Substitute $r = 5$ into $A = 2\pi r^2 + \frac{500\pi}{r}$

$A = 2\pi(5)^2 + \frac{500\pi}{5}$

$A = 150\pi$

Substituting $r = 5$ into $\frac{d^2A}{dr^2} = 4\pi + \frac{1000\pi}{r^3}$ gives:

$\frac{d^2A}{dr^2} = 4\pi + \frac{1000\pi}{5^3} = 12\pi$ which is > 0

So the stationary point is a minimum point.

9 a The total surface area of a solid is made up of: curved surface of the cylinder + hemispherical curved surface + circular base

$2\pi rh + \frac{4\pi r^2}{2} + \pi r^2$

$2\pi rh + 3\pi r^2 = 288\pi$

$2\pi rh = 288\pi - 3\pi r^2$ divide both sides by $2\pi r$

$h = \frac{144}{r} - \frac{3}{2}r$

b Volume of the solid = volume of the cylinder + volume of the hemisphere

$V = \pi r^2 h + \frac{1}{2}\left(\frac{4}{3}\pi r^3\right)$ substituting for h gives:

$V = \pi r^2\left(\frac{144}{r} - \frac{3}{2}r\right) + \frac{2}{3}\pi r^3$

$V = 144\pi r - \frac{3\pi r^3}{2} + \frac{2\pi r^3}{3}$

$V = 144\pi r - \frac{5}{6}\pi r^3$

c A stationary value of V occurs when $\frac{dV}{dr} = 0$

$\frac{dV}{dr} = 144\pi - \frac{5}{2}\pi r^2$

$144\pi - \frac{5}{2}\pi r^2 = 0$

$\frac{5}{2}\pi r^2 = 144\pi$

$r^2 = \frac{288}{5}$

$r = \frac{12\sqrt{10}}{5}$

$\frac{d^2V}{dr^2} = 144\pi - \frac{5}{2}\pi r^2$

When $r = \frac{12\sqrt{10}}{5}$, $\frac{d^2V}{dr^2} = -5\pi\left(\frac{12\sqrt{10}}{5}\right)^2$

$= -288\pi$ which is < 0

So V is a maximum when $r = \frac{12\sqrt{10}}{5}$

10 a Total length of the wire is $4x + 2\pi r$

$4x + 2\pi r = 50$

$2\pi r = 50 - 4x$

$r = \frac{25 - 2x}{\pi}$

b Total area enclosed is $x^2 + \pi r^2$

$A = x^2 + \pi r^2$ substitute for r

$A = x^2 + \pi\left(\frac{25 - 2x}{\pi}\right)^2$

$A = x^2 + \frac{625 - 100x + 4x^2}{\pi}$

$A = \frac{\pi x^2 + 625 - 100x + 4x^2}{\pi}$

$A = \frac{(\pi + 4)x^2 - 100x + 625}{\pi}$

c A stationary value of A is when $\frac{dA}{dx} = 0$

$A = \frac{1}{\pi}[(\pi + 4)x^2 - 100x + 625]$

$\frac{dA}{dx} = \frac{1}{\pi}[(2\pi + 8)x - 100]$

$\frac{1}{\pi}[(2\pi + 8)x - 100] = 0$ multiply both sides by π

$(2\pi + 8)x - 100 = 0$

$x = \frac{100}{2\pi + 8}$

$x = \frac{50}{\pi + 4}$

$x = 7.00$ (3 significant figures)

$A = \frac{(\pi + 4)x^2 - 100x + 625}{\pi}$

substituting $x = 7.00$ gives:

$A = \frac{(\pi + 4)(7.00)^2 - 100(7.00) + 625}{\pi}$

$= 87.5$ (3 significant figures)

The stationary value is $A = 87.5\,\text{cm}^2$ when $x = 7.00\,\text{cm}$

11 a Using Pythagoras' theorem, $h^2 + r^2 = 5^2$

So $r^2 = 25 - h^2$

$r = \sqrt{25 - h^2}$

b Volume of the cylinder $= \pi r^2 h$ substitute $h = 2h$

$V = \pi r^2(2h)$

$V = 2\pi r^2 h$ substitute $r^2 = 25 - h^2$ gives:

$V = 2\pi h(25 - h^2)$

c A stationary value of V is when $\frac{dV}{dh} = 0$

$V = 50\pi h - 2\pi h^3$

$\frac{dV}{dh} = 50\pi - 6\pi h^2$

$50\pi - 6\pi h^2 = 0$

$6\pi h^2 = 50\pi$

$h = \frac{5}{\sqrt{3}}$ or $\frac{5\sqrt{3}}{3}$ cm

d To find the nature of the stationary value find $\frac{d^2V}{dh^2}$

$\frac{d^2V}{dh^2} = -12\pi h$

When $h = \frac{5\sqrt{3}}{3}$, $\frac{d^2V}{dh^2} = -12\pi\left(\frac{5\sqrt{3}}{3}\right) = -20\pi\sqrt{3}$

which is < 0

So, the stationary value is a maximum.

12 a Using similar triangles:

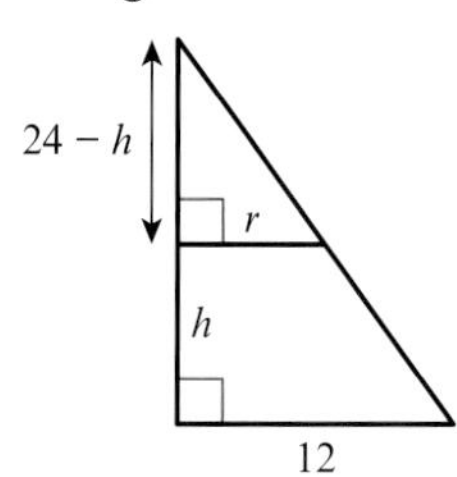

$\frac{24}{12} = \frac{24 - h}{r}$

$2r = 24 - h$

$h = 24 - 2r$

b Volume of the cylinder $= \pi r^2 h$ substitute $h = 24 - 2r$

$V = \pi r^2(24 - 2r)$

$V = 2\pi r^2(12 - r)$

c Find $\frac{dV}{dr} = 48\pi r - 6\pi r^2$

The largest value of V is when there is a stationary value of V, so find the value of V when $\frac{dV}{dr} = 0$.

$48\pi r - 6\pi r^2 = 0$

$6\pi r(8 - r) = 0$

$6\pi r = 0$ or $8 - r = 0$

$r = 0$ (reject) or $r = 8$

Substituting $r = 8$ into $V = 2\pi r^2(12 - r)$ gives:

$V = 2\pi(8)^2(12 - 8) = 512\pi$

To find the largest cylinder, find $\frac{d^2A}{dr^2}$

$\frac{d^2V}{dr^2} = 48\pi - 12\pi r$

When $r = 8$, $\frac{d^2V}{dr^2} = 48\pi - 12\pi(8) = -48\pi$ which is < 0

So 512π cm³ is the volume of the largest cylinder which fits inside the cone.

13 a Let C be the centre of the sphere.

Using Pythagoras' theorem:

$(h - 10)^2 + r^2 = 10^2$

$h^2 - 20h + 100 + r^2 = 100$

$r^2 = 20h - h^2$

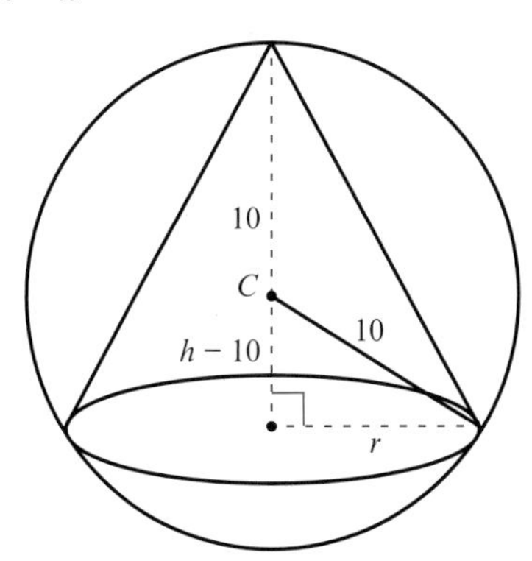

$r = \sqrt{20h - h^2}$

b Volume of the cone $= \frac{1}{3}\pi r^2 h$

$V = \frac{1}{3}\pi(20h - h^2)h$

$V = \frac{1}{3}\pi h^2(20 - h)$

c There is a stationary value for V when $\frac{dV}{dh} = 0$

$$V = \frac{20}{3}\pi h^2 - \frac{1}{3}\pi h^3$$

$$\frac{dV}{dh} = \frac{40}{3}\pi h - \pi h^2$$

$\frac{40}{3}\pi h - \pi h^2 = 0$

$h\left(\frac{40}{3}\pi - \pi h\right) = 0$

$h = 0$ (reject) or $\frac{40}{3}\pi - \pi h = 0$

$\pi h = \frac{40}{3}\pi$

$h = \frac{40}{3}$ or $h = 13\frac{1}{3}$

d To determine the nature of the stationary value, find $\frac{d^2V}{dh^2}$

$\frac{d^2V}{dh^2} = \frac{40}{3}\pi - 2\pi h$

When $h = \frac{40}{3}$, $\frac{d^2V}{dh^2} = \frac{40}{3}\pi - 2\pi\left(\frac{40}{3}\right) = -\frac{40}{3}\pi$

which is < 0

So $h = \frac{40}{3}$ gives a maximum volume.

Substituting $h = \frac{40}{3}$ into $V = \frac{20}{3}\pi h^2 - \frac{1}{3}\pi h^3$ gives:

$V = \frac{20}{3}\pi\left(\frac{40}{3}\right)^2 - \frac{1}{3}\pi\left(\frac{40}{3}\right)^3$

$V = \frac{32000}{27}\pi - \frac{64000}{81}\pi = \frac{32000}{81}\pi$

The maximum value $V = \frac{32000}{81}\pi$ cm³ which occurs when $h = 13\frac{1}{3}$ cm

Chapter 13: Vectors

Exercise 13.1

REMEMBER

A vector of unit length is called a **unit vector**.

1 b $\overrightarrow{AC} = 3\mathbf{i} - 2\mathbf{j}$

h $\overrightarrow{DB} = -3\mathbf{i} - 2\mathbf{j}$

2 c Using Pythagoras, $\sqrt{(5)^2 + (-12)^2} = \sqrt{169} = 13$

g Using Pythagoras, $\sqrt{(-4)^2 + (4)^2} = \sqrt{32} = 4\sqrt{2}$

3 Using Pythagoras, the magnitude of $4\mathbf{i} + 3\mathbf{j}$ is

$\sqrt{(4)^2 + (3)^2} = \sqrt{25} = 5$ units

The magnitude of $\overrightarrow{AB} = 20$ units $= 4 \times 5$
$= 4 \times (4\mathbf{i} + 3\mathbf{j}) = 16\mathbf{i} + 12\mathbf{j}$

4 Using Pythagoras, the magnitude of $12\mathbf{i} - 5\mathbf{j}$ is

$\sqrt{(12)^2 + (-5)^2} = \sqrt{169} = 13$ units

The magnitude of $\overrightarrow{PQ} = 39$ units $= 3 \times 13$
$= 3 \times (12\mathbf{i} - 5\mathbf{j}) = 36\mathbf{i} - 15\mathbf{j}$

5 c First find the length of the vector $-4\mathbf{i} - 3\mathbf{j}$

length$^2 = (-4)^2 + (-3)^2$ using Pythagoras

length = 5

Hence the unit vector in the same direction is:

$\frac{1}{5}(-4\mathbf{i} - 3\mathbf{j})$ or $-\frac{1}{5}(4\mathbf{i} + 3\mathbf{j})$

e First find the length of the vector $3\mathbf{i} + 3\mathbf{j}$

length$^2 = 3^2 + 3^2$ using Pythagoras

length $= 3\sqrt{2}$

Hence the unit vector in the same direction is:

$\frac{1}{3\sqrt{2}}(3\mathbf{i} + 3\mathbf{j}) = \frac{\sqrt{2}}{6}(3\mathbf{i} + 3\mathbf{j}) = \frac{\sqrt{2}}{2}(\mathbf{i} + \mathbf{j})$

6 c $\frac{1}{2}\mathbf{p} - 3\mathbf{r} = \frac{1}{2}(8\mathbf{i} - 6\mathbf{j}) - 3(10\mathbf{i}) = -26\mathbf{i} - 3\mathbf{j}$

d $\frac{1}{2}\mathbf{r} - \mathbf{p} - \mathbf{q} = \frac{1}{2}(10\mathbf{i}) - (8\mathbf{i} - 6\mathbf{j}) - (-2\mathbf{i} + 3\mathbf{j})$

$= -\mathbf{i} + 3\mathbf{j}$

7 a $|\mathbf{p} + \mathbf{q}| = |9\mathbf{i} + 12\mathbf{j} + 3\mathbf{i} - 3\mathbf{j}| = |12\mathbf{i} + 9\mathbf{j}|$

$= \sqrt{(12)^2 + (9)^2} = \sqrt{225} = 15$

b $|\mathbf{p} + \mathbf{q} + \mathbf{r}| = |9\mathbf{i} + 12\mathbf{j} + 3\mathbf{i} - 3\mathbf{j} + 7\mathbf{i} + \mathbf{j}|$

$= |19\mathbf{i} + 10\mathbf{j}| = \sqrt{(19)^2 + (10)^2} = \sqrt{461}$

8 $\lambda\mathbf{p} + \mathbf{q} = 36\mathbf{i} - 13\mathbf{j}$

$\lambda(7\mathbf{i} - 2\mathbf{j}) + (\mathbf{i} + \mu\mathbf{j}) = 36\mathbf{i} - 13\mathbf{j}$

Equating the **i**'s gives

$7\lambda + 1 = 36$

$\lambda = 5$

Equating the **j**'s gives

$-2\lambda + \mu = -13$ substitute for λ

$-2(5) + \mu = -13$

$-10 + \mu = -13$

$\mu = -3$

So $\lambda = 5$, $\mu = -3$.

9 $\mathbf{a} = 5\mathbf{i} - 6\mathbf{j}$, $\mathbf{b} = -\mathbf{i} + 2\mathbf{j}$ and $\mathbf{c} = -13\mathbf{i} + 18\mathbf{j}$.

Find λ and μ such that $\lambda\mathbf{a} + \mu\mathbf{b} = \mathbf{c}$.

$\lambda\mathbf{a} + \mu\mathbf{b} = \mathbf{c}$

$\lambda(5\mathbf{i} - 6\mathbf{j}) + \mu(-\mathbf{i} + 2\mathbf{j}) = -13\mathbf{i} + 18\mathbf{j}$

Equating the **i**'s gives

$5\lambda - \mu = -13$ [1]

Equating the **j**'s gives

$-6\lambda + 2\mu = 18$

$-3\lambda + \mu = 9$ [2]

Adding equations [1] and [2] gives

$2\lambda = -4$

$\lambda = -2$

Substituting for λ in equation [1] gives

$5(-2) - \mu = -13$

$-\mu = -3$

$\mu = 3$

So $\lambda = -2$, $\mu = 3$.

Exercise 13.2

REMEMBER

$\overrightarrow{AB} = \overrightarrow{OB} - \overrightarrow{OA}$ or $\overrightarrow{AB} = \mathbf{b} - \mathbf{a}$

TIP

A vector written in component form $a\mathbf{i} + b\mathbf{j}$ is equivalent to the vector $\begin{pmatrix} a \\ b \end{pmatrix}$. There is no need to convert between forms as they are equivalent, however it is best practice to answer in the same form that the question is given in. In the solutions below you will occasionally see both forms given, however this is only to demonstrate possible solutions – you only need to write one of them.

1 b $A(0, 6)$ and $B(2, -4)$

$\overrightarrow{AB} = \overrightarrow{OB} - \overrightarrow{OA}$ — $\overrightarrow{OB} = 2\mathbf{i} - 4\mathbf{j}$ and $\overrightarrow{OA} = 0\mathbf{i} - 4\mathbf{j}$

$= (2\mathbf{i} - 4\mathbf{j}) - (0\mathbf{i} + 6\mathbf{j})$ — collect $\mathbf{i}$'s and $\mathbf{j}$'s

$\overrightarrow{AB} = 2\mathbf{i} - 10\mathbf{j}$

f $A(5, -6)$ and $B(-1, -7)$

$\overrightarrow{AB} = \overrightarrow{OB} - \overrightarrow{OA}$ — $\overrightarrow{OB} = -\mathbf{i} - 7\mathbf{j}$ and $\overrightarrow{OA} = 5\mathbf{i} - 6\mathbf{j}$

$= (-\mathbf{i} - 7\mathbf{j}) - (5\mathbf{i} - 6\mathbf{j})$ — collect $\mathbf{i}$'s and $\mathbf{j}$'s

$\overrightarrow{AB} = -6\mathbf{i} - \mathbf{j}$

2 a $\overrightarrow{PQ} = 3\mathbf{i} + 5\mathbf{j}$

$\overrightarrow{PQ} = \overrightarrow{OQ} - \overrightarrow{OP}$

$\overrightarrow{OQ} = \overrightarrow{OP} + \overrightarrow{PQ}$ — $\overrightarrow{OP} = \mathbf{i} + 5\mathbf{j}$ and $\overrightarrow{PQ} = 3\mathbf{i} + 5\mathbf{j}$

$= (\mathbf{i} + 5\mathbf{j}) + (3\mathbf{i} + 5\mathbf{j})$ — collect $\mathbf{i}$'s and $\mathbf{j}$'s

$\overrightarrow{OQ} = 4\mathbf{i} + 10\mathbf{j}$

b $\overrightarrow{EF} = \overrightarrow{OF} - \overrightarrow{OE}$

$\overrightarrow{OF} = \overrightarrow{EF} + \overrightarrow{OE}$ — $\overrightarrow{EF} = -2\mathbf{i} + 7\mathbf{j}$ and $\overrightarrow{OE} = -3\mathbf{i} + 4\mathbf{j}$

$= (-2\mathbf{i} + 7\mathbf{j}) + (-3\mathbf{i} + 4\mathbf{j})$ — collect $\mathbf{i}$'s and $\mathbf{j}$'s

$\overrightarrow{OF} = -5\mathbf{i} + 11\mathbf{j}$

c $\overrightarrow{NM} = \overrightarrow{OM} - \overrightarrow{ON}$

$\overrightarrow{ON} = \overrightarrow{OM} - \overrightarrow{NM}$ — $\overrightarrow{OM} = 4\mathbf{i} - 2\mathbf{j}$ and $\overrightarrow{NM} = 3\mathbf{i} - 5\mathbf{j}$

$= 4\mathbf{i} - 2\mathbf{j} - (3\mathbf{i} - 5\mathbf{j})$ — collect $\mathbf{i}$'s and $\mathbf{j}$'s

$\overrightarrow{ON} = \mathbf{i} + 3\mathbf{j}$

3 a The vector $-3\mathbf{i} + 4\mathbf{j}$ has a magnitude

$\sqrt{(-3)^2 + (4)^2} = \sqrt{25} = 5$.

$\overrightarrow{OA}$ has a magnitude 25 units
$= 5 \times 5 = 5 \times (-3\mathbf{i} + 4\mathbf{j}) = -15\mathbf{i} + 20\mathbf{j}$

b The vector $12\mathbf{i} + 5\mathbf{j}$ has a magnitude

$\sqrt{(12)^2 + (5)^2} = \sqrt{169} = 13$.

$\overrightarrow{OB}$ has a magnitude 26 units
$= 2 \times 13 = 2 \times (12\mathbf{i} + 5\mathbf{j}) = 24\mathbf{i} + 10\mathbf{j}$

c $\overrightarrow{AB} = \overrightarrow{OB} - \overrightarrow{OA}$

$= 24\mathbf{i} + 10\mathbf{j} - (-15\mathbf{i} + 20\mathbf{j})$ collect i's and j's

$\overrightarrow{AB} = 39\mathbf{i} - 10\mathbf{j}$

d $|\overrightarrow{AB}| = \sqrt{(39)^2 + (-10)^2} = \sqrt{1621}$

4 a $\overrightarrow{OA} = -7\mathbf{i} - 7\mathbf{j}$

$\overrightarrow{OB} = 9\mathbf{i} + 5\mathbf{j}$

$\overrightarrow{AB} = \overrightarrow{OB} - \overrightarrow{OA}$

$\overrightarrow{AB} = 9\mathbf{i} + 5\mathbf{j} - (-7\mathbf{i} - 7\mathbf{j})$ collect i's and j's

$\overrightarrow{AB} = 16\mathbf{i} + 12\mathbf{j}$

b First find the length of the vector $\overrightarrow{AB} = 16\mathbf{i} + 12\mathbf{j}$

$\text{length}^2 = (16)^2 + (12)^2$ using Pythagoras

length = 20

Hence the unit vector in the same direction is:

$\frac{1}{20}(16\mathbf{i} + 12\mathbf{j})$ or $\frac{1}{5}(4\mathbf{i} + 3\mathbf{j})$

c If $\overrightarrow{AC} = 3\overrightarrow{CB}$ then $\overrightarrow{AC} = \frac{3}{4}\overrightarrow{AB} = 12\mathbf{i} + 9\mathbf{j}$

$\overrightarrow{AC} = \overrightarrow{OC} - \overrightarrow{OA}$

$\overrightarrow{OC} = \overrightarrow{OA} + \overrightarrow{AC}$

$= -7\mathbf{i} - 7\mathbf{j} + 12\mathbf{i} + 9\mathbf{j}$

$\overrightarrow{OC} = 5\mathbf{i} + 2\mathbf{j}$

5 a $\overrightarrow{OP} = -2\mathbf{i} - 4\mathbf{j}$, $\overrightarrow{OQ} = 8\mathbf{i} + 20\mathbf{j}$

$\overrightarrow{PQ} = \overrightarrow{OQ} - \overrightarrow{OP}$

$= 8\mathbf{i} + 20\mathbf{j} - (-2\mathbf{i} - 4\mathbf{j})$ collect i's and j's

$\overrightarrow{PQ} = 10\mathbf{i} + 24\mathbf{j}$

b $|\overrightarrow{PQ}| = \sqrt{(10)^2 + (24)^2} = \sqrt{676} = 26$.

c $|\overrightarrow{PQ}| = 26$

Hence the unit vector in the same direction is:

$\frac{1}{26}(10\mathbf{i} + 24\mathbf{j})$ or $\frac{1}{13}(5\mathbf{i} + 12\mathbf{j})$

d $\overrightarrow{PM} = \frac{1}{2}\overrightarrow{PQ} = 5\mathbf{i} + 12\mathbf{j}$

$\overrightarrow{OM} = \overrightarrow{OP} + \overrightarrow{PM}$

$\overrightarrow{OM} = -2\mathbf{i} - 4\mathbf{j} + 5\mathbf{i} + 12\mathbf{j}$ collect i's and j's

$\overrightarrow{OM} = 3\mathbf{i} + 8\mathbf{j}$

6 $\overrightarrow{OA} = 4\mathbf{i} - 2\mathbf{j}$

$\overrightarrow{OB} = \lambda\mathbf{i} + 2\mathbf{j}$

$\overrightarrow{AB} = \overrightarrow{OB} - \overrightarrow{OA}$

$\overrightarrow{AB} = \lambda\mathbf{i} + 2\mathbf{j} - (4\mathbf{i} - 2\mathbf{j}) = (\lambda - 4)\mathbf{i} + 4\mathbf{j}$

Comparing the unit vector of $\overrightarrow{AB} = 0.3\mathbf{i} + 0.4\mathbf{j}$ with

$\overrightarrow{AB} = (\lambda - 4)\mathbf{i} + 4\mathbf{j}$

$\frac{\lambda - 4}{0.3} = \frac{4}{0.4}$ solve:

$0.4(\lambda - 4) = 4 \times 0.3$

$0.4\lambda - 1.6 = 1.2$

$\lambda = 7$

7 a $\overrightarrow{OA} = -10\mathbf{i} + 10\mathbf{j}$

$\overrightarrow{OB} = 10\mathbf{i} - 11\mathbf{j}$

$\overrightarrow{AB} = \overrightarrow{OB} - \overrightarrow{OA}$

$= (10\mathbf{i} - 11\mathbf{j}) - (-10\mathbf{i} + 10\mathbf{j})$

$\overrightarrow{AB} = 20\mathbf{i} - 21\mathbf{j}$ or $\begin{pmatrix} 20 \\ -21 \end{pmatrix}$

b If $\overrightarrow{AC} = 2\overrightarrow{AB}$ then:

$\overrightarrow{AC} = 2(20\mathbf{i} - 21\mathbf{j})$

$\overrightarrow{AB} = \overrightarrow{BC} = 20\mathbf{i} - 21\mathbf{j}$ or $\begin{pmatrix} 20 \\ -21 \end{pmatrix}$

So C is at $(30, -32)$

The position vector of point C is $30\mathbf{i} - 32\mathbf{j}$

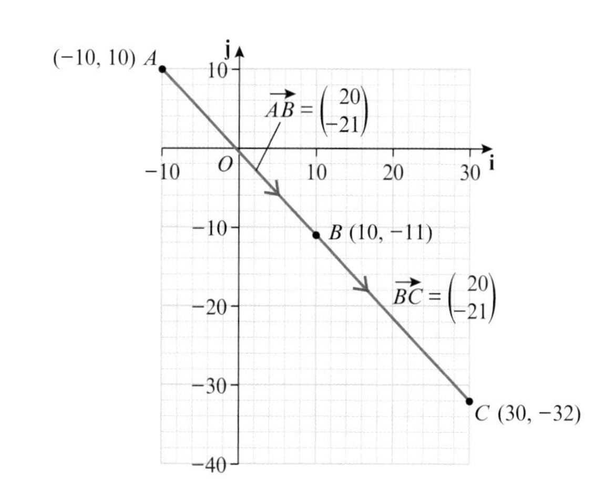

8 a i $\overrightarrow{OA} = \begin{pmatrix} 21 \\ -20 \end{pmatrix} = 21\mathbf{i} - 20\mathbf{j}$

$|21\mathbf{i} - 20\mathbf{j}| = \sqrt{(21)^2 + (-20)^2} = \sqrt{841} = 29$

ii $\overrightarrow{OB} = \begin{pmatrix} 24 \\ 18 \end{pmatrix} = 24\mathbf{i} + 18\mathbf{j}$

$|\overrightarrow{OB}| = \sqrt{(24)^2 + (18)^2} = \sqrt{900} = 30$

iii $\overrightarrow{AB} = \overrightarrow{OB} - \overrightarrow{OA}$

$\overrightarrow{AB} = 24\mathbf{i} + 18\mathbf{j} - (21\mathbf{i} - 20\mathbf{j}) = 3\mathbf{i} + 38\mathbf{j}$

$|\overrightarrow{AB}| = \sqrt{(3)^2 + (38)^2}$

$= \sqrt{1453} = 38.1$ to 3 s.f.

b If $\overrightarrow{AC} = \overrightarrow{CB}$ then AC is parallel to CB and is the same length

Point C is the midpoint of AB.

$\overrightarrow{AC} = \overrightarrow{CB} = 1.5\mathbf{i} + 19\mathbf{j}$

$\overrightarrow{OC} = \overrightarrow{OB} - \overrightarrow{CB}$

$\overrightarrow{OC} = 24\mathbf{i} + 18\mathbf{j} - (1.5\mathbf{i} + 19\mathbf{j})$

$\overrightarrow{OC} = 22.5\mathbf{i} - \mathbf{j}$ or $\begin{pmatrix} 22.5 \\ -1 \end{pmatrix}$

9 a $\overrightarrow{OA} = 3\mathbf{i} - 2\mathbf{j}$

$\overrightarrow{OB} = 15\mathbf{i} + 7\mathbf{j}$

$\overrightarrow{AB} = \overrightarrow{OB} - \overrightarrow{OA}$

$\overrightarrow{AB} = 15\mathbf{i} + 7\mathbf{j} - (3\mathbf{i} - 2\mathbf{j})$

$\overrightarrow{AB} = 12\mathbf{i} + 9\mathbf{j}$

b $\overrightarrow{AC} = \frac{1}{3}\overrightarrow{AB}$

$\overrightarrow{AC} = \frac{1}{3}(12\mathbf{i} + 9\mathbf{j}) = 4\mathbf{i} + 3\mathbf{j}$

$\overrightarrow{OC} = \overrightarrow{OA} + \overrightarrow{AC}$

$\overrightarrow{OC} = 3\mathbf{i} - 2\mathbf{j} + (4\mathbf{i} + 3\mathbf{j})$

$\overrightarrow{OC} = 7\mathbf{i} + \mathbf{j}$

10 a $\overrightarrow{OA} = 6\mathbf{i} + 6\mathbf{j}$

$\overrightarrow{OB} = 12\mathbf{i} - 2\mathbf{j}$

$\overrightarrow{AB} = \overrightarrow{OB} - \overrightarrow{OA}$

$\overrightarrow{AB} = 12\mathbf{i} - 2\mathbf{j} - (6\mathbf{i} + 6\mathbf{j})$

$\overrightarrow{AB} = 6\mathbf{i} - 8\mathbf{j}$

b $\overrightarrow{AC} = \frac{3}{4}\overrightarrow{AB}$

$\overrightarrow{AC} = \frac{3}{4}(6\mathbf{i} - 8\mathbf{j}) = 4.5\mathbf{i} - 6\mathbf{j}$

$\overrightarrow{OC} = \overrightarrow{OA} + \overrightarrow{AC}$

$\overrightarrow{OC} = 6\mathbf{i} + 6\mathbf{j} + (4.5\mathbf{i} - 6\mathbf{j})$

$\overrightarrow{OC} = 10.5\mathbf{i}$

11 $\overrightarrow{OA} = 3\mathbf{i} + 4\mathbf{j}$

$\overrightarrow{OB} = 5\mathbf{i} + 5\mathbf{j}$

If $\overrightarrow{BC} = 2\overrightarrow{AB}$ then A, B and C lie on a straight line

$\overrightarrow{AB} = \overrightarrow{OB} - \overrightarrow{OA}$

$\overrightarrow{AB} = 5\mathbf{i} + 5\mathbf{j} - (3\mathbf{i} + 4\mathbf{j})$

$\overrightarrow{AB} = 2\mathbf{i} + \mathbf{j}$

$\overrightarrow{BC} = 4\mathbf{i} + 2\mathbf{j}$

$\overrightarrow{OC} = \overrightarrow{OB} + \overrightarrow{BC}$

$\overrightarrow{OC} = 5\mathbf{i} + 5\mathbf{j} + 4\mathbf{i} + 2\mathbf{j}$

$\overrightarrow{OC} = 9\mathbf{i} + 7\mathbf{j}$ or $\begin{pmatrix} 9 \\ 7 \end{pmatrix}$

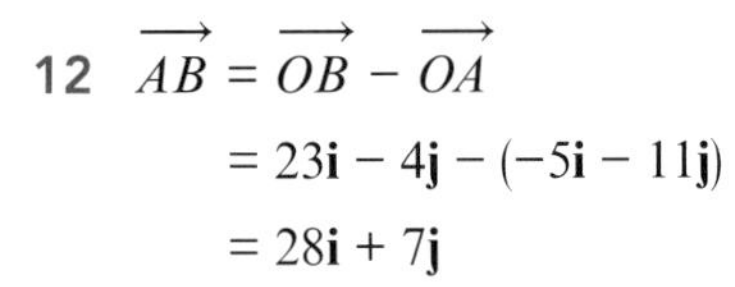

12 $\overrightarrow{AB} = \overrightarrow{OB} - \overrightarrow{OA}$

$= 23\mathbf{i} - 4\mathbf{j} - (-5\mathbf{i} - 11\mathbf{j})$

$= 28\mathbf{i} + 7\mathbf{j}$

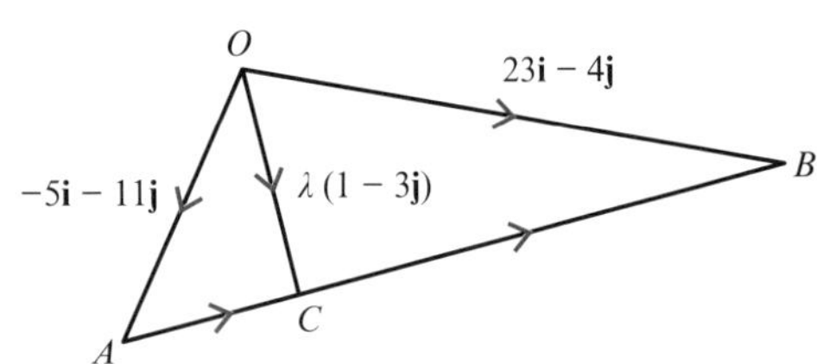

If C lies on AB then $\overrightarrow{AC} = k\overrightarrow{AB}$

$\overrightarrow{AC} = \overrightarrow{OC} - \overrightarrow{OA}$

$= \lambda(\mathbf{i} - 3\mathbf{j}) - (-5\mathbf{i} - 11\mathbf{j})$

$= \lambda\mathbf{i} - 3\lambda\mathbf{j} + 5\mathbf{i} + 11\mathbf{j}$

$\overrightarrow{AC} = (\lambda + 5)\mathbf{i} + (-3\lambda + 11)\mathbf{j}$

$k\overrightarrow{AB} = k(28\mathbf{i} + 7\mathbf{j})$

$= 28k\mathbf{i} + 7k\mathbf{j}$

Hence $(\lambda + 5)\mathbf{i} + (-3\lambda + 11)\mathbf{j} = 28k\mathbf{i} + 7k\mathbf{j}$

Equating the **i**'s gives: $\lambda + 5 = 28k$ (1)

Equating the **j**'s gives: $-3\lambda + 11 = 7k$ (2)

Multiplying (2) by 4 and subtracting from (1) gives:

$\lambda = 3$

13 a $|\overrightarrow{AC}| = 17$ [The AC in the question means the magnitude of AC]

$\overrightarrow{AC} = \overrightarrow{OC} - \overrightarrow{OA}$

$= 6\mathbf{i} + \lambda\mathbf{j} - (-2\mathbf{i} + 7\mathbf{j})$

$= 8\mathbf{i} + (\lambda - 7)\mathbf{j}$

$|\overrightarrow{AC}| = \sqrt{8^2 + (\lambda - 7)^2} = 17$

$8^2 + (\lambda - 7)^2 = 289$

$(\lambda - 7)^2 = 225$

$\lambda - 7 = \pm 15$

$\lambda = -8$ or 22

b When ABC is a straight line, AB is parallel to BC (or AC)

$\overrightarrow{AB} = \overrightarrow{OB} - \overrightarrow{OA}$

$= 2\mathbf{i} - \mathbf{j} - (-2\mathbf{i} + 7\mathbf{j})$

$= 4\mathbf{i} - 8\mathbf{j}$

$\overrightarrow{AC} = 8\mathbf{i} + (\lambda - 7)\mathbf{j}$

If AB is parallel to AC then the coefficients of **i** and **j** should be in the same proportion.

So, $\frac{8}{4} = \frac{\lambda - 7}{-8}$

$-16 = \lambda - 7$

$\lambda = -9$

c If ABC is a right-angle, then AB and BC are perpendicular.

Given the position vectors of A and B, represent points A and B on **i**, **j** coordinate axes.

Draw a line perpendicular to AB at B.

We know that the position vector of C is $\overrightarrow{OC} = 6\mathbf{i} + \lambda\mathbf{j}$

So, C must have coordinates (6, 1)

So, $\lambda = 1$

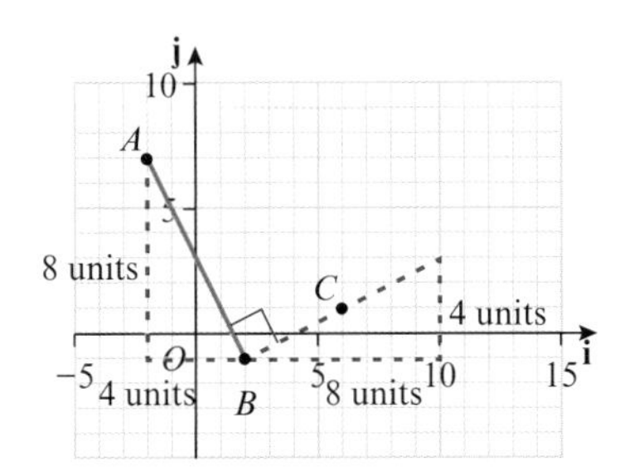

14 $\overrightarrow{OA} = -6\mathbf{i} + 4\mathbf{j}$

$\overrightarrow{OB} = 18\mathbf{i} + 6\mathbf{j}$

$\overrightarrow{OC} = \overrightarrow{OA} + \lambda\overrightarrow{OB}$

$\overrightarrow{OC} = -6\mathbf{i} + 4\mathbf{j} + \lambda(18\mathbf{i} + 6\mathbf{j})$

$= (-6 + 18\lambda)\mathbf{i} + (4 + 6\lambda)\mathbf{j}$

If C lies on the y-axis, $(-6 + 18\lambda) = 0$ so $\lambda = \frac{1}{3}$

$\overrightarrow{OC} = \left(4 + 6 \times \frac{1}{3}\right)\mathbf{j}$

$\overrightarrow{OC} = 6\mathbf{j}$

15 $\overrightarrow{OP} = 8\mathbf{i} + 3\mathbf{j}$

$\overrightarrow{OQ} = -12\mathbf{i} - 7\mathbf{j}$

$\overrightarrow{OR} = \overrightarrow{OP} + \mu\overrightarrow{OQ}$

$\overrightarrow{OR} = 8\mathbf{i} + 3\mathbf{j} + \mu(-12\mathbf{i} - 7\mathbf{j})$

$= (8 - 12\mu)\mathbf{i} + (3 - 7\mu)\mathbf{j}$

If R lies on the x-axis, $(3 - 7\mu) = 0$ so $\mu = \frac{3}{7}$

$\overrightarrow{OR} = \left(8 - 12 \times \frac{3}{7}\right)\mathbf{i}$

$\overrightarrow{OR} = \frac{20}{7}\mathbf{i}$

16 a $\overrightarrow{OP} = -6\mathbf{i} + 8\mathbf{j}$

$\overrightarrow{OQ} = -4\mathbf{i} + 2\mathbf{j}$

$\overrightarrow{OR} = 5\mathbf{i} + 5\mathbf{j}$

i $\overrightarrow{PQ} = \overrightarrow{OQ} - \overrightarrow{OP}$

$= -4\mathbf{i} + 2\mathbf{j} - (-6\mathbf{i} + 8\mathbf{j})$

$= 2\mathbf{i} - 6\mathbf{j}$

$|\overrightarrow{PQ}| = \sqrt{2^2 + (-6)^2} = \sqrt{40} = 2\sqrt{10}$

ii $\overrightarrow{PR} = \overrightarrow{OR} - \overrightarrow{OP}$

$= 5\mathbf{i} + 5\mathbf{j} - (-6\mathbf{i} + 8\mathbf{j})$

$= 11\mathbf{i} - 3\mathbf{j}$

$|\overrightarrow{PR}| = \sqrt{11^2 + (-3)^2} = \sqrt{130}$

iii $\overrightarrow{QR} = \overrightarrow{OR} - \overrightarrow{OQ}$

$= 5\mathbf{i} + 5\mathbf{j} - (-4\mathbf{i} + 2\mathbf{j})$

$= 9\mathbf{i} + 3\mathbf{j}$

$|\overrightarrow{QR}| = \sqrt{9^2 + 3^2} = \sqrt{90} = 3\sqrt{10}$

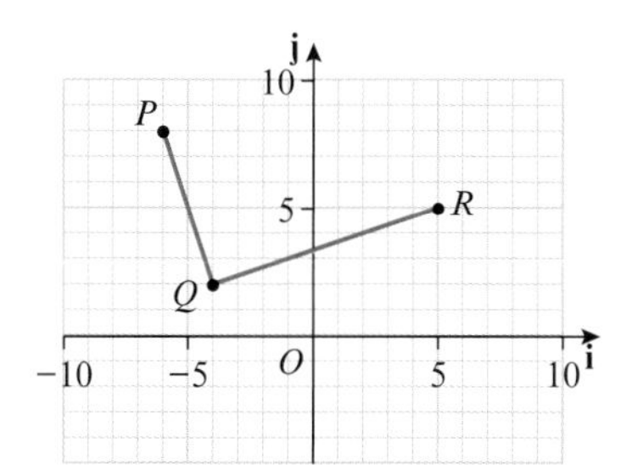

b $PQ = 2\sqrt{10}$ and $QR = 3\sqrt{10}$

Using Pythagoras, $PR^2 = \sqrt{(2\sqrt{10})^2 + (3\sqrt{10})^2}$

$= \sqrt{130}$

From part **a ii**, $PR = \sqrt{130}$ so angle PQR is 90°.

c $\overrightarrow{OP} = \lambda\overrightarrow{OQ} + \mu\overrightarrow{OR}$,

$= \lambda(-4\mathbf{i} + 2\mathbf{j}) + \mu(5\mathbf{i} + 5\mathbf{j})$

$= (-4\lambda + 5\mu)\mathbf{i} + (2\lambda + 5\mu)\mathbf{j}$

Comparing with $\overrightarrow{OP} = -6\mathbf{i} + 8\mathbf{j}$ gives:

$-4\lambda + 5\mu = -6$ (1)

$2\lambda + 5\mu = 8$ (2)

Subtract (2) from (1)

$-6\lambda = -14$

$\lambda = \frac{7}{3}$

Substitute for λ in (2):

$2\left(\frac{7}{3}\right) + 5\mu = 8$

$\mu = \frac{2}{3}$

Exercise 13.3

REMEMBER

Three or more points are **collinear** if they lie on the same straight line.

1

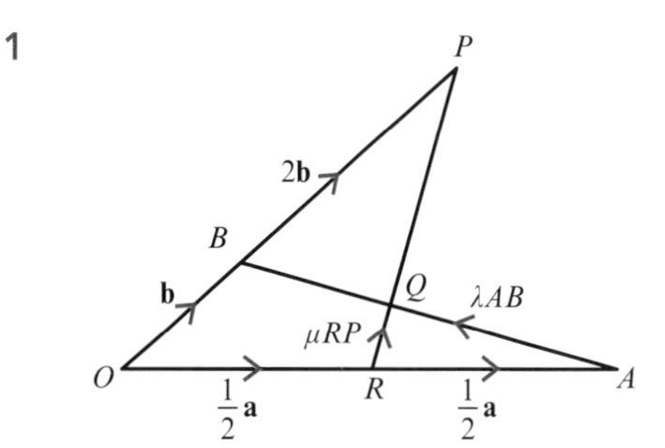

a $\overrightarrow{AB} = \overrightarrow{AO} + \overrightarrow{OB} = -\mathbf{a} + \mathbf{b}$

$\overrightarrow{OQ} = \overrightarrow{OA} + \lambda\overrightarrow{AB}$

$= \mathbf{a} + \lambda(-\mathbf{a} + \mathbf{b})$

$= (1 - \lambda)\mathbf{a} + \lambda\mathbf{b}$

b $\overrightarrow{RP} = \overrightarrow{RO} + \overrightarrow{OP}$

$= -\frac{1}{2}\mathbf{a} + 3\mathbf{b}$

$\overrightarrow{OQ} = \overrightarrow{OR} + \overrightarrow{RQ} = \frac{1}{2}\mathbf{a} + \mu\overrightarrow{RP}$

$= \frac{1}{2}\mathbf{a} + \mu\left(-\frac{1}{2}\mathbf{a} + 3\mathbf{b}\right)$

$= \left(\frac{1}{2} - \frac{1}{2}\mu\right)\mathbf{a} + 3\mu\mathbf{b}$

c Equating the coefficients of **a** and **b** we get:

$1 - \lambda = \frac{1}{2} - \frac{1}{2}\mu$ (1)

$\lambda = 3\mu$ (2)

Using (2), substitute for λ in (1)

$1 - 3\mu = \frac{1}{2} - \frac{1}{2}\mu$

$2 - 6\mu = 1 - \mu$

$\mu = \frac{1}{5}$

So, $\lambda = \frac{3}{5}$

2 a i $\overrightarrow{AC} = \overrightarrow{AB} + \overrightarrow{BC} = 5\mathbf{a} - \mathbf{b}$

$\overrightarrow{AD} = \overrightarrow{AC} + \overrightarrow{CD}$

$= 5\mathbf{a} - \mathbf{b} - 3\mathbf{a}$

$= 2\mathbf{a} - \mathbf{b}$

ii $\overrightarrow{DB} = \overrightarrow{DC} + \overrightarrow{CB}$

$= 3\mathbf{a} + \mathbf{b}$

b i $\overrightarrow{AX} = \lambda\overrightarrow{AC}$

$= \lambda(5\mathbf{a} - \mathbf{b})$

ii $\overrightarrow{DX} = \mu\overrightarrow{DB}$

$= \mu(3\mathbf{a} + \mathbf{b})$

c $\overrightarrow{AD} = \overrightarrow{AX} - \overrightarrow{DX}$

$= \lambda(5\mathbf{a} - \mathbf{b}) - \mu(3\mathbf{a} + \mathbf{b})$

$= (5\lambda - 3\mu)\mathbf{a} - (\lambda + \mu)\mathbf{b}$

$\overrightarrow{AD} = 2\mathbf{a} - \mathbf{b}$

Comparing the coefficients of **a** and **b**:

$5\lambda - 3\mu = 2$ (1)

$\lambda + \mu = 1$ (2)

Multiplying (2) by 3 and adding (1) gives:

$8\lambda = 5$

$\lambda = \frac{5}{8}$

Substitute for λ in (2):

$\mu = \frac{3}{8}$

3 a $\overrightarrow{OY} = \overrightarrow{OP} + \overrightarrow{PY}$

$= \mathbf{a} + 2\mathbf{b}$

$\overrightarrow{OX} = \lambda\,\overrightarrow{OY} = \lambda(\mathbf{a} + 2\mathbf{b})$

b $\overrightarrow{QP} = \overrightarrow{OP} - \overrightarrow{OQ}$

$= \mathbf{a} - 3\mathbf{b}$

$\overrightarrow{QX} = \mu\overrightarrow{QP}$

$= \mu(\mathbf{a} - 3\mathbf{b})$

$\overrightarrow{OX} = \overrightarrow{OQ} + \overrightarrow{QX}$

$= 3\mathbf{b} + \mu(\mathbf{a} - 3\mathbf{b})$

c $\overrightarrow{OX} = \mu\mathbf{a} + (3 - 3\mu)\mathbf{b}$

$\overrightarrow{OX} = \lambda\mathbf{a} + 2\lambda\mathbf{b}$

So, $\mu\mathbf{a} + (3 - 3\mu)\mathbf{b} = \lambda\mathbf{a} + 2\lambda\mathbf{b}$

Equating the coefficients of **a** and **b** gives:

$\mu = \lambda$ (1)

$3 - 3\mu = 2\lambda$ (2)

Using (1), substitute for μ in (2)

$3 - 3\mu = 2\mu$

$\mu = \frac{3}{5}$ and $\lambda = \frac{3}{5}$

4 a $\overrightarrow{OX} = \overrightarrow{OA} + \overrightarrow{AX}$

$= \mathbf{a} + \lambda\overrightarrow{AD}$

$\overrightarrow{AD} = \overrightarrow{AO} + \overrightarrow{OD} = -\mathbf{a} + 2\mathbf{b}$

$\overrightarrow{OX} = \mathbf{a} + \lambda(-\mathbf{a} + 2\mathbf{b})$

$= (1 - \lambda)\mathbf{a} + 2\lambda\mathbf{b}$

b $\overrightarrow{OX} = \overrightarrow{OB} + \overrightarrow{BX}$

$= \mathbf{b} + \mu\overrightarrow{BC}$

$\overrightarrow{BC} = \overrightarrow{BO} + \overrightarrow{OC} = -\mathbf{b} + \frac{5}{3}\mathbf{a}$

$\overrightarrow{OX} = \mathbf{b} + \mu\left(-\mathbf{b} + \frac{5}{3}\mathbf{a}\right)$

$= \frac{5}{3}\mu\mathbf{a} + (1 - \mu)\mathbf{b}$

c So, $(1 - \lambda)\mathbf{a} + 2\lambda\mathbf{b} = \frac{5}{3}\mu\mathbf{a} + (1 - \mu)\mathbf{b}$

Equating the coefficients of **a** and **b** gives:

$1 - \lambda = \frac{5}{3}\mu$ (1)

$2\lambda = 1 - \mu$ (2)

Multiply (1) by 2 and add (2):

$2 = 1 + \frac{7}{3}\mu$

$\mu = \frac{3}{7}$

Substitute for μ in (2) :

$2\lambda = 1 - \frac{3}{7}$

$\lambda = \frac{2}{7}$

5 a i $\overrightarrow{AB} = \overrightarrow{AO} + \overrightarrow{OB}$

$= -\mathbf{a} + \mathbf{b}$

ii $\overrightarrow{AM} = \frac{1}{2}\overrightarrow{AB} = \frac{1}{2}(-\mathbf{a} + \mathbf{b})$

$\overrightarrow{OM} = \overrightarrow{OA} + \overrightarrow{AM}$

$= \mathbf{a} + \frac{1}{2}(-\mathbf{a} + \mathbf{b})$

$= \frac{1}{2}\mathbf{a} + \frac{1}{2}\mathbf{b}$

b $\overrightarrow{OX} = \lambda\overrightarrow{OM} = \lambda\left(\frac{1}{2}\mathbf{a} + \frac{1}{2}\mathbf{b}\right)$

$= \frac{1}{2}\lambda\mathbf{a} + \frac{1}{2}\lambda\mathbf{b}$

c

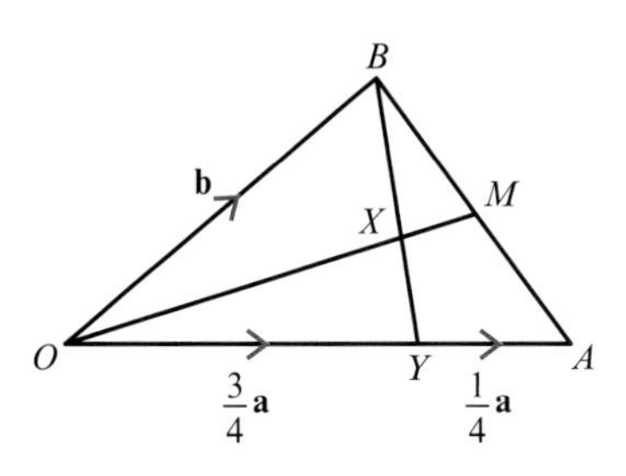

$\overrightarrow{OX} = \overrightarrow{OB} + \overrightarrow{BX}$

$= \mathbf{b} + \mu\overrightarrow{BY}$

$\overrightarrow{BY} = \overrightarrow{BO} + \overrightarrow{OY}$

$= -\mathbf{b} + \frac{3}{4}\mathbf{a}$

$\overrightarrow{OX} = \mathbf{b} + \mu\left(-\mathbf{b} + \frac{3}{4}\mathbf{a}\right)$

$= \frac{3}{4}\mu\mathbf{a} + (1 - \mu)\mathbf{b}$

d So, $\frac{1}{2}\lambda\mathbf{a} + \frac{1}{2}\lambda\mathbf{b} = \frac{3}{4}\mu\mathbf{a} + (1 - \mu)\mathbf{b}$

Equating the coefficients of **a** and **b** gives:

$\frac{1}{2}\lambda = \frac{3}{4}\mu$ (1)

$\frac{1}{2}\lambda = 1 - \mu$ (2)

Subtract (2) from (1) :

$0 = \frac{7}{4}\mu - 1$

$\mu = \frac{4}{7}$

Substitute for μ in (1) gives:

$\lambda = \frac{6}{7}$

6 a $\overrightarrow{BA} = \overrightarrow{BO} + \overrightarrow{OA}$

$= -\mathbf{b} + \mathbf{a}$

$\overrightarrow{BX} = \frac{3}{5}\overrightarrow{BA} = \frac{3}{5}(-\mathbf{b} + \mathbf{a})$

$\overrightarrow{OX} = \overrightarrow{OB} + \overrightarrow{BX}$

$= \mathbf{b} + \frac{3}{5}(-\mathbf{b} + \mathbf{a})$

$= \frac{3}{5}\mathbf{a} + \frac{2}{5}\mathbf{b}$

$\overrightarrow{OP} = \lambda\overrightarrow{OX} = \lambda\left(\frac{3}{5}\mathbf{a} + \frac{2}{5}\mathbf{b}\right)$

$= \frac{3}{5}\lambda\mathbf{a} + \frac{2}{5}\lambda\mathbf{b}$

b $\overrightarrow{BP} = \mu\overrightarrow{BY}$

$\overrightarrow{BY} = \overrightarrow{BO} + \overrightarrow{OY}$

$= -\mathbf{b} + \frac{5}{7}\mathbf{a}$

$\overrightarrow{BP} = \mu\left(-\mathbf{b} + \frac{5}{7}\mathbf{a}\right)$

$\overrightarrow{OP} = \overrightarrow{OB} + \overrightarrow{BP}$

$\overrightarrow{OP} = \mathbf{b} + \mu\left(-\mathbf{b} + \frac{5}{7}\mathbf{a}\right)$

$= \frac{5}{7}\mu\mathbf{a} + (1 - \mu)\mathbf{b}$

c So, $\frac{3}{5}\lambda\mathbf{a} + \frac{2}{5}\lambda\mathbf{b} = \frac{5}{7}\mu\mathbf{a} + (1 - \mu)\mathbf{b}$

Equating the coefficients of **a** and **b** gives:

$\frac{3}{5}\lambda = \frac{5}{7}\mu$ (1)

$\frac{2}{5}\lambda = 1 - \mu$ (2)

Rearranging (2) gives:

$\mu = 1 - \frac{2}{5}\lambda$

Substituting for μ in (1) gives:

$\frac{3}{5}\lambda = \frac{5}{7}\left(1 - \frac{2}{5}\lambda\right)$

$\lambda = \frac{25}{31}$

Substitute for λ in (2):

$\frac{2}{5} \times \frac{25}{31} = 1 - \mu$

$\mu = \frac{21}{31}$

7 a i $\overrightarrow{BX} = \overrightarrow{BO} + \overrightarrow{OX} = -\mathbf{b} + \lambda\mathbf{a}$

$= \lambda\mathbf{a} - \mathbf{b}$

ii $\overrightarrow{AY} = \overrightarrow{AO} + \overrightarrow{OY} = -\mathbf{a} + \mu\mathbf{b}$

b i $5\overrightarrow{BP} = 2(\lambda\mathbf{a} - \mathbf{b})$

$\overrightarrow{BP} = \frac{2}{5}(\lambda\mathbf{a} - \mathbf{b})$

$\overrightarrow{OP} = \overrightarrow{OB} + \overrightarrow{BP}$

$= \mathbf{b} + \frac{2}{5}(\lambda\mathbf{a} - \mathbf{b})$

$\overrightarrow{OP} = \frac{2}{5}\lambda\mathbf{a} + \frac{3}{5}\mathbf{b}$

ii $\overrightarrow{AY} = 4\overrightarrow{PY}$

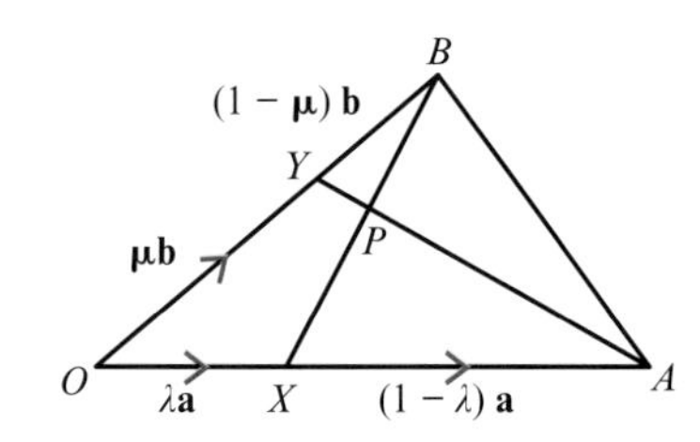

So, $\overrightarrow{PY} = \frac{1}{4}\overrightarrow{AY}$

$\overrightarrow{AY} = \overrightarrow{AO} + \overrightarrow{OY} = -\mathbf{a} + \mu\mathbf{b}$

$\overrightarrow{OP} = \overrightarrow{OY} - \overrightarrow{PY}$

$= \mu\mathbf{b} - \frac{1}{4}\overrightarrow{AY}$

$= \mu\mathbf{b} - \frac{1}{4}(-\mathbf{a} + \mu\mathbf{b})$

$\overrightarrow{OP} = \frac{1}{4}\mathbf{a} + \frac{3}{4}\mu\mathbf{b}$

iii $\frac{2}{5}\lambda\mathbf{a} + \frac{3}{5}\mathbf{b} = \frac{1}{4}\mathbf{a} + \frac{3}{4}\mu\mathbf{b}$

Equating the coefficients of **a** and **b** gives:

$\frac{2}{5}\lambda = \frac{1}{4}$ so $\lambda = \frac{5}{8}$

and $\frac{3}{5} = \frac{3}{4}\mu$ so $\mu = \frac{4}{5}$

8 a i $\overrightarrow{AC} = \overrightarrow{OC} - \overrightarrow{OA}$

$= -2\mathbf{a} + 13\mathbf{b} - (7\mathbf{a} - 5\mathbf{b})$

$\overrightarrow{AC} = -9\mathbf{a} + 18\mathbf{b}$

ii $\overrightarrow{AB} = \overrightarrow{OB} - \overrightarrow{OA}$

$= 2\mathbf{a} + 5\mathbf{b} - (7\mathbf{a} - 5\mathbf{b})$

$\overrightarrow{AB} = -5\mathbf{a} + 10\mathbf{b}$

b $\overrightarrow{AC} = -9\mathbf{a} + 18\mathbf{b} = 9(2\mathbf{b} - \mathbf{a})$

$\overrightarrow{AB} = -5\mathbf{a} + 10\mathbf{b} = 5(2\mathbf{b} - \mathbf{a})$

$\overrightarrow{AC}$ and $\overrightarrow{AB}$ are both vectors of the form $k(2\mathbf{b} - \mathbf{a})$

$\overrightarrow{AC} = \frac{9}{5}\overrightarrow{AB}$

So, AC and AB are parallel lines.

REMEMBER

'Arrows' are needed to describe a **route** using **vector** notation $\overrightarrow{AB}$.

No 'arrows' are needed to describe a **line** AB or the **geometrical properties** of lines.

AC and AB share the same point A.

So, ABC is a straight line with B between A and C.

9 a i Point A divides line OE in 4 parts so $\overrightarrow{OA} = \frac{1}{4}\overrightarrow{OE}$ or $\overrightarrow{OE} = 4\overrightarrow{OA}$

$\overrightarrow{OE} = 4\mathbf{a}$

ii $\overrightarrow{OD} = 2\overrightarrow{OB}$

$\overrightarrow{OD} = 2\mathbf{b}$

iii $\overrightarrow{AB} = \overrightarrow{AO} + \overrightarrow{OB} = -\mathbf{a} + \mathbf{b}$

$\overrightarrow{BC} = 2\overrightarrow{AB} = -2\mathbf{a} + 2\mathbf{b}$

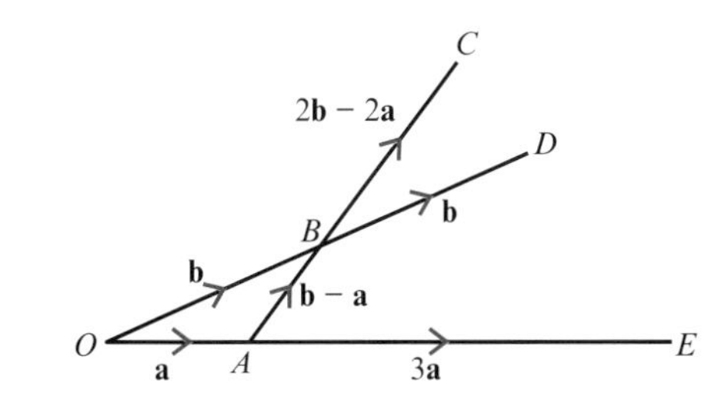

$\overrightarrow{OC} = \overrightarrow{OB} + \overrightarrow{BC}$

$= \mathbf{b} + (-2\mathbf{a} + 2\mathbf{b})$

$= -2\mathbf{a} + 3\mathbf{b}$

b i $\overrightarrow{AE} = 3\mathbf{a}$

$\overrightarrow{AC} = \overrightarrow{AB} + \overrightarrow{BC}$

$= -\mathbf{a} + \mathbf{b} - 2\mathbf{a} + 2\mathbf{b}$

$= -3\mathbf{a} + 3\mathbf{b}$

$\overrightarrow{CA} = 3\mathbf{a} - 3\mathbf{b}$

$\overrightarrow{CE} = \overrightarrow{CA} + \overrightarrow{AE} = 3\mathbf{a} - 3\mathbf{b} + 3\mathbf{a}$

$= 6\mathbf{a} - 3\mathbf{b}$

ii $\overrightarrow{CD} = \overrightarrow{BD} - \overrightarrow{BC}$

$= \mathbf{b} - (-2\mathbf{a} + 2\mathbf{b})$

$= 2\mathbf{a} - \mathbf{b}$

iii $\overrightarrow{DE} = \overrightarrow{DO} + \overrightarrow{OE}$

$= -2\mathbf{b} + 4\mathbf{a}$

$= 4\mathbf{a} - 2\mathbf{b}$

c $\overrightarrow{CE} = 3(2\mathbf{a} - 3\mathbf{b})$

$\overrightarrow{CD} = 1(2\mathbf{a} - 3\mathbf{b})$

$\overrightarrow{CE}$ and $\overrightarrow{CD}$ are both vectors of the form $k(2\mathbf{a} - 3\mathbf{b})$

$\overrightarrow{CE} = 3\overrightarrow{CD}$

So, CE and CD are parallel lines.

CE and CD share the same point C.

So, CDE is a straight line with D between C and E

d $\overrightarrow{CD} = 1(2\mathbf{a} - 3\mathbf{b})$ and $\overrightarrow{CE} = 3(2\mathbf{a} - 3\mathbf{b})$

So, $\overrightarrow{DE} = 3(2\mathbf{a} - 3\mathbf{b}) - 1(2\mathbf{a} - 3\mathbf{b})$

$= 6\mathbf{a} - 9\mathbf{b} - 2\mathbf{a} + 3\mathbf{b}$

$= 4\mathbf{a} - 6\mathbf{b}$

$= 2(2\mathbf{a} - 3\mathbf{b})$

$CD : DE$

$1(2\mathbf{a} - 3\mathbf{b}) : 2(2\mathbf{a} - 3\mathbf{b})$

$1 : 2$

Exercise 13.4

REMEMBER

The formula for an object moving with constant speed:

$$\text{speed} = \frac{\text{distance travelled}}{\text{time taken}}$$

Similarly, the formula for an object moving with constant velocity is:

$$\text{velocity} = \frac{\text{displacement}}{\text{time taken}}$$

If an object has initial position $\mathbf{a}$ and moves with a constant velocity $\mathbf{v}$, the position vector $\mathbf{r}$, at time t, is given by the formula: $\mathbf{r} = \mathbf{a} + t\mathbf{v}$

1 a $\text{velocity} = \dfrac{\text{displacement}}{\text{time taken}}$

$= \dfrac{21\mathbf{i} + 54\mathbf{j}\text{ metres}}{6\text{ seconds}}$

$= 3.5\mathbf{i} + 9\mathbf{j}\,\text{m s}^{-1}$

b displacement = velocity × time taken

$= (5\mathbf{i} - 6\mathbf{j}) \times 6$

$= (30\mathbf{i} - 36\mathbf{j})\,\text{m}$

c $\text{time taken} = \dfrac{\text{displacement}}{\text{velocity}}$

$= \dfrac{-50\mathbf{i} + 50\mathbf{j}\text{ km}}{-4\mathbf{i} + 4\mathbf{j}\text{ km/h}}$

$= 12.5$ hours

2 The displacement from $60\mathbf{i} - 40\mathbf{j}$ **to** $-50\mathbf{i} + 18\mathbf{j}$ is $-110\mathbf{i} + 58\mathbf{j}\,\text{m}$

$\text{velocity vector} = \dfrac{\text{displacement}}{\text{time taken}} = \dfrac{-110\mathbf{i} + 58\mathbf{j}}{5}$

$= -22\mathbf{i} + 11.6\mathbf{j}\,\text{km h}^{-1}$

3 Let the position vector of point Q be $x\mathbf{i} + y\mathbf{j}$

The displacement from P to Q is $(x - 50)\mathbf{i} + (y - 100)\mathbf{j}$

$\text{velocity vector} = \dfrac{\text{displacement}}{\text{time taken}}$

$30\mathbf{i} - 40\mathbf{j} = \dfrac{(x - 50)\mathbf{i} + (y - 100)\mathbf{j}}{2.5}$

$75\mathbf{i} - 100\mathbf{j} = (x - 50)\mathbf{i} + (y - 100)\mathbf{j}$

Equating the coefficients of $\mathbf{i}$ and $\mathbf{j}$:

$x - 50 = 75$ and $y - 100 = -100$

$x = 125 \quad y = 0$

The position vector of Q is $125\mathbf{i}$

4 a The velocity of a particle travelling north-east at $18\sqrt{2}\,\text{km h}^{-1}$ can be written in the form $(a\mathbf{i} + b\mathbf{j})\,\text{km h}^{-1}$:

$\cos 45° = \dfrac{a}{18\sqrt{2}}$ and $\sin 45° = \dfrac{b}{18\sqrt{2}}$

$a = 18\sqrt{2} \times \cos 45°$ $\quad b = 18\sqrt{2} \times \sin 45°$

$a = 18$ $\quad b = 18$

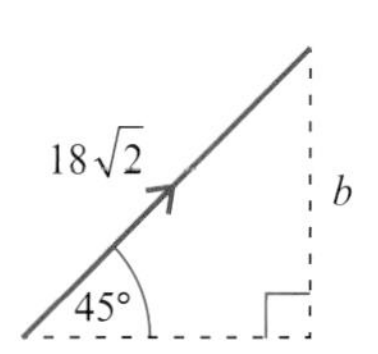

Hence the velocity vector is $(18\mathbf{i} + 18\mathbf{j})\,\text{km h}^{-1}$.

b The velocity of a particle travelling in the direction 030° at $20\,\text{km h}^{-1}$ can be written in the form $(a\mathbf{i} + b\mathbf{j})\,\text{km h}^{-1}$:

$\cos 60° = \dfrac{a}{20}$ and $\sin 60° = \dfrac{b}{20}$

$a = 20 \times \cos 60°$ $\quad b = 20 \times \sin 60°$

$a = 20 \times \dfrac{1}{2} = 10$ $\quad b = 20 \times \dfrac{\sqrt{3}}{2} = 10\sqrt{3}$

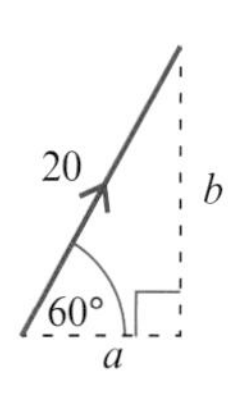

Hence the velocity vector is $(10\mathbf{i} + 10\sqrt{3}\,\mathbf{j})\,\text{km h}^{-1}$.

c The velocity of a particle travelling on a bearing of 240° and speed 100 km h^{-1} can be written in the form $(a\mathbf{i} + b\mathbf{j})$ km h^{-1}:

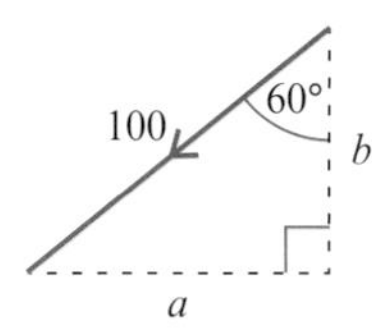

$\sin 60° = \frac{a}{100}$ and $\cos 60° = \frac{b}{100}$

$a = 100 \times \sin 60°$ $\quad b = 100 \times \cos 60°$

$a = 100 \times \frac{\sqrt{3}}{2}$ $\quad b = 50$

Hence the velocity vector is $(-50\sqrt{3}\,\mathbf{i} - 50\mathbf{j})$ km h^{-1}.

5 a Speed $= \sqrt{(12)^2 + (-16)^2}$

$= 20$ m s^{-1}

b i The position vector after 1 second is $-80\mathbf{i} + 60\mathbf{j} + 1(12\mathbf{i} - 16\mathbf{j}) = -68\mathbf{i} + 44\mathbf{j}$ m

ii The position vector after 2 seconds is $-80\mathbf{i} + 60\mathbf{j} + 2(12\mathbf{i} - 16\mathbf{j}) = -56\mathbf{i} + 28\mathbf{j}$ m

iii The position vector after 3 seconds is $-80\mathbf{i} + 60\mathbf{j} + 3(12\mathbf{i} - 16\mathbf{j}) = -44\mathbf{i} + 12\mathbf{j}$ m

c The position vector after t seconds is $-80\mathbf{i} + 60\mathbf{j} + t(12\mathbf{i} - 16\mathbf{j})$ m

or $r = \begin{pmatrix} -80 \\ 60 \end{pmatrix} + t\begin{pmatrix} 12 \\ -16 \end{pmatrix}$

6 a Speed $= \sqrt{(6)^2 + (-8)^2}$

$= 10$ km h^{-1}

b The position vector after 3 hours is $10\mathbf{i} + 38\mathbf{j} + 3(6\mathbf{i} - 8\mathbf{j}) = 28\mathbf{i} + 14\mathbf{j}$ km

c The position vector after t hours is $10\mathbf{i} + 38\mathbf{j} + t(6\mathbf{i} - 8\mathbf{j})$ km

or $r = \begin{pmatrix} 10 \\ 38 \end{pmatrix} + t\begin{pmatrix} 6 \\ -8 \end{pmatrix}$

d $\text{time taken} = \frac{\text{displacement}}{\text{velocity}}$

$= \frac{61\mathbf{i} - 30\mathbf{j} - (10\mathbf{i} + 38\mathbf{j})}{6\mathbf{i} - 8\mathbf{j}}$

$= \frac{51\mathbf{i} - 68\mathbf{j}}{6\mathbf{i} - 8\mathbf{j}}$

$= 8.5$ hours

8.5 hours after 12 noon is 8:30 pm or at 20:30

7 a The velocity of a particle travelling on a bearing of 135° and speed $12\sqrt{2}$ km h^{-1} can be written in the form $(a\mathbf{i} + b\mathbf{j})$ km h^{-1}:

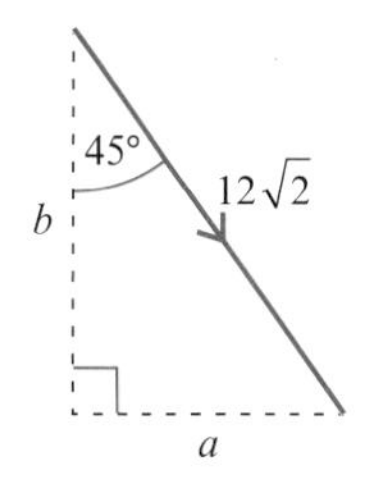

$\sin 45° = \frac{a}{12\sqrt{2}}$ and $\cos 45° = \frac{b}{12\sqrt{2}}$

$a = 12\sqrt{2} \times \sin 45°$ $\quad b = 12\sqrt{2} \times \cos 45°$

$a = 12\sqrt{2} \times \frac{1}{\sqrt{2}} = 12$ $\quad b = 12\sqrt{2} \times \frac{1}{\sqrt{2}} = 12$

135° is an obtuse angle. The cosines of obtuse angles are negative so $b = -12$

Hence the velocity vector is $(12\mathbf{i} - 12\mathbf{j})$ km h^{-1}.

b i The position vector after 2 hours is $5\mathbf{i} + 12\mathbf{j} + 2(12\mathbf{i} - 12\mathbf{j}) = 29\mathbf{i} - 12\mathbf{j}$ km

ii The position vector after 0.75 hours is $5\mathbf{i} + 12\mathbf{j} + 0.75(12\mathbf{i} - 12\mathbf{j}) = 14\mathbf{i} + 3\mathbf{j}$ km

c The position vector after t hours is $5\mathbf{i} + 12\mathbf{j} + t(12\mathbf{i} - 12\mathbf{j})$ km

or $r = \begin{pmatrix} 5 \\ 12 \end{pmatrix} + t\begin{pmatrix} 12 \\ -12 \end{pmatrix}$

8 a The position vector of the boat at point P i.e. when $t = 0$ is:

or $r = \begin{pmatrix} 10 \\ 6 \end{pmatrix} + 0\begin{pmatrix} 5 \\ 12 \end{pmatrix}$

$= \begin{pmatrix} 10 \\ 6 \end{pmatrix}$

$= 10\mathbf{i} + 6\mathbf{j}$

b The velocity vector of the boat is found from the position vector $\mathbf{r} = \begin{pmatrix} 10 \\ 6 \end{pmatrix} + t\begin{pmatrix} 5 \\ 12 \end{pmatrix}$

The velocity vector is $5\mathbf{i} + 12\mathbf{j}$ km h^{-1}

c The speed of the boat $= \sqrt{(5)^2 + (12)^2}$ km h^{-1}

$= 13$ km h^{-1}

d The position vector of the boat from point P when $t = 4$ is:

or $r = \mathbf{r} = \begin{pmatrix} 10 \\ 6 \end{pmatrix} + 4\begin{pmatrix} 5 \\ 12 \end{pmatrix}$

$= \begin{pmatrix} 30 \\ 54 \end{pmatrix}$

$= 30\mathbf{i} + 54\mathbf{j}$

The displacement of the boat from P is then $30\mathbf{i} + 54\mathbf{j} - (10\mathbf{i} + 6\mathbf{j}) = 20\mathbf{i} + 48\mathbf{j}$

Using Pythagoras, the distance from P is $\sqrt{(20)^2 + (48)^2} = 52$ km

9 a The position vector of the submarine at point A is found using:

$\mathbf{r} = \begin{pmatrix} 15 + 8t \\ 20 + 6t \end{pmatrix}$

or $\mathbf{r} = \begin{pmatrix} 15 \\ 20 \end{pmatrix} + t\begin{pmatrix} 8 \\ 6 \end{pmatrix}$ when $t = 0$

$= \begin{pmatrix} 15 \\ 20 \end{pmatrix}$

$= 15\mathbf{i} + 20\mathbf{j}$ km

b The velocity vector of the submarine is found from the position vector $\mathbf{r} = \begin{pmatrix} 15 \\ 20 \end{pmatrix} + t\begin{pmatrix} 8 \\ 6 \end{pmatrix}$

The velocity vector is $8\mathbf{i} + 6\mathbf{j}$ km h^{-1}

c The distance the submarine travels from A to B is 120 km

Each hour, the submarine travels $\sqrt{(8)^2 + (6)^2} = 10$ km

So it takes 12 hours to make the journey.

$\mathbf{r} = \begin{pmatrix} 15 \\ 20 \end{pmatrix} + t\begin{pmatrix} 8 \\ 6 \end{pmatrix}$ so substitute $t = 12$

$= \begin{pmatrix} 111 \\ 92 \end{pmatrix}$

Position vector of $B = 111\mathbf{i} + 92\mathbf{j}$ km

10 a Position vector $\mathbf{r}_A = \begin{pmatrix} -10 \\ 40 \end{pmatrix} + t\begin{pmatrix} 20 \\ 10 \end{pmatrix}$

The position vector of A after 3 hours is $-10\mathbf{i} + 40\mathbf{j} + 3(20\mathbf{i} + 10\mathbf{j}) = 50\mathbf{i} + 70\mathbf{j}$ km

Position vector $\mathbf{r}_B = \begin{pmatrix} 70 \\ 10 \end{pmatrix} + t\begin{pmatrix} -10 \\ 30 \end{pmatrix}$

The position vector of B after 3 hours is $70\mathbf{i} + 10\mathbf{j} + 3(-10\mathbf{i} + 30\mathbf{j}) = 40\mathbf{i} + 100\mathbf{j}$ km

b The distance $AB = \sqrt{(50 - 40)^2 + (70 - 100)^2}$

$= \sqrt{1000}$

$= 31.6$ km (to 3 significant figures)

11 a Position vector $\mathbf{r}_P = \begin{pmatrix} 0 \\ 0 \end{pmatrix} + t\begin{pmatrix} 3 \\ 4 \end{pmatrix}$

The position vector of P after 2 hours is $0\mathbf{i} + 0\mathbf{j} + 2(3\mathbf{i} + 4\mathbf{j}) = 6\mathbf{i} + 8\mathbf{j}$ km

Position vector $\mathbf{r}_Q = \begin{pmatrix} -10 \\ 17 \end{pmatrix} + t\begin{pmatrix} 5 \\ 2 \end{pmatrix}$

The position vector of Q after 2 hours is $-10\mathbf{i} + 17\mathbf{j} + 2(5\mathbf{i} + 2\mathbf{j}) = 0\mathbf{i} + 21\mathbf{j}$ km

b The distance $PQ = \sqrt{(6 - 0)^2 + (8 - 21)^2}$

$= \sqrt{205}$

$= 14.3$ km (to 3 significant figures)

Chapter 14: Calculus – Differentiation 2

Exercise 14.1

REMEMBER

$\frac{d}{dx}(e^x) = e^x$

$\frac{d}{dx}[e^{f(x)}] = f'(x) \times e^{f(x)}$

In particular,

$\frac{d}{dx}[e^{ax+b}] = ae^{ax+b}$

1 h $\frac{d}{dx}(5x - 3e^{\sqrt{x}}) = \frac{d}{dx}(5x - 3e^{x^{0.5}}) = 5 - 3 \times 0.5x^{-0.5}e^{x^{0.5}} = 5 - \frac{3e^{\sqrt{x}}}{2\sqrt{x}}$

k $\frac{d}{dx}\left(\frac{e^x + e^{-x}}{2}\right) = \frac{d}{dx}\left[\frac{1}{2}(e^x + e^{-x})\right] = \frac{d}{dx}\left(\frac{1}{2}e^x + \frac{1}{2}e^{-x}\right)$

$= \frac{d}{dx}\left(\frac{1}{2}e^x\right) + \frac{d}{dx}\left(\frac{1}{2}e^{-x}\right)$

$= \frac{1}{2}e^x - \frac{1}{2}e^{-x}$ or $\frac{e^x - e^{-x}}{2}$

l $\frac{d}{dx}5(x^2 + e^{x^2}) = \frac{d}{dx}(5x^2 + 5e^{x^2})$

$= \frac{d}{dx}(5x^2) + \frac{d}{dx}(5e^{x^2})$

First term: $\frac{d}{dx}(5x^2) = 10x$

Second term: use $\frac{d}{dx}[e^{f(x)}] = f'(x) \times ef(x)$

$\frac{d}{dx}(5e^{x^2}) = 5 \times 2x \times e^{x^2} = 10xe^{x^2}$

Answer: $10x + 10xe^{x^2}$ or $10x(1 + e^{x^2})$

2 b $\frac{d}{dx}(x^2e^{2x}) = x^2 \times \frac{d}{dx}(e^{2x}) + e^{2x} \times \frac{d}{dx}(x^2)$ product rule

$= x^2 \times (2e^{2x}) + e^{2x} \times (2x)$

$= 2x^2e^{2x} + 2xe^{2x}$

i $\frac{d}{dx}\left(\frac{x^2e^x - 5}{e^x + 1}\right) = \frac{(e^x + 1) \times \frac{d}{dx}(x^2e^x - 5) - (x^2e^x - 5) \times \frac{d}{dx}(e^x + 1)}{(e^x + 1)^2}$ (product rule for numerator) and quotient rule

$= \frac{(e^x + 1) \times (x^2e^x + 2xe^x) - (x^2e^x - 5)e^x}{(e^x + 1)^2}$ expand first brackets

$= \frac{e^x(x^2e^x + 2xe^x) + (x^2e^x + 2xe^x) - (x^2e^x - 5)e^x}{(e^x + 1)^2}$ factorise second bracket

$= \frac{e^x(x^2e^x + 2xe^x) + e^x(x^2 + 2x) - (x^2e^x - 5)e^x}{(e^x + 1)^2}$ factorise numerator

$= \frac{e^x[(x^2e^x + 2xe^x) + x^2 + 2x - (x^2e^x - 5)]}{(e^x + 1)^2}$ remove first brackets and expand last brackets

$= \frac{e^x(x^2e^x + 2xe^x + x^2 + 2x - x^2e^x + 5)}{(e^x + 1)^2}$ simplify numerator

$= \frac{e^x(x^2 + 2xe^x + 2x + 5)}{(e^x + 1)^2}$

3 a $y = \frac{5}{e^{2x} + 3}$ at $x = 0$,

$\frac{d}{dx}\left(\frac{5}{e^{2x} + 3}\right) = \frac{(e^{2x} + 3) \times \frac{d}{dx}(5) - (5) \times \frac{d}{dx}(e^{2x} + 3)}{(e^{2x} + 3)^2}$ quotient rule

$= \frac{-5(2e^{2x})}{(e^{2x} + 3)^2}$

$= \frac{-10e^{2x}}{(e^{2x} + 3)^2}$

When $x = 0$, $\frac{dy}{dx} = \frac{-10e^{2(0)}}{(e^{2(0)} + 3)^2} = \frac{-10}{16} = -\frac{5}{8}$

and $y = \frac{5}{e^{2(0)} + 3} = \frac{5}{4}$

The tangent passes through the point $\left(0, \frac{5}{4}\right)$ with gradient $= -\frac{5}{8}$

$y - \frac{5}{4} = -\frac{5}{8}(x - 0)$

$y - \frac{5}{4} = -\frac{5}{8}x$ multiply both sides by 8

$8y - 10 = -5x$

$5x + 8y = 10$

b $y = \sqrt{e^{2x} + 1}$ at $x = \ln 5$,

$y = (e^{2x} + 1)^{\frac{1}{2}}$ chain rule

$\frac{dy}{dx} = \frac{1}{2}(e^{2x} + 1)^{-\frac{1}{2}} \times 2e^{2x}$

$= \frac{e^{2x}}{(e^{2x} + 1)^{\frac{1}{2}}}$

When $x = \ln 5$, $\dfrac{dy}{dx} = \dfrac{e^{2(\ln 5)}}{(e^{2(\ln 5)} + 1)^{\frac{1}{2}}} = \dfrac{e^{\ln 5^2}}{(e^{\ln 5^2} + 1)^{\frac{1}{2}}} = \dfrac{25}{\sqrt{26}}$

and $y = (e^{2x} + 1)^{\frac{1}{2}} = (e^{2\ln 5} + 1)^{\frac{1}{2}} = (e^{\ln 5^2} + 1)^{\frac{1}{2}} = \sqrt{26}$

The tangent passes through the point: $(\ln 5, \sqrt{26})$ with gradient $= \dfrac{25}{\sqrt{26}}$

$y - \sqrt{26} = \dfrac{25}{\sqrt{26}}(x - \ln 5)$

c $y = x^2(1 + e^x)$ product rule

$\dfrac{d}{dx}[x^2(1 + e^x)] = x^2 \times \dfrac{d}{dx}(1 + e^x) + (1 + e^x) \times \dfrac{d}{dx}(x^2)$

$\dfrac{dy}{dx} = x^2e^x + 2x(1 + e^x)$

When $x = 1$, $\dfrac{dy}{dx} = 1^2e^1 + 2(1)(1 + e^1) = 3e + 2$

and $y = 1^2(1 + e^1) = 1 + e$

The tangent passes through the point $(1, 1 + e)$ with gradient $= 3e + 2$

$y - (1 + e) = (3e + 2)(x - 1)$

$y - 1 - e = 3ex - 3e + 2x - 2$

$y = 3ex + 2x - 2e - 1$

4 $y = 5e^{2x} - 4x - 3$

$\dfrac{dy}{dx} = 10e^{2x} - 4$

When $x = 0$, $\dfrac{dy}{dx} = 10e^{2(0)} - 4 = 6$

and $y = 5e^{2(0)} - 4(0) - 3 = 2$

The tangent passes through the point $(0, 2)$ with gradient $= 6$

$y - 2 = 6(x - 0)$

$y = 6x + 2$

The tangent line meets the x-axis at $y = 0$

Substitute $y = 0$ into $y = 6x + 2$

$0 = 6x + 2$

$x = -\dfrac{1}{3}$

The coordinates of A are $\left(-\dfrac{1}{3}, 0\right)$

5 a $y = xe^x$ product rule

$\dfrac{dy}{dx} = x \times \dfrac{d}{dx}(e^x) + e^x \times \dfrac{d}{dx}(x)$

$= xe^x + e^x$

At a stationary point $\frac{dy}{dx} = 0$

$xe^x + e^x = 0$ — factorise

$e^x(x + 1) = 0$

$e^x = 0$ (no solutions) or $x + 1 = 0$

$x = -1$

There is a stationary point at $x = -1$

To find the nature of the stationary point, find $\frac{d^2y}{dx^2}$

$\frac{d^2y}{dx^2} = \frac{d}{dx}(xe^x + e^x) = \frac{d}{dx}(xe^x) + \frac{d}{dx}(e^x) = (xe^x + e^x) + e^x = xe^x + 2e^x$

When $x = -1$, $\frac{d^2y}{dx^2} = 1e^1 + 2e^1 = 3e$ which is >0 so this is a minimum point.

At $x = -1$, $y = (-1)e^{-1} = -\frac{1}{e}$

So $\left(-1, -\frac{1}{e}\right)$ is a minimum point

b $\frac{dy}{dx} = xc^x + e^x$

When $x = 1$, $y = 1e^1 = e$

and $\frac{dy}{dx} = 1e^1 + e^1 = 2e$

The gradient of the tangent × the gradient of the normal = −1

The normal passes through the point (1, e) with gradient $= -\frac{1}{2e}$

The equation of the normal at $P(1, e)$ is $y - e = -\frac{1}{2e}(x - 1)$

c The normal meets the x-axis where $y = 0$

So, $0 - e = -\frac{1}{2e}(x - 1)$

$2e^2 = x - 1$

$x = 2e^2 + 1$

$A = (2e^2 + 1, 0)$

The normal at P meets the y-axis where $x = 0$

So, $y - e = -\frac{1}{2e}(0 - 1)$

$y = \frac{1}{2e} + e$

$B = \left(0, \frac{1}{2e} + e\right)$

As the normal meets the x and y axes at points A and B, the third vertex of triangle AOB is the origin. So, triangle AOB is right-angled at O

The area of triangle $AOB = \frac{1}{2}\left[(2e^2 + 1) \times \left(\frac{1}{2e} + e\right)\right]$

$= \frac{1}{2}\left(e + 2e^3 + \frac{1}{2e} + e\right)$

$= \frac{1}{2}\left(2e^3 + 2e + \frac{1}{2e}\right)$

$\frac{dy}{dx} = \frac{1}{4e}(4e^4 + 4e^2 + 1)$

$= \frac{1}{4e}[(2e^2 + 1)^2]$

$= \frac{(2e^2 + 1)^2}{4e}$

Exercise 14.2

REMEMBER

$\frac{d}{dx}(\ln x) = \frac{1}{x}$

$\frac{d}{dx}[\ln f(x)] = \frac{f'(x)}{f(x)}$

In particular,

$\frac{d}{dx}[\ln (ax + b)] = \frac{a}{ax + b}$

1 e $\frac{d}{dx}[\ln (3x + 1)^2] = \frac{2(3x + 1)^1(3)}{(3x + 1)^2}$ ← 'inside' differentiated ← 'inside'

$= \frac{6}{(3x + 1)}$

l $\frac{d}{dx}[\ln (x^2 + \ln x)] = \frac{2x + \frac{1}{x}}{x^2 + \ln x}$ ← 'inside' differentiated ← 'inside'

$= \frac{2x^2 + 1}{x(x^2 + \ln x)}$

2 e $x^2 \ln (\ln x) = x^2 \times \frac{d}{dx}[\ln (\ln x)] + \ln (\ln x) \times \frac{d}{dx}(x^2)$

use the chain rule to find $\frac{d}{dx}[\ln(\ln x)]$
let $u = \ln x$
then $y = \ln u$

$\frac{du}{dx} = \frac{1}{x}, \frac{dy}{du} = \frac{1}{u}$ and $\frac{dy}{dx} = \frac{dy}{du} \times \frac{du}{dx}$

$\frac{dy}{dx} = \frac{1}{u} \times \frac{1}{x} = \frac{1}{x \ln x}$

So $\frac{d}{dx} = x^2 \times \frac{1}{x \ln x} + \ln (\ln x) \times 2x$

$= \frac{x}{\ln x} + 2x \ln (\ln x)$

i $\frac{d}{dx}\left[\frac{\ln(x^3-1)}{2x+3}\right] = \frac{(2x+3)\times\frac{d}{dx}[\ln(x^3-1)] - \ln(x^3-1)\times\frac{d}{dx}(2x+3)}{(2x+3)^2}$ quotient rule

$= \frac{(2x+3)\times\frac{3x^2}{x^3-1} - \ln(x^3-1)\times(2)}{(2x+3)^2}$

$= \frac{\frac{3x^2(2x+3)}{x^3-1} - 2\ln(x^3-1)}{(2x+3)^2}$ multiply numerator and denominator by $x^3 - 1$

$= \frac{3x^2(2x+3) - 2(x^3-1)\ln(x^3-1)}{(2x+3)^2(x^3-1)}$

3 $y = x^2 \ln 3x$ product rule

$\frac{dy}{dx} = x^2 \times \frac{d}{dx}(\ln 3x) + \ln 3x \times \frac{d}{dx}(x^2)$

$= x^2 \times \frac{3}{3x} + 2x \ln 3x$

$= x + 2x \ln 3x$

At $x = 2$, $\frac{dy}{dx} = 2 + 2(2)\ln(3\times 2) = 2 + 4\ln 6$

$\frac{d^2y}{dx^2} = 1 + 2x \times \frac{d}{dx}(\ln 3x) + \ln(3x) \times \frac{d}{dx}(2x)$ product rule

$= 1 + 2x \times \frac{3}{3x} + \ln 3x \times (2)$

$= 1 + 2 + 2\ln 3x$

$\frac{d^2y}{dx^2} = 3 + 2\ln 3x$

At $x = 2$, $\frac{d^2y}{dx^2} = 3 + 2\ln(3\times 2) = 3 + 2\ln 6$

4 f $\ln\left[\frac{x(x+1)}{x+2}\right] = \ln\frac{(x^2+x)}{(x+2)}$

$= \ln(x^2+x)) - \ln(x+2)$

$\ln\left[\frac{x(x+1)}{x+2}\right] = \frac{2x+1}{x^2+x} - \frac{1}{x+2}$

$= \frac{(2x+1)(x+2)}{(x^2+x)(x+2)} - \frac{(x^2+x)}{(x+2)(x^2+x)}$

$= \frac{(2x+1)(x+2)-(x^2+x)}{(x^2+x)(x+2)}$

$= \frac{x^2+4x+2}{(x^2+x)(x+2)}$

$= \frac{x^2+4x+2}{x(x+1)(x+2)}$

i $\ln\left[\frac{(x+1)(2x-3)}{x(x-1)}\right] = \ln\frac{(2x^2-x-3)}{(x^2-x)}$

$= \ln(2x^2-x-3) - \ln(x^2-x)$

$\ln\left[\frac{(x+1)(2x-3)}{x(x-1)}\right] = \frac{4x-1}{(x+1)(2x-3)} - \frac{2x-1}{x(x-1)}$

$= \frac{x(x-1)(4x-1)}{x(x+1)(2x-3)(x-1)} - \frac{(2x-1)(x+1)(2x-3)}{x(x-1)(x+1)(2x-3)}$

$= \frac{x(x-1)(4x-1)-(2x-1)(x+1)(2x-3)}{x(x-1)(x+1)(2x-3)}$

$= \frac{4x^3-5x^2+x-[(2x^2+x-1)(2x-3)]}{x(x-1)(x+1)(2x-3)}$

$= \frac{4x^3-5x^2+x-[4x^3-6x^2+2x^2-3x-2x+3]}{x(x-1)(x+1)(2x-3)}$

$= \frac{4x^3-5x^2+x-4x^3+6x^2-2x^2+3x+2x-3}{x(x-1)(x+1)(2x-3)}$

$= \frac{-x^2+6x-3}{x(x-1)(x+1)(2x-3)}$

5 a $y = \log_3 x$ use $\log_b a = \frac{\log_c a}{\log_c b}$

$y = \frac{\ln(x)}{\ln 3}$

$y = \frac{1}{\ln 3}(\ln x)$

$\frac{dy}{dx} = \frac{1}{\ln 3} \times \frac{1}{x} = \frac{1}{x\ln 3}$

b $y = \log_2 x^2$ use $\log_b a = \dfrac{\log_c a}{\log_c b}$

$y = \dfrac{\ln(x^2)}{\ln 2}$

$y = \dfrac{1}{\ln 2}(\ln x^2)$

$\dfrac{dy}{dx} = \dfrac{1}{\ln 2} \times \dfrac{2x}{x^2}$

$\dfrac{dy}{dx} = \dfrac{2}{x \ln 2}$

c $y = \log_4(5x - 1)$ use $\log_b a = \dfrac{\log_c a}{\log_c b}$

$y = \dfrac{\ln(5x - 1)}{\ln 4}$

$y = \dfrac{1}{\ln 4}[\ln(5x - 1)]$

$\dfrac{dy}{dx} = \dfrac{1}{\ln 4} \times \dfrac{5}{5x - 1}$

$\dfrac{dy}{dx} = \dfrac{5}{(5x - 1)\ln 4}$

6 a $e^y = 4x^2 - 1$ take $\log_e$ of both sides

$\log_e(e^y) = \log_e(4x^2 - 1)$ power rule of logs

$y\log_e e = \log_e(4x^2 - 1)$ use $\log_e e = \ln e = 1$

$y = \ln(4x^2 - 1)$

$\dfrac{dy}{dx} = \dfrac{8x}{4x^2 - 1}$

b $e^y = 5x^3 - 2x$ take $\log_e$ of both sides

$\log_e(e^y) = \log_e(5x^3 - 2x)$ power rule of logs

$y\log_e e = \log_e(5x^3 - 2x)$ use $\log_e e = \ln e = 1$

$y = \ln(5x^3 - 2x)$

$\dfrac{dy}{dx} = \dfrac{15x^2 - 2}{5x^3 - 2x}$

c $e^y = (x + 3)(x - 4)$ take $\log_e$ of both sides

$\log_e(e^y) = \log_e(x^2 - x - 12)$ power rule of logs

$y\log_e e = \log_e(x^2 - x - 12)$ use $\log_e e = \ln e = 1$

$y = \ln(x^2 - x - 12)$

$\dfrac{dy}{dx} = \dfrac{2x - 1}{x^2 - x - 12}$ or $\dfrac{dy}{dx} = \dfrac{2x - 1}{(x + 3)(x - 4)}$

7

$$x = \frac{1}{2}[e^{y(3x+7)} + 1]$$

$$2x = e^{y(3x+7)} + 1$$

$$2x - 1 = e^{y(3x+7)}$$ take $\log_e$ of both sides

$$\log_e(2x - 1) = \log_e e^{y(3x+7)}$$ power rule of logs

$$\ln(2x - 1) = y(3x + 7)$$

$$y = \frac{\ln(2x - 1)}{3x + 7}$$ quotient rule

$$\frac{dy}{dx} = \frac{(3x + 7) \times \frac{d}{dx}\ln(2x - 1) - \ln(2x - 1) \times \frac{d}{dx}(3x + 7)}{(3x + 7)^2}$$

$$\frac{dy}{dx} = \frac{(3x + 7) \times \frac{2}{2x - 1} - \ln(2x - 1) \times (3)}{(3x + 7)^2}$$

$$\frac{dy}{dx} = \frac{\frac{6x + 14}{2x - 1} - 3\ln(2x - 1)}{(3x + 7)^2}$$

When $x = 1$, $\frac{dy}{dx} = \frac{\frac{6(1) + 14}{2(1) - 1} - 3\ln(2 \times 1 - 1)}{(3 \times 1 + 7)^2} = \frac{20 - 0}{100} = 0.2$

Exercise 14.3

REMEMBER

$$\frac{d}{dx}[\sin(ax + b)] = a\cos(ax + b)$$

$$\frac{d}{dx}[\cos(ax + b)] = -a\sin(ax + b)$$

$$\frac{d}{dx}[\tan(ax + b)] = a\sec^2(ax + b)$$

1 f $\frac{d}{dx}(2\cos 3x - \sin 2x)$

Differentiate $2\cos 3x$ using the chain rule:

Let $y = 2\cos u$ and $u = 3x$

$$\frac{dy}{dx} = \frac{dy}{du} \times \frac{du}{dx}$$

$$= -2\sin u \times 3$$

$$= -6\sin 3x$$

Differentiate $\sin 2x$ using the chain rule:

Let $y = \sin u$ and $u = 2x$

$$\frac{dy}{dx} = \frac{dy}{du} \times \frac{du}{dx}$$

$$= \cos u \times 2$$

$$= 2\cos u$$

$$= 2\cos 2x$$

$$\frac{d}{dx}(2\cos 3x - \sin 2x) = -6\sin 3x - 2\cos 2x$$

i $\frac{d}{dx}\left[2\cos\left(3x - \frac{\pi}{6}\right)\right]$

$$= 2\frac{d}{dx}\left[\cos\left(3x - \frac{\pi}{6}\right)\right]$$

$$= 2 \times -\sin\left(3x - \frac{\pi}{6}\right) \times (3)$$

$$= -6\sin\left(3x - \frac{\pi}{6}\right)$$

2 c $\frac{d}{dx}(\sin^2 x - 2\cos x)$

Differentiate $\sin^2 x$ using the chain rule:

Let $u = \sin x$ and $y = u^2$

$$\frac{dy}{dx} = \frac{dy}{du} \times \frac{du}{dx}$$

$$= 2u \times \cos x$$

So, $\frac{d}{dx}[\sin^2 x] = 2\sin x\cos x$

$$\frac{d}{dx}2\cos x = -2\sin x$$

$$\frac{d}{dx}(\sin^2 x - 2\cos x) = 2\sin x\cos x - -2\sin x$$

$$= 2\sin x\cos x + 2\sin x$$

REMEMBER

$\cos^4 x$ is the same as $(\cos x)^4$ but **not** the same as $\cos x^4$

f $\frac{d}{dx}\left[3\cos^4 x + 2\tan^2\left(2x - \frac{\pi}{4}\right)\right]$

Differentiate $3\cos^4 x$ using the chain rule:

Let $u = \cos x$ and $y = 3u^4$

$$\frac{dy}{dx} = \frac{dy}{du} \times \frac{du}{dx}$$

$$= 12u^3 \times -\sin x$$

So, $\frac{d}{dx}(3\cos^4 x) = -12\sin x\cos^3 x$

Differentiate $2\tan^2\left(2x - \frac{\pi}{4}\right)$

$$= 2\frac{d}{dx}\left[\tan^2\left(2x - \frac{\pi}{4}\right)\right]$$

Differentiate $\tan^2\left(2x - \frac{\pi}{4}\right)$ using the chain rule:

Let $u = 2x - \frac{\pi}{4}$ and $y = \tan^2 u$

$$\frac{dy}{dx} = \frac{dy}{du} \times \frac{du}{dx}$$

$$= 2\tan u\sec^2 u \times 2$$

$$= 4\tan\left(2x - \frac{\pi}{4}\right)\sec^2\left(2x - \frac{\pi}{4}\right)$$

So, $2\frac{d}{dx}\left[\tan^2\left(2x - \frac{\pi}{4}\right)\right]$

$$= 8\tan\left(2x - \frac{\pi}{4}\right)\sec^2\left(2x - \frac{\pi}{4}\right)$$

$$\frac{d}{dx}\left[3\cos 4x + 2\tan^2\left(2x - \frac{\pi}{4}\right)\right]$$

$$= -12\sin x\cos^3 x + 8\tan\left(2x - \frac{\pi}{4}\right)\sec^2\left(2x - \frac{\pi}{4}\right)$$

3 b $\frac{d}{dx}(2\sin 2x\cos 3x) = 2\sin 2x \times \frac{d}{dx}(\cos 3x) + \cos 3x \times \frac{d}{dx}(2\sin 2x)$ product rule

$$= 2\sin 2x \times -3\sin 3x + \cos 3x \times 2 \times 2\cos 2x$$

$$= -6\sin 2x\sin 3x + 4\cos 2x\cos 3x$$

j $\frac{d}{dx}\left(\frac{1}{\sin^3 2x}\right)$

$$\frac{\sin^3 2x \times \frac{d}{dx}(1) - 1 \times \frac{d}{dx}(\sin^3 2x)}{(\sin^3 2x)^2}$$ quotient rule

Differentiate $\sin^3 2x$ using the chain rule:

Let $u = \sin 2x$ and $y = u^3$

$$\frac{dy}{dx} = \frac{dy}{du} \times \frac{du}{dx}$$

$$= 3u^2 \times 2\cos 2x$$

$$= 3\sin^2 2x \times 2\cos 2x$$

$$\frac{d}{dx}(\sin^3 2x) = 6\sin^2 2x\cos 2x$$

So, $\frac{d}{dx}\left(\frac{1}{\sin^3 2x}\right) = \frac{-1 \times 6\sin^2 2x\cos 2x}{(\sin^3 2x)^2}$

$$= \frac{-6\sin^2 2x\cos 2x}{\sin^3 2x \times \sin^3 2x}$$ divide numerator and denominator by $\sin^2 2x$

$$= \frac{-6\cos 2x}{\sin 2x\ \sin^3 2x}$$ write the expression as a product of two fractions

$$= \frac{-6\cos 2x}{\sin 2x} \times \frac{1}{\sin^3 2x}$$ use $\cot x = \frac{\cos x}{\sin x}$ and $\operatorname{cosec} x = \frac{1}{\sin x}$

$$= -6\cot 2x \times \operatorname{cosec}^3 2x$$

$$= -6\cot 2x\operatorname{cosec}^3 2x$$

4 j $\frac{d}{dx}[x^2\ln(\cos x)]$

$$= x^2 \times \frac{d}{dx}[\ln(\cos x)] + [\ln(\cos x)] \times \frac{d}{dx}(x^2)$$ product rule

Differentiate $\ln(\cos x)$ using the chain rule:

Let $y = \ln u$ and $u = \cos x$

$$\frac{dy}{dx} = \frac{dy}{du} \times \frac{du}{dx}$$

$$= \frac{1}{u} \times -\sin x$$

$$= \frac{-\sin x}{\cos x}$$

$$\frac{d}{dx}[\ln(\cos x)] = -\tan x$$

$$\frac{d}{dx}[x^2\ln(\cos x)] = x^2 \times -\tan x + \ln(\cos x) \times 2x$$

$$= -x^2\tan x + 2x\ln(\cos x)$$

$$= x[2\ln(\cos x) - x\tan x]$$

l $\frac{d}{dx}\left[\frac{x\sin x}{e^x}\right]$

$= \frac{e^x \times \frac{d}{dx}(x\sin x) - x\sin x \times \frac{d}{dx}(e^x)}{(e^x)^2}$ quotient rule

$= \frac{e^x[(x \times \frac{d}{dx}(\sin x) + \sin x \times \frac{d}{dx}(x)] - x\sin x \times e^x}{e^{2x}}$

$= \frac{e^x[x\cos x + \sin x] - xe^x \sin x}{e^{2x}}$ divide numerator and denominator by e^x

$= \frac{x\cos x + \sin x - x\sin x}{e^x}$

5 a $y = 2x\cos 3x$

$\frac{dy}{dx} = 2x \times \frac{d}{dx}(\cos 3x) + \cos 3x \times \frac{d}{dx}(2x)$ product rule

$= 2x \times -3\sin 3x + \cos 3x \times 2$

$= -6x\sin 3x + 2\cos 3x$

REMEMBER

It is important to remember that, in calculus, all angles are measured in radians unless a question tells you otherwise.

When $x = \frac{\pi}{3}$, the gradient of the tangent is :

$= -6 \times \frac{\pi}{3} \times \sin 3\left(\frac{\pi}{3}\right) + 2\cos 3\left(\frac{\pi}{3}\right)$

$= -2\pi \times 0 + 2 \times -1$

$= -2$

b $y = \frac{2 - \cos x}{3\tan x}$

$\frac{dy}{dx} = \frac{3\tan x \times \frac{d}{dx}(2 - \cos x) - (2 - \cos x) \times \frac{d}{dx}(3\tan x)}{(3\tan x)^2}$ quotient rule

$= \frac{3\tan x \times \sin x - (2 - \cos x) \times 3\sec^2 x}{(3\tan x)^2}$

$= \frac{3\tan x\sin x - 6\sec^2 x + 3\cos x\sec^2 x}{(3\tan x)^2}$

When $x = \frac{\pi}{4}$, the gradient of the tangent is:

$$= \frac{3\tan\left(\frac{\pi}{4}\right)\sin\left(\frac{\pi}{4}\right) - 6\sec^2\left(\frac{\pi}{4}\right) + 3\cos\left(\frac{\pi}{4}\right)\sec^2\left(\frac{\pi}{4}\right)}{\left(3\tan\left(\frac{\pi}{4}\right)\right)^2}$$

$$= \frac{3 \times 1 \times \frac{\sqrt{2}}{2} - 6 \times 2 + 3 \times \frac{\sqrt{2}}{2} \times 2}{9}$$

$$= \frac{\frac{3\sqrt{2}}{2} - 12 + 3\sqrt{2}}{9}$$

$$= \frac{\frac{9\sqrt{2}}{2} - 12}{9}$$ multiply numerator and denominator by $\frac{2}{3}$

$$= \frac{3\sqrt{2} - 8}{6}$$

6 a $\frac{d}{dx}(\sec x) = \frac{d}{dx}\left(\frac{1}{\cos x}\right)$

$$= \frac{\cos x \times \frac{d}{dx}(1) - 1 \times \frac{d}{dx}(\cos x)}{(\cos x)^2}$$ quotient rule

$$= \frac{\sin x}{\cos^2 x}$$ rewrite the fraction as two separate fractions

$$= \frac{\sin x}{\cos x} \times \frac{1}{\cos x}$$

$$= \tan x \sec x$$

b $\frac{d}{dx}(\operatorname{cosec} x) = \frac{d}{dx}\left(\frac{1}{\sin x}\right)$

$$= \frac{\sin x \times \frac{d}{dx}(1) - 1 \times \frac{d}{dx}(\sin x)}{(\sin x)^2}$$ quotient rule

$$= \frac{-\cos x}{\sin^2 x}$$ rewrite the fraction as two separate fractions

$$= \frac{-\cos x}{\sin x} \times \frac{1}{\sin x}$$

$$= -\cot x \operatorname{cosec} x$$

c $\frac{d}{dx}(\cot x) = \frac{d}{dx}\left(\frac{\cos x}{\sin x}\right)$

$$= \frac{\sin x \times \frac{d}{dx}(\cos x) - \cos x \times \frac{d}{dx}(\sin x)}{\sin^2 x}$$

$= \frac{-\sin x \sin x - \cos x \cos x}{\sin^2 x}$ factorise numerator

$= \frac{-(\sin^2 x + \cos^2 x)}{\sin^2 x}$ use $\sin^2 x + \cos^2 x = 1$

$= \frac{-1}{\sin^2 x}$

$= -\text{cosec}^2 x$

7 a $e^y = \sin 3x$ take $\log_e$ of both sides

$\log_e(e^y) = \log_e(\sin 3x)$ simplify

$y = \ln(\sin 3x)$

Differentiate $\ln(\sin 3x)$ using the chain rule:

Let $u = \sin 3x$ and $y = \ln u$

$\frac{dy}{dx} = \frac{dy}{du} \times \frac{du}{dx}$

$= \frac{1}{u} \times 3\cos 3x$

$\frac{dy}{dx} = \frac{3\cos 3x}{\sin 3x}$

$\frac{dy}{dx} = 3\cot 3x$

b $e^y = 3\cos 2x$ take $\log_e$ of both sides

$\log_e(e^y) = \log_e(3\cos 2x)$ simplify

$y = \ln(3\cos 2x)$

Differentiate $\ln(3\cos 2x)$ using the chain rule:

Let $u = \cos 2x$ and $y = \ln(3u)$

$\frac{dy}{dx} = \frac{dy}{du} \times \frac{du}{dx}$

$\frac{dy}{dx} = \frac{3}{3u} \times -2\sin 2x$

$\frac{dy}{dx} = \frac{-2\sin 2x}{\cos 2x}$

$\frac{dy}{dx} = -2\tan 2x$

8 $y = A\sin x + B\sin 2x$ and substituting $x = \frac{\pi}{2}$ and $y = 3$ gives:

$3 = A\sin\left(\frac{\pi}{2}\right) + B\sin\left(2 \times \frac{\pi}{2}\right)$

$3 = A \times 1 + B \times 0$

$A = 3$

$\frac{dy}{dx} = 3\cos x + 2B\cos 2x$ and substituting $x = \frac{\pi}{3}$ and $\frac{dy}{dx} = \frac{13}{2}$ gives:

$\frac{13}{2} = 3\cos\frac{\pi}{3} + 2B\cos\left(2 \times \frac{\pi}{3}\right)$

$\frac{13}{2} = \frac{3}{2} + 2B \times -\frac{1}{2}$

$\frac{13}{2} = \frac{3}{2} - B$

$B = -5$

Solution: $A = 3$, $B = -5$

9 $y = A\sin x + B\cos 2x$

$\frac{dy}{dx} = A\cos x - 2B\sin 2x$ substitute $x = \frac{\pi}{6}$ and $\frac{dy}{dx} = 5\sqrt{3}$

$5\sqrt{3} = A\cos\frac{\pi}{6} - 2B\sin\left(2 \times \frac{\pi}{6}\right)$

$5\sqrt{3} = A \times \frac{\sqrt{3}}{2} - \frac{2\sqrt{3}}{2}B$ multiply both sides by $2\sqrt{3}$

$30 = 3A - 6B$

$10 = A - 2B$ (1)

$\frac{dy}{dx} = A\cos x - 2B\sin 2x$ substitute $x = \frac{\pi}{4}$ and $\frac{dy}{dx} = 6 + 2\sqrt{2}$

$6 + 2\sqrt{2} = A\cos\frac{\pi}{4} - 2B\sin\left(2 \times \frac{\pi}{4}\right)$

$6 + 2\sqrt{2} = \frac{\sqrt{2}}{2}A - 2B$ multiply both sides by 2

$12 + 4\sqrt{2} = \sqrt{2}A - 4B$ (2)

Multiply (1) by 2 and subtract (2)

$20 - (12 + 4\sqrt{2}) = (2 - \sqrt{2})A$

$8 - 4\sqrt{2} = (2 - \sqrt{2})A$ divide both sides by $2 - \sqrt{2}$

$A = 4$

Substituting $A = 4$ into (1) gives:

$10 = 4 - 2B$

$B = -3$

Exercise 14.4

1 $y = 3\sin\left(2x + \frac{\pi}{2}\right)$

$\frac{dy}{dx} = 3\frac{d}{dx}\left[\sin\left(2x + \frac{\pi}{2}\right)\right]$

$\frac{dy}{dx} = 3 \times \cos\left(2x + \frac{\pi}{2}\right) \times (2)$

$\frac{dy}{dx} = 6\cos\left(2x + \frac{\pi}{2}\right)$

When $x = \frac{\pi}{4}$, $y = 3\sin\left(2 \times \frac{\pi}{4} + \frac{\pi}{2}\right) = 0$

When $x = \frac{\pi}{4}$, $\frac{dy}{dx} = 6\cos\left(2 \times \frac{\pi}{4} + \frac{\pi}{2}\right) = -6$

The gradient of the tangent × the gradient of the normal = −1

The normal passes through the point $\left(\frac{\pi}{4}, 0\right)$ with gradient $= \frac{1}{6}$

$y - 0 = \frac{1}{6}\left(x - \frac{\pi}{4}\right)$

$y = \frac{1}{6}x - \frac{\pi}{24}$

$24y = 4x - \pi$

$4x - 24y = \pi$

2 a $\frac{d}{dx}(x\sin 2x) = x \times \frac{d}{dx}(\sin 2x) + \sin 2x \times \frac{d}{dx}(x)$ product rule

$= x \times (2\cos 2x) + \sin 2x \times (1)$

$= 2x\cos 2x + \sin 2x$

When $x = \frac{\pi}{4}$, $\frac{dy}{dx} = \left(2 \times \frac{\pi}{4}\right)\cos\left(2 \times \frac{\pi}{4}\right) + \sin\left(2 \times \frac{\pi}{4}\right) = 1$

The gradient of the tangent × the gradient of the normal = −1

The normal passes through the point $\left(\frac{\pi}{4}, \frac{\pi}{4}\right)$ with gradient = −1

$y - \frac{\pi}{4} = -1\left(x - \frac{\pi}{4}\right)$

$4y - \pi = -4x + \pi$

$2x + 2y = \pi$

b The normal intersects the x-axis where $y = 0$

So, $2x + 2 \times 0 = \pi$

$x = \frac{\pi}{2}$

$Q = \left(\frac{\pi}{2}, 0\right)$

The normal intersects the y-axis where $x = 0$

So, $2 \times 0 + 2y = \pi$

$y = \frac{\pi}{2}$

$R = \left(0, \frac{\pi}{2}\right)$

c Triangle OQR is right-angled at O, so area of triangle $OQR = \frac{1}{2} \times \frac{\pi}{2} \times \frac{\pi}{2} = \frac{\pi^2}{8}$ units²

3 The curve crosses the y-axis where $x = 0$

So, $y = e^{\frac{1}{2}\times 0} + 1 = 2$

$P = (0, 2)$

$y = e^{\frac{1}{2}x} + 1$ use $\frac{d}{dx}[e^{f(x)}] = f'(x) \times e^{f(x)}$

$\frac{dy}{dx} = \frac{1}{2}e^{\frac{1}{2}x}$

When $x = 0$, $\frac{dy}{dx} = \frac{1}{2}e^{\frac{1}{2}\times 0} = \frac{1}{2}$

The normal passes through the point (0, 2) with gradient $= -2$

$y - 2 = -2(x - 0)$

$y = -2x + 2$ is the equation of the normal.

The normal meets the x-axis where $y = 0$

So, $0 = -2x + 2$

$x = 1$

$Q = (1, 0)$

4 a $y = 5 - e^{2x}$

The curve crosses the x-axis where $y = 0$

So, $0 = 5 - e^{2x}$

$e^{2x} = 5$ take $\log_e$ of both sides

$\log_e e^{2x} = \log_e 5$ use power rule for logs

$2x \log_e e = \log_e 5$

$2x = \ln 5$

$x = \frac{1}{2}\ln 5$

$A = \left(\frac{1}{2}\ln 5, 0\right)$

The curve crosses the y-axis where $x = 0$

$y = 5 - e^{2\times 0}$

$y = 4$

$B = (0, 4)$

b $y = 5 - e^{2x}$ use $\frac{d}{dx}[e^{f(x)}] = f'(x) \times e^{f(x)}$

$\frac{dy}{dx} = -2e^{2x}$

When $x = 0$, $\frac{dy}{dx} = -2e^{2\times 0} = -2$

The normal passes through the point (0, 4) with gradient $= \frac{1}{2}$

$y - 4 = \frac{1}{2}(x - 0)$

The equation of the normal at B is $y = \frac{1}{2}x + 4$

This normal meets the x-axis where $y = 0$

So, $0 = \frac{1}{2}x + 4$

$x = -8$

$C = (-8, 0)$

5 $y = xe^x$

$\frac{d}{dx}(xe^x) = x \times \frac{d}{dx}(e^x) + e^x \times \frac{d}{dx}(x)$ product rule

$= xe^x + e^x$

The gradient of the tangent at $P(1, e)$ i.e. when $x = 1$ is $1e^1 + e^1 = 2e$

The equation of the tangent at P is $y - e = 2e(x - 1)$

$y - e = 2ex - 2e$

$y = 2ex - e$

This tangent meets the y-axis where $x = 0$

So, $y = 2e \times 0 - e$

$y = -e$

$A = (0, -e)$

The gradient of the normal at $P(1, e)$ i.e. when $x = 1$ is $-\frac{1}{2e}$

The equation of the normal at P is $y - e = -\frac{1}{2e}(x - 1)$

$2ey - 2e^2 = -x + 1$

$2ey + x = 2e^2 + 1$

This normal meets the x-axis where $y = 0$

So, $2e \times 0 + x = 2e^2 + 1$

$x = 2e^2 + 1$

$B = (2e^2 + 1, 0)$

Triangle OAB is right-angled at O so area of triangle $OAB = \frac{1}{2} \times (2e^2 + 1) \times e$

$= \frac{1}{2}e(2e^2 + 1)$ units^2

6 $y = \sin 2x$

$\frac{dy}{dx} = 2\cos 2x$

When $x = \frac{\pi}{8}$, $\frac{dy}{dx} = 2\cos\left(2 \times \frac{\pi}{8}\right) = \sqrt{2}$

Using $\frac{\delta y}{\delta x} \approx \frac{dy}{dx}$

$$\frac{\delta y}{p} \approx \sqrt{2}$$

$$\delta y \approx \sqrt{2} \times p$$

$$\delta y \approx \sqrt{2}\,p$$

7 $y = 3 + \ln(2x - 5)$ — use the chain rule to differentiate $\ln(2x - 5)$

$$\frac{d}{dx}[\ln(2x - 5)] = \frac{2}{2x - 5}$$

$$\frac{dy}{dx} = \frac{2}{2x - 5}$$

When $x = 4$, $\frac{dy}{dx} = \frac{2}{2(4) - 5} = \frac{2}{3}$

Using $\frac{\delta y}{\delta x} \approx \frac{dy}{dx}$

$$\frac{\delta y}{p} \approx \frac{2}{3}$$

$$\delta y \approx \frac{2}{3} \times p$$

$$\delta y \approx \frac{2}{3}p$$

8 $y = \frac{\ln x}{x^2 + 3}$ — use the quotient rule

$$\frac{dy}{dx} = \frac{(x^2 + 3) \times \frac{d}{dx}(\ln x) - \ln x \times \frac{d}{dx}(x^2 + 3)}{(x^2 + 3)^2}$$

$$\frac{dy}{dx} = \frac{(x^2 + 3) \times \frac{1}{x} - \ln x \times (2x)}{(x^2 + 3)^2}$$

multiply numerator and denominator by x

$$\frac{dy}{dx} = \frac{(x^2 + 3) - 2x^2 \ln x}{x(x^2 + 3)^2}$$

When $x = 1$, $\frac{dy}{dx} = \frac{(1^2 + 3) - 2(1^2)\ln 1}{1(1^2 + 3)^2} = \frac{1}{4}$

Using $\frac{\delta y}{\delta x} \approx \frac{dy}{dx}$

$$\frac{\delta y}{p} \approx \frac{1}{4}$$

$$\delta y \approx \frac{1}{4} \times p$$

$$\delta y \approx \frac{1}{4}p$$

9 $y = 3 + 2x - 5e^{-x}$

use $\frac{d}{dx}[e^{f(x)}] = f'(x) \times e^{f(x)}$

$\frac{dy}{dx} = 2 + 5e^{-x}$

When $x = \ln 2$, $\frac{dy}{dx} = 2 + 5e^{-\ln 2} = 2 + 5 \times \frac{1}{2} = \frac{9}{2}$

Using $\frac{\delta y}{\delta x} \approx \frac{dy}{dx}$

$\frac{\delta y}{p} \approx \frac{9}{2}$

$\delta y \approx \frac{9}{2} \times p$

$\delta y \approx \frac{9}{2}p$

10 $y = \frac{\ln(x^2 - 2)}{x^2 - 2}$

use the quotient rule to differentiate

$$\frac{dy}{dx} = \frac{(x^2 - 2) \times \frac{d}{dx}[\ln(x^2 - 2)] - \ln(x^2 - 2) \times \frac{d}{dx}(x^2 - 2)}{(x^2 - 2)^2}$$

use the chain rule to find $\frac{d}{dx}[\ln(x^2 - 2)]$

i.e $\frac{d}{dx}[\ln(x^2 - 2)] = \frac{2x}{x^2 - 2}$

So, $\frac{dy}{dx} = \frac{(x^2 - 2) \times \frac{2x}{(x^2 - 2)} - \ln(x^2 - 2) \times (2x)}{(x^2 - 2)^2}$

$\frac{dy}{dx} = \frac{2x - 2x\ln(x^2 - 2)}{(x^2 - 2)^2}$

When $x = \sqrt{3}$, $\frac{dy}{dx} = \frac{2\sqrt{3} - 2\sqrt{3}\ln\left((\sqrt{3})^2 - 2\right)}{\left((\sqrt{3})^2 - 2\right)^2} = 2\sqrt{3}$

Using $\frac{\delta y}{\delta x} \approx \frac{dy}{dx}$

$\frac{\delta y}{p} \approx 2\sqrt{3}$

$\delta y \approx 2\sqrt{3}p$

11 a $y = xe^{\frac{x}{2}}$

product rule

$\frac{dy}{dx} = x \times \frac{d}{dx}\left(e^{\frac{x}{2}}\right) + e^{\frac{x}{2}} \times \frac{d}{dx}(x)$

$\frac{dy}{dx} = \frac{1}{2}xe^{\frac{x}{2}} + e^{\frac{x}{2}}$

At a stationary point, $\frac{dy}{dx} = 0$

$\frac{1}{2}xe^{\frac{x}{2}} + e^{\frac{x}{2}} = 0$ factorise

$e^{\frac{x}{2}}\left(\frac{1}{2}x + 1\right) = 0$

$e^{\frac{x}{2}} = 0$ no solutions or $\frac{1}{2}x + 1 = 0$

$x = -2$

There is a stationary point at $x = -2$

Substituting $x = -2$ into $y = xe^{\frac{x}{2}}$ gives:

$y = -2e^{\frac{-2}{2}} = -2e^{-1}$

The stationary point is at $(-2, -2e^{-1})$

To determine the nature of the stationary point, find $\frac{d^2y}{dx^2}$

$\frac{dy}{dx} = \frac{1}{2}xe^{\frac{x}{2}} + e^{\frac{x}{2}}$ product rule

$\frac{d^2y}{dx^2} = \frac{1}{2}x \times \frac{d}{dx}\left(e^{\frac{x}{2}}\right) + e^{\frac{x}{2}} \times \frac{d}{dx}\left(\frac{1}{2}x\right) + \frac{d}{dx}\left(e^{\frac{x}{2}}\right)$

$\frac{d^2y}{dx^2} = \frac{1}{2}x \times \frac{1}{2}e^{\frac{x}{2}} + \frac{1}{2}e^{\frac{x}{2}} + \frac{1}{2}e^{\frac{x}{2}}$

$\frac{d^2y}{dx^2} = e^{\frac{1}{2}x}\left(\frac{1}{4}x + 1\right)$

Substituting $x = -2$ gives:

$\frac{d^2y}{dx^2} = e^{-1}\left(-\frac{1}{2} + 1\right) = \frac{1}{2}e^{-1}$ which is > 0

$(-2, -2e^{-1})$ is a minimum point.

e $y = (x^2 - 8)e^{-x}$ product rule

$\frac{dy}{dx} = (x^2 - 8) \times \frac{d}{dx}(e^{-x}) + e^{-x} \times \frac{d}{dx}(x^2 - 8)$

$\frac{dy}{dx} = -e^{-x}(x^2 - 8) + 2xe^{-x}$

$\frac{dy}{dx} = -e^{-x}(x^2 - 2x - 8)$

At a stationary point, $\frac{dy}{dx} = 0$

$-e^{-x} = 0$ no solutions or $x^2 - 2x - 8 = 0$

$(x + 2)(x - 4) = 0$

$x = -2$ or $x = 4$

There are stationary points at $x = -2$ and $x = 4$

Substituting $x = -2$ into $y = (x^2 - 8)e^{-x}$ gives:

$y = [(-2)^2 - 8]e^{-(-2)}$

The stationary point is at $(-2, -4e^2)$

Substituting $x = 4$ into $y = (x^2 - 8)e^{-x}$ gives:

$y = (4^2 - 8)e^{-4}$

The stationary point is at $(4, 8e^{-4})$

To determine the nature of the stationary points, find $\frac{d^2y}{dx^2}$

$\frac{dy}{dx} = -e^{-x}(x^2 - 2x - 8)$ product rule

$\frac{d^2y}{dx^2} = -e^{-x} \times \frac{d}{dx}(x^2 - 2x - 8) + (x^2 - 2x - 8) \times \frac{d}{dx}(-e^{-x})$

$\frac{d^2y}{dx^2} = -(2x - 2)e^{-x} + e^{-x}(x^2 - 2x - 8)$

$\frac{d^2y}{dx^2} = e^{-x}(-2x + 2 + x^2 - 2x - 8)$

$\frac{d^2y}{dx^2} = e^{-x}(x^2 - 4x - 6)$

Substituting $x = -2$ gives:

$\frac{d^2y}{dx^2} = e^{-(-2)}[(-2)^2 - 4(-2) - 6] = 6e^2$ which is > 0

$(-2, -4e^2)$ is a minimum point.

Substituting $x = 4$ gives:

$\frac{d^2y}{dx^2} = e^{-4}[4^2 - 4(4) - 6] = -6e^{-4}$ which is < 0

$(4, 8e^{-4})$ is a maximum point.

12 c $y = 5\sin\left(2x + \frac{\pi}{2}\right)$ for $-\frac{\pi}{6} \leqslant x \leqslant \frac{5\pi}{6}$

$\frac{dy}{dx} = 5\frac{d}{dx}\left[\sin\left(2x + \frac{\pi}{2}\right)\right]$

$\frac{dy}{dx} = 5 \times \cos\left(2x + \frac{\pi}{2}\right) \times (2)$

$\frac{dy}{dx} = 10\cos\left(2x + \frac{\pi}{2}\right)$

At a stationary point, $\frac{dy}{dx} = 0$

$10\cos\left(2x + \frac{\pi}{2}\right) = 0$

$\cos\left(2x + \frac{\pi}{2}\right) = 0$ Let $A = \left(2x + \frac{\pi}{2}\right)$

$\cos A = 0$ use your calculator to find $\cos^{-1}(0)$

$A = \frac{\pi}{2}$

As $A = \left(2x + \frac{\pi}{2}\right)$, draw the graph of $y = \cos A$ for $\frac{\pi}{6} \leqslant A \leqslant \frac{13\pi}{6}$

[The domain of A is found by using $-\frac{\pi}{6} \leqslant x \leqslant \frac{5\pi}{6}$.

Substituting $x = -\frac{\pi}{6}$ into $A = \left(2x + \frac{\pi}{2}\right)$, gives $A = \left(2 \times -\frac{\pi}{6} + \frac{\pi}{2}\right) = \frac{\pi}{6}$

Substituting $x = \frac{5\pi}{6}$ into $A = \left(2x + \frac{\pi}{2}\right)$, gives $A = \left(2 \times \frac{5\pi}{6} + \frac{\pi}{2}\right) = \frac{13\pi}{6}$]

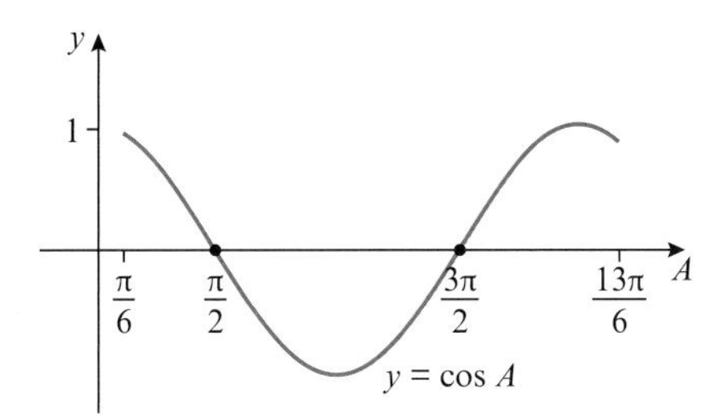

Using the symmetry of the curve:

$A = \frac{\pi}{2}$ and $A = \frac{3\pi}{2}$

As $A = 2x + \frac{\pi}{2}$

$\frac{\pi}{2} = 2x + \frac{\pi}{2}$ and $\frac{3\pi}{2} = 2x + \frac{\pi}{2}$

$x = 0$ and $x = \frac{\pi}{2}$

If $x = 0$, then substituting into $y = 5\sin\left(2x + \frac{\pi}{2}\right)$ gives:

$y = 5\sin\left(2 \times 0 + \frac{\pi}{2}\right) = 5$

One stationary point is at $(0, 5)$

If $x = \frac{\pi}{2}$, then substituting into $y = 5\sin\left(2x + \frac{\pi}{2}\right)$ gives:

$y = 5\sin\left(2 \times \frac{\pi}{2} + \frac{\pi}{2}\right) = -5$

The other stationary point is at $\left(\frac{\pi}{2}, -5\right)$

To determine the nature of the stationary points, find $\frac{d^2y}{dx^2}$

$\frac{dy}{dx} = 10\cos\left(2x + \frac{\pi}{2}\right)$

$\frac{d^2y}{dx^2} = 10\frac{d}{dx}\left[\cos\left(2x + \frac{\pi}{2}\right)\right]$

$= 10 \times -\sin\left(2x + \frac{\pi}{2}\right) \times (2)$

$= -20\sin\left(2x + \frac{\pi}{2}\right)$

When $x = 0$, $\frac{d^2y}{dx^2} = -20\sin\left(2 \times 0 + \frac{\pi}{2}\right) = -20$ which is < 0

So, (0, 5) is a maximum point.

When $x = \frac{\pi}{2}$, $\frac{d^2y}{dx^2} = -20\sin\left(2 \times \frac{\pi}{2} + \frac{\pi}{2}\right) = 20$ which is > 0

So, $\left(\frac{\pi}{2}, -5\right)$ is a minimum point.

e $y = 2\sin x\cos x + 2\cos x$ for $0 \leqslant x \leqslant \pi$ — product rule

$\frac{dy}{dx} = 2\sin x \times \frac{d}{dx}(\cos x) + \cos x \times \frac{d}{dx}(2\sin x) + \frac{d}{dx}(2\cos x)$

$\frac{dy}{dx} = -2\sin^2 x + 2\cos^2 x - 2\sin x$ — use $\sin^2 x + \cos^2 x = 1$

$\frac{dy}{dx} = -2\sin^2 x + 2(1 - \sin^2 x) - 2\sin x$

$\frac{dy}{dx} = -2\sin^2 x + 2 - 2\sin^2 x - 2\sin x$

$\frac{dy}{dx} = -4\sin^2 x - 2\sin x + 2$

At a stationary point, $\frac{dy}{dx} = 0$

$-4\sin^2 x - 2\sin x + 2 = 0$ — multiply both sides by $-\frac{1}{2}$

$2\sin^2 x + \sin x - 1 = 0$ — factorise

$(2\sin x - 1)(\sin x + 1) = 0$ — solve

$2\sin x - 1 = 0$ or $\sin x + 1 = 0$

$\sin x = \frac{1}{2}$ or $\sin x = -1$ (no solutions since $0 \leqslant x \leqslant \pi$)

$x = \frac{\pi}{6}$ and $x = \frac{5\pi}{6}$

If $x = \frac{\pi}{6}$ then substituting into $y = 2\sin x\cos x + 2\cos x$ gives:

$y = 2\sin\frac{\pi}{6}\cos\frac{\pi}{6} + 2\cos\frac{\pi}{6} = \frac{\sqrt{3}}{2} + \sqrt{3} = \frac{3\sqrt{3}}{2}$

So, there is a stationary point at $\left(\frac{\pi}{6}, \frac{3\sqrt{3}}{2}\right)$

If $x = \frac{5\pi}{6}$ then substituting into $y = 2\sin x\cos x + 2\cos x$ gives:

$y = 2\sin\frac{5\pi}{6}\cos\frac{5\pi}{6} + 2\cos\frac{5\pi}{6} = -\frac{\sqrt{3}}{2} - \sqrt{3} = -\frac{3\sqrt{3}}{2}$

So there is a stationary point at $\left(\frac{5\pi}{6}, -\frac{3\sqrt{3}}{2}\right)$

To determine the nature of the stationary points, find $\frac{d^2y}{dx^2}$

Use any of the expressions for $\frac{dy}{dx}$ e.g. $\frac{dy}{dx} = -4\sin^2 x - 2\sin x + 2$

$\frac{d^2y}{dx^2} = -8\sin x\cos x - 2\cos x$

When $x = \frac{\pi}{6}$, $\frac{d^2y}{dx^2} = -8\sin\frac{\pi}{6}\cos\frac{\pi}{6} - 2\cos\frac{\pi}{6} = -3\sqrt{3}$ which is < 0

So, $\left(\frac{\pi}{6}, \frac{3\sqrt{3}}{2}\right)$ is a maximum point.

When $x = \frac{5\pi}{6}$, $\frac{d^2y}{dx^2} = -8\sin\frac{5\pi}{6}\cos\frac{5\pi}{6} - 2\cos\frac{5\pi}{6} = 3\sqrt{3}$ which is > 0

So, $\left(\frac{5\pi}{6}, -\frac{3\sqrt{3}}{2}\right)$ is a minimum point.

13 a $y = Ae^{2x} + Be^{-2x}$

Substituting $x = 0$ and $y = 10$ gives:

$10 = Ae^{2\times 0} + Be^{-2\times 0}$

$A + B = 10$ (1)

$\frac{dy}{dx} = 2Ae^{2x} - 2Be^{-2x}$

Substituting $x = 0$ and $\frac{dy}{dx} = -12$ gives:

$2Ae^{2\times 0} - 2Be^{-2\times 0} = -12$

$A - B = -6$ (2)

Adding (1) and (2) gives:

$2A = 4$

$A = 2$

Substituting $A = 2$ into (1) gives:

$2 + B = 10$

$B = 8$

$y = 2e^{2x} + 8e^{-2x}$

b $\frac{dy}{dx} = 4e^{2x} - 16e^{-2x}$

At a turning point, $\frac{dy}{dx} = 0$

$4e^{2x} - 16e^{-2x} = 0$ multiply both sides by $\frac{1}{4}e^{2x}$

$e^{4x} - 4 = 0$

$e^{4x} = 4$ take $\log_e$ of both sides

$\log_e e^{4x} = \log_e 4$ use power rule for logs

$4x\log_e e = \log_e 4$ $\log_e e = \ln e = 1$

$4x = \ln 4$

$x = \frac{1}{4}\ln 4$

Substitute $x = \frac{1}{4}\ln 4$ into $y = 2e^{2x} + 8e^{-2x}$ gives:

$y = 2e^{2\times\frac{1}{4}\ln 4} + 8e^{-2\times\frac{1}{4}\ln 4}$

$y = 2e^{\ln 4^{\frac{1}{2}}} + 8e^{\ln 4^{-\frac{1}{2}}}$ use power rule for logs i.e $\ln a^m = m \ln a$

$y = 2e^{\ln 2} + 8e^{\ln 2^{-1}}$

$y = 2 \times 2 + 8 \times 2^{-1}$

$y = 8$

There is a turning point at $\left(\frac{1}{4}\ln 4, 8\right)$

To determine the nature of the stationary point, find $\frac{d^2y}{dx^2}$

$\frac{d^2y}{dx^2} = 8e^{2x} + 32e^{-2x}$

When $x = \frac{1}{4}\ln 4$, $\frac{d^2y}{dx^2} = 8e^{2\times\frac{1}{4}\ln 4} + 32e^{-2\times\frac{1}{4}\ln 4} = 40$ which is > 0

So, $\left(\frac{1}{4}\ln 4, 8\right)$ is a minimum point.

14 $y = x \ln x$ crosses the x-axis where $y = 0$

$x \ln x = 0$

$x = 0$ or $\ln x = 0$

$x = 1$

When $x = 0$, $y = 0 \ln 0$ (0 ln 0 is undefined)

When $x = 1$, $y = 1 \ln 1 = 0$

So, $A = (1, 0)$

To find the coordinates of a stationary point on the curve, find $\frac{dy}{dx}$

Use the product rule:

$\frac{dy}{dx} = x \times \frac{d}{dx}(\ln x) + \ln x \times \frac{d}{dx}(x)$

$= 1 + \ln x$

At a stationary point $\frac{dy}{dx} = 0$

$1 + \ln x = 0$

$\ln x = -1$ or $\log_e x = -1$

$x = e^{-1}$

When $x = e^{-1}$, $y = e^{-1}\ln(e^{-1})$

[Using the power rule of logs $\ln e^{-1}$ is the same as $-1 \ln e$ which is -1]

So, $y = e^{-1} \times -1$

The stationary point B is at $(e^{-1}, -e^{-1})$

15 a $y = x^2 e^x$ product rule

$$\frac{dy}{dx} = x^2 \times \frac{d}{dx}(e^x) + e^x \times \frac{d}{dx}(x^2)$$

$$= x^2 \times (e^x) + e^x \times (2x)$$

$$= x^2 e^x + 2xe^x \text{ or } xe^x(x + 2)$$

At a stationary point, $\frac{dy}{dx} = 0$

$xe^x(x + 2) = 0$

So, $x = 0$ or

$e^x = 0$ (no solutions) or

$x + 2 = 0$ (so $x = -2$)

The stationary points have x-coordinates $x = 0$ and $x = -2$

When $x = 0$, $y = x^2 e^x$ so $y = 0^2 e^0 = 0$

When $x = -2$, $y = x^2 e^x$ so $y = (-2)^2 e^{-2} = 4e^{-2}$

The stationary points are at $(0, 0)$ and $(-2, 4e^{-2})$

To determine the nature of the stationary points, find $\frac{d^2y}{dx^2}$

$$\frac{dy}{dx} = x^2 e^x + 2xe^x$$

$$\frac{d^2y}{dx^2} = \frac{d}{dx}(x^2 e^x) + \frac{d}{dx}(2xe^x)$$ product rule

$$\frac{d^2y}{dx^2} = x^2 e^x + 2xe^x + 2xe^x + 2e^x$$

$$\frac{d^2y}{dx^2} = x^2 e^x + 4xe^x + 2e^x$$

When $x = 0$, $\frac{d^2y}{dx^2} = 0^2 e^0 + 4(0)e^0 + 2e^0 = 2$ which is > 0

When $x = -2$, $\frac{d^2y}{dx^2} = (-2)^2 e^{(-2)} + 4(-2)e^{-2} + 2e^{-2} = -2e^{-2}$ which is < 0

So, $P = (0, 0)$ is a minimum point and $Q = (-2, 4e^{-2})$ is a maximum point.

b Find the equation of the tangent at $A(1, e)$

Find the gradient at the point $x = 1$

$\frac{dy}{dx} = x^2e^x + 2xe^x$ substitute $x = 1$

$\frac{dy}{dx} = 1^2e^1 + 2(1)e^1 = 3e$

The tangent at A passes through the point $(1, e)$ with gradient $= 3e$

$y - e = 3e(x - 1)$

$y = 3ex - 2e$

This tangent meets the y-axis at point B where $x = 0$

So, $y = 3e \times 0 - 2e = -2e$

Point B is at $(0, -2e)$

The gradient of the tangent $\times$ the gradient of the normal $= -1$

The normal passes through the point $(1, e)$ with gradient $= -\frac{1}{3e}$

$y - e = -\frac{1}{3e}(x - 1)$

This normal meets the y-axis at point C where $x = 0$

So, $y - e = -\frac{1}{3e}(0 - 1)$

$y = e + \frac{1}{3e}$

Point C is at $\left(0, e + \frac{1}{3e}\right)$

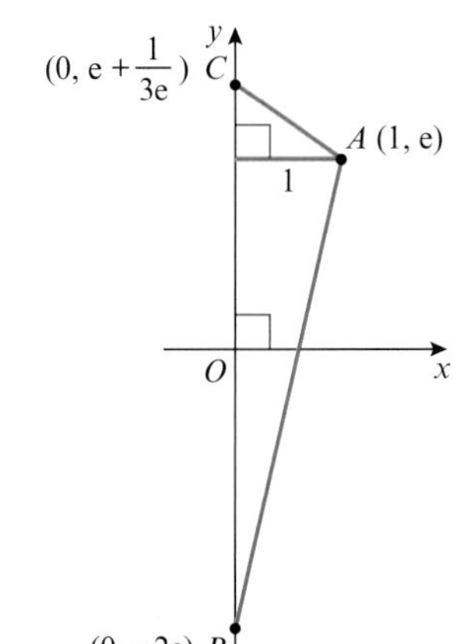

c Area of triangle $ABC = \frac{1}{2} \times$ base $(BC) \times$ perpendicular height

$= \frac{1}{2} \times \left[2e + \left(e + \frac{1}{3e}\right)\right] \times 1$

$= \frac{1}{2}\left(3e + \frac{1}{3e}\right)$ units²

16 a Join G to O (the centre of the semi-circle)

$EO = OG = 6$ centimetres

Angle $GOE = (\pi - 2\theta)$ radians

Angle $GOF = 2\theta$ radians

Shaded area A = area of sector GOF + area of triangle GOE

REMEMBER

Area of a sector $= \frac{1}{2}r^2\theta$ and area of a non right-angled triangle $= \frac{1}{2}ab \sin C$

$= \frac{1}{2} \times 6^2 \times 2\theta + \frac{1}{2} \times 6 \times 6 \times \sin(\pi - 2\theta)$

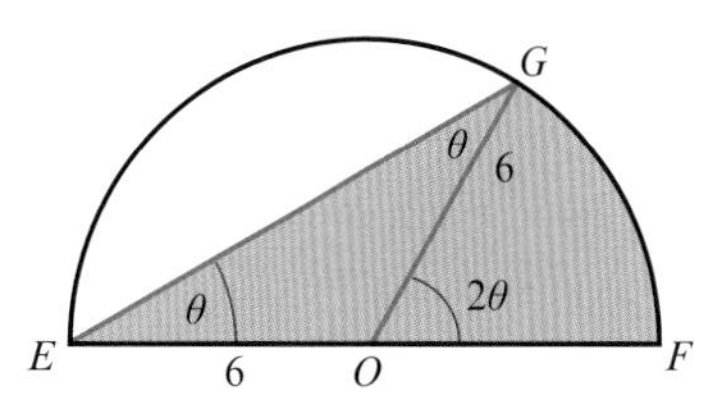

$= 36\theta + 18 \sin(\pi - 2\theta)$

The symmetry of the graph shows why $\sin(\pi - 2\theta)$ is the same as $\sin 2\theta$

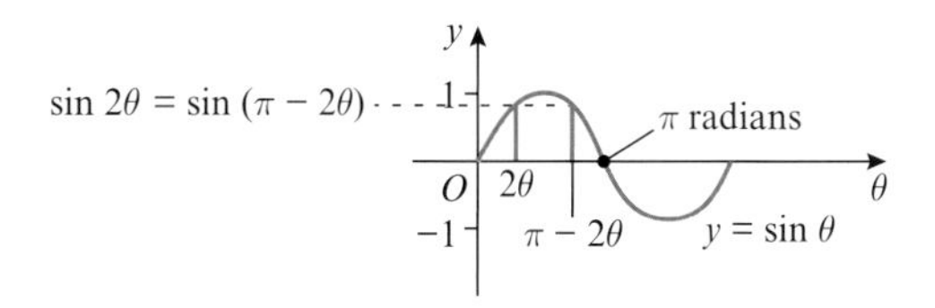

So, $A = 36\theta + 18 \sin 2\theta$

b $\frac{d\theta}{dt} = 0.05$ find $\frac{dA}{dt}$

The chain rule states that $\frac{dA}{dt} = \frac{dA}{d\theta} \times \frac{d\theta}{dt}$

$A = 36\theta + 18 \sin 2\theta$

$\frac{dA}{d\theta} = 36 + 36 \cos 2\theta$

$\frac{dA}{dt} = (36 + 36 \cos 2\theta) \times 0.05$

$\frac{dA}{dt} = 1.8 + 1.8 \cos 2\theta$, so when $\theta = \frac{\pi}{6}$ radians:

$\frac{dA}{dt} = 1.8 + 1.8 \cos\frac{\pi}{3}$

$\frac{dA}{dt}$ = the rate of change of $A = 2.7\,\text{cm}^2$ per second

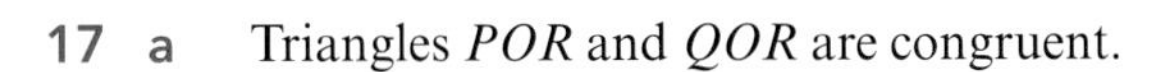

17 a Triangles POR and QOR are congruent.

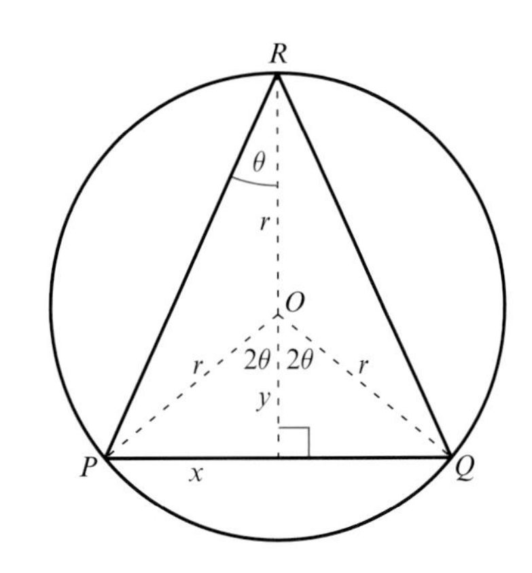

Using the area of a non right-angled triangle $= \frac{1}{2}ab \sin C$:

The area of triangle $OPR = \frac{1}{2} \times r \times r \times \sin(\pi - 2\theta) = \frac{1}{2}r^2 \sin(\pi - 2\theta)$

Angle $POQ = 2\pi - (\pi - 2\theta) - (\pi - 2\theta) = 4\theta$

Divide triangle POQ into 2 equal right-angled triangles (see diagram)

$x = r \sin 2\theta$ and $y = r \cos 2\theta$

Area of left hand triangle $= \frac{1}{2} \times x \times y = \frac{1}{2} \times r \sin 2\theta \times r \cos 2\theta$

$= \frac{1}{2}r^2 \sin 2\theta \cos 2\theta$

Area of triangle $POQ = 2 \times \frac{1}{2}r^2 \sin 2\theta \cos 2\theta = r^2 \sin 2\theta \cos 2\theta$

Shaded area$= \frac{1}{2}r^2 \sin(\pi - 2\theta) + \frac{1}{2}r^2 \sin(\pi - 2\theta) + r^2 \sin 2\theta \cos 2\theta$

The symmetry of the graph shows why $\sin(\pi - 2\theta)$ is the same as $\sin 2\theta$

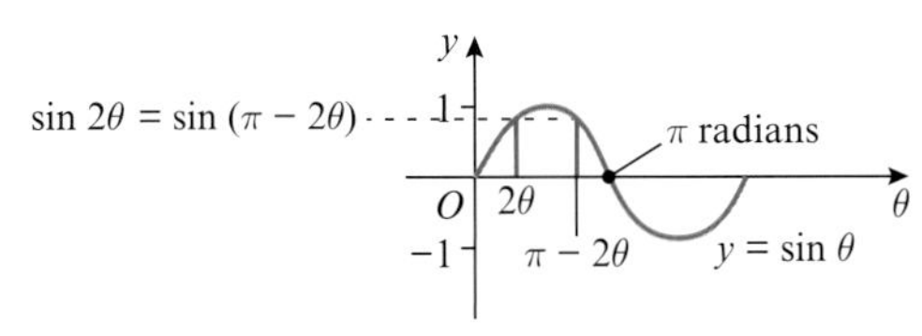

Shaded area $= \frac{1}{2}r^2 \sin 2\theta + \frac{1}{2}r^2 \sin 2\theta + r^2 \sin 2\theta \cos 2\theta$

$A = r^2 \sin 2\theta + r^2 \sin 2\theta \cos 2\theta$

b The radius of the circle is fixed as r cm so it is a constant term.

The angle θ is the variable

$A = r^2[\sin 2\theta(1 + \cos 2\theta)]$

At a stationary point, $\frac{dA}{d\theta} = 0$.

Use the product rule:

$\frac{dA}{d\theta} = r^2[\sin 2\theta \times \frac{d}{d\theta}(1 + \cos 2\theta) + (1 + \cos 2\theta) \times \frac{d}{d\theta}\sin 2\theta]$

$= r^2[\sin 2\theta \times -2 \sin 2\theta + (1 + \cos 2\theta) \times 2 \cos 2\theta]$.

$= r^2(-2 \sin^2 2\theta + 2 \cos 2\theta + 2 \cos^2 2\theta)$ (1)

Use $\sin^2\theta + \cos^2\theta = 1$

So, $\sin^2 2\theta + \cos^2 2\theta = 1$ multiply by 2

$2 \sin^2 2\theta + 2 \cos^2 2\theta = 2$ rearrange

$-2 \sin^2 2\theta = 2 \cos^2 2\theta - 2$

Substitute for $-2\sin^2 2\theta$ into (1)

$$\frac{dA}{d\theta} = r^2(2\cos^2 2\theta - 2 + 2\cos 2\theta + 2\cos^2 2\theta)$$

$$\frac{dA}{d\theta} = r^2(4\cos^2 2\theta + 2\cos 2\theta - 2)$$

$$\frac{dA}{d\theta} = 2r^2(2\cos^2 2\theta + \cos 2\theta - 1) \qquad \text{factorise}$$

$$\frac{dA}{d\theta} = 2r^2(2\cos 2\theta - 1)(\cos 2\theta + 1)$$

At a stationary point, $\frac{dA}{d\theta} = 0$

$2r^2$ is positive providing $r > 0$

$2\cos 2\theta - 1 = 0$ or $\cos 2\theta + 1 = 0$

$\cos 2\theta = 0.5$ or $\cos 2\theta = -1$

$2\theta = \frac{\pi}{3}$ and $\frac{5\pi}{3}$ or $2\theta = \pi$

$\theta = \frac{\pi}{6}$ and $\frac{5\pi}{6}$ or $\theta = \frac{\pi}{2}$

However, as determined from the diagram $\theta < \frac{\pi}{2}$ so there is a stationary point when $\theta = \frac{\pi}{6}$ radians

To determine the nature of the stationary point at $\frac{\pi}{6}$, find the gradient of the curve either side of $\theta = \frac{\pi}{6}$

Now choose values of close to and either side of $\theta = \frac{\pi}{6}$:

Substituting $\theta = \frac{\pi}{9}$ gives $\frac{dA}{d\theta} = 2r^2\left(2\cos 2\left(\frac{\pi}{9}\right) - 1\right)\left(\cos 2\left(\frac{\pi}{9}\right) + 1\right)$ which is positive.

Substituting $\theta = \frac{2\pi}{9}$ gives $\frac{dA}{d\theta} = 2r^2\left(2\cos 2\left(\frac{2\pi}{9}\right) - 1\right)\left(\cos 2\left(\frac{2\pi}{9}\right) + 1\right)$ which is negative.

θ	$\frac{\pi}{9}$	$\frac{\pi}{6}$	$\frac{2\pi}{9}$
$\frac{dA}{d\theta}$	positive	0	negative
Direction of Tangent	/	—	\
Shape of curve		∩	

Therefore, when $\theta = \frac{\pi}{6}$ radians it is a maximum value of A.

Chapter 15: Calculus – Integration

Exercise 15.1

REMEMBER

If $\frac{dy}{dx} = x^n$ then $y = \frac{1}{n+1}x^{n+1} + c$, where c is an arbitrary constant and $n \neq -1$

1 d $\frac{dy}{dx} = \frac{4}{x^3}$ write in index form ready for integration

$\frac{dy}{dx} = 4x^{-3}$

$y = \frac{4}{-3+1}x^{-3+1} + c$

$y = \frac{4}{-2}x^{-2} + c$

$y = -\frac{2}{x^2} + c$

f $\frac{dy}{dx} = \frac{3}{\sqrt{x}}$ write in index form ready for integration

$\frac{dy}{dx} = 3x^{-\frac{1}{2}}$

$y = \frac{3}{-\frac{1}{2}+1}x^{-\frac{1}{2}+1} + c$

$y = \frac{3}{\frac{1}{2}}x^{\frac{1}{2}} + c$

$y = 6\sqrt{x} + c$

2 b $\frac{dy}{dx} = 2x^5 - 3x^3 + 5x$

$y = \frac{2}{6}x^6 - \frac{3}{4}x^4 + \frac{5}{2}x^2 + c$

$= \frac{x^6}{3} - \frac{3}{4}x^4 + \frac{5}{2}x^2 + c$

d $\frac{dy}{dx} = \frac{18}{x^{10}} + \frac{6}{x^7} - 2$ write in index form ready for integration

$= 18x^{-10} + 6x^{-7} - 2x^0$

$y = \frac{18}{-9}x^{-9} + \frac{6}{-6}x^{-6} - \frac{2}{1}x^1 + c$

$= -\frac{2}{x^9} - \frac{1}{x^6} - 2x + c$

3 **c** $\frac{dy}{dx} = (x + 2\sqrt{x})^2$ expand brackets

$\frac{dy}{dx} = (x + 2\sqrt{x})(x + 2\sqrt{x})$

$\frac{dy}{dx} = x^2 + 2x\sqrt{x} + 2x\sqrt{x} + 4x$ write in index form ready for integration

$\frac{dy}{dx} = x^2 + 2x \times x^{\frac{1}{2}} + 2x \times x^{\frac{1}{2}} + 4x$ simplify

$\frac{dy}{dx} = x^2 + 4x^{\frac{3}{2}} + 4x$

$y = \frac{1}{3}x^3 + \frac{4}{\frac{5}{2}}x^{\frac{5}{2}} + 2x^2 + c$

$y = \frac{x^3}{3} + \frac{8}{5}x^{\frac{5}{2}} + 2x^2 + c$

h $\frac{dy}{dx} = \frac{(3x + 5)(x - 2)}{\sqrt{x}}$ expand brackets

$\frac{dy}{dx} = \frac{3x^2 - 6x + 5x - 10}{\sqrt{x}}$

$\frac{dy}{dx} = \frac{3x^2 - x - 10}{x^{\frac{1}{2}}}$

$\frac{dy}{dx} = 3x^{\frac{3}{2}} - x^{\frac{1}{2}} - 10x^{-\frac{1}{2}}$ integrate

$y = \frac{3}{\frac{5}{2}}x^{\frac{5}{2}} - \frac{1}{\frac{3}{2}}x^{\frac{3}{2}} - \frac{10}{\frac{1}{2}}x^{\frac{1}{2}} + c$

$y = \frac{6}{5}x^{\frac{5}{2}} - \frac{2}{3}x^{\frac{3}{2}} - 20x^{\frac{1}{2}} + c$ or $y = \frac{6}{5}x^{\frac{5}{2}} - \frac{2}{3}x^{\frac{3}{2}} - 20\sqrt{x} + c$

4 $\frac{dy}{dx} = 3x^2 - 4x + 1$ integrate

$y = x^3 - 2x^2 + x + c$

When $x = 0$, $y = 5$

$5 = (0)^3 - 2(0)^2 + (0) + c$

$c = 5$

The equation of the curve is $y = x^3 - 2x^2 + x + 5$.

5 $\frac{dy}{dx} = 6x(x - 1)$ expand brackets

$\frac{dy}{dx} = 6x^2 - 6x$ integrate

$y = 2x^3 - 3x^2 + c$

When $x = 1$, $y = -5$

$-5 = 2(1)^3 - 3(1)^2 + c$

$-5 = 2 - 3 + c$

$c = -4$

The equation of the curve is $y = 2x^3 - 3x^2 - 4$.

6 $\frac{dy}{dx} = \frac{2x^3 + 6}{x^2}$ write in index form ready for integration

$\frac{dy}{dx} = 2x + 6x^{-2}$ integrate

$y = x^2 - 6x^{-1} + c$

$y = x^2 - \frac{6}{x} + c$

When $x = -1$, $y = 10$

$10 = (-1)^2 - \frac{6}{-1} + c$

$10 = 1 + 6 + c$

$c = 3$

The equation of the curve is $y = x^2 - \frac{6}{x} + 3$.

7 $\frac{dy}{dx} = \frac{(2 - \sqrt{x})^2}{\sqrt{x}}$

$\frac{dy}{dx} = \frac{(2 - \sqrt{x})(2 - \sqrt{x})}{\sqrt{x}}$

$\frac{dy}{dx} = \frac{4 - 2\sqrt{x} - 2\sqrt{x} + x}{\sqrt{x}}$ write in index form ready for integration

$\frac{dy}{dx} = 4x^{-\frac{1}{2}} - 4 + x^{\frac{1}{2}}$

$y = 8x^{\frac{1}{2}} - 2x - 2x + \frac{2}{3}x^{\frac{3}{2}} + c$

$y = 8x^{\frac{1}{2}} - 4x + \frac{2}{3}x^{\frac{3}{2}} + c$

When $x = 9$, $y = 14$

$14 = 8(9)^{\frac{1}{2}} - 4(9) + \frac{2}{3}(9)^{\frac{3}{2}} + c$

$14 = 24 - 36 + 18 + c$

$c = 8$

The equation of the curve is $y = 8x^{\frac{1}{2}} - 4x + \frac{2}{3}x^{\frac{3}{2}} + 8$

8 $\frac{dy}{dx} = kx^2 - 2x$ integrate

$y = \frac{1}{3}kx^3 - x^2 + c$

When $x = 1$, $y = 6$

$6 = \frac{1}{3}k(1)^3 - (1)^2 + c$

$\frac{1}{3}k + c = 7$ (1)

When $x = -2$, $y = -15$

$-15 = \frac{1}{3}k(-2)^3 - (-2)^2 + c$

$-\frac{8}{3}k + c = -11$ (2)

Subtracting (2) from (1) gives:

$3k = 18$

$k = 6$

Substituting into (1) gives:

$\frac{1}{3} \times 6 + c = 7$

$c = 5$

The equation of the curve is $y = 2x^3 - x^2 + 5$

9 a $\frac{d^2y}{dx^2} = 12x - 12$ integrate

$\frac{dy}{dx} = 6x^2 - 12x + c$

When $x = 2$, $\frac{dy}{dx} = 8$

$8 = 6 \times 2^2 - 12 \times 2 + c$

$c = 8$

$\frac{dy}{dx} = 6x^2 - 12x + 8$ integrate

$y = 2x^3 - 6x^2 + 8x + c$

When $x = 2$, $y = 9$

$9 = 2(2)^3 - 6(2)^2 + 8(2) + c$

$c = 1$

$y = 2x^3 - 6x^2 + 8x + 1$

b $\frac{dy}{dx} = 6x^2 - 12x + 8$

We need to show that $\frac{dy}{dx} = 6x^2 - 12x + 8$ is never less than 2

$\frac{dy}{dx} = 6x^2 - 12x + 8$ complete the square

$\frac{dy}{dx} = 6[x^2 - 2x] + 8$

$\frac{dy}{dx} = 6[(x - 1)^2 - 1^2] + 8$

$\frac{dy}{dx} = 6(x - 1)^2 - 6 + 8$

$\frac{dy}{dx} = 6(x - 1)^2 + 2$

$6(x - 1)^2$ is always $\geqslant 0$

$\frac{dy}{dx} \geqslant 2$

So, the minimum value of the gradient is 2 (which occurs when $x = 1$).

10 $\frac{dy}{dx} = kx - 5$

At $x = 2$, the gradient of the normal is $-\frac{1}{3}$

So the gradient of the tangent to the curve at $x = 2$ is 3

Substitute $x = 2$ and $\frac{dy}{dx} = 3$ into $\frac{dy}{dx} = kx - 5$

$3 = k(2) - 5$

$k = 4$

$\frac{dy}{dx} = 4x - 5$

$y = 2x^2 - 5x + c$

When $x = 2$, $y = -1$

$-1 = 2(2)^2 - 5(2) + c$

$c = 1$

The equation of the curve is $y = 2x^2 - 5x + 1$

Exercise 15.2

REMEMBER

$\int x^n \, dx = \frac{1}{n+1}x^{n+1} + c$, where c is a constant and $n \neq -1$

$\int kf(x) \, dx = k\int f(x) \, dx$, where k is a constant

$\int [f(x) \pm g(x)] \, dx = \int f(x) \, dx \pm \int g(x) \, dx$

1 c $\int 2x^{-3}\,dx$

$= \frac{2x^{-3+1}}{-2} + c$

$= -x^{-2} + c$

$= -\frac{1}{x^2} + c$

f $\int \frac{6}{x^2\sqrt{x}}\,dx$ write in index form ready for integration

$= \int \frac{6}{x^2 \times x^{\frac{1}{2}}}\,dx$

$= \int \frac{6}{x^{\frac{5}{2}}}\,dx$

$= \int 6x^{-\frac{5}{2}}\,dx$ integrate

$= \frac{6}{-\frac{3}{2}}x^{-\frac{3}{2}} + c$

$= -4x^{-\frac{3}{2}} + c$

$= -\frac{4}{x^{\frac{3}{2}}} + c$

$= -\frac{4}{x\sqrt{x}} + c$

2 d $\int (\sqrt{x} + 3)^2\,dx$ expand brackets

$= \int (\sqrt{x} + 3)(\sqrt{x} + 3)\,dx$

$= \int (x + 3\sqrt{x} + 3\sqrt{x} + 9)\,dx$

$= (x + 6\sqrt{x} + 9)\,dx$ write in index form ready for integration

$= \int (x + 6x^{\frac{1}{2}} + 9)\,dx$ integrate

$= \frac{1}{2}x^2 + \frac{6}{\frac{3}{2}}x^{\frac{3}{2}} + 9x + c$

$= \frac{x^2}{2} + 4x^{\frac{3}{2}} + 9x + c$

f $\int \sqrt[3]{x}(x - 4)\,dx$ expand brackets

$= \int (\sqrt[3]{x} \times x^1 - 4\sqrt[3]{x})\,dx$ write in index form ready for integration

$= \int (x^{\frac{4}{3}} - 4x^{\frac{1}{3}})\,dx$

$= \frac{1}{\frac{7}{3}}x^{\frac{7}{3}} - \frac{4}{\frac{4}{3}}x^{\frac{4}{3}} + c$

$= \frac{3}{7}x^{\frac{7}{3}} - 3x^{\frac{4}{3}} + c$

3 c $\displaystyle\int \frac{(x+1)^2}{3x^4}\,dx$ — expand brackets

$\displaystyle = \int \frac{(x+1)(x+1)}{3x^4}\,dx$

$\displaystyle = \int \frac{x^2+2x+1}{3x^4}\,dx$ — write in index form ready for integration

$\displaystyle = \int \left(\frac{1}{3}x^{-2} + \frac{2}{3}x^{-3} + \frac{1}{3}x^{-4}\right)dx$

$\displaystyle = \frac{1}{3\times -1}x^{-1} + \frac{2}{3\times -2}x^{-2} + \frac{1}{3\times -3}x^{-3} + c$

$\displaystyle = -\frac{1}{3x} - \frac{1}{3x^2} - \frac{1}{9x^3} + c$

f $\displaystyle\int \left(\sqrt{x} + \frac{3}{x^2\sqrt{x}}\right)^2 dx$ — expand brackets

$\displaystyle = \int \left(\sqrt{x} + \frac{3}{x^2\sqrt{x}}\right)\left(\sqrt{x} + \frac{3}{x^2\sqrt{x}}\right)dx$

$\displaystyle = \int (x + 3x^{-2} + 3x^{-2} + 9x^{-5})\,dx$

$\displaystyle = \int (x + 6x^{-2} + 9x^{-5})\,dx$ — integrate

$\displaystyle = \frac{1}{2}x^2 + \frac{6}{-1}x^{-1} + \frac{9}{-4}x^{-4} + c$

$\displaystyle = \frac{1}{2}x^2 - \frac{6}{x} - \frac{9}{4x^4} + c$

Exercise 15.3

REMEMBER

$\displaystyle\int (ax+b)^n dx = \frac{1}{a(n+1)}(ax+b)^{n+1} + c,\ n \neq -1$
and $a \neq 0$

1 f $\displaystyle\int \sqrt{(3x-1)^3}\,dx$ — rewrite in index form

$\displaystyle = \int (3x-1)^{\frac{3}{2}}\,dx$ — integrate

$\displaystyle = \frac{1}{3\left(\frac{3}{2}+1\right)}(3x-1)^{\frac{3}{2}+1} + c$

$\displaystyle = \frac{2}{15}(3x-1)^{\frac{5}{2}} + c$

i $\displaystyle\int \frac{3}{2(3-2x)^4}\,dx$ — rewrite

$\displaystyle = \frac{3}{2}\int (3-2x)^{-4}\,dx$ — integrate

$\displaystyle = \frac{3}{2} \times \frac{1}{-2(-4+1)}(3-2x)^{-4+1} + c$

$\displaystyle = \frac{1}{4}(3-2x)^{-3} + c$

$\displaystyle = \frac{1}{4(3-2x)^3} + c$

2 $\displaystyle\frac{dy}{dx} = (4x+1)^4$

$\displaystyle y = \int (4x+1)^4\,dx$ — integrate

$\displaystyle = \frac{1}{4(4+1)}(4x+1)^{4+1} + c$

$\displaystyle = \frac{1}{20}(4x+1)^5 + c$

When $x = 0$, $y = -1.95$

$\displaystyle -1.95 = \frac{1}{20}(4(0)+1)^5 + c$

$c = -2$

The equation of the curve is $\displaystyle y = \frac{(4x+1)^5}{20} - 2$

3 $\frac{dy}{dx} = \sqrt{2x+1}$ write in index form ready for integration

$y = \int (2x+1)^{\frac{1}{2}} dx$ integrate

$= \frac{1}{2\left(\frac{1}{2}+1\right)}(2x+1)^{\frac{1}{2}+1} + c$

$= \frac{1}{3}(2x+1)^{\frac{3}{2}} + c$

When $x = 4$, $y = 11$

$11 = \frac{1}{3}(2 \times 4 + 1)^{\frac{3}{2}} + c$

$c = 2$

$y = \frac{1}{3}(2x+1)^{\frac{3}{2}} + 2$

The equation of the curve is $y = \frac{\sqrt{(2x+1)^3}}{3} + 2$

4 $\frac{dy}{dx} = \frac{1}{\sqrt{10-x}}$ write in index form ready for integration

$y = \int (10-x)^{-\frac{1}{2}} dx$ integrate

$y = \frac{1}{-1\left(-\frac{1}{2}+1\right)}(10-x)^{-\frac{1}{2}+1} + c$

$y = -2(10-x)^{\frac{1}{2}} + c$

When $x = 6$, $y = 1$

$1 = -2(10-6)^{\frac{1}{2}} + c$

$c = 5$

$y = -2(10-x)^{\frac{1}{2}} + 5$

The equation of the curve is $y = 5 - 2\sqrt{10-x}$

5 If the gradient of the normal to the curve at $x = 2$ is $-\frac{1}{8}$ then the gradient of the tangent at $x = 2$ is 8

Substituting $x = 2$, $\frac{dy}{dx} = 8$ into $\frac{dy}{dx} = k(2x-3)^3$ gives:

$8 = k(2 \times 2 - 3)^3$

$k = 8$

So, $\frac{dy}{dx} = 8(2x-3)^3$

$\frac{dy}{dx} = 8(2x-3)^3$ integrate

$y = \frac{8}{2(4)}(2x-3)^4 + c$

$y = (2x-3)^4 + c$

When $x = 2$, $y = 2$

$2 = (2 \times 2 - 3)^4 + c$

$c = 1$

The equation of the curve is $y = (2x-3)^4 + 1$

6 **Method 1**

The 5th row of Pascal's triangle is 1, 5, 10, 10, 5, 1

$(-1 + kx)^5 = 1(-1)^5 + 5(-1)^4(kx) + 10(-1)^3(kx)^2 + 10(-1)^2(kx)^3 + 5(-1)(kx)^4 + 1(kx)^5$

$= -1 + 5kx - 10k^2x^2 + 10k^3x^3 - 5k^4x^4 + k^5x^5$

So, $\frac{dy}{dx} = 2(kx - 1)^5 = -2 + 10kx - 20k^2x^2 + 20k^3x^3 - 10k^4x^4 + 2k^5x^5$ integrate

$y = -2x + 5kx^2 - \frac{20}{3}k^2x^3 + 5k^3x^4 - 2k^4x^5 + \frac{1}{3}k^5x^6 + c$

When $x = 0$, $y = 1$, $c = 1$

When $x = 1$, $y = 8$

$8 = -2(1) + 5k(1)^2 - \frac{20}{3}k^2(1)^3 + 5k^3(1)^4 - 2k^4(1)^5 + \frac{1}{3}k^5(1)^6 + 1$

$0 = 5k - \frac{20}{3}k^2 + 5k^3 - 2k^4 + \frac{1}{3}k^5 - 9$

Let $m = 5k - \frac{20}{3}k^2 + 5k^3 - 2k^4 + \frac{1}{3}k^5 - 9$

Plot the graph of m against k gives $k = 3$ and 0

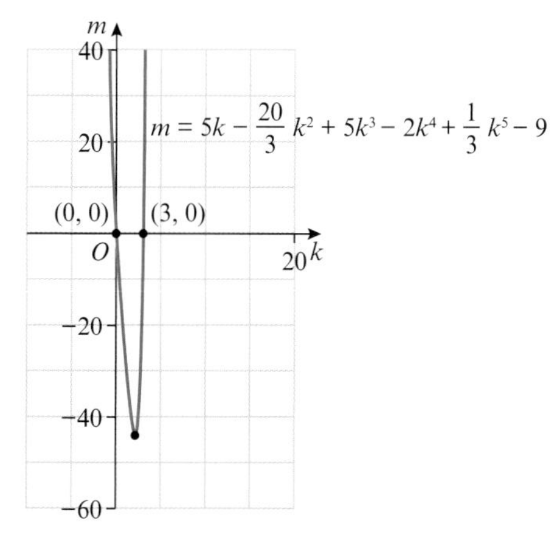

Reject $k = 0$ since integrating and then substituting into

$y = \frac{1}{3k}(kx - 1)^6 + c$ has no meaning

$\frac{dy}{dx} = 2(3x - 1)^5$

$y = \frac{2}{3 \times 6}(3x - 1)^6 + d$

When $x = 0$, $y = 1$

$1 = \frac{1}{9}(3(0) - 1)^6 + d$

$d = \frac{8}{9}$

The equation of the curve is $y = \frac{1}{9}(3x - 1)^6 + \frac{8}{9}$ or $y = \frac{(3x - 1)^6 + 8}{9}$

Method 2

$\frac{dy}{dx} = 2(kx - 1)^5$ integrate

$y = \frac{2}{k(5+1)}(kx - 1)^{5+1} + c$

$y = \frac{1}{3k}(kx - 1)^6 + c$

When $x = 0$, $y = 1$

$1 = \frac{1}{3k}(k \times 0 - 1)^6 + c$

$1 = \frac{1}{3k} + c$

$\frac{1}{3k} + c = 1$ (1)

When $x = 1$, $y = 8$

$\frac{1}{3k}(k \times 1 - 1)^6 + c = 8$

$\frac{1}{3k}(k - 1)^6 + c = 8$ (2)

Subtract (1) from (2)

$\frac{1}{3k}(k - 1)^6 - \frac{1}{3k} = 7$

$\frac{(k-1)^6 - 1}{3k} = 7$

$(k - 1)^6 - 1 = 21k$

$(k - 1)^6 - 21k - 1 = 0$ [3]

Either

Substitute $k = 0$ gives $(0 - 1)^6 - 21(0) - 1 = 0$

However $k \neq 0$ since $y = \frac{1}{3k}(kx - 1)^6 + c$ has no meaning

Substituting $k = 3$ gives $(3 - 1)^6 - 21(3) - 1 = 0$

So $k = 3$ is a solution

Or

Let $u = (k - 1)^6 - 21k - 1$ and plot the graph of u against k.

$k = 3$ is the solution to $(k - 1)^6 - 21k - 1 = 0$

So $\frac{dy}{dx} = 2(3x - 1)^5$

$y = \frac{2}{3 \times 6}(3x - 1)^6 + d$

When $x = 0$, $y = 1$

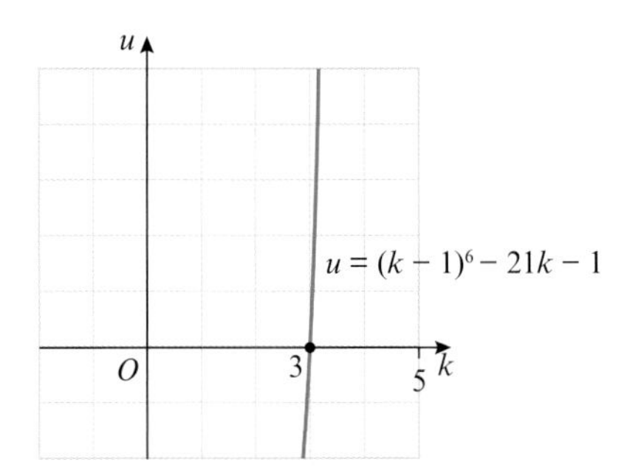

$1 = \frac{1}{9}(3(0) - 1)^6 + d$

$d = \frac{8}{9}$

The equation of the curve is $y = \frac{1}{9}(3x - 1)^6 + \frac{8}{9}$ or $y = \frac{(3x-1)^6 + 8}{9}$

Exercise 15.4

REMEMBER

$\int e^x dx = e^x + c$ $\int e^{ax+b} dx = \frac{1}{a}e^{ax+b} + c$

1 **c** $\int e^{\frac{1}{2}x} dx = \frac{1}{\frac{1}{2}}e^{\frac{1}{2}x} + c = 2e^{\frac{1}{2}x} + c$

i $\int \frac{1}{3}e^{6x-1} dx = \frac{1}{3} \times \frac{1}{6}e^{6x-1} + c = \frac{e^{6x-1}}{18} + c$

2 **c** $\int (3e^x + e^{-x})^2 dx$ expand brackets

$= \int (3e^x + e^{-x})(3e^x + e^{-x}) dx$

$= \int (9e^{2x} + 3e^0 + 3e^0 + e^{-2x}) dx$

$= \int (9e^{2x} + 6 + e^{-2x}) dx$ integrate

$= \frac{9}{2}e^{2x} + 6x + \frac{1}{-2}e^{-2x} + c$

$= \frac{9e^{2x}}{2} + 6x - \frac{e^{-2x}}{2} + c$

f $\int \frac{(e^{4x} - 2e^{x})^2}{e^{3x}} dx$ expand brackets

$= \int \frac{(e^{4x} - 2e^{x})(e^{4x} - 2e^{x})}{e^{3x}} dx$

$= \int \frac{e^{8x} - 2e^{5x} - 2e^{5x} + 4e^{2x}}{e^{3x}} dx$

$= \int \frac{e^{8x} - 4e^{5x} + 4e^{2x}}{e^{3x}} dx$

$= \int (e^{5x} - 4e^{2x} + 4e^{-x}) dx$ integrate

$= \frac{e^{5x}}{5} - 2e^{2x} - 4e^{-x} + c$

3 a $\int \left(2e^{x} + \frac{1}{\sqrt{x}}\right) dx$ rewrite in index form

$\int (2e^{x} + x^{-\frac{1}{2}}) dx$ integrate

$= \left(2e^{x} + \frac{1}{\frac{1}{2}} x^{\frac{1}{2}} + c\right)$

$= 2e^{x} + 2\sqrt{x} + c$

b $\int (x^2 - 3e^{2x+1}) dx$

$= \frac{x^3}{3} - \frac{3e^{2x+1}}{2} + c$

c $\int \frac{3x^2e^{2x} - 4e^{x}}{12x^2e^{x}} dx$ simplify fraction

$= \int \left(\frac{1}{4}e^{x} - \frac{1}{3}x^{-2}\right) dx$ integrate

$= \frac{1}{4}e^{x} - \frac{1}{3 \times -1}x^{-1} + c$

$= \frac{e^{x}}{4} + \frac{1}{3x} + c$

4 $\frac{dy}{dx} = 2e^{2x} + e^{-x}$ integrate

$y = \frac{2}{2}e^{2x} + \frac{1}{-1}e^{-x} + c$

$= e^{2x} - e^{-x} + c$

When $x = 0$, $y = 4$

$4 = e^{2 \times 0} - e^{-0} + c$

$c = 4$

The equation of the curve is $y = e^{2x} - e^{-x} + 4$

5 a $\frac{dy}{dx} = ke^{2-x} + 4x$

At $x = 2$, $\frac{dy}{dx} = 1$

$1 = ke^{2-2} + 4 \times 2$

$k = -7$

b $\frac{dy}{dx} = -7e^{2-x} + 4x$ integrate

$y = \frac{-7}{-1}e^{2-x} + \frac{4}{2}x^2 + c$

$= 7e^{2-x} + 2x^2 + c$

When $x = 2$, $y = 10$

$10 = 7e^{2-2} + 2 \times 2^2 + c$

$c = -5$

The equation of the curve is $y = 7e^{2-x} + 2x^2 - 5$

6 $\frac{d^2y}{dx^2} = 8e^{-2x}$ integrate

$\frac{dy}{dx} = \frac{8}{-2}e^{-2x} + c$

$= -4e^{-2x} + c$

When $x = 0$, $\frac{dy}{dx} = 2$

$2 = -4e^{-2(0)} + c$

$c = 6$

$\frac{dy}{dx} = -4e^{-2x} + 6$ integrate

$y = \frac{-4}{-2}e^{-2x} + 6x + c$

$= 2e^{-2x} + 6x + c$

When $x = 1$, $y = \frac{2}{e^2}$

$\frac{2}{e^2} = 2e^{-2(1)} + 6(1) + c$

$\frac{2}{e^2} = \frac{2}{e^2} + 6 + c$

$c = -6$

The equation of the curve is $y = 2e^{-2x} + 6x - 6$

7 a $\frac{dy}{dx} = 2e^{3-2x}$ integrate

$y = \frac{2}{-2}e^{3-2x} + c$

$= -e^{3-2x} + c$

As P lies on the curve, substitute $x = \frac{3}{2}$, $y = 5$

$5 = -e^{3-2\left(\frac{3}{2}\right)} + c$

$c = 6$

So, $y = -e^{3-2x} + 6$

When $x = 1$, $y = k$

$k = -e^{3-2(1)} + 6$

$k = 6 - e$

b $\dfrac{dy}{dx} = 2e^{3-2x}$

The gradient of the tangent to the curve at

$P\left(\dfrac{3}{2}, 5\right)$ is:

$\dfrac{dy}{dx} = 2e^{3-2\left(\frac{3}{2}\right)}$

$= 2$

The gradient of the normal at P is $-\dfrac{1}{2}$

The equation of the normal at P is found by using $y - y_1 = m(x - x_1)$

$y - 5 = -\dfrac{1}{2}\left(x - \dfrac{3}{2}\right)$ multiply both sides by 4

$4y - 20 = -2x + 3$

$4y + 2x = 23$ (1)

The gradient of the tangent to the curve at $Q\,(1, 6 - e)$ is:

$\dfrac{dy}{dx} = 2e^{3-2(1)}$

$= 2e$

The gradient of the normal at $Q\,(1, 6 - e)$ is $-\dfrac{1}{2e}$

The equation of the normal is found by using $y - y_1 = m(x - x_1)$

$y - (6 - e) = -\dfrac{1}{2e}(x - 1)$

$y - 6 + e = -\dfrac{1}{2e}x + \dfrac{1}{2e}$

$y + \dfrac{1}{2e}x = \dfrac{1}{2e} - e + 6$ multiply both sides by 4

$4y + \dfrac{2}{e}x = \dfrac{2}{e} - 4e + 24$ (2)

Subtract (2) from (1)

$2x - \dfrac{2}{e}x = 23 - \dfrac{2}{e} + 4e - 24$ simplify the right-hand side

$2x - \dfrac{2}{e}x = -\dfrac{2}{e} + 4e - 1$ factorise the left hand side

$x\left(2 - \dfrac{2}{e}\right) = -\dfrac{2}{e} + 4e - 1$

$x = \dfrac{-\dfrac{2}{e} + 4e - 1}{2 - \dfrac{2}{e}}$ multiply numerator and denominator by e

$x = \dfrac{-2 + 4e^2 - e}{2e - 2}$ or $x = \dfrac{4e^2 - e - 2}{2e - 2}$

Substitute for x in (1) gives:

$$4y + 2\left(\frac{4e^2 - e - 2}{2e - 2}\right) = 23$$

$$4y + \frac{8e^2 - 2e - 4}{2e - 2} = 23$$

$$4y = 23 - \frac{8e^2 - 2e - 4}{2e - 2}$$

$$4y = \frac{46e - 46}{2e - 2} - \frac{8e^2 - 2e - 4}{2e - 2}$$

$$4y = \frac{46e - 46 - 8e^2 + 2e + 4}{2e - 2}$$

$$y = \frac{46e - 46 - 8e^2 + 2e + 4}{8e - 8}$$

$$y = \frac{23e - 23 - 4e^2 + e + 2}{4e - 4}$$

$$y = \frac{24e - 4e^2 - 21}{4e - 4}$$

The coordinates of R are $\left(\frac{4e^2 - e - 2}{2e - 2}, \frac{24e - 4e^2 - 21}{4e - 4}\right)$

TIP

Be careful with signs!

Exercise 15.5

REMEMBER

$\int \cos x \, dx = \sin x + c$ $\quad\int [\cos(ax + b)] \, dx = \frac{1}{a}\sin(ax + b) + c$

$\int \sin x \, dx = -\cos x + c$ $\quad\int [\sin(ax + b)] \, dx = -\frac{1}{a}\cos(ax + b) + c$

$\int \sec^2 x \, dx = \tan x + c$ $\quad\int [\sec^2(ax + b)] \, dx = \frac{1}{a}\tan(ax + b) + c$

1 g $\int 2\sec^2(3x) \, dx$

$= 2\int \sec^2(3x) \, dx$

$= 2 \times \frac{1}{3}\tan(3x) + c$

$= \frac{2}{3}\tan 3x + c$

i $\int 5\sin(2 - 3x) \, dx$

$= 5\int \sin(2 - 3x) \, dx$

$= 5 \times -\frac{1}{-3}\cos(2 - 3x) + c$

$= \frac{5}{3}\cos(2 - 3x) + c$

2 c $\int \left(3\cos 2x - \pi\sin\frac{5x}{2}\right) dx$

$= \frac{3}{2}\sin 2x - \pi \times -\frac{1}{\frac{5}{2}}\cos\frac{5x}{2} + c$

$= \frac{3}{2}\sin 2x + \frac{2}{5}\pi\cos\frac{5x}{2} + c$

f $\int \left(\frac{2}{\sqrt{x}} + \sin\frac{x}{2}\right) dx$

$= \int \left(2x^{-\frac{1}{2}} + \sin\frac{1}{2}x\right) dx$

$= 2 \times \frac{1}{\frac{1}{2}}x^{\frac{1}{2}} + -\frac{1}{\frac{1}{2}}\cos\frac{1}{2}x + c$

$= 4\sqrt{x} - 2\cos\frac{x}{2} + c$

3 $\frac{dy}{dx} = \cos x - \sin x$ integrate

$y = \sin x + \cos x + c$

When $x = \frac{\pi}{2}$, $y = 3$

$3 = \sin\frac{\pi}{2} + \cos\frac{\pi}{2} + c$

$3 = 1 + 0 + c$

$c = 2$

The equation of the curve is $y = \sin x + \cos x + 2$

4 $\frac{dy}{dx} = 1 - 4\cos 2x$ integrate

$y = x - \frac{4}{2}\sin 2x + c$

$= x - 2\sin 2x + c$

When $x = \frac{\pi}{4}$, $y = 1$

$1 = \frac{\pi}{4} - 2\sin 2\left(\frac{\pi}{4}\right) + c$

$1 = \frac{\pi}{4} - 2 + c$

$c = 3 - \frac{\pi}{4}$

$y = x - 2\sin 2x + 3 - \frac{\pi}{4}$

5 $\frac{dy}{dx} = 4x - 6\sin 2x$ integrate

$y = 2x^2 - -\frac{6}{2}\cos 2x + c$

$= 2x^2 + 3\cos 2x + c$

When $x = 0$, $y = -2$

$-2 = 2(0)^2 + 3\cos(2 \times 0) + c$

$-2 = 0 + 3 + c$

$c = -5$

The equation of the curve is $y = 2x^2 + 3\cos 2x - 5$

6 $\frac{d^2y}{dx^2} = 45\cos 3x + 2\sin x$ integrate

$\frac{dy}{dx} = \frac{45}{3}\sin 3x + -2\cos x + c$

$= 15\sin 3x - 2\cos x + c$

When $x = 0$, $\frac{dy}{dx} = -2$

$-2 = 15\sin(3 \times 0) - 2\cos 0 + c$

$c = 0$

$\frac{dy}{dx} = 15\sin 3x - 2\cos x$ integrate

$y = -\frac{15}{3}\cos 3x - 2\sin x + c$

$= -5\cos 3x - 2\sin x + c$

When $x = \pi$, $y = -1$

$-1 = -5\cos(3 \times \pi) - 2\sin\pi + c$

$-1 = -5 \times -1 - 0 + c$

$c = -6$

The equation of the curve is
$y = -5\cos 3x - 2\sin x - 6$

7 a $\frac{dy}{dx} = k\cos 3x - 4$

When $x = \pi$, $\frac{dy}{dx} = -10$

$-10 = k\cos 3\pi - 4$

$-10 = k \times -1 - 4$

$k = 6$

b $\frac{dy}{dx} = 6\cos 3x - 4$ integrate

$y = \frac{6}{3}\sin 3x - 4x + c$

$= 2\sin 3x - 4x + c$

The curve passes through the point $(\pi, 2)$

$2 = 2\sin 3\pi - 4 \times \pi + c$

$c = 2 + 4\pi$

The equation of the curve is
$y = 2\sin 3x - 4x + 2 + 4\pi$

8 a $\frac{dy}{dx} = 4\sin\left(2x - \frac{\pi}{2}\right)$ integrate

$y = -\frac{4}{2}\cos\left(2x - \frac{\pi}{2}\right) + c$

$= -2\cos\left(2x - \frac{\pi}{2}\right) + c$

When $x = \frac{\pi}{2}$, $y = 5$

$5 = -2\cos\left(2 \times \frac{\pi}{2} - \frac{\pi}{2}\right) + c$

$5 = -2\cos\left(\frac{\pi}{2}\right) + c$

$c = 5$

$y = -2\cos\left(2x - \frac{\pi}{2}\right) + 5$ or $y = 5 - 2\cos\left(2x - \frac{\pi}{2}\right)$

b The gradient of the curve at $x = \frac{\pi}{3}$ is found by substituting into $\frac{dy}{dx} = 4\sin\left(2x - \frac{\pi}{2}\right)$:

$\frac{dy}{dx} = 4\sin\left(2 \times \frac{\pi}{3} - \frac{\pi}{2}\right)$

$= 2$

The gradient of the tangent at $x = \frac{\pi}{3}$ is 2

The y-coordinate of the point where $x = \frac{\pi}{3}$ is found by substituting $x = \frac{\pi}{3}$ into

$y = 5 - 2\cos\left(2x - \frac{\pi}{2}\right)$

$= 5 - 2\cos\left(2 \times \frac{\pi}{3} - \frac{\pi}{2}\right) = 5 - \sqrt{3}$

The gradient of the normal at $x = \frac{\pi}{3}$ is $-\frac{1}{2}$ (because the gradient of the tangent × the gradient of the normal = −1)

The equation of the normal is found by using $y - y_1 = m(x - x_1)$

$y - (5 - \sqrt{3}) = -\frac{1}{2}\left(x - \frac{\pi}{3}\right)$

$y = -\frac{1}{2}x + \frac{\pi}{6} + 5 - \sqrt{3}$

9 a $\frac{dy}{dx} = 3\cos\left(3x - \frac{\pi}{2}\right)$ integrate

$y = \frac{3}{3}\sin\left(3x - \frac{\pi}{2}\right) + c$

$= \sin\left(3x - \frac{\pi}{2}\right) + c$ (1)

$P\left(\frac{\pi}{3}, 3\right)$ lies on the curve so substitute $x = \frac{\pi}{3}$, $y = 3$ into (1)

$3 = \sin\left(3 \times \frac{\pi}{3} - \frac{\pi}{2}\right) + c$

$3 = 1 + c$

$c = 2$

The curve has equation $y = \sin\left(3x - \frac{\pi}{2}\right) + 2$ (2)

$Q\left(\frac{\pi}{2}, k\right)$ lies on the curve so substitute $x = \frac{\pi}{2}$, $y = k$ into (2)

$k = \sin\left(3 \times \frac{\pi}{2} - \frac{\pi}{2}\right) + 2$

$= 2$

b The gradient of the tangent at $P\left(\frac{\pi}{3}, 3\right)$ is found by substituting $x = \frac{\pi}{3}$ into

$\frac{dy}{dx} = 3\cos\left(3x - \frac{\pi}{2}\right)$

$= 3\cos\left(3 \times \frac{\pi}{3} - \frac{\pi}{2}\right) = 0$

The equation of the tangent at $P\left(\frac{\pi}{3}, 3\right)$ is found by using $y - y_1 = m(x - x_1)$

$y - 3 = 0\left(x - \frac{\pi}{3}\right)$

$y = 3$ (3)

The gradient of the tangent at $Q\left(\frac{\pi}{2}, 2\right)$ is found by substituting $x = \frac{\pi}{2}$ into

$\frac{dy}{dx} = 3\cos\left(3x - \frac{\pi}{2}\right)$

$= 3\cos\left(3 \times \frac{\pi}{2} - \frac{\pi}{2}\right) = -3$

The equation of the tangent at $Q\left(\frac{\pi}{2}, 2\right)$ is found by using $y - y_1 = m(x - x_1)$

$y - 2 = -3\left(x - \frac{\pi}{2}\right)$ (4)

To find R, solve (3) and (4) simultaneously:

Substituting $y = 3$ into (4) gives:

$3 - 2 = -3\left(x - \frac{\pi}{2}\right)$

$\frac{1}{-3} = x - \frac{\pi}{2}$

$x = \frac{\pi}{2} - \frac{1}{3}$ or $\frac{3\pi - 2}{6}$

The y-coordinate is 3

Coordinates of R are $\left(\frac{3\pi - 2}{6}, 3\right)$

10 a $\frac{dy}{dx} = 4\sec^2(3x - \pi)$ integrate

$y = \frac{4}{3}\tan(3x - \pi) + c$ (1)

$T\left(\frac{\pi}{4}, -\frac{4}{3}\right)$ lies on the curve so substitute $x = \frac{\pi}{4}$, $y = -\frac{4}{3}$ into (1)

$-\frac{4}{3} = \frac{4}{3}\tan\left(3 \times \frac{\pi}{4} - \pi\right) + c$

$-\frac{4}{3} = -\frac{4}{3} + c$

$c = 0$

The curve has equation $y = \frac{4}{3}\tan(3x - \pi)$ (2)

$V\left(\frac{\pi}{3}, k\right)$ lies on the curve so substitute $x = \frac{\pi}{3}$, $y = k$ into (2)

$k = \frac{4}{3}\tan\left(3 \times \frac{\pi}{3} - \pi\right)$

$k = 0$

b The gradient of the tangent at $T\left(\frac{\pi}{4}, -\frac{4}{3}\right)$ is found by substituting $x = \frac{\pi}{4}$ into

$\frac{dy}{dx} = 4\sec^2(3x - \pi)$

$= 4\sec^2\left(3 \times \frac{\pi}{4} - \pi\right) = 8$

The equation of the tangent at $T\left(\frac{\pi}{4}, -\frac{4}{3}\right)$ is found by using $y - y_1 = m(x - x_1)$

$y - -\frac{4}{3} = 8\left(x - \frac{\pi}{4}\right)$

$y + \frac{4}{3} = 8x - 2\pi$ (3)

The gradient of the tangent at $V\left(\frac{\pi}{3}, 0\right)$ is found by substituting $x = \frac{\pi}{3}$ into

$\frac{dy}{dx} = 4\sec^2(3x - \pi)$

$= 4\sec^2\left(3 \times \frac{\pi}{3} - \pi\right) = 4$

The equation of the tangent at $V\left(\frac{\pi}{3}, 0\right)$ is found by using $y - y_1 = m(x - x_1)$

$y - 0 = 4\left(x - \frac{\pi}{3}\right)$

$y = 4x - \frac{4\pi}{3}$ (4)

To find W, solve (3) and (4) simultaneously:

Substituting $y = 4x - \frac{4\pi}{3}$ into (3) gives:

$4x - \frac{4\pi}{3} + \frac{4}{3} = 8x - 2\pi$

$\frac{4}{3} - \frac{4\pi}{3} + 2\pi = 4x$

$4x = \frac{4}{3} + \frac{2\pi}{3}$

$x = \frac{1}{3} + \frac{\pi}{6}$ or $\frac{\pi + 2}{6}$

Substituting for x in (4) gives:

$y = 4 \times \left(\frac{\pi + 2}{6}\right) - \frac{4\pi}{3}$

The y-coordinate is $y = \frac{4\pi + 8}{6} - \frac{4\pi}{3}$

$y = \frac{2\pi + 4}{3} - \frac{4\pi}{3}$ or $\frac{2\pi + 4 - 4\pi}{3}$ or $\frac{4 - 2\pi}{3}$

or $\frac{2(2 - \pi)}{3}$

the coordinates of W are $\left(\frac{\pi + 2}{6}, \frac{2(2 - \pi)}{3}\right)$

Exercise 15.6

REMEMBER

$\int \frac{1}{x}\, dx = \ln x + c,\ x > 0$

$\int \frac{1}{ax + b}\, dx = \frac{1}{a}\ln(ax + b) + c,\ ax + b > 0$

1 f $\int \frac{1}{1 - 8x}\, dx = \left(\frac{1}{-8}\right)\ln(1 - 8x) + c$ valid for $1 - 8x > 0$

$= -\frac{1}{8}\ln(1 - 8x) + c,\ x < \frac{1}{8}$

i $\int \frac{5}{2(5x - 1)}\, dx = \frac{5}{2}\int \frac{1}{5x - 1}\, dx = \frac{5}{2}\left(\frac{1}{5}\right)\ln(5x - 1) + c$ valid for $5x - 1 > 0$

$= \frac{1}{2}\ln(5x - 1) + c,\ x > \frac{1}{5}$

2 f $\int\left(3x - \frac{2}{x^2}\right)^2 dx$ expand brackets

$\int\left(3x - \frac{2}{x^2}\right)\left(3x - \frac{2}{x^2}\right)dx = \int\left(9x^2 - \frac{6}{x} - \frac{6}{x} + 4x^{-4}\right)dx$

$\int\left(9x^2 - \frac{12}{x} + 4x^{-4}\right)dx = 3x^3 - 12\ln x - \frac{4}{3}x^{-3} + c = 3x^3 - 12\ln x - \frac{4}{3x^3} + c,\ x > 0$

i $\int\frac{5xe^{4x} - 2e^x}{10xe^x}dx$ split fraction into two fractions

$\int\frac{5xe^{4x}}{10xe^x} - \frac{2e^x}{10xe^x}dx = \int\left(\frac{1}{2}e^{3x} - \frac{1}{5x}\right)dx = \frac{1}{2}\int e^{3x}dx - \frac{1}{5}\int\frac{1}{x}dx$

$= \left(\frac{1}{2} \times \frac{1}{3}\right)e^{3x} - \frac{1}{5}\ln x + c$ valid for $x > 0$

$= \frac{e^{3x}}{6} - \frac{\ln x}{5} + c,\ x > 0$

3 $\frac{dy}{dx} = \frac{5}{2x - 1}$ for $x > -0.5$

$y = \int\frac{5}{2x - 1}dx = 5\int\frac{1}{2x - 1}dx = 5\left(\frac{1}{2}\right)\ln(2x - 1) + c$ valid for $2x - 1 > 0$

$= \frac{5}{2}\ln(2x - 1) + c,\ x > \frac{1}{2}$

Substituting $x = 1$, $y = 3$ gives:

$3 = \frac{5}{2}\ln(2 \times 1 - 1) + c$ so $c = 3$

$y = \frac{5}{2}\ln(2x - 1) + 3$

4 $\frac{dy}{dx} = 2x + \frac{5}{x}$ for $x > 0$

$y = \int\left(2x + \frac{5}{x}\right)dx = x^2 + 5\ln x + c$

Substituting $x = e$, $y = e^2$ gives:

$e^2 = e^2 + 5\ln e + c$

$c = -5$

$y = x^2 + 5\ln x - 5$

5 $\frac{dy}{dx} = \frac{1}{x + e}$ for $x > -e$

$y = \int\frac{1}{x + e}dx = \ln(x + e) + c$

Substituting $x = e$, $y = 2 + \ln 2$

$2 + \ln 2 = \ln(e + e) + c$

$c = 2 + \ln 2 - \ln(2e)$ use product rule for logs

$= 2 + \ln 2 - [\ln 2 + \ln e]$

$= 2 + \ln 2 - [\ln 2 + 1]$

$= 2 + \ln 2 - \ln 2 - 1$

$= 1$

The equation of the curve is $y = 1 + \ln(x + e)$

6 a $\frac{dy}{dx} = 3 - \frac{2}{x}$

$y = \int\left(3 - \frac{2}{x}\right)dx = 3x - 2\ln x + c$

Substituting $x = 1$, $y = -2$ gives:

$-2 = 3(1) - 2\ln 1 + c$

$c = -5$

The equation of the curve is $y = 3x - 2\ln x - 5$

Substituting $x = 2$, $y = k$ gives:

$k = 3(2) - 2\ln 2 - 5$

$= 1 - 2\ln 2$

b The gradient of the tangent at $P(1, -2)$ is

$\frac{dy}{dx} = 3 - \frac{2}{1} = 1$

The equation of the tangent at P is found by using $y - y_1 = m(x - x_1)$

$y - -2 = 1(x - 1)$

$y + 2 = x - 1$

$y = x - 3$ (1)

The gradient of the tangent at Q (2, 1 − 2ln2) is $\frac{dy}{dx} = 3 - \frac{2}{2} = 2$

The equation of the tangent at Q is found by using $y - y_1 = m(x - x_1)$

$y - (1 - 2\ln 2) = 2(x - 2)$

$y - 1 + 2\ln 2 = 2x - 4$

$y = 2x - 3 - 2\ln 2$ (2)

Equating (1) and (2) gives:

$2x - 3 - 2\ln 2 = x - 3$

$x = 2\ln 2$

Substituting for x in (1) gives:

$y = 2\ln 2 - 3$

R is at $(2\ln 2, 2\ln 2 - 3)$

Exercise 15.7

REMEMBER

If $\frac{d}{dx}[F(x)] = f(x)$, then $\int f(x)dx = F(x) + c$

1 a $y = \frac{x + 5}{\sqrt{2x - 1}}$ differentiate using the quotient rule

$\frac{dy}{dx} = \frac{(\sqrt{2x - 1})(1) - (x + 5)\left[\frac{1}{2}(2x - 1)^{-0.5}(2)\right]}{2x - 1}$

$= \frac{\sqrt{2x - 1} - \frac{x + 5}{\sqrt{2x - 1}}}{2x - 1}$ multiply numerator and denominator by $\sqrt{2x - 1}$

$= \frac{2x - 1 - x - 5}{(2x - 1)\sqrt{2x - 1}}$

$= \frac{x - 6}{\sqrt{(2x - 1)^3}}$

b Hence $\int\left(\frac{x - 6}{\sqrt{(2x - 1)^3}}\right)dx = y = \frac{x + 5}{\sqrt{2x - 1}} + c$

2 a $\frac{d}{dx}(3x^2 - 1)^5$ differentiate using the chain rule

$= 5 \times 6x(3x^2 - 1)^4$

$= 30x(3x^2 - 1)^4$

b $\int x(3x^2 - 1)^4\,dx = \frac{1}{30}\int 30x(3x^2 - 1)^4\,dx$

$= \frac{1}{30}(3x^2 - 1)^5 + c$

3 a Find $\frac{d}{dx}(x\ln x)$ using the product rule

$= x \times \frac{1}{x} + \ln x \times (1)$

$= \ln x + 1$

b $\int(1 + \ln x)\,dx = x\ln x$

So, $\int 1\,dx + \int \ln x\,dx = x\ln x$

$\int \ln x\,dx = x\ln x - \int 1\,dx$

$= x\ln x - x + c$

4 a $\frac{d}{dx}\left(\frac{\ln x}{x}\right)$ differentiate using the quotient rule

$= \frac{x \times \frac{1}{x} - \ln x \times (1)}{x^2}$

$= \frac{1 - \ln x}{x^2}$

b $\displaystyle\int\frac{1-\ln x}{x^2}\,dx=\int\frac{1}{x^2}\,dx-\int\frac{\ln x}{x^2}\,dx$

$\displaystyle\int\frac{\ln x}{x^2}\,dx=\int\frac{1}{x^2}\,dx-\int\frac{1-\ln x}{x^2}\,dx$

$\displaystyle=-\frac{1}{x}-\frac{\ln x}{x}+c$

5 **a** $y=x\sqrt{x^2-4}$ differentiate using the product rule

$\displaystyle\frac{dy}{dx}=x\times\frac{1}{2}\times 2x(x^2-4)^{-0.5}+\sqrt{x^2-4}\times(1)$

$=x^2(x^2-4)^{-0.5}+(x^2-4)^{0.5}$

$\displaystyle=\frac{x^2}{\sqrt{x^2-4}}+\frac{\sqrt{x^2-4}}{1}$

$\displaystyle=\frac{x^2}{\sqrt{x^2-4}}+\frac{x^2-4}{\sqrt{x^2-4}}$

$\displaystyle=\frac{2(x^2-2)}{\sqrt{x^2-4}}$

b $\displaystyle\int\frac{x^2-2}{\sqrt{x^2-4}}\,dx=\frac{1}{2}\int\frac{2(x^2-2)}{\sqrt{x^2-4}}\,dx=\frac{1}{2}x\sqrt{x^2-4}+c$

6 **a** $y=(3x+3)\sqrt{x-5}$ differentiate using the product rule

$\displaystyle\frac{dy}{dx}=(3x+3)\times\frac{1}{2}(x-5)^{-0.5}+\sqrt{x-5}\times(3)$

$\displaystyle=\frac{3x+3}{2\sqrt{x-5}}+\frac{3\sqrt{x-5}}{1}$

$\displaystyle=\frac{3x+3}{2\sqrt{x-5}}+\frac{6(x-5)}{2\sqrt{x-5}}$

$\displaystyle=\frac{3x+3+6x-30}{2\sqrt{x-5}}$

$\displaystyle=\frac{9(x-3)}{2\sqrt{x-5}}$

b $\displaystyle\int\frac{(x-3)}{\sqrt{x-5}}\,dx=\frac{2}{9}\int\frac{(x-3)}{\sqrt{x-5}}\,dx=\frac{2}{9}(3x+3)\sqrt{x-5}+c$

$\displaystyle=\frac{2}{3}(x+1)\sqrt{x-5}+c$

7 **a** $\displaystyle\frac{d}{dx}\left(xe^{2x}-\frac{e^{2x}}{2}\right)$

$\displaystyle=[x\times 2e^{2x}+e^{2x}\times(1)]-\frac{2e^{2x}}{2}$

$=2xe^{2x}+e^{2x}-e^{2x}$

$=2xe^{2x}$

b $\displaystyle\int xe^{2x}\,dx=\frac{1}{2}\int 2xe^{2x}\,dx=\frac{1}{2}\left(xe^{2x}-\frac{e^{2x}}{2}\right)+c$

$\displaystyle=\frac{1}{2}xe^{2x}-\frac{1}{4}e^{2x}+c$

8 a $\frac{d}{dx}\left(\frac{\sin x}{1-\cos x}\right) = \frac{(1-\cos x)\times\cos x - \sin x(\sin x)}{(1-\cos x)^2}$

$= \frac{\cos x - \cos^2 x - \sin^2 x}{(1-\cos x)^2}$ use $\sin^2 x + \cos^2 x = 1$

$= \frac{\cos x - 1}{(1-\cos x)^2}$

$= \frac{-(1-\cos x)}{(1-\cos x)^2}$

$= -\frac{1}{1-\cos x}$ or $\frac{1}{\cos x - 1}$ so $k = 1$

b $\int \frac{5}{\cos x - 1}\,dx = 5\int \frac{1}{\cos x - 1}\,dx = \frac{5\sin x}{1-\cos x} + c$

9 a $y = (x+8)\sqrt{x-4}$ differentiate using the product rule

$\frac{dy}{dx} = (x+8)\times\frac{1}{2}(x-4)^{-0.5} + \sqrt{x-4}\times(1)$

$= \frac{x+8}{2\sqrt{x-4}} + \frac{\sqrt{x-4}}{1}$

$= \frac{x+8}{2\sqrt{x-4}} + \frac{2(x-4)}{2\sqrt{x-4}}$

$= \frac{x+8+2(x-4)}{2\sqrt{x-4}}$

$\frac{dy}{dx} = \frac{3x}{2\sqrt{x-4}}$ so $k = \frac{3}{2}$

b $\int \frac{x}{\sqrt{x-4}}\,dx = \frac{2}{3}\int \frac{3x}{2\sqrt{x-4}}\,dx = \frac{2}{3}(x+8)\sqrt{x-4} + c$

10 a Rewrite $y = \frac{1}{x^2-7}$ as $y = (x^2-7)^{-1}$ differentiate using the chain rule

$\frac{dy}{dx} = -1\times 2x(x^2-7)^{-2}$

$= \frac{-2x}{(x^2-7)^2}$ so $k = -2$

b $\int \frac{4x}{(x^2-7)^2}\,dx = -2\int \frac{1}{x^2-7}\,dx = \frac{-2}{x^2-7} + c$

11 a $\frac{d}{dx}(2x^3\ln x) = 2x^3\times\frac{1}{x} + \ln x\times(6x^2)$

$= 2x^2 + 6x^2\ln x$

b $\int (2x^2 + 6x^2\ln x)\,dx = \int 2x^2\,dx + \int 6x^2\ln x\,dx$

So, $\int 6x^2\ln x\,dx = \int (2x^2+6x^2\ln x)\,dx - \int 2x^2\,dx$

$\int x^2\ln x\,dx = \frac{1}{6}\int (2x^2+6x^2\ln x)\,dx - \frac{1}{6}\int 2x^2\,dx$

$= \frac{1}{6}\times 2x^3\ln x - \frac{1}{6}\times\frac{2}{3}x^3 + c$

$= \frac{1}{3}x^3\ln x - \frac{1}{9}x^3 + c$

12 a $\frac{d}{dx}(x\cos x) = -\sin x \times x + \cos x \times (1)$

$= -x\sin x + \cos x$

$= \cos x - x\sin x$

b $\int(\cos x - x\sin x)\,dx = \int\cos x\,dx - \int x\sin x\,dx$

$\int x\sin x\,dx = \int\cos x\,dx - \int(\cos x - x\sin x)\,dx$

$= \sin x - x\cos x + c$

13 a $y = e^{2x}(\sin 2x + \cos 2x)$ differentiate using the product rule

$\frac{dy}{dx} = e^{2x}(2\cos 2x - 2\sin 2x) + (\sin 2x + \cos 2x) \times 2e^{2x}$

$= e^{2x}(2\cos 2x - 2\sin 2x + 2\sin 2x + 2\cos 2x)$

$= e^{2x}(4\cos 2x)$

$= 4e^{2x}\cos 2x$

b $\int e^{2x}\cos 2x\,dx = \frac{1}{4}\int 4e^{2x}\cos 2x\,dx$

$= \frac{1}{4}e^{2x}(\sin 2x + \cos 2x) + c$

14 a $\frac{d}{dx}(x^2\sqrt{2x-7})$ differentiate using the product rule

$= x^2 \times \frac{1}{2} \times 2(2x-7)^{-0.5} + \sqrt{2x-7} \times (2x)$

$\frac{dy}{dx} = \frac{x^2}{\sqrt{2x-7}} + \frac{2x\sqrt{2x-7}}{1}$

$= \frac{x^2}{\sqrt{2x-7}} + \frac{2x(2x-7)}{\sqrt{2x-7}}$

$= \frac{x^2 + 4x^2 - 14x}{\sqrt{2x-7}}$

$= \frac{5x^2 - 14x}{\sqrt{2x-7}}$

b $\int\frac{5x^2 - 14x + 3}{\sqrt{2x-7}}\,dx = \int\frac{5x^2 - 14x}{\sqrt{2x-7}}\,dx + \int\frac{3}{\sqrt{2x-7}}\,dx$

$= x^2\sqrt{2x-7} + 3\int(2x-7)^{-0.5}\,dx$

$= x^2\sqrt{2x-7} + 3 \times \frac{1}{0.5} \times \frac{1}{2}(2x-7)^{0.5} + c$

$= x^2\sqrt{2x-7} + 3\sqrt{2x-7} + c$

$= (x^2 + 3)\sqrt{2x-7} + c$

Exercise 15.8

REMEMBER

$$\int_a^b f(x)\,dx = [F(x)]_a^b = F(b) - F(a)$$

The following rules for definite integrals may also be used.

$$\int_a^b kf(x)\,dx = k\int_a^b f(x)\,dx, \text{ where } k \text{ is a constant}$$

$$\int_a^b [f(x) \pm g(x)]\,dx = \int_a^b f(x)\,dx \pm \int_a^b g(x)\,dx$$

REMEMBER

The formulae for differentiating and integrating these trigonometric functions only apply when x is measured in radians.

1 e

$$\int_{-1}^{2} (5x^2 - 3x)\,dx = \left[\frac{5}{3}x^3 - \frac{3}{2}x^2\right]_{-1}^{2}$$

$$= \left(\frac{5}{3}(2)^3 - \frac{3}{2}(2)^2\right) - \left(\frac{5}{3}(-1)^3 - \frac{3}{2}(-1)^2\right)$$

$$= \left(\frac{40}{3} - 6\right) - \left(-\frac{5}{3} - \frac{3}{2}\right)$$

$$= 10.5$$

l

$$\int_1^4 \left(2\sqrt{x} - \frac{2}{\sqrt{x}}\right)dx = \int_1^4 (2x^{0.5} - 2x^{-0.5})\,dx$$

$$= \left[\frac{2}{1.5}x^{1.5} - \frac{2}{0.5}x^{0.5}\right]_1^4$$

$$= \left[\frac{4}{3}x^{1.5} - 4x^{0.5}\right]_1^4$$

$$= \left(\frac{4}{3}(4)^{1.5} - 4(4)^{0.5}\right) - \left(\frac{4}{3}(1)^3 - 4(1)^{0.5}\right)$$

$$= \left(\frac{32}{3} - 8\right) - \left(\frac{4}{3} - 4\right)$$

$$= 5\frac{1}{3}$$

2 c

$$\int_0^3 \sqrt{(x+1)^3}\,dx = \int_0^3 (x+1)^{\frac{3}{2}}\,dx$$

$$= \left[\frac{1}{\frac{5}{2}}(x+1)^{\frac{5}{2}}\right]_0^3$$

$$= \left[\frac{2}{5}(x+1)^{\frac{5}{2}}\right]_0^3$$

$$= \left(\frac{2}{5}(3+1)^{\frac{5}{2}} - \frac{2}{5}(0+1)^{\frac{5}{2}}\right)$$

$$= 12.4$$

e $$\int_{-1}^{1} \frac{2}{(3x+5)^2}\mathrm{d}x = \int_{-1}^{1} 2(3x+5)^{-2}\mathrm{d}x = \left[\frac{2}{-1} \times \frac{1}{3}(3x+5)^{-1}\right]_{-1}^{1}$$

$$= \left[-\frac{2}{3}(3x+5)^{-1}\right]_{-1}^{1}$$

$$= \left(\left(-\frac{2}{3}(3(1)+5)^{-1}\right) - \left(-\frac{2}{3}(3(-1)+5)^{-1}\right)\right)$$

$$= -\frac{1}{12} - -\frac{1}{3}$$

$$= 0.25$$

3 e $$\int_{0}^{1} \frac{5}{e^{2x-1}}\mathrm{d}x = \int_{0}^{1} 5e^{-(2x-1)}\mathrm{d}x = \int_{0}^{1} 5e^{(1-2x)}\mathrm{d}x$$

$$= \left[\frac{5}{-2}e^{(1-2x)}\right]_{0}^{1}$$

$$= [-2.5e^{(1-2x)}]_{0}^{1}$$

$$= [-2.5e^{1-2(1)} - -2.5e^{1-2(0)}]$$

$$= -2.5e^{-1} + 2.5e^{1}$$

$$= 2.5\left(e^{1} - \frac{1}{e}\right)$$

$$= \frac{5}{2}\left(\frac{e^2}{e} - \frac{1}{e}\right)$$

$$= \frac{5(e^2-1)}{2e}$$

h $$\int_{0}^{1} \left(3e^{x} - \frac{2}{e^{x}}\right)^2 \mathrm{d}x = \int_{0}^{1} \left(3e^{x} - \frac{2}{e^{x}}\right)\left(3e^{x} - \frac{2}{e^{x}}\right)\mathrm{d}x$$

$$= \int_{0}^{1} (9e^{2x} - 6 - 6 + 4e^{-2x})\mathrm{d}x$$

$$= \left[\frac{9}{2}e^{2x} - 6x - 6x + \frac{4}{-2}e^{-2x}\right]_{0}^{1}$$

$$= \left[\frac{9}{2}e^{2x} - 12x - 2e^{-2x}\right]_{0}^{1}$$

$$= \left[\left(\frac{9}{2}e^{2(1)} - 12(1) - 2e^{-2(1)}\right) - \left(\frac{9}{2}e^{2(0)} - 12(0) - 2e^{-2(0)}\right)\right]$$

$$= \left[\left(\frac{9}{2}e^{2} - 12 - \frac{2}{e^{2}}\right) - \left(\frac{9}{2} - 2\right)\right]$$

$$= \frac{9}{2}e^{2} - \frac{2}{e^{2}} - \frac{29}{2}$$

4 c $\int_0^{\frac{\pi}{3}} \sin\left(2x - \frac{\pi}{6}\right) dx = \left[-\frac{1}{2}\cos\left(2x - \frac{\pi}{6}\right)\right]_0^{\frac{\pi}{3}}$

$= -\frac{1}{2}\cos\left(2 \times \frac{\pi}{3} - \frac{\pi}{6}\right) - -\frac{1}{2}\cos\left(2 \times 0 - \frac{\pi}{6}\right)$

$= -\frac{1}{2} \times 0 + \frac{1}{2} \times \frac{\sqrt{3}}{2}$

$= \frac{\sqrt{3}}{4}$

f $\int_{\frac{\pi}{4}}^{\frac{\pi}{2}} (\sin 3x - \cos 2x) dx = \left[-\frac{1}{3}\cos 3x - \frac{1}{2}\sin 2x\right]_{\frac{\pi}{4}}^{\frac{\pi}{2}}$

$= \left(-\frac{1}{3}\cos\frac{3\pi}{2} - \frac{1}{2}\sin\pi\right) - \left(-\frac{1}{3}\cos\frac{3\pi}{4} - \frac{1}{2}\sin\frac{\pi}{2}\right)$

$= (0 - 0) - \left(\frac{1}{3} \times -\frac{\sqrt{2}}{2} - \frac{1}{2}\right)$

$= -\frac{\sqrt{2}}{6} + \frac{1}{2}$

$= \frac{1}{6}(3 - \sqrt{2})$

REMEMBER

$\int \frac{1}{x} dx = \ln|x| + c$ $\int \frac{1}{ax + b} dx = \frac{1}{a}\ln|ax + b| + c$

5 d $\int_{-2}^{-1} \frac{5}{2x + 1} dx = 5\int_{-2}^{-1} \frac{1}{2x + 1} dx = \left[\frac{5}{2}\ln|2x + 1|\right]_{-2}^{-1}$ substitute limits

$= \left[\frac{5}{2}\ln|2 \times (-1) + 1|\right] - \left[\frac{5}{2}\ln|2 \times (-2) + 1|\right]$ simplify

$= \frac{5}{2}\ln|-1| - \frac{5}{2}\ln|-3|$

$= \frac{5}{2}\ln 1 - \frac{5}{2}\ln 3$

$= -\frac{5}{2}\ln 3$

f $\int_{-3}^{-2} \frac{4}{3 - 2x} dx = 4\int_{-3}^{-2} \frac{1}{3 - 2x} dx = \left[\frac{4}{-2}\ln|3 - 2x|\right]_{-3}^{-2}$

$= [-2\ln|3 - 2x|]_{-3}^{-2}$ substitute limits

$= -2\ln|3 - 2(-2)| - -2\ln|3 - 2(-3)|$

$= -2\ln 7 + 2\ln 9$

$= 2\ln 9 - 2\ln 7$

$= 2\ln\frac{9}{7}$

6 a $\int_2^4 \left(1 + \frac{2}{3x-1}\right) dx = \int_2^4 1\, dx + \int_2^4 \frac{2}{3x-1} dx$

$= [x]_2^4 + 2\int_2^4 \frac{1}{3x-1} dx$

$= [x]_2^4 + \left[\frac{2}{3}\ln|3x-1|\right]_2^4$ substitute limits

$= 4 - 2 + \frac{2}{3}\ln 11 - \frac{2}{3}\ln 5$

$= 2 + \frac{2}{3}\ln\frac{11}{5}$

b $\int_1^3 \left(\frac{2}{x} - \frac{1}{2x+1}\right) dx = \int_1^3 \left(\frac{2}{x}\right) dx - \int_1^3 \frac{1}{2x+1} dx$

$= [2\ln x]_1^3 - \left[\frac{1}{2}\ln|2x+1|\right]_1^3$

$= 2\ln 3 - 2\ln 1 - \left[\frac{1}{2}\ln 7 - \frac{1}{2}\ln 3\right]$ use the division law for logs

$= 2\ln 3 - \frac{1}{2}\ln\frac{7}{3}$

$= \frac{1}{2}\left[4\ln 3 - \ln\frac{7}{3}\right]$

$= \frac{1}{2}\left[\ln 3^4 - \ln\frac{7}{3}\right]$

$= \frac{1}{2}\ln\frac{243}{7}$

c $\int_0^1 \left(3 + \frac{1}{5-2x} - 2x\right) dx = \int_0^1 3\, dx + \int_0^1 \frac{1}{5-2x} dx - \int_0^1 2x\, dx$

$= \left[3x + \frac{1}{-2}\ln|5-2x| - x^2\right]_0^1$ substitute limits

$= \left[3 - \frac{1}{2}\ln 3 - 1^2\right] - \left[0 - \frac{1}{2}\ln 5 - 0^2\right]$

$= 2 - \frac{1}{2}\ln 3 + \frac{1}{2}\ln 5$ use the division law

$= 2 + \frac{1}{2}\ln\frac{5}{3}$

7 $\int_1^k \left(\frac{2}{3x-1}\right) dx = 2\int_1^k \frac{1}{3x-1} dx = \left[\frac{2}{3}\ln|3x-1|\right]_1^k$

$= \frac{2}{3}\ln(3k-1) - \frac{2}{3}\ln 2$

So, $\frac{2}{3}\ln 7 = \frac{2}{3}\ln(3k-1) - \frac{2}{3}\ln 2$ divide both sides by $\frac{2}{3}$

$\ln 7 = \ln(3k-1) - \ln 2$ use the division law

$\ln 7 = \ln\frac{3k-1}{2}$

$7 = \frac{3k-1}{2}$

$3k - 1 = 14$

$k = 5$

8 a $2 + \frac{A}{2x+3} = \frac{2(2x+3)}{2x+3} + \frac{A}{2x+3}$

$= \frac{4x+6+A}{2x+3}$

So, $\frac{4x}{2x+3} = \frac{4x+6+A}{2x+3}$

$4x = 4x + 6 + A$

$A = -6$

b $\int_0^1 \left(\frac{4x}{2x+3}\right) dx = \int_0^1 2\,dx + \int_0^1 \frac{-6}{2x+3} dx$

$= \left[2x + \frac{-6}{2}\ln|2x+3|\right]_0^1$

$= (2 - 3\ln 5) - (0 - 3\ln 3)$

$= 2 - 3\ln 5 + 3\ln 3$

$= 2 - 3(\ln 5 - \ln 3)$

$= 2 - 3\ln\frac{5}{3}$

9 a

$$\begin{array}{r} 2x+1 \\ 2x+1\overline{)4x^2+4x} \\ \underline{4x^2+2x} \\ 2x \\ \underline{2x+1} \\ -1 \end{array}$$

$2x + 1 - \frac{1}{2x+1}$ means that the quotient is $2x + 1$ and the remainder is -1

b $\int_0^1 \frac{4x^2+4x}{2x+1} dx = \int_0^1 \left[(2x+1) - \left(\frac{1}{2x+1}\right)\right] dx$

$= \left[(x^2 + x) - \frac{1}{2}\ln|2x+1|\right]_0^1$

$= \left[(1^2+1) - \frac{1}{2}\ln 3\right] - \left[(0^2+0) - \frac{1}{2}\ln 1\right]$

$= 2 - \frac{1}{2}\ln 3$

10

$$\begin{array}{r} 3x-2.5 \\ 2x-1\overline{)6x^2-8x} \\ \underline{6x^2-3x} \\ -5x \\ \underline{-5x+2.5} \\ -2.5 \end{array}$$

So, $\frac{6x^2-8x}{2x-1} = 3x - 2.5 - \frac{2.5}{2x-1}$

$\int_1^2 \frac{6x^2-8x}{2x-1} dx = \int_1^2 \left[(3x-2.5) - 2.5\left(\frac{1}{2x-1}\right)\right] dx$

$= \left[\left(\frac{3}{2}x^2 - 2.5x\right) - \frac{2.5}{2}\ln|2x-1|\right]_1^2$

$= \left[\left(\frac{3}{2} \times 2^2 - 2.5 \times 2\right) - 1.25\ln 3\right] - \left[\left(\frac{3}{2} \times 1^2 - 2.5 \times 1\right) - 1.25\ln 1\right]$

$= 1 - \frac{5}{4}\ln 3 - [-1 - 0]$

$= 2 - \frac{5}{4}\ln 3$

Exercise 15.9

1 a $y = (x+1)\sqrt{2x-1}$

$y = (x+1)(2x-1)^{\frac{1}{2}}$ differentiate by using the product rule

$$\frac{dy}{dx} = (x+1)\left(\frac{1}{2} \times 2(2x-1)^{-\frac{1}{2}}\right) + (2x-1)^{\frac{1}{2}}(1)$$

$$= (x+1)(2x-1)^{-\frac{1}{2}} + (2x-1)^{\frac{1}{2}}$$

$$= \frac{x+1}{(2x-1)^{\frac{1}{2}}} + \frac{(2x-1)^{\frac{1}{2}}}{1}$$

$$= \frac{x+1}{(2x-1)^{\frac{1}{2}}} + \frac{2x-1}{(2x-1)^{\frac{1}{2}}}$$

$$= \frac{x+1+2x-1}{(2x-1)^{\frac{1}{2}}}$$

$$= \frac{3x}{(2x-1)^{\frac{1}{2}}} \text{ or } \frac{3x}{\sqrt{2x-1}}$$

b $$\int_1^5 \frac{x}{\sqrt{2x-1}}\,dx = \frac{1}{3}\int_1^5 \frac{3x}{\sqrt{2x-1}}\,dx = \frac{1}{3}\left[(x+1)\sqrt{2x-1}\right]_1^5$$

$$= \frac{1}{3}\left[(5+1)\sqrt{2(5)-1}\right] - \frac{1}{3}\left[(1+1)\sqrt{2(1)-1}\right]$$

$$= \frac{1}{3}[18] - \frac{1}{3}[2]$$

$$= 5\frac{1}{3}$$

2 a $y = x\sqrt{3x^2+4}$

$y = x(3x^2+4)^{\frac{1}{2}}$ differentiate by using the product rule

$$\frac{dy}{dx} = x\left(\frac{1}{2} \times 6x(3x^2+4)^{-\frac{1}{2}}\right) + (3x^2+4)^{\frac{1}{2}}(1)$$

$$= 3x^2(3x^2+4)^{-\frac{1}{2}} + (3x^2+4)^{\frac{1}{2}}$$

$$= \frac{3x^2}{(3x^2+4)^{\frac{1}{2}}} + \frac{(3x^2+4)^{\frac{1}{2}}}{1}$$

$$= \frac{3x^2}{(3x^2+4)^{\frac{1}{2}}} + \frac{3x^2+4}{(3x^2+4)^{\frac{1}{2}}}$$

$$= \frac{(3x^2+3x^2+4)}{(3x^2+4)^{\frac{1}{2}}}$$

$$= \frac{6x^2+4}{\sqrt{3x^2+4}}$$

b $$\int_0^2 \frac{3x^2+2}{\sqrt{3x^2+4}}\,dx = \frac{1}{2}\int_0^2 \frac{6x^2+4}{\sqrt{3x^2+4}}\,dx = \frac{1}{2}\left[x\sqrt{3x^2+4}\right]_0^2$$

$$= \left[\frac{1}{2}[2\sqrt{3\times 2^2+4}]\right] - \left[\frac{1}{2}[0\sqrt{3\times 0^2+4}]\right]$$

$$= 4$$

3 a $y = \dfrac{1}{x^2 + 5}$

$y = (x^2 + 5)^{-1}$ — differentiate using the chain rule

$\dfrac{dy}{dx} = -1 \times 2x(x^2 + 5)^{-2}$

$= -\dfrac{2x}{(x^2 + 5)^2}$

b $\displaystyle\int_1^2 \frac{4x}{(x^2+5)^2}\,dx = -2\int_1^2 -\frac{2x}{(x^2+5)^2}\,dx = \left[-2 \times \frac{1}{x^2+5}\right]_1^2$

$= \dfrac{-2}{2^2 + 5} - \dfrac{-2}{1^2 + 5}$

$= \dfrac{1}{9}$

4 a $y = \dfrac{x + 2}{\sqrt{3x + 4}}$

$y = (x + 2)(3x + 4)^{-\frac{1}{2}}$ — differentiate by using the product rule

$\dfrac{dy}{dx} = (x + 2) \times -\dfrac{1}{2} \times 3(3x + 4)^{-\frac{3}{2}} + (3x + 4)^{-\frac{1}{2}} \times (1)$

$= -\dfrac{3}{2}(x + 2)(3x + 4)^{-\frac{3}{2}} + (3x + 4)^{-\frac{1}{2}}$

$= \dfrac{-3(x + 2)}{2(3x + 4)^{\frac{3}{2}}} + \dfrac{1}{(3x + 4)^{\frac{1}{2}}}$

$= \dfrac{-3(x + 2)}{2(3x + 4)^{\frac{3}{2}}} + \dfrac{2(3x + 4)}{2(3x + 4)^{\frac{3}{2}}}$

$= \dfrac{-3x - 6 + 6x + 8}{2(3x + 4)^{\frac{3}{2}}}$

$= \dfrac{3x + 2}{2\sqrt{(3x + 4)^3}}$

b $\displaystyle\int_0^4 \frac{6x + 4}{\sqrt{(3x+4)^3}}\,dx = 4\int_0^4 \frac{3x + 2}{2\sqrt{(3x+4)^3}}\,dx = 4\left[\frac{x + 2}{\sqrt{3x + 4}}\right]_0^4$

$= 4\left[\dfrac{4 + 2}{\sqrt{3(4) + 4}} - \dfrac{0 + 2}{\sqrt{3(0) + 4}}\right]$

$= 4[1.5 - 1]$

$= 2$

5 a $\dfrac{d}{dx}\left(\dfrac{x}{\cos x}\right)$ — differentiate using the quotient rule

$= \dfrac{\cos x \times (1) - x \times (-\sin x)}{\cos^2 x}$

$= \dfrac{\cos x + x\sin x}{\cos^2 x}$

b $$\int_0^{\frac{\pi}{4}} \frac{\cos x + x\sin x}{5\cos^2 x}\,dx = \frac{1}{5}\int_0^{\frac{\pi}{4}} \frac{\cos x + x\sin x}{\cos^2 x}\,dx = \frac{1}{5}\left[\frac{x}{\cos x}\right]_0^{\frac{\pi}{4}}$$

$$= \frac{1}{5}\left[\frac{\frac{\pi}{4}}{\cos\frac{\pi}{4}} - \frac{0}{\cos 0}\right]$$

$$= \frac{1}{5}\left[\frac{\frac{\pi}{4}}{\frac{1}{\sqrt{2}}} - \frac{0}{1}\right]$$

$$= \frac{1}{5} \times \frac{\pi\sqrt{2}}{4}$$

$$= \frac{\pi\sqrt{2}}{20}$$

6 a $\frac{d}{dx}(x\sin x)$ — differentiate using the product rule

$= x \times \cos x + \sin x \times (1)$

$= x\cos x + \sin x$

b $$\int_0^{\frac{\pi}{2}} (x\cos x + \sin x)\,dx = \int_0^{\frac{\pi}{2}} x\cos x\,dx + \int_0^{\frac{\pi}{2}} \sin x\,dx$$ — rearrange

$$\int_0^{\frac{\pi}{2}} x\cos x\,dx = \int_0^{\frac{\pi}{2}} (x\cos x + \sin x)\,dx - \int_0^{\frac{\pi}{2}} \sin x\,dx$$

$$= [x\sin x]_0^{\frac{\pi}{2}} - [-\cos x]_0^{\frac{\pi}{2}}$$

$$= \left[\frac{\pi}{2}\sin\frac{\pi}{2} - 0\right] - \left[-\cos\frac{\pi}{2} - -\cos 0\right]$$

$$= \frac{\pi}{2} - [0 + 1]$$

$$= \frac{1}{2}(\pi - 2)$$

7 a $\frac{d}{dx}(x^2\ln x)$ — differentiate using the product rule

$= x^2 \times \frac{1}{x} + 2x\ln x$

$= x + 2x\ln x$

b $$\int_1^{e} (x + 2x\ln x)\,dx = \int_1^{e} x\,dx + \int_1^{e} 2x\ln x\,dx$$ — rearrange

$$\int_1^{e} 2x\ln x\,dx = \int_1^{e} (x + 2x\ln x)\,dx - \int_1^{e} x\,dx$$

$$2\int_1^{e} 2x\ln x\,dx = 2\int_1^{e} (x + 2x\ln x)\,dx - 2\int_1^{e} x\,dx$$

$$\int_1^{e} 4x\ln x\,dx = 2\int_1^{e} (x + 2x\ln x)\,dx - 2\int_1^{e} x\,dx$$

$$= [2(x^2\ln x)]_1^{e} - \left[2 \times \frac{1}{2}x^2\right]_1^{e}$$

$$= [2x^2\ln x]_1^{e} - [x^2]_1^{e}$$

$$= [(2e^2\ln e) - (2 \times 1^2\ln 1)] - [e^2 - 1^2]$$

$$= 2e^2 - e^2 + 1$$

$$= 1 + e^2$$

8 a $y = x\sin 3x$ differentiate using the product rule

$$\frac{dy}{dx} = x \times 3\cos 3x + \sin 3x \times (1)$$

$$\frac{dy}{dx} = 3x\cos 3x + \sin 3x$$

b $\int_0^{\frac{\pi}{6}} (3x\cos 3x + \sin 3x)\,dx = \int_0^{\frac{\pi}{6}} (3x\cos 3x)\,dx + \int_0^{\frac{\pi}{6}} (\sin 3x)\,dx$ rearrange

$$\int_0^{\frac{\pi}{6}} (3x\cos 3x)\,dx = \int_0^{\frac{\pi}{6}} (3x\cos 3x + \sin 3x)\,dx - \int_0^{\frac{\pi}{6}} (\sin 3x)\,dx$$

$$3\int_0^{\frac{\pi}{6}} (x\cos 3x)\,dx = \int_0^{\frac{\pi}{6}} (3x\cos 3x + \sin 3x)\,dx - \int_0^{\frac{\pi}{6}} (\sin 3x)\,dx$$

$$\int_0^{\frac{\pi}{6}} (x\cos 3x)\,dx = \frac{1}{3}\int_0^{\frac{\pi}{6}} (3x\cos 3x + \sin 3x)\,dx - \frac{1}{3}\int_0^{\frac{\pi}{6}} (\sin 3x)\,dx$$

$$= \frac{1}{3}[x\sin 3x]_0^{\frac{\pi}{6}} - \frac{1}{3}\left[-\frac{1}{3}\cos 3x\right]_0^{\frac{\pi}{6}}$$

$$= \frac{1}{3}\left[\left(\frac{\pi}{6}\sin\frac{3\pi}{6}\right) - (0\sin 0)\right] - \frac{1}{3}\left[\left(-\frac{1}{3}\cos\frac{3\pi}{6}\right) - \left(-\frac{1}{3}\cos 0\right)\right]$$

$$= \frac{\pi}{18} - \frac{1}{3}\left[0 + \frac{1}{3}\right]$$

$$= \frac{\pi}{18} - \frac{1}{9} \text{ or } \frac{1}{18}(\pi - 2)$$

Exercise 15.10

REMEMBER

Area $= \int_a^b f(x)\,dx$, where $f(x) \geqslant 0$

1 c The required area is above the x-axis.

$$\text{Area} = \int_1^3 (3x + 6x^{-2} - 5)\,dx$$

$$= \left[\frac{3}{2}x^2 - 6x^{-1} - 5x\right]_1^3$$

$$= \left[\frac{3}{2}x^2 - \frac{6}{x} - 5x\right]_1^3$$

$$= \left(\frac{27}{2} - \frac{6}{3} - 15\right) - \left(\frac{3}{2} - \frac{6}{1} - 5\right)$$

$= 6$ units^2

d The required area is above the x-axis.

$$\text{Area} = \int_0^1 (e^x + 2e^{-x})\,dx$$

$$= \left[e^x + \frac{2}{-1}e^{-x}\right]_0^1$$

$$= [e^x - 2e^{-x}]_0^1$$

$$= (e^1 - 2e^{-1}) - (e^0 - 2e^{-(0)})$$

$= e - \frac{2}{e} + 1$ units^2

REMEMBER

If the required area between $y = f(x)$ and the x-axis lies below the x-axis, then $\int_a^b f(x)\,dx$ will be a negative value. Hence, for a region that lies below the x-axis, the area is given as $\left|\int_a^b f(x)\,dx\right|$.

2 b The required area is below the x-axis.

$$= \left[\frac{1}{2}x^2 - \frac{5}{\frac{1}{2}}\sin\frac{x}{2}\right]_{\frac{\pi}{3}}^{\frac{\pi}{2}}$$

$$= \left[\frac{1}{2}x^2 - 10\sin\frac{x}{2}\right]_{\frac{\pi}{3}}^{\frac{\pi}{2}}$$

$$= \left[\frac{1}{2}\left(\frac{\pi}{2}\right)^2 - 10\sin\frac{\frac{\pi}{2}}{2}\right] - \left[\frac{1}{2}\left(\frac{\pi}{3}\right)^2 - 10\sin\frac{\frac{\pi}{3}}{2}\right]$$

$$= \left[\frac{\pi^2}{8} - 10 \times \frac{\sqrt{2}}{2}\right] - \left[\frac{\pi^2}{18} - 5\right]$$

$$= \frac{\pi^2}{8} - \frac{\pi^2}{18} - 5\sqrt{2} + 5$$

$= \frac{5\pi^2}{72} - 5\sqrt{2} + 5$ this works out as -1.39 to 3 significant figures.

The negative sign is consistent with the area being below the x-axis.

We need $\left|\frac{5\pi^2}{72} - 5\sqrt{2} + 5\right| = -\frac{5\pi^2}{72} + 5\sqrt{2} - 5$

Area $= 5\sqrt{2} - 5 - \frac{5\pi^2}{72}$ units^2

d Area $= \int_{-1}^{1}\left(x + \frac{2}{2x+3}\right)dx$

$$= \left[\frac{1}{2}x^2 + \frac{2}{2}\ln(2x+3)\right]_{-1}^{1}$$

$$= \left[\frac{1}{2} \times 1^2 + \ln(2 \times 1 + 3)\right] - \left[\frac{1}{2} \times (-1)^2 + \ln(2 \times -1 + 3)\right]$$

$$= \frac{1}{2} + \ln 5 - \frac{1}{2} - \ln 1$$

$= \ln 5$ units^2

3 Area $= \int_{-2}^{-1}(x+2)(x+1)(x-1)\,dx + \int_{-1}^{1}(x+2)(x+1)(x-1)\,dx$

$(x+2)(x+1)(x-1) = (x^2+3x+2)(x-1)$

$= x^3 - x^2 + 3x^2 - 3x + 2x - 2$

$= x^3 + 2x^2 - x - 2$

$$\text{Area} = \underbrace{\int_{-2}^{-1}(x^3+2x^2-x-2)\,dx}_{A} + \underbrace{\int_{-1}^{1}(x^3+2x^2-x-2)\,dx}_{B}$$ Area A is above the x-axis Area B is below the x-axis

$$= \underbrace{\left[\frac{1}{4}x^4 + \frac{2}{3}x^3 - \frac{1}{2}x^2 - 2x\right]_{-2}^{-1}}_{A} + \underbrace{\left[\frac{1}{4}x^4 + \frac{2}{3}x^3 - \frac{1}{2}x^2 - 2x\right]_{-1}^{1}}_{B}$$

$$= \left[\left(\frac{1}{4}(-1)^4 + \frac{2}{3}(-1)^3 - \frac{1}{2}(-1)^2 - 2(-1)\right) - \left(\frac{1}{4}(-2)^4 + \frac{2}{3}(-2)^3 - \frac{1}{2}(-2)^2 - 2(-2)\right)\right]$$

$$+ \left[\left(\frac{1}{4}(1)^4 + \frac{2}{3}(1)^3 - \frac{1}{2}(1)^2 - 2(1)\right) - \left(\frac{1}{4}(-1)^4 + \frac{2}{3}(-1)^3 - \frac{1}{2}(-1)^2 - 2(-1)\right)\right]$$

$= \left[\left(\frac{1}{4} - \frac{2}{3} - \frac{1}{2} + 2\right) - \left(4 - \frac{16}{3} - 2 + 4\right)\right] + \left[\left(\frac{1}{4} + \frac{2}{3} - \frac{1}{2} - 2\right) - \left(\frac{1}{4} - \frac{2}{3} - \frac{1}{2} + 2\right)\right]$

$= \left[\frac{13}{12} - \left(4 - \frac{16}{3} - 2 + 4\right)\right] + \left[\left(-\frac{19}{12}\right) - \left(\frac{13}{12}\right)\right]$

$= \left(\frac{13}{12} - \frac{2}{3}\right) + \left(-\frac{19}{12} - \frac{13}{12}\right)$

$= \frac{5}{12} + \left|-\frac{32}{12}\right|$

$= \frac{5}{12} + \frac{32}{12}$

$= 3\frac{1}{12}$

4 c $y = x(x^2 - 4)$ can be written as $y = x(x + 2)(x - 2)$

The curve represents a positive cubic

To find where the graph intersects the x- axis, substitute $y = 0$

$x(x + 2)(x - 2) = 0$

$x = 0, x = -2, x = 2$ the curve crosses the x-axis at $(0, 0)$ $(-2, 0)$ $(2, 0)$

To find where the graph crosses the y-axis, substitute $x = 0$

$y = 0(0 + 2)(0 - 2)$

$y = 0$

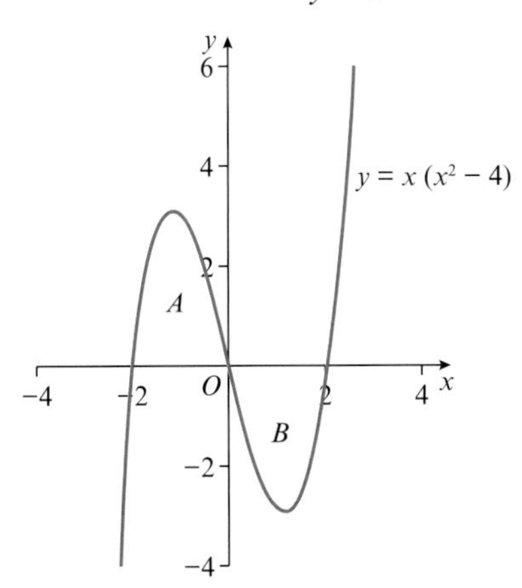

Area A (above the x-axis) $= \int_{-2}^{0} x(x^2 - 4)\,dx = \int_{-2}^{0} (x^3 - 4x)\,dx$

$= \left[\frac{1}{4}x^4 - 2x^2\right]_{-2}^{0}$

$= \left[\left(\frac{1}{4} \times 0^4 - 2(0)^2\right) - \left(\frac{1}{4} \times (-2)^4 - 2(-2)^2\right)\right]$

$= -(4 - 8)$

$= 4$

Area B (beneath the x-axis) $= \int_{0}^{2} x(x^2 - 4)\,dx = \int_{0}^{2} (x^3 - 4x)\,dx$

$$= \left[\frac{1}{4}x^4 - 2x^2\right]_0^2$$

$$= \left[\left(\frac{1}{4} \times 2^4 - 2(2)^2\right) - \left(\frac{1}{4} \times (0)^4 - 2(0)^2\right)\right]$$

$$= -4$$

Area of B = |−4| = 4

The total area bounded by the curve and the x-axis is 4 + 4 = 8 units²

f $y = x^2(4 - x)$ which can be written as $(x + 0)(x + 0)(4 - x)$ or $4 - x^3$

The curve represents a negative cubic

To find where the graph intersects the x-axis, substitute $y = 0$

$(x + 0)(x + 0)(4 - x) = 0$

$x = 0$, $x = 0$ $x = 4$ the curve **crosses** the x-axis at (4, 0)

$x = 0$ is a repeated root. This means that the curve **touches** the x-axis at $x = 0$

To find where the graph crosses the y-axis, substitute $x = 0$

$y = (0 + 0)(0 + 0)(4 - 0)$

$= 4$

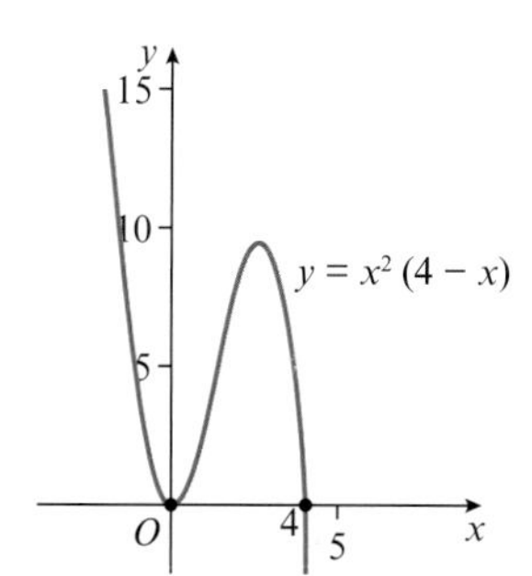

The area bounded by the curve and the x-axis is:

$$= \int_0^4 x^2(4 - x)\,dx$$

$$= \int_0^4 (4x^2 - x^3)\,dx$$

$$= \left[\frac{4}{3}x^3 - \frac{1}{4}x^4\right]_0^4$$

$$= \left[\left(\frac{4}{3} \times 4^3 - \frac{1}{4}(4)^4\right) - \left(\frac{1}{4} \times (0)^4 - \frac{1}{4}(0)^4\right)\right]$$

$$= 21\frac{1}{3} \text{ units}^2$$

5 The graph of $y = \frac{6}{\sqrt{x}}$ lies above the x-axis

(since $x > 0$ so $\frac{6}{\sqrt{x}} > 0$ therefore $y > 0$)

[$x \neq 0$, because $\frac{6}{\sqrt{0}}$ is not defined]

The required area is:

$$\int_4^9 \frac{6}{\sqrt{x}}\,dx \text{ or } \int_4^9 6x^{-\frac{1}{2}}\,dx = \left[\frac{6}{\frac{1}{2}}x^{\frac{1}{2}}\right]_4^9$$

$$= \left[12x^{\frac{1}{2}}\right]_4^9$$

$$= 12 \times 9^{\frac{1}{2}} - 12 \times 4^{\frac{1}{2}}$$

$$= 12 \text{ units}^2$$

6 a The graph of $y = \frac{12}{x^2}$ lies above the x-axis since

$x^2 > 0$ so $\frac{12}{x^2} > 0$ therefore $y > 0$.

[$x \neq 0$, because $\frac{12}{0^2}$ is not defined]

The required area is:

$$\int_1^4 \frac{12}{x^2}\,dx$$

$$= \int_1^4 12x^{-2}\,dx$$

$$= \left[\frac{12}{-1}x^{-1}\right]_1^4$$

$$= \left[\frac{-12}{x}\right]_1^4$$

$$= -\frac{12}{4} - \left(\frac{-12}{1}\right)$$

$$= 9 \text{ units}^2$$

b $1 < p < 4$

If the areas are equal then:

$$\int_1^p 12x^{-2}\,\mathrm{d}x = \int_p^4 12x^{-2}\,\mathrm{d}x$$

$$\left[\frac{-12}{x}\right]_1^p = \left[\frac{-12}{x}\right]_p^4$$

$$\left[\frac{-12}{p} - \frac{-12}{1}\right] = \left[\frac{-12}{4} - \frac{-12}{p}\right]$$

$$\frac{-12}{p} + 12 = -3 + \frac{12}{p}$$ multiply both sides by p

$$-12 + 12p = -3p + 12$$

$$15p = 24$$

$$p = 1.6$$

7 **a** $\frac{\mathrm{d}}{\mathrm{d}x}(xe^x - e^x) = xe^x + e^x \times (1) - e^x$

$= xe^x$

b $\int_0^2 xe^x\,\mathrm{d}x = [xe^x - e^x]_0^2$

$= (2e^2 - e^2) - (0e^0 - e^0)$

$= e^2 + 1$ units^2

8 Shaded area $= 8 = \int_1^k \frac{4}{2x-1}\mathrm{d}x\, k > 1$

$$8 = 4\int_1^k \frac{1}{2x-1}\,\mathrm{d}x$$

$$8 = \left[\frac{4}{2}\ln(2x-1)\right]_1^k$$ the shaded region is above the x-axis

$$8 = [2\ln(2k-1)] - [2\ln(2 \times 1 - 1)]$$

$$8 = 2\ln(2k-1) - 0$$

$$4 = \ln(2k-1)$$

or $4 = \log_e(2k-1)$

$$2k - 1 = e^4$$

$$k = \frac{1}{2}(e^4 + 1)$$

9 **a** $\frac{\mathrm{d}}{\mathrm{d}x}(x\ln x) = x \times \frac{1}{x} + \ln x \times (1)$

$= 1 + \ln x$

b $\int_1^5 (1 + \ln x)\,\mathrm{d}x = \int_1^5 1\,\mathrm{d}x + \int_1^5 \ln x\,\mathrm{d}x$ rearrange

$$\int_1^5 \ln x\,\mathrm{d}x = \int_1^5 (1 + \ln x)\,\mathrm{d}x - \int_1^5 1\,\mathrm{d}x$$

$= [x\ln x]_1^5 - [x]_1^5$

$= [5\ln 5 - 1\ln 1] - [5 - 1]$

$= 5\ln 5 - 4$ units^2

10 a $\frac{d}{dx}(x\cos x) = x \times -\sin x + \cos x \times (1)$

$= -x\sin x + \cos x$

$= \cos x - x\sin x$

b $\int_{\frac{\pi}{2}}^{\pi} (\cos x - x\sin x)\,dx = \int_{\frac{\pi}{2}}^{\pi} \cos x\,dx - \int_{\frac{\pi}{2}}^{\pi} x\sin x\,dx$ rearrange

$\int_{\frac{\pi}{2}}^{\pi} x\sin x\,dx = \int_{\frac{\pi}{2}}^{\pi} \cos x\,dx - \int_{\frac{\pi}{2}}^{\pi} (\cos x - x\sin x)\,dx$

$= [\sin x]_{\frac{\pi}{2}}^{\pi} - [x\cos x]_{\frac{\pi}{2}}^{\pi}$

$= \left[\sin\pi - \sin\frac{\pi}{2}\right] - \left[\pi\cos\pi - \frac{\pi}{2}\cos\frac{\pi}{2}\right]$

$= [0 - 1] - [-\pi - 0]$

$= -1 + \pi$

$= \pi - 1$ units^2

Exercise 15.11

REMEMBER

If two functions $f(x)$ and $g(x)$ intersect at $x = a$ and $x = b$, then the area, A, enclosed between the two curves is given by

$$A = \int_a^b f(x)\,dx - \int_a^b g(x)\,dx$$

1 Let A and B be the intersection points of $y = 1 + \cos x$ and $y = 1$

Solve $y = 1 + \cos x$ and $y = 1$ simultaneously to find the coordinates of A and B:

$1 + \cos x = 1$

$\cos x = 0$ remember to use radians

$x = \frac{\pi}{2}$ and $x = -\frac{\pi}{2}$

$A\left(-\frac{\pi}{2}, 1\right)$, $B\left(\frac{\pi}{2}, 1\right)$

Method 1

$f(x) = 1 + \cos x$ and $g(x) = 1$

Area = area under curve − area of rectangle $ABCD$

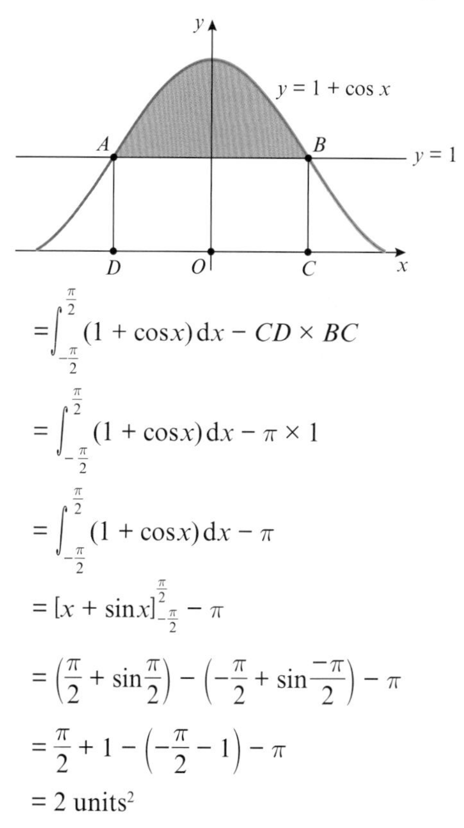

$= \int_{-\frac{\pi}{2}}^{\frac{\pi}{2}} (1 + \cos x)\,dx - CD \times BC$

$= \int_{-\frac{\pi}{2}}^{\frac{\pi}{2}} (1 + \cos x)\,dx - \pi \times 1$

$= \int_{-\frac{\pi}{2}}^{\frac{\pi}{2}} (1 + \cos x)\,dx - \pi$

$= [x + \sin x]_{-\frac{\pi}{2}}^{\frac{\pi}{2}} - \pi$

$= \left(\frac{\pi}{2} + \sin\frac{\pi}{2}\right) - \left(-\frac{\pi}{2} + \sin\frac{-\pi}{2}\right) - \pi$

$= \frac{\pi}{2} + 1 - \left(-\frac{\pi}{2} - 1\right) - \pi$

$= 2$ units^2

Method 2

Use $A = \int_a^b f(x)\,dx - \int_a^b g(x)\,dx$ where

$f(x) = 1 + \cos x$ and $g(x) = 1$

$$\text{Area} = \int_{-\frac{\pi}{2}}^{\frac{\pi}{2}} f(x)\,dx - \int_{-\frac{\pi}{2}}^{\frac{\pi}{2}} g(x)\,dx$$

$$= \int_{-\frac{\pi}{2}}^{\frac{\pi}{2}} (1 + \cos x)\,dx - \int_{-\frac{\pi}{2}}^{\frac{\pi}{2}} 1\,dx$$

$$= \int_{-\frac{\pi}{2}}^{\frac{\pi}{2}} (1 + \cos x - 1)\,dx \text{ or } \int_{-\frac{\pi}{2}}^{\frac{\pi}{2}} \cos x\,dx$$

$$= [\sin x]_{-\frac{\pi}{2}}^{\frac{\pi}{2}}$$

$$= \sin\frac{\pi}{2} - \sin\left(-\frac{\pi}{2}\right)$$

$$= 1 - -1$$

$$= 2 \text{ units}^2$$

2 $f(x) = 2 + 3x - x^2$ and $g(x) = 2$

Area = area under curve − area of rectangle A

$$= \int_0^2 (2 + 3x - x^2)\,dx - 2 \times 2$$

$$= \int_0^2 (2 + 3x - x^2)\,dx - 4$$

$$= \left[2x + \frac{3}{2}x^2 - \frac{1}{3}x^3\right]_0^2 - 4$$

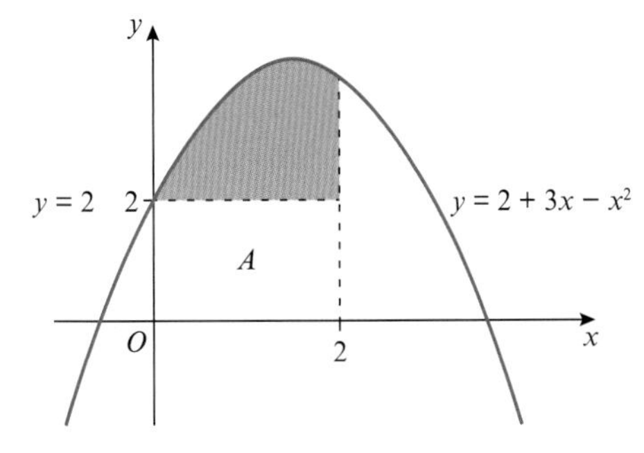

$$= \left(2(2) + \frac{3}{2}(2)^2 - \frac{1}{3}(2)^3\right) - \left(2(0) + \frac{3}{2}(0)^2 - \frac{1}{3}(0)^3\right) - 4$$

$$= \left(4 + 6 - \frac{8}{3}\right) - 0 - 4$$

$$= 3\frac{1}{3} \text{ units}^2$$

3 Solve $y = 3x^2 + 2$ and $y = 14$ simultaneously to find the intersection point of the line and the curve.

$$3x^2 + 2 = 14$$

$$3x^2 = 12$$

$$x^2 = 4$$

$$x = \pm 2 \qquad \text{reject } x = -2$$

$$x = 2$$

$f(x) = 3x^2 + 2$ and $g(x) = 14$

Area = area of rectangle between the curve and the x-axis − area under curve

$$= 2 \times 14 - \int_0^2 (3x^2 + 2)\,dx$$

$$= 28 - \int_0^2 (3x^2 + 2)\,dx$$

$$= 28 - [x^3 + 2x]_0^2$$

$$= 28 - (2^3 + 2 \times 2) - (0^3 + 2 \times 0)$$

$$= 28 - 12 - 0$$

$$= 16 \text{ units}^2$$

4 Area = area under curve − area of the triangle with vertices $(0, 0)$, $\left(\frac{\pi}{2}, 0\right)$ and $(0, 3)$

$$= \int_0^{\frac{\pi}{2}} (2\sin 2x + 3\cos x)\,dx - \frac{1}{2} \times \frac{\pi}{2} \times 3$$

$$= \int_0^{\frac{\pi}{2}} (2\sin 2x + 3\cos x)\,dx - \frac{3\pi}{4}$$

$$= [-\cos 2x + 3\sin x]_0^{\frac{\pi}{2}} - \frac{3\pi}{4}$$

$$= (-(-1) + 3) - (-1 + 0) - \frac{3\pi}{4}$$

$$= 4 + 1 - \frac{3\pi}{4}$$

$$= 5 - \frac{3\pi}{4} \text{ units}^2$$

5 c Solve $y = \sqrt{x}$ and $y = \frac{1}{2}x$ simultaneously to find the intersection point of the line and the curve.

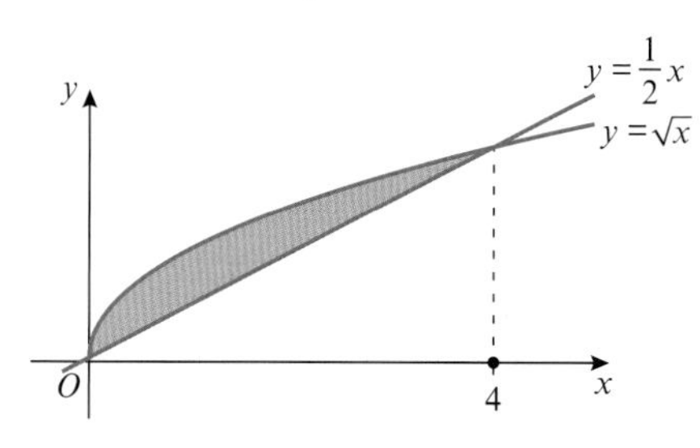

$x^{\frac{1}{2}} = \frac{1}{2}x$ multiply both sides by 2

$2x^{\frac{1}{2}} = x$ rearrange

$2x^{\frac{1}{2}} - x = 0$ factorise

$x^{\frac{1}{2}}(2 - x^{\frac{1}{2}}) = 0$

$x^{\frac{1}{2}} = 0$ and $2 - x^{\frac{1}{2}} = 0$

$x = 0$ and $x^{\frac{1}{2}} = 2$

$x = 4$

Substitute $x = 4$ into $y = \frac{1}{2} \times 4 = 2$

The intersection point is at (4, 2)

Now consider $f(x) = \sqrt{x}$ and $g(x) = \frac{1}{2}x$

Area = area under curve − area of the triangle with vertices (0, 0), (4, 2) and (4, 0)

$$= \int_0^4 \sqrt{x}\,dx - \frac{1}{2} \times 4 \times 2$$

$$= \int_0^4 x^{\frac{1}{2}}\,dx - 4$$

$$= \left[\frac{2}{3}x^{\frac{3}{2}}\right]_0^4 - 4$$

$$= \frac{2}{3} \times 4^{\frac{3}{2}} - 0 - 4$$

$$= \frac{4}{3} = 1\frac{1}{3} \text{ units}^2$$

d $y = 4x - x^2$ is an '∩' shaped parabola which intersects the x-axis where $y = 0$.

So, $0 = 4x - x^2$

$0 = x(4 - x)$

$x = 0$ and $4 - x = 0$ so $x = 4$

The parabola intersects the x-axis at (0, 0) and (4, 0)

The line $2x + y = 0$ or $y = -2x$ passes through (0, 0) and has a gradient −2

Solve $y = 4x - x^2$ and $y = -2x$ simultaneously to find the intersection points A and B of the line and the curve.

$4x - x^2 = -2x$ rearrange

$x^2 - 6x = 0$ factorise

$x(x - 6) = 0$

$x = 0$ or $x = 6$

Substituting $x = 0$ into $2x + y = 0$ gives:

$2(0) + y = 0$

$y = 0$

$A = (0, 0)$

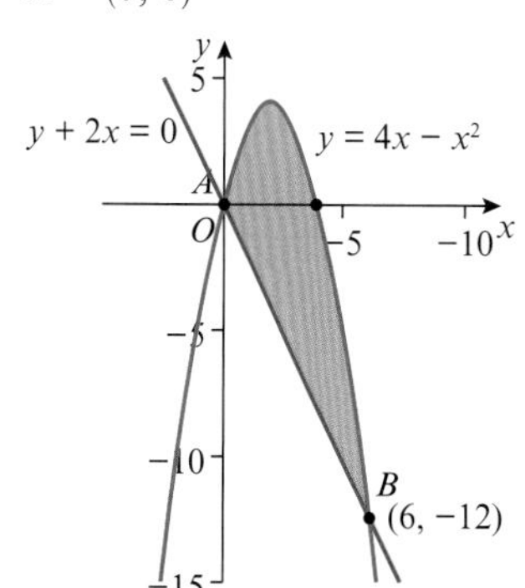

Substituting $x = 6$ into $2x + y = 0$ gives:

$2(6) + y = 0$

$y = -12$

$B = (6, -12)$

Now consider $f(x) = 4x - x^2$ and $g(x) = -2x$

$$\text{Area} = \int_0^6 (4x - x^2)\,dx - \int_0^6 -2x\,dx$$

$$= \int_0^6 (4x - x^2 - (-2x))\,dx$$

$$= \int_0^6 (6x - x^2)\,dx$$

$$= \left[3x^2 - \frac{1}{3}x^3\right]_0^6$$

$$= \left[3(6)^2 - \frac{1}{3}(6)^3\right] - \left[3(0)^2 - \frac{1}{3}(0)^3\right]$$

$= 108 - 72$

$= 36 \text{ units}^2$

6 a $y = x(2 - x)$ or $y = 2x - x^2$ is an '∩' shaped parabola which intersects the x-axis where $y = 0$.

So, $0 = 2x - x^2$

$0 = x(2 - x)$

$x = 0$ and $2 - x = 0$ so $x = 2$

The parabola $y = 2x - x^2$ intersects the x-axis at (0, 0) and (2, 0)

$y = x^2$ is a '∪' shaped parabola that touches the x-axis at (0, 0)

Solve $y = 2x - x^2$ and $y = -2x$ simultaneously to find the intersection points of the line and the curve and

$2x - x^2 = x^2$ rearrange

$2x^2 - 2x = 0$ factorise

$2x(x - 1) = 0$

$x = 0$ or $x = 1$

Substituting $x = 0$ into $y = x^2$ gives:

$y = 0^2$

$y = 0$

$A = (0, 0)$

Substituting $x = 1$ into $y = x^2$ gives:

$y = 1^2$

$y = 1$

$B = (1, 1)$

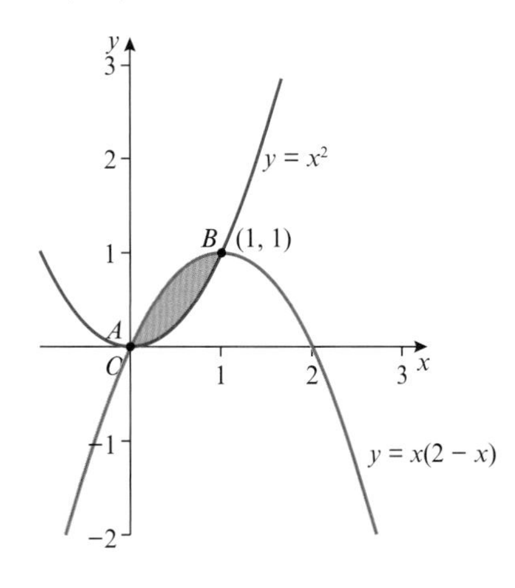

Now consider $f(x) = 2x - x^2$ and $g(x) = x^2$

$$\text{Area} = \int_0^1 (2x - x^2)\,dx - \int_0^1 x^2\,dx$$

$$= \int_0^1 (2x - x^2 - x^2)\,dx$$

$$= \int_0^1 (2x - 2x^2)\,dx$$

$$= \left[x^2 - \frac{2}{3}x^3\right]_0^1$$

$$= \left[(1)^2 - \frac{2}{3}(1)^3\right] - \left[(0)^2 - \frac{2}{3}(0)^3\right]$$

$$= 1 - \frac{2}{3}$$

$$= \frac{1}{3}\text{ units}^2$$

b $y = 4x - 3x^2$ is an '∩' shaped parabola which intersects the x-axis where $y = 0$.

So, $0 = 4x - 3x^2$

$0 = x(4 - x)$

$x = 0$ and $4 - x = 0$ so $x = 4$

The parabola intersects the x-axis at (0, 0) and (4, 0)

$y = x^3$ is a positive cubic curve.

It passes through the x-axis at (0, 0)

Solve $y = 4x - 3x^2$ and $y = x^3$ simultaneously to find the intersection points A, B and C of the line and the curve.

$4x - 3x^2 = x^3$ rearrange

$x^3 + 3x^2 - 4x = 0$ factorise

$x(x^2 + 3x - 4) = 0$

$x(x + 4)(x - 1) = 0$

$x = 0$ or $x = -4$ or $x = 1$

Substituting $x = 0$ into $y = x^3$ gives:

$y = 0^3 = 0$

$A = (0, 0)$

Substituting $x = -4$ into $y = x^3$ gives:

$y = (-4)^3 = -64$

$B = (-4, -64)$

Substituting $x = 1$ into $y = x^3$ gives:

$y = 1^3 = 1$

$C = (1, 1)$

Now consider $f(x) = 4x - 3x^2$ and $g(x) = x^3$

Ignoring point B (because $x \geqslant 0$), the required area is:

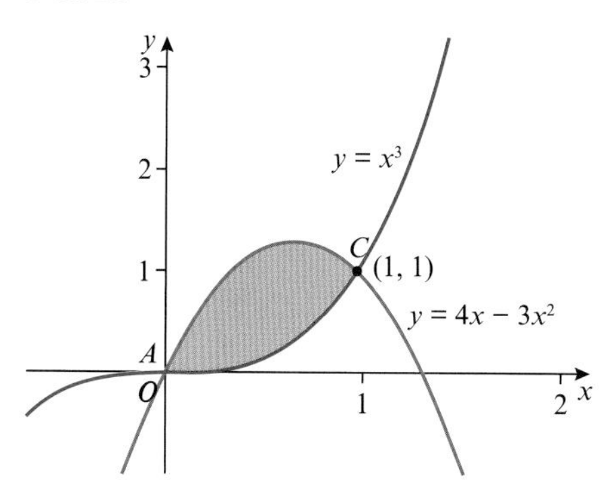

$$\text{Area} = \int_0^1 (4x - 3x^2)\,dx - \int_0^1 x^3\,dx$$

$$= \int_0^1 (4x - 3x^2 - x^3)\,dx$$

$$= \left[2x^2 - x^3 - \frac{1}{4}x^4\right]_0^1$$

$$= \left[2(1)^2 - (1)^3 - \frac{1}{4}(1)^4\right] - \left[2(0)^2 - (0)^3 - \frac{1}{4}(0)^4\right]$$

$$= 1 - \frac{1}{4}$$

$$= \frac{3}{4}\text{ units}^2$$

7 Solve $y = 3\sqrt{x}$ and $y = 10 - x$ simultaneously to find the intersection point of the line and the curve.

$3\sqrt{x} = 10 - x$

$3x^{\frac{1}{2}} = 10 - x$ rearrange

$x + 3x^{\frac{1}{2}} - 10 = 0$

Let $u = x^{\frac{1}{2}}$

$u^2 + 3u - 10 = 0$ factorise

$(u + 5)(u - 2) = 0$

$u = -5$ or $u = 2$

$x^{\frac{1}{2}} = -5$ (no solutions) or $x^{\frac{1}{2}} = 2$ so, $x = 4$

Substitute $x = 4$ into $y = 10 - x$

$y = 10 - 4$

$y = 6$

The curve and the line intersect at $(4, 6)$

The line $y = 10 - x$ intersects the x-axis where $y = 0$

$0 = 10 - x$

$x = 10$

The line intersects the x-axis at $(10, 0)$

Now consider $f(x) = 3\sqrt{x}$ and $g(x) = 10 - x$

Required area $= \int_0^4 3\sqrt{x}\,dx$ + Area of the right-angled triangle with vertices $(4, 6)$, $(10, 0)$, $(4, 0)$

$$= \int_0^4 3x^{\frac{1}{2}}\,dx + \frac{1}{2} \times 6 \times 6$$

$$= \left[\frac{3}{\frac{3}{2}}x^{\frac{3}{2}}\right]_0^4 + 18$$

$$= \left[2x^{\frac{3}{2}}\right]_0^4 + 18$$

$$= \left[2(4)^{\frac{3}{2}}\right] - \left[2(0)^{\frac{3}{2}}\right] + 18$$

$$= 16 + 18$$

$$= 34\text{ units}^2$$

8 a To find the coordinates of P, find the equation of the tangent line to $y = 6x - x^2$ at $(2, 8)$.

$y = 6x - x^2$

$\frac{dy}{dx} = 6 - 2x$

The gradient of the tangent line when $x = 2$ is $\frac{dy}{dx} = 6 - 2(2) = 2$

The equation of the tangent line at $(2, 8)$ is found by using $y - y_1 = m(x - x_1)$

$y - 8 = 2(x - 2)$

$y = 2x - 4 + 8$

$= 2x + 4$

The tangent crosses the x-axis where $y = 0$ so:

$0 = 2x + 4$

$x = -2$

P is at $(-2, 0)$

b Shaded area $= \int_2^6 (6x - x^2)\,dx$ + Area of the right-angled triangle with vertices $(2, 0)$, $(-2, 0)$, $(2, 8)$

$$= \int_2^6 (6x - x^2)\,dx + \frac{1}{2} \times 4 \times 8$$

$$= \int_2^6 (6x - x^2)\,dx + 16$$

$$= \left[3x^2 - \frac{1}{3}x^3\right]_2^6 + 16$$

$= \left[3(6)^2 - \frac{1}{3}(6)^3\right] - \left[3(2)^2 - \frac{1}{3}(2)^3\right] + 16$

$= 108 - 72 - 12 + \frac{8}{3} + 16$

$= 42\frac{2}{3}$ units^2

9 To find the coordinates of R, find the equation of the tangent line to $y = \sqrt{2x+1}$ at (12, 5).

$y = (2x+1)^{\frac{1}{2}}$

$\frac{dy}{dx} = \frac{1}{2} \times 2(2x+1)^{-\frac{1}{2}}$

$\frac{dy}{dx} = (2x+1)^{-\frac{1}{2}}$

The gradient of the tangent line when $x = 12$ is $\frac{dy}{dx} = (2 \times 12 + 1)^{-\frac{1}{2}} = \frac{1}{5}$

The equation of the tangent line at (12, 5) is found by using $y - y_1 = m(x - x_1)$

$y - 5 = \frac{1}{5}(x - 12)$

$5y - 25 = x - 12$

$5y = x + 13$

The tangent crosses the y-axis where $x = 0$ so:

$5y = 0 + 13$

$y = \frac{13}{5}$

R is at $\left(0, \frac{13}{5}\right)$

Shaded area $PQR = \Big[$Area of trapezium with vertices at $(0, 0), \left(0, \frac{13}{5}\right), (12, 5), (12, 0)\Big] - \int_0^{12} \sqrt{2x+1}\,dx$

$= \frac{1}{2}(OR + 5) \times 12 - \int_0^{12} (2x+1)^{\frac{1}{2}}\,dx$

$= \frac{1}{2}\left(\frac{13}{5} + 5\right) \times 12 - \left[\frac{1}{\frac{3}{2}} \times \frac{1}{2}(2x+1)^{\frac{3}{2}}\right]_0^{12}$

$= \frac{228}{5} - \left\{\left[\frac{1}{3}(2 \times 12 + 1)^{\frac{3}{2}}\right] - \left[\frac{1}{3}(2 \times 0 + 1)^{\frac{3}{2}}\right]\right\}$

$= \frac{228}{5} - \frac{125}{3} + \frac{1}{3}$

$= 4\frac{4}{15}$ units^2

10 **Method 1**

Area between the curve $y = 2 + \cos 2x$ and the x-axis (i.e Area of $A + B + D$) is:

$= \int_0^{\pi} (2 + \cos 2x)\,dx$

$= \left[2x + \frac{1}{2}\sin 2x\right]_0^{\pi}$

$= \left(2\pi + \frac{1}{2}\sin 2\pi\right) - \left(0 + \frac{1}{2}\sin 0\right)$

$= 2\pi$

Area of $A + B = \int_0^{\frac{\pi}{3}} (1 + 2\cos 2x)\,dx + \int_{\frac{2\pi}{3}}^{\pi} (1 + 2\cos 2x)\,dx$

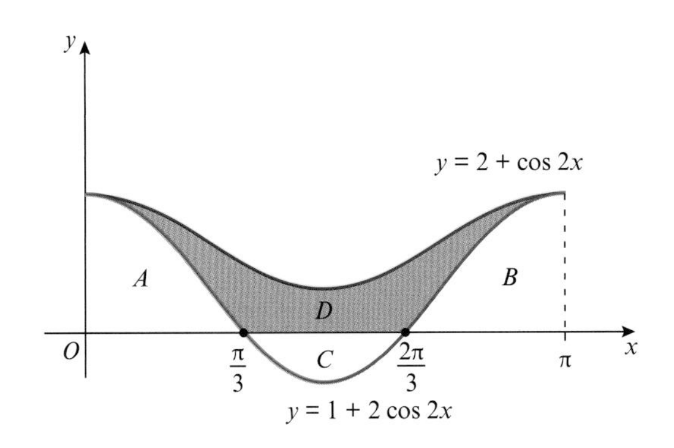

$$= [x + \sin 2x]_0^{\frac{\pi}{3}} + [x + \sin 2x]_{\frac{2\pi}{3}}^{\pi}$$

$$= \left[\left(\frac{\pi}{3} + \sin\frac{2\pi}{3}\right) - (0 + \sin 0)\right] + \left[(\pi + \sin 2\pi) - \left(\frac{2\pi}{3} + \sin\frac{4\pi}{3}\right)\right]$$

$$= \frac{\pi}{3} + \frac{\sqrt{3}}{2} + \pi - \frac{2\pi}{3} + \frac{\sqrt{3}}{2}$$

$$= \frac{2\pi}{3} + \sqrt{3}$$

Area $D = 2\pi - \left(\frac{2\pi}{3} + \sqrt{3}\right) = \frac{4\pi}{3} - \sqrt{3}$

Area $C = \int_{\frac{\pi}{3}}^{\frac{2\pi}{3}} (1 + 2\cos 2x)\, dx = [x + \sin 2x]_{\frac{\pi}{3}}^{\frac{2\pi}{3}}$

$$= \left(\frac{2\pi}{3} + \sin\frac{4\pi}{3}\right) - \left(\frac{\pi}{3} + \sin\frac{2\pi}{3}\right)$$

$$= \frac{2\pi}{3} - \frac{\sqrt{3}}{2} - \left(\frac{\pi}{3} + \frac{\sqrt{3}}{2}\right)$$

$$= \frac{\pi}{3} - \sqrt{3}$$

Area $C = \left|\frac{\pi}{3} - \sqrt{3}\right| = -\frac{\pi}{3} + \sqrt{3}$

Area $C + D = -\frac{\pi}{3} + \sqrt{3} + \frac{4\pi}{3} - \sqrt{3}$

$= \pi$ units^2

Method 2

$f(x) = 2 + \cos 2x$ and $g(x) = 1 + 2\cos 2x$

Using $A = \int_a^b f(x)\, dx - \int_a^b g(x)\, dx$

Required area is $= \int_0^{\pi} (2 + \cos 2x)\, dx - \int_0^{\pi} (1 + 2\cos 2x)\, dx$

$$= \int_0^{\pi} |(2 + \cos 2x - 1 - 2\cos 2x)|\, dx$$

$$= \int_0^{\pi} (1 - \cos 2x)\, dx$$

$$= \left[x - \frac{1}{2}\sin 2x\right]_0^{\pi}$$

$$= \left(\pi - \frac{1}{2}\sin 2\pi\right) - \left(0 - \frac{1}{2}\sin 0\right)$$

$= \pi$ units^2

11 Solve $y = \dfrac{6}{x+3}$ and $y = 4 - x$ simultaneously to find the intersection points of the curve and the line.

$$\frac{6}{x+3} = 4 - x$$

$$6 = (4 - x)(x + 3)$$

$$6 = 4x + 12 - x^2 - 3x$$

$$x^2 - x - 6 = 0 \qquad \text{factorise}$$

$$(x - 3)(x + 2) = 0$$

$x = 3$ or $x = -2$

The x-coordinates of the intersection points are: $x = 3$ and $x = -2$

Now consider $f(x) = 4 - x$ and $g(x) = \dfrac{6}{x+3}$

Using $A = \displaystyle\int_a^b f(x)\,dx - \int_a^b g(x)\,dx$

$$\text{Area} = \int_{-2}^{3} (4 - x)\,dx - \int_{-2}^{3} \left(\frac{6}{x+3}\right)dx$$

$$= \int_{-2}^{3} \left(4 - x - \frac{6}{x+3}\right)dx$$

$$= \left[4x - \frac{1}{2}x^2 - 6\ln|x+3|\right]_{-2}^{3}$$

$$= [4(3) - \frac{1}{2}(3)^2 - 6\ln|3+3|)] - [4(-2) - \frac{1}{2}(-2)^2 - 6\ln|-2+3|]$$

$$= 12 - \frac{9}{2} - 6\ln 6 + 8 + 2$$

$$= \frac{35}{2} - 6\ln 6 \text{ units}^2$$

Chapter 16: Kinematics

Exercise 16.1

REMEMBER

If a particle moves in a straight line, with displacement function $s(t)$, then the rate of change of displacement with respect to time, $\frac{ds}{dt}$, is the **velocity**, v, of the particle at time t.

$$v = \frac{ds}{dt}$$

If the velocity function is $v(t)$, then the rate of change of velocity with respect to time, $\frac{dv}{dt}$, is the **acceleration**, a, of the particle at time t.

$$a = \frac{dv}{dt} = \frac{d^2s}{dt^2}$$

1 a $v = \frac{50}{(3t + 2)^2}$

The particle passes through O when $t = 0$

Substituting into $v = \frac{50}{(3t + 2)^2}$ gives:

$$= \frac{50}{(3 \times 0 + 2)^2}$$

$$= 12.5\,\text{m s}^{-1}$$

b Solve $0.125 = \frac{50}{(3t + 2)^2}$

$$\frac{1}{8} = \frac{50}{(3t + 2)^2}$$

$(3t + 2)^2 = 400$ square root both sides

$3t + 2 = \pm 20$

$3t + 2 = 20$ or $3t + 2 = -20$

$3t = 18$ or $3t = -22$

$t = 6$ or $t = -\frac{22}{3}$ (reject)

So, $t = 6$

c $a = \frac{dv}{dt}$

$v = \frac{50}{(3t + 2)^2}$

$= 50(3t + 2)^{-2}$ differentiate using the chain rule

$\frac{dv}{dt} = 50 \times -2 \times 3(3t + 2)^{-3}$

$a = -300(3t + 2)^{-3}$

Substituting $t = 1$ gives :

$a = -300(3 \times 1 + 2)^{-3}$

$= \frac{-300}{5^3}$

$= -2.4$

The acceleration is $-2.4\,\text{m s}^{-2}$

2 a To find the initial velocity substitute $t = 0$

$v = 6e^{2t} - 2t$

$= 6e^{2(0)} - 2(0)$

$= 6$

The initial velocity is $6\,\text{m s}^{-1}$

b $v = 6e^{2t} - 2t$

$a = \frac{dv}{dt} = 12e^{2t} - 2$

To find the initial acceleration substitute $t = 0$

$a = 12e^{2(0)} - 2$

$= 10$

The initial acceleration is $10\,\text{m s}^{-2}$

3 a Substituting $t = \ln 100$ into $v = 5(1 - e^{-t})$ gives:

$v = 5(1 - e^{-\ln 100})$

$= 5(1 - 0.01)$

$= 4.95$

Velocity is $4.95\,\text{m s}^{-1}$

b $v = 5(1 - e^{-t})$

$= 5\left(1 - \frac{1}{e^t}\right)$

As t becomes very large, e^t becomes very large and $\frac{1}{e^t}$ becomes very small.

So $1 - \frac{1}{e^t}$ approaches 1

v approaches 5

c When $v = 4$,

$5(1 - e^{-t}) = 4$ divide both sides by 5

$1 - \frac{1}{e^t} = 0.8$ rearrange and simplify

$\frac{1}{e^t} = 0.2$

$e^t = 5$ take logs of both sides

$\ln e^t = \ln 5$ power rule for logs

$t \ln e = \ln 5$

$t = \ln 5$

$a = \frac{dv}{dt}$

$v = 5(1 - e^{-t})$ or $v = 5 - 5e^{-t}$

$a = \frac{dv}{dt} = 5e^{-t}$

To find the acceleration substitute $t = \ln 5$

$a = 5e^{-\ln 5}$

$= 5 \times 0.2$

$= 1$

The acceleration is $1\,\text{m s}^{-2}$

d

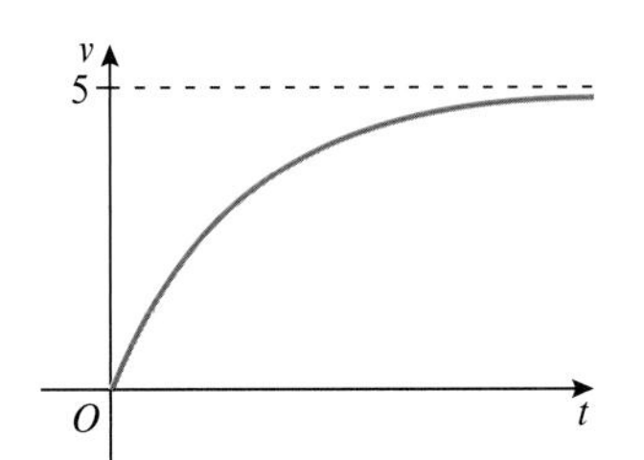

4 a Solve $36 = 9[\ln(3t + 2)]$ divide both sides by 9

$4 = \ln(3t + 2)$

$= \log_e(3t + 2)$

$3t + 2 = e^4$

$t = \frac{1}{3}(e^4 - 2)$

b $s = 9[\ln(3t + 2)]$

$v = \frac{ds}{dt} = 9 \times \frac{3}{(3t + 2)}$

$= \frac{27}{3t + 2}$

When $t = 1$, the velocity is $\frac{27}{3(1) + 2} = 5.4$

The velocity is $5.4\,\text{m s}^{-1}$

c $a = \frac{dv}{dt}$

$v = \frac{27}{3t + 2}$ or $v = 27(3t + 2)^{-1}$

$a = \frac{dv}{dt} = -1 \times 27 \times 3(3t + 2)^{-2}$

$= -\frac{81}{(3t + 2)^2}$

To find the initial acceleration substitute $t = 0$

$$a = -\frac{81}{(3(0) + 2)^2}$$

$$= -20.25\,\text{m s}^{-2}$$

As t increases, $(3t + 2)^2$ becomes larger so $\frac{81}{(3t + 2)^2}$ becomes smaller, $-\frac{81}{(3t + 2)^2}$ is always negative and represents a deceleration for all values of $t \geqslant 0$

5 a $s = \ln(1 + 2t)$

$v = \frac{ds}{dt} = \frac{2}{1 + 2t}$ substituting $v = 0.4$ gives:

$$0.4 = \frac{2}{1 + 2t}$$

$$0.4(1 + 2t) = 2$$

$$0.4 + 0.8t = 2$$

$$t = 2$$

b The 1st second is between $t = 0$ and $t = 1$

The 2nd second is between $t = 1$ and $t = 2$

The 3rd second is between $t = 2$ and $t = 3$

When $t = 2$, $s = \ln(1 + 2 \times 2) = \ln 5$

The **displacement** is $\ln 5$ metres

When $t = 3$, $s = \ln(1 + 2 \times 3) = \ln 7$

The **displacement** is $\ln 7$ metres

When $t = 0$, the **displacement** from O is 0 metres.

Since $v = \frac{2}{1 + 2t}$, $v \geqslant 0$ for $t > 0$, there is no change of direction of motion of the particle

The graph of $s = \ln(1 + 2t)$ shows that the particle is continuing to travel away from O between $t = 2$ and $t = 3$

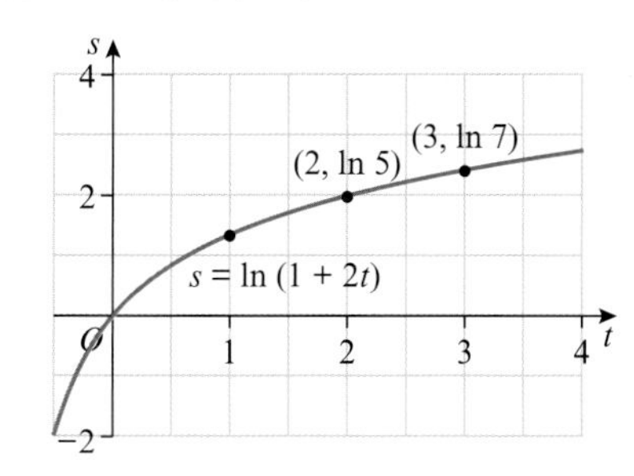

The **distance** that the particle travels in the 3rd second is $\ln 7 - \ln 5$ or $\ln\left(\frac{7}{5}\right)$ metres

c $v = \frac{2}{1 + 2t}$ or $v = 2(1 + 2t)^{-1}$

$$a = \frac{dv}{dt} = -1 \times 2 \times 2(1 + 2t)^{-2} = -\frac{4}{(1 + 2t)^2}$$

$$= -\frac{4}{(1 + 2t)^2}$$

Substituting $t = 1.5$ gives:

$$a = -\frac{4}{(1 + 2 \times 1.5)^2}$$

$$= -0.25$$

The acceleration is $-0.25\,\text{m s}^{-2}$.

6 a $v = 8\cos\left(\frac{t}{4}\right)$

$$4 = 8\cos\left(\frac{t}{4}\right)$$

$$\cos\left(\frac{t}{4}\right) = 0.5$$

$$\cos^{-1}0.5 = \frac{t}{4}$$

Remembering the cosine curve for angles greater than zero radians, $\frac{\pi}{3}$ is the smallest angle whose cosine is 0.5

So, $\frac{t}{4} = \frac{\pi}{3}$

$$t = \frac{4\pi}{3}$$

b $a = \frac{dv}{dt} = \frac{1}{4} \times 8 \times -\sin\left(\frac{t}{4}\right)$

$$= -2\sin\left(\frac{t}{4}\right)$$

Substituting $t = 5$ gives:

$a = -2\sin\left(\frac{5}{4}\right)$ remember to use radians

$$= -2\sin 1.25$$

$= -1.90$ to 3 significant figures

The acceleration is $-1.90\,\text{m s}^{-2}$

c Sketch $a = -2\sin\frac{1}{4}t$

Start with $a = \sin t$ reflecting in the t-axis gives:

$a = -\sin t$ stretching from the t-axis stretch factor 2 gives:

$a = -2\sin t$ stretching from the a-axis stretch factor 4 gives:

$a = -2\sin\frac{1}{4}t$

The period of the graph is $\dfrac{2\pi}{\frac{1}{4}} = 8\pi$

The amplitude is 2

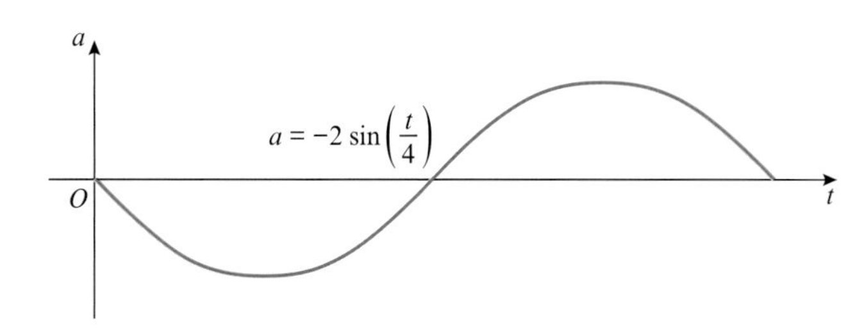

7 a $v = \cos 3t + \sin 3t$

'At rest' means stationary i.e., $v = 0$

$\cos 3t + \sin 3t = 0$ divide both sides by $\cos 3t$

$1 + \dfrac{\sin 3t}{\cos 3t} = 0$

$\tan 3t = -1$ let $x = 3t$

$\tan x = -1$ use a calculator to find $\tan^{-1}(-1)$

$x = -\dfrac{\pi}{4}$

Using the symmetry of the curve:

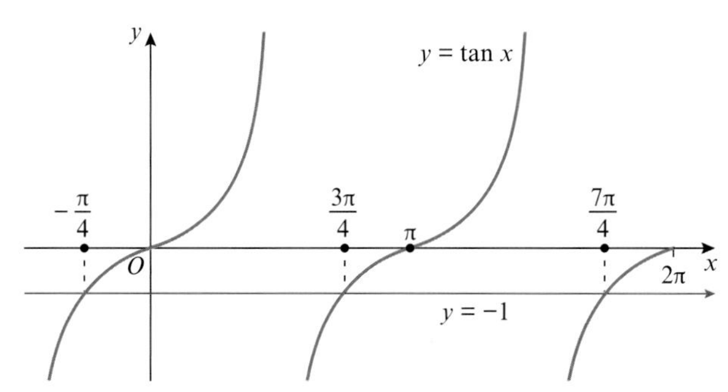

$x = -\dfrac{\pi}{4}$ $\quad x = \left(-\dfrac{\pi}{4} + \pi\right) = \dfrac{3\pi}{4}$ $\quad x = \left(\dfrac{3\pi}{4} + \pi\right) = \dfrac{7\pi}{4}$

Using $x = 3t$

$3t = -\dfrac{\pi}{4}$ $\quad 3t = \dfrac{3\pi}{4}$ $\quad 3t = \dfrac{7\pi}{4}$

$t = -\frac{\pi}{12}$ $t = \frac{\pi}{4}$ $t = \frac{7\pi}{12}$

The particle is first instantaneously at rest when $t = \frac{\pi}{4}$ seconds.

b $v = \cos 3t + \sin 3t$

$a = \frac{dv}{dt} = -3\sin 3t + 3\cos 3t$

Substituting $t = \pi$ gives:

$a = -3\sin 3\pi + 3\cos 3\pi$

$= 0 - 3$

The acceleration is $-3\,\text{m}\,\text{s}^{-2}$

8 **a** $s = 2 - 2\cos 2t$

$v = \frac{ds}{dt} = 4\sin 2t$

$v = 4\sin 2t$

$a = \frac{dv}{dt} = 8\cos 2t$

b $v = 0$

$4\sin 2t = 0$

$\sin 2t = 0$

Let $x = 2t$

$\sin x = 0$ — use a calculator to find $\sin^{-1}(0)$

$x = 0$ — other values of x are π, 2π, 3π etc

So $2t = 0$ $2t = \pi$ $2t = 2\pi$ etc.

$t = 0$ $t = \frac{\pi}{2}$ $t = \pi$ etc.

The particle first comes to rest when $t = \frac{\pi}{2}$ seconds.

When $t = \frac{\pi}{2}$, the distance of the particle from O is $s = 2 - 2\cos 2\left(\frac{\pi}{2}\right) = 4\,\text{m}$

9 **a** $s = 50[e^{-2t} - e^{-4t}]$ or $s = 50e^{-2t} - 50e^{-4t}$.

$v = \frac{ds}{dt} = (-2 \times 50)e^{-2t} - (-4 \times 50)e^{-4t}$

$v = -100e^{-2t} + 200e^{-4t}$

The time when the particle is instantaneously at rest is found by solving for $v = 0$

$-100e^{-2t} + 200e^{-4t} = 0$ — factorise

$100e^{-4t}(-e^{2t} + 2) = 0$ — solve

$100e^{-4t} = 0$ (no solutions)

or $-e^{2t} + 2 = 0$

$e^{2t} = 2$ — take logs of both sides

$\ln(e^{2t}) = \ln 2$ power rule for logs

$2t \ln e = \ln 2$

$2t = \ln 2$

$t = \frac{1}{2}\ln 2$

b When $t = 2$, the displacement $s = 50[e^{-2(2)} - e^{-4(2)}]$

$= 50[e^{-4} - e^{-8}]$

$= 0.899$ m to 3 significant figures.

c We know that when $t = 0$, the displacement from O is

$s = 50[e^{-2\times 0} - e^{-4\times 0}]$

$s = 50(1 - 1)$

$s = 0$

When $t = \frac{1}{2}\ln 2$, the particle is instantaneously at rest.

Its displacement from O is:

$s = 50\left(e^{-2\times\frac{1}{2}\ln 2} - e^{-4\times\frac{1}{2}\ln 2}\right)$

$s = 50\left(\frac{1}{2} - \frac{1}{4}\right)$

$s = 12.5$ m

Immediately after $t = \frac{1}{2}\ln 2$, the particle changes direction.

[When $t = \frac{1}{2}\ln 2$ (≈ 0.377 seconds), $s = 12.5$ m, substituting $t = 0.4$ gives $s = 12.4$ m]

When $t = 2$, the displacement $s = 50(e^{-2\times 2} - e^{-4\times 2}) = 0.899$ m

The displacement of the particle from O for the first 2 seconds is represented by the following sketch:

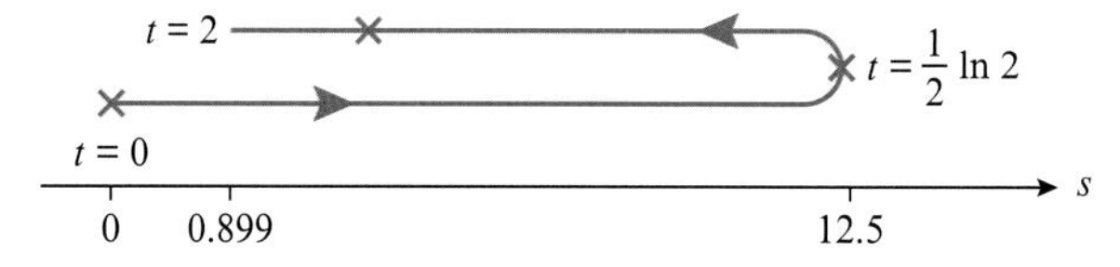

The total distance travelled during the first 2 seconds is $12.5 + (12.5 - 0.899) = 24.1$ m (3 s.f.)

10 a Substitute $t = 0$ into $s = 2t + 2\cos 2t$ to find the initial position of the particle:

$s = 2(0) + 2\cos 2(0)$

$s = 2$ m away from O

b $v = \frac{ds}{dt} = 2 - 4\sin 2t$

$a = \frac{dv}{dt} = -8\cos 2t$

c The time when the particle is instantaneously at rest is found by solving for $v = 0$

$2 - 4\sin 2t = 0$

$\sin 2t = 0.5$

Let $x = 2t$

$\sin x = 0.5$ use a calculator to find $\sin^{-1}(0.5)$

$x = \frac{\pi}{6}$ $\left[\text{the next value of } x \text{ is } \frac{5\pi}{6}\right]$

So $2t = \frac{\pi}{6}$

$t = \frac{\pi}{12}$

The particle first comes to rest when $t = \frac{\pi}{12}$ seconds

Substitute $t = \frac{\pi}{12}$ into $s = 2t + 2\cos 2t$ to find the displacement at that time.

$s = 2\left(\frac{\pi}{12}\right) + 2\cos 2\left(\frac{\pi}{12}\right)$

$s = \frac{\pi}{6} + \sqrt{3}$ m

d Solve $-8\cos 2t = 0$

$\cos 2t = 0$

Let $x = 2t$

$\cos x = 0$ use a calculator to find $\cos^{-1}(0)$

$x = \frac{\pi}{2}$

So $2t = \frac{\pi}{2}$

At $t = \frac{\pi}{4}$ seconds, the acceleration of the particle is zero for the first time.

Substitute $t = \frac{\pi}{4}$ into $s = 2t + 2\cos 2t$

$s = 2\left(\frac{\pi}{4}\right) + 2\cos 2\left(\frac{\pi}{4}\right)$

The distance of the particle from O at this instant is $\frac{\pi}{2}$ m

11 a The time when the particle is instantaneously at rest is found by solving for $v = 0$

$k\cos 4t = 0$

$\cos 4t = 0$

Let $x = 4t$

$\cos x = 0$ use a calculator to find $\cos^{-1}(0)$

$x = \frac{\pi}{2}$

So $4t = \frac{\pi}{2}$

$t = \frac{\pi}{8}$ seconds

b $a = \frac{dv}{dt} = -4k \sin 4t$

c $a = -4k \sin 4t$ substituting $a = 10$, $t = \frac{7\pi}{24}$ gives:

$10 = -4k \sin 4\left(\frac{7\pi}{24}\right)$

$= -4k \sin \frac{7\pi}{6}$

$= -4k \times -0.5$

$k = 5$

12 a $s = 2t$ for $0 \leqslant t \leqslant 4$

$s = 8 + 2\ln(t - 3)$ for $t > 4$

To find the initial velocity of the particle, use $s = 2t$ because $0 \leqslant t \leqslant 4$

$v = \frac{ds}{dt} = 2$

The initial velocity is $2\,\text{m s}^{-1}$

b i When $t = 2$ use $s = 2t$ because $0 \leqslant t \leqslant 4$

$v = \frac{ds}{dt} = 2$ so the velocity at $t = 2$ is still $2\,\text{m s}^{-1}$

ii When $t = 6$ use $s = 8 + 2\ln(t - 3)$ because $t > 4$

$v = \frac{ds}{dt} = \frac{2}{t - 3}$

Substitute $t = 6$ gives:

$v = \frac{2}{6 - 3} = \frac{2}{3}\,\text{m s}^{-1}$

c i The velocity does not change for $0 \leqslant t \leqslant 4$, so the acceleration is $0\,\text{m s}^{-2}$

ii $v = \frac{2}{t - 3}$ or $v = 2(t - 3)^{-1}$

$a = \frac{dv}{dt} = -1 \times 2(t - 3)^{-2}$

$= -\frac{2}{(t - 3)^2}$

Now substitute $t = 6$

$a = -\frac{2}{(6 - 3)^2} = -\frac{2}{9}$

The acceleration is $-\frac{2}{9}\,\text{m s}^{-2}$

d The graph of s against t has two sections

For $0 \leqslant t \leqslant 4$, the graph is a straight line with gradient 2. The end point is (4, 8)

For $t > 4$, the graph is a curve. The gradient at any point on the curve can be found by substituting value of $t > 4$ into the equation for v. The gradient at any point on the curve, represents the velocity at that instant in time. The velocity is always positive for $t > 4$ but becomes smaller as t increases.

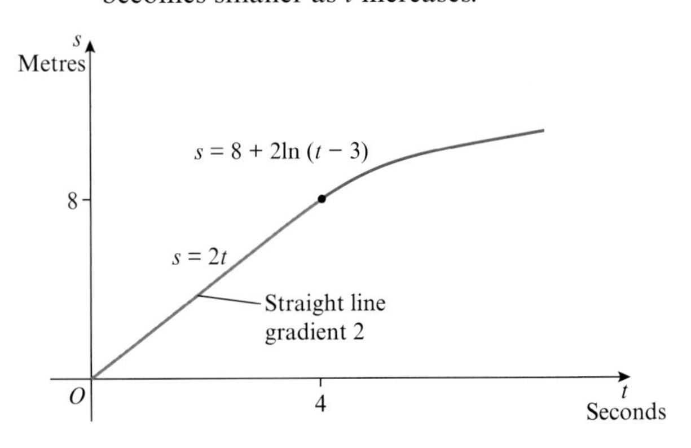

e The eighth second is between $t = 7$ and $t = 8$ seconds.

From the graph, the particle does not change direction at any time as the gradient of the graph (i.e., the velocity) is always positive.

Substituting $t = 7$ into $s = 8 + 2\ln(t - 3)$ gives:

$s = 8 + 2\ln(7 - 3)$

$= 8 + 2\ln 4 = 10.7725\ldots$

Substituting $t = 8$ into $s = 8 + 2\ln(t - 3)$

$s = 8 + 2\ln 5 = 11.2188\ldots$

In the 8th second the particle travels:

$(8 + 2\ln 5) - (8 + 2\ln 4)$ or $2\ln\left(\frac{5}{4}\right)$ m or

$11.2188\ldots - 10.7725\ldots = 0.446\,\text{m}$ (3 s.f.)

13 a At X, $t = 0$

$s = 2t^3 - 17t^2 + 40t - 2$

Substitute $t = 0$

$s = 2(0)^3 - 17(0)^2 + 40(0) - 2$

$s = -2$

The distance OX is 2 metres

b The particle is at rest when $v = 0$

$v = \frac{ds}{dt} = 6t^2 - 34t + 40$

$6t^2 - 34t + 40 = 0$ divide both sides by 2

$3t^2 - 17t + 20 = 0$ factorise

$(3t - 5)(t - 4) = 0$

$t = \frac{5}{3}$ or $t = 4$

$\frac{5}{3} < 4$ so the particle is at rest for the first time when $t = \frac{5}{3}$ seconds

c The velocity is positive when $v > 0$

From part **b**, we know $v = 0$ when $t = \frac{5}{3}$ or $t = 4$

So the t- axis crossing points are $\frac{5}{3}$ and 4

The velocity–time graph of $6t^2 - 34t + 40 > 0$ is a 'U' shaped parabola. We need to find the range of values for t for which the curve is positive (above the t-axis). i.e. $(6t - 10)(t - 4) > 0$

Velocity is positive for $0 \leqslant t < \frac{5}{3}$ and $t > 4$.

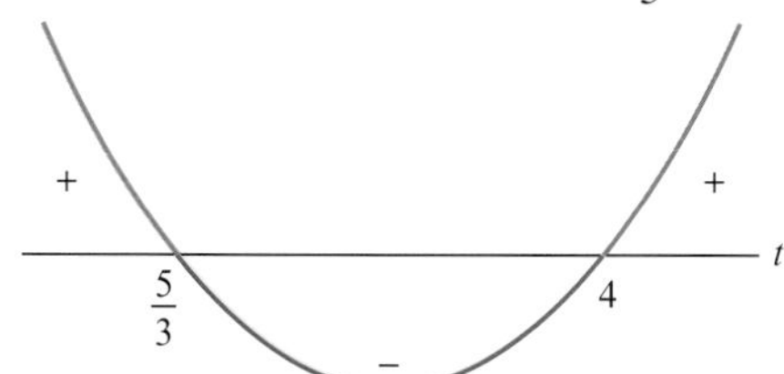

d The values of t for which the velocity is negative is the part of the curve that is below the t-axis.

This is when $\frac{5}{3} < t < 4$

Exercise 16.2

REMEMBER

If a particle moves in a straight line where the acceleration of the particle is a then

$v = \int a\,dt$

and $s = \int v\,dt$

1 a $v = 10t - t^2$

$a = \frac{dv}{dt} = 10 - 2t$

Substituting $a = 6$ gives:

$6 = 10 - 2t$

$t = 2$

Substituting $t = 2$ into $v = 10t - t^2$ gives:

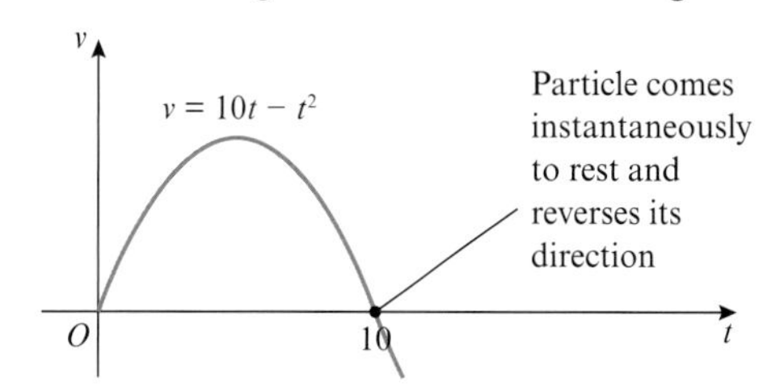

$v = 10(2) - 2^2$

$= 16\,\text{m s}^{-1}$

b $s = \int v\,dt$

$= \int (10t - t^2)\,dt$

$= 5t^2 - \frac{1}{3}t^3 + c$

Using $s = 0$ when $t = 0$, gives $c = 0$

$s = 5t^2 - \frac{1}{3}t^3$

The **displacement**, s metres, is given by

$s = 5t^2 - \frac{1}{3}t^3$

The particle returns to O when $s = 0$

$5t^2 - \frac{1}{3}t^3 = 0$ factorise

$t^2\left(5 - \frac{1}{3}t\right) = 0$ solve

$t^2 = 0$ or $5 - \frac{1}{3}t = 0$

$t = 0$ or $t = 15$

The time taken is 15 seconds

c Since $v > 0$ for $0 < t < 10$, there is no change in the direction of motion in the 2nd second i.e between $t = 1$ and $t = 2$

Substituting $t = 1$ into $s = 5t^2 - \frac{1}{3}t^3$ gives:

$s = 5(1)^2 - \frac{1}{3}(1)^3 = \frac{14}{3}$ m

Substituting $t = 2$ into $s = 5t^2 - \frac{1}{3}t^3$ gives:

$s = 5(2)^2 - \frac{1}{3}(2)^3 = \frac{52}{3}$ m

Distance travelled in the 2nd second $= \frac{52}{3} - \frac{14}{3}$

$= \frac{38}{3} = 12\frac{2}{3}$ m

d The particle comes to instantaneous rest when $v = 0$

$10t - t^2 = 0$ factorising

$t(10 - t) = 0$

$t = 0$ and $10 - t = 0$

$t = 0$ (reject as the particle is at O)

$t = 10$

The particle comes to instantaneous rest when $t = 10$

$s = 5(10)^2 - \frac{1}{3}(10)^3 = 166\frac{2}{3}$ m

TIP

Always read the question carefully. The distance is the same as displacement IF the particle has not changed direction during the relevant time interval.

The particle comes to instantaneous rest when $t = 10$ seconds, and has travelled $166\frac{2}{3}$ m

e When $t = 10$, the particle is instantaneously at rest, immediately afterwards, it reverses its direction of motion.

So, you cannot use $\int_0^{12} (10t - t^2)dt$ to find the **distance** travelled between $t = 0$ and $t = 12$.

The total **distance** travelled between $t = 0$ and $t = 12$ is :

$= \int_0^{10} (10t - t^2)dt + \int_{10}^{12} (10t - t^2)dt$

$= \left[5t^2 - \frac{1}{3}t^3\right]_0^{10} + \left[5t^2 - \frac{1}{3}t^3\right]_{10}^{12}$

$= \left[\left(5(10)^2 - \frac{1}{3}(10)^3\right) - \left(5(0)^2 - \frac{1}{3}(0)^3\right)\right] + \left[\left|\left(5(12)^2 - \frac{1}{3}(12)^3\right) - \left(5(10)^2 - \frac{1}{3}(10)^3\right)\right|\right]$

REMEMBER

The total **distance** that the particle travels is independent of its direction of travel at all stages in its journey. So, we need to add the distances as positive values. Therefore use modulus signs.

$= \left[166\frac{2}{3} - 0\right] + \left[\left|144 - 166\frac{2}{3}\right|\right]$

$= 166\frac{2}{3} + 22\frac{2}{3}$

$= 189\frac{1}{3}$ m

2 **a** $v = \dfrac{32}{(t+2)^2}$ or $v = 32(t+2)^{-2}$

$a = \dfrac{dv}{dt} = -2 \times 32(t+2)^{-3}$ or $-\dfrac{64}{(t+2)^3}$

When $t = 2$, $a = -\dfrac{64}{(2+2)^3} = -1$

When $t = 2$, acceleration is $-1\,\text{m s}^{-2}$.

b $v = \dfrac{32}{(t+2)^2}$ or $32(t+2)^{-2}$

$s = \int v\,dt$

$= \int 32(t+2)^{-2}\,dt$

$= \dfrac{32}{-1}(t+2)^{-1} + c$

Using $s = 0$ when $t = 0$, gives:

$-32(0+2)^{-1} + c = 0$

$c = 16$

$s = -\dfrac{32}{t+2} + 16 = \dfrac{-32 + 16(t+2)}{t+2}$

The displacement, s metres, is given by $s = \dfrac{16t}{t+2}$

c Since $v > 0$ for all values of t, there is no change in the direction of motion of the particle.

'In the 3rd second' means between $t = 2$ and $t = 3$

When $t = 2$, $s = \dfrac{16(3)}{3+2} = 9.6$

When $t = 2$, $s = \dfrac{16(2)}{2+2} = 8$

Distance travelled during the 3rd second $= 9.6 - 8 = 1.6\,\text{m}$

Alternative method

Since there is no change in direction of motion:

$s = \int v\,dt$

$= \int_2^3 (32(t+2)^{-2})\,dt$

$= \left[\dfrac{16t}{t+2}\right]_2^3$

$= (9.6) - (8)$

$= 1.6\text{m}$

3 **a** $v = 4e^{2t} + 2t$

$a = \dfrac{dv}{dt} = 8e^{2t} + 2$

When $t = 1$, $a = 8e^{2(1)} + 2 = 2(4e^2 + 1)$

Its acceleration when $t = 1$ is $8e^2 + 2$ or $2(4e^2 + 1)\,\text{m s}^{-2}$.

b $v = 4e^{2t} + 2t$

$s = \int v\,dt$

$= \int (4e^{2t} + 2t)\,dt$ or $\left(\dfrac{4}{2}e^{2t} + t^2\right)$

$= 2e^{2t} + t^2 + c$

Using $s = 0$ when $t = 0$, gives:

$0 = 2e^{2(0)} + 0^2 + c$

$c = -2$

The displacement, s metres is given by $s = 2e^{2t} + t^2 - 2$

c Since $v > 0$ for all values of t, there is no change in the direction of motion of the particle.

When $t = 0$, $s = 0$

When $t = 2$, $s = 2e^{2(2)} + (2)^2 - 2 = 2e^4 + 2$

Distance travelled during the first 2 seconds $= 2e^4 + 2 \approx 111\,\text{m}$ (to 3 significant figures)

4 $v = t + 2\cos\left(\dfrac{t}{3}\right)$

$s = \int v\,dt$

$= \dfrac{1}{2}t^2 + \dfrac{2}{\frac{1}{3}}\sin\left(\dfrac{t}{3}\right) + c$

$= \dfrac{1}{2}t^2 + 6\sin\left(\dfrac{t}{3}\right) + c$

When $t = 0$, $s = 0$ and $0 = \dfrac{1}{2}(0)^2 + 6\sin 0 + c$, so $c = 0$

$s = \dfrac{1}{2}t^2 + 6\sin\left(\dfrac{t}{3}\right)$

When $t = \dfrac{3\pi}{2}$, the displacement from O is

$s = \dfrac{1}{2}\left(\dfrac{3\pi}{2}\right)^2 + 6\sin\left(\dfrac{3\pi}{6}\right) = \left(\dfrac{9\pi^2}{8} + 6\right)\text{m}$

The acceleration of the particle is:

$a = \dfrac{dv}{dt} = 1 - \dfrac{2}{3}\sin\left(\dfrac{t}{3}\right)$

When $t = \dfrac{3\pi}{2}$, $a = 1 - \dfrac{2}{3}\sin\left(\dfrac{3\pi}{6}\right) = \dfrac{1}{3}\text{m s}^{-2}$

The acceleration is $\dfrac{1}{3}\text{m s}^{-2}$

5 a $v = 4e^{2t} + 6e^{-3t}$

$= 4e^{2t} + \frac{6}{e^{3t}}$

When $t = 0$, $v = 4e^{2(0)} + \frac{6}{e^{3(0)}}$ so $v = 10$ i.e. positive

As t increases, $4e^{2t}$ increases and is always positive

As t increases, $\frac{6}{e^{3t}}$ is always positive and decreasing but it never reaches zero (because zero is the only value that e^{3t} cannot be).

So, $v = 4e^{2t} + \frac{6}{e^{3t}}$ is never zero

b $a = \frac{dv}{dt} = 8e^{2t} - 18e^{-3t} = 8e^{2t} - \frac{18}{e^{3t}}$

Substituting $t = \ln 2$ into $a = 8e^{2t} - \frac{18}{e^{3t}}$

$a = 8e^{2\ln 2} - \frac{18}{e^{3\ln 2}}$

$= 8 \times 4 - \frac{18}{8} = 29.75$

The acceleration is $29.75\,\text{m s}^{-2}$

c The displacement of the particle from O is

$s = \int v\,dt$

$= \int (4e^{2t} + 6e^{-3t})\,dt = 2e^{2t} - 2e^{-3t} + c$

When $t = 0$, $s = 0$ and $c = 0$

$s = 2e^{2t} - 2e^{-3t}$

Substituting $t = 2$ gives:

$s = 2e^{2(2)} - 2e^{-3(2)} = 109\,\text{m}$ to the nearest metre

6 $v = pt^2 + qt - 12$

$a = \frac{dv}{dt} = 2pt + q$

Substituting $t = 2$, $a = 18$ gives:

$18 = 2p(2) + q$

$4p + q = 18$ (1)

The displacement of the particle from O is $s = \int v\,dt$

$s = \int (pt^2 + qt - 12)dt = \frac{1}{3}pt^3 + \frac{1}{2}qt^2 - 12t + c$

When $t = 0$, $s = 0$ and $c = 0$

So $s = \frac{1}{3}pt^3 + \frac{1}{2}qt^2 - 12t$

When $t = 4$, $s = 32$ so:

$\frac{1}{3}p(4)^3 + \frac{1}{2}q(4)^2 - 12(4) = 32$

$\frac{64}{3}p + 8q - 48 = 32$ divide both sides by 8 and simplify

$\frac{8}{3}p + q = 10$ (2)

Solve (1) and (2) simultaneously:

Subtract (2) from (1)

$\frac{4}{3}p = 8$

$p = 6$

Substituting $p = 6$ into (1) gives:

$4(6) + q = 18$

$q = -6$

7 a $v = \int a\,dt = 3t - t^2 + c$

When $t = 0$, $v = 10$ so:

$10 = 0 - 0 + c$

$c = 10$

$v = 3t - t^2 + 10$

The particle is instantaneously at rest when $v = 0$

$3t - t^2 + 10 = 0$

$t^2 - 3t - 10 = 0$ factorise

$(t + 2)(t - 5) = 0$

$t = -2$ (reject)

$t - 5 = 0$ so $t = 5$

The particle is instantaneously at rest when $t = 5$ seconds

b The velocity/time graph of $v = -t^2 + 3t + 10$ is a '∩' shaped parabola.

The v-intercept is $10\,\text{m s}^{-1}$

The t-intercept (when $v = 0$) is $t = 5$

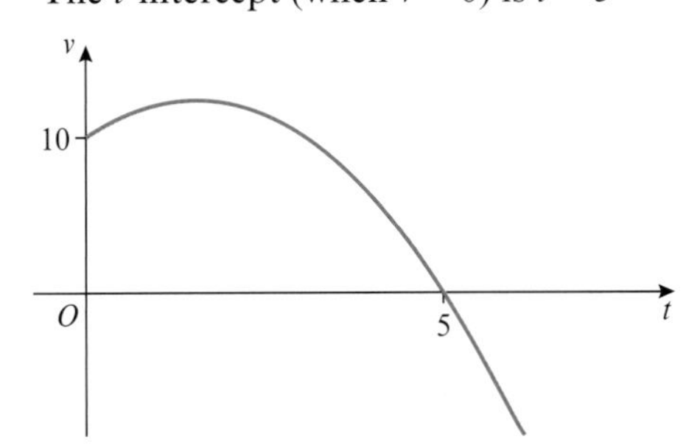

c From the graph, the particle changes direction immediately after $t = 5$

So total distance travelled in the first 7 seconds is:

$$\int_0^5 (-t^2 + 3t + 10)\mathrm{d}t + \int_5^7 (-t^2 + 3t + 10)\mathrm{d}t$$

$$= \left[-\frac{1}{3}t^3 + \frac{3}{2}t^2 + 10t\right]_0^5 + \left[-\frac{1}{3}t^3 + \frac{3}{2}t^2 + 10t\right]_5^7$$

$$= \left[\left(-\frac{1}{3}(5)^3 + \frac{3}{2}(5)^2 + 10(5)\right) - (0)\right] + \left[\left(-\frac{1}{3}(7)^3 + \frac{3}{2}(7)^2 + 10(7)\right) - \left(-\frac{1}{3}(5)^3 + \frac{3}{2}(5)^2 + 10(5)\right)\right]$$

$$= \left[-\frac{125}{3} + \frac{75}{2} + 50\right] + \left[\left(-\frac{343}{3} + \frac{147}{2} + 70\right) - \left(-\frac{125}{3} + \frac{75}{2} + 50\right)\right]$$

$$= \frac{275}{6} + \left|\frac{175}{6} - \frac{275}{6}\right|$$

$$= \frac{275}{6} + \frac{50}{3}$$

$$= 62.5\,\text{m}$$

8 a $v = \int a\,\mathrm{d}t = \frac{3}{2}t^2 - 12t + c$

Substituting $t = 0$, $v = 18$ gives:

$$\frac{3}{2}(0)^2 - 12(0) + c = 18$$

$$c = 18$$

$$v = \frac{3}{2}t^2 - 12t + 18$$

The particle is instantaneously at rest when $v = 0$

$\frac{3}{2}t^2 - 12t + 18 = 0$ multiply both sides by $\frac{2}{3}$

$$t^2 - 8t + 12 = 0$$

$$(t - 6)(t - 2) = 0$$

$$t = 6 \text{ or } 2$$

The particle is instantaneously at rest when $t = 2$ and $t = 6$

b 'In the 4th second' means between $t = 3$ and $t = 4$

We need to find out if there is a change in direction of the particle between these two times.

The graph of $v = \frac{3}{2}t^2 - 12t + 18$ is a 'U' shaped parabola that intersects the t- axis at $t = 0$ and $t = 6$.

For $t < 2$ and $t > 6$ the graph is above the t-axis and the velocity is positive.

Between these times, the graph is below the t-axis which indicates that the velocity is negative.

A change in sign for the velocity indicates a change in direction of the particle's travel.

Between $t = 3$ and $t = 4$ the particle does not change direction so the distance that it travels is:

$$s = \int_3^4 \left(\frac{3}{2}t^2 - 12t + 18\right)\mathrm{d}t = \left[\frac{1}{2}t^3 - 6t^2 + 18t\right]_3^4$$

$$= \left[\frac{1}{2}(4)^3 - 6(4)^2 + 18(4)\right] - \left[\frac{1}{2}(3)^3 - 6(3)^2 + 18(3)\right]$$

$$= 8 - 13.5$$

$$= -5.5$$

The graph between $t = 3$ and $t = 4$ is under the t-axis so the distance travelled is $|-5.5| = 5.5\,\text{m}$

c The total distance travelled in the first 10 seconds is made up of three stages:

Distance between $t = 0$ and $t = 2$

Distance between $t = 2$ and $t = 6$

Distance between $t = 6$ and $t = 10$

$$\int_0^2 \left(\frac{3}{2}t^2 - 12t + 18\right)dt + \int_2^6 \left(\frac{3}{2}t^2 - 12t + 18\right)dt + \int_6^{10} \left(\frac{3}{2}t^2 - 12t + 18\right)dt$$

$$= \left[\frac{1}{2}t^3 - 6t^2 + 18t\right]_0^2 + \left[\frac{1}{2}t^3 - 6t^2 + 18t\right]_2^6 + \left[\frac{1}{2}t^3 - 6t^2 + 18t\right]_6^{10}$$

$$= [(4 - 24 + 36) - (0)] + [|(108 - 216 + 108) - (4 - 24 + 36)|] + [(500 - 600 + 180) - (108 - 216 + 108)]$$

$$= 16 + |-16| + 80$$

$$= 112\,\text{m}$$

---

9 a $a = \frac{dv}{dt} = -12\sin 2t$

To sketch the graph of $a = -12\sin 2t$, transform the graph of $a = \sin t$

Start with the graph of $a = \sin t$ [Period 2π and amplitude 1]

Stretch the graph from the a-axis with stretch factor $\frac{1}{2}$ [Period $\frac{2\pi}{2} = \pi$, amplitude 1] ($a = \sin 2t$)

Stretch the graph from the t-axis stretch factor 12 [Period π, amplitude 12]

Reflect the graph in the t-axis
$a = -12\sin 2t$ [Period π, amplitude 12]

So, the graph of a against is t:

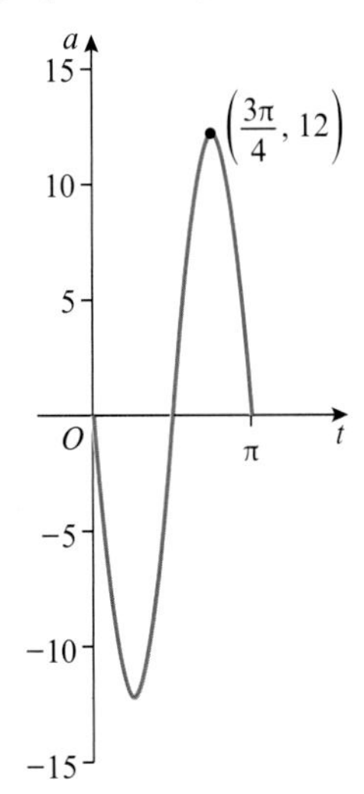

The range of values of the acceleration is
$-12 \leqslant a \leqslant 12$

b The particle first comes instantaneously to rest when $v = 0$

$3 + 6\cos 2t = 0$

$\cos 2t = -0.5$

The cosine curve for $t > 0$

$2t = \cos^{-1}(-0.5)$

$2t = \frac{2}{3}\pi$

$t = \frac{1}{3}\pi$

The particle first comes to rest when $t = \frac{\pi}{3}$

The distance it has travelled between $t = 0$ and $t = \frac{\pi}{3}$ is found by using $s = \int v\,dt$

Between $t = 0$ and $t = \frac{\pi}{3}$,

$$s = \int_0^{\frac{\pi}{3}} (3 + 6\cos 2t)dt = [3t + 3\sin 2t]_0^{\frac{\pi}{3}}$$

$$= \left[\frac{3\pi}{3} + 3\sin\frac{2\pi}{3}\right] - [3(0) + 3\sin 2(0)]$$

$$= \pi + 3 \times \frac{\sqrt{3}}{2}$$

Distance = 5.74 m (3 significant figures)

10 a $v = 8 - 8e^{-2t}$

$a = \frac{dv}{dt} = 16e^{-2t}$

Substituting $t = \ln 5$ gives:

$a = 16e^{-2\ln 5}$

$= \frac{16}{25}$ or $0.64\,\text{m s}^{-2}$

b We need to find out if the particle changes direction in the period $t = 0$ and $t = 2$

The graph of $v = 8 - 8e^{-2t}$ or $v = 8 - \frac{8}{e^{2t}}$

When $t = 0$, $v = 8 - \frac{8}{e^0}$ so $v = 8 - \frac{8}{1}$, $v = 0$

As t increases, $v = 8 - \frac{8}{e^{2t}}$ increases (because $\frac{8}{e^{2t}}$ becomes smaller as t increases).

The velocity is always positive between $t = 0$ and $t = 2$

$s = \int v\,dt$ so $s = 8t + 4e^{-2t} + c$

When $t = 0$, $s = 0$ so $c = -4$

When $t = 2$, $s = 8(2) + 4e^{-2(2)} - 4$

$s = 16 + 4e^{-4} - 4 = 12.0732...$

So distance AO is $= 12.1$ m

11 a The particle first comes instantaneously to rest when $v = 0$

$$2\cos\left(\frac{1}{2}t\right) - 1 = 0$$

$$\cos\frac{1}{2}t = 0.5$$

The cosine curve for $t > 0$

$$\frac{1}{2}t = \cos^{-1}(0.5)$$

$$\frac{1}{2}t = \frac{1}{3}\pi$$

$$t = \frac{2}{3}\pi$$

The particle first comes to rest when $t = \frac{2\pi}{3}$

b We need to find out if the particle changes direction in the period $t = 0$ and $t = 2\pi$.

We need to sketch the graph of

$v = 2\cos\left(\frac{1}{2}t\right) - 1.$

Start with the graph of $v = \cos t$ [Period 2π and amplitude 1]

Stretch the graph from the v-axis with stretch factor 2 [Period $\frac{2\pi}{\frac{1}{2}} = 4\pi$, amplitude 1] ($v = \cos\frac{1}{2}t$)

Stretch the graph from the t-axis stretch factor 2 [Period 4π, amplitude 2] $\left(v = 2\cos\frac{1}{2}t\right)$

Translate the graph by the vector $\begin{pmatrix} 0 \\ -1 \end{pmatrix}$

[Period 4π, amplitude 2] $\left(v = 2\cos\frac{1}{2}t - 1\right)$

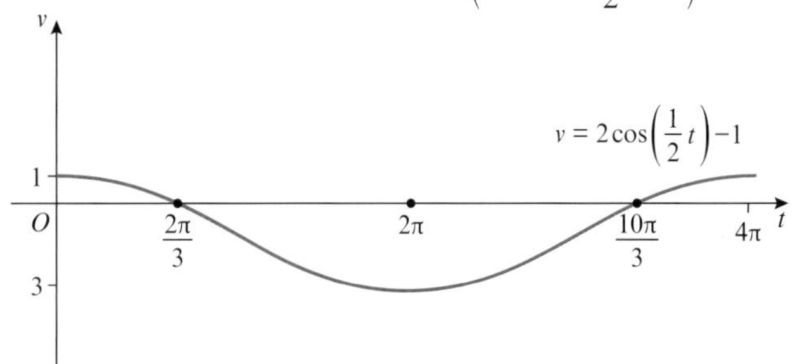

The particle changes direction at $t = \frac{2\pi}{3}$.

The total distance travelled between $t = 0$ and $t = 2\pi$ is made up of two stages:

$t = 0$ to $t = \frac{2\pi}{3}$ and $t = \frac{2\pi}{3}$ to $t = 2\pi$

The total distance s is:

$$s = \int_0^{\frac{2\pi}{3}} \left(2\cos\left(\frac{1}{2}t\right) - 1\right)dt + \left|\int_{\frac{2\pi}{3}}^{2\pi} \left(2\cos\left(\frac{1}{2}t\right) - 1\right)dt\right|$$

$$s = \left[4\sin\frac{1}{2}t - t\right]_0^{\frac{2\pi}{3}} + \left|\left[4\sin\frac{1}{2}t - t\right]_{\frac{2\pi}{3}}^{2\pi}\right|$$

$$s = \left[\left(2\sqrt{3} - \frac{2\pi}{3}\right) - (0)\right] + \left|\left[(0 - 2\pi) - \left(2\sqrt{3} - \frac{2\pi}{3}\right)\right]\right|$$

$s = 1.3697... + 7.6529... = 9.02$ m (3 s.f.)

or $s = \left(2\sqrt{3} - \frac{2\pi}{3}\right) + \left|-2\pi - 2\sqrt{3} + \frac{2\pi}{3}\right|$

$$s = \left(2\sqrt{3} - \frac{2\pi}{3}\right) + 2\pi + 2\sqrt{3} - \frac{2\pi}{3}$$

$$s = 2\sqrt{3} - \frac{2\pi}{3} + 2\pi + 2\sqrt{3} - \frac{2\pi}{3}$$

$$s = \left(4\sqrt{3} + \frac{2\pi}{3}\right)\text{m}$$

12 a Substituting $t = 0$, $a = -2$ into $a = pt + q$ gives:

$-2 = p(0) + q$

$q = -2$

So, $a = pt - 2$

$v = \int a\,dt = \frac{1}{2}pt^2 - 2t + c$

Substitute $t = 0$, $v = 3$

$3 = \frac{1}{2}p(0)^2 - 2(0) + c$

$c = 3$

$v = \frac{1}{2}pt^2 - 2t + 3$

The particle first comes to rest when $v = 0$ and $t = 2$

$0 = \frac{1}{2}p(2)^2 - 2(2) + 3$ multiply both sides by 2 and rearrange

$2p = 1$

$p = \frac{1}{2}$

b $v = \frac{1}{4}t^2 - 2t + 3$

$s = \int v \, dt = \int \left(\frac{1}{4}t^2 - 2t + 3\right) dt = \frac{1}{12}t^3 - t^2 + 3t + c$

When $t = 0$, $s = 0$ so:

$0 = \frac{1}{12}(0)^3 - (0)^2 + 3(0) + c$

$c = 0$

The displacement of the particle is: $s = \frac{1}{12}t^3 - t^2 + 3t$

c The particle next comes to rest when $\frac{1}{4}t^2 - 2t + 3 = 0$

$\frac{1}{4}t^2 - 2t + 3 = 0$ multiply both sides by 4

$t^2 - 8t + 12 = 0$ factorise

$(t - 2)(t - 6) = 0$

$t = 2$ or $t = 6$

The particle next comes to rest when $t = 6$

d The 4th second is between $t = 3$ and $t = 4$.

We need to find out if the particle changes direction in the period $t = 3$ and $t = 4$.

We need to consider the graph of v against t

$v = \frac{1}{4}t^2 - 2t + 3$ is a 'U' shaped parabola that intersects the t-axis twice at $t = 2$ and $t = 6$

For the period $0 \leqslant t < 2$ the velocity is positive

At $t = 2$, and $t = 6$,the velocity is zero

For the period $2 < t < 6$ the velocity is negative.

So, the particle does not change direction in the 4th second.

The distance travelled between $t = 3$ and $t = 4$ is:

$s = \int_3^4 v \, dt = \int_3^4 \left(\frac{1}{4}t^2 - 2t + 3\right) dt = \left[\frac{1}{12}t^3 - t^2 + 3t\right]_3^4$

$= \left(\frac{1}{12}(4)^3 - (4)^2 + 3(4)\right) - \left(\frac{1}{12}(3)^3 - (3)^2 + 3(3)\right)$

$= \frac{4}{3} - \frac{9}{4}$

$= -\frac{11}{12}$

The graph between $t = 3$ and $t = 4$ is under the t-axis so the distance travelled is $\left|-\frac{11}{12}\right| = \frac{11}{12}$ m

13 a Use the product rule to differentiate the following:

$s = 2t\sin\frac{\pi}{3}t$

The velocity $\frac{ds}{dt} = 2t \times \frac{\pi}{3}\cos\frac{\pi}{3}t + \sin\frac{\pi}{3}t \times (2)$

$$v = \frac{2\pi}{3}t\cos\frac{\pi}{3}t + 2\sin\frac{\pi}{3}t$$

The acceleration $a = \frac{dv}{dt}$

$$a = \left(\frac{2\pi}{3}t \times -\frac{\pi}{3}\sin\frac{\pi}{3}t + \cos\frac{\pi}{3}t \times \frac{2\pi}{3}\right) + \frac{\pi}{3} \times 2\cos\frac{\pi}{3}t$$

$$= -\frac{2\pi^2 t}{9}\sin\frac{\pi}{3}t + \frac{2\pi}{3}\cos\frac{\pi}{3}t + \frac{2\pi}{3}\cos\frac{\pi}{3}t$$

$$= -\frac{2\pi^2 t}{9}\sin\frac{\pi t}{3} + \frac{4\pi}{3}\cos\frac{\pi t}{3}$$

b $18(vt - s) = 18t\left(\frac{2\pi}{3}t\cos\frac{\pi}{3}t + 2\sin\frac{\pi}{3}t\right) - 18\left(2t\sin\frac{\pi}{3}t\right)$

$$= 12t^2\pi\cos\frac{\pi}{3}t + 36t\sin\frac{\pi}{3}t - 36t\sin\frac{\pi}{3}t$$

$$= 12t^2\pi\cos\frac{\pi}{3}t$$

$$t^2(9a + \pi^2 s) = 9t^2\left(-\frac{2\pi^2 t}{9}\sin\frac{\pi t}{3} + \frac{4\pi}{3}\cos\frac{\pi t}{3}\right) + 2t^3\pi^2\sin\frac{\pi}{3}t$$

$$= -2t^3\pi^2\sin\frac{\pi t}{3} + 12t^2\pi\cos\frac{\pi t}{3} + 2t^3\pi^2\sin\frac{\pi}{3}t$$

$$= 12t^2\pi\cos\frac{\pi}{3}t$$

So both sides of the equation are equal.